W9-DIV-567

Discovering Computers 2008
Introductory

Discovering Computers 2008

Introductory

Gary B. Shelly

Thomas J. Cashman

Misty E. Vermaat

Contributing Authors

Jeffrey J. Quasney

Susan L. Sebok

Jeffrey J. Webb

Steven M. Freund

Gary C. Kessler

THOMSON COURSE TECHNOLOGY

25 THOMSON PLACE

BOSTON MA 02210

Australia • Canada • Denmark • Japan • Mexico • New Zealand • Philippines • Puerto Rico • Singapore
South Africa • Spain • United Kingdom • United States

Discovering Computers 2008
Introductory

Gary B. Shelly
Thomas J. Cashman
Misty E. Vermaat

Executive Editor:
Alexandra Arnold

Senior Product Manager:
Reed Curry

Associate Product Manager:
Klenda Martinez

Editorial Assistant:
Jon Farnham

Senior Marketing Manager:
Joy Stark-Vancs

Marketing Coordinator:
Julie Schuster

Print Buyer:
Julio Esperas

**Thomson Course Technology
Production Contact:**
Marissa Falco

Researcher:
F. William Vermaat

Development Editor:
Lyn Markowicz

Proofreader:
Nancy Lamm

Final Reader:
Kim Kosmatka

Management Services:
Pre-PressPMG

Interior Designer:
Pre-PressPMG

Art Director:
Bruce Bond

Cover and Text Design:
Joel Sadagursky

Cover Photos:
Jon Chomitz

Illustrator:
Pre-PressPMG

Compositor:
Pre-PressPMG

Printer:
Banta Menasha

COPYRIGHT © 2008 Thomson Course Technology, a division of Thomson Learning, Inc. Thomson Learning™ is a trademark used herein under license.

Printed in USA

2 3 4 5 6 7 8 9 10 BM 08 07

For more information, contact Thomson Course Technology
25 Thomson Place
Boston, Massachusetts 02210

Or find us on the World Wide Web at:
www.course.com

ALL RIGHTS RESERVED. No part of this work covered by the copyright hereon may be reproduced or used in any form or by any means — graphic, electronic, or mechanical, including photocopying, recording, taping, Web distribution, or information storage and retrieval systems — without the written permission of the publisher.

For permission to use material from this text or product, submit a request online at **www.thomsonrights.com**

Any additional questions about permissions can be submitted by e-mail to **thomsonrights@thomson.com**

Thomson Course Technology, the Course Technology logo, the Shelly Cashman Series® and **Custom Edition**® are registered trademarks used under license. All other names used herein are for identification purposes only and are trademarks of their respective owners.

Thomson Course Technology reserves the right to revise this publication and make changes from time to time in its content without notice.

ISBN 13: 978-1-4239-1204-7
ISBN 10: 1-4239-1204-0

Contents

Special Feature

MAKING USE OF THE WEB 116

CHAPTER 3

Application Software 132

CHAPTER 4

The Components of the System Unit 182

CHAPTER 5

Input

Special Feature

BUYER'S GUIDE 2008   444

CHAPTER 9

Communications and Networks 458

CHAPTER 10

Database Management 512

CHAPTER 11

Computer Security, Ethics, and Privacy 554

Discover Computers
and make concepts real with . . .

Online Companion

Use the Online Companion at scsite.com/
dc2008 to bring unparalleled currency to the
learning experience. Access additional information about important topics and make use
of online learning games, practice tests, and
additional reinforcement. Gain access to this
dynamic site through CoursePort, Thomson
Course Technology's login page.

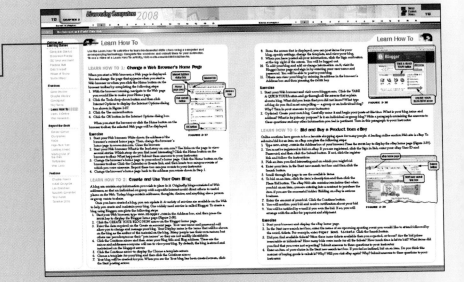

Learn How To

Apply the concepts presented
in the chapter to everyday life
with these hands-on activities.
See the Learn How To activities in action with videos on
the Online Companion.

Ethics and Issues

Ethics and Issues boxes raise controversial, computer-related topics
of the day, challenging readers to
consider closely general concerns
of computers in society.

Case Studies

Exercise your mind and construct
creative solutions to the thought-
provoking case studies presented in
each chapter. The Case Study exercises are constructed for class discussion, independent research, or
examination in a team environment.

practical, hands-on elements.

High-Tech Talk

The High-Tech Talk article at the end of each chapter expands on a topic covered in the chapter and presents a more technical discussion.

Career Corner

Each chapter ends with a Career Corner feature that introduces a computer-career opportunity relating to a topic covered in the chapter.

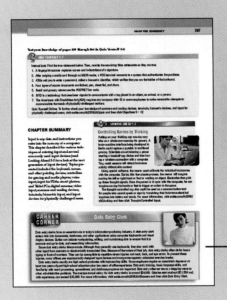

Companies on the Cutting Edge

Everyone who interacts with computers should be aware of the key computer-related companies. Each chapter profiles two of these key companies.

Technology Trailblazers

The Technology Trailblazers section in each chapter offers a glimpse into the life and times of the more famous leaders of the computer industry.

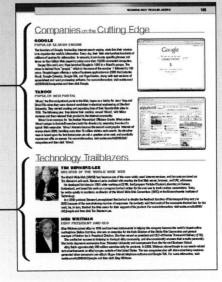

Discover Computers
and make concepts real with . . .

Web Link

Obtain current information and a different perspective about key terms and concepts by visiting the Web addresses in the Web Links found in the margins throughout the book.

Looking Ahead

The Looking Ahead boxes offer a glimpse at the latest advances in computer technology that will be available, usually within five years.

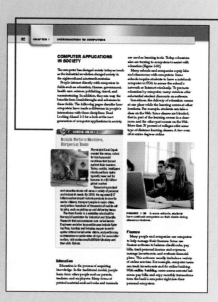

FAQ

FAQ (frequently asked questions) boxes offer common questions and answers about subjects related to the topic at hand.

Learn It Online

The Learn It Online exercises, which include brand-new At the Movies online videos, practice tests, interactive labs, learning games, and Web-based activities offer a wealth of online reinforcement.

interactive Web elements.

Web Research

Each Web Research exercise references an element in the book, requires follow-up research on the Web, and suggests writing a short article or presenting the findings of the research to the class.

Quiz Yourself

Three Quiz Yourself boxes per chapter help ensure retention by reinforcing sections of the chapter material, rather than waiting for the end of the chapter to test. Use Appendix B for a quick check of the answers, and access additional Quiz Yourself quizzes on the Online Companion for interactivity and easy use.

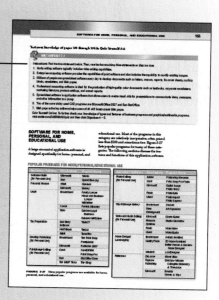

Primary and Secondary Key Terms

Before taking a test, use the Key Terms page as a checklist of terms to know. In the text, primary key terms appear in bold font and secondary key terms appear in italic font. Visit a Key Terms page on the Online Companion and click any term for additional information.

Discover Computers
and make concepts real with . . .

Picture Yourself

Picture yourself using the concepts presented in each chapter. This section at the beginning of each chapter bridges the gap between the chapter-specific material and everyday life using computers.

Chapter Objectives and Table of Contents

Before reading the chapter, carefully read through the Objectives and Contents to discover knowledge that will be gleaned from the chapter.

Step Figures

Each chapter includes numerous step figures that present the more complex computer concepts using a step-by-step pedagogy.

Checkpoint

Use these three pages of label-the-figure, multiple choice, true/false, matching, and short answer exercises to reinforce understanding of the topics presented in the chapter. Visit the Online Companion to complete an interactive version of the Checkpoint exercises.

Initial Chapter Figure

Carefully study the first figure in each chapter because it provides an easy-to-follow overview of the major purpose of the chapter.

pedagogical elements.

Chapter Review

Use the two-page Chapter Review before taking an examination to ensure familiarity with the computer concepts presented. This section includes each objective, followed by a one- or two-paragraph summary. Visit a Chapter Review page on the Online Companion, and click the Audio button to listen to the Chapter Review.

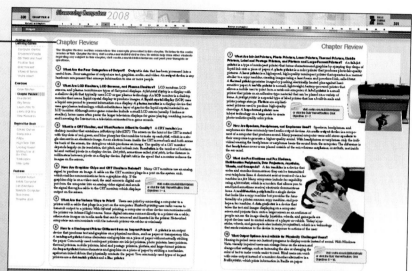

Special Features

Six special features following Chapters 1, 2, 5, 6, 8, and 11 encompass topics from the history of computers, to what's hot on the Web, to a buyer's guide, to the latest in new technology.

Preface

The Shelly Cashman Series® offers the finest textbooks in computer education. We are proud of the fact that the previous twelve editions of this textbook have been the most widely used in computer education. With each new edition of the book, we have implemented significant improvements based on current computer trends and comments made by instructors and students. *Discovering Computers 2008* continues with the innovation, quality, and reliability you have come to expect from the Shelly Cashman Series.

In *Discovering Computers 2008*, you will find an educationally sound, highly visual, and easy-to-follow pedagogy that presents an in-depth treatment of introductory computer subjects. Students will finish the course with a solid understanding of computers, how to use computers, and how to access information on the World Wide Web.

OBJECTIVES OF THIS TEXTBOOK

Discovering Computers 2008, Introductory is intended for use as a stand-alone textbook or in combination with an applications, Internet, or programming textbook in a full-semester introductory computer course. No experience with computers is assumed. The objectives of this book are to:

- Present the most-up-to-date technology in an ever-changing discipline
- Give students an in-depth understanding of why computers are essential components in business and society
- Teach the fundamentals of computers and computer nomenclature, particularly with respect to personal computer hardware and software, and the World Wide Web
- Present the material in a visually appealing and exciting manner that motivates students to learn
- Assist students in planning a career
- Provide exercises and lab assignments that allow students to interact with a computer and learn by actually using the computer and the World Wide Web
- Present strategies for purchasing a desktop computer, a notebook computer, a Tablet PC, and a personal mobile device
- Provide alternative learning techniques and reinforcement via the Web
- Offer distance-education providers a textbook with a meaningful and exercise-rich Online Companion

NEW TO THIS EDITION

Discovering Computers 2008 includes exciting new features, certain to engage and challenge students, making learning with *Discovering Computers 2008* an enriched experience. These new features include:

- Comprehensive updates for currency, including coverage of Microsoft Office 2007, Windows Vista, and Internet Explorer 7.
- Brand new At the Movies videos, Video and Audio: You Review It, and Vista Exercises engage students with exciting and timely activities.
- Revised chapter features such as Ethics and Issues, Looking Ahead, FAQ, Web Links, Companies on the Cutting Edge, and Technology Trailblazers include the most relevant and interesting examples to students.
- New Learn How To exercises and online videos provide a hands-on approach to learning fundamental skills.
- Updated Checkpoint exercises reinforce students' understanding of key concepts presented in the chapters.

DISTINGUISHING FEATURES

To date, more than six million students have learned about computers using a *Discovering Computers* textbook. With the additional World Wide Web integration and interactivity, streaming up-to-date audio and video, extraordinary step-by-step visual drawings and photographs, unparalleled currency, and the Shelly and Cashman touch, this book will make your computer concepts course exciting and dynamic. Distinguishing features of the Shelly Cashman Series *Discovering Computers* books include:

A Proven Pedagogy
Careful explanations of complex concepts, educationally-sound elements, and reinforcement highlight this proven method of presentation.

A Visually Appealing Book that Maintains Student Interest

The latest technology, pictures, drawings, and text are combined artfully to produce a visually appealing and easy-to-understand book. Many of the figures include a step-by-step presentation (see page 196), which simplifies the more complex computer concepts. Pictures and drawings reflect the latest trends in computer technology. This combination of pictures, step-by-step drawings, and easy-to-read text layout sets the standard for computer textbook design.

Latest Technologies and Terms

The technologies and terms your students see in this book are those they will encounter when they start using computers. Only the latest application software is shown throughout the book. New topics and terms include social networking Web site, video blog, vodcast, blogosphere, ccTLD, digital rights management (DRM), gTLD, hypermedia, hypertext, media sharing Web site, UMPC, online community, online social network, participatory Web, tabbed browsing, vlog, vlogger, vlogosphere, VoIP, Web 2.0, e-learning, media player, Web application, Web-based software, Centrino Duo Core, eSATAport, ExpressCard, ExpressCard slot, external SATA, FireWire 800, form factor, front side bus (FSB), massively parallel processing, PCI Express bus, SETI@home, U3 smart drive, vPro technology, air mouse, dance pad, game controller, laser mouse, light gun, motion-sensing game controllers, Wii Remote, aspect ratio, PictBridge, UXGA, WQXGA, WSXGA, WUXGA, WXGA, BD-R, BD-RE, Blu-ray Disc-ROM (BD-ROM), HD DVD-R, HD DVD-ROM disc, HD DVD-RW, LightScribe technology, pocket hard drive, thumb drive, U3 smart drive, video CD (VCD), BlackBerry, Disk Cleanup, Explorers, Flip 3D, folder, index, Live CD, Live USB, media player, Music Explorer, Picture Explorer, Problem Reports and Solutions, search utility, Windows Aero, Windows Defender, Windows Photo Gallery, Windows Sidebar, Windows SideShow, Windows Vista Basic, Windows Vista Business, Windows Vista Enterprise, Windows Vista Home Basic, Windows Vista Home Premium, Windows Vista Ultimate, camera phone, collaborative software, common short code (CSC), EVDO, FTTB, FTTH, picture phone, switch, UWB (ultra-wideband), video phone, collaborative databases, GIS, biometric payment, BitLocker, bot, botnet, e-mail spoofing, Encrypting File System, IP spoofing, SSID, and zombie army.

World Wide Web Enhanced

This book uses the World Wide Web as a major supplement. The purpose of integrating the World Wide Web into the book is to (1) offer students additional information and currency on important topics; (2) use its interactive capabilities to offer creative reinforcement and online quizzes; (3) make available alternative learning techniques with Web-based learning games, practice tests, and interactive labs; (4) underscore the relevance of the World Wide Web as a basic information tool that can be used in all facets of society; (5) introduce students to doing research on the Web; and (6) offer instructors the opportunity to organize and administer their traditional campus-based or distance-education-based courses on the Web using the Blackboard platform. This textbook, however, does not depend on Web access to be used successfully. The Web access adds to the already complete treatment of topics within the book.

Extensive End-of-Chapter Materials

A notable strength of the *Discovering Computers* textbooks is the extensive student activities at the end of each chapter. Well-structured student activities can make the difference between students merely participating in a class and students retaining the information they learn. The activities in the *Discovering Computers 2008* books include: Chapter Review, Key Terms, Checkpoint, Learn It Online, Learn How To, Web Research, and Case Studies.

ORGANIZATION OF THIS TEXTBOOK

Discovering Computers 2008, Introductory provides a thorough introduction to computers. The material is divided into eleven chapters, six special features, three appendices, and a glossary/index.

Chapter 1 – Introduction to Computers   In Chapter 1, students are introduced to basic computer concepts, such as what a computer is, how it works, and what makes it a powerful tool.

Special Feature – Timeline 2008 Milestones in Computer History   In this special feature, students learn about the major computer technology developments during the past 71 years.

Chapter 2 – The Internet and World Wide Web   In Chapter 2, students learn about the Internet, World Wide Web, browsers, e-mail, FTP, and instant messaging.

Special Feature – Making Use of the Web   In this special feature, more than 150 popular up-to-date Web sites are listed and described. Now includes a section on Online Social Networks and Media Sharing. Basic searching techniques also are introduced.

Chapter 3 – Application Software   In Chapter 3, students are introduced to a variety of business software, graphics and multimedia software, home/personal/educational software, and communications software.

Chapter 4 – The Components of the System Unit   In Chapter 4, students are introduced to the components of the system unit; how memory stores data, instructions, and information; and how the system unit executes an instruction.

Chapter 5 – Input   Chapter 5 describes the various techniques of input and commonly used input devices.

Special Feature – Personal Mobile Devices   In this special feature, students receive a detailed presentation of personal mobile device operating systems, built-in personal mobile device software, personal mobile device application software and services, and how to obtain and install personal mobile device software. Also included is a personal mobile device buyer's guide.

Chapter 6 – Output   Chapter 6 describes the various methods of output and commonly used output devices.

Special Feature – Digital Imaging and Video Technology   In this special feature, students are introduced to using a personal computer, digital camera, and digital video camera to manipulate and distribute photographs and video.

Chapter 7 – Storage   In Chapter 7, students learn about various storage media and storage devices.

Chapter 8 – Operating Systems and Utility Programs   In Chapter 8, students learn about a variety of stand-alone operating systems, network operating systems, and embedded operating systems.

Special Feature – Buyer's Guide 2008: How to Purchase a Personal Computer   In this special feature, students are introduced to purchasing a desktop computer, notebook computer, and Tablet PC.

Chapter 9 – Communications and Networks   Chapter 9 provides students with an overview of communications technology and applications.

Chapter 10 – Database Management   Chapter 10 presents students with the advantages of organizing data in a database and describes various types of data.

Chapter 11 – Computer Security, Ethics, and Privacy   In Chapter 11, students learn about computer and Internet risks, ethical issues surrounding information accuracy, intellectual property rights, codes of conduct, information privacy, and computer-related health issues.

Special Feature – Computer Forensics   This special feature introduces students to the scope of, process, and tools involved in computer forensics work. The feature underlines the importance of computer forensics in our increasingly digital world.

Appendix A – Coding Schemes and Number Systems   Appendix A presents the ASCII, EBCDIC, and Unicode coding schemes.

Appendix B – Quiz Yourself Answers   Appendix B provides the answers for the Quiz Yourself questions in the text.

Appendix C – Computer Acronyms   Appendix C summarizes the computer acronyms discussed in the book.

Glossary/Index   The Glossary/Index includes a definition and page references for every key term presented in the book.

SHELLY CASHMAN SERIES INSTRUCTOR RESOURCES

The Shelly Cashman Series is dedicated to providing you with all of the tools you need to make your class a success. The contents of the Instructor Resources and Course Presenter CD-ROMs (1-4239-1212-8) are described below. Information on all supplementary materials is available through your Course Technology representative or by calling one of the following telephone numbers: Colleges and Universities, 1-800-648-7450; High Schools, 1-800-824-5179; Private Career Colleges, 1-800-477-3692 ; Canada, 1-800-268-2222; Corporations with IT Training Centers, 1-800-477-3692; and Government Agencies, Health-Care Organizations, and Correctional Facilities, 1-800-477-3692.

Instructor Resources CD-ROM

The Instructor Resources CD-ROM includes both teaching and testing aids.

Instructor's Manual   The Instructor's Manual is made up of Microsoft Word files, which include lecture notes that summarize the sections of the chapters, figures and boxed elements found in every chapter, teacher tips, classroom activities, lab activities, and quick quizzes.

Syllabus   Sample syllabi, which can be customized easily to a course, are included. The syllabi cover policies, assignments, exams, and other course information.

Figure Files   Illustrations for every figure in the textbook are available in electronic form. Use this ancillary to present a slide show in lecture or to print transparencies for use in lecture with an overhead projector. If you have a personal computer and LCD device, this ancillary can be an effective tool for presenting lectures.

Solutions to Exercises   Solutions are included for end-of-chapter exercises.

Test Bank & Test Engine   The ExamView test bank includes 220 questions for every chapter (80 multiple-choice, 50 true/false, and 40 completion) and features new objective-based question types (10 modified multiple-choice, 10 modified true/false, and 20 matching) and Critical Thinking questions (6 essays and 2 cases with 2 questions each). The test bank also includes page number references, and when appropriate, figure references. Each question also is identified by objective and type of term (primary or secondary). The test bank comes with a copy of the test engine, ExamView, the ultimate tool for your objective-based testing needs.

Printed Test Bank   A Rich Text Format (.rtf) version of the test bank you can print also is included.

Test Out/Final Exam   Use this objective-based exam to test students out of your course, or use it as a final examination. A master answer sheet is included.

Pretest/Posttest   Use these carefully prepared tests at the beginning and the end of the semester to measure student progress. A master answer sheet is included.

Data Files for Students   All the files that are required by students to complete the exercises are included. You can distribute the files on the Instructor Resources CD-ROM to your students over a network, or you can have them follow the instructions on the inside back cover of this book to obtain a copy of the files.

Course Presenter

Course Presenter is a one-click-per-slide presentation system on CD-ROM that provides PowerPoint slides for every subject in each chapter. Use this presentation system to give interesting, well-organized, and knowledge-based lectures. Several brand new computer-related video clips are available for optional presentation. Course Presenter provides consistent coverage for multiple lecturers.

Student Edition Labs

Our Web-based interactive labs help students master hundreds of computer concepts, including input and output devices, file management and desktop applications, computer ethics, virus protection, and much more. Featuring up-to-the-minute content, eye-popping graphics, and rich animation, the highly interactive Student Edition Labs offer students an alternative way to learn through dynamic observation, step-by-step practice, and challenging review questions. Access the free Student Edition Labs from the *Discovering Computers 2008* Online Companion at scsite.com/dc2008 or see the Student Edition Lab exercises on the Learn It Online pages at the end of each chapter. Also available on CD at an additional cost.

Online Content

Blackboard is the leading distance learning solution provider and class-management platform today. Thomson Course Technology has partnered with Blackboard to bring you premium online content. Instructors: Content for use with *Discovering Computers 2008* is available in a Blackboard Course Cartridge and includes topic reviews, case projects, review questions, test banks, practice tests, custom syllabus, and more. Thomson Course Technology also has solutions for several other learning management systems. Please visit http://www.course.com today to see what's available for this title.

Blackboard

SUPPLEMENTS

The following supplements can be used in combination with this textbook.

SAM Computer Concepts

Add more flexibility to your course with SAM Computer Concepts.

SAM (Skills Assessment Manager) Computer Concepts helps you energize your training assignments by allowing students to train and test on important computer skills in an active, hands-on environment. By adding SAM Computer Concepts to your curriculum, you can:

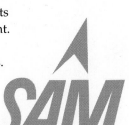

- Reinforce your students' knowledge of key computer concepts with hands-on application exercises.
- Allow your students to "learn by listening" with rich audio in their computer labs.
- Build computer concepts exams from a test bank of more than 50,000 objective-based questions or even create your own custom questions.
- Schedule your students' computer concepts training and testing assignments with powerful administrative tools.
- Track student exam grades and training progress using more than one dozen student and classroom reports.

SAM also features assessment, training, and project-grading solutions for skills in both Microsoft Office 2003 and Office 2007. Let SAM save you time in grading, while students get hands-on practice on valuable real-world skills.

Study Guide

This highly popular *Study Guide* (ISBN 1-4239-1208-X) includes a variety of activities that help students recall, review, and master introductory computer concepts. The *Study Guide* complements the end-of-chapter material with a guided chapter outline; a self-test consisting of true/false, multiple-choice, short answer, fill-in, and matching questions; an entertaining puzzle; and other challenging exercises.

CourseCasts — Learning on the Go. Always available. . . always relevant.

COURSECASTS

Want to keep up with the latest technology trends relevant to you? Visit our site to find a library of podcasts, CourseCasts, featuring a "CourseCast of the Week", and download them to your mp3 player at http://coursecasts.course.com

Our fast-paced world is driven by technology. You know because you're an active participant —always on the go, always keeping up with technological trends, and always learning new ways to embrace technology to power your life.

Ken Baldauf, a faculty member of the Florida State University Computer Science Department, is responsible for teaching technology classes to thousands of FSU students each year. He knows what you know; he knows what you want to learn. He's also an expert in the latest technology and will sort through and aggregate the most pertinent news and information so you can spend your time enjoying technology, rather than trying to figure it out.

Visit us at http://coursecasts.course.com to learn on the go!

About Our New Cover Look

Learning styles of students have changed, but the Shelly Cashman Series' dedication to their success has remained steadfast for over 30 years. We are committed to continually updating our approach and content to reflect the way today's students learn and experience new technology.

This focus on the user is reflected in our bold new cover design, which features photographs of real students using the Shelly Cashman Series in their courses. Each book features a different user, reflecting the many ages, experiences, and backgrounds of all of the students learning with our books. When you use the Shelly Cashman Series, you can be assured that you are learning computer skills using the most effective courseware available.

We would like to thank the administration and faculty at the participating schools for their help in making our vision a reality. Most of all, we'd like to thank the wonderful students from all over the world who learn from our texts and now appear on our covers.

Discovering Computers 2008

CHAPTER ONE

Introduction to Computers

Picture Yourself Taking a Computer Course

Before the lecture begins on the first day of your Introduction to Computers class, you hear several classmates announce they will be gathering in the student lounge after class to talk about homework and form study groups. A few of them confess they know little about computers and are looking forward to learning more. As they talk, you think about your experiences with computers. You had a beginning programming class in high school. You use the Internet and instant messaging regularly to communicate with friends. With your digital camera, you take pictures and e-mail them to family members. Most of your friends and family consider you to be rather computer savvy, so you are confident you will not need a study group.

During the lecture, the instructor reads several computer advertisements to the class. The ads use computer terms and acronyms you have never heard, like eSATA, Blu-ray, Vista, Core 2 Duo, VoIP, Web 2.0, router, Office 2007, U3, and earbud. As he reads, you quickly realize you know less than you thought. When he finishes reading, the instructor tells the class not to worry if some or most of the words in the ads are unfamiliar. "By the time this course is over," he says, "you will learn everything you need to know to buy a computer and will understand how computers are used in society." Excited by the prospect of gaining new knowledge, you decide to join the study group after all.

Read Chapter 1 to become familiar with some of the terms mentioned in the advertisement, discover practical uses of computers, and set a foundation for your further learning throughout this book.

OBJECTIVES

After completing this chapter, you will be able to:

1. Recognize the importance of computer literacy
2. Define the term, computer
3. Identify the components of a computer
4. Discuss the advantages and disadvantages of using computers
5. Recognize the purpose of a network
6. Discuss the uses of the Internet and World Wide Web
7. Distinguish between system software and application software
8. Describe the categories of computers
9. Identify the elements of an information system
10. Describe the various types of computer users
11. Discuss various computer applications in society

CONTENTS

A WORLD OF COMPUTERS

Computers are everywhere: at work, at school, and at home. Many daily activities either involve the use of or depend on information from a computer. As shown in Figure 1-1, people use all types and sizes of computers for a variety of reasons and in a range of places. Some computers sit on top of a desk or on the floor; others are small enough to carry.

Computers are a primary means of local and global communication for billions of people. Consumers use computers to correspond with businesses, employees with other employees and customers, students with classmates and teachers, and family members and military personnel with friends and other family members. In addition to sending text-based messages, people use computers to share pictures, drawings, journals, music, and videos.

Through computers, society has instant access to information from around the globe. Local and national news, weather reports, sports scores, airline schedules, telephone directories, maps and directions, job listings, credit reports, and countless forms of educational material always are accessible. From the computer, you can make a telephone call, meet new friends, share opinions or life stories, book flights, shop, fill prescriptions, file taxes, or take a course.

At home or while on the road, people use computers to manage schedules, balance checkbooks, pay bills, transfer funds, and buy or sell stocks. Banks place automated teller machines (ATMs) all over the world, making it easy for customers to deposit or withdraw funds at anytime. At the grocery store, a computer tracks

FIGURE 1-1   People use all types and sizes of computers in their daily activities.

purchases, calculates the amount of money due, and often generates coupons customized to buying patterns. Vehicles include onboard navigation systems that provide directions, call for emergency services, and track the vehicle if it is stolen.

In the workplace, employees use computers to create correspondence such as e-mail messages, memos, and letters; calculate payroll; track inventory; and generate invoices. Some applications such as automotive design and weather forecasting use computers to perform complex mathematical calculations. At school, teachers use computers to assist with classroom instruction. Students complete assignments and do research on computers in lab rooms, at home, or elsewhere.

People also spend hours of leisure time using a computer. They play games, listen to music or radio broadcasts, watch or compose videos and movies, read books and magazines, share stories, research genealogy, retouch photographs, and plan vacations.

As technology continues to advance, computers are becoming more a part of everyday life. Thus, many people believe that computer literacy is vital to success in today's world. **Computer literacy** involves having a knowledge and understanding of computers and their uses.

This book presents the knowledge you need to be computer literate. As you read this first chapter, keep in mind it is an overview. Many of the terms and concepts introduced in this chapter will be discussed in more depth later in the book.

WHAT IS A COMPUTER?

A **computer** is an electronic device, operating under the control of instructions stored in its own memory, that can accept data, process the data according to specified rules, produce results, and store the results for future use.

Data and Information

Computers process data into information. **Data** is a collection of unprocessed items, which can include text, numbers, images, audio, and video. **Information** conveys meaning and is useful to people.

As shown in Figure 1-2, for example, computers process several data items to print information in the form of a grade report.

FAQ 1-1

Is data a singular or plural word?

The word data is plural for datum. With respect to computers, however, it is accepted and common practice to use the word data in both the singular and plural context. For more information, visit scsite.com/dc2008/ch1/faq and then click Data.

A **FAQ** (frequently asked question) helps you find answers to commonly asked questions. Web sites often post an FAQ section, and each chapter in this book includes FAQ boxes related to topics in the text.

Information Processing Cycle

Computers process data (input) into information (output). A computer often holds data, information, and instructions in storage for future use. *Instructions* are the steps that tell the computer how to perform a particular task. Some people refer to the series of input, process, output, and storage activities as the *information processing cycle*.

Most computers today can communicate with other computers. As a result, communications also has become an essential element of the information processing cycle.

FIGURE 1-2 A computer processes data into information. In this simplified example, the student identification number, semester, course codes, and course grades all represent data. The computer processes the data to produce the grade report (information).

THE COMPONENTS OF A COMPUTER

A computer contains many electric, electronic, and mechanical components known as **hardware**. These components include input devices, output devices, a system unit, storage devices, and communications devices. Figure 1-3 shows some common computer hardware components.

Input Devices

An **input device** is any hardware component that allows you to enter data and instructions into a computer. Six widely used input devices are the keyboard, mouse, microphone, scanner, digital camera, and PC video camera (Figure 1-3).

A computer keyboard contains keys you press to enter data into the computer. For security purposes, some keyboards have a built-in fingerprint scanner, which allows you to work with the computer only if your fingerprint is recognized.

A mouse is a small handheld device. With the mouse, you control movement of a small symbol on the screen, called the pointer, and you make selections from the screen.

A microphone allows you to speak into the computer. A scanner converts printed material (such as text and pictures) into a form the computer can use.

With a digital camera, you take pictures and then transfer them to the computer or printer instead of storing the images on traditional film. A PC video camera is a digital video camera that allows you to create movies or take still pictures electronically.

WEB LINK 1-1

Input Devices
For more information, visit scsite.com/dc2008/ch1/weblink and then click Input Devices.

printer
(output device)

portable media player
(output device)

monitor
(output device)

screen

PC video camera
(input device)

CD/DVD drive
(storage device)

speakers
(output device)

hard disk drive
(storage device)

system unit
(processor, memory, and storage devices)

keyboard
(input device)

mouse
(input device)

scanner
(input device)

digital camera
(input device)

microphone
(input device)

external hard disk
(storage device)

modem
(communications device)

card reader/writer
(storage device)

USB flash drive
(storage device)

FIGURE 1-3 Common computer hardware components include a keyboard, mouse, microphone, scanner, digital camera, PC video camera, printer, monitor, speakers, portable media player, system unit, hard disk drive, external hard disk, USB flash drive, card reader/writer, and modem.

Output Devices

An **output device** is any hardware component that conveys information to one or more people. Four commonly used output devices are a printer, a monitor, speakers, and a portable media player (Figure 1-3 on the previous page).

A printer produces text and graphics on a physical medium such as paper. A monitor displays text, graphics, and videos on a screen. Speakers allow you to hear music, voice, and other audio (sounds). You can transfer audio, video, and digital images from your computer to a portable media player and then listen to the audio, watch the video, or view the images on the media player.

WEB LINK 1-2

Output Devices

For more information, visit scsite.com/dc2008/ch1/weblink and then click Output Devices.

System Unit

The **system unit** is a case that contains the electronic components of the computer that are used to process data (Figure 1-3). The circuitry of the system unit usually is part of or is connected to a circuit board called the motherboard.

Two main components on the motherboard are the processor and memory. The *processor* is the electronic component that interprets and carries out the basic instructions that operate the computer. *Memory* consists of electronic components that store instructions waiting to be executed and data needed by those instructions. Although some forms of memory are permanent, most memory keeps data and instructions temporarily, which means its contents are erased when the computer is shut off.

FAQ 1-2

What is a CPU?

The processor. Most people in the computer industry use the terms *CPU* (*central processing unit*) and processor to mean the same. A CPU is not the same as a computer; a computer contains a CPU. For more information, visit scsite.com/dc2008/ch1/faq and then click CPU.

Storage Devices

Storage holds data, instructions, and information for future use. For example, computers can store hundreds or millions of customer names and addresses. Storage holds these items permanently.

A computer keeps data, instructions, and information on **storage media**. Examples of storage media are USB flash drives, hard disks, CDs, DVDs, and memory cards. A **storage device** records (writes) and/or retrieves (reads) items to and from storage media. Drives and readers/writers, which are types of storage devices (Figure 1-3), accept a specific kind of storage media. For example, a DVD drive (storage device) accepts a DVD (storage media). Storage devices often function as a source of input because they transfer items from storage to memory.

A USB flash drive is a portable storage device that is small and lightweight enough to be transported on a keychain or in a pocket (Figure 1-3). The average USB flash drive can hold about 500 million characters. You plug a USB flash drive in a special, easily accessible opening on the computer.

A hard disk provides much greater storage capacity than a USB flash drive. The average hard disk can hold more than 250 billion characters. Hard disks are enclosed in an airtight, sealed case. Although some are portable, most are housed inside the system unit (Figure 1-4).

FIGURE 1-4 Hard disks are self-contained devices. The hard disk shown here must be installed in the system unit before it can be used.

Portable hard disks are either external or removable. An external hard disk is a separate, free-standing unit, whereas you insert and remove a removable hard disk from the computer or a device connected to the computer.

A compact disc is a flat, round, portable metal disc with a plastic coating. One type of compact disc is a CD-ROM, which can hold from 650 million to 1 billion characters. You can access a CD-ROM using most CD and DVD drives (Figure 1-5). Another type of compact disc is a DVD-ROM, some of which have enough storage capacity to store two full-length movies or 17 billion characters. To use a DVD-ROM, you need a DVD drive.

Some portable devices, such as digital cameras, use memory cards as the storage media. You then can transfer the stored items, such as digital photographs, from the memory card to a computer or printer using a card reader/writer (Figure 1-3 on page 7).

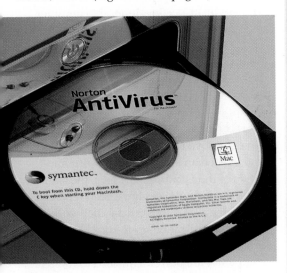

FIGURE 1-5 To use a CD or DVD, you need a CD or DVD drive.

Communications Devices

A **communications device** is a hardware component that enables a computer to send (transmit) and receive data, instructions, and information to and from one or more computers. A widely used communications device is a modem (Figure 1-3).

Communications occur over cables, telephone lines, cellular radio networks, satellites, and other transmission media. Some transmission media, such as satellites and cellular radio networks, are wireless, which means they have no physical lines or wires.

ADVANTAGES AND DISADVANTAGES OF USING COMPUTERS

Society has reaped many benefits from using computers. Both business and home users can make well-informed decisions because they have instant access to information from anywhere in the world. A **user** is anyone who communicates with a computer or utilizes the information it generates. Students, another type of user, have more tools to assist them in the learning process. Read Looking Ahead 1-1 for a look at the next generation of benefits from using computers.

LOOKING AHEAD 1-1

Medical Implants Can Enhance Lifestyles

Cellular phone manufacturers tout their small and powerful products, but the ultimate technology is the tiny cellular-phone-on-a-chip device. By implanting this processor directly into the brain and connecting electrodes to the brain's speech center, people would have the ability to communicate on any wireless network. While this technology might seem extreme, it illustrates the emergence of electronics inside the body to improve human life.

Other possible surgeries might implant a rechargeable electrical stimulator to treat pain or muscle dysfunction or to zap the stomach or nerves with electric current to boost metabolism. A brain computer interface may monitor and treat diseases, such as epilepsy and depression, that affect brain activity. A body-scanning machine might evaluate patients' pain when they cannot communicate.

In addition, a retinal prosthesis system with a light-sensing chip implanted in the eye might help patients with degenerative retinal diseases. For more information, visit scsite.com/dc2008/ch1/looking and then click Computer Implants.

WEB LINK 1-3

Communications Devices

For more information, visit scsite.com/dc2008/ch1/weblink and then click Communications Devices.

ADVANTAGES OF USING COMPUTERS Benefits of computers are possible because computers have the advantages of speed, reliability, consistency, storage, and communications.

- **Speed**: When data, instructions, and information flow along electronic circuits in a computer, they travel at incredibly fast speeds. Many computers process billions or trillions of operations in a single second. Processing involves computing (adding, subtracting, etc.), sorting (e.g., alphabetizing), organizing, displaying pictures, recording audio clips, playing music, and showing a movie or video. For a technical discussion about how computers process data, read the High-Tech Talk article on page 38.
- **Reliability**: The electronic components in modern computers are dependable and reliable because they rarely break or fail.
- **Consistency**: Given the same input and processes, a computer will produce the same results — consistently. A computing phrase — known as *garbage in, garbage out* — points out that the accuracy of a computer's output depends on the accuracy of the input. For example, if you do not use the flash on a digital camera when indoors, the resulting pictures that are displayed on the computer screen may be unusable because they are too dark.
- **Storage**: A computer can transfer data quickly from storage to memory, process it, and then store it again for future use. Many computers store enormous amounts of data and make this data available for processing anytime it is needed.
- **Communications**: Most computers today can communicate with other computers, often wirelessly. Computers with this capability can share any of the four information processing cycle operations — input, process, output, and storage — with another computer or a user.

DISADVANTAGES OF USING COMPUTERS Some disadvantages of computers relate to the violation of privacy, public safety, the impact on the labor force, health risks, and the impact on the environment.

- **Violation of Privacy**: Nearly every life event is stored in a computer somewhere…in medical records, credit reports, tax records, etc. In many instances, where personal and confidential records were not properly protected, individuals have found their privacy violated and identities stolen. Read Ethics & Issues 1-1 for a related discussion.
- **Public Safety**: Adults, teens, and children around the world are using computers to share publicly their photos, videos, journals, music, and other personal information. Some of these unsuspecting, innocent computer users have fallen victim to crimes committed by dangerous strangers. Protect yourself and your dependents from these criminals by being cautious. For example, do not share information that would allow others to identify or locate you.
- **Impact on Labor Force**: Although computers have improved productivity in many ways and created an entire industry with hundreds of thousands of new jobs, the skills of millions of employees have been replaced by computers. Thus, it is crucial that workers keep their education up-to-date. A separate impact on the labor force is that some companies are outsourcing jobs to foreign countries instead of keeping their homeland labor force employed.

ETHICS & ISSUES 1-1

What Should Be Done about Identity Theft?

Using e-mail and other techniques on the Internet, scam artists are employing a technique known as *phishing* to try to steal your personal information, such as credit card numbers, banking information, and passwords. For example, an e-mail message may appear to be a request from your credit card company to verify your Social Security number and online banking password. Instead, the information you submit ends up in the hands of the scammer, who then uses the information for a variety of unethical and illegal acts. Sadly, the result often is identity theft. You can help to deter identity theft in several ways: 1) shred your financial documents before discarding them, 2) do not click links in unsolicited e-mail messages, and 3) enroll in a credit monitoring service. Consumer advocates often blame credit card companies and credit bureaus for lax security standards. Meanwhile, the companies blame consumers for being too gullible and forthcoming with private information. Both sides blame the government for poor privacy laws and light punishments for identity thieves. But while the arguments go on, law enforcement agencies bear the brunt of the problem by spending hundreds of millions of dollars responding to complaints and finding and processing the criminals. Under current laws, who is responsible for Internet identity theft? Why? Should laws be changed to stop it, or should consumers change behavior? What is an appropriate punishment for identity thieves? Given the international nature of the Internet, how can foreign identity thieves be handled?

- **Health Risks**: Prolonged or improper computer use can lead to injuries or disorders of the hands, wrists, elbows, eyes, neck, and back. Computer users can protect themselves from these health risks through proper workplace design, good posture while at the computer, and appropriately spaced work breaks. Another health risk, called computer addiction, occurs when someone becomes obsessed with using the computer. Once recognized, computer addiction is a treatable disorder.
- **Impact on Environment**: Computer manufacturing processes and computer waste are depleting natural resources and polluting the environment. When computers are discarded in landfills, they release toxic materials and potentially dangerous levels of lead, mercury, and flame retardants. Strategies that can help protect the environment include recycling, regulating manufacturing processes, extending the life of computers, and immediately donating replaced computers. When you purchase a new computer, some retailers offer to dispose of your old computer properly.

Test your knowledge of pages 4 through 11 in Quiz Yourself 1-1.

QUIZ YOURSELF 1-1

Instructions: Find the true statement below. Then, rewrite the remaining false statements so they are true.

1. A computer is a motorized device that processes output into input.

2. A storage device records (reads) and/or retrieves (writes) items to and from storage media.

3. An output device is any hardware component that allows you to enter data and instructions into a computer.

4. Computer literacy involves having a knowledge and understanding of computers and their uses.

5. Computers have the disadvantages of fast speeds, high failure rates, producing consistent results, storing small amounts of data, and communicating with others.

6. Four commonly used input devices are a printer, a monitor, speakers, and a portable media player.

Quiz Yourself Online: To further check your knowledge of computer literacy, computers and their components, and the advantages and disadvantages of computers, visit scsite.com/dc2008/ch1/quiz and then click Objectives 1 – 4.

NETWORKS AND THE INTERNET

A **network** is a collection of computers and devices connected together, often wirelessly, via communications devices and transmission media. When a computer connects to a network, it is **online**.

Networks allow computers to share *resources*, such as hardware, software, data, and information. Sharing resources saves time and money. In many networks, one or more computers act as a server. The server controls access to the resources on a network. The other computers on the network, each called a client or workstation, request resources from the server (Figure 1-6). The major differences between the server and client computers are that the server ordinarily has more power, more storage space, and expanded communications capabilities.

Many homes and most businesses and schools network their computers and devices. Most allow users to connect their computers wirelessly to the network. Home networks usually are small, existing within a single structure. Business and school networks can be small, such as in a room or building, or widespread, connecting computers across a city, country, or the globe. The world's largest computer network is the Internet.

FIGURE 1-6 A server manages the resources on a network, and clients access the resources on the server. This network enables three separate computers to share the same printer, one wirelessly.

The Internet

The **Internet** is a worldwide collection of networks that connects millions of businesses, government agencies, educational institutions, and individuals (Figure 1-7).

More than one billion people around the world use the Internet daily for a variety of reasons, including the following:

- Communicate with and meet other people
- Access a wealth of information, news, and research findings
- Shop for goods and services
- Bank and invest
- Take a class
- Access sources of entertainment and leisure, such as online games, music, videos, books, and magazines
- Download music and video
- Share information

Figure 1-8 shows examples in each of these areas.

People connect to the Internet to exchange information with others around the world. E-mail allows you to send messages to other users. With instant messaging, you can have a live conversation with another connected user. In a chat room, you can communicate with multiple users at the same time — much like a group discussion. With Internet telephony, you can use the Internet to make a telephone call.

Businesses, called access providers, offer users and companies access to the Internet free or for a fee. By subscribing to an access provider, you can use your computer and a communications device, such as a modem, to connect to the many services of the Internet.

The Web, short for World Wide Web, is one of the more popular services on the Internet. Think of the Web as a global library of information available to anyone connected to the Internet. The **Web** contains billions of documents called Web pages. A **Web page** can contain text, graphics, audio, and video. The eight screens shown in Figure 1-8 are examples of Web pages. Web pages often have built-in connections, or links, to other documents, graphics, other Web pages, or Web sites. A Web site is a collection of related Web pages. Some Web sites allow users to access music and videos that can be downloaded, or transferred to storage media in a computer or portable media player, and then listen to the music through speakers, headphones, or earphones, or view the videos on a display device.

WEB LINK 1-4

The Internet
For more information, visit scsite.com/dc2008/ch1/weblink and then click Internet.

FIGURE 1-7
The Internet is the largest computer network, connecting millions of computers around the world.

communicate

access information

shop

bank and invest

take a class

entertainment

download music

share information

FIGURE 1-8 Users access the Internet for a variety of reasons.

In addition to accessing and using information on the Web, many people use the Web as a means to share personal information, photographs, videos, or artwork with the world. Anyone can create a Web page and then make it available, or *publish* it, on the Internet for others to see (read Ethics & Issues 1-2 for a related discussion). Millions of people worldwide join online communities, each called a **social networking Web site**, that encourage members to share their interests, ideas, stories, photos, music, and videos with other registered users (Figure 1-9). Some social networking Web sites are college oriented, some business oriented, others are more focused. A **photo sharing community**, for example, is a specific type of social networking Web site that allows users to create an online photo album and store their electronic photographs. Some Web sites provide publishing services free.

Hundreds of thousands of people today also use blogs to publish their thoughts on the Web. A *blog* is an informal Web site consisting of time-stamped articles in a diary or journal format, usually listed in reverse chronological order. As others read the articles in a blog, they reply with their own thoughts. A blog that contains video clips is called a *video blog*.

Podcasts are a popular way people verbally share information on the Web. A *podcast* is recorded audio stored on a Web site that can be downloaded to a computer or a portable media player such as an iPod. A video podcast, or *vodcast*, is a podcast that contains video and

WEB LINK 1-5

Social Networking Web Sites

For more information, visit scsite.com/dc2008/ch1/weblink and then click Social Networking Web Sites.

usually audio. At a convenient time and location, the user listens to the downloaded podcast or watches the downloaded vodcast.

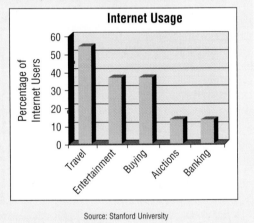

FAQ 1-3

What Web sites do users visit on the Internet?

A recent survey found that users visit various types of Web sites, as shown in the chart below. For more information, visit scsite.com/dc2008/ch1/faq and then click Web Sites.

Internet Usage

Source: Stanford University

ETHICS & ISSUES 1-2

Who Is Responsible for the Accuracy of Web Pages?

Since the dawn of the Web, some groups have used Web sites to try to convince people that the Holocaust in World War II did not occur. Using fake research papers and authoritative looking Web pages, these groups hope to revise history to their liking. In response, other groups have created Web sites to counter those claims and provide evidence of the truth. Many people think that anything in print is true, even what they read on the Web. Yet, authors with a wide range of expertise, authority, motives, and biases create Web pages. Web pages can be as accurate as the most scholarly journal, or no truer than the most disreputable supermarket tabloid. The Web makes it easy to obtain information, but Web page readers must make an extra effort to determine the quality of that information. In evaluating a Web page, experts suggest that you consider such factors as the purpose, scope, sponsor, timeliness, presentation, author, and permanence of the page. Ultimately, who is responsible for the accuracy of information on the Web? Why? What factors are most important in evaluating the accuracy of a Web page? Why? Should people be held accountable for what they publish on the Web? If so, by whom?

FIGURE 1-9 MySpace is a popular social networking Web site.

COMPUTER SOFTWARE

Software, also called a **program**, consists of a series of instructions that tells the computer what to do and how to do it.

You interact with a program through its user interface. The user interface controls how you enter data and instructions and how information is displayed on the screen. Software today often has a graphical user interface. With a **graphical user interface** (**GUI** pronounced gooey), you interact with the software using text, graphics, and visual images such as icons (Figure 1-10). An *icon* is a miniature image that represents a program, an instruction, or some other object. You can use the mouse to select icons that perform operations such as starting a program.

The two categories of software are system software and application software. The following sections describe these categories of software.

System Software

System software consists of the programs that control or maintain the operations of the computer and its devices. System software serves as the interface between the user, the application software, and the computer's hardware. Two types of system software are the operating system and utility programs.

OPERATING SYSTEM   An *operating system* is a set of programs that coordinates all the activities among computer hardware devices. It provides a means for users to communicate with the computer and other software. Many of today's computers use Windows XP or Vista (Figure 1-10), which are two of Microsoft's operating systems, or Mac OS X, Apple's operating system.

When a user starts a computer, portions of the operating system load into memory from the computer's hard disk. It remains in memory while the computer is on.

FIGURE 1-10   The graphical user interface of Windows Vista.

UTILITY PROGRAM A *utility program* allows a user to perform maintenance-type tasks usually related to managing a computer, its devices, or its programs. Most operating systems include several utility programs for managing disk drives, printers, and other devices and media. You also can buy utility programs that allow you to perform additional computer management functions.

Application Software

Application software consists of programs designed to make users more productive and/or assist them with personal tasks. A widely used type of application software related to communications is a Web browser, which allows users with an Internet connection to access and view Web pages. Other popular application software includes word processing software, spreadsheet software, database software, and presentation graphics software.

Many other types of application software exist that enable users to perform a variety of tasks. These include personal information management, note taking, project management, accounting, document management, computer-aided design, desktop publishing, paint/image editing, audio and video editing, multimedia authoring, Web page authoring, personal finance, legal, tax preparation, home design/landscaping, education, reference, and entertainment (e.g., games or simulations, etc.). As shown in Figure 1-11, you can purchase application software from a store that sells computer products. Read Ethics & Issues 1-3 for a related discussion.

WEB LINK 1-6

Application Software

For more information, visit scsite.com/dc2008/ch1/weblink and then click Application Software.

ETHICS & ISSUES 1-3

Do Computer Games Do More Harm than Good?

Grand Theft Auto: San Andreas is one of today's most popular computer games. In the game, players advance through the mafia by conveying secret packages, following alleged snitches, and planting car bombs. Consumers have bought millions of copies of Grand Theft Auto. Purchasers praise the game's vivid graphics and wide range of allowable behaviors. After it was released, the game was found to contain hidden adult content accessible by using a special code. Despite investigations, the company was not fined or punished for the content. Some parents and politicians condemn the game's explicit violence and the rewards it gives players for participating in illegal acts. They fear that games like Grand Theft Auto eventually could lead to antisocial or criminal behavior. Even worse, critics fear that the game's popularity may influence future developers of computer games aimed at younger children. Despite the fears, research has shown that playing violent games has no impact on behavior or increased crime. In fact, in the time in which gaming has become popular, violent crime has decreased by 50 percent in America. Some researchers and parents note the positive aspects of gaming, such as increased dexterity for players, use of critical thinking skills to solve problems in games, meeting goals, and following rules. What impact, if any, do violent computer games or games that include unacceptable acts have on individual behavior? On balance, is computer gaming good or bad for people? Why? What other motivations might parents have who limit their children's computer gaming?

FIGURE 1-11 Stores that sell computer products have shelves stocked with software for sale.

Installing and Running Programs

The instructions in a program are stored on storage media such as a hard disk or compact disc. When purchasing software from a computer store, you typically receive a box that includes a CD(s) or DVD(s) that contains the program. You also may receive a manual or printed instructions explaining how to install and use the software.

Installing is the process of setting up software to work with the computer, printer, and other hardware components. When you buy a computer, it usually has some software pre-installed on its hard disk. This enables you to use the computer the first time you turn it on. To begin installing additional software from a CD or DVD, insert the program disc in a CD or DVD drive. The computer then copies all or part of the program from the disc to the computer's hard disk.

Once software is installed, you can use, or **run**, it. When you instruct the computer to run an installed program, the computer *loads* it, which means the program is copied from storage to memory. Once in memory, the computer can carry out, or *execute*, the instructions in the program. Figure 1-12 illustrates the steps that occur when a user installs and runs a greeting card program.

FAQ 1-4

How do I know if computer software will run on my computer?

When you buy a computer, the box or the order summary will list the computer's specifications. Similarly, when you buy software, the software box lists specifications. Your computer's specifications should be the same as or greater than the software specifications. For more information, visit scsite.com/dc2008/ch1/faq and then click Computer Software.

FIGURE 1-12 INSTALLING AND RUNNING A COMPUTER PROGRAM

Step 1: INSTALL
When you insert a greeting card program disc in the CD drive for the first time, the computer begins the procedure of installing the greeting card program on the hard disk.

Step 2: RUN
Once installed, you can instruct the computer to run the greeting card program. The computer transfers instructions from the hard disk to memory.

instructions transfer to memory

CD-ROM

Step 3: USE
The greeting card program executes. Using this program, you can create custom greeting cards.

Software Development

A *programmer*, sometimes called a computer programmer or *developer*, is someone who develops software or writes the instructions that direct the computer to process data into information. When writing instructions, a programmer must be sure the program works properly so the computer generates the desired results. Complex programs can require thousands to millions of instructions.

Programmers use a programming language or program development tool to create computer programs. Popular programming languages include C++, Java, JavaScript, Visual C#, and Visual Basic. Figure 1-13 shows some of the instructions a programmer may write to create a Web application.

Test your knowledge of pages 11 through 18 in Quiz Yourself 1-2.

QUIZ YOURSELF 1-2

Instructions: Find the true statement below. Then, rewrite the remaining false statements so they are true.

1. A resource is a collection of computers and devices connected together via communications devices and transmission media.

2. Installing is the process of setting up software to work with the computer, printer, and other hardware components.

3. Popular system software includes Web browsers, word processing software, spreadsheet software, database software, and presentation graphics software.

4. The Internet is one of the more popular services on the Web.

5. Two types of application software are the operating system and utility programs.

Quiz Yourself Online: To further check your knowledge of networks, the Internet and Web, and system software versus application software, visit scsite.com/dc2008/ch1/quiz and then click Objectives 5 – 7.

CATEGORIES OF COMPUTERS

Industry experts typically classify computers in seven categories: personal computers, mobile computers and mobile devices, game consoles, servers, mainframes, supercomputers, and embedded computers. A computer's size, speed, processing power, and price determine the category it best fits. Due to rapidly changing technology, however, the distinction among categories is not always clear-cut. Still, many people refer to these categories when discussing computers.

Figure 1-14 summarizes the seven categories of computers. The following pages discuss computers and devices that fall in each category.

FIGURE 1-13 The top figure illustrates some of the instructions a programmer writes in JavaScript to create the Web application shown in the bottom figure.

CATEGORIES OF COMPUTERS

Category	Physical Size	Number of Simultaneously Connected Users	General Price Range
Personal computers (desktop)	Fits on a desk	Usually one (can be more if networked)	Several hundred to several thousand dollars
Mobile computers and mobile devices	Fits on your lap or in your hand	Usually one	Less than a hundred dollars to several thousand dollars
Game consoles	Small box or handheld device	One to several	Several hundred dollars or less
Servers	Small cabinet	Two to thousands	Several hundred to a million dollars
Mainframes	Partial room to a full room of equipment	Hundreds to thousands	$300,000 to several million dollars
Supercomputers	Full room of equipment	Hundreds to thousands	$500,000 to several billion dollars
Embedded computers	Miniature	Usually one	Embedded in the price of the product

FIGURE 1-14 This table summarizes some of the differences among the categories of computers. These should be considered general guidelines only because of rapid changes in technology.

PERSONAL COMPUTERS

A **personal computer** is a computer that can perform all of its input, processing, output, and storage activities by itself. A personal computer contains a processor, memory, and one or more input, output, and storage devices. They also often contain a communications device.

Two popular styles of personal computers are the PC (Figure 1-15) and the Apple (Figure 1-16). The term, *PC-compatible*, refers to any personal computer based on the original IBM personal computer design. Companies such as Dell, Gateway, Hewlett-Packard, and Toshiba sell PC-compatible computers. PC and PC-compatible computers use different operating systems. PC and PC-compatible computers usually use a Windows operating system. Apple computers usually use a Macintosh operating system (Mac OS X).

Two types of personal computers are desktop computers and notebook computers. The next section discusses desktop personal computers. Notebook computers are discussed in the mobile computers section.

WEB LINK 1-7

Personal Computers

For more information, visit scsite.com/dc2008/ch1/weblink and then click Personal Computers.

FIGURE 1-15 The PC and PC-compatible computers usually use a Windows operating system.

FIGURE 1-16 Apple computers, such as the iMac, usually use a Macintosh operating system.

Desktop Computers

A **desktop computer** is designed so the system unit, input devices, output devices, and any other devices fit entirely on or under a desk or table (Figures 1-15 and 1-16 on the previous page). In many models, the system unit is a tall and narrow *tower*, which can sit on the floor vertically — if desktop space is limited.

Some desktop computers function as a server on a network. Others, such as a gaming desktop computer and Media Center PC, target a specific audience. The *gaming desktop computer* offers high-quality audio, video, and graphics with optimal performance for sophisticated single-user and networked or Internet multi-player games. A *Media Center PC* is a home entertainment desktop computer that provides a means of accessing television programs, radio broadcasts, photographs, and videos, as well as basic computing capabilities. These high-end computers cost much more than the basic desktop computer.

Another expensive, powerful desktop computer is the workstation, which is geared for work that requires intense calculations and graphics capabilities. An architect uses a workstation to design buildings and homes. A graphic artist uses a workstation to create computer-animated special effects for full-length motion pictures and video games.

FAQ 1-5

Does the term, workstation, have two meanings?

Yes. In the computer industry, a *workstation* can be a high-powered computer or a client computer on a network. For more information, visit scsite.com/dc2008/ch1/faq and then click Workstation.

MOBILE COMPUTERS AND MOBILE DEVICES

A **mobile computer** is a personal computer you can carry from place to place. Similarly, a **mobile device** is a computing device small enough to hold in your hand.

The most popular type of mobile computer is the notebook computer. The following sections discuss the notebook computer and widely used mobile devices.

Notebook Computers

A **notebook computer**, also called a **laptop computer**, is a portable, personal computer designed to fit on your lap. Notebook computers are thin and lightweight, yet they can be as powerful as the average desktop computer. Notebook computers usually are more expensive than desktop computers with equal capabilities.

On a typical notebook computer, the keyboard is on top of the system unit, and the monitor attaches to the system unit with hinges (Figure 1-17). These computers weigh on average between 2.5 and 9 pounds, which allows users easily to transport the computers from place to place. Most notebook computers can operate on batteries or a power supply or both.

FAQ 1-6

Are sales for notebook computers or desktop computers higher?

For the first time in history, notebook computer sales are consistently higher than desktop computer sales — a sure sign that we have entered an era of mobile computing. For more information, visit scsite.com/dc2008/ch1/faq and then click Computer Sales.

display

CD or DVD drive

hinge

keyboard

FIGURE 1-17   On a typical notebook computer, the keyboard is on top of the system unit, and the display attaches to the system unit with hinges.

TABLET PC Resembling a letter-sized slate, the **Tablet PC** is a special type of notebook computer that allows you to write or draw on the screen using a digital pen (Figure 1-18). With a *digital pen*, users write or draw by pressing the pen on the screen, and issue instructions to the Tablet PC by tapping on the screen. For users who prefer typing instead of handwriting, some Tablet PC designs have an attached keyboard; others allow you to connect a separate keyboard to the device. Tablet PCs also support voice input so users can enter text and issue instructions by speaking into the computer.

Tablet PCs are useful especially for taking notes in lectures, at meetings, conferences, and other forums where the standard notebook computer is not practical. With a cost of about $1,000 or more, some users may find Tablet PCs more appropriate for their needs than traditional notebook computers.

FIGURE 1-18 A Tablet PC combines the features of a traditional notebook computer with the simplicity of pencil and paper.

Mobile Devices

Mobile devices, which are small enough to carry in a pocket, usually do not have disk drives. Instead, these devices store programs and data permanently on special memory inside the system unit or on small storage media such as memory cards. You often can connect a mobile device to a personal computer to exchange information between the computer and the mobile device.

Some mobile devices are **Internet-enabled**, meaning they can connect to the Internet wirelessly. With an Internet-enabled device, users can chat, send e-mail and instant messages, and access the Web.

Three popular types of mobile devices are handheld computers, PDAs, and smart phones. Some combination mobile devices also are available, for example, a PDA/smart phone.

HANDHELD COMPUTER A **handheld computer**, sometimes referred to as an *ultra personal computer* (*uPC*), an *Ultra-Mobile PC* (*UMPC*), or a *handtop computer*, is a computer small enough to fit in one hand (Figure 1-19). Because of their reduced size, the screens on handheld computers are small. Many handheld computers communicate wirelessly with other devices or computers and also include a digital pen or stylus for input. Similar to a digital pen, a *stylus* is a small metal or plastic device that looks like a ballpoint pen but uses pressure instead of ink to write, draw, or make selections.

Some handheld computers have miniature or specialized keyboards. Many handheld computers are industry-specific and serve the needs of mobile employees, such as meter readers and parcel delivery people, whose jobs require them to move from place to place.

FIGURE 1-19 This handheld computer is a full PC that fits in your hand and weighs less than two pounds.

PDA A **PDA** (*personal digital assistant*) provides personal organizer functions such as a calendar, an appointment book, an address book, a calculator, and a notepad (Figure 1-20). Most PDAs also offer a variety of other application software such as word processing, spreadsheet, personal finance, and games.

The primary input device of a PDA is a stylus. Some PDAs have a built-in miniature keyboard. If you prefer to type on a PDA that does not have a keyboard, you can insert the PDA in a special separate keyboard. Some PDAs also support voice input and have built-in cameras.

FIGURE 1-20 PDAs provide personal information management functions as well as Internet access and telephone capabilities.

Many PDAs are Internet-enabled so users can check e-mail and access the Web. Some also provide telephone capabilities. Because of all the added features, increasingly more people are replacing their pocket-sized appointment books with PDAs or smart phones.

SMART PHONE Offering the convenience of one-handed operation, a **smart phone** is an Internet-enabled telephone that usually also provides PDA capabilities. In addition to basic telephone capabilities, a smart phone allows you to send and receive e-mail messages and access the Web. Most models have color screens and many play music and include built-in cameras so you can share photographs or videos with others as soon as you capture the image (Figure 1-21).

As smart phones and PDAs continue a trend of offering similar functions, it is becoming increasingly difficult to differentiate between the two devices. This trend, known as *convergence*, has led manufacturers to refer to PDAs and smart phones simply as *handhelds*. Some factors that affect a consumer's purchasing decision include the device's size, screen size, and capabilities of available software.

CONSOLES

A **game console** is a mobile computing device designed for single-player or multiplayer video games (Figure 1-22). Standard game consoles use a handheld controller(s) as an input device(s); a television screen as an output device; and hard disks, CDs, DVDs, and/or memory cards for storage. Weighing on average between five and nine pounds, the compact size of game consoles make them easy to use at home, in the car, in a hotel, any location that has an electrical outlet. Three popular models are Microsoft's Xbox 360, Nintendo's Wii, and Sony's PlayStation 3.

A handheld game console is small enough to in one hand, making it more portable than the standard game console. With the handheld game console, the controls, screen, and speakers are built into the device. Because of their reduced si the screens are small — three to four inches. Sor models use cartridges to store games; others use miniature type of CD or DVD. Many handheld game consoles can communicate wirelessly with other similar consoles for multiplayer gaming. Two popular models are Nintendo DS Lite and Sony's PlayStation Portable (PSP).

In addition to gaming, many console models allow users to listen to music, watch movies, an connect to the Internet. Game consoles can cost from a few hundred dollars to more than $500.

FIGURE 1-21 In addition to basic telephone functionality, smart phones allow you to check e-mail, access the Web, listen to music, and share photos and videos.

handheld game console

game consol

FIGURE 1-22
Game consoles provide hours of video game entertainment.

WEB LINK 1-8

Smart Phones

For more information, visit scsite.com/dc2008/ch1/weblink and then click Smart Phones.

SERVERS

A **server** controls access to the hardware, software, and other resources on a network and provides a centralized storage area for programs, data, and information (Figure 1-23). Servers can support from two to several thousand connected computers at the same time.

In many cases, one server accesses data, information, and programs on another server. In other cases, people use personal computers or terminals to access data, information, and programs on a server. A terminal is a device with a monitor, keyboard, and memory.

FIGURE 1-23
A server controls access to resources on a network.

MAINFRAMES

A **mainframe** is a large, expensive, powerful computer that can handle hundreds or thousands of connected users simultaneously (Figure 1-24). Mainframes store tremendous amounts of data, instructions, and information. Most major corporations use mainframes for business activities. With mainframes, large businesses are able to bill millions of customers, prepare payroll for thousands of employees, and manage thousands of items in inventory. One study reported that mainframes process more than 83 percent of transactions around the world.

Mainframes also can act as servers in a network environment. Servers and other mainframes can access data and information from a mainframe. People also can access programs on the mainframe using terminals or personal computers.

FIGURE 1-24
Mainframe computers can handle thousands of connected computers and process millions of instructions per second.

SUPERCOMPUTERS

A **supercomputer** is the fastest, most powerful computer — and the most expensive (Figure 1-25). The fastest supercomputers are capable of processing more than 135 trillion instructions in a single second. With weights that exceed 100 tons, these computers can store more than 20,000 times the data and information of an average desktop computer.

Applications requiring complex, sophisticated mathematical calculations use supercomputers. Large-scale simulations and applications in medicine, aerospace, automotive design, online banking, weather forecasting, nuclear energy research, and petroleum exploration use a supercomputer.

FIGURE 1-25 This supercomputer simulates various environmental occurrences such as global climate changes, pollution, and earthquakes.

EMBEDDED COMPUTERS

An **embedded computer** is a special-purpose computer that functions as a component in a larger product. Embedded computers are everywhere — at home, in your car, and at work. The following list identifies a variety of everyday products that contain embedded computers.

- Consumer Electronics: mobile and digital telephones, digital televisions, cameras, video recorders, DVD players and recorders, answering machines
- Home Automation Devices: thermostats, sprinkling systems, security monitoring systems, appliances, lights
- Automobiles: antilock brakes, engine control modules, airbag controller, cruise control

- Process Controllers and Robotics: remote monitoring systems, power monitors, machine controllers, medical devices
- Computer Devices and Office Machines: keyboards, printers, faxes, copiers

Because embedded computers are components in larger products, they usually are small and have limited hardware. These computers perform various functions, depending on the requirements of the product in which they reside. Embedded computers in printers, for example, monitor the amount of paper in the tray, check the ink or toner level, signal if a paper jam has occurred, and so on. Figure 1-26 shows some of the many embedded computers in cars.

Advanced airbag systems have crash-severity sensors that determine the appropriate level to inflate the airbag, reducing the chance of airbag injury in low-speed accidents.

Adaptive cruise control systems detect if cars in front of you are too close and, if necessary, adjust the vehicle's throttle, may apply brakes, and/or sound an alarm.

Tire pressure monitoring systems send warning signals if tire pressure is insufficient.

Cars equipped with wireless communications capabilities, called *telematics*, include such features as navigation systems and Internet access.

Drive-by-wire systems sense pressure on the gas pedal and communicate electronically to the engine how much and how fast to accelerate.

FIGURE 1-26 Some of the embedded computers designed to improve your safety, security, and performance in today's automobiles.

ELEMENTS OF AN INFORMATION SYSTEM

To be valuable, information must be accurate, organized, timely, accessible, useful, and cost-effective to produce. Generating information from a computer requires the following five elements:

- Hardware
- Software
- Data
- People
- Procedures

Together, these elements (hardware, software, data, people, and procedures) comprise an *information system*. Figure 1-27 shows how each of the elements of an information system in a large business might interact.

The hardware must be reliable and capable of handling the expected workload. The software must be developed carefully and tested thoroughly. The data entered into the computer must be accurate.

Most companies with mid-sized and large computers have an IT (information technology) department. Staff in the IT department should be skilled and up-to-date on the latest technology. IT staff also should train users so they understand how to use the computer properly. Today's users also work closely with IT staff in the development of computer applications that relate to their areas of work.

Finally, all the IT applications should have readily available documented procedures that address operating the computer and using its applications.

FIGURE 1-27   HOW THE ELEMENTS OF AN INFORMATION SYSTEM IN A LARGE BUSINESS MIGHT INTERACT

Step 1:
IT staff (people) develop processes (procedures) for tabulating time cards (data).

Step 2:
Employees (people) in the payroll department use a program (software) to enter the time cards (data) in the computer.

Step 3:
The computer (hardware) performs calculations required to process the payroll and stores the results on storage media such as a hard disk (hardware).

Step 4:
Paychecks, the information, print on a corporate printer (hardware).

WEB LINK 1-9

Women in Technology

For more information, visit scsite.com/ dc2008/ch1/weblink and then click Women in Technology.

WEB LINK 1-10

Minorities in Technology

For more information, visit scsite.com/ dc2008/ch1/weblink and then click Minorities in Technology.

EXAMPLES OF COMPUTER USAGE

Every day, people around the world rely on different types of computers for a variety of applications. To illustrate the range of uses for computers, this section takes you on a visual and narrative tour of five categories of users:

- Home user
- Small office/home office (SOHO) user
- Mobile user
- Power user
- Large business user

The following pages discuss the types of hardware and software required by each category of user.

Home User

In an increasing number of homes, the computer no longer is a convenience. Instead, it is a basic necessity. Each family member, or **home user**, spends time on the computer for different reasons that include budgeting and personal financial management, Web access, communications, and entertainment (Figure 1-28).

FIGURE 1-28a (personal financial management)

FIGURE 1-28b (Web access)

FIGURE 1-28c (communications)

FIGURE 1-28d (entertainment)

FIGURE 1-28 The home user spends time on a computer for a variety of reasons.

On the Internet, home users access a huge amount of information, take college classes, pay bills, manage investments, shop, listen to the radio, watch movies, read books, play games, file taxes, book airline reservations, and make telephone calls. They also communicate with others around the world through e-mail, blogs, instant messaging, and chat rooms using personal computers, PDAs, and smart phones. Home users share ideas, interests, photos, music, and videos on social networking Web sites, or online social networks (read Ethics & Issues 1-4 for a related discussion). With a digital camera, home users take photographs and then send the electronic images to others (Figure 1-29). Using a PC video camera, which costs less than $100, home users easily have live video calls with friends, family members, and others.

Many home users have a portable media player, so they can download music or podcasts, and listen to the music and/or audio at a later time through earphones attached to the player. They also usually have one or more game consoles to play video games individually or with friends and family members.

Today's homes also typically have one or more desktop computers. Many home users network multiple desktop computers throughout the house, often wirelessly. These small networks allow family members to share an Internet connection and a printer.

To meet their needs, home users have a variety of software. They type letters, homework assignments, and other documents with word processing software. Personal finance software helps the home user with personal finances, investments, and family budgets.

Other software assists with preparing taxes, keeping a household inventory, and setting up maintenance schedules.

Reference software, such as encyclopedias, medical dictionaries, or a road atlas, provides valuable information for everyone in the family. With entertainment software, the home user can play games, compose music, research genealogy, or create greeting cards. Educational software helps adults learn to speak a foreign language and youngsters to read, write, count, and spell.

FAQ 1-7

Can I watch a DVD on my computer?

Yes, in most cases. Simply insert the DVD in the computer's DVD drive. Within a few seconds, you should see the DVD begin to play on your computer's screen. If the DVD does not play, it is possible you need to run a program that starts the DVD. For more information, visit scsite.com/dc2008/ch1/faq and then click DVDs.

FIGURE 1-29 Home users take and view photographs on a digital camera.

ETHICS & ISSUES 1-4

Who Should Monitor Online Social Networks?

In recent years, online social networks such as MySpace exploded as a new means of communicating and socializing for teens and young adults. Not surprisingly, the problems associated with these online networks mirror some problems in society in general. Problems include bullying, smear campaigns against individuals, and inappropriate contact between adults and minors. Recently, a high-school-aged girl secretly left the country with the intent of marrying an adult in the foreign country whom she met on a social networking site. Fortunately, authorities in the foreign country intercepted her at the airport and sent her home. Some parents claim that the social networking sites should better monitor and report inappropriate behavior. While the sites have stepped up monitoring, they often claim that they are just providing a forum, and parents and authorities should be responsible for the inappropriate actions of its members. Many teens and young adults feel that the problems are simply a matter of personal responsibility and using care when online. Should providers of online social networks be required to monitor and stop inappropriate or socially unacceptable behavior? Why or why not? What role should parents play in overseeing a child's involvement in online social networks? Why? Should police or other government authorities be responsible for maintaining order in online social networks in the same way they are charged with maintaining order in society in general? Why or why not?

Small Office/Home Office User

Computers assist small business and home office users in managing their resources effectively. A **small office/home office** (*SOHO*) includes any company with fewer than 50 employees, as well as the self-employed who work from home. Small offices include local law practices, accounting firms, travel agencies, and florists. SOHO users typically have a desktop computer to perform some or all of their duties. Many also have PDAs or smart phones to manage appointments and contact information.

SOHO users access the Internet — often wirelessly — to look up information such as addresses, directions (Figure 1-30a), postal codes, flights, and package shipping rates or to make telephone calls. Nearly all SOHO users communicate with others through e-mail.

Many are entering the *e-commerce* arena and conduct business on the Web. Their Web sites advertise products and services and may provide a means for taking orders. Small business Web sites sometimes use a *Web cam*, which is a video camera that displays its output on a Web page. A Web cam allows SOHO users to show the world a live view of some aspect of their business.

To save money on hardware and software, small offices often network their computers. For example, the small office connects one printer to a network for all employees to share.

SOHO users often have basic business software such as word processing and spreadsheet software to assist with document preparation and finances (Figure 1-30b). They are likely to use other industry-specific types of software. A candy shop, for example, will have software that allows for taking orders and payments, updating inventory, and paying vendors.

FIGURE 1-30a   (Web access)

FIGURE 1-30b   (spreadsheet program)

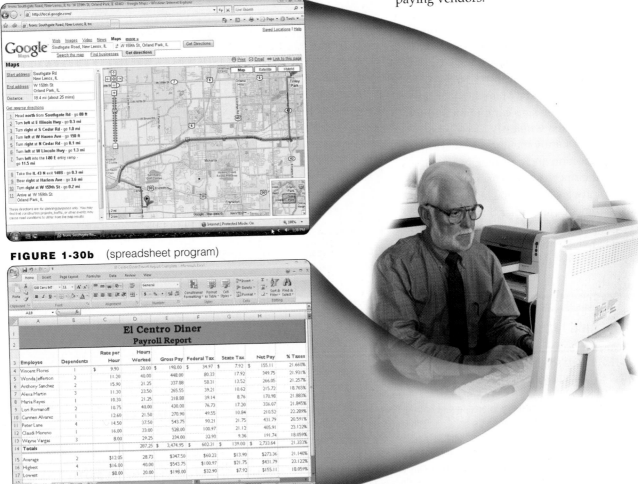

FIGURE 1-30   People with a home office and employees in small offices typically use a personal computer for some or all of their duties.

Mobile User

Today, businesses and schools are expanding to serve people across the country and around the world. Thus, increasingly more employees and students are **mobile users**, who work on a computer while away from a main office or school (Figure 1-31). Examples of mobile users are sales representatives, real estate agents, insurance agents, meter readers, package delivery people, journalists, consultants, and students.

Mobile users often have a notebook computer, Tablet PC, Internet-enabled PDA, or smart phone. With these computers and devices, the mobile user connects to other computers on a network or the Internet, often wirelessly accessing services such as e-mail and the Web. Mobile users can transfer information between their mobile device and another computer, such as one at the main office or school.

The mobile user works with basic business software such as word processing and spreadsheet software. With presentation graphics software, the mobile user can create and deliver presentations to a large audience by connecting a mobile computer or device to a video projector that displays the presentation on a full screen. Many scaled-down programs are available for mobile devices such as PDAs and smart phones.

FIGURE 1-31 Mobile users have notebook computers, Tablet PCs, PDAs, and smart phones so they can work, do homework, send messages, or connect to the Internet while away from a wired connection.

Power User

Another category of user, called a **power user**, requires the capabilities of a workstation or other type of powerful computer (Figure 1-32). Examples of power users include engineers, scientists, architects, desktop publishers, and graphic artists. Power users often work with *multimedia*, combining text, graphics, audio, and video into one application. These users need computers with extremely fast processors because of the nature of their work.

The power user's workstation contains industry-specific software. For example, engineers and architects use software to draft and design floor plans, mechanical assemblies, or vehicles. A desktop publisher uses software to prepare marketing literature such as newsletters, brochures, and annual reports. A geologist uses software to study the earth's surface. This software usually is expensive because of its specialized design.

Power users exist in all types of businesses. Some work at home. Their computers typically have network connections and Internet access.

FIGURE 1-32 This graphic artist uses a powerful computer to edit video.

Large Business User

A large business has hundreds or thousands of employees or customers that work in or do business with offices across a region, the country, or the world. Each employee or customer who uses a computer in the large business is a **large business user** (Figure 1-33).

Many large companies use the words, *enterprise computing*, to refer to the huge network of computers that meets their diverse computing needs. The network facilitates communications among employees at all locations. Users access the network of servers or mainframes through desktop computers, mobile computers, PDAs, and smart phones.

Large businesses use computers and the computer network to process high volumes of transactions in a single day. Although they may differ in size and in the products or services offered, all generally use computers for basic business activities. For example, they bill millions of customers, prepare payroll for thousands of employees, and manage thousands of items in inventory. Some large businesses use blogs to open communications among employees, customers, and/or vendors.

Large businesses typically have e-commerce Web sites, allowing customers and vendors to conduct business online. The Web site also showcases products, services, and other company information. Customers, vendors, and other interested parties can access this information on the Web. Once an order is placed, computers update inventory records to reflect goods sold and goods purchased.

The marketing department in a large business uses desktop publishing software to prepare marketing literature. The accounting department uses software for accounts receivable, accounts payable, billing, general ledger, and payroll activities.

The employees in the *information technology (IT) department* keep the computers and the network running. They determine when the company requires new hardware or software.

Large business users work with word processing, spreadsheet, database, and presentation graphics software. They also may use calendar programs to post their schedules on the network. And, they might use PDAs or smart phones to maintain contact information. E-mail and Web browsers enable communications among employees, vendors, and customers.

Some large businesses place kiosks in public locations. A *kiosk* is a freestanding computer, usually with a touch screen (Figure 1-34). Some kiosks provide information such as maps, while others are interactive, allowing users to place orders, search records, print tickets, vote, and complete registrations.

Many employees of large businesses telecommute. **Telecommuting** is a work arrangement in which employees work away from a company's standard workplace and often communicate with the office through the computer. Employees who telecommute have flexible work schedules so they can combine work and personal responsibilities, such as child care.

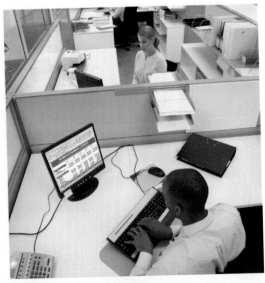

FIGURE 1-33 A large business can have hundreds or thousands of users in offices across a region, the country, or the world.

FIGURE 1-34 Airline travelers check in using this self-service kiosk.

Putting It All Together

The previous pages discussed the hardware and software requirements for the home user, small office/home office user, mobile user, power user, and large business user. The table in Figure 1-35 summarizes these requirements.

CATEGORIES OF USERS

User	Hardware	Software
HOME	• Desktop or notebook computer • PDA or smart phone • Game consoles	• Business (e.g., word processing) • Personal information manager • Personal finance, online banking, tax preparation • Web browser • E-mail, blogging, instant messaging, and chat rooms • Internet telephone calls • Photo editing • Reference (e.g., encyclopedias, medical dictionaries, road atlas) • Entertainment (e.g., games, music composition, greeting cards) • Educational (e.g., tutorials, children's math and reading software)
SMALL OFFICE/ HOME OFFICE	• Desktop computer • PDA or smart phone • Shared network printer	• Business (e.g., word processing, spreadsheet, database) • Personal information manager • Company specific (e.g., accounting, legal reference) • Network management • Web browser • E-mail • Internet telephone calls
MOBILE	• Notebook computer equipped with a wireless modem, or a Tablet PC • Video projector • PDA or smart phone	• Business (e.g., word processing, spreadsheet, note taking, presentation graphics) • Personal information manager • Web browser • E-mail
POWER	• Workstation or other powerful computer with multimedia capabilities • PDA or smart phone	• Desktop publishing • Multimedia authoring • Computer-aided design • Photo, audio, and video editing • Personal information manager • Web browser • E-mail
LARGE BUSINESS	• Server or mainframe • Desktop or notebook computer • Industry-specific handheld computer • PDA or smart phone • Kiosk	• Business (e.g., word processing, spreadsheet, database, presentation graphics) • Personal information manager • Accounting • Network management • Web browser • E-mail • Blogging

FIGURE 1-35 Today, computers are used by millions of people for work tasks, school assignments, and leisure activities. Different computer users require different kinds of hardware and software to meet their needs effectively.

COMPUTER APPLICATIONS IN SOCIETY

The computer has changed society today as much as the industrial revolution changed society in the eighteenth and nineteenth centuries.

People interact directly with computers in fields such as education, finance, government, health care, science, publishing, travel, and manufacturing. In addition, they can reap the benefits from breakthroughs and advances in these fields. The following pages describe how computers have made a difference in people's interactions with these disciplines. Read Looking Ahead 1-2 for a look at the next generation of computer applications in society.

LOOKING AHEAD 1-2

Robots Perform Mundane, Dangerous Tasks

Playwright Karel Capek created the name, robot, for his humanoid machines that turned against their creators. Today, mobile, intelligent robots perform tasks typically reserved for humans in a $5 billion global market.

Tomorrow's practical and versatile robots will serve a variety of personal and industrial needs. By 2010, the expected $17 billion market should include products to care for senior citizens, transport people in major cities, and perform hundreds of thousands of mobile utility jobs, such as picking up and delivering items.

The Anna Konda is a snakelike robot built by Norway's Foundation for Industrial and Scientific Research that can maneuver over varied terrain. Engineers envision its possible uses include fighting fires, locating and bringing oxygen to earthquake victims buried under debris, and performing maintenance on underwater oil rigs. For more information, visit scsite.com/dc2008/ch1/looking and then click Robots.

Education

Education is the process of acquiring knowledge. In the traditional model, people learn from other people such as parents, teachers, and employers. Many forms of printed material such as books and manuals are used as learning tools. Today, educators also are turning to computers to assist with education (Figure 1-36).

Many schools and companies equip labs and classrooms with computers. Some schools require students to have a notebook computer or PDA to access the school's network or Internet wirelessly. To promote education by computer, many vendors offer substantial student discounts on software.

Sometimes, the delivery of education occurs at one place while the learning occurs at other locations. For example, students can take a class on the Web. Some classes are blended; that is, part of the learning occurs in a classroom and the other part occurs on the Web. More than 70 percent of colleges offer some type of distance learning classes. A few even offer entire degrees online.

FIGURE 1-36   In some schools, students have notebook computers on their desks during classroom lectures.

Finance

Many people and companies use computers to help manage their finances. Some use finance software to balance checkbooks, pay bills, track personal income and expenses, manage investments, and evaluate financial plans. This software usually includes a variety of online services. For example, computer users can track investments and do online banking. With **online banking**, users access account balances, pay bills, and copy monthly transactions from the bank's computer right into their personal computers.

Many financial institutions' Web sites also offer online banking (Figure 1-37). When using a Web site instead of finance software on your computer, all your account information is stored on the bank's computer. The advantage is you can access your financial records from anywhere in the world.

Investors often use **online investing** to buy and sell stocks and bonds — without using a broker. With online investing, the transaction fee for each trade usually is much less than when trading through a broker.

Government

A government provides society with direction by making and administering policies. To provide citizens with up-to-date information, most government offices have Web sites. People in the United States access government Web sites to file taxes, apply for permits and licenses, pay parking tickets, buy stamps, report crimes, apply for financial aid, and renew vehicle registrations and driver's licenses.

Employees of government agencies use computers as part of their daily routine. North American 911 call centers use computers to dispatch calls for fire, police, and medical assistance. Military and other agency officials use the U.S. Department of Homeland Security's network of information about domestic security threats to help protect against terrorist attacks. Law enforcement officers have online access to the FBI's National Crime Information Center (NCIC) through in-vehicle notebook computers, fingerprint scanners, and PDAs (Figure 1-38). The NCIC contains more than 52 million missing persons and criminal records, including names, fingerprints, parole/probation records, mug shots, and other information. Read Ethics & Issues 1-5 for a related discussion.

FIGURE 1-37   Many financial institutions' Web sites offer online banking.

FIGURE 1-38   Law enforcement officials have in-vehicle computers and PDAs to access emergency, missing person, and criminal records in computer networks in local, state, and federal agencies.

ETHICS & ISSUES 1-5

Should the Government Be Able to Perform Surveillance on All Electronic Communications?

In the years following the terrorist attacks of September 11, 2001, the federal government began several electronic surveillance initiatives. Some activists say that the words snooping or eavesdropping better describe the programs. By law, government agencies are prohibited from spying on United States citizens. In special cases, agencies such as the CIA (Central Intelligence Agency) or NSA (National Security Agency) can obtain a warrant to monitor communications between a citizen and a foreigner. One controversial program called the Terrorist Surveillance Program allowed warrantless monitoring of electronic communications, such as phone calls and Internet communications. Another program involved the gathering of telephone records of tens of millions of Americans who were not suspects in any criminal acts. This program may have involved what some activists call fishing techniques, that is, gathering huge amounts of data and then sifting through it for patterns that may suggest illegal activity. Proponents of the programs say that they are necessary to protect the public and should be allowed in a time of war. Detractors of the programs claim that the programs are unconstitutional, are ineffective, and violate civil liberties. How much leeway should the government have when it comes to listening in on electronic communications? Why? Given the threat posed by terrorists, should the government be able to engage in warrantless searches of electronic communications? Why or why not? Who should oversee the government's behavior in these activities?

Health Care

Nearly every area of health care uses computers. Whether you are visiting a family doctor for a regular checkup, having lab work or an outpatient test, or being rushed in for emergency surgery, the medical staff around you will be using computers for various purposes:

- Hospitals and doctors use computers to maintain patient records.
- Computers monitor patients' vital signs in hospital rooms and at home.
- Computers and computerized devices assist doctors, nurses, and technicians with medical tests (Figure 1-39).
- Doctors use the Web and medical software to assist with researching and diagnosing health conditions.
- Doctors use e-mail to correspond with patients.
- Pharmacists use computers to file insurance claims.
- Surgeons implant computerized devices, such as pacemakers, that allow patients to live longer.
- Surgeons use computer-controlled devices to provide them with greater precision during operations, such as for laser eye surgery and robot-assisted heart surgery.

Many Web sites provide up-to-date medical, fitness, nutrition, or exercise information. These Web sites also maintain lists of doctors and dentists to help you find the one that suits your needs. They have chat rooms, so you can talk to others diagnosed with similar conditions. Some Web sites even allow you to order prescriptions online.

An exciting development in health care is telemedicine, which is a form of long-distance health care. Through *telemedicine*, health-care professionals in separate locations conduct live conferences on the computer. For example, a doctor at one location can have a conference with a doctor at another location to discuss a bone X-ray. Live images of each doctor, along with the X-ray, are displayed on each doctor's computer.

Science

All branches of science, from biology to astronomy to meteorology, use computers to assist them with collecting, analyzing, and modeling data. Scientists also use the Internet to communicate with colleagues around the world.

Breakthroughs in surgery, medicine, and treatments often result from scientists' use of computers. Tiny computers now imitate functions of the central nervous system, retina of the eye, and cochlea of the ear. A cochlear implant allows a deaf person to listen. Electrodes implanted in the brain stop tremors associated with Parkinson's disease. Cameras small enough to swallow — sometimes called a camera pill — take pictures inside your body to detect polyps, cancer, and other abnormalities (Figure 1-40).

A *neural network* is a system that attempts to imitate the behavior of the human brain. Scientists create neural networks by connecting thousands of processors together much like the neurons in the brain are connected. The capability of a personal computer to recognize spoken words is a direct result of scientific experimentation with neural networks.

FIGURE 1-39 Doctors, nurses, technicians, and other medical staff use computers while performing tests on patients.

FIGURE 1-40 HOW A CAMERA PILL WORKS

Step 1:
A patient swallows a tiny capsule that contains a miniature disposable camera, lights, a transmitter, and batteries. The camera is positioned at the clear end of the capsule.

Step 2:
As the capsule moves through the inside of the patient's body, the camera snaps about 50,000 pictures, which are transmitted to a recording device worn as a belt on the patient's waist.

Step 3:
The doctor transfers the data on the recording device to a computer so it can be processed and analyzed.

Publishing

Publishing is the process of making works available to the public. These works include books, magazines, newspapers, music, film, and video. Special software assists graphic designers in developing pages that include text, graphics, and photographs; artists in composing and enhancing songs; filmmakers in creating and editing film; and journalists and mobile users in capturing and modifying video clips.

Many publishers make their works available online (Figure 1-41). Some Web sites allow you to copy the work, such as a book or music, to your desktop computer, handheld computer, PDA, or smart phone.

FIGURE 1-41 Many magazine and newspaper publishers make the content of their publications available online.

Travel

Whether traveling by car or airplane, your goal is to arrive safely at your destination. As you make the journey, you may interact with some of the latest technology.

Vehicles manufactured today often include some type of onboard navigation system. Many mobile devices such as PDAs and smart phones have built-in navigation systems. Some mobile users prefer to carry specialized hand-held navigation devices (Figure 1-42).

In preparing for a trip, you may need to reserve a car, hotel, or flight. Many Web sites offer these services to the public. For example, you can order airline tickets on the Web. If you plan to drive somewhere and are unsure of the road to take to your destination, you can print directions and a map from the Web.

WEB LINK 1-11

Handheld Navigation Devices

For more information, visit scsite.com/dc2008/ch1/weblink and then click Handheld Navigation Devices.

FAQ 1-8

Do home users book travel on the Web?

Yes, it is estimated that nearly 22 percent ($53 billion) of the travel industry's revenues stem from leisure travel bookings. As shown in the chart, computer users of all ages visit travel agency Web sites. For more information, visit scsite.com/dc2008/ch1/faq and then click Travel Bookings.

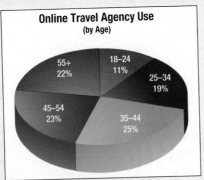

Online Travel Agency Use
(by Age)

- 18–24 11%
- 25–34 19%
- 35–44 25%
- 45–54 23%
- 55+ 22%

Source: The ClickZ Network

Manufacturing

Computer-aided manufacturing (*CAM*) refers to the use of computers to assist with manufacturing processes such as fabrication and assembly. Industries use CAM to reduce product development costs, shorten a product's time to market, and stay ahead of the competition.

Often, robots carry out processes in a CAM environment. CAM is used by a variety of industries, including oil drilling, power generation, food production, and automobile manufacturing. Automobile plants, for example, have an entire line of industrial robots that assemble a car (Figure 1-43).

Special computers on the shop floor record actual labor, material, machine, and computer time used to manufacture a particular product. The computers process this data and automatically update inventory, production, payroll, and accounting records on the company's network.

FIGURE 1-43 Automotive factories use industrial robots to weld car bodies.

FIGURE 1-42 This handheld navigation device gives users turn-by-turn voice-prompted directions to a destination.

Test your knowledge of pages 18 through 36 in Quiz Yourself 1-3.

QUIZ YOURSELF 1-3

Instructions: Find the true statement below. Then, rewrite the remaining false statements so they are true.

1. A desktop computer is a portable, personal computer designed to fit on your lap.

2. A personal computer contains a processor, memory, and one or more input, output, and storage devices.

3. Each large business user spends time on the computer for different reasons that include budgeting and personal financial management, Web access, communications, and entertainment.

4. A home user requires the capabilities of a workstation or other powerful computer.

5. Mainframes are the fastest, most powerful computers — and the most expensive.

6. The elements of an information system are hardware, e-mail, data, people, and the Internet.

7. With embedded computers, users access account balances, pay bills, and copy monthly transactions from the bank's computer right into their personal computers.

Quiz Yourself Online: To further check your knowledge of categories of computers, information system elements, computer users, and computer applications in society, visit scsite.com/dc2008/ch1/quiz and then click Objectives 8 – 11.

CHAPTER SUMMARY

Chapter 1 introduced you to basic computer concepts such as what a computer is, how it works, and its advantages and disadvantages. You learned about the components of a computer. Next, the chapter discussed networks, the Internet, and computer software. The many different categories of computers, computer users, and computer applications in society also were presented.

This chapter is an overview. Many of the terms and concepts introduced will be discussed further in later chapters. For a history of hardware and software developments, read the Timeline 2008 that follows this chapter.

CAREER CORNER   Personal Computer Salesperson

When you decide to buy or upgrade a personal computer, the most important person with whom you interact probably will be a personal computer salesperson. This individual will be a valuable resource to you in providing the information and expertise you need to select a computer that meets your requirements.

Computer manufacturers and retailers that sell several types of personal computers need competent salespeople. A *personal computer salesperson* must be computer literate and have a specific knowledge of the computers he or she sells. The salesperson also must have a working knowledge of computer peripherals (printers, scanners, cameras, etc.). In addition, a successful salesperson has a friendly, outgoing personality that helps customers feel comfortable. Through open-ended questions, the salesperson can determine a customer's needs and level of experience. With this information, the salesperson can choose the best computer for the customer and explain the features of the computer in language the customer will understand. Most computer salespeople also can recommend a qualified installer for your computer or qualified service technician.

Computer salespeople typically have at least a high school diploma. Before reaching the sales floor, however, salespeople usually complete extensive company training programs. These programs often consist of self-directed, self-paced Web-training classes. Most salespeople also participate in training updates, often on a monthly basis.

Personal computer salespeople generally earn a guaranteed amount plus a commission for each sale. A computer salesperson can earn about $45,000 a year. Top salespeople can be among a company's more highly compensated employees, earning in excess of $90,000 including commissions. For more information, visit scsite.com/dc2008/ch1/careers and then click Personal Computer Salesperson.

High-Tech Talk

ANALOG VERSUS DIGITAL: MAKING THE CONVERSION

Data is processed in one of two ways: analog or digital. People generally process *analog* data — that is, continuous wave patterns. The sight and sound of a traveling subway car transmits to your eyes and ears as light and sound waves, or smooth up-and-down patterns (Figure 1-44a). A computer, by contrast, is *digital*, which means computers process data in two discrete states: positive (on, or 1) and non-positive (off, or 0) as shown in Figure 1-44b. The 1 and 0 represent the two digits used by the binary number system. While this system is at the heart of digital computing, binary digital impulses appear as long strings of 1s and 0s.

If sound and light waves are analog and a computer is digital, how does a computer record audio clips, play music, or show a movie? How can a digital computer use an analog telephone line to dial up to access the Internet?

The key lies in analog-to-digital and digital-to-analog conversions. For example, the computer allows you to record sounds and playback sounds. The computer performs these conversions to record a digital audio clip of your analog voice. The microphone, which is an analog input source, connects directly to the computer. The diaphragm in the microphone converts the analog sound waves into an analog electrical signal. This signal flows to the computer's *analog-to-digital converter (ADC)*, which converts the signal into digital data. The digital data flows to the *digital signal processor (DSP)*, compressing the data to save space. Finally, the compressed data is stored in an audio file format.

To play a recorded sound, the computer reverses the process. The processor retrieves and sends the digital data to the DSP to be decompressed. The DSP sends the decompressed digital data to the computer's *digital-to-analog converter (DAC)*, which converts the digital data back to an analog voltage for output via a speaker or headphones. In other words, a DAC takes that long binary number string of 1s and 0s and turns it into an electronic signal that the sound output devices can decode and use.

Similarly, a video card allows you to record a video or play a movie on a DVD. A camera and microphone capture and send the analog picture and sound signals to a video card. The video card's ADC converts the signals into digital data. The digital data is compressed and saved in a file format such as AVI (audio/video interleave) or MPEG (Moving Picture Experts Group). When playing a movie, the computer decompresses and separates the video and audio data. It then sends the signals to the video card's DAC. The DAC translates the digital data into analog signals and sends them to the monitor and speakers, where they are displayed as your movie.

The modem in a computer also links the analog and digital worlds. When using a dial-up modem, the computer does not transmit digital data directly across analog telephone lines. Instead, the modem converts the computer's digital signals to analog signals (called *modulation*) to be sent over telephone lines. When the analog signal reaches its destination, another modem recreates the original digital signal (*demodulation*). This allows the receiving computer to process the data. The next time you dial up using a modem, pick up the telephone. The loud, screeching noise you hear is the sound of digital data after being converted to analog sound waves. For more information, visit scsite.com/dc2008/ch1/tech and then click Analog versus Digital.

FIGURE 1-44a (analog signal)

FIGURE 1-44b (digital signal)

FIGURE 1-44 Analog versus digital signals.

Companies on the Cutting Edge

DELL
DIRECT BUSINESS COMPUTER MANUFACTURER

As a leading manufacturer of personal computers, *Dell* prides itself on its direct approach to computer sales. The company hosts one of the world's largest volume e-commerce Web sites where customers can configure and price computers and electronic components, order systems, and track their orders online.

Founded by Michael Dell in 1984, the company sells more computers globally than any computer company, placing it 25th on the FORTUNE 500.

The company set the industry standard for global recycling in 2006 when it provided free recycling of any Dell product for consumers throughout the world. Dell also has partnered with the National Cristina Foundation to distribute donated equipment to disabled and economically disadvantaged children and adults. For more information, visit scsite.com/dc2008/ch1/companies and then click Dell.

APPLE COMPUTER
INTRODUCING INNOVATIVE TECHNOLOGIES

Millions of computer users in more than 120 countries loyally use *Apple Computer*'s hardware and software with a passion usually reserved for sports teams and musical groups.

Steven Jobs and Stephen Wozniak founded Apple in 1976 when they marketed the Apple I, a circuit board they had developed in Jobs's garage. In 1977, Apple Computer incorporated and introduced the Apple II, the first mass-marketed personal computer. Apple introduced the Macintosh product line in 1984, which featured a graphical user interface.

Under Jobs's direction as CEO, Apple introduced award-winning desktop and notebook computers, the OS X operating system, iLife, and professional applications. The iPod is the world's most popular portable media player, and the iTunes Music Store is the number one online music store. More than 70 percent of 2007-model U.S. vehicles offer iPod integration. For more information, visit scsite.com/dc2008/ch1/companies and then click Apple Computer.

Technology Trailblazers

BILL GATES
MICROSOFT'S FOUNDER

Bill Gates, the founder of Microsoft Corporation, suggests that college students should learn how to learn by getting the best education they can. Because he is considered by many as the most powerful person in the computing industry, it might be wise to listen to him.

Gates learned to program computers when he was 13. Early in his career, he developed the BASIC programming language for the MITS Altair, one of the first microcomputers. He founded Microsoft in 1975 with Paul Allen, and five years later, they provided the first operating system, called MS-DOS, for the IBM PC. Today, Microsoft's Windows and Office products dominate the software market.

In July 2008, Gates plans to step out of his day-to-day role in the company. He will continue as chairman and advisor while devoting more time to his philanthropic efforts. For more information, visit scsite.com/dc2008/ch1/people and then click Bill Gates.

ANNE MULCAHY
XEROX CEO

Color printing and consulting services are the two areas where the Xerox Corporation can make a difference, according to *Anne Mulcahy*, the company's CEO and chairman of the board. She should know the nature of the business, having started her career with the Stamford, Connecticut-based corporation more than 30 years ago as a field sales representative.

One of Mulcahy's first decisions after landing the top job in 2001 was eliminating the corporation's tagline, "The Document Company." She believes the company's name, standing solo, speaks for itself in the printing, copying, and services worlds. Her ethical and values-based leadership decisions to revamp the company have revolved around Xerox's roots of innovation and customer care. She is a member of the boards of directors of Target Corporation, Citigroup, and Catalyst, a not-for-profit organization supporting women in business. For more information, visit scsite.com/dc2008/ch1/people and then click Anne Mulcahy.

Chapter Review

The Chapter Review section summarizes the concepts presented in this chapter. To listen to the audio version of this Chapter Review, visit scsite.com/dc2008/ch1/review. To obtain help from other students regarding any subject in this chapter, visit scsite.com/dc2008/ch1/forum and post your thoughts or questions.

(1) Why Is Computer Literacy Important? **Computer literacy** involves having knowledge and understanding of computers and their uses. As computers become more a part of everyday life, many people believe that computer literacy is vital to success.

(2) What Is a Computer? A **computer** is an electronic device, operating under the control of instructions stored in its own memory, that can accept data, process the data according to specified rules, produce results, and store the results for future use.

(3) What Are the Components of a Computer? The electric, electronic, and mechanical components of a computer, or **hardware**, include input devices, output devices, a system unit, storage devices, and communications devices. An **input device** allows you to enter data or instructions into a computer. An **output device** conveys information to one or more people. The **system unit** is a case that contains the electronic components of a computer that are used to process data. A **storage device** records and/or retrieves items to and from **storage media**. A **communications device** enables a computer to send and receive data, instructions, and information to and from one or more computers.

(4) What Are the Advantages and Disadvantages of Using Computers? Computers have the advantages of speed, reliability, consistency, storage, and communications. They perform operations at incredibly fast speeds, are dependable and reliable, consistently generate error-free results, can store enormous amounts of data, and can share processing with other computers. Disadvantages of computers relate to the violation of privacy, public safety, the impact on the labor force, health risks, and the impact on the environment.

connect Visit scsite.com/dc2008/ch1/quiz or click the Quiz Yourself button. Click Objectives 1 – 4.

(5) What Is the Purpose of a Network? A **network** is a collection of computers and devices connected together, often wirelessly, via communications devices and transmission media. Networks allow computers to share *resources*, such as hardware, software, data, and information.

(6) How Are the Internet and World Wide Web Used? The **Internet** is a worldwide collection of networks that connects millions of businesses, government agencies, educational institutions, and individuals. People use the Internet to communicate with and meet other people, access news and information, shop for goods and services, bank and invest, take classes, for entertainment and leisure, download music and video, and share information. The **Web**, short for World Wide Web, is a global library of documents containing information that is available to anyone connected to the Internet.

(7) How Is System Software Different from Application Software? **Software**, also called a **program**, is a series of instructions that tells the computer what to do and how to do it. **System software** consists of the programs that control or maintain the operations of a computer and its devices. Two types of system software are the *operating system*, which coordinates activities among computer hardware devices, and *utility programs*, which perform maintenance-type tasks usually related to managing a computer, its devices, or its programs. **Application software** assists users with personal tasks. Popular application software includes Web browsers, word processing software, spreadsheet software, database software, and presentation graphics software.

connect Visit scsite.com/dc2008/ch1/quiz or click the Quiz Yourself button. Click Objectives 5 – 7.

Chapter Review

⑧ What Are the Categories of Computers? Industry experts typically classify computers in seven categories: personal computers, mobile computers and mobile devices, game consoles, servers, mainframes, supercomputers, and embedded computers. A **personal computer** is a computer that can perform all of its input, processing, output, and storage activities by itself. A **mobile computer** is a personal computer you can carry from place to place, and a **mobile device** is a computing device small enough to hold in your hand. A **game console** is a mobile computing device designed for single-player or multiplayer video games. A **server** controls access to the hardware, software, and other resources on a network and provides a centralized storage area for programs, data, and information. A **mainframe** is a large, expensive, powerful computer that can handle hundreds or thousands of connected users simultaneously and can store tremendous amounts of data, instructions, and information. A **supercomputer** is the fastest, most powerful, and most expensive computer and is used for applications requiring complex, sophisticated mathematical calculations. An **embedded computer** is a special-purpose computer that functions as a component in a larger product.

⑨ What Are the Elements of an Information System? An *information system* combines hardware, software, data, people, and procedures to produce timely and useful information. People in an *information technology (IT) department* develop procedures for processing data. Following these procedures, people use hardware and software to enter the data into a computer. Software processes the data and directs the computer hardware to store changes on storage media and produce information in a desired form.

⑩ What Are the Types of Computer Users? Computer users can be separated into five categories: home user, small office/home office user, mobile user, power user, and large business user. A **home user** is a family member who uses a computer for a variety of reasons, such as budgeting and personal financial management, Web access, communications, and entertainment. A **small office/home office** (*SOHO*) user is a small company or self-employed individual who works from home. SOHO users access the Internet to look up information and use basic business software and sometimes industry-specific software. **Mobile users** are employees and students who work on a computer while away from a main office or school. A **power user** uses a workstation or other powerful computer to work with industry-specific software. Power users exist in all types of businesses. A **large business user** works in a company with many employees and uses a computer and computer network to process high volumes of transactions.

⑪ What Computer Applications Are Used in Society? People interact directly with computers in fields such as education, finance, government, health care, science, publishing, travel, and manufacturing. In education, students use computers and software to assist with learning or take distance learning classes. In finance, people use computers for **online banking** and **online investing**. Government offices have Web sites to provide citizens with up-to-date information, and government employees use computers as part of their daily routines. In health care, computers are used to maintain patient records, monitor patients, assist with medical tests and research, correspond with patients, file insurance claims, provide greater precision during operations, and as implants. All branches of science use computers to assist with collecting, analyzing, and modeling data and to communicate with colleagues around the world. Publishers use computers to assist in designing pages and make the content of their works available online. Many vehicles use some type of online navigation system to help people travel more quickly and safely. Manufacturers use **computer-aided manufacturing** (*CAM*) to assist with manufacturing processes.

Connect
Visit scsite.com/dc2008/ch1/quiz or click the Quiz Yourself button. Click Objectives 8 – 11.

Quizzes and Learning Games

Computer Genius
Crossword Puzzle
DC Track and Field
Practice Test
Quiz Yourself
Wheel of Terms
You're Hired!

Exercises

Case Studies
Chapter Review
Checkpoint
▸ Key Terms
Learn How To
Learn It Online
Web Research

Beyond the Book

Career Corner
Companies
FAQs
High-Tech Talk
Looking Ahead
Making Use of the Web
Trailblazers
Web Links

Features

Chapter Forum
Install Computer
Lab Exercises
Maintain Computer
Tech News
Timeline 2008

Key Terms

You should know the Primary Terms and be familiar with the Secondary Terms. Use the list below to help focus your study. To further enhance your understanding of the Key Terms in this chapter, visit scsite.com/dc2008/ch1/terms. See an example of and a definition for each term, and access current and additional information about the term from the Web.

Primary Terms

(shown in bold-black characters in the chapter)

application software (16)
communications device (9)
computer (6)
computer literacy (5)
computer-aided manufacturing (36)
data (6)
desktop computer (20)
embedded computer (24)
FAQ (6)
game console (22)
graphical user interface (GUI) (15)
handheld computer (21)
hardware (7)
home user (26)
information (6)
input device (7)
installing (17)
Internet (12)
Internet-enabled (21)
laptop computer (20)
large business user (30)
mainframe (23)
mobile computer (20)
mobile device (20)
mobile users (29)
network (11)
notebook computer (20)
online (11)
online banking (32)

online investing (33)
output device (8)
PDA (21)
personal computer (19)
photo sharing community (14)
power user (29)
program (15)
run (17)
server (23)
small office/home office (28)
smart phone (22)
social networking Web site (14)
software (15)
storage device (8)
storage media (8)
supercomputer (23)
system software (15)
system unit (8)
Tablet PC (21)
telecommuting (30)
user (9)
Web (12)
Web page (12)

Secondary Terms

(shown in italic characters in the chapter)

blog (14)
CAM (36)
convergence (22)
developer (18)
digital pen (21)
e-commerce (28)
enterprise computing (30)
execute (17)
gaming desktop computer (20)
garbage in, garbage out (10)
handhelds (22)
handtop computer (21)
icon (15)
information processing cycle (6)
information system (25)
information technology (IT) department (30)
instructions (6)
kiosk (30)
loads (17)
Media Center PC (20)
memory (8)
multimedia (29)
neural network (34)
operating system (15)
PC-compatible (19)
personal digital assistant (21)
podcast (14)
processor (8)
programmer (18)

publish (14)
resources (11)
SOHO (28)
stylus (21)
telematics (24)
telemedicine (34)
tower (20)
ultra personal computer (uPC) (21)
Ultra-Mobile PC (UMPC) (21)
utility program (16)
video blog (14)
vodcast (14)
Web cam (28)

Checkpoint

Use the Checkpoint exercises to check your knowledge level of the chapter. The Beyond the Book exercises will help broaden your understanding of the concepts presented in this chapter. To complete the Checkpoint exercises interactively, visit scsite.com/dc2008/ch1/check.

Label the Figure

Identify these common computer hardware components.

a. card reader/writer (storage)

b. CD/DVD drive (storage)

c. portable media player (output)

d. digital camera (input)

e. external hard disk (storage)

f. internal hard disk drive (storage)

g. keyboard (input)

h. microphone (input)

i. modem (communications)

j. monitor (output)

k. mouse (input)

l. PC video camera (input)

m. printer (output)

n. scanner (input)

o. speaker (output)

p. system unit (processor, memory, storage)

q. USB flash drive (storage)

True/False

Mark T for True and F for False. (See page numbers in parentheses.)

_____ 1. Many people believe that computer literacy is vital to success in today's world. (5)

_____ 2. Hardware consists of a series of instructions that tells the computer what to do and how to do it. (7)

_____ 3. The circuitry of the system unit usually is part of or is connected to a circuit board called the server. (8)

_____ 4. The computing phrase, garbage in, garbage out, points out that the accuracy of a computer's input depends on the accuracy of the output. (10)

_____ 5. A network is a collection of computers and devices connected together, often wirelessly, via communications devices and transmission media. (11)

_____ 6. Businesses, called access providers, offer users and companies access to the Internet free or for a fee. (12)

_____ 7. A blog that contains video clips is called a video blog. (14)

_____ 8. A PDA provides personal organizer functions such as a calendar, an appointment book, an address book, a calculator, and a notepad. (21)

_____ 9. An information system consists of hardware, software, data, people, and procedures. (25)

_____ 10. Telecommuting is a work arrangement in which employees work away from a company's standard workplace and often communicate with the office through the computer. (30)

_____ 11. With online investing, the transaction fee for each trade usually is much more than when trading through a broker. (33)

Checkpoint

 Multiple Choice   Select the best answer. (See page numbers in parentheses.)

1. Computer literacy involves having a knowledge and understanding of _____. (5)
   a. computer programming
   b. computers and their uses
   c. computer repair
   d. all of the above

2. A computer can _____. (6)
   a. accept data
   b. process data according to specified rules
   c. produce and store results
   d. all of the above

3. The series of input, process, output, and storage sometimes is referred to as the _____ cycle. (6)
   a. computer programming
   b. information processing
   c. data entering
   d. Web browsing

4. Commonly used _____ devices are a keyboard, a mouse, and a microphone. (7)
   a. input
   b. storage
   c. output
   d. mobile

5. A _____ controls access to the resources on a network. (11)
   a. server
   b. workstation
   c. client
   d. tower

6. Millions of people worldwide join online communities, each called a _____, that encourage members to share their interests, ideas, stories, photos, music, and videos with other registered users. (14)
   a. podcast
   b. social networking Web site
   c. vodcast
   d. blog

7. A _____ is a specific type of social networking Web site that allows users to create an online photo album and store their electronic photographs. (14)
   a. vodcast
   b. blog
   c. chat room
   d. photo sharing community

8. A _____ is recorded audio stored on a Web site that can be downloaded to a computer or portable media player. (14)
   a. podcast
   b. social networking Web site
   c. blog
   d. speaker

9. Two types of _____ are desktop computers and notebook computers. (19)
   a. embedded computers
   b. supercomputers
   c. servers
   d. personal computers

10. A _____ is a special type of notebook computer that is useful for taking notes in lectures, at meetings, and other forums where the standard notebook computer is not practical. (21)
    a. smart phone
    b. PDA
    c. game console
    d. Tablet PC

11. As smart phones and PDAs continue a trend of offering similar functions, it is becoming increasingly difficult to differentiate between the two devices, which is a trend known as _____. (22)
    a. installing
    b. mobile computing
    c. convergence
    d. telematics

12. Examples of the _____ category of computer users include engineers, scientists, architects, desktop publishers, and graphic artists. (29)
    a. power user
    b. large business user
    c. mobile user
    d. small office/home office user

13. When using _____, users access account balances, pay bills, and copy monthly transactions from a bank's computer right to their personal computers. (32)
    a. e-commerce
    b. personal finance software
    c. online banking
    d. accounting software

14. _____ is a system that attempts to imitate the behavior of the human brain. (34)
    a. Telemedicine
    b. A kiosk
    c. E-commerce
    d. A neural network

Checkpoint

Matching

Match the terms with their definitions. (See page numbers in parentheses.)

_____ 1. processor (8)

_____ 2. memory (8)

_____ 3. vodcast (14)

_____ 4. install (17)

_____ 5. execute (17)

_____ 6. stylus (21)

_____ 7. mainframe (23)

_____ 8. supercomputer (23)

_____ 9. multimedia (29)

_____ 10. kiosk (30)

a. interprets and carries out basic instructions that operate a computer

b. carry out the instructions in a computer program

c. combines text, graphics, audio, and video into one application

d. large, expensive, powerful computer that can handle hundreds or thousands of connected users simultaneously

e. fastest, most powerful computer — and the most expensive

f. collection of computers and devices connected together

g. mobile device that can connect to the Internet wirelessly

h. metal or plastic device that uses pressure to write, draw, or make selections

i. freestanding computer, usually with a touch screen

j. set up software to work with a computer and other hardware components

k. stores instructions waiting to be executed and the data needed

l. a podcast that contains video and also usually audio

Short Answer

Write a brief answer to each of the following questions.

1. How is data different from information? _____ What is the information processing cycle? _____

2. How can the use of computers lead to a violation of privacy? _____ How can the use of computers cause a public safety problem? _____

3. How is hardware different from software? _____ What is a programmer? _____

4. What are seven categories of computers? _____ What determines how a computer is categorized? _____

5. How do Web sites benefit individuals' health care? _____ How can telemedicine benefit health care? _____

Beyond the Book

Read the following book elements, learn more about each using the Web, and then write a brief report.

1. Ethics & Issues — What Should Be Done about Identity Theft? (10), Who Is Responsible for the Accuracy of Web Pages? (14), Do Computer Games Do More Harm than Good? (16), Who Should Monitor Online Social Networks? (27), Should the Government Be Able to Perform Surveillance on All Electronic Communications? (33)

2. Career Corner — Personal Computer Salesperson (37)

3. Companies on the Cutting Edge — Dell or Apple Computer (39)

4. FAQs (6, 8, 14, 17, 20, 27, 36)

5. High-Tech Talk — Analog versus Digital: Making the Conversion (38)

6. Looking Ahead — Medical Implants Can Enhance Lifestyles (9) or Robots Perform Mundane, Dangerous Tasks (32)

7. Making Use of the Web — Fun and Entertainment (117)

8. Picture Yourself Taking a Computer Course (2)

9. Technology Trailblazers — Bill Gates or Anne Mulcahy (39)

10. Timeline 2008 (52)

11. Web Links (7, 8, 9, 12, 14, 16, 19, 22, 26, 36)

Learn It Online

Use the Learn It Online exercises to reinforce your understanding of the chapter concepts. To access the Learn It Online exercises, visit scsite.com/dc2008/ch1/learn.

(1) At the Movies — Try a Free Operating System

To view the Try a Free Operating System movie, click the number 1 button. Locate your video and click the corresponding High-Speed or Dial-Up link, depending on your Internet connection. Watch the movie and then complete the exercise by answering the questions that follow. Learn how to try Ubuntu Linux operating system on your own computer without installing a thing. Explain the process by which you can try Linux's Ubuntu operating system on your computer without installing it. What is a downside to running your system from your CD-ROM?

(2) Video and Audio: You Review It — Social Networking

In this chapter you learned about social networking. Click the number 2 button to view the suggested links and begin your search for videos, podcasts, or vodcasts related to social networking. Choose a video, podcast, or vodcast that discusses social networking and is of interest to you, and then write a description of its contents. Explain why you chose this piece, what you liked about it, what you disliked about it, and whether you would recommend it to a fellow student. Finish your review by giving the video, podcast, or vodcast a rating of 1-5 stars. Submit your review in the format requested by your instructor.

(3) Student Edition Labs — Using Input Devices

Click the number 3 button. A new browser window will open, displaying the Student Edition Labs (screen shown in the figure below). Follow the on-screen instructions to complete the Using Input Devices Lab. When finished, click the Exit button. If required, submit your results to your instructor.

(4) Student Edition Labs — Using Windows

Click the number 4 button. A new browser window will open, displaying the Student Edition Labs. Follow the on-screen instructions to complete the Using Windows Lab. When finished, click the Exit button. If required, submit your results to your instructor.

(5) Practice Test

Click the number 5 button. Answer each question. When completed, enter your name and click the Grade Test button to submit the quiz for grading. Make a note of any missed questions. If required, submit your score to your instructor.

Learn It Online

⑥ Who Wants To Be a Computer Genius²?

Click the number 6 button to find out if you are a computer genius. Directions about how to play the game will be displayed. When you are ready to play, click the Play button. Submit your score to your instructor.

⑦ Wheel of Terms

Click the number 7 button to reinforce important terms you learned in this chapter by playing the Shelly Cashman Series version of this popular game. Directions about how to play the game will be displayed. When you are ready to play, click the Play button. Submit your score to your instructor.

⑧ DC Track and Field

Click the number 8 button to use what you have learned in this chapter to compete against other students in three track and field events. Directions about how to play the game will be displayed. When you are ready to play, click the start first event button. If required, submit your score to your instructor.

⑨ You're Hired!

Click the number 9 button to use what you have learned in this chapter to embark on the path to a career in computers. Directions about how to play the game will be displayed. When you are ready to play, click the begin game button. If required, submit your score to your instructor.

⑩ Crossword Puzzle Challenge

Click the number 10 button, and then click the Crossword Puzzle Challenge link. Directions about how to play the game will be displayed. Complete the puzzle to reinforce skills you learned in this chapter. When you are ready to play, click the Continue button. Submit the completed puzzle to your instructor.

⑪ Vista Exercises

Click the number 11 button. When the Vista Exercises menu appears, click the exercise assigned by your instructor. A new browser window will open. Follow the on-screen instructions to complete the exercise. When finished, click the Exit button. If required, submit your results to your instructor.

⑫ Learn the Web

No matter how much computer experience you have, navigating the Web for the first time can be intimidating. How do you get started? Click the number 12 button and click the links to discover how you can find out everything you want to know about the Internet.

⑬ Chapter Discussion Forum

Select an objective from this chapter on page 3 about which you would like more information. Click the number 13 button and post a short message listing a meaningful message title accompanied by one or more questions concerning the selected objective. In two days, return to the threaded discussion by clicking the number 13 button. Submit to your instructor your original message and at least one response to your message.

⑭ Google Maps

Click the number 14 button to learn how to locate businesses in your area, view a location's surroundings via satellite, and find directions from one location to another. Print a copy of the Google Maps page and then step through the exercise. If required, submit your results to your instructor.

Learn How To

Use the Learn How To activities to learn fundamental skills when using a computer and accompanying technology. Complete the exercises and submit them to your instructor. To see a video of a Learn How To activity, visit scsite.com/dc2008/ch1/howto.

LEARN HOW TO 1: Start and Close an Application

An application accomplishes tasks on a computer. You can start any application by using the Start button.

Complete these steps to start the Web browser application called Internet Explorer:
1. Click the Start button (⊞) at the left of the Windows taskbar on the bottom of the screen to display the Start menu.
2. Click All Programs on the Start menu to display the All Programs list (Figure 1-45).
3. Click the program name, Internet Explorer, in the All Programs list to open the Internet Explorer browser window (Figure 1-46).

An item in the All Programs list might have an open folder icon next to it. When this occurs, click the item and another list will appear. Click the application name in this list to start the application. Some application names might appear on the Start menu itself. If so, click any of these names to start the corresponding application.

Below the line on the left side of the Start menu, Windows displays the names of the applications recently opened on the computer. You can start any of these applications by clicking the name of the application.

FIGURE 1-45

FIGURE 1-46

To close an application, click the Close button (▣) in the upper-right corner of the window. If you have created but not saved a document, Windows will ask if you want to save the document. If you do not want to save it, click the No button in the displayed dialog box. If you want to save it, refer to Learn How To number 1 in Chapter 3 on page 178.

Exercise

1. Using the Start button, start the application named WordPad found in the Accessories list of the All Programs list. WordPad is a word processing application. Type the following: `To start an application, click the application name in the All Programs list` and then type your name. Click the Print button (🖶) on the toolbar. Submit the printout to your instructor.
2. Close the WordPad application. If you are asked if you want to save changes to the document, click the No button. Start the WordPad application again, type some new text, and then close the WordPad application. When the dialog box is displayed, click the Cancel button. What happened? Now, close the WordPad window without saving the document. Submit your answer to your instructor.
3. Using the Start button, start the e-mail program on the computer. What is the name of the e-mail program? In the program window, what menu names are displayed on the menu bar at the top of the window? Close the e-mail program. Submit your answers to your instructor.

Learn How To

LEARN HOW TO 2: Use the Discovering Computers 2008 Online Companion (scsite.com/dc2008)

The Discovering Computers 2008 Online Companion provides a variety of activities and exercises. To use the site, you first must register and establish a user name and password. Perform the following steps to register:
1. Start the Web browser.
2. Type scsite.com/dc2008 in the Address box of the Web browser. Press the ENTER key.
3. When the registration page is displayed, click the New User Registration link.
4. Follow the on-screen instructions to complete registration.

When you first type a Web address to display a page from the dc2008 site, you must enter your user name and password to gain access to the site. When you are done using the site, close the browser so no one else can visit the site with your user name and password.

Exercise
1. Start the Web browser on your computer.
2. Type scsite.com/dc2008/ch1/howto in the Address box of the browser and then press the ENTER key.
3. If the registration page is displayed and you have not yet registered, complete the steps above. If you are registered, enter your user name and password, and then click the Enter button.
4. Navigate to the Chapter 1 home page.
5. Visit each of the Exercises Web pages (Case Studies, Chapter Review, Checkpoint, Key Terms, Learn How To, Learn It Online, and Web Research). Use the navigation bar on the left of the screen to display these pages.
6. Click the browser's Close button to close the application.
7. Write a report that describes the use of each of the Exercises pages you visited. Which page do you think will prove the most valuable to you when using the book and the Web site? Why? Which will be the least useful? Why? Submit your report to your instructor.

LEARN HOW TO 3: Find Out About Your Computer

By following these steps, you can find out about your computer:
1. Click the Start button on the Windows taskbar.
2. Click All Programs on the Start menu, click Accessories in the All Programs list, and then click System Tools in the Accessories list.
3. Click System Information in the System Tools list. Windows displays a system summary in the right side of the window, and an index of categories in the left side of the window (Figure 1-47).

To determine more information about your computer, click any of the plus signs in the left side of the window. Then, click the item about which you want more information.

index of categories   system summary

FIGURE 1-47

Exercise
1. Submit the answers to the following questions about your computer:
   a. What type of operating system (OS Name) is in use?
   b. What company manufactured the computer?
   c. How much RAM (physical memory) is on the computer?
   d. How much data can you store on the C: drive?
   e. What is the name of a CD or DVD drive found on the computer?

Web Research

Use the Internet-based Web Research exercises to broaden your understanding of the concepts presented in this chapter. Visit scsite.com/dc2008/ch1/research to obtain more information pertaining to each exercise. To discuss any of the Web Research exercises in this chapter with other students, post your thoughts or questions at scsite.com/dc2008/ch1/forum.

① Scavenger Hunt   Use one of the <u>search engines</u> listed in Figure 2-10 in Chapter 2 on page 78 or your own favorite search engine to find the answers to the questions below. Copy and paste the Web address from the Web page where you found the answer. Some questions may have more than one answer. If required, submit your answers to your instructor. (1) What bank was the first to use a computer for its accounting and check handling systems in 1959? (2) Two National Science Foundation (NSF) programs were established in 1997 to interconnect 50 university and scientific computing sites. What colleges host these two sites? What were the locations of the five original NSF-financed supercomputer centers? (3) Personal finance software helps you balance your checkbook and manage your finances. What is the name of a popular personal finance software program? (4) What is the name of the first spreadsheet program? (5) A programming language developed by the U.S. Department of Defense was named to honor a famous woman mathematician. What is the name of this programming language?

② Search Sleuth   Visit the <u>Google Web site</u> (google.com) and then click the About Google link at the bottom of the page. Using your word processing program, answer the following questions and then, if required, submit your answers to your instructor. (1) Below Our Company, click Corporate Info. What is Google's mission? (2) Click the Culture link on the left side of the page. Provide a summary of the Googleplex environment. (3) Click your browser's Back button twice or press the BACKSPACE key two times to return to the About Google page. Below the Products heading, click the Services & Tools link. Click the Finance link and list two stories in the Today's Headlines section. What are the NASDAQ's opening and closing figures? (4) Click your browser's Back button two times to return to the Google home page. In the Google Search text box, type `banking` and click the Google Search button. Approximately how many hits resulted? Do any definitions appear? If so, list the definitions. How much time did it take to complete the search? (5) In the Google Search text box, type `online banking` and click the Search button. Compare this to your earlier search. Are there more or fewer hits? How much time did it take to complete the second search? (6) Click one of the resulting online banking links and review the information. Write a 50-word summary. Using the information contained within the Web site, do you think you have sufficient knowledge to manage your accounts online?

③ Newsgroups   One of the more popular topics for <u>newsgroups</u> is the Internet. Find three newsgroups, such as those listed in CyberFiber (cyberfiber.com/internet.htm) or Google Groups, that discuss an aspect of the Internet. Read the newsgroup postings and post a reply to one message. Summarize three topics under discussion and your reply to a message.

④ Journaling   Respond to your readings in this chapter by writing at least one page about your reactions, evaluations, and reflections about computer usage in your daily life. For example, how many hours do you spend each week using computers at home, school, and work? What steps do you take to avoid <u>identity theft</u>? What storage devices do you use? Have you recycled or discarded unwanted computer equipment? You also can write about the new terms you learned by reading this chapter. If required, submit your journal to your instructor.

⑤ Ethics in Action   The Internet has increased the ease with which students can plagiarize material for research paper assignments. Teachers are using online services, such as Turnitin.com, to help detect plagiarized papers and to help students understand how to cite sources correctly. Visit the <u>Turnitin site</u> (turnitin.com) and then write a summary of how this service is used. How prevalent is plagiarism on your campus? What action should an instructor take when a student submits a plagiarized paper? If required, submit your summary to your instructor.

Case Studies

Use the Case Studies to apply the concepts presented in the chapter to real-world situations. Visit scsite.com/dc2008/ch1/cases to obtain more information pertaining to each exercise. To discuss the Case Studies in this chapter with other students, visit scsite.com/dc2008/ch1/forum and post your thoughts or questions.

CASE STUDY 1 — Class Discussion   Virtually everyone who works with computers has experienced problems with <u>computer software</u>. Problems can range from not being able to load the software to your computer to getting the software loaded and having it produce unanticipated results. Depending on the situation and time these problems may occur, it can place a great amount of stress on the user. Some people compare these types of problems to a craftsman's tools malfunctioning in the middle of a project. On the other hand, many people feel reactions to computer software problems tend to be more extreme than reactions to problems with other tools they use. Write a brief report about how you have seen people react to computer software problems. Include ideas on how they can reduce their frustration when dealing with such problems. Be prepared to discuss your findings.

CASE STUDY 2 — Class Discussion   You are a member of your local school district's board of education. Over the past year, the number of computers purchased by the district increased by 85 percent, while the supply of library books declined by almost 10 percent. School officials claim that computers extend learning opportunities and develop the <u>computer literacy</u> needed in today's technological world. Yet, some parents are complaining that computer purchases represent frivolous, status-seeking spending. Notebook computers are purchased for teachers, while textbooks and library books are too old, too worn, and too scarce. Use the Web and/or print media to learn how computers are being used in schools. As a school board member, draft a proposal recommending the percentage of the instructional materials budget that should be spent on computers versus the percentage that should be spent on library books and textbooks. Note the factors that influenced your decision. Be prepared to discuss your recommendations.

CASE STUDY 3 — Research   Computers are everywhere. Watching television, driving a car, using a charge card, even ordering fast food all involve computers, not to mention browsing the Web on your personal computer. Your car computer is an <u>embedded computer</u> that can be described as special-purpose, because it only accepts specific input and performs limited functions. Your personal computer, on the other hand, is general-purpose, meaning it accepts a wide range of input and can perform a variety of tasks. For one day, make a list of each computer you encounter (be careful not to limit yourself just to the computers you see). How is the computer used? Is the computer special-purpose or general-purpose? Why? How was the task the computer performs accomplished before computers? Write a brief report or use PowerPoint to create a presentation and share your findings.

CASE STUDY 4 — Research   You are an assistant manager at a local computer store. Your manager suspects that for cultural, financial, or societal reasons, certain groups of people are more likely to buy computers than others. To increase the impact of the store's promotions, your manager has asked you to discover if computers are purchased by individuals from a broad spectrum, or if a certain type exists that represents most <u>computer buyers</u>. Use the Web and/or print media to learn more about the demographics of computer buyers. What gender are most buyers? In what age range do they fall? What seems to be the typical educational level? What is the approximate average income of a typical buyer? Do buyers tend to share any other characteristics? If you discover any trends, what reasons might be behind the results? Write a brief report or use PowerPoint to create a presentation and share your findings.

CASE STUDY 5 — Team Challenge   People use computers in a variety of fields, including education, finance, government, health care, science, publishing, travel, and manufacturing. Although the way people use computers varies, each use of a computer involves <u>computer hardware</u>, computer software, and normally some type of communications capability over networks, such as the Internet. Form a three-member team and choose a field in which you all are interested. Using the Web and/or print media, assign one member of your team to investigate hardware used in the field, another member to investigate software used in the field, and the third member to investigate communications capabilities used in the field. After your investigation, characterize a hypothetical business or organization in the field. Based on your investigation, prepare a report that recommends specific hardware, software, and networking capabilities that would be best for the business or organization; explain your recommendations in the report.

Timeline 2008

MILESTONES IN COMPUTER HISTORY

Dr. John V. Atanasoff and Clifford Berry design and build the first electronic digital computer. Their machine, the Atanasoff-Berry-Computer, or ABC, provides the foundation for advances in electronic digital computers.

John von Neumann poses in front of the electronic computer built at the Institute for Advanced Study. This computer and its von Neumann architecture served as the prototype for subsequent stored program computers worldwide.

William Shockley, John Bardeen, and Walter Brattain invent the transfer resistance device, eventually called the transistor. The transistor would revolutionize computers, proving much more reliable than vacuum tubes.

| 1937 | 1943 | 1945 | 1946 | 1947 | 195 |

During World War II, British scientist Alan Turing designs the Colossus, an electronic computer created for the military to break German codes. The computer's existence is kept secret until the 1970s.

Dr. John W. Mauchly and J. Presper Eckert, Jr. complete work on the first large-scale electronic, general-purpose digital computer. The ENIAC (Electronic Numerical Integrator And Computer) weighs 30 tons, contains 18,000 vacuum tubes, occupies a 30 × 50 foot space, and consumes 160 kilowatts of power. The first time it is turned on, lights dim in an entire section of Philadelphia.

The first commercially available electronic digital computer, the UNIVAC I (UNIVersal Automatic Computer), is introduced by Remington Rand. Public awareness of computers increases when the UNIVAC I, after analyzing only five percent of the popular vote, correctly predicts that Dwight D. Eisenhower will win the presidential election.

Dr. Grace Hopper considers the concept of reusable software in her paper, "The Education of a Computer." The paper describes how to program a computer with symbolic notation instead of the detailed machine language that had been used.

The IBM 305 RAMAC system is the first to use magnetic disk for external storage. The system provides storage capacity similar to magnetic tape that previously was used, but offers the advantage of semi-random access capability.

Fortran (FORmula TRANslation), an efficient, easy-to-use programming language, is introduced by John Backus.

More than 200 programming languages have been created.

IBM introduces two smaller, desk-sized computers: the IBM 1401 for business and the IBM 1620 for scientists. The IBM 1620 initially is called the CADET, but IBM drops the name when campus wags claim it is an acronym for, Can't Add, Doesn't Even Try.

1952　1953　1957　1958　1959　1960

The IBM model 650 is one of the first widely used computers. Originally planning to produce only 50 machines, the system is so successful that eventually IBM manufactures more than 1,000. With the IBM 700 series of machines, the company will dominate the mainframe market for the next decade.

Core memory, developed in the early 1950s, provides much larger storage capacity than vacuum tube memory.

Jack Kilby of Texas Instruments invents the integrated circuit, which lays the foundation for high-speed computers and large-capacity memories. Computers built with transistors mark the beginning of the second generation of computer hardware.

COBOL, a high-level business application language, is developed by a committee headed by Dr. Grace Hopper. COBOL uses English-like phrases and runs on most business computers, making it one of the more widely used programming languages.

Dr. John Kemeny of Dartmouth leads the development of the BASIC programming language. BASIC will be widely used on personal computers.

Computer Science Corporation becomes the first software company listed on the New York Stock Exchange.

Under pressure from the industry, IBM announces that some of its software will be priced separately from the computer hardware. This unbundling allows software firms to emerge in the industry.

Digital Equipment Corporation (DEC) introduces the first minicomputer, the PDP-8. The machine is used extensively as an interface for time-sharing systems.

In a letter to the editor titled, "GO TO Statements Considered Harmful," Dr. Edsger Dijsktra introduces the concept of structured programming, developing standards for constructing computer programs.

The ARPANET network, a predecessor of the Internet, is established.

1964　**1965**　　**1968**　**1969**　**1970**

The number of computers has grown to 18,000. Third-generation computers, with their controlling circuitry stored on chips, are introduced. The IBM System/360 computer is the first family of compatible machines, merging science and business lines.

Alan Shugart at IBM demonstrates the first regular use of an 8-inch floppy (magnetic storage) disk.

Fourth-generation computers, built with chips that use LSI (large-scale integration) arrive. While the chips used in 1965 contained as many as 1,000 circuits, the LSI chip contains as many as 15,000.

IBM introduces the term word processing for the first time with its Magnetic Tape/Selectric Typewriter (MT/ST). The MT/ST was the first reusable storage medium that allowed typed material to be edited without having to retype the document.

MITS, Inc. advertises one of the first microcomputers, the Altair. Named for the destination in an episode of *Star Trek*, the Altair is sold in kits for less than $400. Although initially it has no keyboard, no monitor, no permanent memory, and no software, 4,000 orders are taken within the first three months.

VisiCalc, a spreadsheet program written by Bob Frankston and Dan Bricklin, is introduced. Originally written to run on Apple II computers, VisiCalc will be seen as the most important reason for the acceptance of personal computers in the business world.

The IBM PC is introduced, signaling IBM's entrance into the personal computer marketplace. The IBM PC quickly garners the largest share of the personal computer market and becomes the personal computer of choice in business.

Ethernet, the first local area network (LAN), is developed at Xerox PARC (Palo Alto Research Center) by Robert Metcalf. The LAN allows computers to communicate and share software, data, and peripherals. Initially designed to link minicomputers, Ethernet will be extended to personal computers.

The first public online information services, CompuServe and the Source, are founded.

1971   1975   1976   1979   1980   1981

IBM offers Microsoft Corporation cofounder, Bill Gates, the opportunity to develop the operating system for the soon-to-be announced IBM personal computer. With the development of MS-DOS, Microsoft achieves tremendous growth and success.

Dr. Ted Hoff of Intel Corporation develops a microprocessor, or microprogrammable computer chip, the Intel 4004.

The first computer virus, Elk Cloner, is spread via Apple II floppy disks, which contained the operating system. A short rhyme would appear on the screen when the user pressed Reset after the 50th boot of an infected disk.

Steve Jobs and Steve Wozniak build the first Apple computer. A subsequent version, the Apple II, is an immediate success. Adopted by elementary schools, high schools, and colleges, for many students, the Apple II is their first contact with the world of computers.

Alan Shugart presents the Winchester hard drive, revolutionizing storage for personal computers.

Special Feature

scsite.com/dc2008/ch1/timeline

3.275 Million

3,275,000 personal computers are sold, almost 3,000,000 more than in 1981.

Apple introduces the Macintosh computer, which incorporates a unique, easy-to-learn, graphical user interface.

COMPAQ

Compaq, Inc. is founded to develop and market IBM-compatible PCs.

Microsoft

Microsoft has public stock offering and raises approximately $61 million. Within 20 years, Microsoft's stock is worth nearly $350 billion or 5,735 times the amount raised in the initial public stock offering.

Hayes introduces the 300 bps smart modem. The modem is an immediate success.

Hewlett-Packard announces the first LaserJet printer for personal computers.

1982 — 1983 — 1984 — 1986 — 1988

Instead of choosing a person for its annual award, *TIME* magazine names the computer Machine of the Year for 1982, acknowledging the impact of computers on society.

Lotus Development Corporation is founded. Its spreadsheet software, Lotus 1-2-3, which combines spreadsheet, graphics, and database programs in one package, becomes the best-selling program for IBM personal computers.

Microsoft surpasses Lotus Development Corporation to become the world's top software vendor.

While working at CERN, Switzerland, Tim Berners-Lee invents an Internet-based hypermedia enterprise for information sharing. Berners-Lee will call this innovation the World Wide Web.

World Wide Web Consortium releases standards that describe a framework for linking documents on different computers.

Several companies introduce computers using the Pentium processor from Intel. The Pentium chip is the successor to the Intel 486 processor. It contains 3.1 million transistors and is capable of performing 112,000,000 instructions per second.

Microsoft releases Microsoft Office 3 Professional, the first version of Microsoft Office.

1989 **1991** **1992** **1993**

The Intel 486 becomes the world's first 1,000,000 transistor microprocessor. It crams 1.2 million transistors on a .4" x .6" sliver of silicon and executes 15,000,000 instructions per second — four times as fast as its predecessor, the 80386 chip.

The White House launches its Web site, which includes an interactive citizens' handbook and White House history and tours.

Microsoft releases Windows 3.1, the latest version of its Windows operating system. Windows 3.1 offers improvements such as TrueType fonts, multimedia capability, and object linking and embedding (OLE). In two months, 3,000,000 copies of Windows 3.1 are sold.

U.S. Robotics introduces PalmPilot, a handheld personal organizer. The PalmPilot's user friendliness and low price make it a standout next to more expensive personal digital assistants (PDAs).

Sun Microsystems launches Java, an object-oriented programming language that allows users to write one application for a variety of computer platforms. Java becomes one of the hotter Internet technologies.

Microsoft releases Windows NT 4.0, an operating system for client-server networks. Windows NT's management tools and wizards make it easier for developers to build and deploy business applications.

Jim Clark and Marc Andreessen found Netscape and launch Netscape Navigator 1.0, a browser for the World Wide Web.

1994

1995

1996

Linus Torvalds creates the Linux kernel, a UNIX-like operating system that he releases free across the Internet for further enhancement by other programmers.

Microsoft releases Windows 95, a major upgrade to its Windows operating system. Windows 95 consists of more than 10,000,000 lines of computer instructions developed by 300 person-years of effort. More than 50,000 individuals and companies test the software before it is released.

Two out of three employees in the United States have access to a personal computer, and one out of every three homes has a personal computer. Fifty million personal computers are sold worldwide and more than 250,000,000 are in use.

Apple and Microsoft sign a joint technology development agreement. Microsoft buys $150,000,000 of Apple stock.

More than 10,000,000 people take up telecommuting, which is the capability of working at home and communicating with an office via computer. Increasingly more firms embrace telecommuting to help increase productivity, reduce absenteeism, and provide greater job satisfaction.

Apple Computer introduces the iMac, the next version of its popular Macintosh computer. The iMac abandons such conventional features as a floppy disk drive but wins customers with its futuristic design, see-through case, and easy setup. Consumer demand outstrips Apple's production capabilities, and some vendors are forced to begin waiting lists.

DVD, the next generation of optical disc storage technology, is introduced. DVD can store computer, audio, and video data in a single format, with the capability of producing near-studio quality. By year's end, 500,000 DVD players are shipped worldwide.

1997

1998

Intel introduces the Pentium II processor with 7.5 million transistors. The new processor, which incorporates MMX technology, processes video, audio, and graphics data more efficiently and supports applications such as movie editing, gaming, and more.

E-commerce, or electronic commerce — the marketing of goods and services over the Internet — booms. Companies such as Dell, E*TRADE, and Amazon.com spur online shopping, allowing buyers to obtain everything from hardware and software to financial and travel services, insurance, automobiles, books, and more.

Microsoft releases Internet Explorer 4.0 and seizes a key place in the Internet arena. This new Web browser is greeted with tremendous customer demand.

Microsoft ships Windows 98, an upgrade to Windows 95. Windows 98 offers improved Internet access, better system performance, and support for a new generation of hardware and software. In six months, more than 10,000,000 copies of Windows 98 are sold worldwide.

Fifty million users are connected to the Internet and World Wide Web.

Special Feature

Governments and businesses frantically work to make their computers Y2K (Year 2000) compliant, spending more than $500 billion worldwide. Y2K noncompliant computers cannot distinguish whether 01/01/00 refers to 1900 or 2000, and thus may operate using a wrong date. This Y2K bug can affect any application that relies on computer chips, such as ATMs, airplanes, energy companies, and the telephone system. In the end, the Y2K bug turned out not to be a problem.

U.S. District Judge Thomas Penfield Jackson rules in the antitrust lawsuit brought by the Department of Justice and 19 states that Microsoft used its monopoly power to stifle competition.

Shawn Fanning, 19, and his company, Napster, turn the music industry upside down by developing software that allows computer users to swap music files with one another without going through a centralized file server. The Recording Industry of America, on behalf of five media companies, sues Napster for copyright infringement and wins.

1999   2000

Microsoft introduces Office 2000, its premier productivity suite, offering new tools for users to create content and save it directly to a Web site without any file conversion or special steps.

E-commerce achieves mainstream acceptance. Annual e-commerce sales exceed $100 billion, and Internet advertising expenditures reach more than $5 billion.

Open source software, such as the Linux operating system and the Apache Web server created by unpaid volunteers, begin to gain wide acceptance among computer users.

Dot-com companies (Internet based) go out of business at a record pace — nearly one per day — as financial investors withhold funding due to the companies' unprofitability.

Microsoft ships Windows 2000 and Windows Me. Windows 2000 offers improved behind-the-scenes security and reliability. Windows Me is designed for home users and lets them edit home movies, share digital photos, index music, and create a home network.

According to the U.S. Department of Commerce, Internet traffic is doubling every 100 days, resulting in an annual growth rate of more than 700 percent. It has taken radio and television 30 years and 15 years, respectively, to reach 60 million people. The Internet has achieved the same audience base in 3 years.

Intel unveils its Pentium 4 chip with clock speeds starting at 1.4 GHz. The Pentium 4 includes 42 million transistors, nearly twice as many contained on its predecessor, the Pentium III.

Microsoft releases major operating system updates with Windows XP for the desktop and servers, and Pocket PC 2002 for handheld computers. Windows XP is significantly more reliable than previous versions, features a 32-bit computing architecture, and offers a new look and feel. Pocket PC 2002 offers the handheld computer user a familiar Windows interface and consistent functionality.

2000

2001

Microsoft introduces Office XP, the next version of the world's leading suite of productivity software. Features include speech and handwriting recognition, smart tags, and task panes.

Telemedicine uses satellite technology and videoconferencing to broadcast consultations and to perform distant surgeries. Robots are used for complex and precise tasks. Computer-aided surgery uses virtual reality to assist with training and planning procedures.

Avid readers enjoy e-books, which are digital texts read on compact computer screens. E-books can hold the equivalent of 10 traditional books containing text and graphics. Readers can search, highlight text, and add notes.

Special Feature

After several years of negligible sales, the Tablet PC is reintroduced as the next-generation mobile PC. The lightweight device, the size of a three-ring notebook, is ideal for people on the go.

Digital video cameras, DVD writers, easy-to-use video editing software, and improvements in storage capabilities allow the average computer user to create Hollywood-like videos with introductions, conclusions, scenes rearranged, music, and voice-over.

Wireless computers and devices, such as keyboards, mouse devices, home networks, and wireless Internet access points become commonplace. Latest operating systems include support for both the Wi-Fi (wireless fidelity) and Bluetooth standards. Wireless capabilities are standard on many PDAs and Tablet PCs.

2002

2003

Microsoft launches its .NET strategy, which is a new environment for developing and running software applications featuring ease of development of Web-based services.

Microsoft ships Office 2003, the latest version of its flagship Office suite. More than 400 million people in 175 nations and 70 languages are using a version of Office.

DVD writers begin to replace CD writers (CD-RW). DVDs can store up to eight times as much data as CDs. Uses include storing home movies, music, photos, and backups.

Intel ships its revamped Pentium 4 chip with the 0.13 micron processor and Hyper-Threading (HT) Technology, operating at speeds of 3.06 GHz. This new development eventually will enable processors with a billion transistors to operate at 20 GHz.

In an attempt to maintain their current business model of selling songs, the Recording Industry Association of America (RIAA) files over 250 lawsuits against individual computer users who offer copyrighted music over peer-to-peer networks.

Companies such as RealNetworks, Microsoft, Sony, and Wal-Mart stake out turf in the online music store business started by Apple Computer. In the previous year, Apple's iTunes Music Store Web site sold nearly 20 million songs for 99 cents each.

USB flash drives become a cost-effective way to transport data and information from one computer to another.

Video-Pod

Apple releases the latest version of its popular pocket-sized iPod portable media player. First it played songs, then photos, then podcasts, and now, in addition, up to 150 hours of music videos and TV shows on a 2.5" color display.

Microsoft introduces Visual Studio 2005. The product includes Visual Basic, Visual C#, Visual J#, Visual C++, and SQL Server. Microsoft also releases a Visual Studio 2005 Express Edition for hobbyists, students, and nonprofessionals.

Flat-panel LCD monitors overtake bulky CRT monitors as the popular choice of computer users. Flat-panel LCD monitors offer several advantages including physical size, weight, true display size, better power consumption, and no radiation emission.

Major retailers begin requiring suppliers to include radio frequency identification (RFID) tags or microchips with antennas, which can be as small as 1/3 of a millimeter across, in the goods they sell. RFIDs eventually may eliminate long checkout lines.

Spam, spyware, phishing, pharming, spim, and spit take center stage, along with viruses, as major nuisances to the 801 million computer users worldwide.

Spyware
Spam **Pharming**
Phishing
Spim **Spit**

2004

2005

106 million, or 53 percent, of the 200 million online population in America accesses the Internet via speedy broadband.

Linux, the open source operating system, makes major inroads into the server market as a viable alternative to Microsoft Windows, Sun's Solaris, and the UNIX operating systems.

The smart phone overtakes the PDA as the personal mobile device of choice. A smart phone offers the user a cellular phone, full personal information management and e-mail functionality, a Web browser, instant message capabilities, and even the ability to listen to music, watch and record video, play games, and take pictures.

Microsoft unveils Windows XP Media Center Edition 2005. This operating system allows users to access the routine capabilities of a Windows XP-based PC while focusing on delivering media content such as music, digital photography, movies, and television.

Blogging
Podcasting

Blogging and podcasting become mainstream methods for distributing information via the Web.

Linux

Apple Computer introduces the sleek iMac G5. The new computer's display device contains the system unit.

Microsoft releases the Xbox 360, its latest game console. Features include the capability to play music, display photos, and network with computers and other Xbox games.

Sony launches its PlayStation 3. New features include a Blu-ray disc player, high-definition capabilities, and always-on online connectivity. Sony hopes to continue its advantage over Microsoft. Since the release of Microsoft's Xbox 360 in 2005, Sony's PS2 has outsold the Xbox 360 by nearly a 2-to-1 margin. Nintendo releases Wii, featuring the wireless Wii Remote that allows users to control the game using physical gestures as well as traditional button presses through the use of motion detection technology.

Microsoft and Mozilla release new versions of their respective Web browsers. Microsoft's Internet Explorer 7 and Mozilla's Firefox 2 offer easier browsing through the use of tabs and allow search capabilities directly from the toolbar. They also offer enhanced security features to protect from phishing and to help defend against malware.

San Francisco and Philadelph are among municipalities acr the United States deploying low-cost, high-speed, broadb wireless connectivity to all po within their jurisdiction. Citize access the Internet at broadband spee using wireless desktop computers, no book computers, or mobile devices to connect to Wi-Fi access points.

facebook

Web 2.0, a term coined in 2004, becomes household term with the popularity of soc networking sites such as MySpace, Faceb and YouTube. MySpace reaches 80 million registered users, m between the ages of 18 and 40. Facebook surpasses 13 million registered users and becomes the number one photo sharing s on the Web. YouTube becomes the most popular video sharing Web site with people watching and sharing more than 70 milli videos a day.

2006

Google, founded in 1998, is the most used search engine, capturing 54 percent of the market over Yahoo! and MSN. It is estimated that Google receives approximately 1 billion search requests per day.

Intel introduces its Core 2 Duo processor family. Boasting record-breaking performance while using less power, the family consists of five desktop computer processors and five mobile computer processors. The desktop processor includes 291 million transistors, yet uses 40 percent less power than the Pentium processor.

IBM produces the fastest supercomputer called Blue Gene/L. It can perform approximately 28 trillion calculations in the time it takes to blink your eye, or about one-t of a second. They also start a proje called the World Community Grid that li nearly 100,000 personal computers worldwide. Computer owners volunteer the use of their computers when the computers otherwise woul be sitting idle. The Blue Gene/L primarily is used to explore hydrodynamics, quantum chemistry, molecular dynamics, climate modeling, and fina modeling, while the World Community Grid will be used, among other projects, to maintain an up-to-date HIV/AIDS database as the virus evolv into drug-resistant forms.

Apple begins selling Macintosh computers with Intel microprocessors.

In response to Apple's popular iPod, Microsoft unveils the Zune. Among its features is a 30 GB portable media player; the Zune Marketplace music service; wireless technology; a built-in FM tuner; and a bright, 3″ screen.

the popularity of YouTube has
own, so have video blogs, or vlogs.
ogs allow users to video their
essage instead of entering text via
regular blog. The growth in the
pularity of vlogs can be attributed
several factors, including the use
video portable media players.
dcasting also has increased in
pularity for the same reasons. A
dcast is distinguished from other
gital audio formats by its capability
be downloaded automatically.

Intel introduces Clovertown, a four-core processor made for
dual-processor servers. Multiplying the number of cores
cuts down energy consumption for equivalent levels of
performance. Intel projects that processors with tens of
cores will be available by the end of the decade, and
processors with hundreds of cores possible within 10 years.

CINEMANOW

CinemaNow, the leading Internet provider of
premium videos, offers Burn to DVD service for movie downloads.
The service allows users to legally download a complete DVD and
burn one copy of the movie to a blank DVD. CinemaNow offers
downloads for more than 4,000 feature-length films and television
shows. TiVo introduces a new service for users of its set-top boxes
to allow them to download videos from the Internet and watch them
from their television sets.

Voice over Internet Protocol (VoIP)
providers expand usage to include
Wi-Fi telephones. The telephones
enable high-quality service through
a Wireless-G network and high-speed
Internet connection.

Notebook computer sales continue to
rise, overtaking desktop computers. Advances
in technology, plus notebook computer prices
reaching a low point have businesses as well as
individuals rapidly replacing desktop computers
with more mobile notebook computers.

2007

Microsoft releases the latest version of its
flagship Office suite. New features include the
most significant update to the user interface
in more than a decade, including the
introduction of the Ribbon, which replaces
the toolbars in most of the programs, and
the capability to save documents in XML
and PDF formats.

Blu-ray and HD DVD increase in popularity.
While a Blu-ray Disc (BD) can hold more data
than an HD DVD disc, the HD DVD players
are much less expensive and still have
enough capacity to hold a high-definition
movie. A Blu-ray disc can store about 9
hours of high-definition (HD) video on a
50 GB disc and about 23 hours of standard-
definition (SD) video. HD DVD capacity is
limited to a maximum of 45 GB.

Microsoft Office

Microsoft ships the latest version of its
widely used operating system, Windows
Vista™. Windows Vista focuses on
greatly improving security, deployment,
manageability, and performance. Vista
offers a Basic interface and the Aero
interface, which offers several graphic
features including translucent
windows. Internet Explorer 7 is
included with Windows Vista.

Windows Vista

CHAPTER TWO

The Internet and World Wide Web

Picture Yourself in an Online Social Network

You have accepted a summer internship in a city about 300 miles from home. While thrilled with this opportunity, your feelings are mixed, because you will not see your friends all summer. At your going away party, everyone agrees to stay in touch over the summer via instant messaging, e-mail, and text messaging. Your friend, Derek, says, "We can do better than that on MySpace, a popular online social network." He will send an e-mail message explaining how to get started, along with some tips about using MySpace safely. Intrigued, you agree.

Once settled in your new city, you visit MySpace.com, create a profile, and designate your space as private, so that only friends and people you know can access it. You add a short video of you and your friends, digital pictures from your going away party, some music, and a personalized background. Referring to Derek's safety tips, you do not include any personal information that would make you easy to identify. When you sort MySpace members to see who lives nearby, you are excited to see Tina, an ex-classmate. You send her a request to be included in her friends on MySpace and she agrees. In her self-portrait, you see that she is in a band, which is playing in a concert this weekend. Tina alerts you to two of her friends with whom you might like to chat in a MySpace chat room and invites you to her concert. Suddenly, it seems the summer will not be long or lonely, after all.

To learn how technology enables you to communicate with people worldwide, read Chapter 2 and discover features of the Internet and World Wide Web.

OBJECTIVES

After completing this chapter, you will be able to:

1. Discuss the history of the Internet

2. Explain how to access and connect to the Internet

3. Analyze an IP address

4. Identify the components of a Web address

5. Explain the purpose of a Web browser

6. Search for information on the Web

7. Describe the types of Web sites

8. Recognize how Web pages use graphics, animation, audio, video, virtual reality, and plug-ins

9. Identify the steps required for Web publishing

10. Describe the types of e-commerce

11. Explain how e-mail, FTP, newsgroups and message boards, mailing lists, chat rooms, instant messaging, and Internet telephony work

12. Identify the rules of netiquette

CONTENTS

THE INTERNET

One of the major reasons business, home, and other users purchase computers is for Internet access. Through the Internet, society has access to global information and instant communications. Further, access to the Internet can occur anytime from a computer anywhere: at home, at work, at school, in a restaurant, on an airplane, and even at the beach.

The **Internet**, also called the *Net*, is a worldwide collection of networks that links millions of businesses, government agencies, educational institutions, and individuals. Each of the networks on the Internet provides resources that add to the abundance of goods, services, and information accessible via the Internet.

Today, more than one billion users around the world access a variety of services on the Internet, some of which are shown in Figure 2-1. The World Wide Web and e-mail are two of the more widely used Internet services. Other services include FTP (File Transfer Protocol), newsgroups, chat rooms, instant messaging, and Internet telephony. To enhance your understanding of these services, the chapter begins by discussing the history of the Internet and how the Internet works and then explains each of these services.

FIGURE 2-1a (Web)

FIGURE 2-1b (e-mail)

FIGURE 2-1 People around the world use a variety of Internet services in daily activities. Internet services allow users to access the Web, send e-mail messages, transfer documents and photographs, post messages, chat with a group, or have a private conversation with an online friend(s) or family member(s).

HISTORY OF THE INTERNET

The Internet has its roots in a networking project started by the Pentagon's Advanced Research Projects Agency (*ARPA*), an agency of the U.S. Department of Defense. ARPA's goal was to build a network that (1) allowed scientists at different physical locations to share information and work together on military and scientific projects and (2) could function even if part of the network were disabled or destroyed by a disaster such as a nuclear attack. That network, called *ARPANET*, became functional in September 1969, linking scientific and academic researchers across the United States.

The original ARPANET consisted of four main computers, one each located at the University of California at Los Angeles, the University of California at Santa Barbara, the Stanford Research Institute, and the University of Utah. Each computer served as a host on the network. A *host*, more commonly known today as a server, is any computer that provides services and connections to other computers on a network. Hosts often use high-speed communications to transfer data and messages over a network.

As researchers and others realized the great benefit of using ARPANET's e-mail to share data and information, ARPANET underwent phenomenal growth. By 1984, ARPANET had more than 1,000 individual computers linked as hosts. Today, more than 350 million hosts connect to the Internet.

Some organizations connected entire networks to ARPANET to take advantage

FIGURE 2-1c (FTP – File Transfer Protocol)

FIGURE 2-1d (newsgroup)

FIGURE 2-1e (chat room)

FIGURE 2-1f (instant messaging)

FIGURE 2-1g (Internet telephony)

of the high-speed communications it offered. In 1986, the National Science Foundation (NSF) connected its huge network of five super-computer centers, called *NSFnet*, to ARPANET. This configuration of complex networks and hosts became known as the Internet.

Until 1995, NSFnet handled the bulk of the communications activity, or **traffic**, on the Internet. In 1995, NSFnet terminated its network on the Internet and resumed its status as a research network.

Today, the Internet consists of many local, regional, national, and international networks. Numerous corporations, commercial firms, and other companies such as IBM provide networks to handle the Internet traffic. Both public and private organizations own networks on the Internet. These networks, along with telephone companies such as Verizon and AT&T, cable and satellite companies, and the government, all contribute toward the internal structure of the Internet. Read Looking Ahead 2-1 for a look at the next generation of the Internet.

Even as the Internet grows, it remains a public, cooperative, and independent network. Each organization on the Internet is responsible only for maintaining its own network. No single person, company, institution, or government agency controls or owns the Internet. The *World Wide Web Consortium* (W3C), however, oversees research and sets standards and guidelines for many areas of the Internet. The mission of the W3C is to contribute to the growth of the Web. Nearly 400 organizations from around the world are members of the W3C. They advise, define standards, and address other issues.

WEB LINK 2-1

W3C

For more information, visit scsite.com/ dc2008/ch2/weblink and then click W3C.

LOOKING AHEAD 2-1

Internet Speeds into the Future

The Internet of the future will be much larger and faster. According to some Internet experts, in the next 20 years, Web surfers will be able to browse more than 250 million Web sites.

This increase in volume will be based, in part, on *Internet2*. This not-for-profit project connects more than 206 educational and 60 research institutions via a high-speed private network. When used solely as a research tool, Internet2 applications process massive amounts of data, such as linking observatories atop Hawaii's tallest mountains and video conferences from 20 remote sites across the world.

Schools have used the Internet2 for interactive video conferences linking authors with readers, music composers with conductors, and operating room doctors with medical students. For more information, visit scsite.com/dc2008/ch2/looking and then click Internet2.

HOW THE INTERNET WORKS

Data sent over the Internet travels via many networks and communications media. The following sections present various ways to connect to these networks on the Internet.

Connecting to the Internet

Employees and students often connect to the Internet through a business or school network. In this case, the computers usually are part of a network that connects to an Internet access provider through a high-speed connection.

Some homes use dial-up access to connect to the Internet. **Dial-up access** takes place when the modem in your computer uses a standard telephone line to connect to the Internet. A dial-up connection, however, is slow-speed technology.

Many home and small business users are opting for higher-speed *broadband* Internet connections through DSL, cable television networks, radio signals, or satellite.

- **DSL** (digital subscriber line) is a technology that provides high-speed Internet connections using regular copper telephone lines.
- A **cable modem** allows access to high-speed Internet services through the cable television network.
- *Fixed wireless* high-speed Internet connections use a dish-shaped antenna on your house or business to communicate with a tower location via radio signals.
- A *Wi-Fi* (wireless fidelity) network uses radio signals to provide Internet connections to wireless computers and devices.
- A *satellite modem* communicates with a satellite dish to provide high-speed Internet connections via satellite.

In most cases, broadband Internet access is always on. That is, it is connected to the Internet the entire time the computer is running. With dial-up access, by contrast, you must establish the connection to the Internet. Usually a modem dials the telephone number to the Internet access provider.

Mobile users access the Internet using a variety of technologies. Most hotels and airports provide dial-up or broadband Internet connections. Wireless Internet access technologies, such as Wi-Fi networks, allow mobile users to connect easily to the Internet with notebook computers, Tablet PCs, PDAs, and smart phones while away from a telephone, cable, or other wired connection. Many public locations, such as airports, hotels, schools, shopping malls, and coffee shops, are *hot spots* that provide Wi-Fi Internet connections to users with mobile computers or devices. Some cities and counties provide free Wi-Fi Internet connections to all residents.

Access Providers

An **access provider** is a business that provides individuals and companies access to the Internet free or for a fee. For example, some Wi-Fi networks provide free access while others charge a

per use fee. Other access providers often charge a fixed amount for an Internet connection, usually about $7 to $25 per month for dial-up, $13 to $40 for DSL, $20 to $45 for cable, $35 to $70 for fixed wireless, and $60 to $99 for satellite. To attract more customers, some access providers also offer Web publishing services. Web publishing is discussed later in the chapter.

Users access the Internet through regional or national ISPs, online service providers, and wireless Internet service providers (Figure 2-2).

FAQ 2-1

Is bandwidth important?

Yes. *Bandwidth* is a measure of how fast data and information travel over transmission media. Thus, higher-speed broadband Internet connections have a higher bandwidth than dial-up connections. For more information, visit scsite.com/dc2008/ch2/faq and then click Bandwidth.

FIGURE 2-2 Common ways to access the Internet are through a regional or national Internet service provider, an online service provider, or a wireless Internet service provider.

An **ISP** (**Internet service provider**) is a regional or national access provider. A *regional ISP* usually provides Internet access to a specific geographic area. A *national ISP* is a business that provides Internet access in cities and towns nationwide. For dial-up access, some national ISPs provide both local and toll-free telephone numbers. Due to their larger size, national ISPs usually offer more services and have a larger technical support staff than regional ISPs. Examples of national ISPs are AT&T Worldnet Service and EarthLink.

In addition to providing Internet access, an **online service provider** (**OSP**) also has many members-only features. These features include special content and services such as news, weather, legal information, financial data, hardware and software guides, games, travel guides, e-mail, photo communities, online calendars, and instant messaging. Some even have their own built-in Web browser. The fees for using an OSP sometimes are slightly higher than fees for an ISP. The two more popular OSPs are AOL (America Online) and MSN (Microsoft Network). AOL differs from many OSPs in that it provides gateway functionality to the Internet, meaning it regulates the Internet services to which members have access. AOL also provides free access to its services to any user with a broadband Internet connection.

With dial-up Internet access, the telephone number you dial connects you to an access point on the Internet, called a *point of presence* (*POP*). When selecting an ISP or OSP, ensure it provides at least one local POP telephone number. Otherwise, long-distance telephone charges will apply for the time you connect to the Internet.

A **wireless Internet service provider** (*WISP*) is a company that provides wireless Internet access to computers and mobile devices, such as smart phones and PDAs, with built-in wireless capability or to computers with wireless modems or wireless access devices. An antenna on or built into the computer or device typically sends signals through the airwaves to communicate with a wireless Internet service provider. Some examples of wireless Internet service providers include Boingo Wireless, Cingular Wireless, T-Mobile, and Verizon Wireless.

WEB LINK 2-2

Wireless Internet Service Providers

For more information, visit scsite.com/dc2008/ch2/weblink and then click Wireless Internet Service Providers.

FAQ 2-2

Is free Internet access becoming more popular?

Free Internet access is growing in popularity. Internet access providers such as NetZero and AOL provide free Internet access and rely on revenue from advertisers to cover the costs associated with providing the free Internet service. For this reason, customers using a free Internet access provider may notice more advertisements. For more information, visit scsite.com/dc2008/ch2/faq and then click Free Internet Access.

How Data Travels the Internet

Computers connected to the Internet work together to transfer data and information around the world using servers and clients. On the Internet, your computer is a client that can access data, information, and services on a variety of servers.

The inner structure of the Internet works much like a transportation system. Just as interstate highways connect major cities and carry the bulk of the automotive traffic across the country, several main transmission media carry the heaviest amount of traffic on the Internet. These major carriers of network traffic are known collectively as the *Internet backbone*.

In the United States, the transmission media that make up the Internet backbone exchange data at several different major cities across the country. That is, they transfer data from one network to another until it reaches its final destination (Figure 2-3).

FAQ 2-3

How do I find the right access provider?

The Web provides many comprehensive lists of access providers. These lists often use the terms ISP and OSP interchangeably. One of the more popular lists on the Web is called The List. For more information, visit scsite.com/dc2008/ch2/faq and then click The List.

FIGURE 2-3 HOW A HOME USER'S DATA MIGHT TRAVEL THE INTERNET USING A CABLE MODEM CONNECTION

Step 1: You initiate an action to request data from the Internet. For example, you request to display a Web page on your computer screen.

Step 2: A cable modem transfers the computer's digital signals to the cable television line in your house.

Step 3: Your request (digital signals) travels through cable television lines to a central cable system, which is shared by up to 500 homes in a neighborhood.

Step 4: The central cable system sends your request over high-speed fiber-optic lines to the cable operator, who often also is the ISP.

Step 5: The ISP routes your request through the Internet backbone to the destination server (in this example, the server that contains the requested Web site).

Step 6: The server retrieves the requested Web page and sends it back through the Internet backbone to your computer.

Internet Addresses

The Internet relies on an addressing system much like the postal service to send data to a computer at a specific destination. An **IP address**, short for *Internet Protocol address*, is a number that uniquely identifies each computer or device connected to the Internet. The IP address usually consists of four groups of numbers, each separated by a period. The number in each group is between 0 and 255. For example, the numbers 216.239.39.99 are an IP address. In general, the first portion of each IP address identifies the network and the last portion identifies the specific computer.

These all-numeric IP addresses are difficult to remember and use. Thus, the Internet supports the use of a text name that represents one or more IP addresses. A **domain name** is the text version of an IP address. Figure 2-4 shows an IP address and its associated domain name.

As with an IP address, the components of a domain name are separated by periods.

In Figure 2-4, the com portion of the domain name is called the top-level domain. Every domain name contains a *top-level domain (TLD)*, which is the last section of the domain name. A generic TLD (*gTLD*), such as the one in Figure 2-4, identifies the type of organization associated with the domain. *Dot-com* is the term sometimes used to describe organizations with a TLD of com.

IP address ⟶ 216.239.39.99

Domain name ⟶ www.google.com

top-level domain

FIGURE 2-4 The IP address and domain name for the Google Web site.

The group that assigns and controls top-level domains is the *Internet Corporation for Assigned Names and Numbers (ICANN* pronounced EYE-can). Figure 2-5 lists some generic TLDs. For international Web sites outside the United States, the domain name also includes a country code TLD (*ccTLD*), which is a two-letter country code, such as au for Australia or fr for France. For example, www.philips.com.au is the domain name for Philips Australia.

The *domain name system (DNS)* is the method that the Internet uses to store domain names and their corresponding IP addresses. When you specify a domain name, a **DNS server** translates the domain name to its associated IP address so data can be routed to the correct computer. A DNS server is an Internet server that usually is associated with an Internet access provider.

For a more technical discussion about Internet addresses, read the High-Tech Talk article on page 102.

EXAMPLES OF GENERIC TOP-LEVEL DOMAINS

Original Generic TLD	Intended Purpose
com	Commercial organizations, businesses, and companies
edu	Educational institutions
gov	Government agencies
mil	Military organizations
net	Network providers and commercial companies
org	Nonprofit organizations
Newer Generic TLD	**Intended Purpose**
aero	Aviation community members
biz	Businesses of all sizes
cat	Catalan cultural community
coop	Business cooperatives such as credit unions and rural electric co-ops
info	Businesses, organizations, or individuals providing general information
jobs	Employment or human resource businesses
mobi	Delivery and management of mobile Internet services
museum	Accredited museums
name	Individuals or families
pro	Certified professionals such as doctors, lawyers, and accountants
tel	Internet communications
travel	Travel industry

FIGURE 2-5   In addition to the TLDs listed above, the Internet Corporation for Assigned Names and Numbers (ICANN) continually evaluates proposals for new TLDs.

FAQ 2-4

How does a person or company get a domain name?

For top-level domains such as biz, com, info, name, net, and org, you register for a domain name from a *registrar*, which is an organization that sells and manages domain names. In addition to determining prices and policies for domain name registration, a registrar may offer additional services such as Web site hosting. For more information, visit scsite.com/dc2008/ch2/faq and then click Registrar.

Test your knowledge of pages 68 through 74 in Quiz Yourself 2-1.

QUIZ YOURSELF 2-1

Instructions: Find the true statement below. Then, rewrite the remaining false statements so they are true.

1. An access provider is a business that provides individuals and companies access to the Internet free or for a fee.

2. A WISP is a number that uniquely identifies each computer or device connected to the Internet.

3. An IP address, such as www.google.com, is the text version of a domain name.

4. Dial-up access takes place when the modem in your computer uses the cable television network to connect to the Internet.

5. The World Wide Web Consortium (W3C) oversees research and owns the Internet.

Quiz Yourself Online: To further check your knowledge of Internet history, accessing and connecting to the Internet, and Internet addresses, visit scsite.com/dc2008/ch2/quiz and then click Objectives 1 – 3.

THE WORLD WIDE WEB

Although many people use the terms World Wide Web and Internet interchangeably, the World Wide Web actually is a service of the Internet. While the Internet was developed in the late 1960s, the World Wide Web emerged in the early 1990s. Since then, it has grown phenomenally to become one of the more widely used Internet services.

The **World Wide Web** (*WWW*), or **Web**, consists of a worldwide collection of electronic documents. Each electronic document on the Web is called a **Web page**, which can contain text, graphics, audio, and video. Additionally, Web pages usually have built-in connections to other documents.

Some Web pages are static (fixed); others are dynamic (changing). Visitors to a *static Web page* all see the same content. With a *dynamic Web page*, by contrast, visitors can customize some or all of the viewed content such as desired stock quotes, weather for a region, or ticket availability for flights.

A **Web site** is a collection of related Web pages and associated items, such as documents and pictures, stored on a Web server. A **Web server** is a computer that delivers requested Web pages to your computer. The same Web server can store multiple Web sites. Some industry experts use the terms **Web 2.0** and *participatory Web* to refer to Web sites that allow users to modify Web site content, provide a means for users to share personal information, and have application software built into the site for visitors to use.

The following pages discuss how to browse the Web, use a Web address, search for information on the Web, and recognize types of Web sites. Also discussed are multimedia on the Web and Web publishing.

Browsing the Web

A **Web browser**, or **browser**, is application software that allows users to access and view Web pages. To browse the Web, you need a computer that is connected to the Internet and has a Web browser. The more widely used Web browsers for personal computers are Internet Explorer, Netscape, Firefox, Opera, and Safari.

With an Internet connection established, you start a Web browser. The browser retrieves and displays a starting Web page, sometimes called the browser's home page. Figure 2-6 shows how a Web browser displays a home page. The initial home page that is displayed

FIGURE 2-6   HOW A WEB BROWSER DISPLAYS A HOME PAGE

Step 1:
Click the Web browser program name to start the Web browser software.

Internet Explorer Web browser name

Step 2:
Behind the scenes, the Web browser looks up its home page setting. For illustration purposes only, the screen below shows the home page setting is msn.com.

msn.com

Step 3:
The Web browser communicates with a server maintained by your Internet access provider. The server translates the domain name of the home page to an IP address and then sends the IP address to your computer.

207.68.172.234

Step 4:
The Web browser uses the IP address to contact the Web server associated with the home page and then requests the home page from the server. The Web server sends the home page to the Web browser, which formats the page for display on your screen.

is one selected by your Web browser. You can change your browser's home page at anytime.

The more common usage of the term, **home page**, refers to the first page that a Web site displays. Similar to a book cover or a table of contents for a Web site, the home page provides information about the Web site's purpose and content. Often it provides connections to other documents, Web pages, or Web sites. Many Web sites allow you to personalize the home page so it contains areas of interest to you.

Many current Web browsers support *tabbed browsing*, where the top of the browser displays a tab (similar to a file folder tab) for each Web page you open. To move from one open Web page to another, you *click* the tab in the Web browser; that is, point to the tab and then press the left mouse button.

Internet-enabled mobile devices such as PDAs and smart phones use a special type of browser, called a *microbrowser*, which is designed for their small screens and limited computing power. Many Web sites design Web pages specifically for display on a microbrowser (Figure 2-7).

For a computer or mobile device to display a Web page, the page must be downloaded. **Downloading** is the process of a computer receiving information, such as a Web page, from a server on the Internet. While a browser downloads a Web page, it typically displays an animated logo or icon in the top-right corner of the browser window. The animation stops when the download is complete. Depending on the speed of your Internet connection and the amount of graphics involved, a Web page download can take from a few seconds to several minutes.

Web Addresses

A Web page has a unique address, called a **URL** (*Uniform Resource Locator*) or **Web address**. For example, the home page for the US National Parks Travel Guide Web site has http://www.us-parks.com as its Web address. A Web browser retrieves a Web page using its Web address.

If you know the Web address of a Web page, you can type it in the Address box at the top of the browser window. For example, if you type the Web address http://www.us-parks.com/grand_canyon/scenic_vistas.html in the Address box and then press the ENTER key, the browser downloads and displays the Web page shown in Figure 2-8.

A Web address consists of a protocol, domain name, and sometimes the path to a specific Web page or location on a Web page. Many Web page addresses begin with http://. The *http*, which stands for *Hypertext Transfer Protocol*, is a set of rules that defines how pages transfer on the Internet. The first portion of the domain name identifies the type of Internet server. For example, www indicates a Web server.

To help minimize errors, many browsers and Web sites do not require you enter the http:// portion of the Web address. For example, typing www.us-parks.com/grand_canyon/scenic_vistas.html, instead of the entire address, still accesses the Web site. If you enter an incorrect Web address, the browser may display a list of similar addresses from which you can select. Many Web sites also allow users to eliminate the www from the Web page name.

When you enter the Web address, http://www.us-parks.com/grand_canyon/scenic_vistas.html in the Web browser, it sends a request to the Web server that contains the us-parks.com Web site. The server then retrieves the Web page named scenic_vistas.html in the grand_canyon path and delivers it to your browser, which then displays the Web page on the screen.

When you enter a Web address in a browser, you request, or *pull*, information from a Web server. Some Web servers also can *push* content to your computer at regular intervals or whenever updates are made to the site. For example, some Web servers provide the capability of displaying current sporting event scores or weather reports on your computer screen.

For information about useful Web sites and their associated Web addresses, read the Making Use of the Web feature that follows this chapter.

FIGURE 2-7 Sample microbrowser screens.

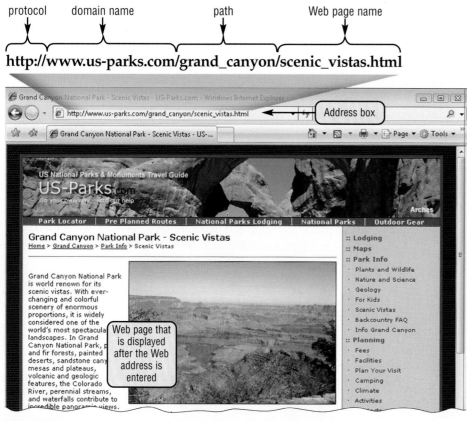

protocol   domain name   path   Web page name

http://www.us-parks.com/grand_canyon/scenic_vistas.html

FIGURE 2-8   After entering the Web address http://www.us-parks.com/grand_canyon/scenic_vistas.html in the Address box, this Web page at the US National Parks Travel Guide Web site is displayed.

FAQ 2-5

Which Web browser currently has the highest market share?

Microsoft's Internet Explorer (IE) currently is the most popular browser, with approximately 76 percent of the market share. The chart below illustrates the market share of the more popular Web browsers. For more information, visit scsite.com/dc2008/ch2/faq and then click Browser Market Share.

■ IE □ Netscape
■ Firefox □ Other

Source: Janco Associates, Inc.

Navigating Web Pages

Most Web pages contain hypertext or hypermedia links. A **link**, short for *hyperlink*, is a built-in connection to another related Web page or part of a Web page. *Hypertext* refers to links in text-based documents, whereas *hypermedia* combines text-based links with graphic, audio, and video links. Links allow you to obtain information in a nonlinear way. That is, instead of accessing topics in a specified order, you move directly to a topic of interest. Branching from one related topic to another in a nonlinear fashion is what makes links so powerful. Some people use the phrase, **surfing the Web**, to refer to the activity of using links to explore the Web.

Text links may be underlined and/or displayed in a color different from other text on the Web page. Pointing to, or positioning the pointer on, a link on the screen typically changes the shape of the pointer to a small hand with a pointing index finger. The Web page shown in Figure 2-9 contains a variety of link types, with the pointer on one of the links.

Each link on a Web page corresponds to another Web address. To activate a link, you click it. Clicking a link causes the Web page

associated with the link to be displayed on the screen. The linked object might be on the same Web page, a different Web page at the same Web site, or a separate Web page at a different Web site in another city or country. To remind you visually that you have clicked a link, a text link often changes color after you click it.

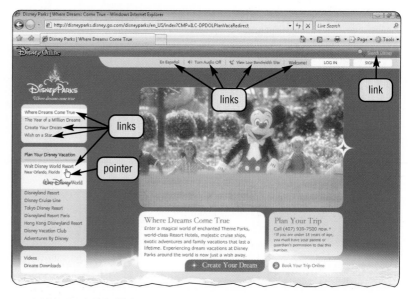

FIGURE 2-9   This Web page contains various types of links: text that is underlined, text in a different color, and images.

Searching for Information on the Web

The Web is a global resource of information. One primary use of the Web is to search for specific information, including text, graphics, audio, and video. The first step in successful searching is to identify the main idea or concept in the topic about which you are seeking information. Determine any synonyms, alternate spellings, or variant word forms for the topic. Then, use a search tool to locate the information.

The two most commonly used search tools are subject directories and search engines. A **subject directory** classifies Web pages in an organized set of categories, such as sports or shopping, and related subcategories. A **search engine** is a program that finds Web sites, Web pages, images, videos, news, and other information.

Some Web sites offer the functionality of both a subject directory and a search engine. Yahoo! and Google, for example, are widely used search engines that also provide a subject directory. To use Yahoo! or Google, you enter the Web address (yahoo.com or google.com) in the Address box in a browser window. The table in Figure 2-10 lists the

Web addresses of several popular general-purpose subject directories and search engines.

SUBJECT DIRECTORIES   A subject directory provides categorized lists of links arranged by subject. Figure 2-11 shows how to use Yahoo!'s

FIGURE 2-11   HOW TO USE A SUBJECT DIRECTORY

Step 1:
Type the subject directory's Web address (in this case, dir.yahoo.com) in the Address box in the Web browser.

Address box

Step 6:
Click the Podcast.net link to display the Podcast.net Web page. Scroll down, if necessary, and then point to the Hardware link in the Computers & Internet cate

Hardware link

Compute
Internet ca

Step 7:
Click the Hardware link to display a list of Hardware podcasts. Scroll throu the list of podcasts, if necessary, and then point to the Mobile Media Deve link.

Mobile Media
Developer link

WIDELY USED SEARCH TOOLS

Search Tool	Web Address	Subject Directory	Search Engine
A9.com	a9.com		X
AlltheWeb	alltheweb.com		X
AltaVista	altavista.com		X
AOL Search	search.aol.com	X	X
Ask.com	ask.com		X
Dogpile	dogpile.com		X
Excite	excite.com	X	X
Gigablast	gigablast.com	X	X
Google	google.com	X	X
Live Search	live.com		X
LookSmart	looksmart.com	X	X
Lycos	lycos.com		X
MSN	msn.com	X	X
Netscape Search	search.netscape.com		X
Open Directory Project	dmoz.org	X	X
Overture	overture.com		X
WebCrawler	webcrawler.com		X
Yahoo!	yahoo.com	X	X

FIGURE 2-10   Many subject directories and search engines allow searching about any topic on the Web.

subject directory to search for podcasts (audio broadcasts) that discuss mobile media. As shown in the figure, you locate a particular topic by clicking links through different levels, moving from the general to the specific. Each time you click a category link, the subject directory displays a list of subcategory links, from which you again choose. You continue in this fashion until the search tool displays a list of Web pages about the desired topic.

The major problem with a subject directory is deciding which categories to choose as you work through the menus of links presented.

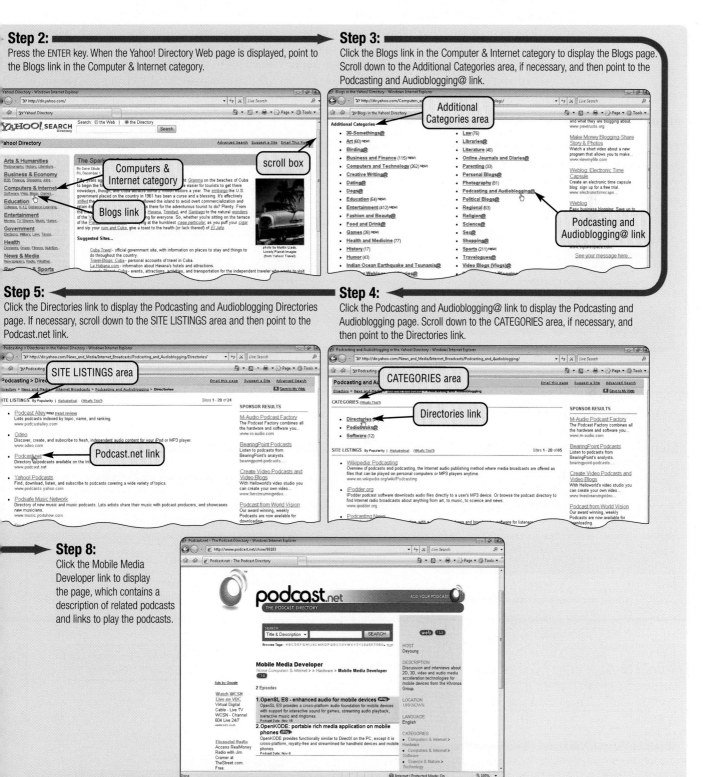

Step 2:
Press the ENTER key. When the Yahoo! Directory Web page is displayed, point to the Blogs link in the Computer & Internet category.

Step 3:
Click the Blogs link in the Computer & Internet category to display the Blogs page. Scroll down to the Additional Categories area, if necessary, and then point to the Podcasting and Audioblogging@ link.

Step 5:
Click the Directories link to display the Podcasting and Audioblogging Directories page. If necessary, scroll down to the SITE LISTINGS area and then point to the Podcast.net link.

Step 4:
Click the Podcasting and Audioblogging@ link to display the Podcasting and Audioblogging page. Scroll down to the CATEGORIES area, if necessary, and then point to the Directories link.

Step 8:
Click the Mobile Media Developer link to display the page, which contains a description of related podcasts and links to play the podcasts.

SEARCH ENGINES A search engine is particularly helpful in locating Web pages about certain topics or in locating specific Web pages, images, videos, news, and other information for which you do not know the exact Web address. Thousands of search engines are available. Some are general and perform searches on any topic; others are restricted to certain subjects, such as finding people, job hunting, or locating real estate.

Instead of clicking through links, search engines require that you enter a word or phrase, called **search text** or *keywords*, that define the item about which you want information. Search engines often respond with results that include thousands of links to Web pages, many with little or no bearing on the information you are seeking. You can eliminate the superfluous pages by carefully crafting a keyword that limits the search.

Figure 2-12 shows how to use the Google search engine to search for the phrase, BBC news digital world podcast. The results of the search, called *hits*, shown in Step 3 include more than two million links to Web pages that reference BBC news digital world podcast. Each hit in the list has a link that, when clicked, displays an associated Web site or Web page.

FIGURE 2-12 HOW TO USE A SEARCH ENGINE

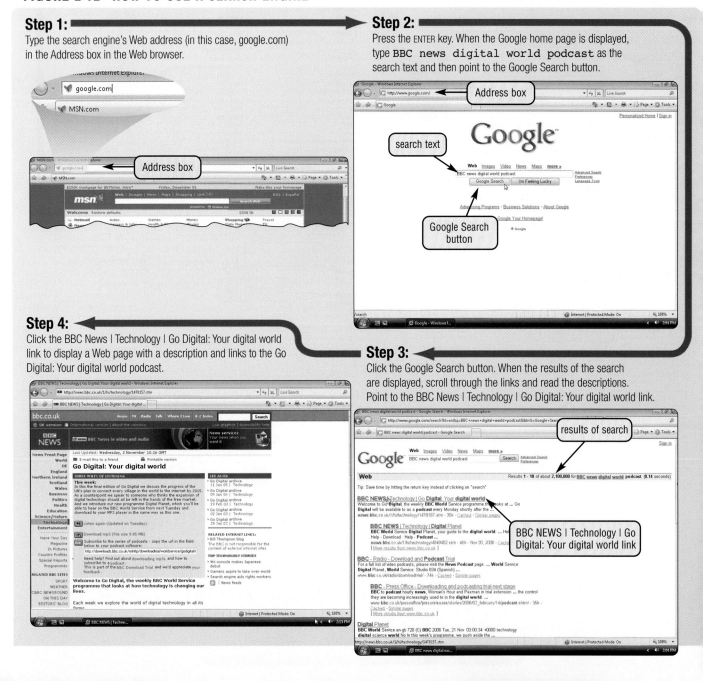

Step 1:
Type the search engine's Web address (in this case, google.com) in the Address box in the Web browser.

Step 2:
Press the ENTER key. When the Google home page is displayed, type BBC news digital world podcast as the search text and then point to the Google Search button.

Step 4:
Click the BBC News | Technology | Go Digital: Your digital world link to display a Web page with a description and links to the Go Digital: Your digital world podcast.

Step 3:
Click the Google Search button. When the results of the search are displayed, scroll through the links and read the descriptions. Point to the BBC News | Technology | Go Digital: Your digital world link.

Most search engines sequence the hits based on how close the words in the search text are to one another in the Web page titles and their descriptions. Thus, the first few links probably contain more relevant information.

If you enter a phrase with spaces between the words in the search text, most search engines display results (hits) that include all of the words, except for common words (e.g., to, the, and). The table in Figure 2-13 lists some common operators you can include in your search text to refine your search. Other techniques you can use to improve your Web searches include the following:

- Use specific nouns and put the most important terms first in the search text.
- List all possible spellings, for example, email, e-mail.
- Before using a search engine, read its Help information.

- If the search is unsuccessful with one search engine, try another.

Many search engines use a program called a *spider* to build and maintain lists of words found on Web sites. When you enter search text, the search engine scans this prebuilt list for hits. The more sophisticated the search engine combined with precise search criteria, the more rapid the response and effective the search.

In addition to searching for Web pages, many search engines allow you to search for images, news articles, and local businesses. Read Looking Ahead 2-2 for a look at the next generation of searching techniques.

FAQ 2-6

How do Google and Yahoo! make money?

Google and Yahoo! are able to offer their services free to the public by charging a fee to companies that wish to advertise on their Web site. Advertisements can be very effective, because they often are related to your search results. For more information, visit scsite.com/dc2008/ch2/faq and then click Online Advertisements.

SEARCH ENGINE OPERATORS

Operator	Description	Examples	Explanation
Space or +	Use the space or plus operator (+) when you want search results to display hits that include specific words.	art + music art music	Results have both words art and music — in any order.
OR	Use the OR operator when you want search results to display hits that include only one word from a list.	dog OR puppy dog OR puppy OR canine	Results have either the word dog or puppy. Results have the word dog or puppy or canine.
-	Use the minus operator (-) when you want to exclude a word from your search results.	automobile -convertible	Results include automobile but do not include convertible.
" "	Use the quotation marks operator when you want to search for an exact phrase in a certain order.	"19th century literature"	Results include only hits that have the exact phrase, 19th century literature.
*	Use the asterisk operator (*) when you want search results to substitute characters in place of the asterisk.	writer*	Results include any word that begins with writer (e.g., writer, writers, writer's).

FIGURE 2-13 Use search engine operators to help refine a search.

 LOOKING AHEAD 2-2

Facing Up to Search Technology

If you think a face looks familiar but you cannot recall the person's name, people-searching tools on the Internet may help solve the identity question. *Facial-recognition technology* being developed could identify pictures based on facial features, such as blue eyes or dimples. Once an individual is identified, the search engine then could search for other pictures of that person stored on a computer or on the Internet.

Other search engines being created are locating 3-D images for engineers and designers who use millions of inventoried parts at large industrial companies. When these employees need to locate a particular item based on a shape, not a part or model number, the search engines analyze shapes based on patterns and contours.

Researchers predict image searches will be common on the Internet in less than 15 years and will include a voice interface, a thesaurus, and customized results based on the researcher's background. For more information, visit scsite.com/dc2008/ch2/looking and then click Search Engines.

Types of Web Sites

Twelve types of Web sites are portal, news, informational, business/marketing, educational, entertainment, advocacy, blog, wiki, online social network, content aggregator, and personal (Figure 2-14). Many Web sites fall in more than one of these categories.

PORTAL　A **portal** is a Web site that offers a variety of Internet services from a single, convenient location (Figure 2-14a). Most portals offer the following free services: search engine and/or subject directory; news; sports and weather; Web publishing; reference tools such as yellow pages, stock quotes, and maps; shopping; and e-mail and other forms of online communications.

Many portals have online communities. An **online community** is a Web site that joins a specific group of people with similar interests or relationships. These communities may offer online photo albums, chat rooms, and other services to facilitate communications among members.

Popular portals include AltaVista, AOL, Excite, GO.com, LookSmart, Lycos, MSN, NBCi, Netscape, and Yahoo!. A *wireless portal* is a portal designed for Internet-enabled mobile devices.

NEWS　A news Web site contains newsworthy material including stories and articles relating to current events, life, money, sports, and the weather (Figure 2-14b). Many magazines and newspapers sponsor Web sites that provide summaries of printed articles, as well as articles not included in the printed versions. Newspapers and television and radio stations are some of the media that maintain news Web sites.

INFORMATIONAL　An informational Web site contains factual information (Figure 2-14c). Many United States government agencies have informational Web sites providing information such as census data, tax codes, and the congressional budget. Other organizations provide information such as public transportation schedules and published research findings.

BUSINESS/MARKETING　A business/marketing Web site contains content that promotes or sells products or services (Figure 2-14d). Nearly every business has a business/marketing Web site. Allstate Insurance Company, Dell Inc., General Motors Corporation, Kraft Foods Inc., and Walt Disney Company all have business/marketing Web sites. Many of these companies also allow you to purchase their products or services online.

EDUCATIONAL　An educational Web site offers exciting, challenging avenues for formal and informal teaching and learning (Figure 2-14e). On the Web, you can learn how airplanes fly or how to cook a meal. For a more structured learning experience, companies provide online training to employees; and colleges offer online classes and degrees. Instructors often use the Web to enhance classroom teaching by publishing course materials, grades, and other pertinent class information.

ENTERTAINMENT　An entertainment Web site offers an interactive and engaging environment (Figure 2-14f). Popular entertainment Web sites offer music, videos, sports, games, ongoing Web episodes, sweepstakes, chats, and more. Sophisticated entertainment Web sites often partner with other technologies. For example, you can cast your vote about a topic on a television show.

ADVOCACY　An advocacy Web site contains content that describes a cause, opinion, or idea (Figure 2-14g). These Web sites usually present views of a particular group or association. Sponsors of advocacy Web sites include the Democratic National Committee, the Republican National Committee, the Society for the Prevention of Cruelty to Animals, and the Society to Protect Human Rights.

BLOG　A **blog**, short for *Weblog*, is an informal Web site consisting of time-stamped articles, or posts, in a diary or journal format, usually listed in reverse chronological order (Figure 2-14h). A blog that contains video clips is called a video blog, or *vlog*. The term *blogosphere* refers to the worldwide collection of blogs, and the *vlogosphere* refers to all vlogs worldwide.

Blogs reflect the interests, opinions, and personalities of the author, called the *blogger* or *vlogger* (for vlog author), and sometimes site visitors.

Blogs have become an important means of worldwide communication. Businesses create blogs to communicate with employees, customers, and vendors. Teachers create blogs to collaborate with other teachers and students. Home users create blogs to share aspects of their personal life with family, friends, and others.

WIKI　A **wiki** is a collaborative Web site that allows users to create, add to, modify, or delete the Web site content via their Web browser. Most wikis are open to modification by the general

FIGURE 2-14a (portal)

FIGURE 2-14b (news)

FIGURE 2-14c (informational)

FIGURE 2-14d (business/marketing)

FIGURE 2-14e (educational)

FIGURE 2-14f (entertainment)

FIGURE 2-14g (advocacy)

FIGURE 2-14h (blog)

FIGURE 2-14i (wiki)

FIGURE 2-14j (social network)

FIGURE 2-14k (content aggregator)

FIGURE 2-14l (personal)

FIGURE 2-14
Types of Web sites.

public. Wikis usually collect recent edits on a Web page so someone can review them for accuracy. The difference between a wiki and a blog is that users cannot modify original posts made by the blogger. A popular wiki is Wikipedia, a free Web encyclopedia (Figure 2-14i on the previous page). Read Ethics & Issues 2-1 for a related discussion.

ONLINE SOCIAL NETWORKS An **online social network**, also called a **social networking Web site**, is a Web site that encourages members in its online community to share their interests, ideas, stories, photos, music, and videos with other registered users (Figure 2-14j). Most include chat rooms, newsgroups, and other communications services. Popular social networking Web sites include Facebook, Friendster, and MySpace, which alone has more than 12 million visitors each day. A **media sharing Web site** is a specific type of online social network that enables members to share media such as photos, music, and videos. Flickr, Fotki, and Webshots are popular photo sharing communities; Google Video and YouTube are popular video sharing communities.

CONTENT AGGREGATOR A *content aggregator* is a business that gathers and organizes Web content and then distributes, or feeds, the content to subscribers for free or a fee. Examples of distributed content include news, music, video, and pictures. Subscribers select content in which they are interested. Whenever this content changes, it is downloaded automatically (pushed) to the subscriber's computer or mobile device.

    RSS 2.0, which stands for *Really Simple Syndication*, is a specification that content aggregators use to distribute content to subscribers (Figure 2-14k). *Atom* is another specification sometimes used by content aggregators to distribute content.

WEB LINK 2-3

MySpace
For more information, visit scsite.com/dc2008/ch2/weblink and then click MySpace.

PERSONAL A private individual or family not usually associated with any organization may maintain a personal Web site or just a single Web page (Figure 2-14l). People publish personal Web pages for a variety of reasons. Some are job hunting. Others simply want to share life experiences with the world.

Evaluating a Web Site

Do not assume that information presented on the Web is correct or accurate. Any person, company, or organization can publish a Web page on the Internet. No one oversees the content of these Web pages. Figure 2-15 lists guidelines for assessing the value of a Web site or Web page before relying on its content.

GUIDELINES FOR EVALUATING THE VALUE OF A WEB SITE

Evaluation Criteria	Reliable Web Sites
Affiliation	A reputable institution should support the Web site without bias in the information.
Audience	The Web site should be written at an appropriate level.
Authority	The Web site should list the author and the appropriate credentials.
Content	The Web site should be well organized and the links should work.
Currency	The information on the Web page should be current.
Design	The pages at the Web site should download quickly and be visually pleasing and easy to navigate.
Objectivity	The Web site should contain little advertising and be free of preconceptions.

FIGURE 2-15 Criteria for evaluating a Web site's content.

ETHICS & ISSUES 2-1

Should You Trust a Wiki for Academic Research?

As wikis have grown in number, size, and popularity, some educators and librarians have shunned the sites as valid sources of research. While many wikis are tightly controlled with a limited number of contributors and expert editors, these usually focus on narrowly-defined, specialized topics. Large online wikis, such as Wikipedia, often involve thousands of editors, many of whom remain anonymous. Recently, an entry on Wikipedia was maliciously altered to suggest that a prominent journalist was involved in the assassination of John F. Kennedy. Editors corrected the information several months later after a friend of the journalist notified him of the errors. In other situations, rival political factions falsified or embellished wiki entries in an attempt to give their candidate an advantage. Some wiki supporters argue that most wikis provide adequate controls to quickly correct false or misleading content and to punish those who submit it. Some propose that wikis should be used as a starting point for researching a fact, but that the fact should be verified using traditional sources. Should wikis be allowed as valid sources for academic research? Why or why not? Would you submit a paper to your instructor that cites a wiki as a source? An encyclopedia? Why or why not? What policies could wikis enforce that could garner more confidence from the public?

Multimedia on the Web

Most Web pages include more than just formatted text and links. The more exciting Web pages use multimedia. **Multimedia** refers to any application that combines text with graphics, animation, audio, video, and/or virtual reality. Multimedia brings a Web page to life, increases the types of information available on the Web, expands the Web's potential uses, and makes the Internet a more entertaining place to explore. Multimedia Web pages often require proper hardware and software and take more time to download because they contain large graphics files and video or audio clips.

The sections that follow discuss how the Web uses graphics, animation, audio, video, and virtual reality.

FAQ 2-7

What is a file?

A *file* is a unit of storage. When you want the computer to store items (e.g., data, information, programs, graphics, audio clips, or video clips), it places them in files on storage media such as a hard disk. File sizes vary depending on items being stored. For example, graphics files usually consume more storage space than data files. For more information, visit scsite.com/dc2008/ch2/faq and then click Files.

GRAPHICS A **graphic**, or *graphical image*, is a digital representation of nontext information such as a drawing, chart, or photograph. Today, many Web pages use colorful graphical designs and images to convey messages (Figure 2-16).

The Web contains countless images about a variety of subjects. You can download many of these images at no cost and use them for non-commercial purposes. Recall that downloading is the process of transferring an object from the Web to your computer. For example, you can insert images into greeting cards, announcements, and other documents.

Of the graphics formats that exist on the Web (Figure 2-17), the two more common are JPEG and GIF formats. *JPEG* (pronounced JAY-peg) is a format that compresses graphics to reduce their file size, which means the file takes up less storage space. Smaller file sizes result in faster downloading of Web pages because small files transmit faster than large files. The

more compressed the file, the smaller the image and the lower the quality. The goal with JPEG graphics is to reach a balance between image quality and file size. Digital photographs often use the JPEG format.

GIF (pronounced jiff) graphics also use compression techniques to reduce file sizes. The GIF format works best for images that have only a few distinct colors, such as company logos. The newer *PNG* (pronounced ping) graphics format improves upon the GIF format, and thus may eventually replace the GIF format.

The BMP and TIFF formats listed in Figure 2-17 may require special viewer software, and they have larger file sizes. Thus, these formats are not used on the Web as frequently as JPEG, GIF, and PNG formats.

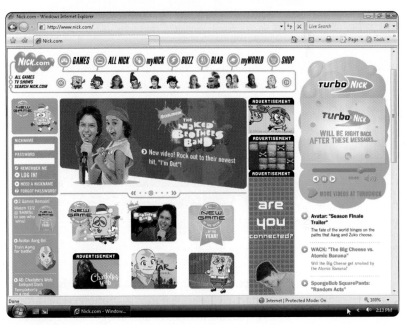

FIGURE 2-16 This Web page uses colorful graphical designs and images to convey its messages.

GRAPHICS FORMATS USED ON THE WEB

Abbreviation	Name	Uses
BMP	Bit Map	Desktop background, scanned images
GIF	Graphics Interchange Format	Simple diagrams, shapes, images with few colors
JPEG	Joint Photographic Experts Group	Digital camera photographs
PNG	Portable Network Graphics	Web graphics
TIFF	Tagged Image File Format	Photographs used by printing industry

FIGURE 2-17 The Web uses graphics file formats for images.

Some Web sites use thumbnails on their pages because graphics can be time-consuming to display. A *thumbnail* is a small version of a larger graphic. You usually can click a thumbnail to display a larger image (Figure 2-18).

FIGURE 2-18
Clicking the thumbnail in the top screen displays a larger image in a separate window.

ANIMATION Many Web pages use **animation**, which is the appearance of motion created by displaying a series of still images in sequence. Animation can make Web pages more visually interesting or draw attention to important information or links. For example, text that animates by scrolling across the screen can serve as a ticker to display stock updates, news, sports scores, weather, or other information. Web-based games often use animation.

Web page developers add animation to Web pages using a variety of techniques. Web page authoring programs, such as Adobe Flash, enable Web site developers to combine animation and interactivity in Web pages. Developers unfamiliar with Web page authoring programs can create an *animated GIF*, which combines several GIF images in a single GIF file.

AUDIO On the Web, you can listen to audio clips and live audio. **Audio** includes music, speech, or any other sound. Simple applications consist of individual audio files available for download to a computer. Once downloaded, you can play (listen to) the contents of these files. Some common Web audio file formats are listed in Figure 2-19. Audio files are compressed to reduce their file sizes. For example, the **MP3** format reduces an audio file to about one-tenth its original size, while preserving much of the original quality of the sound.

Some music publishers have Web sites that allow users to download sample tracks free to persuade them to buy the entire CD. Other Web sites allow a user to purchase and download an entire CD (Figure 2-20). It is legal to download copyrighted music only if the song's copyright holder has granted permission for users to download and play the song. Copyright issues led to the development of *digital rights management (DRM)*, a strategy designed to prevent illegal distribution of music and other digital content. Read Ethics & Issues 2-2 for a related discussion.

To listen to an audio file on your computer, you need special software called a **player**. Most current operating systems contain a player. Popular players include iTunes, RealPlayer, and Windows Media Player. You can download the players free from the Web.

Some applications on the Web use streaming audio. **Streaming** is the process of transferring data in a continuous and even flow. Streaming allows users to access and use a file while it is transmitting. For example, *streaming audio* enables you to listen to music as it downloads to your computer. Many radio and television stations use streaming audio to broadcast music, interviews, talk shows, sporting events, music videos, news, live concerts, and other segments.

Podcasting is another popular method of distributing audio. A *podcast* is recorded audio, usually an MP3 file, stored on a Web site that can be downloaded to a computer or a portable media player such as an iPod. Examples of podcasts include music, radio shows, news stories, classroom lectures, political messages, and television commentaries. Podcasters register their podcasts with content aggregators. Subscribers select podcast feeds they want to be downloaded automatically whenever they connect. Some Web sites, such as podcast.net, specialize in podcast distribution. Others, such as National Public Radio, have incorporated a podcast component in their existing Web site.

AUDIO WEB FILE FORMATS

Format	Description	Format	Description
AAC	Advanced Audio Coding	WAV	Windows waveform
AIFF	Audio Interchange File Format	WMA	Windows Media Audio (part of Windows Media framework)
ASF	Advanced Streaming (or Systems) Format (part of Windows Media framework)	RA	RealAudio sound file (supported by RealPlayer)
		QT	QuickTime audio, video, or 3-D animation
MP3	Moving Pictures Experts Group Audio Layer 3 (MPEG-3)		

FIGURE 2-19 Popular Web audio file formats.

FIGURE 2-20 HOW TO PURCHASE AND DOWNLOAD MUSIC

Step 1: Display the music Web site on the screen. Search for, select, and pay for the music you want to purchase from the music Web site.

Step 2: Download the music from the Web site's server to your computer's hard disk.

Step 3a: Listen to the music from your computer's hard disk.

Step 3b: Download music from your computer's hard disk to a portable media player. Listen to the music through earphones attached to the portable media player.

 ETHICS & ISSUES 2-2

Who Should Control the Content of Your CDs, DVDs, and Media Files?

When you purchase a CD, a DVD, or media files online, you are not purchasing the songs or movies they contain. You actually are purchasing a license to listen to or watch the digital content in a certain manner. The license limits what you can do with the CDs, DVDs, or media files. For example, you cannot play the music or movies in a public forum, nor can you copy and distribute the digital content. Some media companies now employ electronic means of digital rights management (DRM), which automatically restricts what you can do with digital content. Media companies claim that DRM helps them to stem the tide of piracy and the sharing of content. Consumers argue that DRM restrictions infringe on their rights of fair use, and that oftentimes DRM makes playing the content in certain devices impossible. In some cases, DRM prevents users from making backup copies of the content or copying the content to their computers or other devices. Some people have worked around DRM restrictions, but the *Digital Millennium Copyright Act* (DMCA) makes any attempt to circumvent DRM an illegal activity. Because you already own a license to the content, if you scratch or lose a CD or DVD, should you be able to obtain a free or low-cost replacement for the content? Why or why not? If you already purchased a license for music by purchasing a CD, is it fair that you should pay full price again if you also would like the music in MP3 format? Why? How can the rights of media companies and consumers best be balanced?

Web publishing is the development and maintenance of Web pages. To develop a Web page, you do not have to be a computer programmer. For the small business or home user, Web publishing is fairly easy as long as you have the proper tools. The five major steps to Web publishing are as follows: (1) plan a Web site, (2) analyze and design a Web site, (3) create a Web site, (4) deploy a Web site, and (5) maintain a Web site. Figure 2-24 illustrates these steps with respect to a personal Web site.

FIGURE 2-24 HOW TO PUBLISH YOUR RESUME ON THE WEB

Step 1:
Plan a Web site.
Think about issues that could affect the design of the Web site.

Step 2:
Analyze and design a Web site. Design the layout of the elements of the Web site.

Step 3:
Create a Web site. Use word processing software or Web page authoring software to create the Web site.

Step 4:
Deploy a Web site. Save the Web site on a Web server.

Step 5:
Maintain a Web site. Visit your Web site regularly to be sure it is working and current.

Test your knowledge of pages 75 through 90 in Quiz Yourself 2-2.

QUIZ YOURSELF 2-2

Instructions: Find the true statement below. Then, rewrite the remaining false statements so they are true.

1. A blog is a Web site that uses a regularly updated journal format to reflect the interests, opinions, and personalities of the author and sometimes site visitors.

2. A Web browser classifies Web pages in an organized set of categories, such as sports or shopping, and related subcategories.

3. Audio and video files are downloaded to reduce their file sizes.

4. Popular portals include iTunes, RealPlayer, and Windows Media Player.

5. The more widely used search engines for personal computers are Internet Explorer, Netscape, Firefox, Opera, and Safari.

6. To develop a Web page, you have to be a computer programmer.

7. To improve your Web searches, use general nouns and put the least important terms first in the search text.

Quiz Yourself Online: To further check your knowledge of Web addresses, Web browsers, searching, types of Web sites, elements of a Web page, and Web publishing, visit scsite.com/dc2008/ch2/quiz and then click Objectives 4 – 9.

E-COMMERCE

E-commerce, short for *electronic commerce*, is a business transaction that occurs over an electronic network such as the Internet. Anyone with access to a computer, an Internet connection, and a means to pay for purchased goods or services can participate in e-commerce (Figure 2-25).

In the past, e-commerce transactions were conducted primarily using desktop computers. Today, many mobile computers and devices, such as PDAs and smart phones, also access the Web wirelessly. Some people use the term *m-commerce* (mobile commerce) to identify e-commerce that takes place using mobile devices.

Popular uses of e-commerce by consumers include shopping, investing, and banking. Users can purchase just about any product or service on the Web. Some examples include flowers, books, computers, prescription drugs, music, movies, cars, airline tickets, and concert tickets. Through online investing, individuals buy and sell stocks or bonds without using a broker.

Three different types of e-commerce are business-to-consumer, consumer-to-consumer, and business-to-business. *Business-to-consumer (B2C) e-commerce* consists of the sale of goods

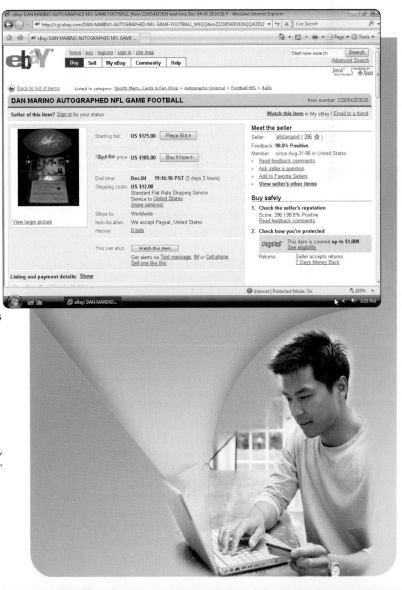

FIGURE 2-25 E-commerce activities include shopping for goods at an online auction, such as eBay.

and services to the general public. For example, Dell has a B2C Web site. Instead of visiting a computer store to purchase a computer, customers can order one that meets their specifications directly from the Dell Web site.

A customer (consumer) visits an online business through an **electronic storefront**, which contains product descriptions, graphics, and a shopping cart. The **shopping cart** allows the customer to collect purchases. When ready to complete the sale, the customer enters personal data and the method of payment, preferably through a secure Internet connection. Read Looking Ahead 2-3 for a look at the next generation of shopping carts.

Instead of purchasing from a business, consumers can purchase from each other. For example, with an **online auction**, users bid on an item being sold by someone else. The highest bidder at the end of the bidding period purchases the item. *Consumer-to-consumer (C2C) e-commerce* occurs when one consumer sells directly to another, such as in an online auction. eBay is one of the more popular online auction Web sites.

Most e-commerce, though, actually takes place between businesses, which is called *business-to-business (B2B) e-commerce*. Businesses often provide goods and services to other businesses, such as online advertising, recruiting, credit, sales, market research, technical support, and training. For example, some MasterCard and Visa credit card companies provide corporations with Web-based purchasing, tracking, and transaction downloading capabilities.

As an alternative to entering credit card, bank account, or other financial information online,

some shopping and auction Web sites allow consumers to use an online payment service such as PayPal or Google Checkout. To use an online payment service, you create an account that is linked to your credit card or funds at a financial institution. When you make a purchase, you use your online payment service account, which transfers money for you without revealing your financial information.

FAQ 2-8

Is it safe to shop online?

Not always. It always is best to conduct online transactions with well-established companies. If possible, research these companies and read about others' online shopping experiences before making a purchase. If you never have heard of a particular online business, do not entrust them with your credit card information. For more information, visit scsite.com/dc2008/ch2/faq and then click Online Shopping.

OTHER INTERNET SERVICES

The Web is only one of the many services on the Internet. The Web and other Internet services have changed the way we communicate. We can send e-mail messages to the president, have a discussion with experts about the stock market, chat with someone in another country about genealogy, and talk about homework assignments with classmates via instant messages. Many times, these communications take place completely in writing — without the parties ever meeting each other.

At home, work, and school, people use computers and Internet-enabled mobile devices so they always have instant access to e-mail, FTP (File Transfer Protocol), newsgroups and message boards, mailing lists, chat rooms, instant messaging, and Internet telephony. The following pages discuss each of these Internet services.

E-Mail

E-mail (short for *electronic mail*) is the transmission of messages and files via a computer network. E-mail was one of the original services on the Internet, enabling scientists and researchers working on government-sponsored projects to communicate with colleagues at other locations. Today, e-mail is a primary

WEB LINK 2-5

PayPal

For more information, visit scsite.com/dc2008/ch2/weblink and then click PayPal.

LOOKING AHEAD 2-3

Grocery Shopping with a Buddy

Finding items in the local grocery store may become quick and easy with the help of IBM's Shopping Buddy, a portable computer attached to a shopping cart.

Shoppers access the system by using their preferred customer card or a key. Once logged in, a miniature global positioning satellite system identifies their location in the store. As they roll down each aisle, the Shopping Buddy flashes an alert of sale items and favorite products. If they are looking for a particular item, they can type its name or select it from a list, and the computer will display a map showing the item's location.

Shoppers can scan each item's bar code with a detachable wand, and the Shopping Buddy will keep a running total. They also can order deli items without standing in line and bag their items as they shop. For more information, visit scsite.com/dc2008/ch2/looking and then click Shopping Buddy.

communications method for both personal and business use.

You use an **e-mail program** to create, send, receive, forward, store, print, and delete e-mail messages. Outlook and Outlook Express are two popular e-mail programs. The steps in Figure 2-26 illustrate how to send an e-mail message using Outlook. The message can be simple text or can include an attachment such as a word processing document, a graphic, an audio clip, or a video clip.

FIGURE 2-26 HOW TO SEND AN E-MAIL MESSAGE

Step 1:
Start an e-mail program and point to the New Mail Message button.

New Mail Message button

Step 2:
Click the New Mail Message button to display the Message window.

Step 3:
Enter the recipient's e-mail address, the subject, and the message in the Message window.

Step 4:
Click the Attach File button to attach a JPEG file containing a picture to the message. Click the Send button to send the message.

Attach File button

Send button

icon for JPG file attached to message

Step 5:
When Carly receives the e-mail message, she opens the JPEG file to view the picture.

Internet access providers typically supply an e-mail program as a standard part of their Internet access services. Some Web sites, such as Google Gmail, MSN Hotmail, and Yahoo! Mail, provide free e-mail services. To use these Web-based e-mail programs, you connect to the Web site and set up an e-mail account, which typically includes an e-mail address and a password. Read Ethics & Issues 2-3 for a related discussion.

Just as you address a letter when using the postal system, you must address an e-mail message with the e-mail address of your intended recipient. Likewise, when someone sends you a message, they must have your e-mail address. An **e-mail address** is a combination of a user name and a domain name that identifies a user so he or she can receive Internet e-mail (Figure 2-27).

A **user name** is a unique combination of characters, such as letters of the alphabet and/or numbers, that identifies a specific user. Your user name must be different from the other user names in the same domain. For example, a user named Carly Martinez whose server has a domain name of scsite.com might want to select CMartinez as her user name. If scsite.com already has a CMartinez (for Carlos Martinez), Carly will have to select a different user name, such as carlymartinez or carly_martinez.

Sometimes, companies decide user names for employees. In many cases, however, users select their own user names, often selecting a nickname or any other combination of characters for their user name. Many users select a combination of their first and last names so others can remember it easily.

In an Internet e-mail address, an @ (pronounced at) symbol separates the user name from the domain name. Your service provider supplies the domain name. Using the example in Figure 2-27, a possible e-mail address for Carly Martinez would be carlymartinez@scsite.com, which would be read as follows: Carly Martinez at s c site dot com. Most e-mail programs allow you to create an **address book**, which contains a list of names and e-mail addresses.

When you send an e-mail message, an outgoing mail server that is operated by your Internet access provider determines how to route the message through the Internet and then sends the message. *SMTP* (simple mail transfer protocol) is a communications protocol used by some outgoing mail servers.

ETHICS & ISSUES 2-3

E-Mail: Irritant or Liberator?

E-mail is one of the more popular services on the Internet. Worldwide, approximately 1 billion people send and receive e-mail messages. E-mail makes business managers more productive by allowing them to share information, ideas, and opinions easily. But ironically, this easy sharing also can make managers less productive. Every day, managers wade through rivers of e-mail messages. Some of the messages are important, but many are copies of messages sent to others, notes on minor matters, or observations once shared in brief telephone calls or on walks to the water cooler. Most messages expect a quick reply, so hours can be spent dealing with e-mail. The constant flow of e-mail steals the time and interrupts the concentration needed for everyday work activities. Even worse, as managers become accustomed to the brief, rapid thinking demanded for e-mail, they can become unused to the creative, contemplative, persistent thought processes required for complex projects. Managers use a variety of measures to dam the flood of e-mail, including limiting the amount of time spent on messages, having colleagues telephone when they send important messages, and using filtering software to prioritize messages. What is the best way to deal with e-mail? Why? In terms of productivity, how can a company maximize the advantages of e-mail and minimize the disadvantages? Would you trust an automated tool to sort and organize your e-mail for you? Why or why not?

carlymartinez@scsite.com

FIGURE 2-27 An e-mail address is a combination of a user name and a domain name.

As you receive e-mail messages, an incoming mail server — also operated by your Internet access provider — holds the messages in your mailbox until you use your e-mail program to retrieve them. *POP3*, the latest version of POP (*Post Office Protocol*), is a communications protocol used by some incoming mail servers. Most e-mail programs have a mail notification alert that informs you via a message and/or sound when you receive new mail. Figure 2-28 illustrates how an e-mail message may travel from a sender to a receiver.

WEB LINK 2-6

E-Mail
For more information, visit scsite.com/dc2008/ch2/weblink and then click E-Mail.

 FAQ 2-9

Can my computer get a virus through e-mail?

Yes. A *virus* is a computer program that can damage files and the operating system. One way that virus authors attempt to spread a virus is by sending virus-infected e-mail attachments. If you receive an e-mail attachment, you should use an antivirus program to verify that it is virus free.

For more information, read the High-Tech Talk article on page 168, the section about viruses and antivirus programs in Chapter 8, and visit scsite.com/dc2008/ch2/faq and then click Viruses.

FIGURE 2-28   HOW AN E-MAIL MESSAGE MAY TRAVEL FROM A SENDER TO A RECEIVER

FTP

FTP (*File Transfer Protocol*) is an Internet standard that permits file uploading and downloading (transferring) with other computers on the Internet. Uploading is the opposite of downloading; that is, **uploading** is the process of transferring documents, graphics, and other objects from your computer to a server on the Internet. Web page authors, for example, often use FTP to upload their Web pages to a Web server.

Many operating systems include FTP capabilities (Figure 2-29). If yours does not, you can download FTP programs from the Web, usually for a small fee.

An *FTP server* is a computer that allows users to upload and/or download files using FTP. An FTP site is a collection of files including text, graphics, audio clips, video clips, and program files that reside on an FTP server. Many FTP sites have *anonymous FTP*, whereby anyone can transfer some, if not all, available

files. Some FTP sites restrict file transfers to those who have authorized accounts (user names and passwords) on the FTP server.

Large files on FTP sites often are compressed to reduce storage space and download time. Before you can use a compressed (zipped) file, you must uncompress (unzip) it. Chapter 8 discusses utilities that zip and unzip files.

Newsgroups and Message Boards

A **newsgroup** is an online area in which users have written discussions about a particular subject (Figure 2-30). To participate in a discussion, a user sends a message to the newsgroup, and other users in the newsgroup read and reply to the message. The entire collection of Internet newsgroups is called *Usenet*, which contains tens of thousands of newsgroups about a multitude of topics. Some major topic areas include news, recreation, society, business, science, and computers.

A computer that stores and distributes newsgroup messages is called a *news server*. Many universities, corporations, Internet access providers, and other large organizations have a news server. Some newsgroups require you to enter a user name and password to participate in the discussion. Only authorized members can use this type of newsgroup. For example, a newsgroup for students taking a college course may require a user name and password to access the newsgroup. This ensures that only students in the course participate in the discussion.

To participate in a newsgroup, typically you use a program called a *newsreader*. Outlook Express includes a newsreader. You also can download newsreaders free or for a fee on the Web. Instead of using your own newsreader, some Web sites that sponsor newsgroups have a built-in newsreader. A newsreader enables you to access a newsgroup to read previously entered messages, called *articles*. You can *post*, or add, articles of your own. The newsreader also keeps track of which articles you have and have not read.

Newsgroup members frequently post articles as a reply to another article — either to

WEB LINK 2-7

FTP

For more information, visit scsite.com/dc2008/ch2/weblink and then click FTP.

FIGURE 2-29a (FTP site being added to My Network Places folder)

FIGURE 2-29b (FTP site link is displayed in My Network Places folder)

FIGURE 2-29 Many operating systems, such as Windows Vista, have built-in FTP capabilities.

WEB LINK 2-8

Newsgroups and Message Boards

For more information, visit scsite.com/ dc2008/ch2/weblink and then click Newsgroups and Message Boards.

FIGURE 2-30 Users in a newsgroup read and reply to other users' messages.

answer a question or to comment on material in the original article. These replies may cause the author of the original article, or others, to post additional articles related to the original article. A *thread* or *threaded discussion* consists of the original article and all subsequent related replies. A thread can be short-lived or continue for some time, depending on the nature of the topic and the interest of the participants.

Using a newsreader, you can search for newsgroups discussing a particular subject such as a type of musical instrument, brand of sports equipment, or employment opportunities. If you like the discussion in a particular newsgroup, you can subscribe to it, which means its location is saved in your newsreader for easy future access.

In some newsgroups, posted articles are sent to a moderator instead of immediately displaying on the newsgroup. The *moderator* reviews the contents of the article and then posts it, if appropriate. With a *moderated newsgroup*, the moderator decides if the article is relevant to the discussion. The moderator may choose to edit or discard inappropriate articles. For this reason, the content of a moderated newsgroup is considered more valuable.

A popular Web-based type of discussion group that does not require a newsreader is a **message board**. Many Web sites use message boards instead of newsgroups because they are easier to use.

Mailing Lists

A **mailing list** is a group of e-mail names and addresses given a single name. When a message is sent to a mailing list, every person on the list receives a copy of the message in his or her mailbox. To add your e-mail name and address to a mailing list, you **subscribe** to it (Figure 2-31). To remove your name, you **unsubscribe** from the mailing list. Some mailing lists are called *LISTSERVs*, named after a popular mailing list program.

FIGURE 2-31 When you join a mailing list, you and all others on the mailing list receive e-mail messages from the Web site.

WEB LINK 2-9

Mailing Lists

For more information, visit scsite.com/ dc2008/ch2/weblink and then click Mailing Lists.

Thousands of mailing lists exist about a variety of topics in areas of entertainment, business, computers, society, culture, health, recreation, and education. To locate a mailing list dealing with a particular topic, search for the keywords, mailing list or LISTSERV, in a search engine. Many vendors use mailing lists to communicate with their customer base.

Chat Rooms

A **chat** is a real-time typed conversation that takes place on a computer. **Real time** means that you and the people with whom you are conversing are online at the same time. A **chat room** is a location on an Internet server that permits users to chat with each other. Anyone in the chat room can participate in the conversation, which usually is specific to a particular topic.

As you type on your keyboard, a line of characters and symbols is displayed on the computer screen. Others connected to the same chat room server also see what you have typed (Figure 2-32). Some chat rooms support voice chats and video chats, in which people hear or see each other as they chat.

WEB LINK 2-10

Chat Rooms

For more information, visit scsite.com/ dc2008/ch2/weblink and then click Chat Rooms.

To start a chat session, you connect to a chat server through a program called a *chat client*. Today's browsers usually include a chat client. If yours does not, you can download a chat client from the Web. Some Web sites allow users to conduct chats without a chat client.

Once you have installed a chat client, you can create or join a conversation on the chat server to which you are connected. The chat room should indicate the discussion topic. The person who creates a chat room acts as the operator and has responsibility for monitoring the conversation and disconnecting anyone who becomes disruptive. Operator status can be shared or transferred to someone else.

Instant Messaging

Instant messaging (IM) is a real-time Internet communications service that notifies you when one or more people are online and then allows you to exchange messages or files or join a private chat room with them. Some IM services support voice and video conversations (Figure 2-33). Many IM services also can alert you to information such as calendar appointments, stock quotes, weather, or sports scores. They also allow you to send pictures or other documents to a recipient. For IM to work, both parties must be online at the same time. Also, the receiver of a message must be willing to accept messages.

People use IM on all types of computers, including desktop computers and mobile computers and devices, such as smart phones. To use IM, you may have to install *instant messenger* software on the computer or device you plan to use. Some operating systems, such as Windows Vista, include an instant messenger. Popular IM software includes AIM (AOL Instant Messenger), Google Talk, Windows Live Messenger, and Yahoo! Messenger. No standards currently exist for IM. To ensure successful communications, all individuals on the contact list need to use the same or a compatible instant messenger.

FIGURE 2-32 As you type, the words and symbols you enter are displayed on the computer screens of other people in the same chat room.

FIGURE 2-33   AN EXAMPLE OF INSTANT MESSAGING

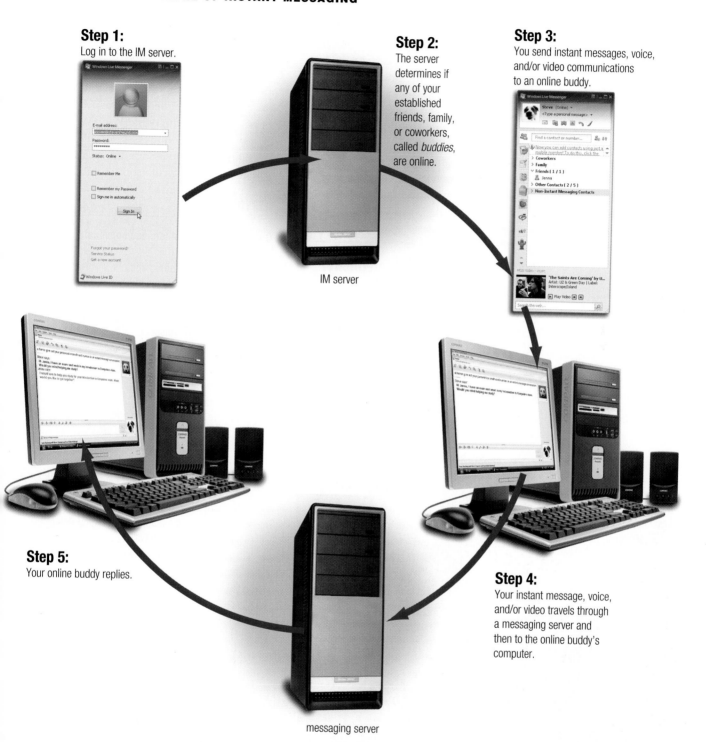

Step 1:
Log in to the IM server.

Step 2:
The server determines if any of your established friends, family, or coworkers, called *buddies*, are online.

Step 3:
You send instant messages, voice, and/or video communications to an online buddy.

IM server

Step 5:
Your online buddy replies.

Step 4:
Your instant message, voice, and/or video travels through a messaging server and then to the online buddy's computer.

messaging server

Internet Telephony

Internet telephony, also called *Voice over IP* (Internet Protocol) or *VoIP*, enables users to speak to other users over the Internet. That is, Internet telephony uses the Internet (instead of the public switched telephone network) to connect a calling party to one or more local or long-distance called parties.

To place an Internet telephone call, you need a high-speed Internet connection (e.g., via DSL or cable modem); Internet telephone service; a microphone or telephone, depending on the Internet telephone service; and Internet telephone software or a telephone adapter, depending on the Internet telephone service. Calls to other parties with the same Internet telephone service often are free, while calls that connect to the telephone network typically cost about $15 to $25 per month.

WEB LINK 2-11

Internet Telephony
For more information, visit scsite.com/ dc2008/ch2/weblink and then click Internet Telephony.

As you speak in a microphone connected to your computer or a telephone connected to the telephone adapter, the Internet telephone software and the computer's sound card or the telephone adapter convert your spoken words (analog signals) to digital signals and then transmit the digitized audio over the Internet to the called parties. Software and equipment at the receiving end reverse the process so the receiving parties can hear what you have said. Figure 2-34 illustrates a user's equipment configuration for Internet telephony.

FAQ 2-10

How popular is Internet telephony?

Vonage, a leader in Internet telephony service, recently indicated that it has more than 2 million subscriber lines. For more information, visit scsite.com/dc2008/ch2/faq and then click Internet Telephony.

FIGURE 2-34   Equipment configuration for a user making a call via Internet telephony.

NETIQUETTE

Netiquette, which is short for Internet etiquette, is the code of acceptable behaviors users should follow while on the Internet; that is, it is the conduct expected of individuals while online. Netiquette includes rules for all aspects of the Internet, including the World Wide Web, e-mail, FTP, newsgroups and message boards, chat rooms, and instant messaging. Figure 2-35 outlines some of the rules of netiquette.

NETIQUETTE

Golden Rule: Treat others as you would like them to treat you.

1. In e-mail, newsgroups, and chat rooms:
   - Keep messages brief. Use proper grammar, spelling, and punctuation.
   - Be careful when using sarcasm and humor, as it might be misinterpreted.
   - Be polite. Avoid offensive language.
   - Read the message before you send it.
   - Use meaningful subject lines.
   - Avoid sending or posting *flames,* which are abusive or insulting messages. Do not participate in *flame wars,* which are exchanges of flames.
   - Avoid sending spam, which is the Internet's version of junk mail. *Spam* is an unsolicited e-mail message or newsgroup posting sent to many recipients or newsgroups at once.
   - Do not use all capital letters, which is the equivalent of SHOUTING!
   - Use **emoticons** to express emotion. Popular emoticons include

:)	Smile	:\	Undecided
:(	Frown	:o	Surprised
:l	Indifference		

   - Use abbreviations and acronyms for phrases:

BTW	by the way
FYI	for your information
FWIW	for what it's worth
IMHO	in my humble opinion
TTFN	ta ta for now
TYVM	thank you very much

   - Clearly identify a *spoiler,* which is a message that reveals a solution to a game or ending to a movie or program.
2. Read the *FAQ* (frequently asked questions), if one exists. Many newsgroups and Web pages have an FAQ.
3. Do not assume material is accurate or up-to-date. Be forgiving of other's mistakes.
4. Never read someone's private e-mail.

FIGURE 2-35   Some of the rules of netiquette.

Test your knowledge of pages 91 through 100 in Quiz Yourself 2-3.

QUIZ YOURSELF 2-3

Instructions: Find the true statement below. Then, rewrite the remaining false statements so they are true.

1. A chat room is a location on an Internet server that permits users to chat with each other.

2. An e-mail address is a combination of a user name and an e-mail program that identifies a user so he or she can receive Internet e-mail.

3. Business-to-consumer e-commerce occurs when one consumer sells directly to another, such as in an online auction.

4. FTP is an Internet standard that permits file reading and writing with other computers on the Internet.

5. Spam uses the Internet (instead of the public switched telephone network) to connect a calling party to one or more called parties.

6. Netiquette is the code of unacceptable behaviors while on the Internet.

7. On a newsgroup, a subscription consists of the original article and all subsequent related replies.

Quiz Yourself Online: To further check your knowledge of e-commerce, e-mail, FTP, newsgroups and message boards, mailing lists, chat rooms, instant messaging, Internet telephony, and netiquette, visit scsite.com/dc2008/ch2/quiz and then click Objectives 10 – 12.

CHAPTER SUMMARY

This chapter presented the history and structure of the Internet. It discussed the World Wide Web at length, including topics such as browsing, navigating, searching, Web publishing, and e-commerce (read Ethics & Issues 2-4 for a related discussion). It also introduced other services available on the Internet, such as e-mail, FTP, newsgroups and message boards, chat rooms, instant messaging, and Internet telephony. Finally, the chapter listed rules of netiquette.

ETHICS & ISSUES 2-4

Should Companies Be Able to Track Your Online Habits?

When you visit a Web site that includes an advertisement, someone probably is recording the fact that you visited that Web site and viewed the advertisement with your browser. Over time, companies that specialize in tracking who views which online advertisements can amass an enormous amount of information about your online Web surfing habits. This collection of information is considered to be part of your *online profile*. One company claims that through the use of advertisements on Web pages, it can track well over one billion Web page views per day. Through tracking the Web sites a user visits, the products they buy, and the articles they read, a company may attempt to profile the visitor's beliefs, associations, and habits. Although a user may think he or she is anonymous while navigating the Web, the company can attempt through various means to link the user's true identity with the user's online profile. The company can sell online profiles, with or without the user's true identity, to other advertisers or organizations. Should organizations be allowed to track your Web surfing habits? Why or why not? Should organizations be allowed to associate your real identity with your online identity and profit from the information? Should companies give you the option of not being tracked? What are the benefits and dangers of online tracking?

CAREER CORNER

Web Developer

If you are looking for a job working with the latest Internet technology, then Web developer could be the career for you. A *Web developer* analyzes, designs, develops, implements, and supports Web applications and functionality. Specialized programming skills required include HTML, JavaScript, Java, Perl, C++, and VBScript. Developers also need multimedia knowledge, including Photoshop, Flash, and Dreamweaver. Developers must be aware of emerging technologies and know how they can be used to enhance a Web presence.

A Web developer must be able to appreciate a client's needs, recognize the technologies involved to meet those needs, and explain those technologies to the client. For example, if the client is a large corporation seeking to set up an online store, a Web developer must understand e-commerce and be able to explain requirements, probable costs, and possible outcomes in a way the client can understand.

Educational requirements vary from company to company and can range from a high school education to a four-year degree. Many companies place heavy emphasis on certifications. Two of the more popular certifications are available through the International Webmasters Association (IWA) and the World Organization of Webmasters (WOW). A wide salary range exists — from $40,000 to $80,000 — depending on educational background and location. For more information, visit scsite.com/dc2008/ch2/careers and then click Web Developer.

High-Tech Talk

A COMPUTER'S INTERNET PROTOCOL (IP) ADDRESS

Every computer on the Internet has a unique address, called an IP address, that distinguishes it from other computers on the Internet. An IP address has two parts that identify a specific computer: one part to identify the network where that computer resides and a second part to pinpoint the specific computer or host within that network.

A typical IP address — such as 216.239.39.99 — has four groups of numbers that range from 0 through 255. This form of the IP address sometimes is called a *dotted decimal number* or *dotted quad*. The four groups of numbers in the dotted quad are called octets, because they each have 8 bits when viewed in binary form for a total of 32 bits in the IP address. For instance, the binary form of 216.239.39.99 is 11011000.11101111.00101001.01100011 (Figure 2-36). For more information about how the binary system works, see Appendix A.

Because each of the 8 bits can be 1 or 0, the total possible combinations per octet are 2^8, or 256. Combining the four octets of an IP address provides a possible 2^{32} or 4,294,967,296 unique values. The actual number of available addresses is about 3 billion, because some values are reserved for special use and are, therefore, off limits.

To request data such as a Web page from a computer on the Internet, you need only an IP address. For instance, if you type the Web address, http://216.239.39.99, your browser will display the home page on the machine hosting the Google Web site. Of course, remembering one IP address out of billions is a little overwhelming — so you probably would just type the domain name, www.google.com, in your browser. Your browser then contacts a domain name server (DNS) to resolve the human-readable domain name into a machine-readable IP address. Each

FIGURE 2-36
Components of an IP address.

domain name server houses a simple database that maps domain names to IP addresses. The DNS would resolve the human-readable domain name, www.google.com, into a machine-readable IP address, 216.239.39.99.

Domain names are helpful because they are easier for people to remember than IP addresses. You can learn more about a domain using the whois form at the Network Solutions Web site (www.netsol.com and then click the WHOIS link). If you type a domain name, such as google.com, the form displays the registration information for that domain, including its IP address.

Like all other computers, your computer must have an IP address to connect to the Internet or another computer that has an IP address. Servers generally have *static IP addresses*, because they usually are connected to the Internet and their IP addresses do not change often. When you connect to the Internet using your home computer, you most likely are using a temporary or *dynamic IP address*. Your access provider uses the *Dynamic Host Configuration Protocol (DHCP)* to assign your computer a temporary dynamic IP address from a pool of IP addresses. The dynamic IP address is unique only for that session. Once you disconnect, the DHCP server puts that IP address back in the IP address pool so it can assign it to the next requesting computer. Even if you immediately reconnect, the DHCP server might not assign you the same IP address. Using DHCP and dynamic IP addresses means an Internet service provider needs only one IP address for each modem it supports, rather than one for each of its millions of customers.

Billions of IP addresses sounds like a lot. But, because so many computers connected to the Internet need unique IP addresses, a growing shortage of IP addresses exists. A new IP addressing scheme, called *IPv6* or *IPng (IP Next Generation)* will lengthen IP addresses from 32 bits to 128 bits and increase the number of available IP addresses to a whopping 3.4×10^{38}, or 340,000,000,000,000,000,000,000,000,000,000,000,000.

Do you want to know the IP address currently assigned to your computer?

- With Windows Vista, click the Start button on the Windows taskbar and then click Control Panel. Click Network and Internet, and then click View Network Status and Tasks. Finally, click View status, and then click Details.
- With Windows 2000/XP, click the Start button on the taskbar and then click Run. Type cmd to open the MS-DOS window. Type ipconfig and then press the ENTER key.

If you are using an older version of AOL, the IP address might read 0.0.0.0 because AOL uses a proprietary method to assign IP addresses. For more information, visit scsite.com/dc2008/ch2/tech and then click IP Addresses.

Companies on the Cutting Edge

GOOGLE
POPULAR SEARCH ENGINE

The founders of *Google*, the leading Internet search engine, state that their mission is to organize the world's information. Every day, their Web site handles hundreds of millions of queries for information. In seconds, it can locate specific phrases and terms on four billion Web pages by using more than 10,000 connected computers.

Sergey Brin and Larry Page launched Google in 1998 in a friend's garage. The name is derived from "googol," which is the name of the number 1 followed by 100 zeros. Google began offering a suite of business applications in 2006 that includes Gmail, Google Calendar, Google Talk, and Page Creator, along with test versions of spreadsheet and word processing software. For more information, visit scsite.com/dc2008/ch2/companies and then click Google.

YAHOO!
POPULAR WEB PORTAL

Yahoo!, the first navigational portal to the Web, began as a hobby for Jerry Yang and David Filo when they were doctoral candidates in electrical engineering at Stanford University. They started creating and organizing lists of their favorite Web sites in 1994. The following year, they shared their creation, named Yahoo!, with fellow students and then released their product to the Internet community.

Yahoo! is an acronym for Yet Another Hierarchical Officious Oracle. What makes Yahoo! unique is that staff members build the directory by assuming the role of a typical Web researcher. Yahoo! Answers became the second most popular Internet reference site in 2006, handling more than 12 million visitors each month. Its attractiveness is based upon the fact that anyone can ask a question at no cost, and practically anyone can offer an answer. For more information, visit scsite.com/dc2008/ch2/companies and then click Yahoo!.

Technology Trailblazers

TIM BERNERS-LEE
CREATOR OF THE WORLD WIDE WEB

The World Wide Web (WWW) has become one of the more widely used Internet services, and its roots are based on *Tim Berners-Lee's* work. Berners-Lee is credited with creating the first Web server, browser, and URL addresses.

He developed his ideas in 1989 while working at CERN, the European Particle Physics Laboratory in Geneva, Switzerland, and based his work on a program he had written for his own use to track random associations. Today, he works quietly in academia as director of the World Wide Web Consortium (W3C) at the Massachusetts Institute of Technology.

In a 2006 podcast, Berners-Lee explained that he had to disable the feedback function of his inaugural blog entry in 2005 because of the overwhelming number of responses. He modestly said that most of the comments thanked him for his work; he, in turn, thanked the Web users for their support of his product. For more information, visit scsite.com/dc2008/ch2/people and then click Tim Berners-Lee.

MEG WHITMAN
EBAY PRESIDENT AND CEO

Meg Whitman joined eBay in 1998 and has been instrumental in helping the company become the world's largest online marketplace. Before that time, she was an executive for the Keds Division of the Stride Rite Corporation and general manager of Hasbro Inc.'s Preschool Division. She then served as president and CEO of Florists Transworld Delivery (FTD).

She credits her success to listening to the loyal eBay community, and she occasionally answers their e-mails personally. She holds degrees in economics from Princeton University and management from the Harvard Business School.

eBay fields approximately 350 million searches daily for products. In 2006, Whitman chose Google to run search-related text advertisements on eBay's pages outside of the United States. The two companies also will share advertising revenues generated when consumers use eBay's Skype Internet telephone software and Google Talk. For more information, visit scsite.com/dc2008/ch2/people and then click Meg Whitman.

Chapter Review

The Chapter Review section summarizes the concepts presented in this chapter. To listen to the audio version of this Chapter Review, visit scsite.com/dc2008/ch2/review. To obtain help from other students regarding any subject in this chapter, visit scsite.com/dc2008/ch2/forum and post your thoughts or questions.

① What Is the History of the Internet? The **Internet** is a worldwide collection of networks that links millions of businesses, government agencies, educational institutions, and individuals. The Internet has its roots in *ARPANET*, a network started in 1969 to link researchers across the United States. In 1986, the National Science Foundation connected its huge network, called *NSFnet*, to ARPANET, creating a configuration of complex networks and hosts that became known as the Internet.

② How Can You Access and Connect to the Internet? Employees and students often connect to the Internet through a business or school network. The networks usually use a high-speed line. Some home and small businesses connect to the Internet with **dial-up access**, which uses a modem in the computer and a standard telephone line. Many home and small business users opt for higher-speed *broadband* connections, such as DSL, cable television networks, radio signals, or satellite. **DSL** provides Internet connections using regular copper telephone lines. A **cable modem** allows access to Internet services through the cable television network. *Fixed wireless* connections use a dish-shaped antenna to communicate via radio signals. A *Wi-Fi* network uses radio signals. A *satellite modem* communicates with a satellite dish. An **access provider** is a business that provides access to the Internet free or for a fee. An **ISP** (**Internet service provider**) is a regional or national access provider. An **online service provider** (**OSP**) provides Internet access in addition to members-only features. A **wireless Internet service provider** (*WISP*) provides wireless Internet access to computers and mobile devices with built-in wireless capabilities or access devices.

③ What Is an IP Address? An **IP address** (*Internet Protocol address*) is a number that uniquely identifies each computer or device connected to the Internet. The Internet relies on IP addresses to send data to computers at specific locations. A **domain name** is the text version of an IP address.

> connect
> Visit scsite.com/dc2008/ch2/c
> or click the Quiz Yourself button. Click
> Objectives 1 – 3.

④ What Are the Components of a Web Address? The **World Wide Web** (*WWW*), or **Web**, consists of a worldwide collection of electronic documents. Each electronic document is called a **Web page**. A **URL** (*Uniform Resource Locator*), or **Web address**, is a unique address for a Web page. A Web address consists of a protocol, a domain name, and sometimes the path to a specific Web page or location on a Web page.

⑤ What Is the Purpose of a Web Browser? A **Web browser**, or **browser**, is application software that allows users to access and view Web pages. When you type a Web address in the Address box of a browser window, a computer called a **Web server** delivers the requested Web page to your computer. Most Web pages contain links. A **link** is a built-in connection that, when clicked, displays a related Web page or part of a Web page.

⑥ How Can You Search for Information on the Web? Two commonly used search tools are subject directories and search engines. A **subject directory** classifies Web pages in an organized set of categories. By clicking links, you move through categories to display a list of Web pages about a desired topic. A **search engine** is a program that finds Web sites, Web pages, images, videos, news, and other information. To use a search engine, you enter a word or phrase, called **search text**, that defines the item about which you want information. The search engine displays a list of *hits*. When clicked, each hit displays an associated Web site or Web page.

Chapter Review

(7) What Are the Types of Web Sites? A **portal** is a Web site that offers a variety of Internet services from a single location. A news Web site contains newsworthy material. An informational Web site contains factual information. A business/marketing Web site promotes or sells products or services. An educational Web site offers avenues for teaching and learning. An entertainment Web site provides an interactive and engaging environment. An advocacy Web site describes a cause, opinion, or idea. A **blog** is an informal Web site consisting of time-stamped articles, or posts, in a diary or journal format, usually listed in reverse chronological order. A **wiki** is a collaborative Web site that allows users to create, add to, modify, or delete the Web site content via their Web browser. An **online social network**, or **social networking Web site**, encourages members to share their interests, ideas, stories, photos, music, and videos with other registered users. A *content aggregator* is a business that gathers and organizes Web content and then distributes, or feeds, the content to subscribers for free or a fee. A personal Web site is maintained by a private individual or family.

(8) How Do Web Pages Use Graphics, Animation, Audio, Video, Virtual Reality, and Plug-Ins?
Some Web pages use **multimedia**, which combines text with graphics, animation, audio, video, and/or virtual reality. A **graphic** is a digital representation of nontext information such as a drawing or photograph. **Animation** is the appearance of motion created by displaying a series of still images. **Audio** includes music, speech, or any other sound. **Video** consists of full-motion images. **Virtual reality (VR)** is the use of computers to simulate an environment that appears as three-dimensional space. A **plug-in** is a program that extends a browser's capability to display multimedia elements.

(9) What Are the Steps Required for Web Publishing? Web publishing is the development and maintenance of Web pages. The five major steps to Web publishing are: (1) plan a Web site, (2) analyze and design a Web site, (3) create a Web site, (4) deploy a Web site, and (5) maintain a Web site.

connect Visit scsite.com/dc2008/ch2/quiz or click the Quiz Yourself button. Click Objectives 4 – 9.

(10) What Are the Types of E-Commerce? **E-commerce**, short for *electronic commerce*, is a business transaction that occurs over an electronic network such as the Internet. *Business-to-consumer (B2C) e-commerce* consists of the sale of goods and services to the general public. *Consumer-to-consumer (C2C) e-commerce* occurs when one consumer sells directly to another, such as an **online auction**. *Business-to-business (B2B) e-commerce* takes place between businesses that exchange goods and services.

(11) How Do E-Mail, FTP, Newsgroups and Message Boards, Mailing Lists, Chat Rooms, Instant Messaging, and Internet Telephony Work? **E-mail** (short for *electronic mail*) is the transmission of messages and files via a computer network. **FTP** (*File Transfer Protocol*) is an Internet standard that permits file **uploading** and **downloading** with other computers. A **newsgroup** is an online area in which users have written discussions. A **message board** is a Web-based type of discussion group that is easier to use than a newsgroup. A **mailing list** is a group of e-mail names and addresses given a single name, so that everyone on the list receives a message sent to the list. A **chat room** is a location on an Internet server that permits users to conduct real-time typed conversations. **Instant messaging (IM)** is a real-time Internet communications service that notifies you when one or more people are online. **Internet telephony** enables users to speak to other users over the Internet.

(12) What Are the Rules of Netiquette? **Netiquette**, which is short for Internet etiquette, is the code of acceptable behaviors users should follow while on the Internet. Netiquette rules include: keep messages short, be polite, avoid sending *flames* or *spam*, use **emoticons** and acronyms, read the *FAQ*, do not assume material is accurate or up-to-date, and never read someone's private e-mail.

connect Visit scsite.com/dc2008/ch2/quiz or click the Quiz Yourself button. Click Objectives 10 – 12.

Discovering Computers 2008

Key Terms

You should know the Primary Terms and be familiar with the Secondary Terms. Use the list below to help focus your study. To further enhance your understanding of the Key Terms in this chapter, visit scsite.com/dc2008/ch2/terms. See an example of and a definition for each term, and access current and additional information about the term from the Web.

Primary Terms

(shown in bold-black characters in the chapter)

access provider (71)
address book (94)
animation (86)
audio (86)
blog (82)
browser (75)
cable modem (70)
chat (98)
chat room (98)
dial-up access (70)
DNS server (74)
domain name (73)
downloading (76)
DSL (70)
e-commerce (91)
electronic storefront (92)
e-mail (92)
e-mail address (94)
e-mail program (93)
emoticons (100)
FTP (96)
graphic (85)
home page (76)
instant messaging (IM) (98)
Internet (68)
Internet telephony (99)
IP address (73)
ISP (Internet service provider) (72)
link (77)
mailing list (97)
media sharing Web site (84)
message board (97)
MP3 (86)
multimedia (85)
netiquette (100)
newsgroup (96)
online auction (92)

online community (82)
online service provider (OSP) (72)
online social network (84)
player (86)
plug-in (89)
portal (82)
real time (98)
RSS 2.0 (84)
search engine (78)
search text (80)
shopping cart (92)
social networking Web site (84)
streaming (86)
subject directory (78)
subscribe (97)
surfing the Web (77)
traffic (70)
unsubscribe (97)
uploading (96)
URL (76)
user name (94)
video (88)
video blog (82)
virtual reality (VR) (88)
Web (75)
Web 2.0 (75)
Web address (76)
Web browser (75)
Web page (75)
Web publishing (90)
Web server (75)
Web site (75)
wiki (82)
wireless Internet service provider (72)
World Wide Web (75)

Secondary Terms

(shown in italic characters in the chapter)

ARPA (69)
animated GIF (86)
anonymous FTP (96)
ARPANET (69)
articles (96)
Atom (84)
blogger (82)
blogosphere (82)
broadband (70)
buddies (99)
business-to-business (B2B) e-commerce (92)
business-to-consumer (B2C) e-commerce (91)
ccTLD (74)
chat client (98)
click (76)
consumer-to-consumer (C2C) e-commerce (92)
content aggregator (84)
digital rights management (DRM) (86)
domain name system (DNS) (74)
dot-com (73)
dynamic Web page (75)
electronic commerce (91)
electronic mail (92)
FAQ (100)
File Transfer Protocol (96)
fixed wireless (70)
flame wars (100)
flames (100)
FTP server (96)
GIF (85)
graphical image (85)
gTLD (73)
hits (80)
host (69)
hot spots (71)
http (76)
hyperlink (77)
hypermedia (77)
hypertext (77)
Hypertext Transfer Protocol (76)
instant messenger (98)
Internet backbone (72)
Internet Corporation for Assigned Names and Numbers (ICANN) (74)
Internet Protocol address (73)
JPEG (85)
keywords (80)

LISTSERVs (97)
m-commerce (91)
microbrowser (76)
moderated newsgroup (97)
moderator (97)
MPEG (88)
MP4 (88)
MPEG-4 (88)
national ISP (72)
Net (68)
news server (96)
newsreader (96)
NSFnet (70)
participatory Web (75)
PNG (85)
podcast (86)
point of presence (POP) (72)
POP3 (95)
post (96)
Post Office Protocol (95)
pull (76)
push (76)
Really Simple Syndication (84)
regional ISP (72)
satellite modem (70)
SMTP (94)
spam (100)
spider (81)
spoiler (100)
static Web page (75)
streaming audio (86)
streaming video (88)
tabbed browsing (76)
thread (97)
threaded discussion (97)
thumbnail (86)
top-level domain (TLD) (73)
Uniform Resource Locator (76)
Usenet (96)
vlog (82)
vlogger (82)
vlogosphere (82)
Voice over IP (99)
VoIP (99)
VR world (88)
Weblog (82)
Wi-Fi (70)
wireless portal (82)
WISP (72)
World Wide Web Consortium (W3C) (70)
WWW (75)

Checkpoint

Use the Checkpoint exercises to check your knowledge level of the chapter. The Beyond the Book exercises will help broaden your understanding of the concepts presented in this chapter. To complete the Checkpoint exercises interactively, visit scsite.com/dc2008/ch2/check.

Label the Figure
Identify the types of Web sites.

a. advocacy

b. blog

c. business/marketing

d. content aggregator

e. educational

f. entertainment

g. informational

h. news

i. online social network

j. personal

k. portal

l. wiki

True/False
Mark T for True and F for False. (See page numbers in parentheses.)

_____ 1. A single government agency owns and controls the Internet. (70)

_____ 2. DSL is a technology that provides high-speed Internet connections over the cable television network. (70)

_____ 3. In general, the first portion of each IP address identifies the specific computer and the last portion identifies the network. (73)

_____ 4. A Web 2.0 Web site may include application software built into the site for visitors to use. (75)

_____ 5. Tabbed browsing refers to the practice of Web sites keeping tabs on their visitors. (76)

_____ 6. Hypertext combines text-based links with graphic, audio, and video links. (77)

_____ 7. A major problem with a subject directory is deciding which categories to choose as you work through the menus of links presented. (79)

_____ 8. Most social networking Web sites include chat rooms, newsgroups, and other communications services. (84)

_____ 9. A podcast is a collaborative Web site that allows users to add to, modify, or delete the Web site content via their Web browser. (86)

_____ 10. To develop a Web page, you do not have to be a computer programmer. (90)

_____ 11. An online auction is an example of business-to-consumer (B2C) e-commerce. (92)

_____ 12. A flame is an unsolicited e-mail message or newsgroup posting sent to many recipients or newsgroups at once. (100)

Checkpoint

 Multiple Choice   Select the best answer. (See page numbers in parentheses.)

1. The Internet has its roots in _____, which was a networking project started by an agency of the U.S. Department of Defense. (69)
   a. ICANN
   b. NSFnet
   c. WISP
   d. ARPANET

2. A Wi-Fi network uses _____ to provide Internet connections to wireless computers and devices. (70)
   a. copper telephone lines
   b. the cable television network
   c. radio signals
   d. a dish-shaped antenna

3. As with an IP address, the components of a domain name are separated by _____. (73)
   a. commas
   b. semicolons
   c. colons
   d. periods

4. Many Web page addresses begin with _____, which stands for a set of rules that defines how pages transfer on the Internet. (76)
   a. W3C
   b. http
   c. hits
   d. pop

5. _____ combines text-based links with graphic, audio, and video links. (77)
   a. Hypertext
   b. Multi-linking
   c. Hypermedia
   d. Tabbed Browsing

6. All of the following techniques can be used to improve Web searches except _____. (81)
   a. list all possible spellings
   b. read a search engine's Help information
   c. use general nouns and put the most important terms last
   d. if a search is unsuccessful, try another search engine

7. _____ may offer online photo albums, chat rooms, and other services to facilitate communications among members. (82)
   a. Online communities
   b. Informational Web sites
   c. Advocacy Web sites
   d. Wikis

8. A _____ is a specific type of online social network that enables members to share photos, music, and videos. (84)
   a. blog
   b. wiki
   c. podcast
   d. media sharing Web site

9. A(n) _____ is a business that gathers and organizes Web content and then distributes, or feeds, the content to subscribers for free or a fee. (84)
   a. WISP
   b. ISP
   c. content aggregator
   d. blogger

10. A _____ is recorded audio stored on a Web site that can be downloaded to a computer or a portable media player. (86)
    a. blog
    b. wiki
    c. portal
    d. podcast

11. _____ is a strategy designed to prevent illegal distribution of music and other digital content. (86)
    a. A threaded discussion
    b. Internet telephony
    c. Digital rights management
    d. Podcasting

12. _____ is the process of transferring data in a continuous and even flow, allowing users to access and use a file while it is transmitting. (86)
    a. Linking
    b. Streaming
    c. Surfing
    d. Clicking

13. At a consumer-to-consumer (C2C) Web site, a(n) _____ allows users to purchase from other consumers. (92)
    a. news server
    b. online auction
    c. wireless portal
    d. shopping cart

14. Use _____, such as :) for smile and :(for frown, to express emotions in e-mail, newsgroups, and chat rooms. (100)
    a. emoticons
    b. spam
    c. spoilers
    d. flames

Checkpoint

Matching

Match the terms with their definitions. (See page numbers in parentheses.)

_____ 1. gTLD (73)
_____ 2. ccTLD (74)
_____ 3. home page (76)
_____ 4. link (77)
_____ 5. spider (81)
_____ 6. MP3 (86)
_____ 7. player (86)
_____ 8. plug-in (89)
_____ 9. address book (94)
_____ 10. VoIP (99)

a. browser designed for the small screens and limited power of PDAs and smart phones
b. program that extends the capability of a browser
c. enables users to speak to other users over the Internet
d. software used to listen to an audio file on a computer
e. a two-letter country code for international Web sites outside the United States
f. built-in connection to a related Web page or part of a Web page
g. first page that a Web site displays
h. identifies the type of organization associated with a domain
i. copy a program from storage to memory
j. contains a list of names and e-mail addresses
k. format that reduces an audio file to about one-tenth its original size
l. program used to build and maintain lists of words found on Web sites

Short Answer

Write a brief answer to each of the following questions.

1. How is a regional ISP different from a national ISP? _____ How is an ISP different from a WISP? _____
2. How is a static Web page different from a dynamic Web page? _____ What is a Web site? _____.
3. What are two types of specifications used by content aggregators to distribute content? _____ How might you evaluate the accuracy of a Web site? _____
4. What three graphics formats are used frequently on the Web? _____ How are they different? _____
5. When might you use an online payment system? _____ How does the service work? _____

Beyond the Book

Read the following book elements, learn more about each using the Web, and then write a brief report.

1. Ethics & Issues — Should You Trust a Wiki for Academic Research? (84), Who Should Control the Content of Your CDs, DVDs, and Media Files? (87), E-Mail: Irritant or Liberator? (94), or Should Companies Be Able to Track Your Online Habits? (101)
2. Career Corner — Web Developer (101)
3. Companies on the Cutting Edge — Google or Yahoo! (103)
4. FAQs (71, 72, 74, 77, 81, 85, 92, 95, 100)
5. High-Tech Talk — A Computer's Internet Protocol (IP) Address (102)
6. Looking Ahead — Internet Speeds into the Future (70), Facing Up to Search Technology (81), or Grocery Shopping with a Buddy (92)
7. Making Use of the Web — Travel (118)
8. Picture Yourself in an Online Social Network (66)
9. Technology Trailblazers — Tim Berners-Lee or Meg Whitman (103)
10. Web Links (70, 72, 84, 88, 92, 95, 96, 97, 98, 99)

Learn It Online

Use the Learn It Online exercises to reinforce your understanding of the chapter concepts. To access the Learn It Online exercises, visit scsite.com/dc2008/ch2/learn.

1 At the Movies — Tell Your Stories Via Vlog

To view the Tell Your Stories Via Vlog movie, click the number 1 button. Locate your video and click the corresponding High-Speed or Dial-Up link, depending on your Internet connection. Watch the movie and then complete the exercise by answering the question that follows. If jotting down your diary in text is not appealing, try a simple and free video blog. Explain briefly how to create a vlog.

2 Video and Audio: You Review It — Internet Telephony

In this chapter you learned about Internet telephony. Click the number 2 button to view the suggested links and begin your search for videos, podcasts, or vodcasts related to Internet telephony. Choose a video, podcast, or vodcast that discusses Internet telephony and is of interest to you, and then write a description of its contents. Explain why you chose this piece, what you liked about it, what you disliked about it, and whether you would recommend it to a fellow student. Finish your review by giving the video, podcast, or vodcast a rating of 1 – 5 stars. Submit your review in the format requested by your instructor.

3 Student Edition Labs — Connecting to the Internet

Click the number 3 button. A new browser window will open, displaying the Student Edition Labs. Follow the on-screen instructions to complete the Connecting to the Internet Lab. When finished, click the Exit button. If required, submit your results to your instructor.

4 Student Edition Labs — Getting the Most out of the Internet

Click the number 4 button. A new browser window will open, displaying the Student Edition Labs. Follow the on-screen instructions to complete the Getting the Most out of the Internet Lab. When finished, click the Exit button. If required, submit your results to your instructor.

5 Student Edition Labs — E-mail

Click the number 5 button. A new browser window will open, displaying the Student Edition Labs. Follow the on-screen instructions to complete the E-mail Lab. When finished, click the Exit button. If required, submit your results to your instructor.

6 Practice Test

Click the number 6 button. Answer each question. When completed, enter your name and click the Grade Test button to submit the quiz for grading. Make a note of any missed questions. If required, submit your score to your instructor.

7 Who Wants To Be a Computer Genius^2?

Click the number 7 button to find out if you are a computer genius. Directions about how to play the game will be displayed. When you are ready to play, click the Play button. Submit your score to your instructor.

Learn It Online

8 Wheel of Terms

Click the number 8 button to reinforce important terms you learned in this chapter by playing the Shelly Cashman Series version of this popular game. Directions about how to play the game will be displayed. When you are ready to play, click the Play button. Submit your score to your instructor.

9 DC Track and Field

Click the number 9 button to use what you have learned in this chapter to compete against other students in three track and field events. Directions about how to play the game will be displayed. When you are ready to play, click the start first event button. If required, submit your score to your instructor.

10 You're Hired!

Click the number 10 button to use what you have learned in this chapter to embark on the path to a career in computers. Directions about how to play the game will be displayed. When you are ready to play, click the begin game button. If required, submit your score to your instructor.

11 Crossword Puzzle Challenge

Click the number 11 button, then click the Crossword Puzzle Challenge link. Directions about how to play the game will be displayed. Complete the puzzle to reinforce skills you learned in this chapter. When you are ready to play, click the Continue button. Submit the completed puzzle to your instructor.

12 Vista Exercises

Click the number 12 button. When the Vista Exercises menu appears, click the exercise assigned by your instructor. A new browser window will open. Follow the on-screen instructions to complete the exercise. When finished, click the Exit button. If required, submit your results to your instructor.

13 In the News

In her book, *Caught in the Net*, Kimberly S. Young contends that the Internet can be addictive. Young's methodology and conclusions have been questioned by several critics, but Young remains resolute. She points out that at one time, no one admitted to the existence of alcoholism. Click the number 13 button and read a news article about the impact of Internet use on human behavior. What effect did the Internet have? Why? In your opinion, is the Internet's influence positive or negative? Why?

14 Chapter Discussion Forum

Select an objective from this chapter on page 67 about which you would like more information. Click the number 14 button and post a short message listing a meaningful message title accompanied by one or more questions concerning the selected objective. In two days, return to the threaded discussion by clicking the number 14 button. Submit to your instructor your original message and at least one response to your message.

15 Google Earth

Click the number 15 button to download Google Earth. Once you have downloaded Google Earth, use it to fly to your home, school, Grand Canyon, Baghdad, Paris, and Moscow. At each location, use the buttons to change the view. Print a copy of the map showing your school, handwrite on the map the school's elevation, and submit the map to your instructor.

Learn How To

Use the Learn How To activities to learn fundamental skills when using a computer and accompanying technology. Complete the exercises and submit them to your instructor. To see a video of a Learn How To activity, visit scsite.com/dc2008/ch2/howto.

LEARN HOW TO 1: Change a Web Browser's Home Page

When you start a Web browser, a Web page is displayed. You can change the page that appears when you start a Web browser or when you click the Home button on the browser toolbar by completing the following steps:

1. With the browser running, navigate to the Web page you would like to make your Home page.
2. Click the Tools drop-down button and then click Internet Options to display the Internet Options dialog box shown in Figure 2-37.
3. Click the Use current button.
4. Click the OK button in the Internet Options dialog box.

When you start the browser or click the Home button on the browser toolbar, the selected Web page will be displayed.

FIGURE 2-37

Exercise

1. Start your Web browser. Write down the address of the browser's current home page. Then, change the browser's home page to www.cnn.com. Close the browser.
2. Start your Web browser. What is the lead story on cnn.com? Use links on the page to view several stories. Which story do you find most interesting? Click the Home button on the browser toolbar. What happened? Submit these answers to your instructor.
3. Change the browser's home page to your school's home page. Click the Home button on the browser toolbar. Click the Calendar or Events link, and then locate two campus events of which you were unaware. Report these two campus events to your instructor.
4. Change the browser's home page back to the address you wrote down in Step 1.

LEARN HOW TO 2: Create and Use Your Own Blog

A blog can contain any information you wish to place in it. Originally, blogs consisted of Web addresses, so that an individual or group with a specific interest could direct others to useful places on the Web. Today, blogs contain addresses, thoughts, diaries, and anything else a person or group wants to share.

Once you have created a blog, you can update it. A variety of services are available on the Web to help you create and maintain your blog. One widely used service is called Blogger. To create a blog using Blogger, complete the following steps:

1. Start your Web browser, type www.blogger.com in the Address box, and then press the ENTER key to display the Blogger home page (Figure 2-38).
2. Click the CREATE YOUR BLOG NOW arrow on the Blogger home page.
3. Enter the data required on the Create an account page. Your user name and password will allow you to change and manage your blog. Your Display name is the name that will be shown on the blog as the author of the material on the blog. Many people use their own names, but others use pseudonyms as their "pen names" so they are not readily identifiable.
4. Click the Continue arrow and then enter your Blog title and Blog address. These are the names and addresses everyone will use to view your blog. By default, the blog is stored and maintained on the blogspot server.
5. Click the Continue arrow to display the Choose a template screen.
6. Choose a template for your blog and then click the Continue arrow.
7. Your blog will be created for you. When you see the Your blog has been created screen, click the Start posting arrow.

Learn How To

8. From the screen that is displayed, you can post items for your blog, specify settings, change the template, and view your blog.
9. When you have posted all your information, click the Sign out button at the top right of the screen. You will be logged out.
10. To edit your blog and add or change information on it, visit the Blogger home page and sign in by entering your user name and password. You will be able to post to your blog.
11. Others can view your blog by entering its address in the browser's Address box and then pressing the ENTER key.

Exercise

1. Start your Web browser and visit www.blogger.com. Click the TAKE A QUICK TOUR button and go through all the screens that explain about a blog. What did you learn that you did not know? What type of blog do you find most compelling — a group or an individual blog? Why? Turn in your answers to your instructor.

TAKE A QUICK TOUR button

CREATE YOUR BLOG NOW arrow

FIGURE 2-38

2. Optional: Create your own blog. Carefully name it and begin your posts at this time. What is your blog name and address? What is its primary purpose? Is it an individual or group blog? Write a paragraph containing the answers to these questions and any other information you feel is pertinent. Turn in this paragraph to your instructor.

LEARN HOW TO 3: Bid and Buy a Product from eBay

Online auctions have grown to be a favorite shopping space for many people. A leading online auction Web site is eBay. To submit a bid for an item on eBay, complete the following steps:

1. Type www.ebay.com in the Address box of your browser. Press the ENTER key to display the eBay home page (Figure 2-39).
2. You must be registered to bid on eBay. If you are registered, click the Sign in link, enter your eBay User ID and Password, and then click the Submit button. If not, click the register link and follow the instructions.
3. Pick an item you find interesting and on which you might bid.
4. Enter your item in the Start new search text box and then click the Search button.
5. Scroll through the page to see the available items.
6. To bid on an item, click the item's description and then click the Place Bid button. The eBay Web site contains reminders that when you bid on an item, you are entering into a contract to purchase the item if you are the successful bidder. Bidding on eBay is serious business.
7. Enter the amount of your bid. Click the Continue button.
8. You will confirm your bid and receive notification about your bid.
9. You will be notified by e-mail if you won the bid. If so, you will arrange with the seller for payment and shipment.

eBay home page

Search button

Start new search text box

FIGURE 2-39

Exercise

1. Start your browser and display the eBay home page.
2. In the Start new search text box, enter the name of an upcoming sporting event you would like to attend followed by the word, tickets. For example, enter Super Bowl tickets. Click the Search button.
3. Did you find available tickets? Were there more tickets available than you expected, or fewer? Are the bid prices reasonable or ridiculous? How many bids were made for all the tickets? How much time is left to bid? What items did you find that you were not expecting? Submit answers to these questions to your instructor.
4. Enter an item of your choice in the Start new search text box. If you feel so inclined, bid on an item. Do you think this manner of buying goods is valuable? Why? Will you visit eBay again? Why? Submit answers to these questions to your instructor.

Quizzes and Learning Games

Computer Genius
Crossword Puzzle
DC Track and Field
Practice Test
Quiz Yourself
Wheel of Terms
You're Hired!

Exercises

Case Studies
Chapter Review
Checkpoint
Key Terms
Learn How To
Learn It Online
▶ Web Research

Beyond the Book

Career Corner
Companies
FAQs
High-Tech Talk
Looking Ahead
Making Use of the Web
Trailblazers
Web Links

Features

Chapter Forum
Install Computer
Lab Exercises
Maintain Computer
Tech News
Timeline 2008

Web Research

Use the Internet-based Web Research exercises to broaden your understanding of the concepts presented in this chapter. Visit scsite.com/dc2008/ch2/research to obtain more information pertaining to each exercise. To discuss any of the Web Research exercises in this chapter with other students, post your thoughts or questions at scsite.com/dc2008/ch2/forum.

① Scavenger Hunt Use one of the search engines listed in Figure 2-10 in Chapter 2 on page 78 or your own favorite search engine to find the answers to the questions below. Copy and paste the Web address from the Web page where you found the answer. Some questions may have more than one answer. If required, submit your answers to your instructor. (1) The World Wide Web Consortium (W3C) sets Internet standards. Who is the current CEO of the W3C? (2) What cable company was established in 1858 to carry instantaneous communications across the ocean that eventually would be used for Internet communications? (3) What American president in 1957 created both the interstate highway system and the Advanced Research Projects Agency (ARPA)? (4) What was eBay's original name, and what was the first item offered for auction? (5) How many Web pages is Google currently searching?

② Search Sleuth The Internet has provided the opportunity to access encyclopedias online. One of the more comprehensive encyclopedia research sites is **Encyclopedia.com**. Visit this Web site and then use your word processing program to answer the following questions. Then, if required, submit your answers to your instructor. (1) On the site's home page you can search or browse encyclopedia articles alphabetically. Click the letter, W. Click the Wom-Wz link. Scroll down to the World Wide Web entry and then click this link. What is the definition of the World Wide Web according to the first sentence of this article? Who is the American computer consultant who promoted the idea of linking documents via hypertext during the 1960s? What words are hyperlinks within this article? (2) Type "Web browser" as the keyword in the Search text box and then press the ENTER key or click the Research button. How many articles discussing Web browsers are found on the Encyclopedia.com Web site? (3) In the search results list, click the link to find newspaper and magazine articles related to this term. How many articles are listed? (4) Type multimedia as the keyword in the Search text box and then press the ENTER key or click the Research button. In the search results list, click the multimedia link. What hardware typically is required to work with multimedia according to this article? What are some optional hardware devices? (5) Type "personal computer" as the keyword in the Search text box and then press the ENTER key or click the Research button. Click one of the personal computer links, review the material, and, if required, submit to your instructor a 50-word summary of the information you read.

③ Newsgroups One of the more popular topics for **newsgroups** is netiquette. Read the information Borland Software Corporation (info.borland.com/newsgroups/netiquette.html) provides on general newsgroup conduct. Then find three newsgroups, such as those listed in CyberFiber (cyberfiber.com/internet.htm) or Google Groups, that discuss this topic. Read the information and then summarize the advice provided.

④ Journaling Respond to your readings in this chapter by writing at least one page about your reactions, evaluations, and reflections about using the **Internet**. For example, do you prefer to use e-mail or instant messaging (IM) when communicating with friends? Have you downloaded music files or shopped online? Which Web sites do you visit frequently? Do you have a blog? You also can write about the new terms you learned by reading this chapter. If required, submit your journal to your instructor.

⑤ Ethics in Action **Web cams** are video cameras that display their output on a Web page. The feasibility of installing Web cams in 47,000 locations susceptible to terrorist threats, such as nuclear and chemical plants, national airports, and gas storage facilities, is being explored. Citizens would monitor the cameras and report suspicious activity. Critics of this proposal state that the constant surveillance is an invasion of privacy. Visit the USHomeGuard Web site (ushomeguard.org) and then write a summary of the citizen corps' roles in this project. Then locate other Web sites that oppose this plan and summarize their views. If required, submit your summary to your instructor.

Case Studies

Use the Case Studies to apply the concepts presented in the chapter to real-world situations. Visit scsite.com/dc2008/ch2/cases to obtain more information pertaining to each exercise. To discuss the Case Studies in this chapter with other students, visit scsite.com/dc2008/ch2/forum and post your thoughts or questions.

CASE STUDY 1 — Class Discussion   Although Internet Explorer may be the most widely used <u>Web browser</u>, it is not the only Web browser program in use. Use the Internet or print media to compare reviews of other Web browsers such as Netscape, Opera, or Firefox with Internet Explorer. Prepare a brief report explaining any major differences between the browsers you researched and Internet Explorer. Include in your report which browser you would recommend and the reasons for your recommendation. Be prepared to discuss your findings.

CASE STUDY 2 — Class Discussion   Many retailers, such as Sports Authority, Barnes and Noble, and Toys R Us, are <u>brick-and-click businesses</u>. That is, they allow customers to conduct complete transactions at a physical location as well as online at a Web site. Choose a local brick-and-click business in which you have shopped at the physical location and visit the Web site of the business. Compare the type, availability, and cost (include tax and shipping) of products or services available. Prepare a report that summarizes the advantages and disadvantages of dealing with the physical location versus the Web site of a brick-and-click business. Would you rather shop at the physical location or at the Web site? Why? Does the answer depend on the business, the product, or some other factor? Be prepared to share your findings in class.

CASE STUDY 3 — Research   Web <u>search engines</u> use different techniques for searching Web resources. If you were designing a search engine, what would you have the engine look for when determining whether a Web page successfully matches the keywords? Visit the Help page of Google, Ask.com, MSN Search, and Yahoo! to get an idea of what criteria they use. Compile a list containing the criteria you would have your search engine use to determine whether a Web page is a successful match for keywords. Include a short explanation for each criterion. Write a brief report or use PowerPoint to create a presentation and share your ideas with your class.

CASE STUDY 4 — Research   <u>The Internet</u> has had a tremendous impact on business. For some businesses, that influence has not been positive. For example, surveys suggest that as a growing number of people order products online, traditional brick-and-mortar businesses are seeing fewer customers. Use the Web and/or print media to learn more about businesses that have been affected negatively by the Internet. What effect has the Internet had? How can the business compete with the Internet? How has the Internet changed business in positive ways? Write a brief report or use PowerPoint to create a presentation and share your findings with your class.

CASE STUDY 5 — Team Challenge   Mr. Steve Sandberg is vice president of operations for a major luxury hotel chain. He and three of his associates want to start a new chain of discount hotels called Sleepy Hollow. They have made a plan that includes opening hotels initially in Chicago, St. Louis, Denver, and Houston. They plan to offer comfortable rooms, high-speed Internet access, and continental breakfast. Besides offering reservations over the telephone, they want to develop a Web site that will allow customers to negotiate a nightly rate as their check-in time approaches. Form a three-member team and assist Mr. Sandberg in evaluating existing major hotel Web sites by listing the advantages and disadvantages of each. Assign each member the task of evaluating three of the following hotel chains: Marriot, Hilton, Holiday Inn, Ramada, Super 8, Motel 6, Days Inn, Fairfield Inn, and Radisson. Make sure every hotel chain listed is assigned to at least one team member. Have each member print the <u>home page</u> of the hotel chain he or she is assigned. In evaluating the Web sites, each member should pay particular attention to the following areas: (1) design of Web site, (2) ease of use, (3) reservations, (4) awards programs, (5) specials, (6) online Help, (7) about the hotel, and (8) contact the hotel. Meet with your team to share each member's findings and then write a final report or create a PowerPoint presentation that summarizes the team's conclusions and ranks the sites in terms of their effectiveness.

Special Feature

Making Use of the Web

A wealth of information is available on the World Wide Web. The riches are yours if you know where to find this material. Locating useful Web sites may be profitable for your educational and professional careers, as the resources may help you research class assignments and make your life more fulfilling and manageable.

Because the World Wide Web does not have an organizational structure to assist you in locating reliable material, you need additional resources to guide you in searching. To help you find useful Web sites, this Special Feature describes specific information about a variety of Web pages, and it includes tables of Web addresses, so you can get started. The material is organized in several areas of interest.

AREAS OF INTEREST	
Fun and Entertainment	Learning
Travel	Science
Finance	Environment
Online Social Networks and Media Sharing	Health
Blogs	Research and Resources
Government	Careers
Shopping and Auctions	Arts and Literature
Weather, Sports, and News	

Web Exercises at the end of each category will reinforce the material and help you discover Web sites that may add a treasure trove of knowledge to your life.

Fun and Entertainment
THAT'S ENTERTAINMENT

Rock 'n' Roll on the Web

Consumers place great significance on buying entertainment products for fun and recreation. Nearly 10 percent of the United States's economy is spent on attending concerts and buying DVDs, CDs, reading materials, sporting goods, and toys.

Many Web sites supplement our cravings for fun and entertainment. For example, you can see and hear the musicians inducted into the Rock and Roll Hall of Fame and Museum (Figure 1). If you need an update on your favorite reality-based television program or a preview of an upcoming movie, E! Online and Entertainment Tonight provide the latest features on television and movie stars. The Internet Movie Database contains credits and reviews of more than 849,000 titles.

Watch the surfers riding the waves in Washington and romp with pandas at the San Diego Zoo. Web cams, which are video cameras that display their output on Web pages, take armchair travelers across the world for views of natural attractions, historical monuments, colleges, and cities. Many Web sites featuring Web cams are listed in the table in Figure 2.

FIGURE 1 Visitors exploring the Rock and Roll Hall of Fame and Museum Web site will find history, exhibitions, programs, and the names and particulars of the latest inductees.

FUN AND ENTERTAINMENT WEB SITES

Web Cams	Web Address
AfriCam Virtual Game Reserve	africam.com
CamVista.com	camvista.com
Discovery Kids — Live Cams	kids.discovery.com/cams/cams.html
EarthCam — Webcam Network	earthcam.com
Iowa State Insect Zoo Live Camera	zoocam.ent.iastate.edu
NOAA ESRL Global Monitoring Division — South Pole Live Camera	www.cmdl.noaa.gov/obop/spo/livecamera.html
Panda Cam San Diego Zoo	sandiegozoo.org/zoo/ex_panda_station.html
Westport, Washington Surfcam	westportlodging.com/westport_web_cams.html
Wild Birds Unlimited Bird FeederCam	wbu.com/feedercam_home.htm
WorldLIVE	worldlive.cz/en/webcams

Entertainment	Web Address
AMG All Music Guide	allmusic.com
E! Online	eonline.com
Entertainment Weekly's EW.com	ew.com/ew
The Internet Movie Database (IMDb)	imdb.com
MSN Entertainment	entertainment.msn.com
Old Time Radio (OTR) — Radio Days: A Soundbite History	otr.com
Rock and Roll Hall of Fame and Museum	rockhall.com
World Radio Network (WRN)	wrn.org
Yahoo! Entertainment	et.tv.yahoo.com

For more information about fun and entertainment Web sites, visit scsite.com/dc2008/ch2/web.

FIGURE 2 When you visit Web sites offering fun and entertainment resources, you can be both amused and informed.

FUN AND ENTERTAINMENT WEB EXERCISES

1 Visit the WorldLIVE site listed in Figure 2. View two of the Web cams closest to your hometown, and describe the scenes. Then, visit the Discovery Kids — Live Cams Web site and view one of the animal cams in the Live Cams. What do you observe? Visit another Web site listed in Figure 2 and describe the view. What are the benefits of having Web cams at these locations throughout the world?

2 What are your favorite movies? Use The Internet Movie Database Web site listed in Figure 2 to search for information about two of these films, and write a brief description of the biographies of the major stars and director for each movie. Then, visit one of the entertainment Web sites and describe three of the featured stories. At the Rock and Roll Hall of Fame and Museum Web site, view the information about Elvis and one of your favorite musicians. Write a paragraph describing the information available about these rock stars.

Travel
GET PACKING!

Explore the World without Leaving Home

When you are ready to arrange your next travel adventure or just want to explore destination possibilities, the Internet provides ample resources to set your plans in motion.

To discover exactly where your destination is on this planet, cartography Web sites, including MapQuest and Maps.com, allow you to pinpoint your destination. View your exact destination using satellite imagery with Google Maps (Figure 3) and Windows Live Local.

Some good starting places are general travel Web sites such as Expedia Travel, Cheap Tickets, and Travelocity, which is owned by the electronic booking service travel agents use. These all-encompassing Web sites, including those in Figure 4, have tools to help you find the lowest prices and details on flights, car rentals, cruises, and hotels.

FIGURE 3 Google Maps provides location information and satellite imagery for many regions on this planet.

TRAVEL WEB SITES

General Travel	Web Address
Cheap Tickets	cheaptickets.com
Expedia Travel	expedia.com
Orbitz	orbitz.com
PlanetRider Travel Directory	planetrider.com
Travelocity	travelocity.com
Cartography	**Web Address**
Google Maps	maps.google.com
MapQuest	mapquest.com
Maps.com	maps.com
Windows Live Local	local.live.com
Travel and City Guides	**Web Address**
Frommers	frommers.com
Greatest Cities	greatestcities.com
U.S.-Parks US National Parks Adventure Travel Guide	us-parks.com
VirtualTourist.com	virtualtourist.com

For more information about travel Web sites, visit scsite.com/dc2008/ch2/web.

FIGURE 4 These travel resources Web sites offer travel information to exciting destinations throughout the world.

TRAVEL WEB EXERCISES

1 Visit one of the cartography Web sites listed in Figure 4 and obtain the directions from your campus to one of these destinations: the White House in Washington, D.C.; Elvis's home in Memphis, Tennessee; Walt Disney World in Orlando, Florida; or the Grand Old Opry in Nashville, Tennessee. How many miles is it to your destination? What is the estimated driving time? Then, visit one of the general travel Web sites listed in the table and plan a flight from the nearest major airport to one of the four destinations for the week after finals and a return trip one week later. What is the lowest economy coach fare for this round-trip flight? What airline, flight numbers, and departure and arrival times did you select?

2 Visit one of the travel and city guides Web sites listed in Figure 4, and choose a destination for a getaway this coming weekend. Write a one-page paper giving details about this location, such as popular hotels and lodging, expected weather, population, local colleges and universities, parks and recreation, ancient and modern history, and tours. Include a map or satellite photograph of this place. Why did you select this destination? How would you travel there and back? What is the breakdown of expected costs for this weekend, including travel expenditures, meals, lodging, and tickets to events and activities? What Web addresses did you use to complete this exercise?

Finance
MONEY MATTERS

Cashing In on Financial Advice

You can manage your money with advice from financial Web sites that offer online banking, tax help, personal finance, and small business and commercial services.

If you do not have a personal banker or a financial planner, consider a Web adviser to guide your investment decisions. The Yahoo! Finance Web site (Figure 5) provides financial news and investment information.

If you are ready to ride the ups and downs of the NASDAQ and the Dow, an abundance of Web sites listed in Figure 6, including Reuters and Morningstar.com, can help you pick companies that fit your interests and financial needs.

Claiming to be the fastest, easiest tax publication on the planet, the Internal Revenue Service Web site contains procedures for filing tax appeals and contains IRS forms, publications, and legal regulations.

FIGURE 5 Yahoo! Finance Web site contains charting features that graphically depict information related to financing and investing.

FINANCE WEB SITES

Advice and Education	Web Address
Bankrate.com	bankrate.com
LendingTree	lendingtree.com
Loan.com	loan.com
The Motley Fool	fool.com
MSN Money	moneycentral.msn.com
Wells Fargo	wellsfargo.com
Yahoo! Finance	finance.yahoo.com
Stock Market	**Web Address**
AIG VALIC	valic.com
E*TRADE Financial	us.etrade.com
Financial Engines	financialengines.com
Merrill Lynch Direct	mldirect.ml.com
Morningstar.com	morningstar.com
Reuters	investor.reuters.com
Vanguard	vanguard.com
Taxes	**Web Address**
H&R Block	hrblock.com
Internal Revenue Service	irs.gov
Jackson Hewitt	jacksonhewitt.com
Liberty Tax Service	libertytax.com

For more information about finance Web sites, visit scsite.com/ dc2008/ch2/web.

FIGURE 6 Financial resources Web sites offer general information, stock market analyses, and tax advice, as well as guidance and money-saving tips.

FINANCE WEB EXERCISES

1 Visit three advice and education Web sites listed in Figure 6 and read their top business world reports. Write a paragraph about each, summarizing these stories. Which stocks or mutual funds do these Web sites predict as being sound investments today? What are the current market indexes for the DJIA (Dow Jones Industrial Average), S&P 500, and NASDAQ, and how do these figures compare with the previous day's numbers?

2 Using two of the stock market Web sites listed in Figure 6, search for information about Microsoft, Adobe Systems, and one other software vendor. Write a paragraph about each of these stocks describing the revenues, net incomes, total assets for the previous year, current stock price per share, highest and lowest prices of each stock during the past year, and other relevant investment information.

Online Social Networks and Media Sharing
CHECK OUT MY NEW PHOTOS

Online Social Networks and Media Sharing Web Sites More Popular than Ever

Do you ever wonder what your friends are doing? What about your friends' friends? Over the past two years, the popularity of online social networks has increased dramatically. Online social networks such as MySpace and AIM Pages allow you to create a personalized profile that others are able to view online. These profiles may include information about you such as your hometown, your age, your hobbies, and pictures. You also may create links to your friends' pages, post messages for individual friends, or bulletins for all of your friends to see. Online social networks are great places not only to keep in touch with your friends, but to reconnect with old friends and meet new friends!

If you would like to post pictures and videos and do not require the full functionality of an online social network, you might consider a media sharing Web site, which is a type of online social network. Media sharing Web sites such as YouTube and Phanfare (Figure 7) allow you to post media, including photos and videos, for others to view, print, and/or download. Media sharing Web sites, which may be free or charge a fee, provide a quick, efficient way to share photos of your last vacation or videos of your brother's high school graduation.

FIGURE 7 The Phanfare Web site allows subscribers to share their photos and videos with others.

ONLINE SOCIAL NETWORKS AND MEDIA SHARING

Online Social Networks	Web Address
AIM Pages Social Network	aimpages.com
Facebook	facebook.com
Friendster	friendster.com
MySpace — a place for friends	myspace.com
Media Sharing	**Web Address**
flickr	flickr.com
iFeeder Media Sharing Portal	ifeeder.com
Phanfare	phanfare.com
Picasa Web Albums	picasa.com
Shutterfly * Shutterfly Studio	shutterfly.com
Twango	twango.com
Yahoo! Video	video.yahoo.com
YouTube	youtube.com

For more information about online social networks and media sharing Web sites, visit scsite.com/dc2008/ch2/web.

FIGURE 8 Online social networks and media sharing Web sites are popular ways to keep in touch with friends, meet new people, and share media.

ONLINE SOCIAL NETWORKS AND MEDIA SHARING WEB EXERCISES

1. Many individuals now use online social networks. Visit two online social networks listed in Figure 8. If you are attempting to access an online social network from your classroom and are unable to do so, your school may have restricted use of social networking Web sites. Compare and contrast these two sites by performing the following actions and recording your findings. First, create a profile on each of these sites. If you find a Web site that charges a fee to sign up, choose another Web site. How easy is the sign-up process? Does either Web site ask for any personal information you are uncomfortable sharing? If so, what information? Once you sign up, make a list of five of your closest friends, and search for their profiles on each of these two sites. What site contains more of your friends? Browse each site and make a list of its features. In your opinion, what site is better? Explain why.

2. Media sharing Web sites make it extremely easy to share photos and videos with friends, family, and colleagues. Before choosing an online media sharing Web site to use, you should do some research. Visit two media sharing Web sites in Figure 8. Is there a fee to post media to these Web sites? If so, how much? Are these Web sites supported by advertisements? Locate the instructions for posting media to these Web sites. Are the instructions straightforward? Do these Web sites impose a limit on the number and/or size of media files you can post? Summarize your responses to these questions in two or three paragraphs.

Blogs
EXPRESS YOURSELF

Blogosphere Growing Swiftly

Internet users are feeling the need to publish their views, and they are finding Weblogs, or blogs for short, the ideal vehicle. The blogosphere began as an easy way for individuals to express their opinions on the Web. Today, this communication vehicle has become a powerful tool, for individuals, groups, and corporations are using blogs to promote their ideas and advertise their products. It is not necessary to have a background in Web design to be able to post to a blog.

Bloggers generally update their Web sites frequently to reflect their views. Their posts range from a paragraph to an entire essay and often contain links to other Web sites. The more popular blogs discuss politics, lifestyles, and technology.

Individuals easily may set up a blog free or for a fee, using Web sites such as Blogger, Cooeey (Figure 9), and TypePad. In addition, online social networks may have a built-in blogging feature. Be cautious of the information you post on your blog, especially if it is accessible to everyone online.

Corporate blogs, such as The GM FastLane Blog, discuss all aspects of the company's products, whereas all-encompassing blogs, such as the Metafilter Community Weblog and others in Figure 10, are designed to keep general readers entertained and informed.

Blogs are affecting the manner in which people communicate, and some experts predict they will one day become our primary method of sharing information.

BLOGS WEB SITES

BLOG	Web Address
A List Apart	alistapart.com
Blog Top Sites — Internet Blogs	blogtopsites.com/internet
Blog.com	blog.com
Blogger	blogger.com
Bloglines	bloglines.com
Blogstream	blogstream.com
Boing Boing: A Directory of Wonderful Things	boingboing.net
Cooeey	www.cooeey.com
Davenetics * Politics + Media + Musings	davenetics.com
Geek News Central	geeknewscentral.com
GM FastLane Blog	fastlane.gmblogs.com
kottke.org: home of fine hypertext products	kottke.org
MetaFilter Community Weblog	metafilter.com
Scripting News	scripting.com
TypePad	typepad.com

For more information about blogs Web sites, visit scsite.com/dc2008/ch2/web.

FIGURE 10 These blogs offer information about technology, news, politics, and entertainment.

BLOGS WEB EXERCISES

1 Visit three of the blog Web sites listed in Figure 10. Make a table listing the blog name, its purpose, the author, its audience, and advertisers, if any, who sponsor the blog. Then, write a paragraph that describes the information you found on each of these blogs.

2 Many Internet users read the technology blogs to keep abreast of the latest developments. Visit the Geek News Central and Scripting News blogs listed in Figure 10 and write a paragraph describing the top story in each blog. Read the posted comments, if any. Then, write another paragraph describing two other stories found on these blogs that cover material you have discussed in this course. Write a third paragraph discussing which one is more interesting to you. Would you add reading blogs to your list of Internet activities? Why or why not?

FIGURE 9 The Cooeey Web site allows members to share their insights by posting to their personal blogs.

Government
STAMP OF APPROVAL

Making a Federal Case for Useful Information

When it is time to buy stamps to mail your correspondence, you no longer need to wait in long lines at your local post office. The U.S. Postal Service has authorized several corporations to sell stamps online.

You can recognize U.S. Government Web sites on the Internet by their .gov top-level domain abbreviation. For example, The Library of Congress Web site is loc.gov. Government and military Web sites offer a wide range of information, and some of the more popular sites are listed in Figure 12. The Time Service Department Web site will provide you with the correct time. If you are looking for a federal document, FedWorld (Figure 11) lists thousands of documents distributed by the government on its Web site. For access to the names of your congressional representatives, visit the extensive Hieros Gamos Web site.

GOVERNMENT RESOURCES WEB SITES

Postage	Web Address
Endicia	endicia.com
Pitney Bowes	pb.com
Stamps.com	stamps.com

Government	Web Address
FedWorld	www.fedworld.gov
Hieros Gamos — Worldwide Legal Directories	hg.org
The Library of Congress	loc.gov
National Agricultural Library	nal.usda.gov
The National Archives	archives.gov
THOMAS Legislative Information	thomas.loc.gov
Time Service Department	tycho.usno.navy.mil
U.S. Department of Education	ed.gov
United States Department of the Treasury	treas.gov
U.S. Government Printing Office	www.access.gpo.gov
United States National Library of Medicine	www.nlm.nih.gov
United States Patent and Trademark Office	www.uspto.gov
USAJOBS	usajobs.opm.gov
The White House	whitehouse.gov

For more information about government Web sites, visit scsite.com/dc2008/ch2/web.

FIGURE 12 These Web sites offer information about buying U.S.-approved postage online and researching federal agencies.

FIGURE 11 The FedWorld Web site contains a wealth of information disseminated by the federal government.

GOVERNMENT WEB EXERCISES

1 View the three postage Web sites listed in Figure 12. Compare and contrast the available services on each one. Consider postage cost, necessary equipment, shipping services, security techniques, and tracking capability. Explain why you would or would not like to use this service.

2 Visit the Hieros Gamos Web site listed in Figure 12. What are the names, addresses, and telephone numbers of your two state senators and your local congressional representative? On what committees do they serve? Who is the chief justice of the Supreme Court, and what has been this justice's opinion on two recently decided cases? Who are the members of the president's cabinet? Then, visit two other Web sites listed in Figure 12. Write a paragraph about each Web site describing its content and features.

Shopping and Auctions
BARGAINS GALORE

Let Your Mouse Do Your Shopping

From groceries to clothing to computers, you can buy just about everything you need with just a few clicks of your mouse. Electronic retailers (e-tailers) are cashing in on cybershoppers' purchases. Books, computer software and hardware, and music are the hottest commodities.

The two categories of Internet shopping Web sites are those with physical counterparts, such as Wal-Mart and Best Buy, and those with only a Web presence, such as Amazon.com and Buy.com (Figure 13). Popular Web shopping sites are listed in Figure 14.

Another method of shopping for the items you need, and maybe some you really do not need, is to visit auction Web sites, including those listed in Figure 14. Categories include antiques and collectibles, automotive, computers, electronics, music, sports, sports cards and memorabilia,

and toys. Online auction Web sites can offer unusual items, including *Star Wars* props and memorabilia and a round of golf with Tiger Woods. eBay is one of thousands of Internet auction Web sites and is the world's largest personal online trading community.

SHOPPING AND AUCTIONS WEB SITES

Auctions	Web Address
craigslist	craigslist.org
eBay®	ebay.com
Sotheby's	sothebys.com
uBid.com	ubid.com
Yahoo! Auctions	auctions.yahoo.com
Books and Music	**Web Address**
Amazon.com	amazon.com
Barnes & Noble.com	bn.com
BookFinder.com	bookfinder.com
Computers and Electronics	**Web Address**
BestBuy	bestbuy.com
Buy.com	buy.com
Crutchfield	crutchfield.com
Miscellaneous	**Web Address**
drugstore.com	drugstore.com
Froogle	froogle.com
Sharper Image	sharperimage.com
Walmart.com	walmart.com

For more information about shopping and auctions Web sites, visit scsite.com/dc2008/ch2/web.

FIGURE 13 Buy.com is a popular electronic retailer that sells a variety of products.

FIGURE 14 Making online purchases can help ease the burden of driving to and fighting the crowds in local malls.

SHOPPING AND AUCTIONS WEB EXERCISES

1 Visit two of the computers and electronics and two of the miscellaneous Web sites listed in Figure 14. Write a paragraph describing the features these Web sites offer compared with the same offerings from stores. In another paragraph, describe any disadvantages of shopping at these Web sites instead of actually visiting a store. Then, describe their policies for returning unwanted merchandise and for handling complaints.

2 Using one of the auction Web sites listed in Figure 14, search for two objects pertaining to your hobbies. For example, if you are a sports fan, you can search for a complete set of Upper Deck cards. If you are a car buff, search for your dream car. Describe these two items. How many people have bid on these items? Who are the sellers? What are the opening and current bids?

Weather, Sports, and News
WHAT'S NEWS?

Weather, Sports, and News Web Sites Score Big Hits

Rain or sun? Hot or cold? Weather is the leading online news item, with at least 10,000 Web sites devoted to this field. Millions of people view the WX.com Web site (Figure 15) each month.

Baseball may be the national pastime, but sports aficionados yearn for everything from auto racing to cricket. The Internet has more than one million pages of multimedia sports news, entertainment, and merchandise.

The Internet has emerged as a major source for news, with one-third of Americans going online at least once a week and 15 percent going online daily for reports of major news events. Many of these viewers are using Really Simple Syndication (RSS) technology to be notified when new stories about their favorite topics are available on the Internet. Popular weather, sports, and news Web sites are listed in Figure 16.

FIGURE 15 Local, national, and international weather conditions and details about breaking weather stories are available on WX.com.

WEATHER, SPORTS, AND NEWS WEB SITES

Weather	Web Address
Infoplease Weather	infoplease.com/weather.html
Intellicast.com	intellicast.com
National Weather Service	www.crh.noaa.gov
STORMFAX	stormfax.com
The Weather Channel	weather.com
WX.com	wx.com

Sports	Web Address
CBS SportsLine.com	cbs.sportsline.com
ESPN.com	espn.com
NCAAsports.com	ncaasports.com
OFFICIAL WEBSITE OF THE OLYMPIC MOVEMENT	olympic.org
SIRC — A World of Sport Information	sirc.ca
Sporting News Radio	radio.sportingnews.com

News	Web Address
Google News	news.google.com
MSNBC	msnbc.com
New York Post Online Edition	nypost.com
onlinenewspapers.com	onlinenewspapers.com
Privacy.org	privacy.org
SiliconValley.com	siliconvalley.com
Starting Page	startingpage.com/html/news.html
USATODAY.com	usatoday.com
washingtonpost.com	washingtonpost.com

For more information about weather, sports, and news Web sites, visit scsite.com/dc2008/ch2/web.

FIGURE 16 Keep informed about the latest weather, sports, and news events with these Web sites.

WEATHER, SPORTS, AND NEWS EXERCISES

1 Visit two of the sports Web sites in Figure 16 and write a paragraph describing the content these Web sites provide concerning your favorite sport. Visit news.google.com and then search for stories about this sport team or athlete. Then, create a customized news page with stories about your sports interests. Include RSS feeds to get regularly updated summaries on this subject.

2 Visit the onlinenewspapers.com and Starting Page Web sites listed in Figure 16 and select two newspapers from each site. Write a paragraph describing the top national news story featured in each of these four Web pages. Then, write another paragraph describing the top international news story displayed at each Web site. In the third paragraph, discuss which of the four Web sites is the most interesting in terms of story selection, photographs, and Web page design.

Environment
THE FATE OF THE ENVIRONMENT

Protecting the Planet's Ecosystem

From the rain forests of Africa to the marine life in the Pacific Ocean, the fragile ecosystem is under extreme stress. Many environmental groups have developed Web sites, including those listed in Figure 21, in attempts to educate worldwide populations and to increase resource conservation. The GreenNet Web site (Figure 22) contains

information for people who would like to help safeguard the environment.

On an international scale, the Environmental Sites on the Internet Web page developed by the Royal Institute of Technology in Stockholm, Sweden, has been rated as one of the better ecological Web sites. Its comprehensive listing of environmental concerns range from aquatic ecology to wetlands.

The U.S. federal government has a number of Web sites devoted to specific environmental concerns. For example, the U.S. Environmental Protection Agency (EPA) provides pollution data, including ozone levels and air pollutants, for specific areas. Its AirData Web site displays air pollution emissions and monitoring data from the entire United States and is the world's most extensive collection of air pollution data.

ENVIRONMENT WEB SITES

NAME	Web Address
Central African Regional Program for the Environment (CARPE)	carpe.umd.edu
Earthjustice	earthjustice.org
EarthTrends: The Environmental Information Portal	earthtrends.wri.org
Environmental Defense	edf.org
Environmental Sites on the Internet	www.ima.kth.se/im/envsite/envsite.htm
EPA AirData — Access to Air Pollution Data	epa.gov/air/data
Global Change and Environmental Education Resources	gcrio.org/educ.html
GreenNet	gn.apc.org
New American Dream	newdream.org
University of Wisconsin — Milwaukee Environmental Health and Safety Resources	www.uwm.edu/Dept/EHSRM/EHSLINKS
USGS Acid rain data and reports	bqs.usgs.gov/acidrain
World-Wide Web Virtual Library: Botany / Plant Biology	ou.edu/cas/botany-micro/www-vl/

For more information about environment Web sites, visit scsite.com/dc2008/ch2/web.

FIGURE 21 Environment Web sites provide vast resources for ecological data and action groups.

FIGURE 22 A visit to the GreenNet Web site provides information about people who work to support the environment.

ENVIRONMENT WEB EXERCISES

1 The New American Dream Web site encourages consumers to reduce the amount of junk mail sent to their homes. Using the table in Figure 21, visit the Web site and write a paragraph stating how many trees are leveled each year to provide paper for these mailings, how many garbage trucks are needed to haul this waste, and other statistics. Read the letters that you can use to eliminate your name from bulk mail lists. To whom would you mail these letters? How long does it take to stop these unsolicited letters?

2 Visit the EPA AirData Web site. What is the highest ozone level recorded in your state this past year? Where are the nearest air pollution monitoring Web sites, and what are their levels? Where are the nearest sources of air pollution? Read two reports about two different topics, such as acid rain and air quality, and summarize their findings. Include information about who sponsored the research, who conducted the studies, when the data was collected, and the impact of this pollution on the atmosphere, water, forests, and human health. Whom would you contact for further information regarding the data and studies?

Health
NO PAIN, ALL GAIN

Store Personal Health Records Online

More than 70 million consumers use the Internet yearly to search for health information, so using the Web to store personal medical data is a natural extension of the Internet's capabilities. Internet health services and portals are available online to store your personal health history, including prescriptions, lab test results, doctor visits, allergies, and immunizations. Web sites such as MedlinePlus (Figure 23) provide free health information to consumers.

In minutes, you can register with a health Web site by choosing a user name and password. Then, you create a record to enter your medical history. You also can store data for your emergency contacts, primary care physicians,

specialists, blood type, cholesterol levels, blood pressure, and insurance plan. No matter where you are in the world, you and medical personnel can obtain records via the Internet or fax machine. Some popular online health database management systems are shown in Figure 24.

HEALTH WEB SITES

Medical History	Web Address
PersonalMD	personalmd.com
Practice Solutions	practicesolutions.ca
Records for Living, Inc — Personal Health and Living Management	recordsforliving.com
WebMD	webmd.com
General Health	**Web Address**
Centers for Disease Control and Prevention	www.cdc.gov
familydoctor.org	familydoctor.org
healthfinder	healthfinder.gov
HealthWeb	healthweb.org
Medical Library Association Consumer and Patient Health Information Section (CAPHIS)	caphis.mlanet.org/consumer
MedlinePlus	medlineplus.gov
PEC: Health and Nutrition Web Sites	pecentral.org/websites/healthsites.html
www.health.gov	health.gov
For more information about health Web sites, visit scsite.com/dc2008/ch2/web.	

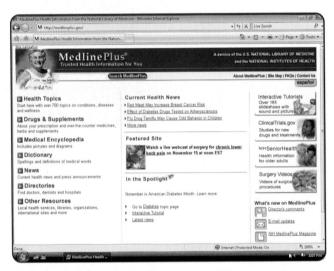

FIGURE 23 The MedLine Plus Web site provides health information from the U.S. Library of Medicine and the National Institutes of Health.

FIGURE 24 These health Web sites allow you to organize your medical information and store it in an online database and also obtain information about a variety of medical conditions and treatments.

HEALTH WEB EXERCISES

1 Access one of the health Web sites listed in Figure 24. Register yourself or a family member, and then enter the full health history. Create an emergency medical card if the Web site provides the card option. Submit this record and emergency card to your instructor. If you feel uncomfortable disclosing medical information for yourself or a family member, you may enter fictitious information.

2 Visit three of the health Web sites listed in Figure 24. Describe the features of each. Which of the three is the most user-friendly? Why? Describe the privacy policies of these three Web sites. Submit your analysis of these Web sites to your instructor.

Research and Resources
SEARCH AND YE SHALL FIND

Info on the Web

A recent Web Usability survey conducted by the Nielsen Norman Group found that 88 percent of people log onto a computer and then use a search engine as their first action. Search engines require users to type words and phrases that characterize the information being sought. Yahoo! (Figure 25), Google, and AltaVista are some of the more popular search engines. The key to effective searching on the Web is composing search queries that narrow the search results and place the most relevant Web sites at the top of the results list.

Keep up with the latest developments by viewing online dictionaries and encyclopedias that add to their collections of computer and product terms on a regular basis. Shopping for a new computer can be a daunting experience, but many online guides can help you select the components that best fit your needs and budget. If you are not confident in your ability to solve a problem alone, turn to online technical support. Web sites often provide streaming how-to video lessons, tutorials, and real-time chats with experienced technicians. Hardware and software reviews, price comparisons, shareware, technical questions and answers, and breaking technology news are found on comprehensive portals. Figure 26 lists popular research and resources Web sites.

RESEARCH AND RESOURCES WEB SITES

Research	Web Address
A9.com	a9.com
AlltheWeb	alltheweb.com
AltaVista	altavista.com
Ask.com	ask.com
Google	google.com
HotBot	hotbot.com
Overture	overture.com
Windows Live	live.com
Yahoo!	yahoo.com
Resources	**Web Address**
CNET.com	cnet.com
eHow	ehow.com
PC911	pcnineoneone.com
TechBargains	techbargains.com
Webopedia	webopedia.com
ZDNet	zdnet.com

For more information about research and resources Web sites, visit scsite.com/dc2008/ch2/web.

FIGURE 25 The Yahoo! News search results for the phrase, computer, lists more than 26,000 stories.

FIGURE 26 Web users can find information by using research and resources Web sites.

RESEARCH AND RESOURCE WEB EXERCISES

1 Use two of the search engines listed in the Research category in Figure 26 to find three Web sites that review the latest digital cameras from Sony and Kodak. Make a table listing the search engines, Web site names, and the cameras' model numbers, suggested retail price, megapixels, memory, and features.

2 Visit the Webopedia Web site. Search this site for five terms. Create a table with two columns: one for the cyberterm and one for the Web definition. Then, create a second table listing five recently added or updated words and their definitions on this Web site. Next, visit the TechBargains Web site to choose the components you would buy if you were building a customized desktop computer and notebook computer. Create a table for both computers, listing the computer manufacturer, processor model name or number and manufacturer, clock speed, RAM, cache, number of expansion slots, and number of bays.

Careers
IN SEARCH OF THE PERFECT JOB

Web Helps Career Hunt

While your teachers give you valuable training to prepare you for a career, they rarely teach you how to begin that career. You can broaden your horizons by searching the Internet for career information and job openings.

First, examine some of the job search Web sites. These resources list thousands of openings in hundreds of fields, companies, and locations. For example, the U.S. Department of Labor Web site, shown in Figure 27, allows you to find information for different types of jobs. This information may include the training and education required, salary data, working conditions, job descriptions, and more.

When a company contacts you for an interview, learn as much about it and the industry as possible before the interview. Many of the Web sites listed in Figure 28 include detailed company profiles and links to their corporate Web sites.

CAREER WEB SITES

Job Search	Web Address
BestJobsUSA.com	bestjobsusa.com
CareerBuilder	careerbuilder.com
CareerNet	careernet.com
CAREERXCHANGE	careerexchange.com
College Grad Job Hunter	collegegrad.com
EmploymentGuide.com	employmentguide.com
Job.com	job.com
JobBank USA	jobbankusa.com
JobWeb.com	www.jobweb.com
Monster	monster.com
Spherion	spherion.com
USAJOBS	usajobs.opm.gov
VolunteerMatch	volunteermatch.org
Yahoo! HotJobs	hotjobs.yahoo.com
Company/Industry Information	**Web Address**
Career ResourceCenter.com	resourcecenter.com
Forbes.com	forbes.com/careers
FORTUNE	fortune.com
Hoover's	hoovers.com
Occupational Outlook Handbook	stats.bls.gov/oco

For more information about career Web sites, visit scsite.com/dc2008/ch2/web.

FIGURE 27 The Occupational Outlook Handbook provides career information to those searching for jobs.

FIGURE 28 Career Web sites provide a variety of job openings and information about major companies worldwide.

CAREERS WEB EXERCISES

1 Use two of the job search Web sites listed in Figure 28 to find three companies with job openings in your field. Make a table listing the Web site name, position available, description, salary, location, desired education, and desired experience.

2 It is a good idea to acquire information before graduation about the industry in which you would like to work. Are you interested in the automotive manufacturing industry, the restaurant service industry, or the financial industry? Use two of the company/industry information Web sites listed in Figure 28 to research a particular career related to your major. Write a paragraph naming the Web sites and the specific information you found, such as the nature of the work, recommended training and qualifications, employment outlook, and earnings. Then, use two other Web sites to profile three companies with positions available in this field. Write a paragraph about each of these companies, describing the headquarters' location, sales and earnings for the previous year, total number of employees, working conditions, perks, and competitors.

Arts and Literature
FIND SOME CULTURE

Get Ready to Read, Paint, and Dance

Brush up your knowledge of Shakespeare, grab a canvas, and put on your dancing shoes. Visual arts and literature Web sites, including those in Figure 29, are about to sweep you off your cyberfeet.

ARTS AND LITERATURE WEB SITES

Arts	Web Address
accessplace arts	accessplace.com/arts.htm
Art News — absolutearts.com	absolutearts.com
The Children's Museum of Indianapolis	childrensmuseum.org
GalleryGuide.com	galleryguide.com
The Getty	getty.edu
Louvre Museum	louvre.fr
Montreal Museum of Fine Arts	mmfa.qc.ca
The New York Times: Arts	nytimes.com/pages/arts/index.html
Virtual Library museums pages (VLmp)	vlmp.museophile.com
Literature	**Web Address**
Bartleby.com	bartleby.com
Bibliomania	bibliomania.com
Fantastic Fiction	fantasticfiction.co.uk
Literary History	literaryhistory.com
The Modern Library eBook List	randomhouse.com/modernlibrary/ebookslist.html
Project Gutenberg	gutenberg.org
William Shakespeare at eNotes	shakespeare.com

For more information about arts and literature Web sites, visit scsite.com/dc2008/ch2/web.

FIGURE 29 Discover culture throughout the world by visiting these arts and literature Web sites.

The full text of hundreds of books is available online from the Bibliomania and Project Gutenberg Web sites. Shakespeare.com provides in-depth reviews and news of the world's most famous playwright and his works. The Bartleby.com Web site features biographies, definitions, quotations, dictionaries, and indexes.

When you are ready to absorb more culture, you can turn to various art Web sites. Many museums have images of their collections online. Among them are the Getty Museum in Los Angeles (Figure 30), the Montreal Museum of Fine Arts, and the Louvre Museum in Paris.

The accessplace arts and The New York Times Web sites focus on the arts and humanities and provide fascinating glimpses into the worlds of dance, music, performance, cinema, and other topics pertaining to creative expression.

FIGURE 30 Permanent and temporary exhibitions, educational activities, and a bookstore are featured on the Getty Museum Web site.

ARTS AND LITERATURE WEB EXERCISES

1 Visit The Modern Library eBook List Web site listed in Figure 29 and view one book in the 20th CENTURY NOVELS, 19th CENTURY NOVELS, BRITISH LITERATURE, and HISTORY sections. Create a table with columns for the book name, author, cost, online store, local store, and description. Then, read the excerpt from each of the four books and write a paragraph describing which of these four books is the most interesting to you. What are the advantages and disadvantages of reading classic literature electronically?

2 Using the arts Web sites listed in Figure 29, search for three temporary exhibitions in galleries throughout the world. Describe the venues, the artists, and the works. What permanent collections are found in these museums? Some people shop for gifts in the museums' stores. View and describe three items for sale.

CHAPTER THREE

Application Software

Picture Yourself Using Software

This is a busy semester for you. Besides a full load of classes, you have joined your school's Hospitality Club. In addition, your brother has enlisted you to help plan your grandparents' fiftieth anniversary party, a job that entails retouching some of their old photographs and tracking the party's budget. You plan to use software on your notebook computer and PDA to assist with these tasks.

In the student lounge before geography class, you check e-mail on your notebook computer. You have a message from a fellow club member asking if you have finished the flyer for the Hospitality Club's upcoming dance, along with a reminder for tomorrow's meeting. Using word processing software, you put the finishing touches on the flyer and then respond to the e-mail message, including the flyer as an attachment. You enter the meeting date in your appointment calendar in your PDA and then return to your notebook computer. You then start your photo editing software and finish retouching your grandparents' wedding photograph. Next, you use personal finance software to enter the latest figures for your grandparents' party. Deciding you have worked enough today, you spend some time creating a blog about the party and designing a spectacular roller coaster.

Read Chapter 3 to learn more about word processing software, e-mail programs, photo editing software, desktop publishing software, PDA application software, personal finance software, and entertainment software, and discover many other types of application software.

After completing this chapter, you will be able to:

1. Identify the categories of application software

2. Explain ways software is distributed

3. Explain how to work with application software

4. Identify the key features of widely used business programs

5. Identify the key features of widely used graphics and multimedia programs

6. Identify the key features of widely used home, personal, and educational programs

7. Identify the types of application software used in communications

8. Describe the function of several utility programs

9. Discuss the advantages of using Web-based software

10. Describe the learning aids available for application software

CONTENTS

APPLICATION SOFTWARE

With the proper software, a computer is a valuable tool. Software allows users to create letters, memos, reports, and other documents; design Web pages and diagrams; draw and alter images; record and enhance audio and video clips; prepare and file taxes; play single player or multiplayer games; compose e-mail messages and instant messages; and much more. To accomplish these and many other tasks, users work with application software. **Application software** consists of programs designed to make users more productive and/or assist them with personal tasks. Application software has a variety of uses:

1. To make business activities more efficient
2. To assist with graphics and multimedia projects
3. To support home, personal, and educational tasks
4. To facilitate communications

The table in Figure 3-1 categorizes popular types of application software by their general use. Although many types of communications software exist, the ones listed in Figure 3-1 are application software oriented. Successful use of application software often requires the use of one or more of the utility programs identified in Figure 3-1.

The categories in Figure 3-1 are not mutually exclusive. Software listed in one category may be used in other categories. For example, desktop publishing programs, which are categorized as graphics and multimedia software, often are used for business or personal reasons.

Application software is available in a variety of forms: packaged, custom, Web-based, open source, shareware, freeware, and public domain.

- **Packaged software** is mass-produced, copyrighted retail software that meets the needs of a wide variety of users, not just a single user or company. Word processing and spreadsheet software are examples of packaged software. Packaged software is available in retail stores or on the Web.

- **Custom software** performs functions specific to a business or industry. Sometimes a company cannot find packaged software that meets its unique requirements. In this case, the company may use programmers to develop tailor-made custom software, which usually costs more than packaged software.

CATEGORIES OF APPLICATION SOFTWARE

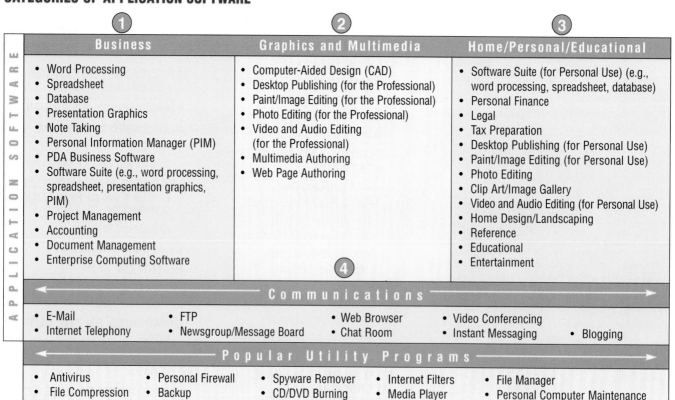

Business	**Graphics and Multimedia**	**Home/Personal/Educational**
• Word Processing • Spreadsheet • Database • Presentation Graphics • Note Taking • Personal Information Manager (PIM) • PDA Business Software • Software Suite (e.g., word processing, spreadsheet, presentation graphics, PIM) • Project Management • Accounting • Document Management • Enterprise Computing Software	• Computer-Aided Design (CAD) • Desktop Publishing (for the Professional) • Paint/Image Editing (for the Professional) • Photo Editing (for the Professional) • Video and Audio Editing (for the Professional) • Multimedia Authoring • Web Page Authoring	• Software Suite (for Personal Use) (e.g., word processing, spreadsheet, database) • Personal Finance • Legal • Tax Preparation • Desktop Publishing (for Personal Use) • Paint/Image Editing (for Personal Use) • Photo Editing • Clip Art/Image Gallery • Video and Audio Editing (for Personal Use) • Home Design/Landscaping • Reference • Educational • Entertainment

Communications

• E-Mail • Internet Telephony	• FTP • Newsgroup/Message Board	• Web Browser • Chat Room	• Video Conferencing • Instant Messaging • Blogging

Popular Utility Programs

• Antivirus • File Compression	• Personal Firewall • Backup	• Spyware Remover • CD/DVD Burning	• Internet Filters • Media Player	• File Manager • Personal Computer Maintenance

FIGURE 3-1 The four major categories of popular application software are outlined in this table. Communications software often is bundled with other application or system software. Also identified in the table are widely used utility programs.

- **Web-based software** refers to programs hosted by a Web site. Users access and interact with Web-based software from any computer or device that is connected to the Internet. Many Web sites provide free access to their programs; some charge a fee. Examples of Web-based software include e-mail, word processing, tax preparation, and game programs. Web-based programs are discussed in more depth later in the chapter.
- **Open source software** is software provided for use, modification, and redistribution. This software has no restrictions from the copyright holder regarding modification of the software's internal instructions and redistribution of the software. Open source software usually can be downloaded from the Internet, sometimes at no cost.
- **Shareware** is copyrighted software that is distributed at no cost for a trial period. To use a shareware program beyond that period, you send payment to the program developer. Shareware developers trust users to send payment if software use extends beyond the stated trial period. In some cases, a scaled-down version of the software is distributed free, and payment entitles the user to the fully functional product.
- **Freeware** is copyrighted software provided at no cost by an individual or a company that retains all rights to the software. Thus, programmers typically cannot incorporate freeware in applications they intend to sell. The word, free, in freeware indicates the software has no charge.
- **Public-domain software** has been donated for public use and has no copyright restrictions. Anyone can copy or distribute public-domain software to others at no cost.

Thousands of shareware, freeware, and public-domain programs are available on the Internet for users to download. Examples include communications programs, graphics programs, and games. These programs usually have fewer capabilities than retail programs.

After you purchase or download software, you install it. During installation, the program may ask you to register and/or activate the software. Registering the software is optional and usually involves submitting your name and other personal information to the software manufacturer or developer. Registering the software often entitles you to product support. *Product activation* is a technique that some software manufacturers use

to ensure the software is not installed on more computers than legally licensed. Usually, the software does not function or has limited functionality until you activate it via the Internet or telephone. Thus, activation is a required process for programs requesting it. Registering and/or activating the software also usually entitles you to free program updates for a specified time period, such as a year.

The Role of System Software

System software serves as the interface between the user, the application software, and the computer's hardware (Figure 3-2). To use application software, such as a word processing program, your computer must be running system software — specifically, an operating system. Four popular personal computer operating systems are Windows Vista, Windows XP, Linux, and Mac OS X.

Each time you start a computer, the operating system is *loaded* (copied) from the computer's hard disk into memory. Once the operating system is loaded, it coordinates all the activities of the computer. This includes starting application software and transferring data among input and output devices and memory. While the computer is running, the operating system remains in memory.

Application Software

System Software

FIGURE 3-2 A user does not communicate directly with the computer hardware. Instead, system software is the interface between the user, the application software, and the hardware. For example, when a user instructs the application software to print, the application software sends the print instruction to the system software, which in turn sends the print instruction to the hardware.

Working with Application Software

To use application software, you must instruct the operating system to start the program. The steps in Figure 3-3 illustrate how to start and interact with the Paint program, which is included with the Windows Vista operating system. The following paragraphs explain the steps in Figure 3-3.

Personal computer operating systems often use the concept of a desktop to make the computer easier to use. The **desktop** is an on-screen work area that has a graphical user interface (read Looking Ahead 3-1 for a look at the next generation of user interfaces). Step 1 of Figure 3-3 shows icons, a button, a pointer, and a menu on the Windows Vista desktop. An **icon** is a small image displayed on the screen that represents a program, a document, or some other object. A **button** is a graphical element that you activate to cause a specific action to take place. One way to activate a button is to click it. To **click** a button on the screen requires moving the pointer to the button and then pressing and releasing a button on the mouse (usually the left mouse button). The **pointer** is a small symbol displayed on the screen that moves as you move the mouse. Common pointer shapes are an I-beam (I), a block arrow (�), and a pointing hand (☝).

FIGURE 3-3 HOW TO START A PROGRAM FROM WINDOWS VISTA

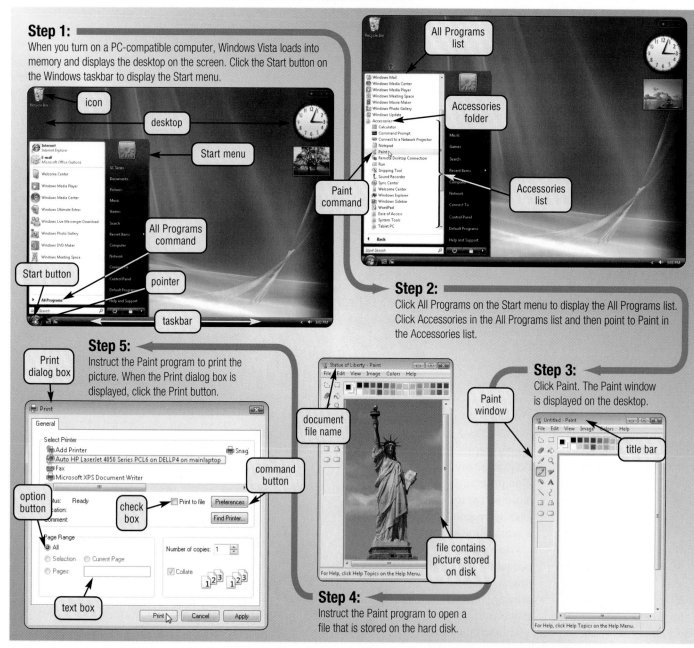

Step 1:
When you turn on a PC-compatible computer, Windows Vista loads into memory and displays the desktop on the screen. Click the Start button on the Windows taskbar to display the Start menu.

Step 2:
Click All Programs on the Start menu to display the All Programs list. Click Accessories in the All Programs list and then point to Paint in the Accessories list.

Step 3:
Click Paint. The Paint window is displayed on the desktop.

Step 4:
Instruct the Paint program to open a file that is stored on the hard disk.

Step 5:
Instruct the Paint program to print the picture. When the Print dialog box is displayed, click the Print button.

LOOKING AHEAD 3-1

Touch Drive Your Computer Screen

Computer users soon may discard the mouse and let their fingers do the work with an innovative user interface system that displays images in thin air.

The virtual touch screen uses a rear projector system to create images that look three dimensional and appear to float in midair. Users interact with projected objects with their hands, so there is no need for a mouse, monitor, physical surface, or special gloves or eyeglasses. In specialized environments, users also can use a scalpel, scissors, pen, or pencil to move objects.

The only hardware required to project these images is a standard video source, such as a computer, television, DVD player, or video game console. The projected images can be as large as 30 inches diagonally and are viewed best against a black background to emphasize the color contrast. For more information, visit scsite.com/dc2008/ch3/looking and then click Gesture Recognition.

The Windows Vista desktop contains a Start button on the lower-left corner of the taskbar. When you click the Start button, the Start menu is displayed on the desktop. A **menu** contains a list of commands from which you make selections. A **command** is an instruction that causes a program to perform a specific action.

As illustrated in Steps 1 and 2 of Figure 3-3, when you click the Start button and click the All Programs command on the Start menu, the All Programs list is displayed on the Start menu. Clicking the Accessories folder in the All Programs list displays the Accessories list.

To start a program, you can click its program name on a menu or in a list. This action instructs the operating system to start the program, which means the program's instructions load from a storage medium (such as a hard disk) into memory. For example, when you click Paint in the Accessories list, Windows Vista loads the Paint program instructions from the computer's hard disk into memory.

Once loaded into memory, the program is displayed in a window on the desktop (Step 3 of Figure 3-3). A **window** is a rectangular area of the screen that displays data and information. The top of a window has a **title bar**, which is a horizontal space that contains the window's name.

With the program loaded, you can create a new file or open an existing one. A *file* is a named collection of stored data, instructions, or information. A file can contain text, images, audio, and video. To distinguish among various files, each file has a file name. A *file name* is a unique combination of letters of the alphabet, numbers, and other characters that identifies a file. The title bar of the document window usually displays a document's file name. Step 4 of Figure 3-3 shows the contents of the file, Statue of Liberty,

displaying in the Paint window. The file contains an image photographed with a digital camera.

In some cases, when you instruct a program to perform an activity such as printing, the program displays a dialog box. A *dialog box* is a window that provides information, presents available options, or requests a response. Dialog boxes, such as the one shown in Step 5 of Figure 3-3, often contain option buttons, text boxes, check boxes, and command buttons. Clicking the Print button in the dialog box instructs the computer to print the picture.

FAQ 3-1

What programs are included with Windows Vista?

Every version of Windows Vista includes Calculator, Notepad, WordPad, Internet Explorer, Windows Photo Gallery, Windows Mail, Windows Calendar, and a variety of games. For more information, visit scsite.com/dc2008/ch3/faq and then click Windows Vista Programs.

Test your knowledge of pages 134 through 137 in Quiz Yourself 3-1.

QUIZ YOURSELF 3-1

Instructions: Find the true statement below. Then, rewrite the remaining false statements so they are true.

1. Application software is used to make business activities more efficient; assist with graphics and multimedia projects; support home, personal, and educational tasks; and facilitate communications.

2. Public-domain software is mass-produced, copyrighted retail software that meets the needs of a wide variety of users, not just a single user or company.

3. To use system software, your computer must be running application software.

4. When a program is started, its instructions load from memory into a storage medium.

Quiz Yourself Online: To further check your knowledge of application software categories, ways software is distributed, and working with application software, visit scsite.com/dc2008/ch3/quiz and then click Objectives 1 – 3.

BUSINESS SOFTWARE

Business software is application software that assists people in becoming more effective and efficient while performing their daily business activities. Business software includes programs such as word processing, spreadsheet, database, presentation graphics, note taking, personal information manager software, PDA business software, software suites, project management, accounting, document management, and enterprise computing software. Figure 3-4 lists popular programs for each of these categories.

The following sections discuss the features and functions of business software. Word processing and spreadsheet software have a heavier emphasis because of their predominant use.

Word Processing Software

Word processing software is one of the more widely used types of application software. **Word processing software**, sometimes called a *word processor*, allows users to create and manipulate documents containing mostly text and sometimes graphics (Figure 3-5). Millions of people use word processing software every day to develop documents such as letters, memos, reports, fax cover sheets, mailing labels, newsletters, and Web pages.

Word processing software has many features to make documents look professional and visually appealing. Some of these features include the capability of changing the shape and size of characters, changing the color of characters, applying special effects such as three-dimensional shadows, and organizing text in newspaper-style columns. When using colors for characters, however, they will print as black or gray unless you have a color printer.

Most word processing software allows users to incorporate many types of graphical images, such as digital pictures and clip art, in documents. **Clip art** is a collection of drawings,

POPULAR BUSINESS PROGRAMS

Application Software	Manufacturer	Program Name
Word Processing	Microsoft	Word 2007
	Sun	StarOffice Writer
	Corel	WordPerfect
Spreadsheet	Microsoft	Excel 2007
	Sun	StarOffice Calc
	Corel	Quattro Pro
Database	Microsoft	Access 2007
	Sun	StarOffice Base
	Corel	Paradox
	Microsoft	Visual FoxPro SQL Server
	Oracle	Oracle Database
	MySQL AB	MySQL
Presentation Graphics	Microsoft	PowerPoint 2007
	Sun	StarOffice Impress
	Corel	Presentations
Note Taking	Microsoft	OneNote 2007
	Agilix	GoBinder
	Corel	Grafigo
Personal Information Manager (PIM)	Microsoft	Outlook 2007
	IBM	Organizer
	Palm	Desktop
PDA Business Software	CNetX	Pocket SlideShow
	Microsoft	Pocket Word Pocket Excel Pocket Outlook
	Mobile Systems	MobiSystems Office Suite Professional
	Mozilla	Thunderbird
	Ultrasoft	Money

Application Software	Manufacturer	Program Name
Software Suite (for the Professional)	Microsoft	Office 2007 Office for Mac
	Sun	StarOffice Office Suite
	Corel	WordPerfect Office
	IBM	Lotus SmartSuite
Project Management	Microsoft	Project 2007
	Primavera	SureTrak Project Manager
Accounting	Intuit	QuickBooks
	Sage Software	Peachtree
Document Management	Adobe	Acrobat
	Enfocus	PitStop
	Nuance	PDF Converter PaperPort
Enterprise Computing Software	Oracle	PeopleSoft Enterprise Human Resources
	Sage Software	Sage MAS 500
	MSC Software	MSC.SimManager
	Oracle	Oracle Manufacturing
	SAP	mySAP Customer Relationship Management
	NetSuite	NetERP
	Apropos Technology	Apropos Interaction Management Suite

FIGURE 3-4 Popular business software.

photographs, and other images that you can insert in documents. In Figure 3-5, a user inserted an image of a lake in the document. Word processing software usually includes public-domain images. You can find additional public-domain and proprietary images on the Web or purchase them on CD or DVD.

All word processing software provides at least some basic capabilities to help users create and modify documents. Defining the size of the paper on which to print and specifying the *margins* — that is, the portion of the page outside the main body of text, including the top, the bottom, and both sides of the paper — are examples of some of these capabilities. If you type text that extends beyond the right page margin, the word processing software automatically positions text at the beginning of the next line. This feature, called *wordwrap*, allows users to type words in a paragraph continually without pressing the ENTER key at the end of each line. When you modify paper size or margins, the word processing software automatically rewraps text so it fits in the adjusted paper size and margins.

As you type more lines of text than can be displayed on the screen, the top portion of the document moves upward, or scrolls, off the screen. *Scrolling* is the process of moving different portions of the document on the screen into view.

A major advantage of using word processing software is that users easily can change what they have written. For example, a user can

insert, delete, or rearrange words, sentences, paragraphs, or entire sections. The find, or *search,* feature allows you to locate all occurrences of a certain character, word, or phrase. This feature, in combination with the *replace* feature, allows you to substitute existing characters or words with new ones.

Word processing software includes a *spelling checker,* which reviews the spelling of individual words, sections of a document, or the entire document. The spelling checker compares the words in the document with an electronic dictionary that is part of the word processing software. You can customize the electronic dictionary by adding words such as

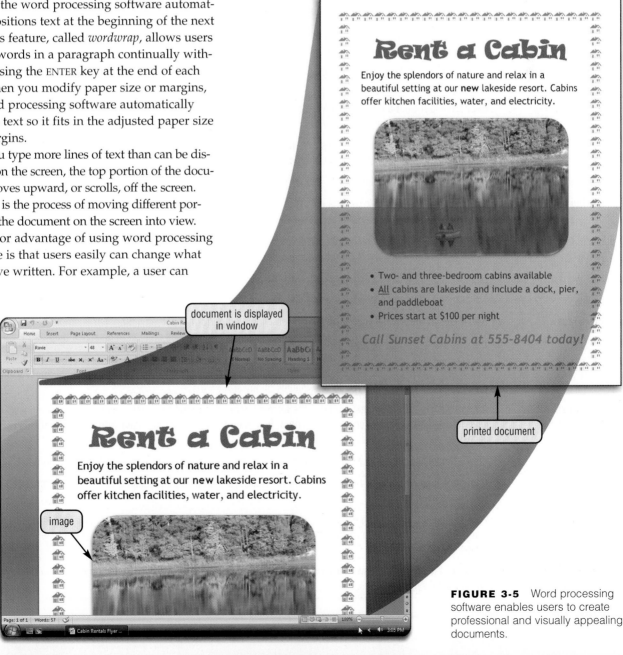

document is displayed in window

image

printed document

FIGURE 3-5 Word processing software enables users to create professional and visually appealing documents.

WEB LINK 3-1

Word Processing Software

For more information, visit scsite.com/ dc2008/ch3/weblink and then click Word Processing Software.

companies, streets, cities, and personal names, so the software can check the spelling of those words too.

Another benefit of word processing software is the capability to insert headers and footers in a document. A *header* is text that appears at the top of each page, and a *footer* is text that appears at the bottom of each page. Page

numbers, company names, report titles, and dates are examples of items often included in headers and footers.

In addition to these basic capabilities, most current word processing programs provide numerous additional features, which are listed in the table in Figure 3-6.

ADDITIONAL WORD PROCESSING FEATURES

AutoCorrect	As you type words, the AutoCorrect feature corrects common spelling errors. AutoCorrect also corrects capitalization mistakes.
AutoFormat	As you type, the AutoFormat feature automatically applies formatting to the text. For example, it automatically numbers a list or converts a Web address to a hyperlink.
Collaboration	Collaboration includes discussions and online meetings. Discussions allow multiple users to enter comments in a document and read and reply to each other's comments. Through an online meeting, users share documents with others in real time and view changes as they are being made.
Columns	Most word processing software can arrange text in two or more columns to look like text in a newspaper or magazine. The text from the bottom of one column automatically flows to the top of the next column.
Grammar Checker	The grammar checker proofreads documents for grammar, writing style, sentence structure errors, and reading statistics.
Ink Input	Supports input from a digital pen. Word processing software that supports ink input incorporates user's handwritten text and drawings in a word processing document. Ink input is popular on Tablet PCs.
Macros	A *macro* is a sequence of keystrokes and instructions that a user records and saves. When you want to execute the same series of instructions, execute the macro instead.
Mail Merge	Creates form letters, mailing labels, and envelopes.
Reading Layout	For those users who prefer reading on the screen, reading layout increases the readability and legibility of an on-screen document by hiding unnecessary buttons, increasing the size of displayed characters, and providing navigation tools.
Research	Some word processing software allows you to search through various forms of online and Internet reference information — based on selected text in a document. Research services available include a thesaurus, English and bilingual dictionaries, encyclopedias, and Web sites that provide information such as stock quotes, news articles, and company profiles.
Smart Tags	*Smart tags* automatically appear on the screen when you perform a certain action. For example, typing an address causes a smart tag to appear. Clicking this smart tag provides options to display a map of the address or driving directions to or from the address.
Tables	Tables organize information into rows and columns. In addition to evenly spaced rows and columns, some word processing programs allow you to draw tables of any size or shape.
Templates	A *template* is a document that contains the formatting necessary for a specific document type. Templates usually exist for memos, fax cover sheets, and letters. In addition to templates provided with the software, users have access to many online templates through the manufacturer's Web site.
Thesaurus	With a thesaurus, a user looks up a synonym (word with the same meaning) for a word in a document.
Tracking Changes	If multiple users work with a document, the word processing software highlights or color-codes changes made by various users.
Voice Recognition	With some word processing programs, users can speak into the computer's microphone and watch the spoken words appear on the screen as they talk. With these programs, users edit and format the document by speaking or spelling an instruction.
Web Page Development	Most word processing software allows users to create, edit, format, and convert documents to be displayed on the World Wide Web.

FIGURE 3-6 Many additional features are included with word processing software.

Developing a Document

With application software, such as word processing, users create, edit, format, save, and print documents. During the process of developing a document, users likely will switch back and forth among all of these activities.

When you **create** a document, you enter text or numbers, insert images, and perform other tasks using an input device such as a keyboard, mouse, or digital pen. If you are using Microsoft Office Word 2007 to design a flyer, for example, you are creating a document.

To **edit** a document means to make changes to its existing content. Common editing tasks include inserting, deleting, cutting, copying, and pasting. Inserting text involves adding text to a document. Deleting text means that you are removing text or other content. Cutting is the process of removing a portion of the document and storing it in a temporary storage location, sometimes called a *clipboard*. A clipboard also contains items that you copy (duplicate) in a document. *Pasting* is the process of transferring an item from a clipboard to a specific location in a document. Read Ethics & Issues 3-1 for a related discussion.

When users **format** a document, they change its appearance. Formatting is important because the overall look of a document significantly can affect its ability to communicate clearly. Examples of formatting tasks are changing the font, font size, or font style of text.

A **font** is a name assigned to a specific design of characters. Two basic types of fonts are serif and sans serif. A *serif font* has short decorative lines at the upper and lower ends of the characters. Sans means without. Thus, a *sans serif font* does not have the short decorative lines at the upper and lower ends of the characters. Times New Roman is an example of a serif font. Arial is an example of a sans serif font.

Font size indicates the size of the characters in a particular font. Font size is gauged by a measurement system called points. A single *point* is about 1/72 of an inch in height. The text you are reading in this book is about 10 point. Thus, each character is about 5/36 (10/72) of an inch in height. A *font style* adds emphasis to a font. Bold, italic, and underline are examples of font styles. Figure 3-7 illustrates fonts, font sizes, and font styles.

ETHICS & ISSUES 3-1

How Should Schools Deal with Internet Plagiarism?

A high school teacher failed 28 students for plagiarizing, or copying, material from the Internet. When parents complained, the school board passed the students, and the teacher resigned. Word processing software and the Internet make plagiarism easier than ever. Students can use term paper Web sites, such as CheatHouse.com, to copy complete papers on a variety of topics. According to one survey, half of those who responded said that cheating does not or may not matter in the long run, and 60 percent had plagiarized in the past. Students who plagiarize blame peer pressure, classroom competition, the "busy work" nature of some assignments, and the permissive attitude that pervades the Internet. Teachers have several tools to catch plagiarists, including a variety of Internet-based services, such as Turnitin, that compare suspected papers to papers found on the Internet and produce an originality report highlighting text that may have been copied. Some instructors, however, are reluctant to investigate the integrity of a student's work and possibly ruin an academic career, but more and more schools require instructors to do such checking using paid services to check papers. How should educators deal with plagiarism? Should a school's response to plagiarism depend on such factors as the material copied, the assignment for which it was copied, or the reason it was copied? Why or why not?

FIGURE 3-7 The Times New Roman and Arial fonts are shown in two font sizes and a variety of font styles.

During the process of creating, editing, and formatting a document, the computer holds it in memory. To keep the document for future use requires that you save it. When you **save** a document, the computer transfers the document from memory to a storage medium such as a USB flash drive, hard disk, or CD. Once saved, a document is stored permanently as a file on the storage medium.

When you **print** a document, the computer places the contents of the document on paper or some other medium. One of the benefits of word processing software is the ability to print the same document many times, with each copy looking just like the first. Instead of printing a document and physically distributing it, some users e-mail the document to others on a network such as the Internet.

Spreadsheet Software

Spreadsheet software is another widely used type of application software. **Spreadsheet software** allows users to organize data in rows and columns and perform calculations on the data. These rows and columns collectively are called a *worksheet*. For years, people used paper to organize data and perform calculations by hand. In an electronic worksheet, you organize data in the same manner, and the computer performs the calculations more quickly and accurately (Figure 3-8). Because of spreadsheet software's logical approach to organizing data, many people use this software to organize and present nonfinancial data, as well as financial data.

As with word processing software, most spreadsheet software has basic features to help users create, edit, and format worksheets. Spreadsheet software also incorporates many of the features found in word processing software such as macros, checking spelling, changing fonts and font sizes, adding colors, tracking changes, inserting audio and video clips, providing research capabilities, recognizing handwritten text and drawings, and creating Web pages from existing spreadsheet documents.

The following sections describe the features of most spreadsheet programs.

FAQ 3-2

How often should I save a document?

Saving at regular intervals ensures that the majority of your work will not be lost in the event of a power loss or system failure. Many programs have an AutoSave feature that automatically saves open documents at specified time intervals, such as every 10 minutes. For more information, visit scsite.com/dc2008/ch3/faq and then click Saving Documents.

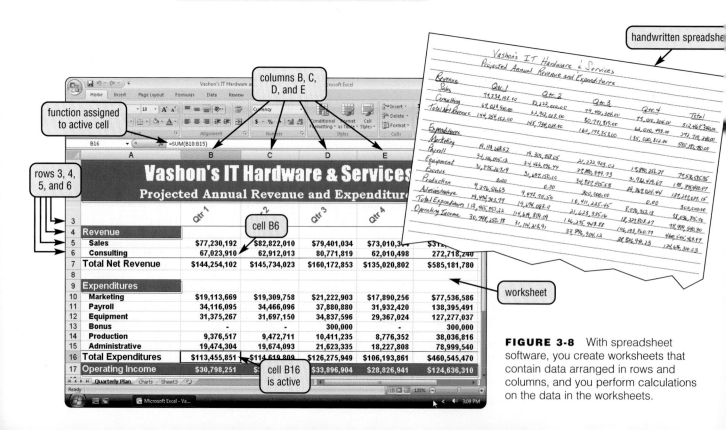

FIGURE 3-8 With spreadsheet software, you create worksheets that contain data arranged in rows and columns, and you perform calculations on the data in the worksheets.

SPREADSHEET ORGANIZATION A spreadsheet file is similar to a notebook that can contain more than 1,000 related individual worksheets. Data is organized vertically in columns and horizontally in rows on each worksheet (Figure 3-8). Each worksheet usually can have more than 16,000 columns and 1 million rows. One or more letters identify each column, and a number identifies each row. Only a small fraction of the columns and rows are displayed on the screen at one time. Scrolling through the worksheet displays different parts of it on the screen.

A *cell* is the intersection of a column and row. Each worksheet has more than 17 billion cells in which you can enter data. The spreadsheet software identifies cells by the column and row in which they are located. For example, the intersection of column B and row 6 is referred to as cell B6. As shown in Figure 3-8, cell B6 contains the number, 67,023,910, which represents the consulting revenue for the first quarter.

Cells may contain three types of data: labels, values, and formulas. The text, or *label*, entered in a cell identifies the worksheet data and helps organize the worksheet. Using descriptive labels, such as Total Net Revenue and Total Expenditures, helps make a worksheet more meaningful.

CALCULATIONS Many of the worksheet cells shown in Figure 3-8 contain a number, called a *value*, that can be used in a calculation. Other cells, however, contain formulas that generate values. A *formula* performs calculations on the data in the worksheet and displays the resulting value in a cell, usually the cell containing the formula. When creating a worksheet, you can enter your own formulas.

In many spreadsheet programs, you begin a formula with an equal sign, a plus sign, or a minus sign. Next, you enter the formula, separating cell references (e.g., B10) with operators. Common operators are + for addition, − for subtraction, * for multiplication, and / for division. In Figure 3-8, for example, cell B16 could contain the formula =B10+B11+B12+B13 +B14+B15, which would add together (sum) the contents of cells B10, B11, B12, B13, B14, and B15. That is, this formula calculates the total expenditures for the first quarter. A more efficient way to sum the contents of cells, however, is to use a special type of formula, called a function.

A *function* is a predefined formula that performs common calculations such as adding the values in a group of cells or generating a value such as the time or date. For example, instead of using the formula =B10+B11+B12+B13+B14+B15 to calculate the total expenditures for the first quarter, you could use the SUM function. This function requires you to identify the starting cell and the ending cell in a group to be summed, separating these two cell references with a colon. For example, the function =SUM(B10:B15) instructs the spreadsheet program to add all of the numbers in cells B10 through B15. Figure 3-9 lists functions commonly included in spreadsheet programs.

SPREADSHEET FUNCTIONS

Financial	
FV (rate, number of periods, payment)	Calculates the future value of an investment
NPV (rate, range)	Calculates the net present value of an investment
PMT (rate, number of periods, present value)	Calculates the periodic payment for an annuity
PV (rate, number of periods, payment)	Calculates the present value of an investment
RATE (number of periods, payment, present value)	Calculates the periodic interest rate of an annuity
Date and Time	
DATE	Returns the current date
NOW	Returns the current date and time
TIME	Returns the current time
Mathematical	
ABS (number)	Returns the absolute value of a number
INT (number)	Rounds a number down to the nearest integer
LN (number)	Calculates the natural logarithm of a number
LOG (number, base)	Calculates the logarithm of a number to a specified base
ROUND (number, number of digits)	Rounds a number to a specified number of digits
SQRT (number)	Calculates the square root of a number
SUM (range)	Calculates the total of a range of numbers
Statistical	
AVERAGE (range)	Calculates the average value of a range of numbers
COUNT (range)	Counts how many cells in the range have numeric entries
MAX (range)	Returns the maximum value in a range
MIN (range)	Returns the minimum value in a range
STDEV (range)	Calculates the standard deviation of a range of numbers
Logical	
IF (logical test, value if true, value if false)	Performs a test and returns one value if the result of the test is true and another value if the result is false

FIGURE 3-9 Functions typically found in spreadsheet software.

RECALCULATION One of the more powerful features of spreadsheet software is its capability of recalculating the rest of the worksheet when data in a worksheet changes. When you enter a new value to change data in a cell, any value affected by the change is updated automatically and instantaneously. In Figure 3-8 on page 142, for example, if you change the consulting revenue for the first quarter from 67,023,910 to 67,523,910, the total net revenue in cell B7 automatically changes from $144,254,102 to $144,754,102.

Spreadsheet software's capability of recalculating data also makes it a valuable budgeting, forecasting, and decision making tool. Most spreadsheet software includes a *what-if analysis* feature, where you change certain values in a spreadsheet to reveal the effects of those changes.

CHARTING Another standard feature of spreadsheet software is *charting*, which depicts the data in graphical form. A visual representation of data through charts often makes it easier for users to see at a glance the relationship among the numbers.

Three popular chart types are line charts, column charts, and pie charts. Figure 3-10 shows examples of these charts that were plotted from the data in Figure 3-8. A *line chart* shows a trend during a period of time, as indicated by a rising or falling line. For example, a line chart could show the total expenses for the four quarters. A *column chart*, also called a *bar chart*, displays bars of various lengths to show the relationship of data. The bars can be horizontal, vertical, or stacked on top of one another. For example, a column chart might show the total quarterly expenditures, with each bar representing a different category of expenditure. A *pie chart*, which has the shape of a round pie cut into slices, shows the relationship of parts to a whole. For example, you might use a pie chart to show the percentage each expenditure category contributed to the total expenditures.

When you modify data in a worksheet, any associated charts automatically update to reflect the worksheet changes. Charts, as well as any other part of a workbook, can be linked to or embedded in a word processing document.

WEB LINK 3-2

Spreadsheet Software

For more information, visit scsite.com/ dc2008/ch3/weblink and then click Spreadsheet Software.

FIGURE 3-10 Three basic types of charts provided with spreadsheet software are line charts, column charts, and pie charts. The charts shown here were created from the data in the worksheet in Figure 3-8.

Database Software

A **database** is a collection of data organized in a manner that allows access, retrieval, and use of that data. In a manual database, you might record data on paper and store it in a filing cabinet. With a computerized database, such as the one shown in Figure 3-11, the computer stores the data in an electronic format on a storage medium such as a hard disk.

Database software is application software that allows users to create, access, and manage a database. Using database software, you can add, change, and delete data in a database; sort and retrieve data from the database; and create forms and reports using the data in the database.

With most popular personal computer database programs, a database consists of a collection of tables, organized in rows and columns. Each row, called a *record*, contains data about a given person, product, object, or event. Each column, called a *field*, contains a specific category of data within a record.

The Sports Store database shown in Figure 3-11 consists of two tables: an Item table and a Supplier table. The Item table contains nine records (rows), each storing data about one item. The item data is grouped into six fields (columns): Item Number, Description, On Hand, Cost, Selling Price, and Supplier Code. The On Hand field, for instance, contains the quantity on hand in inventory. The Item and Supplier tables relate to one another through a common field, Supplier Code.

Users run queries to retrieve data. A *query* is a request for specific data from the database. For example, a query might request items that are low on hand. Database software can take the results of a query and present it in a window on the screen or send it to the printer.

FAQ 3-3

How big is the largest database?

According to a recent survey, the world's largest database holds more than 100 trillion characters. In the next few years, the size of the largest database is expected to exceed 5 quadrillion characters. For more information, visit scsite.com/dc2008/ch3/faq and then click Enterprise Databases.

FIGURE 3-11 This database contains two tables: one for the items and one for the suppliers. The Item table has nine records and six fields; the Supplier table has three records and three fields.

Presentation Graphics Software

Presentation graphics software is application software that allows users to create visual aids for presentations to communicate ideas, messages, and other information to a group. The presentations can be viewed as slides, sometimes called a *slide show*, that are displayed on a large monitor or on a projection screen (Figure 3-12).

Presentation graphics software typically provides a variety of predefined presentation formats that define complementary colors for backgrounds, text, and graphical accents on the slides. This software also provides a variety of layouts for each individual slide such as a title slide, a two-column slide, and a slide with clip art, a picture, a chart, a table, a diagram (Figure 3-13), or animation. In addition, you can enhance any text, charts, and graphical images on a slide with 3-D and other special effects such as shading, shadows, and textures.

When building a presentation, users can set the slide timing so the presentation automatically displays the next slide after a preset delay. Presentation graphics software allows you to apply special effects to the transition between slides. One slide, for example, might fade away as the next slide is displayed.

To help organize the presentation, you can view thumbnail versions of all the slides similarly to how 35mm slides look on a photographer's light table.

Presentation graphics software typically includes a clip gallery that provides images, pictures, video clips, and audio clips to enhance multimedia presentations. Users with an artistic ability can create their own graphics using paint/image editing software (discussed later in the chapter) and then *import* (bring in) the graphics into the slide. Some audio and video editing programs work with presentation graphics software, providing users with an easy means to record and insert video, music, and audio commentary in a presentation.

Presentation graphics software incorporates some of the features found in word processing software such as checking spelling, formatting, providing research capabilities, recognizing handwritten text and drawings, and creating Web pages from existing slide shows.

WEB LINK 3-3

Presentation Graphics Software

For more information, visit scsite.com/dc2008/ch3/weblink and then click Presentation Graphics Software.

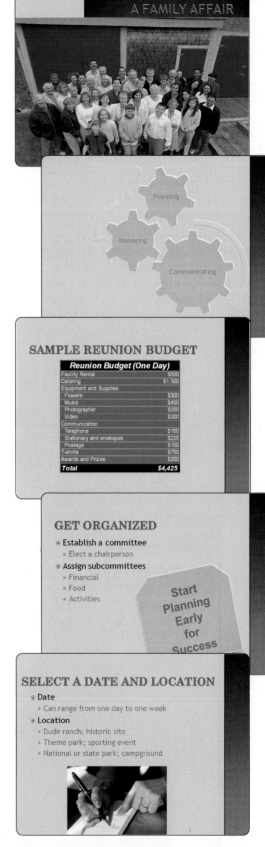

FIGURE 3-12   This presentation created with presentation graphics software consists of five slides.

FIGURE 3-13 In presentation graphics software, users can change the design and layout of any slide in a presentation.

Note Taking Software

Note taking software is application software that enables users to enter typed text, handwritten comments, drawings, or sketches anywhere on a page and then save the page as part of a notebook (Figure 3-14). The software can convert handwritten comments to typed text or store the notes in handwritten form. Users also can include audio recordings as part of their notes.

Once the notes are captured (entered and saved), users easily can organize them, reuse them, and share them. This software allows users to search through saved notes for specific text. It even can search through an entire notebook. Users also can flag important notes with color, highlights, and shapes.

On a desktop or notebook computer, users enter notes primarily via the keyboard or microphone. On a Tablet PC, however, the primary input device is a digital pen. Users find note taking software convenient during meetings, class lectures, conferences, in libraries, and other settings that previously required a pencil and tablet of paper for recording thoughts and discussions.

Note taking software incorporates many of the features found in word processing software such as checking spelling, changing fonts and font sizes, adding colors, inserting audio and video clips, and providing research capabilities.

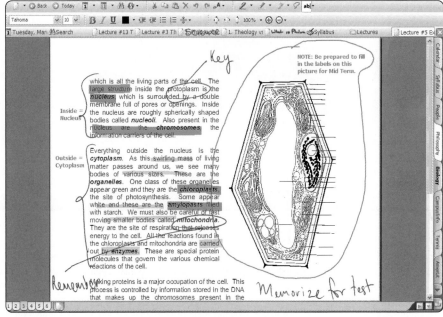

FIGURE 3-14 With note taking software, students and other mobile users can handwrite notes, draw sketches, and type text.

Personal Information Manager Software

A **personal information manager** (**PIM**) is application software that includes an appointment calendar, address book, notepad, and other features to help users organize personal information. With a PIM, you can take information previously tracked in a weekly or daily calendar, and organize and store it on your computer. The appointment calendar allows you to schedule activities for a particular day and time. With the address book, you can enter and maintain names, addresses, telephone numbers, and e-mail addresses of customers, coworkers, family members, and friends. You can use the notepad to record ideas, reminders, and other important information.

Most PDAs and many smart phones today include, among many other features, PIM functionality. Using a PDA or smart phone, you can synchronize, or coordinate, information so that both the PDA or smart phone and your personal computer and/or organization's server have the latest version of the information. Some PDAs and smart phones synchronize with the computer wirelessly. With others, you connect the PDA or smart phone to the computer with a cable, or you insert the device in a cradle, which has a cable that plugs in the computer (Figure 3-15).

FIGURE 3-15 With most PDAs and smart phones, you can synchronize or transfer information from the device to a desktop computer, so the updated important information always is available.

PDA Business Software

In addition to PIM software, a huge variety of business software is available for PDAs. Although some PDAs have software built in, most have the capability of accessing software on miniature storage media such as memory cards. Business software for PDAs allows users to create documents and worksheets, manage databases and lists, create slide shows, take notes, manage budgets and finances, view and edit photographs, read electronic books, plan travel routes, compose and read e-mail messages, send instant messages, and browse the Web. For additional information about software for PDAs, read the Personal Mobile Devices feature that follows Chapter 5.

Software Suite

A **software suite** is a collection of individual programs sold as a single package. Business software suites typically include, at a minimum, the following programs: word processing, spreadsheet, e-mail, and presentation graphics. Two of the more widely used software suites are Microsoft Office 2007 and Sun StarOffice.

Software suites offer two major advantages: lower cost and ease of use. Buying a collection of programs in a software suite usually costs significantly less than purchasing them individually. Software suites provide ease of use because the programs in a software suite normally use a similar interface and share features such as clip art and spelling checker. For example, once you learn how to print using the software suite's word processing program, you can apply the same skill to the spreadsheet and presentation graphics programs in the software suite.

 FAQ 3-4

How popular are handheld devices?

During the past year, the overall popularity of handheld devices, including smart phones and PDAs, has been increasing at an average rate of approximately 55 percent. Smart phones have experienced a growth of approximately 75 percent, while the use of PDAs declined by approximately 33 percent. The following table illustrates the market shares for the more popular companies in the handheld device market. For more information, visit scsite.com/dc2008/ch3/faq and then click Handheld Devices.

Market Share

- Nokia
- Motorola
- RIM
- Sharp
- Palm
- Other

Source: Canalys.com

Project Management Software

Project management software allows a user to plan, schedule, track, and analyze the events, resources, and costs of a project (Figure 3-16). Project management software helps users manage project variables, allowing them to complete a project on time and within budget. An engineer, for example, might use project management software to manage new product development to schedule product screening, market evaluation, technical product evaluation, and manufacturing processes.

FIGURE 3-16 Shown here is project management software, which allows you to track, control, and manage the events, resources, and costs of a project.

Accounting Software

Accounting software helps companies record and report their financial transactions (Figure 3-17). With accounting software, business users perform accounting activities related to the general ledger, accounts receivable, accounts payable, purchasing, invoicing, and payroll functions. Accounting software also enables users to write and print checks, track checking account activity, and update and reconcile balances on demand.

Newer accounting software supports online credit checks, billing, direct deposit, and payroll services. Some accounting software offers more complex features such as job costing and estimating, time tracking, multiple company reporting, foreign currency reporting, and forecasting the amount of raw materials needed for products. The cost of accounting software for small businesses ranges from less than one hundred to several thousand dollars. Accounting software for large businesses can cost several hundred thousand dollars.

FIGURE 3-17 Accounting software helps companies record and report their financial transactions.

Document Management Software

Document management software provides a means for sharing, distributing, and searching through documents by converting them into a format that can be viewed by any user (Figure 3-18). The converted document, which mirrors the original document's appearance, can be viewed and printed without the software that created the original document. A popular file format used by document management software to save converted documents is *PDF* (Portable Document Format), developed by Adobe Systems. To view and print a PDF file, you need Acrobat Reader software, which can be downloaded free from Adobe's Web site.

Many businesses use document management software to share and distribute company brochures, literature, and other documents electronically. Home users distribute fliers, announcements, and graphics electronically. Some document management software allows users to edit and add comments to the converted document.

WEB LINK 3-4

Document Management Software

For more information, visit scsite.com/dc2008/ch3/weblink and then click Document Management Software.

Enterprise Computing Software

A large organization, commonly referred to as an enterprise, requires special computing solutions because of its size and large geographic distribution. A typical enterprise consists of a wide variety of departments, centers, and divisions — collectively known as functional units. Nearly every enterprise has the following functional units: human resources, accounting and finance, engineering or product development, manufacturing, marketing, sales, distribution, customer service, and information technology. Each of these functional units has specialized software requirements, as outlined below.

- Human resources software manages employee information such as benefits, personal information, performance evaluations, training, and vacation time.
- Accounting software manages everyday transactions, such as sales and payments to suppliers. Financial software helps managers budget, forecast, and analyze.
  - Engineering or product development software allows engineers to develop plans for new products and test their product designs.
  - Manufacturing software assists in the assembly process, as well as in scheduling and managing the inventory of parts and products.
  - Marketing software allows marketing personnel to create marketing campaigns and track their effectiveness.
  - Sales software enables the sales force to manage contacts, schedule meetings, log customer interactions, manage product information, and take customer orders.
  - Distribution software analyzes and tracks inventory and manages product shipping status.
  - Customer service software manages the day-to-day interactions with customers, such as telephone calls, e-mail messages, Web interactions, and instant messaging sessions.
  - Information technology staff use a variety of software to maintain and secure the hardware and software in an enterprise.

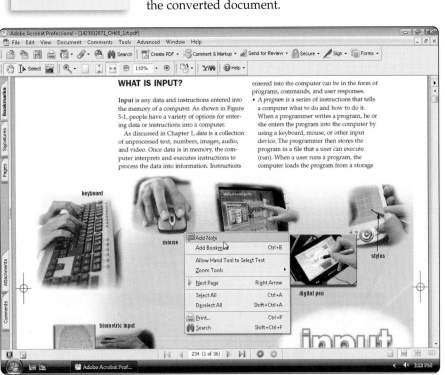

FIGURE 3-18   Adobe Acrobat allows users to create and edit PDF files.

GRAPHICS AND MULTIMEDIA SOFTWARE

In addition to business software, many people work with software designed specifically for their field of work. Power users such as engineers, architects, desktop publishers, and graphic artists often use sophisticated software that allows them to work with graphics and multimedia. This software includes computer-aided design, desktop publishing, paint/image editing, photo editing, video and audio editing, multimedia authoring, and Web page authoring. Figure 3-19 lists some popular programs in each of these categories, specifically designed for professional or more technically astute users. These programs often cost several hundred dollars or more. Many of these programs incorporate user-friendly interfaces and/or have scaled-down versions, making it possible for the home and small business users to create documents using these programs. The following sections discuss the features and functions of graphics and multimedia software.

POPULAR GRAPHICS AND MULTIMEDIA SOFTWARE

Application Software	Manufacturer	Program Name
Computer-Aided Design (CAD)	Autodesk	AutoCAD
	Chief Architect	Chief Architect
	Microsoft	Visio 2007
Desktop Publishing (for the Professional)	Adobe	InDesign
	Corel	Ventura
	Quark	QuarkXPress
Paint/Image Editing (for the Professional)	Adobe	Freehand Illustrator
	Corel	Painter
	Microsoft	Expression Graphic Designer
Photo Editing (for the Professional)	Adobe	Photoshop
	Nik Software	Nik Sharpener Pro
Video and Audio Editing (for the Professional)	Adobe	Audition Encore DVD Premiere Pro
	Avid Technology	Avid Xpress Pro
	Cakewalk	SONAR
	Sony	ACID Pro
	Ulead	MediaStudio Pro DVD Workshop
Multimedia Authoring	Adobe	Authorware Director
	SumTotal Systems	ToolBook Instructor
Web Page Authoring	Adobe	Dreamweaver Fireworks Flash GoLive
	Microsoft	SharePoint Designer 2007

FIGURE 3-19 Popular graphics and multimedia programs — for the professional.

Computer-Aided Design

Computer-aided design (CAD) software is a sophisticated type of application software that assists a professional user in creating engineering, architectural, and scientific designs. For example, engineers create design plans for vehicles (Figure 3-20) and security systems. Architects design building structures and floor plans. Scientists design drawings of molecular structures.

CAD software eliminates the laborious manual drafting that design processes can require. Three-dimensional CAD programs allow designers to rotate designs of 3-D objects to view them from any angle. Some CAD software even can generate material lists for building designs.

FIGURE 3-20 Architects use CAD software to create vehicle components.

Desktop Publishing Software (for the Professional)

Desktop publishing (DTP) software enables professional designers to create sophisticated documents that contain text, graphics, and many colors (Figure 3-21). Professional DTP software is ideal for the production of high-quality color documents such as textbooks, corporate newsletters, marketing literature, product catalogs, and annual reports. Today's DTP software allows designers to convert a color document into a format for use on the World Wide Web.

Although many word processing programs have some of the capabilities of DTP software, professional designers and graphic artists use DTP software because it supports page layout. *Page layout* is the process of arranging text and graphics in a document on a page-by-page basis. DTP software includes color libraries to assist in color selections for text and graphics. A *color library* is a standard set of colors used by designers and printers to ensure that colors will print exactly as specified. Designers and graphic artists can print finished publications on a color printer, take them to a professional printer, or post them on the Web.

Paint/Image Editing Software (for the Professional)

Graphic artists, multimedia professionals, technical illustrators, and desktop publishers use paint software and image editing software to create and modify graphical images such as those used in DTP documents and Web pages. **Paint software**, also called *illustration software*, allows users to draw pictures, shapes, and other graphical images with various on-screen tools such as a pen, brush, eyedropper, and paint bucket (Figure 3-22). **Image editing software** provides the capabilities of paint software and also includes the capability to enhance and modify existing images and pictures. Modifications can include adjusting or enhancing image colors, adding special effects such as shadows and glows, and creating animations.

FIGURE 3-22   With paint software, artists can create and modify any type of graphical image.

Photo Editing Software (for the Professional)

Professional photo editing software is a type of image editing software that allows photographers, videographers, engineers, scientists, and other high-volume digital photo users to edit and customize digital photographs (Figure 3-23). Professional photo editing software allows users to save images in a wide variety of file formats. With professional photo editing software, users can retouch photos, crop images, remove red-eye, change image shapes, color-correct images, straighten images, remove or rearrange objects in a photo, and apply filters. Read Ethics & Issues 3-2 for a related discussion.

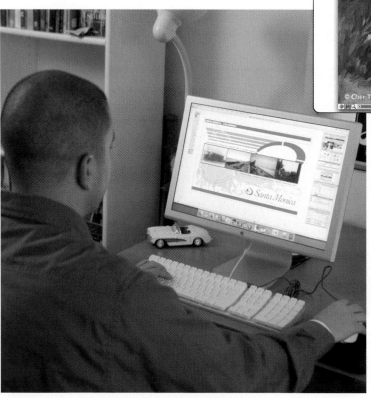

FIGURE 3-21   Professional designers and graphic artists use DTP software to produce sophisticated publications such as marketing literature.

Video.psd @ 95% (RGB/8) [scaled]

FIGURE 3-23 With professional photo editing software, users can edit and customize digital photographs.

ETHICS & ISSUES 3-2

Altering Digital Photographs — Art or Fraud?

In several recent high-profile cases, major news sources have published purposefully altered photographs. The alterations were more than just touching up a bad-hair day; rather, they were attempts to alter the facts. Typically, those responsible for the deception are fired from their jobs. Many commercial artists, photojournalists, and creators of cartoons, book covers, and billboards use photo editing software to alter photographs. With this software, an artist can convert photographs to a digital form that can be colorized, stretched, squeezed, texturized, or otherwise altered. For example, tabloid newspapers or dubious online sources may alter a photograph by switching a head on a body in a photo with someone else's head. The National Press Photographers Association, however, has expressed reservations about digital altering and endorses the following: "As [photo] journalists we believe the guiding principle of our profession is accuracy; therefore, we believe it is wrong to alter the content of a photograph in any way … that deceives the public." Yet, some insist that the extent to which a photo "deceives the public" is in the eye of the beholder. Is it ethical to alter digital photographs? Why or why not? Does the answer depend on the reason for the alteration, the extent of the alteration, or some other factor? If some alteration is accepted, can photographic integrity still be guaranteed? Why or why not?

Video and Audio Editing Software (for the Professional)

Video editing software (Figure 3-24) allows professionals to modify a segment of a video, called a clip. For example, users can reduce the length of a video clip, reorder a series of clips, or add special effects such as words that move horizontally across the screen.

Video editing software typically includes audio editing capabilities. **Audio editing software** lets users modify audio clips, produce studio-quality soundtracks, and add audio to video clips. Audio editing software usually includes *filters*, which are designed to enhance audio quality. For example, a filter might remove a distracting background noise from the audio clip.

FIGURE 3-24 With video editing software, users modify video images.

Multimedia Authoring Software

Multimedia authoring software allows users to combine text, graphics, audio, video, and animation in an interactive application (Figure 3-25). With this software, users control the placement of text and images and the duration of sounds, video, and animation. Once created, multimedia presentations often take the form of interactive computer-based presentations or Web-based presentations designed to facilitate learning, demonstrate product functionality, and elicit direct-user participation. Training centers, educational institutions, and online magazine publishers all use multimedia authoring software to develop interactive applications. These applications may be available on a CD or DVD, over a local area network, or via the Internet.

FAQ 3-5

How do I know which program to buy?

Many companies, such as Adobe Systems and Corel, offer downloadable *trial versions* of their software that allow you to use the software free for a limited time. Try a few. Read computer magazines and Web sites for reviews of various products. For more information, visit scsite.com/dc2008/ch3/faq and then click Trial Versions.

Web Page Authoring Software

Web page authoring software helps users of all skill levels create Web pages that include graphical images, video, audio, animation, and other special effects with interactive content (Figure 3-26). In addition, many Web page authoring programs allow users to organize, manage, and maintain Web sites.

Application software, such as Word and Excel, often includes Web page authoring features. This allows home users to create basic Web pages using application software they already own. For more sophisticated Web pages, users work with Web page authoring software. Many Web page developers also use multimedia authoring software along with, or instead of, Web page authoring software for Web page development.

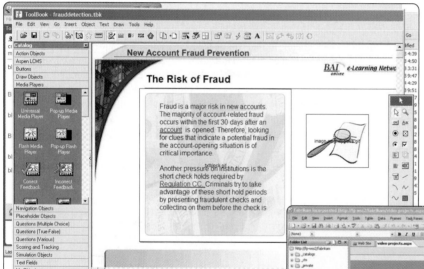

FIGURE 3-25   Multimedia authoring software allows you to create dynamic presentations that include text, graphics, video, sound, and animation.

FIGURE 3-26   With Web page authoring software, users create sophisticated Web pages.

Test your knowledge of pages 138 through 154 in Quiz Yourself 3-2.

QUIZ YOURSELF 3-2

Instructions: Find the true statement below. Then, rewrite the remaining false statements so they are true.

1. Audio editing software typically includes video editing capabilities.

2. Enterprise computing software provides the capabilities of paint software and also includes the capability to modify existing images.

3. Millions of people use spreadsheet software every day to develop documents such as letters, memos, reports, fax cover sheets, mailing labels, newsletters, and Web pages.

4. Professional accounting software is ideal for the production of high-quality color documents such as textbooks, corporate newsletters, marketing literature, product catalogs, and annual reports.

5. Spreadsheet software is application software that allows users to create visual aids for presentations to communicate ideas, messages, and other information to a group.

6. Two of the more widely used CAD programs are Microsoft Office 2007 and Sun StarOffice.

7. Web page authoring software helps users of all skill levels create Web pages.

Quiz Yourself Online: To further check your knowledge of types and features of business programs and graphics/multimedia programs, visit scsite.com/dc2008/ch3/quiz and then click Objectives 4 – 5.

SOFTWARE FOR HOME, PERSONAL, AND EDUCATIONAL USE

A large amount of application software is designed specifically for home, personal, and educational use. Most of the programs in this category are relatively inexpensive, often priced less than $100 and sometimes free. Figure 3-27 lists popular programs for many of these categories. The following sections discuss the features and functions of this application software.

POPULAR PROGRAMS FOR HOME/PERSONAL/EDUCATIONAL USE

Application Software	Manufacturer	Program Name
Software Suite (for Personal Use)	Microsoft	Works
	Sun	OpenOffice.org
Personal Finance	Intuit	Quicken
	Microsoft	Money
Legal	Broderbund	Family Lawyer Home and Business Lawyer WillWriter
	Cosmi	Perfect Attorney
	Nolo	Quicken Legal Business Quicken WillMaker
Tax Preparation	2nd Story Software	TaxACT
	H&R Block	TaxCut
	Intuit	TurboTax
Desktop Publishing (for Personal Use)	Broderbund	The Print Shop PrintMaster
	Microsoft	Publisher 2007
Paint/Image Editing (for Personal Use)	Corel	CorelDRAW Paint Shop Pro
	Sun	StarOffice Draw
	The GIMP Team	The Gimp

Application Software	Manufacturer	Program Name
Photo Editing (for Personal Use)	Adobe	Photoshop Elements
	Corel	Paint Shop Pro Photo
	Microsoft	Digital Image Photo Story
	Roxio	PhotoSuite
	Ulead	PhotoImpact Photo Express
Clip Art/Image Gallery	Broderbund	ClickArt
	Nova Development	Art Explosion
Video and Audio Editing (for Personal Use)	Microsoft	Movie Maker
	Pinnacle Systems	Studio MovieBox
	Roxio	VideoWave
	Ulead	VideoStudio
Home Design/ Landscaping	Broderbund	Instant Architect
	Quality Plans	3D Home Architect Better Homes & Gardens Home Designer
	ValuSoft	LandDesigner
Reference	DeLorme	Street Atlas
	Fogware Publishing	Merriam-Webster Collegiate Dictionary & Thesaurus
	Microsoft	Encarta Streets & Trips

FIGURE 3-27 Many popular programs are available for home, personal, and educational use.

Software Suite (for Personal Use)

A software suite (for personal use) combines application software such as word processing, spreadsheet, database, and other programs in a single, easy-to-use package. Many computer vendors install a software suite for personal use, such as Microsoft Works, on new computers sold to home users.

As mentioned earlier, the programs in a software suite use a similar interface and share some common features. The programs in software suites for personal use typically are available only through the software suite; that is, you cannot purchase them individually. These programs may not have all the capabilities of business application software. For many home users, however, the capabilities of software suites for personal use more than meet their needs.

Personal Finance Software

Personal finance software is a simplified accounting program that helps home users and small office/home office users balance their checkbooks, pay bills, track personal income and expenses, set up budgets, manage home inventory (Figure 3-28), track investments, and evaluate financial plans. Personal finance software helps determine where, and for what purpose, you are spending money so you can manage your finances. Reports can summarize transactions by category (such as dining), by payee (such as the electric company), or by time (such as the last two months). Financial planning features include analyzing home and personal loans, preparing income taxes, and managing retirement savings.

Most of these personal finance programs also offer a variety of online services, which require access to the Internet. For example, users can track investments online, compare insurance rates from leading insurance companies, and bank online. **Online banking** offers access to account balances, provides bill paying services, and allows you to download monthly transactions and statements from the Web directly to your computer.

FIGURE 3-28 Personal finance software assists home users with tracking personal income and expenses.

FAQ 3-6

How many people bank online?

Currently, about 40 million people bank online. By 2010, this number is expected to grow to 50 million. The chart below depicts popular online banking activities. For more information, visit scsite.com/dc2008/ch3/faq and then click Online Banking.

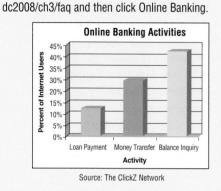

Online Banking Activities

Source: The ClickZ Network

Legal Software

Legal software assists in the preparation of legal documents and provides legal information to individuals, families, and small businesses (Figure 3-29). Legal software provides standard contracts and documents associated with buying, selling, and renting property; estate planning; marriage and divorce; and preparing a will or living trust. By answering a series of questions or completing a form, the legal software tailors the legal document to specific needs.

Once the legal document is created, you can file the paperwork with the appropriate agency, court, or office; or take the document to your attorney for his or her review and signature. Before using one of these software programs to create a document, you may want to check with your local bar association for its legality.

Tax Preparation Software

Tax preparation software is used to guide individuals, families, or small businesses through the process of filing federal taxes (Figure 3-30). These programs forecast tax liability and offer money-saving tax tips, designed to lower your tax bill. After you answer a series of questions and complete basic forms, the software creates and analyzes your tax forms to search for potential errors and deduction opportunities. Once the forms are complete, you can print any necessary paperwork, and then they are ready for filing. Instead of mailing forms through the postal service, the IRS allows taxpayers to file their taxes online.

FAQ 3-7

What are the benefits of filing taxes online?

More than 72 million taxpayers *e-file*, or use tax software and/or tax preparation Web sites to file state and federal tax returns electronically. Filing your taxes online not only increases the accuracy of your return, but also decreases its processing time. If you are expecting a refund, online filing will ensure you receive your refund as quickly as possible. For more information, visit scsite.com/dc2008/ch3/faq and then click E-Filing Taxes.

WEB LINK 3-5

Legal Software

For more information, visit scsite.com/dc2008/ch3/weblink and then click Legal Software.

FIGURE 3-29 Legal software provides legal information to individuals, families, and small businesses and assists in record keeping and the preparation of legal documents.

FIGURE 3-30 Tax preparation software guides individuals, families, or small businesses through the process of filing federal taxes.

Desktop Publishing Software (for Personal Use)

Instead of using professional DTP software (as discussed earlier in this chapter), many home and small business users work with simpler, easy-to-understand DTP software designed for smaller-scale desktop publishing projects (Figure 3-31). **Personal DTP software** helps home and small business users create newsletters, brochures, advertisements, post-cards, greeting cards, letterhead, business cards, banners, calendars, logos, and Web pages.

Personal DTP programs provide hundreds of thousands of graphical images. You also can import (bring in) your own digital photographs into the documents. These programs typically guide you through the development of a document by asking a series of questions, offering numerous predefined layouts, and providing standard text you can add to documents. Then, you can print a finished publication on a color printer or post it on the Web.

Many personal DTP programs also include paint/image editing software and photo editing software.

WEB LINK 3-6

Personal DTP Software

For more information, visit scsite.com/ dc2008/ch3/weblink and then click Personal DTP Software.

Paint/Image Editing Software (for Personal Use)

Personal paint/image editing software provides an easy-to-use interface, usually with more simplified capabilities than its professional counterpart, including functions tailored to meet the needs of the home and small business user.

As with the professional versions, personal paint software includes various simplified tools that allow you to draw pictures, shapes, and other images (Figure 3-32). Personal image editing software provides the capabilities of paint software and the ability to modify existing graphics and photos. These products also include many templates to assist you in adding an image to documents such as greeting cards, banners, calendars, signs, labels, business cards, and letterhead.

FAQ 3-8

How do I print my pictures from my digital camera?

Your digital camera may connect with a cable directly to your computer or to a kiosk at a store. You also may be able to remove the media card from the digital camera and transfer pictures from the card to your computer and/or printer for print-ing. Online services also are available that allow you to transfer your pictures to them electroni-cally, and they will mail you the prints. For more information, visit scsite.com/dc2008/ch3/faq and then click Printing Digital Pictures.

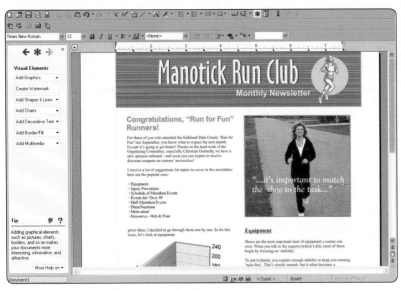

FIGURE 3-31 With desktop publishing software, home and small business users can create professional-looking newsletters.

FIGURE 3-32 Home users can purchase affordable paint/image editing programs that enable them to draw images.

Photo Editing Software

Instead of professional photo editing software, many home and small business users work with easier-to-use personal photo editing software. **Personal photo editing software** allows users to edit digital photographs by removing red-eye, erasing blemishes, restoring aged photos, adding special effects (Figure 3-33), or creating electronic photo albums. When you purchase a digital camera, it usually includes photo editing software. You can print edited photographs on labels, calendars, business cards, and banners; or post them on a Web page. Some photo editing software allows users to send digital photographs to an online print service, which will deliver high-resolution printed images through the postal service. Many online print services have a photo community where users can post photographs on the Web for others to view.

FIGURE 3-33 Personal photo editing software enables home users to edit digital photographs.

Clip Art/Image Gallery

Application software often includes a **clip art/image gallery**, which is a collection of clip art and photographs. Some applications have links to additional clips available on the Web. You also can purchase clip art/image gallery software that contains hundreds of thousands of images (Figure 3-34).

In addition to clip art, many clip art/image galleries provide fonts, animations, sounds, video clips, and audio clips. You can use the images, fonts, and other items from the clip art/image gallery in all types of documents, including word processing, desktop publishing, spreadsheet, and presentation graphics.

FIGURE 3-34 Clip art/image gallery software contains hundreds of thousands of images.

FAQ 3-9

Is it legal to use pictures I find on the Internet?

Not always. Before deciding to use a picture you find on the Internet, you first should check whether the image is protected by a copyright. You may find a copyright symbol (©) or notice, either on the image itself or elsewhere. Contact the person or company hosting the Web site to obtain permission to use any pictures if you are unsure whether they are protected by a copyright. For more information, visit scsite.com/dc2008/ch3/faq and then click Online Pictures.

Video and Audio Editing Software (for Personal Use)

Many home users work with easy-to-use video and audio editing software, which is much simpler to use than its professional counterpart, for small-scale movie making projects (Figure 3-35). With these programs, home users can edit home movies, add music or other sounds to the video, and share their movies on the Web. Some operating systems include video editing and audio editing software.

FIGURE 3-35 With personal video and audio editing software, home users can edit their home movies.

Home Design/Landscaping Software

Homeowners or potential homeowners can use **home design/landscaping software** to assist them with the design, remodeling, or improvement of a home, deck, or landscape (Figure 3-36). Home design/landscaping software includes hundreds of predrawn plans that you can customize to meet your needs. These programs show changes to home designs and landscapes, allowing homeowners to preview proposed modifications. Once designed, many home design/landscaping programs print a materials list outlining costs and quantities for the entire project.

FIGURE 3-36 Home design/landscaping software can help you design or remodel a home, deck, or landscape.

WEB LINK 3-7

Home Design/Landscaping Software

For more information, visit scsite.com/ dc2008/ch3/weblink and then click Home Design/Landscaping Software.

Reference and Educational Software

Reference software provides valuable and thorough information for all individuals (Figure 3-37). Popular reference software includes encyclopedias, dictionaries, health/ medical guides, maps, and travel directories.

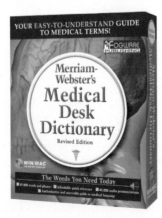

FIGURE 3-37 This reference dictionary gives text definitions and audio pronunciations of medical terms.

WEB LINK 3-8

Reference Software

For more information, visit scsite.com/dc2008/ ch3/weblink and then click Reference Software.

Educational software is software that teaches a particular skill. Educational software exists for just about any subject, from learning how to type to learning how to cook. Preschool to high-school learners use educational software to assist them with subjects such as reading and math or to prepare them for class or college entry exams. Educational software often includes games and other content to make the learning experience more fun.

Many educational programs use a computer-based training approach. **Computer-based training** (**CBT**), also called computer-aided instruction (CAI), is a type of education in which students learn by using and completing exercises with instructional software. CBT typically consists of self-directed, self-paced instruction about a topic. Beginning athletes, for example, use CBT programs to learn the intricacies of baseball, football, soccer, tennis, and golf. The military and airlines use CBT simulations to train pilots to fly in various conditions and environments. Schools use CBT to teach students math, language, and software skills.

Entertainment Software

Entertainment software for personal computers includes interactive games, videos, and other programs designed to support a hobby or provide amusement and enjoyment. For example, you might use entertainment software to play games (Figure 3-38) individually or with others online, make a family tree, listen to music, or fly an aircraft.

FIGURE 3-38 Entertainment software can provide hours of recreation.

APPLICATION SOFTWARE FOR COMMUNICATIONS

One of the main reasons people use computers is to communicate and share information with others. Some communications software is considered system software because it works with hardware and transmission media.

Other communications software makes users more productive and/or assists them with personal tasks, and thus, is considered application software. Chapter 2 presented a variety of application software for communications, which is summarized in the table in Figure 3-39. Read Ethics & Issues 3-3 for a related discussion.

APPLICATION SOFTWARE FOR COMMUNICATIONS

E-Mail
- Messages and files sent via a network such as the Internet
- Requires an e-mail program
  - Integrated in many software suites and operating systems
  - Available free at portals on the Web
  - Included with paid Internet access service
  - Can be purchased separately from retailers

FTP
- Method of uploading and downloading files with other computers on the Internet
- May require an FTP program
  - Integrated in some operating systems
  - Available for download on the Web for a small fee

Web Browser
- Allows users to access and view Web pages on the Internet
- Requires a Web browser program
  - Integrated in some operating systems
  - Available for download on the Web free or for a fee

Video Conferencing
- Meeting between geographically separated people who use a network such as the Internet to transmit video/audio
- Requires video conferencing software, a microphone, speakers, and sometimes a video camera attached to your computer

Internet Telephony (VoIP)
- Allows users to speak to other users over the Internet
- Requires Internet connection, Internet telephone service, microphone or telephone, and Internet telephone software or telephone adapter

Newsgroup/Message Board
- Online area where users have written discussions
- Newsgroup may require a newsreader program
  - Integrated in some operating systems, e-mail programs, and Web browsers; built into some Web sites
  - Available for download on the Web, usually at no cost
  - Included with some paid Internet access services

Chat Room
- Real-time, online typed conversation
- Requires chat client software
  - Integrated in some operating systems, e-mail programs, and Web browsers
  - Available for download on the Web, usually at no cost
  - Included with some paid Internet access services
  - Built into some Web sites

Instant Messaging
- Real-time exchange of messages, files, audio, and/or video with another online user
- Requires instant messenger software
  - Integrated in some operating systems
  - Available for download on the Web, usually at no cost
  - Included with some paid Internet access services

Blogging
- Time-stamped articles, or posts, in a diary or journal format, usually listed in reverse chronological order
- Blogger needs *blog software*, or *blogware*, to create/maintain blog
  - Some Web sites do not require installation of blog software

FIGURE 3-39 A summary of application software for home and business communications.

ETHICS & ISSUES 3-3

Should Companies Monitor Employees' E-Mail and Internet Traffic?

According to one survey, more than 42 percent of all companies monitor (after transmission) or intercept (during transmission) employees' e-mail. Employers can use software to find automatically personal or offensive e-mail messages that have been sent or received, and intercept and filter messages while they are being sent or received. Companies also monitor other Internet traffic such as Web sites visited by employees and how much time employees spend instant messaging and visiting chat rooms. Companies perform this monitoring to improve productivity, increase security, reduce misconduct, and control liability risks. Few laws regulate employee monitoring, and courts have given employers a great deal of leeway in watching work on company-owned computers. In one case, an employee's termination for using her office e-mail system to complain about her boss was upheld, even though the company allowed e-mail use for personal communications. The court decreed that the employee's messages were inappropriate for workplace communications. Executives have not escaped scrutiny, either. Prominent leaders, such as Bill Gates, have had e-mail messages they sent used against them in court. Many employees believe that monitoring software violates their privacy rights. State laws usually favor the privacy of the employee, while federal laws tend to favor the employer's right to perform such monitoring. To reduce employee anxiety about monitoring and to follow some state laws, legal experts suggest that companies publish written policies and accept employee feedback, provide clear descriptions of acceptable and unacceptable behavior, respect employee needs and time, and establish a balance between security and privacy. Should companies monitor or intercept employees' Internet communications? Why or why not? How can a company balance workplace security and productivity with employee privacy? If a company monitors Internet use, what guidelines should be followed to maintain worker morale? Why? Is intercepting and filtering e-mail more offensive than monitoring e-mail? Why?

POPULAR UTILITY PROGRAMS

Utility programs are considered system software because they assist a user with controlling or maintaining the operation of a computer, its devices, or its software. Some utility programs are included with the operating system, and others are available as stand-alone programs.

Utility programs typically offer features that provide an environment conducive to successful use of application software. One of the more important utility programs protects a computer against viruses. A computer *virus* is a potentially damaging computer program that affects, or infects, a computer negatively by altering the way the computer works without the user's knowledge or permission. For a technical discussion about viruses, read the High-Tech Talk article on page 168.

Other features of utility programs include protecting a computer against unauthorized intrusions; removing spyware from a computer; filtering e-mail messages, Web content, and advertisements; managing files and disks; compressing files; backing up; playing media files; burning (recording on) a CD or DVD; and maintaining a personal computer. The table in Figure 3-40 briefly describes several utility programs. Chapter 8 discusses them in more depth.

FAQ 3-10

How much does a computer virus attack cost a company?

A recent survey found that it typically costs an enterprise about $10,000 to recover from a computer virus attack. When the virus attacks multiple servers, however, the costs can exceed $100,000. For more information, visit scsite.com/dc2008/ch3/faq and then click Computer Virus Attacks.

WEB LINK 3-9

Antivirus Programs

For more information, visit scsite.com/dc2008/ch3/weblink and then click Antivirus Programs.

WIDELY USED UTILITY PROGRAMS

Utility Program	Description
Antivirus Program	An *antivirus program* protects a computer against viruses by identifying and removing any computer viruses found in memory, on storage media, or in incoming files.
Personal Firewall	A *personal firewall* detects and protects a personal computer from unauthorized intrusions.
Spyware Remover	A *spyware remover* detects and deletes spyware, adware, and other similar programs on your computer.
Internet Filters • Anti-Spam Program	An *anti-spam program* attempts to remove spam (Internet junk mail) before it reaches your e-mail inbox.
• Web Filter	A *Web filter* restricts access to specified Web sites.
• Pop-Up Blocker	A *pop-up blocker* stops advertisements from displaying on Web pages and disables pop-up windows.
File Manager	A *file manager* provides functions related to file management.
File Compression	A *file compression utility* shrinks the size of a file(s), so the file takes up less storage space than the original file.
Backup	A *backup utility* allows users to copy selected files or an entire hard disk to another storage medium.
Media Player	A *media player* allows you to view images and animation, listen to audio, and watch video files.
CD/DVD Burning	A *CD/DVD burner* writes text, graphics, audio, and video files on a recordable or rewritable CD or DVD.
Personal Computer Maintenance	A *personal computer maintenance utility* identifies and fixes operating system problems, detects and repairs disk problems, and includes the capability of improving a computer's performance.

FIGURE 3-40 A summary of widely used utility programs.

WEB-BASED SOFTWARE

As discussed earlier in this chapter, users can purchase application software from a software vendor, retail store, or Web-based business. Users typically install purchased application software on a computer before they run it. Installed software has two disadvantages: (1) it requires disk space on your computer, and (2) it can be costly to upgrade as vendors release new versions. As an alternative, some users opt to access Web-based software.

As previously mentioned, Web-based software refers to programs hosted by a Web site. Users often interact with Web-based software, sometimes called a *Web application*, directly at the host's Web site. Some Web sites, however, require you download the software to your local computer or device. Web-based software sites often store users' data and information on their servers. Users concerned with data security may shy away from this type of Web-based software. For this reason, some Web-based software sites provide users with an option of storing data locally on their own personal computer or mobile device.

Many of the previously discussed types of application software have Web-based options. For example, word processing, e-mail, personal information manager, software suite, photo editing, Web page authoring, tax preparation, clip art/image gallery, reference, educational, and entertainment programs are available as Web-based software.

Some Web sites provide free access to their Web-based software. For example, one site creates a map and driving directions when a user enters a starting and destination point. Others offer part of their Web-based software free and charge for access to a more comprehensive program (Figure 3-41). Another type allows you to use the program free and pay a fee when a certain action occurs. For example,

you can prepare your tax return free using TurboTax for the Web, but if you elect to print it or file it electronically, you pay a minimal fee.

Web 2.0

Experts often use the term Web 2.0 to describe Web sites that offer Web-based software. Recall that Web 2.0, or participatory Web, refers to Web sites that provide users with a means to share and/or store personal information through Web-based software and may allow users to modify Web site content. Several types of Web 2.0 sites have emerged:

- Web-based software that focuses on user communications — i.e., e-mail, instant messaging, and Internet telephony software
- Web-based software you download from the Web site — i.e., mapping software
- Web-based software you download from the Web site that also has a Web component that offers additional features — i.e., word processing software that allow others to access documents, media player programs that connect to an online store for downloading media
- Web-based software you interact with only through the Web site that provides users with an online community for user input and/or collaboration — i.e., social networks, photo sharing, wikis

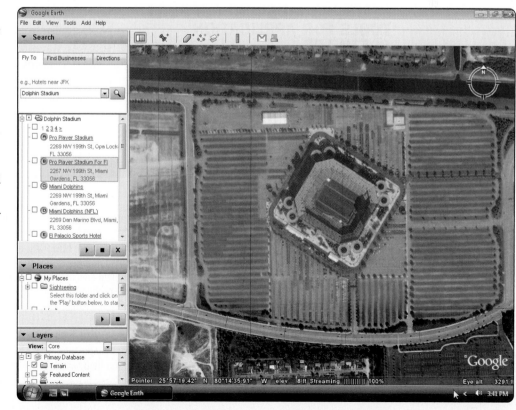

FIGURE 3-41 This program displays three-dimensional maps, satellite images, and aerial photography of the entire earth.

Application Service Providers

Storing and maintaining programs can be a costly investment for businesses. Thus, some have elected to outsource one or more facets of their information technology (IT) needs to an application service provider. An *application service provider (ASP)* is a third-party organization that manages and distributes software and services on the Web.

The five categories of ASPs are:

1. *Enterprise ASP*: customizes and delivers high-end business applications, such as finance and database
2. *Local/Regional ASP*: offers a variety of software applications to a specific geographic region
3. *Specialist ASP*: delivers applications to meet a specific business need, such as human resources or project management
4. *Vertical Market ASP*: provides applications for a particular industry, such as construction, health care, or retail
5. *Volume Business ASP*: supplies prepackaged applications, such as accounting, to businesses

A variety of payment schemes are available. Some rent use of the application on a monthly basis or charge based on the number of user accesses. Others charge a one-time fee.

LEARNING AIDS AND SUPPORT TOOLS FOR APPLICATION SOFTWARE

Learning how to use application software effectively involves time and practice (read Looking Ahead 3-2 for a look at how effective use of software potentially can help the medical field). To assist in the learning process, many programs provide online Help, Web-based Help, and templates.

Online Help is the electronic equivalent of a user manual (Figure 3-42a). It usually is integrated in a program. In most programs, a function key or a button on the screen starts the Help feature. When using a program, you can use the Help feature to ask a question or access the Help topics in subject or alphabetical order.

Most online Help also links to Web sites that offer *Web-based Help*, which provides updates and more comprehensive resources to respond to technical issues about software (Figure 3-42b). Many can search for answers to questions you enter in complete sentences. Some Web sites contain chat rooms, in which a user can talk directly with a technical support person or join a conversation with other users who may be able to answer questions or solve problems.

A *template* is a document that contains the formatting necessary for a specific document type (Figure 3-42c). Many programs include templates. For example, word processing software contains templates for memorandums, meeting agendas, fax cover sheets, flyers, letters, and resumes. Spreadsheet software includes templates for invoices and purchase orders.

If you want to learn more about a particular program from a printed manual, many books are available to help you learn to use the features of personal computer programs. These books typically are available in bookstores and software stores (Figure 3-43).

Many colleges and schools provide training on several of the applications discussed in this chapter. For more information, contact your local school for a list of class offerings.

LOOKING AHEAD 3-2

3-D Scans May Reduce Surgeries

When commercial software developers collaborate with computer scientists, the results can benefit users as diverse as doctors and moviemakers.

Doctors using Live Surface software can turn data from MRI, CAT, or other medical scans into 3-D images of any part of a patient's body. Created by computer scientists at Brigham Young University, the software uses a paint-by-number approach to isolate specific areas, such as the heart, so doctors more closely can examine and better diagnose medical problems.

Using the software may eliminate the need for some exploratory surgeries and provide visual roadmaps to guide surgeries. The software tools also can be used by moviemakers to pull 3-D images of specific objects or a single actor from video clips. Adobe Systems funded the research for Live Surface and previously supported the development of a program manipulating two-dimensional objects that is now part of Adobe Photoshop. For more information, visit scsite.com/dc2008/ch3/looking and then click 3-D Scans.

FIGURE 3-42a (online Help)

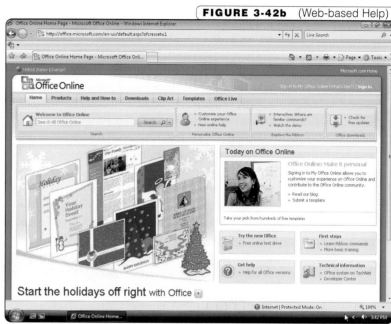

FIGURE 3-42b (Web-based Help)

FIGURE 3-42 Many programs include online Help, Web-based Help, and templates.

FIGURE 3-42c (template)

FIGURE 3-43 Bookstores often sell trade books to help you learn to use the features of personal computer application software.

Web-Based Training

Web-based training (*WBT*) is a type of CBT (computer-based training) that uses Internet technology and consists of application software on the Web. Similar to CBT, WBT typically consists of self-directed, self-paced instruction about a topic. WBT is popular in business, industry, and schools for teaching new skills or enhancing existing skills of employees, teachers, or students. When using a WBT product, students actively become involved in the learning process instead of remaining passive recipients of information.

Many Web sites offer WBT to the general public. Such training covers a wide range of topics, from how to change a flat tire to creating documents in Word. Many of these Web sites are free. Others require registration and payment to take the complete Web-based course.

WBT often is combined with other materials for distance learning and e-learning. **Distance learning (DL)** is the delivery of education at one location while the learning takes place at other locations. DL courses provide time, distance, and place advantages for students who live far from a college campus or work full time. These courses enable students to attend class from anywhere in

WEB LINK 3-10

E-Learning
For more information, visit scsite.com/dc2008/ch3/weblink and then click E-Learning.

the world and at times that fit their schedules. Many national and international companies offer DL training. These training courses eliminate the costs of airfare, hotels, and meals for centralized training sessions.

E-learning, short for electronic learning, is the delivery of education via some electronic method such as the Internet, networks, or CDs/DVDs. To enhance communications, e-learning systems also may include video conferencing, e-mail, blogs, wikis, newsgroups, chat rooms, and groupware. Read Ethics & Issues 3-4 for a related discussion.

E-learning providers often specialize in presenting instructors with the tools for preparation, distribution, and management of DL courses (Figure 3-44). These tools enable instructors to create rich, educational Web-based training sites and allow the students to interact with a powerful Web learning environment. Through the training site, students can check their progress, take practice tests, search for topics, send e-mail messages, and participate in discussions and chats.

FIGURE 3-44 Using Blackboard Academic Suite, instructors can communicate online with their students.

ETHICS & ISSUES 3-4

Will Patents Endanger E-Learning?

Approximately 90 percent of colleges use e-learning systems. Recently, a provider of a popular e-learning system declared it had been awarded a patent on some of the most fundamental aspects of e-learning. The company immediately filed a lawsuit against one of its largest competitors for patent infringement, claiming they simply are protecting a great investment that they have made in developing the technology. They are not trying to stop any companies from selling similar software; they just expect a small royalty from the other companies for using the patents. Critics point out that the United States Patent and Trademark Office may have erred because it is not allowed to grant patents for obvious ideas, and e-learning systems are rather obvious. Critics also claim that due to its importance in education, this technology should be given special consideration. In fact, the technology was invented as part of a research project at a respected university. In Europe and the U.S., there are political movements against the patenting of any software. Should companies be able to patent software? Why or why not? Should a higher standard apply in granting patents for systems directly related to academia? Why or why not? In what ways do you think the e-learning provider should be able to protect the investments it has made in the technology? Are e-learning systems an obvious idea to you?

Test your knowledge of pages 155 through 166 in Quiz Yourself 3-3.

QUIZ YOURSELF 3-3

Instructions: Find the true statement below. Then, rewrite the remaining false statements so they are true.

1. An anti-spam program protects a computer against viruses by identifying and removing any computer viruses found in memory, on storage media, or in incoming files.

2. Computer-based training is a type of Web-based training that uses Internet technology and consists of application software on the Web.

3. E-mail and Web browsers are examples of communications software that are considered application software.

4. Legal software is a simplified accounting program that helps home users and small office/home office users balance their checkbooks, pay bills, track investments, and evaluate financial plans.

5. Personal DTP software is a popular type of image editing software that allows users to edit digital photographs.

Quiz Yourself Online: To further check your knowledge of types and features of home, personal, educational, and communications programs, utility programs, Web-based software, and software learning aids, visit scsite.com/dc2008/ch3/quiz and then click Objectives 6 – 10.

CHAPTER SUMMARY

This chapter illustrated how to start and use application software. It then presented an overview of a variety of business software, graphics and multimedia software, home/personal/educational software, and communications software (read Ethics & Issues 3-5 for a related discussion).

The chapter also described widely used utility programs and discussed Web-based software. Finally, learning aids and support tools for application software were presented.

ETHICS & ISSUES 3-5

Copying Software — A Computer Crime!

Usually, when you buy software, you legally can make one copy of the software for backup purposes. Despite the law, many people make multiple copies, either to share or to sell. Often, the sharing is done online. In a recent survey, more than 50 percent of students and 25 percent of instructors admitted that they had illegally copied, or would illegally copy, software. Microsoft, a leading software manufacturer, estimates that almost 25 percent of software in the United States has been copied illegally. Among small businesses, the rate may be even higher. The Business Software Alliance, an industry trade association, believes that 40 percent of small U.S. businesses use illegally copied software and that cutting the amount of illegal software by 10 percent would add $125 billion to the U.S. economy. Illegally copied software costs the software industry billions a year in lost revenues, and the law allows fines up to $150,000 for each illegal copy of software. People and companies copy software illegally for a variety of reasons, insisting that software prices are too high, software often is copied for educational or other altruistic purposes, copied software makes people more productive, no restrictions should be placed on the use of software after it is purchased, and everyone copies software. What should be the penalty for copying software? Why? Can you counter the reasons people give for copying software illegally? How? Would you copy software illegally? Why or why not?

CAREER CORNER

Help Desk Specialist

A Help Desk specialist position is an entryway into the information technology (IT) field. A *Help Desk specialist* deals with problems in hardware, software, or communications systems. Job requirements may include the following: solve procedural and software questions both in person and over the telephone, develop and maintain Help Desk operations manuals, and assist in training new Help Desk personnel.

Usually, a Help Desk specialist must be knowledgeable about the major programs in use. Entry-level positions primarily involve answering calls from people with questions. Other positions provide additional assistance and assume further responsibilities, often demanding greater knowledge and problem-solving skills that can lead to more advanced IT positions. This job is ideal for people who must work irregular hours, because many companies need support people to work evenings, weekends, or part-time.

Educational requirements are less stringent than they are for other jobs in the computer field. In some cases, a high school diploma is sufficient. Advancement requires a minimum of a two-year degree, while management generally requires a bachelor's degree in IT or a related field. Certification is another way Help Desk specialists can increase their attractiveness in the marketplace. Entry-level salaries range from $38,000 to $60,000 per year. Managers range from $55,000 to $95,000. For more information, visit scsite.com/dc2008/ch3/careers and then click Help Desk Specialist.

High-Tech Talk

COMPUTER VIRUSES:
DELIVERY, INFECTION, AND AVOIDANCE

Klez. Melissa. Netsky. Nimda. Like the common cold, virtually countless variations of computer viruses exist. Unlike the biological viruses that cause the common cold, people create computer viruses. To create a virus, an unscrupulous programmer must code and then test the virus code to ensure the virus can replicate itself, conceal itself, monitor for certain events, and then deliver its *payload* — the destructive event or prank the virus was created to deliver. Despite the many variations of viruses, most have two phases to their execution: infection and delivery.

To start the infection phase, the virus must be activated. Today, the most common way viruses spread is by people running infected programs disguised as e-mail attachments. During the infection phase, viruses typically perform three actions:

1. First, a virus replicates by attaching itself to program files. A *macro virus* hides in the macro language of an application, such as Word. A *boot sector virus* targets the master boot record and executes when the computer boots up. A *file virus* attaches itself to program files. The file virus, Win32.Hatred, for example, replicates by first infecting Windows executable files for the Calculator, Notepad, Help, and other programs on the hard disk. The virus then scans the computer to locate .exe files on other drives and stores this information in the system registry. The next time an infected file is run, the virus reads the registry and continues infecting another drive.

2. Viruses also conceal themselves to avoid detection. A *stealth virus* disguises itself by hiding in fake code sections, which it inserts within working code in a file. A *polymorphic virus* actually changes its code as it infects computers. Win32.Hatred uses both concealment techniques. The virus writes itself to the last file section, while modifying the file header to hide the increased file size. It also scrambles and encrypts the virus code as it infects files.

3. Finally, viruses watch for a certain condition or event and activate when that condition or event occurs. The event might be booting up the computer or hitting a date on the system clock. A *logic bomb* activates when it detects a specific condition (say, a name deleted from the employee list). A *time bomb* is a logic bomb that activates on a particular date or time. Win32.Hatred, for instance, unleashes its destruction when the computer clock hits the seventh day of any month. If the triggering condition does not exist, the virus simply replicates.

During the delivery phase, the virus unleashes its payload, which might be a harmless prank that displays a meaningless message — or it might be destructive, corrupting or deleting data and files. When Win32.Hatred triggers, it displays the author's message and then covers the screen with black dots. The virus also deletes several antivirus files as it infects the system. The most dangerous viruses do not have an obvious payload, instead they quietly modify files. A virus, for example, could randomly change numbers in an inventory program or introduce delays to slow a computer.

Other kinds of electronic annoyances exist in addition to viruses. While often called viruses, worms and Trojan horse applications actually are part of a broader category called *malicious-logic programs*.

- A *worm*, such as the CodeRed or Sircam worm, resides in active memory and replicates itself over a network to infect machines, using up the system resources and possibly shutting the system down.

- A *Trojan horse* is a destructive program disguised as a real application, such as a screen saver. When a user runs a seemingly innocent program, a Trojan horse hiding inside can capture information, such as user names and passwords, from your system or open up a backdoor that allows a hacker remotely to control your computer. Unlike viruses, Trojan horses do not replicate themselves.

As with the common cold, every computer user is susceptible to a computer virus. In 1995, the chance that a virus would infect your computer was 1 in 1,000; by 2004, the odds were only 1 in 7. Even with better antivirus software, viruses are tough to avoid, as deceitful programmers craft new electronic maladies to infect your computer. Due to the increasing threat of viruses attacking your computer, it is more important than ever to protect your computer from viruses. Figure 3-45 lists steps you can follow to protect your computer from a virus infection. For more information, visit scsite.com/dc2008/ch3/tech and then click Computer Viruses.

STEPS TO VIRUS PROTECTION

1. Install the latest Microsoft updates.
2. Purchase a good antivirus program.
3. After installing an antivirus program, scan your entire computer to be sure your system is clean.
4. Update your antivirus definitions regularly.
5. Be suspicious of any and all unsolicited e-mail attachments.
6. Stay informed about viruses and virus hoaxes.
7. Install a personal firewall program.
8. Download software only if you are sure the Web site is legitimate.
9. Avoid as best you can visiting unscrupulous Web sites.

FIGURE 3-45 Guidelines to keep your computer virus free.

Companies on the Cutting Edge

ADOBE SYSTEMS
DIGITAL IMAGING LEADER

Practically every image seen on a computer and in print has been shaped by software developed by *Adobe Systems, Inc.* The company, based in San Jose, California, is one of the world's largest application software corporations and is committed to helping people communicate effectively.

Adobe's acquisition of Macromedia in 2005 expanded its product line. Print, Internet, and mobile publishers use the software included in Creative Suite, such as Photoshop, Illustrator, and InDesign. Web page designers also use the Studio programs, which include Dreamweaver, Flash, Fireworks, Contribute, and FlashPaper. Acrobat software is used to share documents electronically; the free Reader has been downloaded more than 600 million times in 26 different languages, and the full-featured version accounts for approximately 20 percent of sales.

Adobe was named the greenest corporate building in the United States in 2006 for reducing electricity consumption by 35 percent and natural gas consumption by 41 percent since 2001. For more information, visit scsite.com/dc2008/ch3/companies and then click Adobe Systems.

MICROSOFT
REALIZING POTENTIAL WITH BUSINESS SOFTWARE

Microsoft's mission is "to enable people and businesses throughout the world to realize their potential." As the largest software company in the world, *Microsoft* has indeed helped computer users in every field reach their goals.

When Microsoft was incorporated in 1975, the company had three programmers, one product, and revenues of $16,000. Thirty years later, the company employs more than 1,000 people, produces scores of software titles with Office and Windows leading the industry, and has annual revenue of approximately $50 billion.

The Zune portable media player, Windows Vista operating system, and Office 2007 expand the corporation's offerings in the consumer and business marketplace. For more information, visit scsite.com/dc2008/ch3/companies and then click Microsoft.

Technology Trailblazers

DAN BRICKLIN
VISICALC DEVELOPER

When *Dan Bricklin* was enrolled at the Harvard Business School in the 1970s, he often used his calculator to determine the effect of changing one value on a balance sheet. He recognized the need to develop a program that would perform a series of calculations automatically when the first number was entered.

He named his creation VisiCalc, short for Visible Calculator. He and a friend formed a company called Software Arts and programmed the VisiCalc prototype using Apple Basic on an Apple II computer. The small program was the first piece of application software that provided a reason for businesses to buy Apple computers. It laid the foundation for the development of other spreadsheets and included many of the features found in today's spreadsheet software.

As president of Software Garden, Inc., a small consulting and software-development firm, one of his latest projects was producing a training video explaining copyright law basics to software developers. For more information, visit scsite.com/dc2008/ch3/people and then click Dan Bricklin.

MASAYOSHI SON
SOFTBANK PRESIDENT AND CEO

Many students carry photographs of family and friends in their wallets and book bags. As a 16-year-old student in the 1970s, *Masayoshi Son* carried a picture of a microchip. He predicted that the microchip was going to change people's lives, and he wanted to be part of that trend.

While majoring in economics at the University of California, Berkeley, he earned his first million dollars by importing arcade games from Japan to the campus, developing new computer games, and selling a patent for a multilingual pocket translator to Sharp Corporation.

At age 23 he founded Softbank, which is Japan's second-largest broadband Internet service and telephone provider. In 2006, he was named to Asiamoney's list of the most powerful and influential people in business and finance in the Asia Pacific region. For more information, visit scsite.com/dc2008/ch3/people and then click Masayoshi Son.

Chapter Review

The Chapter Review section summarizes the concepts presented in this chapter. To listen to the audio version of this Chapter Review, visit scsite.com/dc2008/ch3/review. To obtain help from other students regarding any subject in this chapter, visit scsite.com/dc2008/ch3/forum and post your thoughts or questions.

① What Are the Categories of Application Software? **Application software** consists of programs designed to make users more productive and/or assist them with personal tasks. The major categories of application software are business software; graphics and multimedia software; home, personal, and educational software; and communications software.

② How Is Software Distributed? Application software is available in a variety of forms. **Packaged software** is mass-produced, copyrighted retail software that meets the needs of a variety of users. **Custom software** performs functions specific to a business or industry. **Web-based software** refers to programs hosted by a Web site. **Open source software** is provided for use, modification, and redistribution. **Shareware** is copyrighted software that is distributed free for a trial period. **Freeware** is copyrighted software provided at no cost by an individual or a company that retains all rights to the software. **Public-domain software** is free software donated for public use and has no copyright restrictions.

③ How Do You Work with Application Software? Personal computer operating systems often use the concept of a **desktop**, which is an on-screen work area that has a graphical user interface. To start an application in Windows Vista, move the **pointer** to the Start **button** on the taskbar and **click** the Start button by pressing and releasing a button on the mouse. Then, click the program name on the **menu** or in a list. Once loaded into memory, the program is displayed in a **window** on the desktop.

connect
Visit scsite.com/dc2008/ch3/
or click the Quiz Yourself button. Click
Objectives 1 – 3.

④ What Are the Key Features of Widely Used Business Programs? **Business software** assists people in becoming more effective and efficient while performing daily business activities. Business software includes the following programs. **Word processing software** allows users to **create** a document by entering text and inserting images, **edit** the document by making changes, and **format** the document by changing its appearance. **Spreadsheet software** allows users to organize data in rows and columns, perform calculations, recalculate when data changes, and chart the data. **Database software** allows users to create a **database**, which is a collection of data organized to allow access, retrieval, and use of that data. **Presentation graphics software** allows users to create a *slide show* that is displayed on a monitor or projection screen. **Note taking software** enables users to enter typed text, handwritten comments, drawings, or sketches on a page and then save the page as part of a notebook. A **personal information manager (PIM)** is software that includes features to help users organize personal information. A **software suite** is a collection of individual programs sold as a single package. **Project management software** allows users to plan, schedule, track, and analyze a project. **Accounting software** helps companies record and report their financial transactions. **Document management software** provides a means for sharing, distributing, and searching through documents by converting them into a format that can be viewed by any user.

⑤ What Are the Key Features of Widely Used Graphics and Multimedia Programs?
Graphics and multimedia software includes the following programs. **Computer-aided design (CAD) software** assists in creating engineering, architectural, and scientific designs. **Desktop publishing (DTP) software** enables professional designers to create sophisticated documents that contain text, graphics, and colors. **Paint software** lets users draw graphical images with various on-screen tools. **Image editing software** provides the capabilities of paint software and includes the capability to modify existing images. **Professional photo editing software** is a type of image editing software that allows high-volume digital photo users to edit and customize digital photographs. **Video editing software** allows professionals to modify segments of a video. **Audio editing software** lets users modify audio clips, produce studio-quality soundtracks, and add audio to video clips.

Chapter Review

Multimedia authoring software allows users to combine text, graphics, audio, video, and animation in an interactive application. **Web page authoring software** helps users create Web pages that include graphical images, video, audio, animation, and other special effects.

Visit scsite.com/dc2008/ch3/quiz or click the Quiz Yourself button. Click Objectives 4 – 5.

(6) **What Are the Key Features of Widely Used Home, Personal, and Educational Programs?** Software for home, personal, and educational use includes the following applications. A software suite (for personal use) combines application software such as word processing, spreadsheet, and database into a single package. **Personal finance software** is an accounting program that helps users balance their checkbooks, pay bills, track income and expenses, track investments, and evaluate financial plans. **Legal software** assists in the preparation of legal documents. **Tax preparation software** guides users through filing federal taxes. **Personal DTP software** helps users create newsletters, brochures, advertisements, greeting and business cards, logos, and Web pages. **Personal paint/image editing software** provides an easy-to-use interface with functions tailored to meet the needs of home and small business users. **Personal photo editing software** is a type of image editing software used to edit digital photographs. Application software often includes a **clip art/image gallery**, which is a collection of clip art and photographs. Video and audio editing software is used to edit home movies, add music or other sounds, and share movies on the Web. **Home design/landscaping software** assists with the design, remodeling, or improvement of a home or landscape. **Reference software** provides valuable and thorough information for all individuals. **Educational software** teaches a particular skill. **Entertainment software** includes interactive games, videos, and other programs to support hobbies or provide amusement.

(7) **What Are the Types of Application Software Used in Communications?** Application software for communications includes e-mail programs to transmit messages via a network; FTP programs to upload and download files on the Internet; Web browsers to access and view Web pages; video conferencing software for meetings on a network; Internet telephony (VoIP), which allows users to speak to other users over the Internet; newsgroup/message board programs that allow online written discussions; chat room software to have real-time, online typed conversations; instant messaging software for real-time exchange of messages or files; and *blog software*, or *blogware*, to create and maintain a blog.

(8) **What Are the Functions of Utility Programs?** Utility programs support the successful use of application software. An *antivirus program* protects a computer against a computer *virus*, which is a potentially damaging computer program. A *personal firewall* detects and protects a personal computer from unauthorized intrusions. A *spyware remover* detects and deletes spyware, adware, and other similar programs. An *anti-spam program* removes spam (Internet junk mail). A *Web filter* restricts access to specified Web sites. A *pop-up blocker* disables pop-up windows. A *file manager* provides functions related to file and disk management. A *file compression utility* shrinks the size of a file. A *backup utility* allows users to copy selected files or an entire hard disk to another storage medium. A *media player* allows you to view images and animation, listen to audio, and watch video. A *CD/DVD burner* writes files on a CD or DVD. A *personal computer maintenance utility* fixes operating system and disk problems.

(9) **What Are the Advantages of Using Web-Based Software?** A *Web application* requires less disk space on a computer than installed software and is less costly to upgrade. An *application service provider (ASP)* is a third-party organization that manages and distributes software and services on the Web.

(10) **What Learning Aids Are Available for Application Software?** To assist in the learning process, many programs offer Help features. **Online Help** is the electronic equivalent of a user manual. Most online Help links to *Web-based help*, which provides updates and more comprehensive resources. A *template* is a document that contains the formatting necessary for a specific document type.

Visit scsite.com/dc2008/ch3/quiz or click the Quiz Yourself button. Click Objectives 6 – 10.

Key Terms

You should know the Primary Terms and be familiar with the Secondary Terms. Use the list below to help focus your study. To further enhance your understanding of the Key Terms in this chapter, visit scsite.com/dc2008/ch3/terms. See an example of and a definition for each term, and access current and additional information about the term from the Web.

Primary Terms

(shown in bold-black characters in the chapter)

accounting software (149)
application software (134)
audio editing software (153)
business software (138)
button (136)
click (136)
clip art (138)
clip art/image gallery (159)
command (137)
computer-aided design (CAD) software (151)
computer-based training (CBT) (160)
create (141)
custom software (134)
database (145)
database software (145)
desktop (136)
desktop publishing (DTP) software (152)
distance learning (DL) (166)
document management software (150)
edit (141)
educational software (160)
entertainment software (160)
font (141)
font size (141)
format (141)
freeware (135)
home design/landscaping software (160)
icon (136)
image editing software (152)
legal software (157)
menu (137)
multimedia authoring software (154)
note taking software (147)

online banking (156)
online Help (164)
open source software (135)
packaged software (134)
paint software (152)
personal DTP software (158)
personal finance software (156)
personal information manager (PIM) (148)
personal paint/image editing software (158)
personal photo editing software (159)
pointer (136)
presentation graphics software (146)
print (142)
professional photo editing software (152)
project management software (149)
public-domain software (135)
reference software (160)
save (142)
shareware (135)
software suite (148)
spreadsheet software (142)
tax preparation software (157)
title bar (137)
video editing software (153)
Web page authoring software (154)
Web-based software (135)
Web-based training (165)
window (137)
word processing software (138)

Secondary Terms

(shown in italic characters in the chapter)

anti-spam program (162)
antivirus program (162)
application service provider (ASP) (164)
backup utility (162)
bar chart (144)
blog software (161)
blogware (161)
CD/DVD burner (162)
cell (143)
charting (144)
clipboard (141)
color library (152)
column chart (144)
dialog box (137)
e-learning (166)
enterprise ASP (164)
field (145)
file (137)
file compression utility (162)
file manager (162)
file name (137)
filters (153)
font style (141)
footer (140)
formula (143)
function (143)
header (140)
illustration software (152)
import (146)
label (143)
line chart (144)
loaded (135)
local/regional ASP (164)
macro (140)
margins (139)
media player (162)

page layout (152)
pasting (141)
PDF (150)
personal computer maintenance utility (162)
personal firewall (162)
pie chart (144)
point (141)
pop-up blocker (162)
product activation (135)
query (145)
record (145)
replace (139)
sans serif font (141)
scrolling (139)
search (139)
serif font (141)
slide show (146)
smart tags (140)
specialist ASP (164)
spelling checker (139)
spyware remover (162)
system software (135)
template (140, 164)
value (143)
vertical market ASP (164)
virus (162)
volume business ASP (164)
WBT (165)
Web-based Help (164)
Web application (163)
Web filter (162)
what-if analysis (144)
word processor (138)
wordwrap (139)
worksheet (142)

Checkpoint

Use the Checkpoint exercises to check your knowledge level of the chapter. The Beyond the Book exercises will help broaden your understanding of the concepts presented in this chapter. To complete the Checkpoint exercises interactively, visit scsite.com/dc2008/ch3/check.

Label the Figure

Identify these elements in the Windows Vista graphical user interface.

a. Accessories folder
b. Accessories list
c. Back command
d. All Programs list
e. Start button
f. Paint program

True/False

Mark T for True and F for False. (See page numbers in parentheses.)

_____ 1. The categories of application software are not mutually exclusive. (134)

_____ 2. Public-domain software is available to the public for a fee. (135)

_____ 3. To click a button on the screen requires moving the pointer away from the button and then pressing and holding down a button on the mouse (usually the right mouse button). (136)

_____ 4. A menu is an instruction that causes a program to perform a specific action. (137)

_____ 5. A font is a name assigned to a specific design of characters. (141)

_____ 6. In a spreadsheet program, a formula performs calculations and displays the resulting value in a cell. (143)

_____ 7. Professional photo editing software is a type of image editing software that allows photographers, videographers, engineers, scientists, and other high-volume digital photo users to edit and customize digital photographs. (152)

_____ 8. Legal software assists in the preparation of legal documents and provides legal information to individuals, families, and small businesses. (157)

_____ 9. Personal DTP programs never include paint/image editing software or photo editing software. (158)

_____ 10. Some communications software is considered system software because it works with hardware and transmission media. (161)

_____ 11. Antivirus programs, personal firewalls, and file managers are all examples of utility programs. (162)

_____ 12. Some Web sites require you to download software in order to run their Web applications. (163)

Checkpoint

 Multiple Choice   Select the best answer. (See page numbers in parentheses.)

1. Examples of _____, which is hosted on a Web site, include e-mail, word processing, tax preparation, and game programs. (135)
   a. shareware
   b. Web-based software
   c. e-learning software
   d. public-domain software

2. In a document window, the _____ usually displays a document's file name. (137)
   a. title bar
   b. status bar
   c. menu
   d. dialog box

3. In word processing, pasting is the process of _____. (141)
   a. moving different portions of the document on the screen into view
   b. transferring an item from the clipboard to a specific location in a document
   c. locating all occurrences of a certain character, word, or phrase
   d. removing a portion of a document and storing it in a temporary storage location

4. Most spreadsheet software includes a what-if analysis feature, where you _____. (144)
   a. depict the data in a spreadsheet in graphical form
   b. enter labels to identify worksheet data and organize the worksheet
   c. change values in a spreadsheet to identify the effects of those changes
   d. review the spelling of individual words and sections of a worksheet

5. With database software, users can run a _____, which is a request for specific data from the database. (145)
   a. record
   b. function
   c. query
   d. field

6. _____ software provides a means for sharing, distributing, and searching through documents by converting them into a format that can be viewed by any user. (150)
   a. Database
   b. Document management
   c. Portable Document Format
   d. Word processing

7. _____ combines application software such as word processing, spreadsheet, database, and other programs in a single, easy-to-use package. (156)
   a. A software suite
   b. Shareware
   c. Packaged software
   d. Custom software

8. _____ helps home users determine where, and for what purpose, they are spending money. (156)
   a. Legal software
   b. Personal DTP software
   c. Personal finance software
   d. Tax preparation software

9. _____ helps home and small business users create newsletters, brochures, advertisements, postcards, greeting cards, letterhead, business cards, banners, calendars, logos, and Web pages. (158)
   a. Blogware
   b. Note taking software
   c. A personal information manager
   d. Personal DTP software

10. _____ is a collection of clip art and photographs. (159)
    a. Professional photo editing software
    b. Personal photo editing software
    c. Clip art/image gallery
    d. Entertainment software

11. A(n) _____ restricts access to specified Web sites. (162)
    a. anti-spam program
    b. antivirus program
    c. spyware remover
    d. Web filter

12. _____ allows you to view images and animation, listen to audio, and watch video files. (162)
    a. A software suite
    b. Video editing software
    c. A media player
    d. A CD/DVD burner

13. An enterprise ASP _____. (164)
    a. supplies packaged applications
    b. provides applications for a particular industry
    c. customizes and delivers high-end business applications
    d. offers a variety of software applications to specific regions

14. _____ is the delivery of education via some electronic method such as the Internet, networks, or CDs/DVDs. (166)
    a. A software wizard
    b. E-learning
    c. Online help
    d. Distance learning

Checkpoint

Matching

Match the terms with their definitions. (See page numbers in parentheses.)

_____ 1. icon (136)

_____ 2. button (136)

_____ 3. window (137)

_____ 4. clip art (138)

_____ 5. format (141)

_____ 6. cell (143)

_____ 7. database (145)

_____ 8. PDF (150)

_____ 9. virus (162)

_____ 10. volume business ASP (164)

a. popular file format used by document management software to save converted documents

b. provides prepackaged applications, such as accounting, to businesses

c. small symbol on the screen that moves as you move the mouse

d. potentially damaging computer program that affects, or infects, a computer negatively by altering the way the computer works without the user's knowledge or permission

e. collection of data organized in a manner that allows access, retrieval, and use of that data

f. collection of drawings, photographs, and other images that can be inserted

g. text that appears at the bottom of every page

h. rectangular area of the screen that displays data and information

i. graphical image activated to cause a specific action to take place

j. change the appearance of a document

k. intersection of a row and column in a spreadsheet

l. small image that represents a program, document, or some other object

Short Answer

Write a brief answer to each of the following questions.

1. What are the features of presentation graphics software? _____ What types of media might a person use to enhance a presentation? _____

2. What are the features of personal information manager software? _____ Where might you find personal information manager software? _____

3. What are disadvantages of installed software? _____ How can you access Web-based software? _____

4. What is Web 2.0? _____ Describe four types of Web 2.0 sites. _____

5. In most programs, how do you start the online Help feature? _____ What are some of the templates included with word processing software? _____

Beyond the Book

Read the following book elements, learn more about each using the Web, and then write a brief report.

1. Ethics & Issues — How Should Schools Deal with Internet Plagiarism? (141), Altering Digital Photographs — Art or Fraud? (153), Should Companies Monitor Employees' E-Mail and Internet Traffic? (161), Will Patents Endanger E-Learning? (166), or Copying Software — A Computer Crime! (167)

2. Career Corner — Help Desk Specialist (167)

3. Companies on the Cutting Edge — Adobe Systems or Microsoft (169)

4. FAQs (137, 142, 145, 148, 154, 157, 158, 159, 162)

5. High-Tech Talk — Computer Viruses: Delivery, Infection, and Avoidance (168)

6. Looking Ahead — Touch Drive Your Computer Screen (137) or 3-D Scans May Reduce Surgeries (164)

7. Making Use of the Web — Finance (119)

8. Picture Yourself Using Software (132)

9. Technology Trailblazers — Dan Bricklin or Masayoshi Son (169)

10. Web Links (140, 144, 146, 150, 157, 158, 160, 162, 166)

Learn It Online

Use the Learn It Online exercises to reinforce your understanding of the chapter concepts. To access the Learn It Online exercises, visit scsite.com/dc2008/ch3/learn.

① At the Movies — Your Very Own Video Game Oracle

To view the Your Very Own Video Game Oracle movie, click the number 1 button. Locate your video and click the corresponding High-Speed or Dial-Up link, depending on your Internet connection. Watch the movie and then complete the exercise by answering the question that follows. Explore Microsoft Game Advisor, a Web site that offers free computer scans that let you know whether or not your computer can handle specific computer games. What are the basic functions of Microsoft's Game Advisor?

② Video and Audio: You Review It — Video Editing Software

In this chapter you learned about video editing software. Click the number 2 button to view the suggested links and begin your search for videos, podcasts, or vodcasts related to video editing software. Choose a video, podcast, or vodcast that discusses video editing software and is of interest to you, and then write a description of its contents. Explain why you chose this piece, what you liked about it, what you disliked about it, and whether you would recommend it to a fellow student. Finish your review by giving the video, podcast, or vodcast a rating of 1-5 stars. Submit your review in the format requested by your instructor.

③ Student Edition Labs — Word Processing

Click the number 3 button. A new browser window will open, displaying the Student Edition

Labs. Follow the on-screen instructions, and complete the Word Processing Lab. When finished, click the Exit button. If required, submit your results to your instructor.

④ Student Edition Labs — Spreadsheets

Click the number 4 button. A new browser window will open, displaying the Student Edition Labs. Follow the on-screen instructions, and complete the Spreadsheets Lab. When finished, click the Exit button. If required, submit your results to your instructor.

⑤ Student Edition Labs — Databases

Click the number 5 button. A new browser window will open, displaying the Student Edition Labs. Follow the on-screen instructions, and complete the Databases Lab. When finished, click the Exit button. If required, submit your results to your instructor.

⑥ Student Edition Labs — Presentation Software

Click the number 6 button. A new browser window will open, displaying the Student Edition Labs. Follow the on-screen instructions, and complete the Presentation Software Lab. When finished, click the Exit button. If required, submit your results to your instructor.

⑦ Practice Test

Click the number 7 button. Answer each question. When completed, enter your name and click the Grade Test button to submit the quiz for grading. Make a note of any missed questions. If required, submit your score to your instructor.

⑧ Who Wants To Be a Computer Genius²?

Click the number 8 button to find out if you are a computer genius. Directions about how to play the game will be displayed. When you are ready to play, click the Play button. Submit your score to your instructor.

Learn It Online

 Wheel of Terms

Click the number 9 button to reinforce important terms you learned in this chapter by playing the Shelly Cashman Series version of this popular game. Directions about how to play the game will be displayed. When you are ready to play, click the Play button. Submit your score to your instructor.

 DC Track and Field

Click the number 10 button to use what you have learned in this chapter to compete against other students in three track and field events. Directions about how to play the game will be displayed. When you are ready to play, click the start first event button. If required, submit your score to your instructor.

 You're Hired!

Click the number 11 button to use what you have learned in this chapter to embark on the path to a career in computers. Directions about how to play the game will be displayed. When you are ready to play, click the begin game button. If required, submit your score to your instructor.

 Crossword Puzzle Challenge

Click the number 12 button, then click the Crossword Puzzle Challenge link. Directions about how to play the game will be displayed. Complete the puzzle to reinforce skills you learned in this chapter. When you are ready to play, click the Continue button. Submit the completed puzzle to your instructor.

 Vista Exercises

Click the number 13 button. When the Vista Exercises menu appears, click the exercise assigned by your instructor. A new browser window will open. Follow the on-screen instructions to complete the exercise. When finished, click the Exit button. If required, submit your results to your instructor.

14 **In the News**

It is a computer user's worst fear — he or she opens an unfamiliar e-mail message or uses a disc of unknown origin and a computer virus is released that damages and/or deletes files. Fortunately, specialized software prevents such things from happening to your computer. Click the number 14 button and read a news article about antivirus programs. Which program does the article recommend? What does it do? Who will benefit from using this software? Why? Where can the software be obtained? Would you be interested in this software? Why or why not?

15 **Chapter Discussion Forum**

Select an objective from this chapter on page 133 about which you would like more information. Click the number 15 button and post a short message listing a meaningful message title accompanied by one or more questions concerning the selected objective. In two days, return to the threaded discussion by clicking the number 15 button. Submit to your instructor your original message and at least one response to your message.

16 **Google Home Page**

Click the number 16 button to learn how to make the Google home page your default home page. Explore the different sections of the Google home page (Images, Groups, News, Froogle, Local, and more). On the News page, use the Customize this page feature to rearrange the page and to add other sections. Print the Google News page and then step through the exercise. If required, submit your results to your instructor.

Select a chapter:

1 2 3 4 5 6 7 8 9 10 11 12 13 14 15

3 | **Application Software**

Learn How To

Use the Learn How To activities to learn fundamental skills when using a computer and accompanying technology. Complete the exercises and submit them to your instructor. To see a video of a Learn How To activity, visit scsite.com/dc2008/ch3/howto.

LEARN HOW TO 1: Save a File in Application Software

When you use application software, usually you either will create a new file or modify an existing file. If you turn off your computer or lose electrical power while working on the file, the file will not be retained. In order to retain the file, you must save it.

To save a new file, you must complete several tasks:
1. Initiate an action indicating you want to save the file, such as selecting Save from the File menu.
2. Designate where the file should be stored. This includes identifying both the device (such as drive C) and the folder (such as Documents).
3. Specify the name of the file.
4. Click the Save button to save the file.

Tasks 2 through 4 normally can be completed using a dialog box such as shown in Figure 3-46.

If you close a program prior to saving a new or modified file, the program may display a dialog box asking if you want to save the file. If you click the Yes button, a modified file will be saved using the same file name in the same location. Saving a new file requires that you complete tasks 2 through 4.

Exercise

1. Start the WordPad program from the Accessories list in the All Programs list.
2. Type Saving a file is the best insurance against losing work.
3. Click the Save button on the WordPad toolbar. What dialog box is displayed? Where will the file be saved? What is the default file name? If you wanted to save the file on the desktop, what would you do? Click the Cancel button in the dialog box. Submit your answers to your instructor.
4. Click the Close button in the WordPad window. What happened? Click the Yes button in the WordPad dialog box. What happened? Connect a USB flash drive to one of the computer's USB ports. Select the USB drive as the location for saving the file. Name the file, Chapter 3 How To 1. Save the file. What happened? Submit your answers to your instructor.

FIGURE 3-46

LEARN HOW TO 2: Install and Uninstall Application Software

When you purchase application software, you must install the software on the computer where you want to run it. The exact installation process varies with each program, but generally you must complete the following steps:
1. Insert the CD-ROM or DVD-ROM containing the application software into a drive.
2. The opening window will appear. If the CD-ROM or DVD-ROM contains more than one program, choose the program you want to install. Click the Continue or Next button.
3. Some file extractions will occur and then an Install Wizard will begin. You normally must accomplish the following steps by completing the directions within the wizard:
   a. Accept the terms of the license agreement.
   b. Identify where on your computer the software will be stored. The software usually selects a default location on drive C, and you normally will accept the default location.
   c. Select any default options for the software.
   d. Click a button to install the software.
4. A Welcome/Help screen often will be displayed. Click a button to finish the installation process.

Learn How To

At some point, you may want to remove software. Most software includes an uninstall program that will remove the program and all its software components. To uninstall a program, complete the following steps:

1. Click the Start button on the Windows taskbar.
2. Click Control Panel on the Start menu.
3. Click Uninstall a program to display the Uninstall or change a program window (Figure 3-47).
4. Select the program you wish to remove. In Figure 3-47, Corel Paint Shop Pro Photo XI is selected as the program to remove.
5. Click the Uninstall button.
6. A dialog box will be displayed informing you that the software is being prepared for uninstall. You then will be informed that the process you are following will remove the program. You will be asked if you want to continue. To uninstall the program, click the Yes button.

The program will be removed from the computer.

FIGURE 3-47

Exercise

1. Optional: Insert the CD-ROM or DVD-ROM containing the software you want to install into a drive and follow the instructions for installing the software. **Warning: If you are using a computer other than your own, particularly in a school laboratory, do not perform this exercise unless you have specific permission from your instructor.**
2. Optional: Follow the steps above to uninstall software you want to remove. Be aware that if you uninstall software, the software will not be available for use until you reinstall it. **Warning: If you are using a computer other than your own, particularly in a school laboratory, do not perform this exercise unless you have specific permission from your instructor.**

LEARN HOW TO 3: Check Application Software Version

Most application software will be modified from time to time by its developer. Each time the software is changed, it acquires a new version number and sometimes an entirely new name. To determine what version of software you have, perform the following steps:

1. Start the application program.
2. Click Help on the menu bar and then click About on the Help menu (the program name often follows the word, About) to open the About window (Figure 3-48).
3. To close the About window, click the OK button.

Depending on the software, in the About window you also might be able to determine further information.

FIGURE 3-48

Exercise

1. Start your Web browser and open the About window for the browser. What is the name of the browser? What version of the browser are you using? What is the product ID? What does the copyright notice say? Submit your answers to your instructor.
2. Start any other application software. Open the About window. What is the name of the program? What is the version number? What information do you find that you did not see in Exercise 1? Which window do you find more useful? Why? Submit your answers to your instructor.

Web Research

Use the Internet-based Web Research exercises to broaden your understanding of the concepts presented in this chapter. Visit scsite.com/dc2008/ch3/research to obtain more information pertaining to each exercise. To discuss any of the Web Research exercises in this chapter with other students, post your thoughts or questions at scsite.com/dc2008/ch3/forum.

① **Scavenger Hunt** Use one of the <u>search engines</u> listed in Figure 2-10 in Chapter 2 on page 78 or your own favorite search engine to find the answers to the questions below. Copy and paste the Web address from the Web page where you found the answer. Some questions may have more than one answer. If required, submit your answers to your instructor. (1) What are some new features in the latest edition of Microsoft Streets and Trips? (2) What was the inspiration for the Pac-Man computer game character? (3) How did Ivan Sutherland influence the development of computer-aided design (CAD) software? (4) What Web site features software that creates a game requiring a player to put numbers in nine rows of nine boxes?

② **Search Sleuth** A <u>virus</u> is a potentially damaging computer program that can harm files and the operating system. The National Institute of Standards and Technology Computer Security Resource Center (csrc.nist.gov/virus/) is one of the more comprehensive Web sites discussing viruses. Visit this Web site and then use your word processing program to answer the following questions. Then, if required, submit your answers to your instructor. (1) The Virus Information page provides general information about viruses and links to various resources that provide more specific details. What two steps does the National Institute recommend to detect and prevent viruses from spreading? (2) Click the Computer Associates' Virus Information Center link in the Virus Resources & Other Areas of Interest section. What viruses are listed in the Top 5 Virus Threats section? (3) Click the link of a Top 5 threat and read the summary information. According to the Method of Distribution section, how does this virus spread? (4) Type bots as the keyword in the Search text box at the top of the page. Click the first results link that answers this question: What is a bot, and what does it do? Review the information you read and then write a 50-word summary.

③ **Journaling** Respond to your readings in this chapter by writing at least one page about your reactions, evaluations, and reflections about the first time you used <u>home, personal, and educational software</u>. For example, do you use software to balance your checkbook, share photos, or play computer games? Which programs do you use most? How do your favorite programs make it easier or more enjoyable for you to perform personal tasks? You also can write about the new terms you learned by reading this chapter. If required, submit your journal to your instructor.

④ **Expanding Your Understanding** Microsoft seeks to help customers use its products by maintaining the <u>Microsoft Help and Support</u> Web site (support.microsoft.com). This Web site has a link to the Knowledge Base, which contains more than 250,000 articles written by Microsoft employees who support the company's products. Also included are software downloads and updates, public newsgroups, methods of getting online or telephone assistance, and the Security Support Center. View this site and then search the Knowledge Base for information on Microsoft Word. Also view the common issues, updates, security issues, and visitors' top links listed on the Web site. Write a report summarizing your findings. If required, submit your report to your instructor.

⑤ **Ethics in Action** A hacker is someone who tries to access a computer or network illegally. Although the activity sometimes is a harmless prank, it sometimes causes extensive damage. Some hackers say their activities give them a sense of excitement and test their skills. Others say their activities are a form of civil disobedience that allows them to challenge authority and force companies to make their products more secure. View online sites such as <u>Hackers: Outlaws & Angels</u> (tlc.discovery.com/convergence/hackers/hackers.html) that provide information about whether hackers provide some benefit to the Internet society. Write a report summarizing your findings and include a table of links to Web sites that provide additional details. If required, submit your report to your instructor.

Case Studies

Use the Case Studies to apply the concepts presented in the chapter to real-world situations. Visit scsite.com/dc2008/ch3/cases to obtain more information pertaining to each exercise. To discuss the Case Studies in this chapter with other students, visit scsite.com/dc2008/ch3/forum and post your thoughts or questions.

CASE STUDY 1 – Class Discussion   The owner of Mel's Hair Salon for Men and Women has decided to obtain a personal desktop computer for use in his business. In addition to using the computer for writing letters, developing advertising pieces, performing basic accounting, and maintaining lists of customers, the owner would like his employees to use a **digital camera** to take pictures of customers after they have had their hair done and create a file of printed full-color pictures of customers for marketing purposes. The owner has asked you to recommend the type of camera, software, and computer he should buy. Prepare a brief report detailing your findings and recommendations. Be prepared to discuss your recommendations in class.

CASE STUDY 2 – Class Discussion   Your manager at Dave's Office Supply Outlet intends to choose a spreadsheet program that the entire company will use. He prefers to learn about software using trade books — written texts that explain the features of a program and how to use it — rather than using online Help or tutorials. He has asked you to evaluate the **spreadsheet** trade books available in bookstores on the Web. Visit a bookstore Web site and other Web sites that sell books to survey the spreadsheet trade books available for Microsoft Excel, Lotus, Quattro Pro, and StarOffice Calc. Which spreadsheet program has the most books available? How difficult would it be to learn each program using the trade books at hand? Which trade book do you think is the best? Why? If you were going to purchase software solely on the basis of the related trade books, which program would you buy? Why? Be prepared to discuss your recommendations in class.

CASE STUDY 3 – Research   Karl's Game Den sells new and used computer and video games. Karl recently purchased a large quantity of children's games; however, they are not selling as he expected. You recently read that 62 percent of **entertainment software** purchases are made by males, and the average age of frequent purchasers is 40. You suggest that Karl may be selling to the wrong demographic. Karl has asked you to investigate what type of games and how many games he should stock. Use the Web and/or print media to determine the top five selling games in the United States. Prepare a brief report that includes your list and answers the following questions. Do males and females favor different types of software? If so, should software developers adapt their products? Why or why not? Is it important to modify educational/entertainment software to meet the interests of different groups? Why?

CASE STUDY 4 – Research   Frank's Custom Design frequently enhances its work with scanned photographs or graphics obtained with **illustration software**. The owner recently read that the Internet is providing a new resource for desktop publishers. Companies such as Corbis, Picture Network International, Muse, and Liaison International are offering archives of artwork and photographs. You have been asked to investigate the feasibility of using this new resource. Information about all four companies can be found on the World Wide Web. Pick two companies that provide digital images and find out more about their product. Prepare a brief report that answers the following questions. What kinds of illustrations are available? How are pictures on a specific subject located? How are the illustrations provided? What fees are involved? Would the cost be different for a high school student creating one paper than for an organization newsletter with a statewide distribution? Which company do you prefer? Why?

CASE STUDY 5 – Team Challenge   The new superintendent of Lisle Elementary School District 205 has recommended that **educational software** play a major role in the learning process at every grade level. In her presentation to the school board, she claimed that educational software is available for a wide variety of skills and subjects. She also indicated that educational software lets students learn at their own pace, shows infinite patience, and usually offers an entertaining approach. The president of the school board is not so sure. Unlike human instructors, educational software often does not recognize unique problems, fails to address individual goals, and provides limited feedback. Form a three-member team and investigate the use of educational software. Have each member of your team visit a software vendor's Web site, or an educational cooperative's Web site and list the advantages and disadvantages of using educational software. Select a program on the Web or from your school's education department library and use it. Note the subject being taught, the audience to which the software is directed, the approach used, and any special features. Then, meet with your team, discuss your findings, prepare a team report or PowerPoint presentation, and share it with your class.

The Components of the System Unit

Picture Yourself Computer Shopping

In the months since paying off your car, you have been saving up for your next large purchase — a personal computer. Your school offers a student discount for computers purchased online, so you hope to realize some savings from that. You have talked to several knowledgeable friends and coworkers about what you need and want in a computer. Armed with this knowledge and your wish list, you are ready to shop.

After visiting several computer vendors' Web sites and comparing prices and features, you finally decide on a model. Because you enjoy computer gaming, you opt for a high-performance video card. You also are staff photographer for your school's newspaper, so you want to have the necessary storage to work with digital photographs. The model you have chosen has an Intel Core 2 Duo processor, 4 GB of dual-channel DDR2 SDRAM, and a 500 GB SATA hard drive. With a DVI port, eight USB 2.0 ports, two FireWire ports, built-in card readers, a headphone jack, speakers, a network card, and a CD/DVD drive, it should more than meet your needs. The computer's preloaded software includes the Microsoft Windows Vista operating system. You are delighted to see that the vendor is offering an online promotion of free shipping and a free upgrade to a flat-panel display. You submit your order and look forward to it being delivered right to your door.

By buying online, you have a computer customized to your needs, but you also know you have much to learn. Read Chapter 4 to learn about drives, adapter cards, processors, ports, RAM, and other components of the system unit.

After completing this chapter, you will be able to:

1. Differentiate among various styles of system units

2. Identify chips, adapter cards, and other components of a motherboard

3. Describe the components of a processor and how they complete a machine cycle

4. Identify characteristics of various personal computer processors on the market today

5. Define a bit and describe how a series of bits represents data

6. Explain how programs transfer in and out of memory

7. Differentiate among the various types of memory

8. Describe the types of expansion slots and adapter cards

9. Explain the differences among a serial port, a parallel port, a USB port, a FireWire port, and other ports

10. Describe how buses contribute to a computer's processing speed

11. Identify components in mobile computers and mobile devices

12. Understand how to clean a system unit

CONTENTS

THE SYSTEM UNIT

Whether you are a home user or a business user, you most likely will make the decision to purchase a new computer or upgrade an existing computer within the next several years. Thus, you should understand the purpose of each component in a computer. As Chapter 1 discussed, a computer includes devices used for input, processing, output, storage, and communications. Many of these components are part of the system unit.

The **system unit** is a case that contains electronic components of the computer used to process data. System units are available in a variety of shapes and sizes. The case of the system unit, sometimes called the *chassis*, is made of metal or plastic and protects the internal electronic components from damage. All computers have a system unit (Figure 4-1).

On desktop personal computers, the electronic components and most storage devices are part of the system unit. Other devices, such as the keyboard, mouse, microphone, monitor, printer, USB flash drive, portable media player, scanner, PC video camera, and speakers, normally occupy space outside the system unit. The trend is toward a smaller *form factor*, or size and shape, of the desktop personal computer system unit.

FIGURE 4-1   All sizes of computers have a system unit.

On notebook computers, the keyboard and pointing device often occupy the area on the top of the system unit, and the display attaches to the system unit by hinges. The location of the system unit on a Tablet PC varies, depending on the design of the Tablet PC. Some models build the system unit behind the display (as shown in Figure 4-1), while others position the system unit below the keyboard (shown later in the chapter). The system unit on an ultra personal computer, a PDA, and a smart phone usually consumes the entire device. On these mobile computers and devices, the display often is built into the system unit.

With game consoles, the input and output devices, such as controllers and a television, reside outside the system unit. On handheld game consoles and portable media players, by contrast, the packaging around the system unit houses the input devices and display.

At some point, you might have to open the system unit on a desktop personal computer to replace or install a new electronic component. For this reason, you should be familiar with the electronic components of a system unit. Figure 4-2 identifies some of these components, which include the processor, memory, adapter cards, drive bays, and the power supply.

The processor interprets and carries out the basic instructions that operate a computer. Memory typically holds data waiting to be processed and instructions waiting to be executed. The electronic components and circuitry of the system unit, such as the processor and memory, usually are part of or are connected to a circuit board called the motherboard. Many current motherboards also integrate sound, video, modem, and networking capabilities.

drive bays

sound card

video card

power supply

memory

processor

FIGURE 4-2 The system unit on a typical personal computer consists of numerous electronic components, some of which are shown in this figure. The sound card and video card are two types of adapter cards.

Adapter cards are circuit boards that provide connections and functions not built into the motherboard or expand on the capability of features integrated into the motherboard. For example, a sound card and a video card are two types of adapter cards found in some desktop personal computers today. Devices outside the system unit often attach to ports on the system unit by a connector on a cable. These devices may include a keyboard, mouse, microphone, monitor, printer, scanner, portable media player, USB flash drive, card reader/writer, digital camera, PC video camera, and speakers. A drive bay holds one or more disk drives. The power supply converts electricity from a power cord plugged in a wall outlet into a form that can be used by the computer.

The Motherboard

The **motherboard**, sometimes called a *system board*, is the main circuit board of the system unit. Many electronic components attach to the

motherboard; others are built into it. Figure 4-3 shows a photograph of a current desktop personal computer motherboard and identifies its expansion slots, processor chip, and memory slots. Memory chips are installed on memory cards (modules) that fit in a slot on the motherboard.

A computer **chip** is a small piece of semiconducting material, usually silicon, on which integrated circuits are etched. An *integrated circuit* contains many microscopic pathways capable of carrying electrical current. Each integrated circuit can contain millions of elements such as resistors, capacitors, and transistors. A *transistor*, for example, can act as an electronic switch that opens or closes the circuit for electrical charges. Most chips are no bigger than one-half-inch square. Manufacturers package chips so the chips can be attached to a circuit board, such as a motherboard or an adapter card. Specific types of chips are discussed later in the chapter.

WEB LINK 4-1

Motherboards

For more information, visit scsite.com/ dc2008/ch4/weblink and then click Motherboards.

expansion slots
for adapter cards

processor chip in
processor slot,
below cooling fan

slots for
memory
modules

motherboard

FIGURE 4-3   Many electronic components attach to the motherboard in a desktop personal computer, including a processor chip, memory modules, and adapter cards.

PROCESSOR

The **processor**, also called the **central processing unit (CPU)**, interprets and carries out the basic instructions that operate a computer. The processor significantly impacts overall computing power and manages most of a computer's operations. On larger computers, such as mainframes and supercomputers, the various functions performed by the processor extend over many separate chips and often multiple circuit boards. On a personal computer, all functions of the processor usually are on a single chip. Some computer and chip manufacturers use the term *microprocessor* to refer to a personal computer processor chip.

Processors contain a control unit and an arithmetic logic unit (ALU). These two components work together to perform processing operations. Figure 4-4 illustrates how other devices connected to the computer communicate with the processor to carry out a task.

The Control Unit

The **control unit** is the component of the processor that directs and coordinates most of the operations in the computer. The control unit has a role much like a traffic cop: it interprets each instruction issued by a program and then initiates the appropriate action to carry out the instruction. Types of internal components that the control unit directs include the arithmetic/logic unit, registers, and buses, each discussed later in this chapter. Read Ethics & Issues 4-1 for a related discussion.

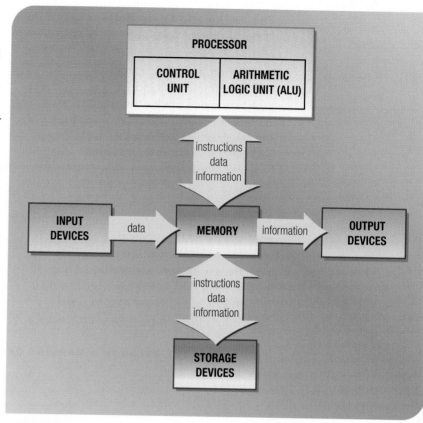

FIGURE 4-4 Most devices connected to the computer communicate with the processor to carry out a task. When a user starts a program, for example, its instructions transfer from a storage device to memory. Data needed by programs enters memory from either an input device or a storage device. The control unit interprets and executes instructions in memory, and the ALU performs calculations on the data in memory. Resulting information is stored in memory, from which it can be sent to an output device or a storage device for future access, as needed.

ETHICS & ISSUES 4-1

Can Computers Think?

Since the dawn of the computing age, people have wondered if a computer ever would be capable of thought. As computer processors and software become more powerful, the question is more hotly debated. People who believe computers can think argue that, if a person had a conversation with a computer and was convinced the computer was really human, then the computer is intelligent. This criteria is known as the Turing Test, named after British mathematician Alan Turing who proposed the test in 1950. If a computer can pass a modern version of the Turing Test, it is considered to be intelligent, and it may win the prestigious $100,000 Loebner Prize. Opponents counter this argument by saying that, if a question written in a foreign language was submitted to a person who can read and write the language and a person who cannot read or write the language but has a list of questions and appropriate answers, it might be impossible to tell the response of one person from the other. But, the person who cannot read or write the language really does not understand it, any more than a computer really can think. Besides, computers lack at least two essential components of human thinking — common sense and emotion. Computers can consider millions of chess moves a second, but humans have the common sense to recognize that some moves are not worthy of consideration. Can computers think? Why or why not? If computers cannot think now, might they be able to think in the future? Why? How important is emotion in the ability to think?

The Arithmetic Logic Unit

The **arithmetic logic unit** (*ALU*), another component of the processor, performs arithmetic, comparison, and other operations.

Arithmetic operations include basic calculations such as addition, subtraction, multiplication, and division. *Comparison operations* involve comparing one data item with another to determine whether the first item is greater than, equal to, or less than the other item. Depending on the result of the comparison, different actions may occur. For example, to determine if an employee should receive overtime pay, software instructs the ALU to compare the number of hours an employee worked during the week with the regular time hours allowed (e.g., 40 hours). If the hours worked are greater than 40, software instructs the ALU to perform calculations that compute the overtime wage.

Machine Cycle

For every instruction, a processor repeats a set of four basic operations, which comprise a *machine cycle* (Figure 4-5): (1) fetching, (2) decoding, (3) executing, and, if necessary, (4) storing. *Fetching* is the process of obtaining a program instruction or data item from memory. The term *decoding* refers to the process of translating the instruction into signals the computer can execute. *Executing* is the process of carrying out the commands. *Storing*, in this context, means writing the result to memory (not to a storage medium).

In some computers, the processor fetches, decodes, executes, and stores only one instruction at a time. In these computers, the processor waits until an instruction completes all four stages of the machine cycle (fetch, decode, execute, and store) before beginning work on the next instruction.

FIGURE 4-5 THE STEPS IN A MACHINE CYCLE

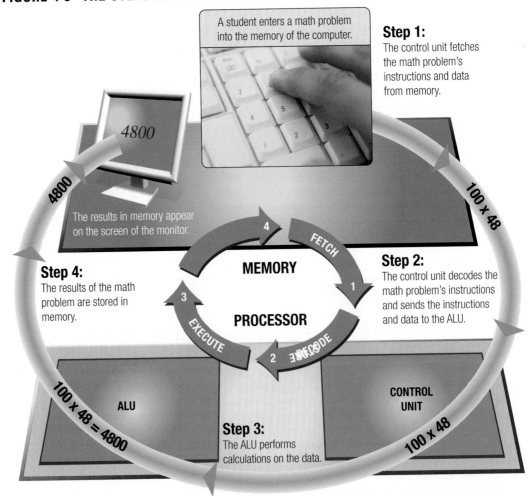

A student enters a math problem into the memory of the computer.

Step 1:
The control unit fetches the math problem's instructions and data from memory.

Step 2:
The control unit decodes the math problem's instructions and sends the instructions and data to the ALU.

Step 3:
The ALU performs calculations on the data.

Step 4:
The results of the math problem are stored in memory.

The results in memory appear on the screen of the monitor.

MEMORY

PROCESSOR

FETCH

DECODE

EXECUTE

ALU

CONTROL UNIT

4800

100 x 48

100 x 48 = 4800

100 x 48

Most of today's personal computers support a concept called pipelining. With *pipelining*, the processor begins fetching a second instruction before it completes the machine cycle for the first instruction. Processors that use pipelining are faster because they do not have to wait for one instruction to complete the machine cycle before fetching the next. Think of a pipeline as an assembly line. By the time the first instruction is in the last stage of the machine cycle, three other instructions could have been fetched and started through the machine cycle (Figure 4-6).

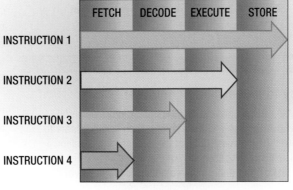

FIGURE 4-6 Most modern personal computers support pipelining. With pipelining, the processor fetches a second instruction before the first instruction is completed. The result is faster processing.

Registers

A processor contains small, high-speed storage locations, called *registers*, that temporarily hold data and instructions. Registers are part of the processor, not part of memory or a permanent storage device. Processors have many different types of registers, each with a specific storage function. Register functions include storing the location from where an instruction was fetched, storing an instruction while the control unit decodes it, storing data while the ALU computes it, and storing the results of a calculation.

The System Clock

The processor relies on a small quartz crystal circuit called the **system clock** to control the timing of all computer operations. Just as your heart beats at a regular rate to keep your body functioning, the system clock generates regular electronic pulses, or ticks, that set the operating pace of components of the system unit.

Each tick equates to a *clock cycle*. In the past, processors used one or more clock cycles to execute each instruction. Processors today often are *superscalar*, which means they can execute more than one instruction per clock cycle.

The pace of the system clock, called the **clock speed**, is measured by the number of ticks per second. Current personal computer processors have clock speeds in the gigahertz range. Giga is

a prefix that stands for billion, and a *hertz* is one cycle per second. Thus, one **gigahertz (GHz)** equals one billion ticks of the system clock per second. A computer that operates at 2.6 GHz has 2.6 billion (giga) clock cycles in one second (hertz).

The faster the clock speed, the more instructions the processor can execute per second. The speed of the system clock has no effect on devices such as a printer or disk drive. The speed of the system clock is just one factor that influences a computer's performance. Other factors, such as the type of processor chip, amount of cache, memory access time, bus width, and bus clock speed, are discussed later in this chapter.

FAQ 4-1

Does the system clock also keep track of the current date and time?

No, a separate battery-backed chip, called the *real-time clock*, keeps track of the date and time in a computer. The battery continues to run the real-time clock even when the computer is off. For more information, visit scsite.com/dc2008/ch4/faq and then click Computer Clock.

Some computer professionals measure a processor's speed according to the number of *MIPS* (*millions of instructions per second*) it can process. Current desktop personal computers can process more than 27,000 MIPS. No real standard for measuring MIPS exists, however, because different instructions require varying amounts of processing time. Read Looking Ahead 4-1 for a look at the next generation of processing speeds.

LOOKING AHEAD 4-1

Hybrid Technology to Power Supercomputer

In the race to build the world's fastest, more powerful computers, IBM is using a combination of processors to power a supercomputer that can process 1 quadrillion calculations per second.

IBM's *Roadrunner* supercomputer features a hybrid design that pairs conventional supercomputer processors with processors designed for Sony's PlayStation 3 and uses commercially available IBM hardware. The supercomputer's more than 16,000 AMD Opteron processors and more than 16,000 processors communicate continuously with each other to handle complex calculations with large numbers of constantly changing, interacting variables, such as those required for weather simulations.

When completed in 2008, the supercomputer will occupy 12,000 square feet at the Los Alamos National Laboratory. Roadrunner was designed in 2006 to reach four times the computing speed of the U.S. government's then fastest machine, IBM's Blue Gene, housed at the Lawrence Livermore National Laboratory.

For more information, visit scsite.com/dc2008/ch4/looking and then click Hybrid Supercomputer.

Dual-Core and Multi-Core Processors

Several processor chip manufacturers now offer dual-core and multi-core processors. A **dual-core processor** is a single chip that contains two separate processors. Similarly, a **multi-core processor** is a chip with two or more separate processors. Each processor on a dual-core/multi-core chip generally runs at a slower clock speed than a single-core processor, but dual-core/multi-core chips typically increase overall performance. Although a dual-core processor does not double the processing speed of a single-core processor, it can approach those speeds. The performance increase is especially noticeable when users are running multiple programs simultaneously such as antivirus software, spyware remover, e-mail program, instant messaging, media player, CD burning software, and photo editing software. Dual-core and multi-core processors also are energy efficient, requiring lower levels of power consumption and emitting less heat in the system unit.

WEB LINK 4-2

Multi-Core Processors

For more information, visit scsite.com/dc2008/ch4/weblink and then click Multi-Core Processors.

Comparison of Personal Computer Processors

The leading processor chip manufacturers for personal computers are Intel, AMD (Advanced Micro Devices), Transmeta, IBM, and Motorola. These manufacturers often identify their processor chips by a model name or model number. Figure 4-7 categorizes the historical development of the personal computer processor and documents the increases in clock speed and number of transistors in chips since 1982. The greater the number of transistors, the more complex and powerful the chip.

With its earlier processors, Intel used a model number to identify the various chips. After learning that processor model numbers could not be trademarked and protected from use by competitors, Intel began identifying its processors with names. Most high-performance PCs today use a processor in the Intel **Core** family or the **Pentium** family. Less expensive, basic PCs use a brand of Intel processor in the **Celeron** family. The **Xeon** and **Itanium** families of processors are ideal for workstations and low-end servers.

Today, AMD is the leading manufacturer of *Intel-compatible processors*, which have an internal design similar to Intel processors, perform the same functions, and can be as powerful, but often are less expensive. Transmeta, also a manufacturer of Intel-compatible processors, specializes in processors for mobile computers and devices. Intel and Intel-compatible processors are used in PCs.

Until recently, Apple computers used only an *IBM processor* or a *Motorola processor*, which had a design different from the Intel-style processor. Today's Apple computers, however, use Intel processors.

In the past, chip manufacturers listed a processor's clock speed in marketing literature and advertisements. As previously mentioned, though, clock speed is only one factor that impacts processing speed in today's computers. To help consumers evaluate various processors, manufacturers such as Intel and AMD now use a numbering scheme that more accurately reflects the processing speed of their chips.

Processor chips include technologies to improve processing performance. For example, many processors today use dual-core or multi-core chips. Some of Intel's processor chips contain *Hyper-Threading* (*HT*) *Technology*, which improves

COMPARISON OF PERSONAL COMPUTER PROCESSORS

* Clock speed is not the only factor that determines processor performance.

	NAME	DATE INTRODUCED/ UPDATED	MANUFACTURER	CLOCK SPEED*	NUMBER OF TRANSISTORS
SERVER PROCESSORS	Xeon	2001/2006	Intel	1.4 – 3.73 GHz	42 – 169 million
	Itanium 2	2003/2006	Intel	1.3 – 1.66 GHz	220 – 410 million
	Itanium	2001	Intel	733 – 800 MHz	25.4 – 60 million
	Pentium III Xeon	1999/2000	Intel	500 – 900 MHz	9.5 – 28 million
	Pentium II Xeon	1998/1999	Intel	400 – 450 MHz	7.5 – 27 million
	Opteron	2003/2006	AMD	1.4 – 3 GHz	233 million
	Athlon MP	2002	AMD	1.53 – 2.25 GHz	54.3 million
DESKTOP PERSONAL COMPUTER PROCESSORS	Core 2 Extreme	2006	Intel	2.93 GHz	291 million
	Core 2 Duo	2006	Intel	1.86 – 2.66 GHz	291 million
	Pentium Extreme Edition	2005/2006	Intel	3.2 – 3.73 GHz	178 million
	Pentium D	2005/2006	Intel	2.66 – 3.6 GHz	376 million
	Pentium 4	2000/2005	Intel	1.3 – 3.8 GHz	42 – 178 million
	Pentium III	1999/2003	Intel	450 MHz – 1.4 GHz	9.5 – 44 million
	Celeron D	2004/2006	Intel	2.13 – 3.46 GHz	26.2 – 125 million
	Celeron	1998/2003	Intel	266 MHz – 2.8 GHz	7.5 – 55 million
	Pentium II	1997/1998	Intel	233 – 450 MHz	7.5 million
	Pentium Pro	1995/1999	Intel	150 – 200 MHz	5.5 million
	Pentium	1993/1997	Intel	75 – 233 MHz	3.3 – 4.5 million
	80486DX	1989/1994	Intel	25 – 100 MHz	1.6 million
	80386	1985/1990	Intel	16 – 33 MHz	275,000
	80286	1982	Intel	6 – 12 MHz	134,000
	Athlon 64 FX/X2	2005	AMD	2 – 2.8 GHz	114 – 233 million
	Sempron	2004	AMD	1.5 – 2 GHz	68.5 million
	Athlon 64	2003/2004	AMD	2 – 2.4 GHz	105.9 – 114 million
	Athlon	1999/2002	AMD	500 MHz – 1.4 GHz	22 – 38 million
	Duron	1999/2001	AMD	600 MHz – 1.3 GHz	25 million
	AMD–K6	1997/1999	AMD	300 – 450 MHz	8.8 – 21.3 million
	PowerPC (G1 to G5)	1994/2005	Motorola/IBM	60 MHz – 2.7 GHz	2.8 – 58 million
	68040	1989	Motorola	25 – 40 MHz	1.2 million
	68030	1987	Motorola	16 – 50 MHz	270,000
	68020	1984	Motorola	16 – 33 MHz	190,000
MOBILE PROCESSORS	Core 2 Duo	2006	Intel	1.66 – 2.33 GHz	291 million
	Core Duo	2006	Intel	1.20 – 2.33 GHz	151 million
	Core Solo	2006	Intel	1.06 – 1.83 GHz	151 million
	Celeron M	2004	Intel	900 MHz – 1.6 GHz	55 million
	Pentium M	2003/2004	Intel	1.10 – 2 GHz	77 – 140 million
	Mobile Celeron	1999/2003	Intel	266 MHz – 2.8 GHz	18.9 million
	Mobile Pentium 4	1997/2002	Intel	200 MHz – 3.46 GHz	55 million
	Turion 64	2005	AMD	1.6 – 2 GHz	114 million
	Mobile Sempron	2004	AMD	1.6 – 1.8 GHz	37.5 million
	Mobile Athlon	2001/2002	AMD	1.4 – 2.2 GHz	37.5 – 105.9 million
	Mobile Duron	2000/2001	AMD	1.3 GHz	25 million
	Efficeon	2003	Transmeta	1 – 1.7 GHz	79 million
	Crusoe	2000	Transmeta	500 MHz – 1 GHz	6.7 million

FIGURE 4-7 A comparison of some processors.

processing power and time by allowing a processor to mimic the power of two processors. Most processors have built-in instructions to improve the performance of multimedia and 3-D graphics.

Processors for notebook computers include technology to integrate wireless capabilities and optimize and extend battery life. For example, Intel's *Centrino* and *Centrino Duo* mobile technology integrates wireless capabilities in notebook computers and Tablet PCs. PDAs and other smaller mobile devices often use a processor that consumes less power yet offers high performance.

Another type of processor, called *system on a chip*, integrates the functions of a processor, memory, and a video card on a single chip. Lower-priced personal computers, Tablet PCs, networking devices, portable media players, and game consoles sometimes have a system-on-a-chip processor. The goal of system-on-a-chip manufacturers is to create processors that have faster clock speeds, consume less power, are small, and are cost effective.

Buying a Personal Computer

If you are ready to buy a new computer, the processor you select should depend on how you plan to use the computer. If you purchase an IBM-compatible PC or Apple computer, you will choose an Intel processor or, in some cases, an Intel-compatible processor (Figure 4-8).

Most users will realize greater processing performance with a dual-core/multi-core processor. Intel's dual-core and multi-core processors also include *vPro technology*, which provides the ability to track computer hardware and software, diagnose and resolve computer problems, and secure computers from outside threats. If you plan to purchase an entertainment desktop computer, you will want it to use Intel's *Viiv technology*, which is designed to enhance digital entertainment through a home computer.

Instead of buying an entirely new computer, you might be able to upgrade your processor to increase the computer's performance. Be certain the processor you buy is compatible with your computer's motherboard; otherwise, you will have to replace the motherboard, too. Replacing a processor is a fairly simple process, whereas replacing a motherboard is much more complicated.

For detailed computer purchasing guidelines, read the Buyer's Guide 2008 feature that follows Chapter 8. Read Ethics & Issues 4-2 for a related discussion.

GUIDELINES FOR SELECTING AN INTEL OR INTEL-COMPATIBLE PROCESSOR

USE			
• Power users with workstations • Low-end servers on a network	Itanium 2	Xeon	Opteron
• Power users or users who design professional drawings; produce and edit videos; record and edit music; participate in video conferences; create professional Web sites; play graphic-intensive multiplayer Internet games • Users who design professional documents containing graphics such as newsletters or number-intensive spreadsheets; produce multimedia presentations; use the Web as an intensive research tool; send documents and graphics via the Web; watch videos; play graphic-intensive games on CD or DVD; create personal Web sites • Home users who manage personal finances; create basic documents with word processing and spreadsheet software; edit photographs; communicate with others on the Web via e-mail, chat rooms, and discussions; shop on the Web; create basic Web pages; use the computer as a digital entertainment unit	Core 2 Duo Athlon 64 FX	Core 2 Extreme Athlon 64 X2	
• Home users who manage personal finances; create basic documents with word processing and spreadsheet software; edit photographs; make greeting cards and calendars; use educational or entertainment CDs; communicate with others on the Web via e-mail, chat rooms, and discussions	Celeron D	Sempron	
• Users with mobile computers or mobile devices	Core 2 Duo	Efficeon	Turion 64

FIGURE 4-8
Determining which processor to obtain when you purchase a computer depends on computer usage.

FAQ 4-2

What is Moore's Law?

Moore's Law is a prediction made by one of the founders of Intel, Gordon Moore, that the number of transistors and resistors placed on computer chips would double every year, with a proportional increase in computing power and decrease in cost. The chart below shows the growth of Intel processors. For more information, read the Technology Trailblazer article on page 219 and visit scsite.com/dc2008/ch4/faq and then click Moore's Law.

Intel Processor Chip Complexity

ETHICS & ISSUES 4-2

Discarded Computer Components: Whose Problem Is It?

Experts estimate that about 1 billion computers will be discarded by 2010. The discarded items often are known as *e-waste*. As technology advances and prices fall, many people think of computers as disposable items. Computers contain several toxic elements, including lead, mercury, and barium. Computers thrown into landfills or burned in incinerators can pollute the ground and the air. A vast amount of e-waste ends up polluting third world countries. One solution is to recycle old computers. Some lawmakers prefer a more aggressive approach, such as setting up a recycling program that would be paid for by adding a $10 fee to a computer's purchase price, or forcing computer makers to be responsible for collecting and recycling their products. California already requires a $6 to $10 recycling fee for any products sold that include a CRT monitor. Manufacturers have taken steps, such as offering to recycle old computers and using energy efficient and environmentally friendly manufacturing techniques, but some claim that consumers should bear the responsibility of disposing of their old computer parts. Several have reduced the amount of toxic material in their products, and manufacturers have set up their own recycling programs, for which users pay a fee. What can be done to ensure that computers are disposed of safely? Should government, manufacturers, or users be responsible for safe disposal? Why? How can computer users be motivated to recycle obsolete equipment?

Heat Sinks, Heat Pipes, and Liquid Cooling

Processor chips generate quite a bit of heat, which could cause the chip to burn up. Although the computer's main fan generates airflow, many of today's processors require additional cooling. A *heat sink* is a small ceramic or metal component with fins on its surface that absorbs and disperses heat produced by electrical components such as a processor (Figure 4-9). Some heat sinks are packaged as part of a processor chip. Others are installed on the top or the side of the chip. Because a heat sink consumes extra space, a smaller device called a *heat pipe* cools processors in notebook computers.

Some computers use liquid cooling technology to reduce the temperature of a processor. *Liquid cooling technology* uses a continuous flow of fluid(s), such as water and glycol, in a process that transfers the heated fluid away from the processor to a radiator-type grill, which cools the liquid, and then returns the cooled fluid to the processor.

Mobile computers and devices often have Low Voltage or Ultra Low Voltage (ULV) processors, which have such low power demands that they do not require additional cooling.

FIGURE 4-9 A heat sink, which is attached to the top of a processor, prevents the chip from overheating. The heat sink fan, which attaches to the top of the heat sink, helps distribute air dissipated by the heat sink.

Parallel Processing

Parallel processing is a method that uses multiple processors simultaneously to execute a single program or task (Figure 4-10). Parallel processing divides a single problem into portions so that multiple processors work on their assigned portion of the problem at the same time. Parallel processing requires special software that recognizes how to divide the problem and then bring the results back together again.

Some personal computers implement parallel processing with dual-core processors or multi-core processors. Others have two or more separate processor chips, respectively called dual processor or multiprocessor computers.

Massively parallel processing is large scale parallel processing that involves hundreds or thousands of processors. Supercomputers use massively parallel processing for applications such as artificial intelligence and weather forecasting. Some applications draw on the idle time of home users' personal computers to achieve parallel processing. For example, the *SETI@home* scientific project runs a program on home users' Internet-connected computers whose purpose is to detect possible intelligent life outside Earth.

Test your knowledge of pages 184 through 194 in Quiz Yourself 4-1.

 QUIZ YOURSELF 4-1

Instructions: Find the true statement below. Then, rewrite the remaining false statements so they are true.

1. A computer chip is a small piece of semiconducting material, usually silicon, on which integrated circuits are etched.

2. Four basic operations in a machine cycle are: (1) comparing, (2) decoding, (3) executing, and, if necessary, (4) pipelining.

3. Processors contain a motherboard and an arithmetic logic unit (ALU).

4. The central processing unit, sometimes called a system board, is the main circuit board of the system unit.

5. The leading processor chip manufacturers for personal computers are Microsoft, AMD, IBM, Motorola, and Transmeta.

6. The pace of the system clock, called the clock speed, is measured by the number of ticks per minute.

7. The system unit is a case that contains mechanical components of the computer used to process data.

Quiz Yourself Online: To further check your knowledge of system unit styles, motherboards, processor components and machine cycles, and characteristics of personal computer processors, visit scsite.com/dc2008/ch4/quiz and then click Objectives 1 – 4.

DATA REPRESENTATION

To understand fully the way a computer processes data, you should know how a computer represents data. People communicate through speech by combining words into sentences. Human speech is **analog** because it uses continuous (wave form) signals that vary in strength and quality. Most computers are **digital**. They recognize only two discrete states: on and off. This is because computers are electronic devices powered by electricity, which also has only two states: on and off.

The two digits, 0 and 1, easily can represent these two states (Figure 4-11). The digit 0 represents the electronic state of off (absence of an electronic charge). The digit 1 represents the electronic state of on (presence of an electronic charge).

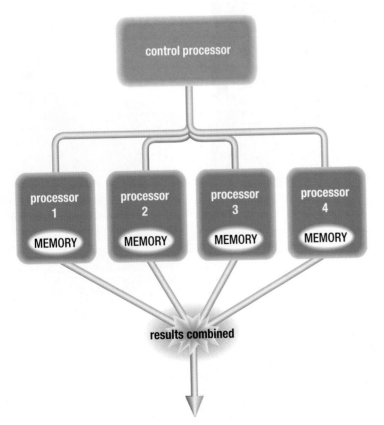

FIGURE 4-10 Parallel processing divides a problem into portions so that multiple processors work on their assigned portion of a problem at the same time. In this illustration, one processor, called the control processor, is managing the operations of four other processors.

When people count, they use the digits in the [de]cimal system (0 through 9). The computer, by [co]ntrast, uses a binary system because it recog[niz]es only two states. The **binary system** is a [nu]mber system that has just two unique digits, [0] and 1, called bits. A **bit** (short for *binary digit*) [is] the smallest unit of data the computer can [pr]ocess. By itself, a bit is not very informative. [W]hen 8 bits are grouped together as a unit, [the]y form a **byte**. A byte provides enough differ[en]t combinations of 0s and 1s to represent 256 [in]dividual characters. These characters include [nu]mbers, uppercase and lowercase letters of the [alp]habet, punctuation marks, and others, such as [the] letters of the Greek alphabet.

The combinations of 0s and 1s that represent [ch]aracters are defined by patterns called a cod[in]g scheme. In one coding scheme, the number [4 i]s represented as 00110100, the number 6 as [00]110110, and the capital letter E as 01000101 [(Fi]gure 4-12). Two popular coding schemes are [AS]CII and EBCDIC (Figure 4-13). The American [Sta]ndard Code for Information Interchange (*ASCII* [pr]onounced ASK-ee) scheme is the most widely [us]ed coding system to represent data. Most [pe]rsonal computers and servers use the ASCII [co]ding scheme. The Extended Binary Coded [De]cimal Interchange Code (*EBCDIC* pronounced [EB]-see-dik) scheme is used primarily on [ma]inframe computers and high-end servers.

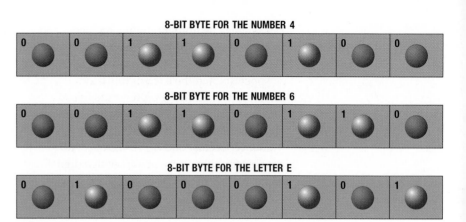

8-BIT BYTE FOR THE NUMBER 4

8-BIT BYTE FOR THE NUMBER 6

8-BIT BYTE FOR THE LETTER E

FIGURE 4-12 Eight bits grouped together as a unit are called a byte. A byte represents a single character in the computer.

The ASCII and EBCDIC coding schemes are sufficient for English and Western European languages but are not large enough for Asian and other languages that use different alphabets. *Unicode* is a 16-bit coding scheme that has the capacity of representing more than 65,000 characters and symbols. The Unicode coding scheme is capable of representing almost all the world's current written languages, as well as classic and historical languages. To allow for expansion, Unicode reserves 30,000 codes for future use and 6,000 codes for private use. Unicode is implemented in several operating systems, including Windows Vista, Windows XP, Mac OS X, and Linux.

BINARY DIGIT (BIT)	ELECTRONIC CHARGE	ELECTRONIC STATE
1		ON
0		OFF

[FI]GURE 4-11 A computer circuit represents the [0 o]r the 1 electronically by the presence or absence [of] an electronic charge.

ASCII	SYMBOL	EBCDIC
00110000	0	11110000
00110001	1	11110001
00110010	2	11110010
00110011	3	11110011
00110100	4	11110100
00110101	5	11110101
00110110	6	11110110
00110111	7	11110111
00111000	8	11111000
00111001	9	11111001
01000001	A	11000001
01000010	B	11000010
01000011	C	11000011
01000100	D	11000100
01000101	E	11000101
01000110	F	11000110
01000111	G	11000111
01001000	H	11001000
01001001	I	11001001
01001010	J	11010001
01001011	K	11010010
01001100	L	11010011
01001101	M	11010100

ASCII	SYMBOL	EBCDIC
01001110	N	11010101
01001111	O	11010110
01010000	P	11010111
01010001	Q	11011000
01010010	R	11011001
01010011	S	11100010
01010100	T	11100011
01010101	U	11100100
01010110	V	11100101
01010111	W	11100110
01011000	X	11100111
01011001	Y	11101000
01011010	Z	11101001
00100001	!	01011010
00100010	"	01111111
00100011	#	01111011
00100100	$	01011011
00100101	%	01101100
00100110	&	01010000
00101000	(	01001101
00101001	)	01011101
00101010	*	01011100
00101011	+	01001110

FIGURE 4-13 Two popular coding schemes are ASCII and EBCDIC.

Unicode-enabled programming languages and software products include Java, XML, Microsoft Office, and Oracle.

Appendix A at the back of this book discusses the ASCII, EBCDIC, and Unicode schemes in more depth, along with the parity bit and number systems.

Coding schemes such as ASCII make it possible for humans to interact with a digital computer that processes only bits. When you press a key on a keyboard, a chip in the keyboard converts the key's electronic signal into a special code that is sent to the system unit. Then, the system unit converts the code into a binary form the computer can process and stores it in memory. Every character is converted to its corresponding byte. The computer then processes the data as bytes, which actually is a series of on/off electrical states. When processing is finished, software converts the byte into a human-recognizable number, letter of the alphabet, or special character that is displayed on a screen or is printed (Figure 4-14). All of these conversions take place so quickly that you do not realize they are occurring.

Standards, such as those defined by ASCII, EBCDIC, and Unicode, also make it possible for components in computers to communicate with each other successfully. By following these and other standards, manufacturers can produce a component and be assured that it will operate correctly in a computer.

FIGURE 4-14 HOW A LETTER IS CONVERTED TO BINARY FORM AND BACK

Step 1:
The user presses the capital letter T (SHIFT+T keys) on the keyboard, which in turn creates a special code for the capital letter T.

Step 2:
The scan code for the capital letter T is sent to the system unit.

Step 3:
The system unit converts the scan code for the capital letter T to its ASCII binary code (01010100) and stores it in memory for processing.

Step 4:
After processing, the binary code for the capital letter T is converted to an image and displayed on the output device.

MEMORY

Memory consists of electronic components that store instructions waiting to be executed by the processor, data needed by those instructions, and the results of processed data (information). Memory usually consists of one or more chips on the motherboard or some other circuit board in the computer.

Memory stores three basic categories of items: (1) the operating system and other system software that control or maintain the computer and its devices; (2) application programs that carry out a specific task such as word processing; and (3) the data being processed by the application programs and resulting information. This role of memory to store both data and programs is known as the *stored program concept*.

Bytes and Addressable Memory

A byte (character) is the basic storage unit in memory. When application program instructions and data are transferred to memory from storage devices, the instructions and data exist as bytes. Each byte resides temporarily in a location in memory that has an *address*. An address simply is a unique number that identifies the location of a byte in memory. The illustration in Figure 4-15 shows how seats in a concert hall are similar to addresses in memory: (1) a seat, which is identified by a unique seat number, holds one person at a time, and a

location in memory, which is identified by a unique address, holds a single byte; and (2) both a seat, identified by a seat number, and a byte, identified by an address, can be empty. To access data or instructions in memory, the computer references the addresses that contain bytes of data.

Memory Sizes

Manufacturers state the size of memory chips and storage devices in terms of the number of bytes the chip or device has available for storage (Figure 4-16). Recall that storage devices hold data, instructions, and information for future use, while most memory holds these items temporarily. A **kilobyte** (**KB** or **K**) is equal to exactly 1,024 bytes. To simplify memory and storage definitions, computer users often round a kilobyte down to 1,000 bytes. For example, if a memory chip can store 100 KB, it can hold approximately 100,000 bytes (characters). A **megabyte** (**MB**) is equal to approximately 1 million bytes. A **gigabyte** (**GB**) equals approximately 1 billion bytes. A **terabyte** (**TB**) is equal to approximately 1 trillion bytes.

MEMORY AND STORAGE SIZES

Term	Abbreviation	Approximate Number of Bytes	Exact Amount of Bytes	Approximate Number of Pages of Text
Kilobyte	KB or K	1 thousand	1,024	1/2
Megabyte	MB	1 million	1,048,576	500
Gigabyte	GB	1 billion	1,073,741,824	500,000
Terabyte	TB	1 trillion	1,099,511,627,776	500,000,000

FIGURE 4-16 Terms commonly used to define memory and storage sizes.

Types of Memory

The system unit contains two types of memory: volatile and nonvolatile. When the computer's power is turned off, *volatile memory* loses its contents. *Nonvolatile memory*, by contrast, does not lose its contents when power is removed from the computer. Thus, volatile memory is temporary and nonvolatile memory is permanent. RAM is the most common type of volatile memory. Examples of nonvolatile memory include ROM, flash memory, and CMOS. The following pages discuss these types of memory.

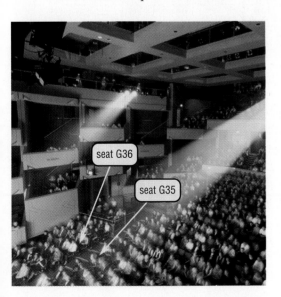

FIGURE 4-15 Seats in a concert hall are similar to addresses in memory: a seat holds one person at a time, and a location in memory holds a single byte; and both a seat and a byte can be empty.

RAM

Users typically are referring to RAM when discussing computer memory. **RAM** (*random access memory*), also called *main memory*, consists of memory chips that can be read from and written to by the processor and other devices. When you turn on power to a computer, certain operating system files (such as the files that determine how the Windows Vista desktop appears) load into RAM from a storage device such as a hard disk. These files remain in RAM as long as the computer has continuous power. As additional programs and data are requested, they also load into RAM from storage.

The processor interprets and executes a program's instructions while the program is in RAM. During this time, the contents of RAM may change (Figure 4-17). RAM can accommodate multiple programs simultaneously.

Most RAM is volatile, which means it loses its contents when the power is removed from the computer. For this reason, you must save any data, instructions, and information you

FIGURE 4-17 HOW PROGRAM INSTRUCTIONS TRANSFER IN AND OUT OF RAM

Step 1:
When you start the computer, certain operating system files are loaded into RAM from the hard disk. The operating system displays the user interface on the screen.

hard disk — RAM — operating system instructions — operating system interface

Step 2:
When you start a Web browser, the program's instructions are loaded into RAM from the hard disk. The Web browser and certain operating system instructions are in RAM. The Web browser window is displayed on the screen.

hard disk — RAM — Web browser instructions — Web browser window

Step 3:
When you start a paint program, the program's instructions are loaded into RAM from the hard disk. The paint program, along with the Web browser and certain operating system instructions, are in RAM. The paint program window is displayed on the screen.

hard disk — RAM — paint program instructions — Web browser and paint program windows

Step 4:
When you quit a program, such as the Web browser, its program instructions are removed from RAM. The Web browser no longer is displayed on the screen.

RAM — Web browser program instructions are removed from RAM — Web browser window no longer is displayed on desktop may need in the future. Saving is the process of copying data, instructions, and information from RAM to a storage device such as a hard disk.

Three basic types of RAM chips exist: dynamic RAM, static RAM, and magnetoresistive RAM.

- *Dynamic RAM* (*DRAM* pronounced DEE-ram) chips must be re-energized constantly or they lose their contents. Many variations of DRAM chips exist, most of which are faster than the basic DRAM. *Synchronous DRAM* (*SDRAM*) chips are much faster than DRAM chips because they are synchronized to the system clock. Double Data Rate SDRAM (*DDR SDRAM*) chips are even faster than SDRAM chips because they transfer data twice for each clock cycle, instead of just once, and DDR2 is even faster than DDR. Dual channel SDRAM is faster than single channel SDRAM because it delivers twice the amount of data to the processor. *Rambus DRAM* (*RDRAM*) is yet another type of DRAM that is much faster than SDRAM because it uses pipelining techniques. Most personal computers today use some form of SDRAM chips or RDRAM chips.

- *Static RAM* (*SRAM* pronounced ESS-ram) chips are faster and more reliable than any variation of DRAM chips. These chips do not have to be re-energized as often as DRAM chips, thus, the term static. SRAM chips, however, are much more expensive than DRAM chips. Special applications such as cache use SRAM chips. A later section in this chapter discusses cache.

- A newer type of RAM, called *magnetoresistive RAM* (*MRAM* pronounced EM-ram), stores data using magnetic charges instead of electrical charges. Manufacturers claim that MRAM has greater storage capacity, consumes less power, and has faster access times than electronic RAM. Also, MRAM retains its contents after power is removed from the computer, which could prevent loss of data for users. As the cost of MRAM declines, experts predict MRAM could replace both DRAM and SRAM.

RAM chips usually reside on a **memory module**, which is a small circuit board. **Memory slots** on the motherboard hold memory modules (Figure 4-18). Three types of memory modules are SIMMs, DIMMs, and RIMMs. A *SIMM* (*single inline memory module*)

has pins on opposite sides of the circuit board that connect together to form a single set of contacts. With a *DIMM* (*dual inline memory module*), by contrast, the pins on opposite sides of the circuit board do not connect and thus form two sets of contacts. SIMMs and DIMMs typically hold SDRAM chips. A *RIMM* (*Rambus inline memory module*) houses RDRAM chips. For a more technical discussion about RAM, read the High-Tech Talk article on page 218 at the end of this chapter.

WEB LINK 4-3

RAM
For more information, visit scsite.com/dc2008/ch4/weblink and then click RAM.

FIGURE 4-18 This photo shows a memory module being inserted in a motherboard.

RAM CONFIGURATIONS The amount of RAM necessary in a computer often depends on the types of software you plan to use. A computer executes programs that are in RAM. Think of RAM as the workspace on the top of your desk. Just as the top of your desk needs a certain amount of space to hold papers, a computer needs a certain amount of memory to store programs, data, and information. The more RAM a computer has, the faster the computer will respond.

A software package typically indicates the minimum amount of RAM it requires. If you want the application to perform optimally, usually you need more than the minimum specifications on the software package.

Generally, home users running Windows Vista and using basic application software such as word processing should have at least 512 MB of RAM. Most business users who work with accounting, financial, or spreadsheet programs, and programs requiring multimedia capabilities should have a minimum of 1 GB of RAM. Users creating professional Web sites or using graphics-intensive applications will want at least 2 GB of RAM.

Figure 4-19a lists guidelines for the amount of RAM for various types of users. Figure 4-19b shows advertisements that match to each user requirement. Advertisements normally list the type of processor, the clock speed of the processor, and the amount of RAM in the computer. The amount of RAM in computers purchased today ranges from 512 MB to 16 GB. In an advertisement, manufacturers specify the maximum amount of RAM a computer can hold, for example, 1 GB expandable to 2 GB. Read Ethics & Issues 4-3 for a related discussion.

FAQ 4-3

Can I add more RAM to my computer?

Check your computer documentation to see how much RAM you can add. RAM modules are relatively inexpensive and usually include easy-to-follow installation instructions. Be sure to purchase RAM compatible with your brand and model of computer. For more information, visit scsite.com/dc2008/ch4/faq and then click Upgrading RAM.

ETHICS & ISSUES 4-3

Should Schools Supply Computers to All Students?

Around the country and around the world, local and national governments have begun to supply school-children with inexpensive notebook computers. Many school districts in the United States purchase a note-book computer priced at approximately $600 for each student when the student enters a particular grade level. The United Nations endorses a plan known as *One Laptop per Child* to supply $100 notebook comput-ers to developing countries, some of which already pledged to purchase millions of the devices for school-children. The device, which recharges with a hand crank, includes Wi-Fi networking and a simple, intuitive user interface. Supporters of these plans maintain that computer literacy and electronic communication are vital skills in today's world, and students should be introduced to computers as early in their school years as possible. Many people oppose plans to equip every student with a computer because they say that the technology detracts from traditional educational sub-jects, such as basic reading and math. They also point out the number of college instructors who ban the use of computers in the classroom. The computers require maintenance, support, and instructional time to teach students how to use the devices. Young children may lack the responsibility to care for and use the comput-ers properly. Should schools supply computers to all students? Why or why not? What is the appropriate grade level at which to require computer literacy? Why? Who should bear the cost of purchasing required computers for students? Why?

FIGURE 4-19a (RAM guidelines)

RAM	512 MB to 1 GB	1 GB to 2 GB	2 GB and up
Use	Home and business users managing personal finances; using standard application software such as word processing; using educational or entertainment CD-ROMs; communicating with others on the Web	Users requiring more advanced multimedia capabilities; running number-intensive accounting, financial, or spreadsheet programs; using voice recognition; working with videos, music, and digital imaging; creating Web sites; participating in video conferences; playing Internet games	Power users creating professional Web sites; running sophisticated CAD, 3-D design, or other graphics-intensive software

FIGURE 4-19b (computers for sale)

Model	A200	I280	A220	I213	I293	A280
Processor	2.00 GHz Sempron processor	2.80 GHz Celeron D processor	2.20 GHz Athlon 64 X2 processor	2.13 GHz Core 2 Duo processor	2.93 GHz Core 2 Extreme processor	2.80 GHz Opteron processor
Memory	512 MB DDR SDRAM	1 GB DDR SDRAM	1 GB DDR2 SDRAM	2 GB DDR2 SDRAM	4 GB DDR2 SDRAM	4 GB DDR2 SDRAM

FIGURE 4-19 Determining how much RAM you need depends on the applications you intend to run on your computer. Advertisements for computers normally list the type of processor, the speed of the processor, and the amount of RAM installed.

Cache

Most of today's computers improve processing times with **cache** (pronounced cash). Two types of cache are memory cache and disk cache. This chapter discusses memory cache. Chapter 7 discusses disk cache.

Memory cache helps speed the processes of the computer because it stores frequently used instructions and data. Most personal computers today have two types of memory cache: L1 cache and L2 cache. Some also have L3 cache.

- *L1 cache* is built directly in the processor chip. L1 cache usually has a very small capacity, ranging from 8 KB to 128 KB. The more common sizes for personal computers are 32 KB or 64 KB.

- *L2 cache* is slightly slower than L1 cache but has a much larger capacity, ranging from 64 KB to 16 MB. When discussing cache, most users are referring to L2 cache. Current processors include *advanced transfer cache* (*ATC*), a type of L2 cache built directly on the processor chip. Processors that use ATC perform at much faster rates than those that do not use it.

Personal computers today typically have from 512 KB to 4 MB of advanced transfer cache. Servers and workstations have from 4 MB to 6 MB of advanced transfer cache.

- *L3 cache* is a cache on the motherboard that is separate from the processor chip. L3 cache exists only on computers that use L2 advanced transfer cache. Personal computers often have up to 2 MB of L3 cache; servers and workstations have from 8 MB to 24 MB of L3 cache.

Cache speeds up processing time because it stores frequently used instructions and data. When the processor needs an instruction or data, it searches memory in this order: L1 cache, then L2 cache, then L3 cache (if it exists), then RAM — with a greater delay in processing for each level of memory it must search (Figure 4-20). If the instruction or data is not found in memory, then it must search a slower speed storage medium such as a hard disk, CD, or DVD.

ROM

Read-only memory (**ROM** pronounced rahm) refers to memory chips storing permanent data and instructions. The data on most ROM chips cannot be modified — hence, the name read-only. ROM is nonvolatile, which means its contents are not lost when power is removed from the computer. In addition to computers, many devices contain ROM chips. For example, ROM chips in printers contain data for fonts.

WEB LINK 4-4

Cache
For more information, visit scsite.com/ dc2008/ch4/weblink and then click Cache.

PROCESSOR CHIP

L1 cache — part of processor

L1 cache - fastest access

L2 cache — part of processor

slower access than L1 cache

L3 cache — separate chip between processor and RAM

slower access than L1 and L2 cache

RAM

slower access than L1, L2, and L3 cache

FIGURE 4-20 Cache helps speed processing times when the processor requests data, instructions, or information.

Manufacturers of ROM chips often record data, instructions, or information on the chips when they manufacture the chips. These ROM chips, called **firmware**, contain permanently written data, instructions, or information.

A *PROM* (*programmable read-only memory*) *chip* is a blank ROM chip on which a programmer can write permanently. Programmers use *microcode* instructions to program a PROM chip. Once a programmer writes the microcode on the PROM chip, it functions like a regular ROM chip and cannot be erased or changed.

A variation of the PROM chip, called an *EEPROM* (electrically erasable programmable read-only memory) *chip*, allows a programmer to erase the microcode with an electric signal.

Flash Memory

Flash memory is a type of nonvolatile memory that can be erased electronically and rewritten, similar to EEPROM. Most computers use flash memory to hold their startup instructions because it allows the computer easily to update its contents. For example, when the computer changes from standard time to daylight savings time, the contents of a flash memory chip (and the real-time clock chip) change to reflect the new time.

Flash memory chips also store data and programs on many mobile computers and devices, such as PDAs, smart phones, printers, digital cameras, automotive devices, portable media players, digital voice recorders, and pagers. When you enter names and addresses in a PDA or smart phone, a flash memory chip stores the data. Some portable media players store music on flash memory chips (Figure 4-21); others store music on tiny hard disks or flash memory cards. A later section in this chapter discusses flash memory cards, which contain flash memory on a removable device instead of a chip.

WEB LINK 4-5

Flash Memory
For more information, visit scsite.com/dc2008/ch4/weblink and then click Flash Memory.

FAQ 4-4

How much music can I store on a portable media player?

Portable media players that store music on flash memory chips can hold up to 2,000 songs. Portable media players with tiny hard disks have a much greater storage capacity — from 1,000 to 20,000 songs. For more information, visit scsite.com/dc2008/ch4/faq and then click Portable Media Players.

FIGURE 4-21   HOW A PORTABLE MEDIA PLAYER MIGHT STORE MUSIC IN FLASH MEMORY

Step 1:
Purchase and download music tracks from a Web site. With one end of a special cable connected to the system unit, connect the other end to the USB port in the portable media player.

Step 2:
Instruct the computer to copy the music tracks to a flash memory chip in the portable media player.

Step 3:
Plug the earphones in the portable media player, push a button on the portable media player, and listen to the music through the earphones.

flash memory chips

USB port

from the computer

portable media player

earphones cable

CMOS

Some RAM chips, flash memory chips, and other types of memory chips use **complementary metal-oxide semiconductor** (**CMOS** pronounced SEE-moss) technology because it provides high speeds and consumes little power. CMOS technology uses battery power to retain information even when the power to the computer is off. Battery-backed CMOS memory chips, for example, can keep the calendar, date, and time current even when the computer is off. The flash memory chips that store a computer's startup information often use CMOS technology.

FAQ 4-5

What should I do if my computer's date and time are wrong?

First, try resetting the date and time. To do this in Windows Vista, double-click the time at the right edge of the taskbar. If the computer continues to lose time or display an incorrect date, you may need to replace the CMOS battery on the motherboard that powers the system clock. For more information, visit scsite.com/dc2008/ch4/faq and then click CMOS Battery.

Memory Access Times

Access time is the amount of time it takes the processor to read data, instructions, and information from memory. A computer's access time directly affects how fast the computer processes data. Accessing data in memory can be more than 200,000 times faster than accessing data on a hard disk because of the mechanical motion of the hard disk.

Today's manufacturers use a variety of terminology to state access times (Figure 4-22). Some use fractions of a second, which for memory occurs in nanoseconds. A **nanosecond** (abbreviated *ns*) is one billionth of a second. A nanosecond is extremely fast (Figure 4-23). In fact, electricity travels about one foot in a nanosecond.

Other manufacturers state access times in MHz; for example, 667 MHz DDR2 SDRAM. If a manufacturer states access time in megahertz, you can convert it to nanoseconds by dividing 1 billion ns by the megahertz number. For example, 667 MHz equals approximately 1.5 ns (1,000,000,000/667,000,000).

The access time (speed) of memory contributes to the overall performance of the computer. Standard SDRAM chips can have access times up to 133 MHz (about 7.5 ns), and access times of the DDR SDRAM chips reach 667 MHz. The higher the megahertz, the faster the access time; conversely, the lower the nanoseconds, the faster the access time. The faster RDRAM chips can have access times up to 1600 MHz (about 0.625 ns). ROM access times range from 25 to 250 ns.

While access times of memory greatly affect overall computer performance, manufacturers and retailers usually list a computer's memory in terms of its size, not its access time. Thus, an advertisement might describe a computer as having 512 MB of SDRAM upgradeable to 4 GB.

ACCESS TIME TERMINOLOGY

Term	Abbreviation	Speed
Millisecond	ms	One-thousandth of a second
Microsecond	µs	One-millionth of a second
Nanosecond	ns	One-billionth of a second
Picosecond	ps	One-trillionth of a second

FIGURE 4-22 Access times are measured in fractions of a second. This table lists the terms used to define access times.

10 million operations = 1 blink

FIGURE 4-23 It takes about one-tenth of a second to blink your eye, which is the equivalent of 100 million nanoseconds. In the time it takes to blink your eye, a computer can perform some operations 10 million times.

Test your knowledge of pages 194 through 203 in Quiz Yourself 4-2.

QUIZ YOURSELF 4-2

Instructions: Find the true statement below. Then, rewrite the remaining false statements so they are true.

1. A computer's memory access time directly affects how fast the computer processes data.
2. A gigabyte (GB) equals approximately 1 trillion bytes.
3. Memory cache helps speed the processes of the computer because it stores seldom used instructions and data.
4. Most computers are analog, which means they recognize only two discrete states: on and off.
5. Most RAM retains its contents when the power is removed from the computer.
6. Read-only memory (ROM) refers to memory chips storing temporary data and instructions.

Quiz Yourself Online: To further check your knowledge of bits, bytes, data representation, and types of memory, visit scsite.com/dc2008/ch4/quiz and then click Objectives 5 – 7.

EXPANSION SLOTS AND ADAPTER CARDS

An **expansion slot** is a socket on the motherboard that can hold an adapter card. An **adapter card**, sometimes called an *expansion card*, is a circuit board that enhances functions of a component of the system unit and/or provides connections to peripherals. A **peripheral** is a device that connects to the system unit and is controlled by the processor in the computer. Examples of peripherals are modems, disk drives, printers, scanners, and keyboards.

Figure 4-24 lists currently used types of adapter cards. Sometimes, all functionality is built in the adapter card. With others, a cable connects the adapter card to a device, such as a digital video camera, outside the system unit. Figure 4-25 shows an adapter card being inserted in an expansion slot on a personal computer motherboard.

Some motherboards include all necessary capabilities and do not require adapter cards. Other motherboards may require adapter cards to provide capabilities such as sound and video. A **sound card** enhances the sound-generating capabilities of a personal computer by allowing sound to be input through a microphone and output through external speakers or headphones. A **video card**, also called a *graphics card*, converts computer output into a video signal that travels through a cable to the monitor, which displays an image on the screen.

WEB LINK 4-6

Sound Cards

For more information, visit scsite.com/ dc2008/ch4/weblink and then click Sound Cards.

TYPES OF ADAPTER CARDS

Adapter Card	Purpose
Disk controller	Connects disk drives
FireWire	Connects to FireWire devices
MIDI	Connects musical instruments
Modem	Connects other computers through telephone or cable television lines
Network	Connects other computers and peripherals
PC-to-TV converter	Connects a television
Sound	Connects speakers or a microphone
TV tuner	Allows viewing of television channels on the monitor
USB 2.0	Connects to USB 2.0 devices
Video	Connects a monitor
Video capture	Connects a camcorder

FIGURE 4-24 Currently used adapter cards and their functions.

FIGURE 4-25 An adapter card being inserted in an expansion slot on the motherboard of a personal computer.

In the past, installing a card was not easy and required you to set switches and other elements on the motherboard. Many of today's computers support **Plug and Play**, which means the computer automatically can configure adapter cards and other peripherals as you install them. Having Plug and Play support means you can plug in a device, turn on the computer, and then immediately begin using the device.

Flash Memory Cards, USB Flash Drives, PC Cards, and ExpressCard Modules

Four widely used types of removable flash memory devices include flash memory cards, USB flash drives, PC Cards, and ExpressCard modules. Unlike adapter cards that require you to open the system unit and install the card on the motherboard, you can change a removable flash memory device without having to open the system unit or restart the computer. This feature, called *hot plugging*, allows you to insert and remove the removable flash memory and other devices while the computer is running.

- A **flash memory card** is a removable flash memory device, usually no bigger than 1.5" in height or width, that you insert and remove from a slot in a computer, mobile device, or card reader/writer (Figure 4-26). Many mobile and consumer devices, such as PDAs, smart phones, digital cameras, and portable media players, use these memory cards. Some printers and computers have built-in card readers/writers or slots that read flash memory cards. In addition, you can purchase an external card reader/writer that attaches to any computer. Flash memory cards are available in a variety of shapes and sizes. The type of flash memory card you have will determine the type of card reader/writer you need. Storage capacities of flash memory cards range from 32 MB to 8 GB.
- A *USB flash drive* is a flash memory storage device that plugs in a USB port on a computer or portable device. (The next section discusses USB ports.) A special type of USB flash drive, called a *U3 smart drive*, includes preinstalled software accessed through a Windows-type interface. Storage capacities of USB flash drives range from 32 MB to 64 GB, with the latter being extremely expensive.
- Many computers have a **PC Card slot** or an **ExpressCard slot**, which is a special type of expansion slot that holds a PC Card or an ExpressCard module, respectively. A **PC Card**

is a thin, credit card-sized removable flash memory device that primarily is used today to enable notebook computers to access the Internet wirelessly. ExpressCard modules, about one-half the size of PC Cards, are the next generation of PC Cards. An **ExpressCard module**, which can be used as a removable flash memory device, adds memory, communications, multimedia, and security capabilities to computers (Figure 4-27). Both PC Cards and ExpressCard modules conform to standards developed by the *Personal Computer Memory Card International Association* (PCMCIA). These standards help to ensure the interchangeability of PC Cards and ExpressCard modules among personal computers.

WEB LINK 4-7

ExpressCard Modules
For more information, visit scsite.com/dc2008/ch4/weblink and then click ExpressCard Modules.

FIGURE 4-26 Removable flash memory devices are available in a range of sizes.

FIGURE 4-27 An ExpressCard module slides in an ExpressCard slot on a computer.

PORTS AND CONNECTORS

A **port** is the point at which a peripheral attaches to or communicates with a system unit so the peripheral can send data to or receive information from the computer. An external device, such as a keyboard, monitor, printer, mouse, and microphone, often attaches by a cable to a port on the system unit. Instead of port, the term **jack** sometimes is used to identify audio and video ports. The front and back of the system unit contain many ports (Figure 4-28).

Ports have different types of connectors. A **connector** joins a cable to a peripheral. One end of a cable attaches to the connector on the system unit, and the other end of the cable attaches to a connector on the peripheral. Most connectors are available in one of two genders: male or female. Male connectors have one or more exposed pins, like the end of an electrical cord you plug in the wall. Female connectors have matching holes to accept the pins on a male connector, like an electrical wall outlet.

Sometimes, you cannot attach a new peripheral to the computer because the connector on the system unit is the same gender as the connector on the cable. In this case, purchasing a gender changer solves this problem. A *gender changer* is a device that enables you to join two connectors that are both female or both male.

Manufacturers often identify the cables by their connector types to assist you with purchasing a cable to connect a computer to a peripheral. Figure 4-29 shows the different types of connectors you may find on a system unit. Notice that many are color-coded to help you match the connector to the correct port. Some system units include these connectors when you buy the computer. You add other connectors by inserting adapter cards on the motherboard. Certain adapter cards have ports that allow you to attach a peripheral to the adapter card.

Desktop personal computers may have a serial port, a parallel port, several USB ports, and a FireWire port. The next section discusses these and other ports.

FIGURE 4-28 A system unit has many ports on its front and back.

CONNECTOR TYPES

Connector Type	Picture	Connector Type	Picture
Audio in		Monitor	
Cable TV		Mouse	
Center Surround Sound/Subwoofer		Network	
Composite video in		Printer	
Digital Video Interface (DVI)		Rear Surround Sound	
eSATA port		Serial	
FireWire		Side Surround Sound	
FM reception		S/PDIF	
HDMI port		Speaker	
Headphones		S-video	
Keyboard		Telephone line in	
Microphone		USB	

FIGURE 4-29   Examples of different types of connectors on a system unit.

Serial Ports

A **serial port** is a type of interface that connects a device to the system unit by transmitting data one bit at a time (Figure 4-30). Serial ports usually connect devices that do not require fast data transmission rates, such as a mouse, keyboard, or modem. The *COM port* (short for communications port) on the system unit is one type of serial port.

Some modems that connect the system unit to a telephone line use a serial port because the telephone line expects the data in a specific frequency. Serial ports conform to either the RS-232 or RS-422 standard, which specifies the number of pins used on the port's connector.

serial transmission of data

byte representation for number 1 (00110001)

byte representation for number 3 (00110011)

byte representation for number 5 (00110101)

connector

port

FIGURE 4-30
A serial port transmits data one bit at a time. One wire sends data, another receives data, and the remaining wires are used for other communications operations.

Parallel Ports

Unlike a serial port, a **parallel port** is an interface that connects devices by transferring more than one bit at a time (Figure 4-31). Originally, parallel ports were developed as an alternative to the slower speed serial ports.

Some printers can connect to the system unit using a parallel port. This parallel port can transfer eight bits of data (one byte) simultaneously through eight separate lines in a single cable.

byte representation for number 1 ⟶ 00110001
byte representation for number 3 ⟶ 00110011
byte representation for number 5 ⟶ 00110101

connector

port

FIGURE 4-31 A parallel port is capable of transmitting more than one bit at a time. The port shown in this figure has eight wires that transmit data; the remaining wires are used for other communications operations.

USB Ports

A **USB port**, short for *universal serial bus port*, can connect up to 127 different peripherals together with a single connector. Devices that connect to a USB port include the following: mouse, printer, digital camera, scanner, speakers, portable media player, CD, DVD, smart phone, PDA, game console, and removable hard disk. Personal computers typically have six to eight USB ports on the front and/or back of the system unit (Figure 4-28 on page 206). The latest version of USB, called *USB 2.0*, is a more advanced and faster USB, with speeds 40 times higher than that of its predecessor.

To attach multiple peripherals using a single USB port, you can daisy chain the devices together outside the system unit. *Daisy chain* means the first USB device connects to the USB port on the computer, the second USB device connects to the first USB device, the third USB device connects to the second USB device, and so on. An alternative to daisy chaining is to use a USB hub. A **USB hub** is a device that plugs in a USB port on the system unit and contains multiple USB ports in which you plug cables from USB devices.

USB also supports hot plugging and Plug and Play, which means you can attach peripherals while the computer is running. With serial and parallel port connections, by contrast, you often must restart the computer after attaching the peripheral.

Some newer peripherals may attach only to a USB port. Others attach to either a serial or parallel port, as well as a USB port.

  FAQ 4-6

Can older USB devices plug in a USB 2.0 port?

Yes. USB 2.0 is *backward compatible*, which means that it supports older USB devices as well as new USB 2.0 devices. Keep in mind, though, that older USB devices do not run any faster in a USB 2.0 port. For more information, visit scsite.com/dc2008/ch4/faq and then click USB 2.0.

FireWire Ports

Previously called an *IEEE 1394 port*, a **FireWire port** is similar to a USB port in that it can connect multiple types of devices that require faster data transmission speeds, such as digital video cameras, digital VCRs, color printers, scanners, digital cameras, and DVD drives, to a single connector. A FireWire port allows you to connect up to 63 devices together. The latest FireWire version, called *FireWire 800*, is much more advanced than its predecessor, FireWire 400.

You can use a FireWire hub to attach multiple devices to a single FireWire port. A **FireWire hub** is a device that plugs in a FireWire port on the system unit and contains multiple FireWire ports in which you plug cables from FireWire devices. The FireWire port supports Plug and Play.

Some newer peripherals may attach only to a FireWire port. Having standard ports and connectors, such as FireWire and USB, greatly simplify the process of attaching devices to a personal computer. For newer computers that do not have a serial or parallel port, users plug the device in a USB or FireWire port — as specified by the device's manufacturer. In general, FireWire has replaced audio, parallel, and SCSI ports, which are discussed in the next section. USB ports have replaced mouse, keyboard, serial, audio, parallel, and SCSI ports. Figure 4-32 shows how FireWire and USB ports are replacing other ports completely.

FAQ 4-7

Why are some of my USB and FireWire cables different?

Some smaller computers and devices, such as digital cameras and game consoles, have a mini-USB or mini-FireWire port that requires the USB or FireWire cable have a mini connector at one end and a standard connector at the other end to attach to the computer. Other devices, such as some smart phones, may require the USB or FireWire cable have a device-specific connector at one end for special uses such as wireless Internet connections. For more information, visit scsite.com/dc2008/ch4/faq and then click USB and FireWire Cables.

Special-Purpose Ports

Five special-purpose ports are MIDI, eSATA, SCSI, IrDA, and Bluetooth. These ports are not included in typical computers. For a computer to have these ports, you often must customize the computer purchase order. The following sections discuss these special-purpose ports.

MIDI PORT A special type of serial port that connects the system unit to a musical instrument, such as an electronic keyboard, is called a **MIDI port**. Short for *Musical Instrument Digital Interface*, MIDI (pronounced MID-dee) is the electronic music industry's standard that defines how devices, such as sound cards and synthesizers, represent sounds electronically. A *synthesizer*, which can be a peripheral or a chip, creates sound from digital instructions.

A system unit with a MIDI port has the capability of recording sounds that have been created by a synthesizer and then processing the sounds (the data) to create new sounds. Nearly every sound card supports the MIDI standard, so you can play and manipulate on one computer sounds that originally were created on another computer.

TRADITIONAL PORTS

FIGURE 4-32 USB and FireWire ports are replacing traditional ports completely.

NEW PORTS

WEB LINK 4-8

FireWire Ports

For more information, visit scsite.com/dc2008/ch4/weblink and then click FireWire Ports.

WEB LINK 4-9

eSATA

For more information, visit scsite.com/ dc2008/ch4/weblink and then click eSATA.

eSATA Port   An **eSATA port**, or *external SATA port*, allows you to connect an external SATA (Serial Advanced Technology Attachment) hard disk to a computer. SATA hard disks are popular because of their fast data transmission speeds. eSATA connections provide up to six times faster data transmission speeds than external hard disks attached to a computer's USB or FireWire port.

SCSI Port   A special high-speed parallel port, called a **SCSI port**, allows you to attach SCSI (pronounced skuzzy) peripherals such as disk drives and printers. Depending on the type of *SCSI*, which stands for small computer system interface, you can daisy chain up to either 7 or 15 devices together. Some computers include a SCSI port. Others have a slot that supports a SCSI card.

IrDA Port   Some devices can transmit data via infrared light waves. For these wireless devices to transmit signals to a computer, both the computer and the device must have an **IrDA port** (Figure 4-33). These ports conform to standards developed by the *IrDA* (Infrared Data Association).

To ensure nothing obstructs the path of the infrared light wave, you must align the IrDA port on the device with the IrDA port on the computer, similarly to the way you operate a television

remote control. Devices that use IrDA ports include a PDA, smart phone, keyboard, mouse, printer, and pager. Several of these devices use a high-speed IrDA port, sometimes called a *fast infrared port*.

Bluetooth Port   An alternative to IrDA, **Bluetooth** technology uses radio waves to transmit data between two devices (Figure 4-34). Unlike IrDA, the Bluetooth devices do not have to be aligned with each other. Many computers, peripherals, PDAs, smart phones, cars, and other consumer electronics are Bluetooth-enabled, which means they contain a small chip that allows them to communicate with other Bluetooth-enabled computers and devices. Bluetooth headsets allow smart phone users to connect their phone to a headset wirelessly. The latest version of Bluetooth, called Bluetooth 2.0, supports higher connection speeds and is backward compatible with its predecessors.

If you have a computer that is not Bluetooth enabled, you can purchase a Bluetooth wireless port adapter that will convert an existing USB port or serial port into a Bluetooth port. Also available are Bluetooth PC Cards and ExpressCard modules for notebook computers and Bluetooth cards for PDAs and smart phones.

TravelMate Series

acer

IrDA ports

notebook computer

smart phone

FIGURE 4-33   Many devices communicate wirelessly with desktop or notebook computers through IrDA ports.

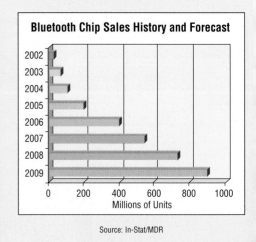

FAQ 4-8

How popular is Bluetooth?

Experts predict Bluetooth chip sales will grow to 866 million units by 2009 with revenues of $3 billion, as shown in the chart below. For more information, visit scsite.com/dc2008/ch4/faq and then click Bluetooth Growth.

Bluetooth Chip Sales History and Forecast

Source: In-Stat/MDR

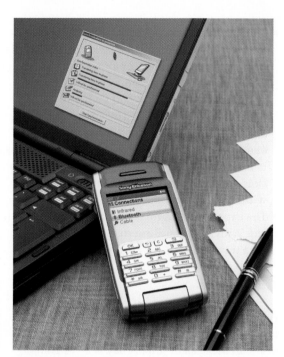

FIGURE 4-34 This smart phone wirelessly communicates with a Bluetooth-enabled notebook computer.

BUSES

As explained earlier in this chapter, a computer processes and stores data as a series of electronic bits. These bits transfer internally within the circuitry of the computer along electrical channels. Each channel, called a **bus**, allows the various devices both inside and attached to the system unit to communicate with each other. Just as vehicles travel on a highway to move from one destination to another, bits travel on a bus (Figure 4-35).

Buses transfer bits from input devices to memory, from memory to the processor, from the processor to memory, and from memory to output or storage devices. Buses consist of two parts: a data bus and an address bus. The *data bus* transfers actual data and the *address bus* transfers information about where the data should reside in memory.

The size of a bus, called the *bus width*, determines the number of bits that the computer can transmit at one time. For example, a 32-bit bus can transmit 32 bits (4 bytes) at a time. On a 64-bit bus, bits transmit from one location to another 64 bits (8 bytes) at a time. The larger the number of bits handled by the bus, the faster the computer transfers data. Using the highway analogy again, assume that one lane on a highway can carry one bit. A 32-bit bus is like a 32-lane highway. A 64-bit bus is like a 64-lane highway.

If a number in memory occupies 8 bytes, or 64 bits, the computer must transmit it in two separate steps when using a 32-bit bus: once for the first 32 bits and once for the second 32 bits. Using a 64-bit bus, the computer can transmit the number in a single step, transferring all 64 bits at once. The wider the bus, the fewer number of transfer steps required and the faster the transfer of data. Most personal computers today use a 64-bit bus.

In conjunction with the bus width, many computer professionals refer to a computer's word size. **Word size** is the number of bits the processor can interpret and execute at a given time. That is, a 64-bit processor can manipulate 64 bits at a time. Computers with a larger word size can process more data in the same amount of time than computers with a smaller word size. In most computers, the word size is the same as the bus width.

FIGURE 4-35 Just as vehicles travel on a highway, bits travel on a bus. Buses transfer bits from input devices to memory, from memory to the processor, from the processor to memory, and from memory to output or storage devices.

Every bus also has a clock speed. Just like the processor, manufacturers state the clock speed for a bus in hertz. Recall that one megahertz (MHz) is equal to one million ticks per second. Most of today's processors have a bus clock speed of 400, 533, 667, 800, or 1066 MHz. The higher the bus clock speed, the faster the transmission of data, which results in applications running faster.

A computer has two basic types of buses: a system bus and an expansion bus. A *system bus*, also called the *front side bus* (*FSB*), is part of the motherboard and connects the processor to main memory. An *expansion bus* allows the processor to communicate with peripherals. When computer professionals use the term bus by itself, they usually are referring to the system bus.

Expansion Bus

Some peripherals outside the system unit connect to a port on an adapter card, which is inserted in an expansion slot on the motherboard. This expansion slot connects to the expansion bus, which allows the processor to communicate with the peripheral attached to the adapter card. Data transmitted to memory or the processor travels from the expansion slot via the expansion bus and the system bus.

The types of expansion buses on a motherboard determine the types of cards you can add to the computer. Thus, you should understand these expansion buses commonly found in today's personal computers: PCI bus, PCI Express bus, AGP bus, USB, FireWire bus, and PC Card bus.

- The *PCI bus* (Peripheral Component Interconnect bus) is a high-speed expansion bus that connects higher speed devices. Types of cards you can insert in a PCI bus expansion slot include video cards, sound cards, SCSI cards, and high-speed network cards.
- The *PCI Express bus* is an expansion bus that expands on and doubles the speed of the original PCI bus. PCI Express is backward compatible with PCI; that is, it will work with devices that use the PCI bus. Nearly all video cards today use the PCI Express bus, as well as many hard disks and network cards. The ExpressCard technology used in notebook computers also works with the PCI Express bus. Experts predict the PCI Express bus eventually will replace the PCI bus completely.
- The *Accelerated Graphics Port* (*AGP*) is a bus designed by Intel to improve the speed with which 3-D graphics and video transmit. With an AGP video card in an AGP bus slot, the AGP bus provides a faster, dedicated interface between the video card and memory. Newer processors support AGP technology.

- The USB (universal serial bus) and *FireWire bus* are buses that eliminate the need to install cards in expansion slots. In a computer with a USB, for example, USB devices connect to each other outside the system unit, and then a single cable attaches to the USB port. The USB port then connects to the USB, which connects to the PCI bus on the motherboard. The FireWire bus works in a similar fashion. With these buses, expansion slots are available for devices not compatible with USB or FireWire.
- The expansion bus for a PC Card is the *PC Card bus*. With a PC Card inserted in a PC Card slot, data travels on the PC Card bus to the PCI bus.

BAYS

After you purchase a computer, you may want to install an additional storage device, such as a disk drive, in the system unit. A **bay** is an opening inside the system unit in which you can install additional equipment. A bay is different from a slot, which is used for the installation of adapter cards. Rectangular openings, called **drive bays**, typically hold disk drives.

Two types of drive bays exist: external and internal. An *external drive bay* allows a user to access the drive from outside the system unit (Figure 4-36). CD drives, DVD drives, and tape drives are examples of devices installed in external drive bays. An *internal drive bay* is concealed entirely within the system unit. Hard disk drives are installed in internal bays.

FIGURE 4-36   External drive bays usually are located beside or on top of one another.

POWER SUPPLY

Many personal computers plug in standard wall outlets, which supply an alternating current (AC) of 115 to 120 volts. This type of power is unsuitable for use with a computer, which requires a direct current (DC) ranging from 5 to 12 volts. The **power supply** is the component of the system unit that converts the wall outlet AC power into DC power. Different motherboards and computers require different wattages on the power supply. If a power supply is not providing the necessary power, the computer will not function properly.

Built into the power supply is a fan that keeps the power supply and other components of the system unit cool. This fan dissipates heat generated by the processor and other components of the system unit. Many newer computers have additional fans near certain components in the system unit such as the processor, hard disk, and ports.

Some external peripherals such as an external modem, speakers, or a tape drive have an **AC adapter**, which is an external power supply. One end of the AC adapter plugs in the wall outlet and the other end attaches to the peripheral. The AC adapter converts the AC power into DC power that the peripheral requires.

FAQ 4-9

How many fans are in a system unit?

Most system units have at least three fans: one in the power supply, one in the case, and one on the processor heat sink. In addition, you also may find a fan on the video card. While some computers contain fans that are designed to be quiet or operate in a quiet mode, others allow you to turn off noisy fans until they are needed. You also can purchase utility programs that slow or stop the fan until the temperature reaches a certain level. For more information, visit scsite.com/dc2008/ch4/faq and then click Computer Fans.

MOBILE COMPUTERS AND DEVICES

As businesses and schools expand to serve people across the country and around the world, increasingly more people need to use a computer while traveling to and from a main office or school to conduct business, communicate, or do homework. As Chapter 1 discussed, users with such mobile computing needs — known as mobile users — often have a mobile computer, such as a notebook computer or Tablet PC, or a mobile device such as a smart phone or PDA (Figure 4-37).

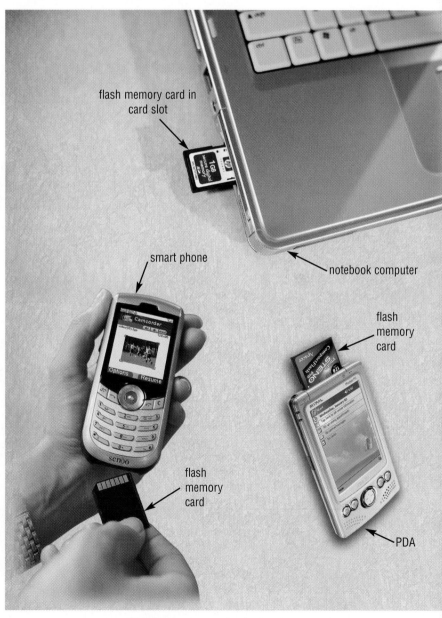

FIGURE 4-37 Users with mobile computing needs often have a notebook computer, PDA, and/or smart phone.

Weighing on average between 2.5 and 9 pounds, notebook computers can run either using batteries or using a standard power supply. Smaller PDAs and smart phones run strictly on batteries. Like their desktop counterparts, mobile computers and devices have a motherboard that contains electronic components that process data.

A notebook computer usually is more expensive than a desktop computer with the same capabilities because it is more costly to miniaturize the components. Notebook computers may have video, modem, network, FireWire, USB, headphones, and microphone ports (Figure 4-38). Read Ethics & Issues 4-4 for a related discussion.

Two basic designs of Tablet PC are available: slate and convertible. With the slate Tablet PC (shown in Figure 4-1 on page 184), all the hardware is behind the display — much like a PDA. Users can attach a removable keyboard to the slate Tablet PC. The display on the convertible Tablet PC, which is attached to a keyboard, can be rotated 180 degrees and folded down over the keyboard. Thus, the convertible Tablet PC can be repositioned to look like either a notebook computer or a slate Tablet PC. Tablet PCs usually include several slots and ports (Figure 4-39).

PDAs and smart phones are quite affordable, usually priced at a few hundred dollars or less.

FIGURE 4-38 Ports on a typical notebook computer.

ETHICS & ISSUES 4-4

Should Notebook Computers Be Banned on Airplanes?

After a series of terrorist threats and other incidents, several international airlines banned the use or possession of notebook computers on their flights. Some worry about the threat of a terrorist smuggling a weapon inside the notebook computer. Others banned certain brands of computers after it was discovered the batteries, in rare circumstances, could cause a fire. Still other airlines are concerned about new wireless technology interfering with critical electronics in their airplanes. Those opposed to such measures argue that the risks associated with notebook computers are extremely minor and no higher than the risk from most other everyday items. No major accidents or incidents have been linked to the use or possession of notebook computers on airplanes. Also, the gain in productivity from the use of computers by passengers in airplanes must be taken into consideration as well, they argue. Many people rely on computers for their work; if good security measures were in place, an outright ban would be unnecessary, and people would be more productive on long flights. Should notebook computers be banned on airplanes? Why or why not? Who should evaluate the risks associated with notebook computers, and what standard, if any, should be set for an acceptable level of risk? Why? If notebook computers are banned on airplanes, what other devices should be banned or regulated? Why?

FIGURE 4-39 Ports and slots on a convertible Tablet PC.

These mobile devices often have an IrDA port or are Bluetooth enabled so users can communicate wirelessly with other computers or devices such as a printer.

PUTTING IT ALL TOGETHER

When you purchase a computer, it is important to understand how the components of the system unit work. Many components of the system unit influence the speed and power of a computer. These include the type of processor, the clock speed of the processor, the amount of RAM, bus width, and the clock speed of the bus. The configuration you require depends on your intended use.

The table in Figure 4-40 lists the suggested minimum processor and RAM requirements based on the needs of various types of computer users. Read Looking Ahead 4-2 for a look at a future use of chips.

LOOKING AHEAD 4-2

Healing Bodies with Nanotechnology

Human organs damaged or destroyed through disease, accidents, or the aging process may regain functionality through recent breakthroughs in *nanotechnology*, which involves the design and manufacture of molecule-sized chips. This

engineering combines a patient's live cells and plastic covered with nanometer-size patterns to stimulate the growth of new tissue.

More than 1,700 companies in 34 countries are pushing the limits of science and engineering by manipulating single atoms, electrons, and lasers in the quest to improve health, protect the environment, provide national security, and speed up the telecommunication industry. For example, researchers are using nanotechnology to store data in record time, with one experiment saving the entire content of the *Encyclopedia Britannica* in approximately one minute. Other scientists are examining breaks in chromosomes in an attempt to identify people's cancer susceptibility.

New materials and more effective chip designs are expected to stimulate the nanotechnology field into becoming a $1 trillion market within the decade. For more information, visit scsite.com/dc2008/ch4/looking and then click Nanotechnology.

SUGGESTED MINIMUM CONFIGURATIONS BY USER

User	Processor and RAM
HOME	Intel Celeron D or AMD Sempron or Intel Core 2 Duo or AMD Athlon 64 FX Minimum RAM: 512 MB
SMALL OFFICE/ HOME OFFICE	Intel Core 2 Duo or AMD Athlon 64 FX Minimum RAM: 1 GB
MOBILE	Intel Core Solo or Intel Core 2 Duo or AMD Turion 64 Minimum RAM: 1 GB
POWER	Intel Itanium 2 or AMD Opteron or Intel Core 2 Extreme or Intel Xeon Minimum RAM: 2 GB
LARGE BUSINESS	Intel Core 2 Duo or AMD Athlon 64 FX Minimum RAM: 1 GB

FIGURE 4-40 Suggested processor and RAM configurations by user.

KEEPING YOUR COMPUTER CLEAN

Over time, the system unit collects dust — even in a clean environment. Built up dust can block airflow in the computer, which can cause it to overheat, corrode, or even stop working. By cleaning your computer once or twice a year, you can help extend its life. This preventive maintenance task requires a few basic products (Figure 4-41):

- can of compressed air — removes dust and lint from difficult-to-reach areas
- lint-free antistatic wipes and swabs
- bottle of rubbing alcohol
- small computer vacuum (or small attachments on your house vacuum)
- antistatic wristband — to avoid damaging internal components with static electricity
- small screwdriver (may be required to open the case or remove adapter cards)

Before cleaning the computer, turn it off, unplug it from the electrical outlet, and unplug all cables from the ports. Blow away any dust from all openings on the computer case, such as drives, slots, and ports. Vacuum the power supply fan on the back of the computer case to remove any dust that has accumulated on it. Next, release short blasts of compressed air on the power supply fan. Then, use an antistatic wipe to clean the exterior of the case.

If you need assistance opening the computer case, refer to the instructions that came with the computer. Once the case is open, put the antistatic wristband on your wrist and attach its clip to the case of the computer. Use the antistatic wipes to clean dust and grime inside the walls of the computer case. Vacuum as much dust as possible from the interior of the case, including the wires, chips, adapter cards, and fan blades. Next, release short blasts of compressed air in areas the vacuum cannot reach. If the motherboard and adapter cards still look dirty, gently clean them with lint-free wipes or swabs lightly dampened with alcohol.

When finished, be sure all adapter cards are set tightly in their expansion slots. Then close the case, plug in all cables, and attach the power cord. Write down the date you cleaned the computer so you have a record for your next cleaning.

If you do not feel comfortable cleaning the system unit yourself, have a local computer company clean it for you.

FAQ 4-10

Is it safe to open my computer case?

Yes, as long as you are careful and wear an antistatic wristband. Before opening the case, though, check with the computer manufacturer to be sure you will not void a warranty if you clean the computer or install additional components. Also, do not handle any internal components unless you intend to repair or replace them, as unnecessary handling may decrease the life of the component(s). For more information, visit scsite.com/dc2008/ch4/faq and then click Computer Cases.

FIGURE 4-41 With a few products, this computer user keeps his computer clean.

Test your knowledge of pages 204 through 216 in Quiz Yourself 4-3.

QUIZ YOURSELF 4-3

Instructions: Find the true statement below. Then, rewrite the remaining false statements so they are true.

1. A bus is the point at which a peripheral attaches to or communicates with a system unit so the peripheral can send data to or receive information from the computer.

2. An AC adapter is a socket on the motherboard that can hold an adapter card.

3. Built into the power supply is a heater that keeps components of the system unit warm.

4. Serial ports can connect up to 127 different peripherals together with a single connector.

5. The higher the bus clock speed, the slower the transmission of data.

6. When cleaning the inside of the system unit, wear an antistatic wristband to avoid damaging internal components with static electricity.

Quiz Yourself Online: To further check your knowledge of expansion slots, adapter cards, ports, buses, components of mobile computers and devices, and cleaning a computer, visit scsite.com/dc2008/ch4/quiz and then click Objectives 8 – 12.

CHAPTER SUMMARY

Chapter 4 presented the components of the system unit; described how memory stores data, instructions, and information; and discussed the sequence of operations that occur when a computer executes an instruction. The chapter included a comparison of various personal computer processors on the market today. It also discussed how to clean a system unit.

CAREER CORNER

Computer Engineer

A *computer engineer* designs and develops the electronic components found in computers and peripheral devices. They also can work as researchers, theorists, and inventors. Companies may hire computer engineers for permanent positions or as consultants, with jobs that extend from a few months to a few years, depending on the project. Engineers in research and development often work on projects that will not be released to the general public for two years.

Responsibilities vary from company to company. All computer engineering work, however, demands problem-solving skills and the ability to create and use new technologies. The ability to handle multiple tasks and concentrate on detail is a key component. Assignments often are taken on as part of a team. Therefore, computer engineers must be able to communicate clearly with both computer personnel and computer users, who may have little technical knowledge.

Before taking in-depth computer engineering design and development classes, students usually take mathematics, physics, and basic engineering. Computer engineering degrees include B.S., M.S., and Ph.D. Because computer engineers employed in private industry often advance into managerial positions, many computer engineering graduates obtain a master's degree in business administration (M.B.A.). Most computer engineers earn between $70,000 and $115,000 annually, depending on their experience and employer, but salaries can exceed $150,000. For more information, visit scsite.com/dc2008/ch4/careers and then click Computer Engineer.

High-Tech Talk

RANDOM ACCESS MEMORY (RAM): THE GENIUS OF MEMORY

Inside your computer, RAM takes the form of separate microchip modules that plug in slots on the computer's motherboard. These slots connect through a line (bus) or set of electrical paths to the computer's processor. Before you turn on a computer, its RAM is a blank slate. As you start and use your computer, the operating system files, applications, and any data currently being used by the processor are written to and stored in RAM so the processor can access them quickly.

How is this data written to and stored in RAM? In the most common form of RAM, dynamic random access memory (DRAM), *transistors* (in this case, acting as switches) and a *capacitor* (as a data storage element) create a *memory cell*, which represents a single bit of data.

Memory cells are etched onto a silicon wafer in a series of columns (bitlines) and rows (wordlines), known as an *array*. The intersection of a column and row constitutes the *address* of the memory cell (Figure 4-42). Each memory cell has a unique address that can be found by counting across columns and then counting down by row. The address of a character consists of a series of memory cell addresses put together.

To write data to RAM, the processor sends the memory controller the address of a memory cell in which to store data. The *memory controller* organizes the request and sends the column and row address in an electrical charge along the appropriate address lines, which are very thin electrical lines etched into the RAM chip. This causes the transistors along those address lines to close.

These transistors act as a switch to control the flow of electrical current in an either closed or open circuit. While the transistors are closed, the software sends bursts of electricity along selected data lines. When the electrical charge traveling down the data line reaches an address line where a transistor is closed, the charge flows through the closed transistor and charges the capacitor.

A capacitor works as electronic storage that holds an electrical charge. Each charged capacitor along the address line represents a 1 bit. An uncharged capacitor represents a 0 bit. The combination of 1s and 0s from eight data lines forms a single byte of data.

The capacitors used in dynamic RAM, however, lose their electrical charge. The processor or memory controller continuously has to recharge all of the capacitors holding a charge (a 1 bit) before the capacitor discharges. During this *refresh operation*, which happens automatically thousands of times per second, the memory controller reads

FIGURE 4-42 An illustration of one type of DRAM. When writing data, switches 1 and 2 in the circuit are closed and switches 3 and 4 are open. When reading data, switches 2, 3, and 4 in the circuit are closed and switch 1 is open. Most DRAM chips actually have arrays of memory cells (upper-left corner of figure) that are 16 rows deep.

memory and then immediately rewrites it. This refresh operation is what gives dynamic RAM its name. Dynamic RAM has to be refreshed continually, or it loses the charges that represent bits of data. A specialized circuit called a counter tracks the refresh sequence to ensure that all of the rows are refreshed.

The process of reading data from RAM uses a similar, but reverse, series of steps. When the processor gets the next instruction it is to perform, the instruction may contain the address of a memory cell from which to read data. This address is sent to the memory controller. To locate the memory cell, the memory controller sends the column and row address in an electrical charge down the appropriate address lines.

This electrical charge causes the transistors along the address line to close. At every point along the address line where a capacitor is holding a charge, the capacitor discharges through the circuit created by the closed transistors, sending electrical charges along the data lines.

A specialized circuit called a *sense amplifier* determines and amplifies the level of charge in the capacitor. A capacitor charge over a certain voltage level represents the binary value 1; a capacitor charge below that level represents a 0. The sensed and amplified value is sent back down the address line to the processor.

As long as a computer is running, data continuously is being written to and read from RAM. As soon as you shut down a computer, RAM loses its data. The next time you turn on a computer, operating system files and other data are again loaded into RAM and the read/write process starts all over. For more information, visit scsite.com/dc2008/ch4/tech and then click Memory.

Companies on the Cutting Edge

AMD
PC PROCESSOR SUPPLIER

Customer needs influence the integrated circuits *Advanced Micro Devices* (*AMD*) develops for the computing, communications, and consumer electronics industries. AMD calls this philosophy "customer-centric innovation."

As a global supplier of PC processors, AMD engineers its technologies at its Submicron Development Center (SDC) in Sunnyvale, California. The technologies are put into production at manufacturing facilities in the United States, Europe, Asia, and Japan.

Among the company's more successful line of processors is the AMD 64 family, which is composed of the AMD Athlon 64 processor for desktop and personal computers, the AMD Opteron processor for servers and workstations, and the AMD Turion mobile technology for notebook computers. The company's memory chips introduced in 2006 use less power and perform 10 percent faster than its older forms of memory. For more information, visit scsite.com/dc2008/ch4/companies and then click AMD.

INTEL
CHIP MAKER DOMINATES THE COMPUTER MARKET

When Gordon Moore and Robert Noyce started *Intel* in 1968, their goal was to replace magnetic core memory with semiconductor memory. Noyce and Moore, together with Andy Grove, refined the process of placing thousands of tiny electronic devices on a silicon chip. In 1971, the company introduced the Intel 4004, the first single-chip microprocessor.

When IBM chose the Intel 8008 chip for its new personal computer in 1980, Intel chips became standard for all IBM-compatible personal computers. Today, Intel's microprocessors are the building blocks in countless personal computers, servers, networks, and communications devices. The company achieved a breakthrough in 2006 by creating lasers on computer chips, which will increase connection speeds and distances dramatically and drop laser prices from $50 to $1. For more information, visit scsite.com/dc2008/ch4/companies and then click Intel.

Technology Trailblazers

JACK KILBY
INTEGRATED CIRCUIT INVENTOR

Jack Kilby was awarded more than 60 patents during his lifetime, but one has changed the world. His integrated circuit, or microchip, invention made microprocessors possible. He was awarded the Nobel Prize in physics in 2000 for his part in the invention of the integrated circuit.

Kilby started his work with miniature electrical components at Centralab, where he developed transistors for hearing aids. He then took a research position with Texas Instruments and developed a working model of the first integrated circuit, which was patented in 1959. Kilby applied this invention to various industrial, military, and commercial applications, including the first pocket calculator, called the Pocketronic.

Kilby is considered one of the more influential people in the world who has had the greatest impact on business computing in the past 50 years. Kilby died in 2005, but his legacy lives on. His first circuit has fostered a worldwide integrated circuit market with sales of nearly $200 billion annually. For more information, visit scsite.com/dc2008/ch4/people and then click Jack Kilby.

GORDON MOORE
INTEL COFOUNDER

More than 40 years ago, *Gordon Moore* predicted that the number of transistors and resistors placed on computer chips would double every year, with a proportional increase in computing power and decrease in cost. This bold forecast, now known as Moore's Law, proved amazingly accurate for 10 years. Then, Moore revised the estimate to doubling every two years.

Convinced of the future of silicon chips, Moore cofounded Intel in 1968. Moore's lifelong interest in technology was kindled at an early age when he experimented with a neighbor's chemistry set. Even then, he displayed the passion for practical outcomes that has typified his work as a scientist and engineer.

He recently starred in a documentary, *The Microprocessor Chronicles*, which traces the history of microprocessor innovations. For more information, visit scsite.com/dc2008/ch4/people and then click Gordon Moore.

Chapter Review

The Chapter Review section summarizes the concepts presented in this chapter. To listen to the audio version of this Chapter Review, visit scsite.com/dc2008/ch4/review. To obtain help from other students regarding any subject in this chapter, visit scsite.com/dc2008/ch4/forum and post your thoughts or questions.

(1) How Are Various Styles of System Units Different? The **system unit** is a case that contains electronic components of the computer used to process data. On desktop personal computers, most storage devices also are part of the system unit. On notebook computers, the keyboard and pointing device often occupy the area on top of the system unit, and the display attaches to the system unit by hinges. On mobile devices, the display often is built into the system unit. With game consoles, the input and output devices, such as controllers and a television, reside outside the system unit. On handheld game consoles and portable media players, by contrast, the packaging around the system unit houses the input devices and display.

(2) What Are Chips, Adapter Cards, and Other Components of the Motherboard? The **motherboard** is the main circuit board of the system unit. The motherboard contains many electronic components including a processor chip, memory chips, expansion slots, and adapter cards. A **chip** is a small piece of semiconducting material, usually silicon, on which integrated circuits are etched. Expansion slots hold adapter cards that provide connections and functions not built into the motherboard.

(3) What Are the Components of a Processor, and How Do They Complete a Machine Cycle? The **processor** interprets and carries out the basic instructions that operate a computer. Processors contain a **control unit** that directs and coordinates most of the operations in the computer and an **arithmetic logic unit** (*ALU*) that performs arithmetic, comparison, and other operations. The *machine cycle* is a set of four basic operations — *fetching, decoding, executing,* and *storing* — that the processor repeats for every instruction. The control unit fetches program instructions and data from memory and decodes the instructions into commands the computer can execute.

(4) What Are the Characteristics of Various Personal Computer Processors? A **dual-core processor** is a single chip that has two separate processors. A **multi-core processor** is a chip with two or more separate processors. Intel produces the **Core** and **Pentium** processor families for high-performance PCs, the **Celeron** processor family for basic PCs, and the **Xeon** and **Itanium** processor families for workstations and low-end servers. AMD manufactures *Intel-compatible processors*, which have an internal design similar to Intel processors. Some devices have a *system on a chip* processor that integrates the functions of a processor, memory, and a video card on a single chip.

> *connect*
> Visit scsite.com/dc2008/ch4/⊕ or click the Quiz Yourself button. Click Objectives 1 – 4.

(5) What Is a Bit, and How Does a Series of Bits Represent Data? Most computers are **digital** and recognize only two discrete states: off and on. To represent these states, computers use the **binary system**, which is a number system that has just two unique digits — 0 (for off) and 1 (for on) — called bits. A **bit** is the smallest unit of data a computer can process. Grouped together as a unit, 8 bits form a **byte**, which provides enough different combinations of 0s and 1s to represent 256 individual characters. The combinations are defined by patterns, called coding schemes, such as *ASCII, EBCDIC,* and *Unicode.*

(6) How Do Programs Transfer In and Out of Memory? When an application program starts, the program's instructions load into **memory** from the hard disk. The program and operating system instructions are in memory, and the program's window is displayed on the screen. When you quit the program, the program instructions are removed from memory, and the program no longer is displayed on the screen.

Chapter Review

(7) What Are the Various Types of Memory?   The system unit contains volatile and nonvolatile memory. *Volatile memory* loses its contents when the computer's power is turned off. *Nonvolatile memory* does not lose its contents when the computer's power is turned off. RAM is the most common type of volatile memory. ROM, flash memory, and CMOS are examples of nonvolatile memory. **RAM** consists of memory chips that can be read from and written to by the processor and other devices. **ROM** refers to memory chips storing permanent data and instructions that usually cannot be modified. **Flash memory** can be erased electronically and rewritten. **CMOS** technology uses battery power to retain information even when the power to the computer is turned off.

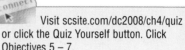
Visit scsite.com/dc2008/ch4/quiz or click the Quiz Yourself button. Click Objectives 5 – 7.

(8) What Are the Types of Expansion Slots and Adapter Cards?   An **expansion slot** is a socket on the motherboard that can hold an adapter card. An **adapter card** is a circuit board that enhances functions of a component of the system unit and/or provides a connection to a **peripheral** such as a modem, disk drive, printer, scanner, or keyboard. Several types of adapter cards exist. A **sound card** enhances the sound-generating capabilities of a personal computer. A **video card** converts computer output into a video signal that displays an image on the screen. Many computers today support **Plug and Play**, which enables the computer to configure adapter cards and peripherals automatically.

(9) How Are a Serial Port, a Parallel Port, a USB Port, a FireWire port, and Other Ports Different?   A **port** is the point at which a peripheral attaches to or communicates with a system unit so it can send data to or receive information from the computer. A **serial port**, which transmits data one bit at a time, usually connects devices that do not require fast data transmission, such as a mouse, keyboard, or modem. A **parallel port**, which transfers more than one bit at a time, sometimes connects a printer to the system unit. A **USB port** can connect up to 127 different peripherals together with a single connector. A **FireWire port** can connect multiple types of devices that require faster data transmission speeds. Five special-purpose ports are MIDI, eSATA, SCSI, IrDA, and Bluetooth. A **MIDI port** connects the system unit to a musical instrument. An **eSATA port** connects an external SATA hard disk to a computer. A **SCSI port** attaches the system unit to SCSI peripherals, such as disk drives. An **IrDA port** and **Bluetooth** technology allow wireless devices to transmit signals to a computer via infrared light waves or radio waves.

(10) How Do Buses Contribute to a Computer's Processing Speed?   A **bus** is an electrical channel along which bits transfer within the circuitry of a computer, allowing devices both inside and attached to the system unit to communicate. The size of a bus, called the *bus width*, determines the number of bits that the computer can transmit at one time. The larger the bus width, the faster the computer transfers data.

(11) What Are the Components in Mobile Computers and Mobile Devices?   In addition to the motherboard, processor, memory, sound card, PC Card slot, and **drive bay**, a mobile computer's system unit also houses devices such as the keyboard, pointing device, speakers, and display. The system unit for a typical notebook computer often has video, modem, network, FireWire, USB, headphone, and microphone ports. Tablet PCs usually include several slots and ports. PDAs and smart phones often have an IrDA port or are Bluetooth enabled so users can communicate wirelessly.

(12) How Do You Clean a System Unit?   Before cleaning a system unit, turn off the computer and unplug it from the wall. Use a small vacuum and a can of compressed air to remove external dust. After opening the case, wear an antistatic wristband and vacuum the interior. Wipe away dust and grime using lint-free antistatic wipes and rubbing alcohol.

Visit scsite.com/dc2008/ch4/quiz or click the Quiz Yourself button. Click Objectives 8 – 12.

Quizzes and Learning Games

Computer Genius
Crossword Puzzle
DC Track and Field
Practice Test
Quiz Yourself
Wheel of Terms
You're Hired!

Exercises

Case Studies
Chapter Review
Checkpoint
▶ Key Terms
Learn How To
Learn It Online
Web Research

Beyond the Book

Career Corner
Companies
FAQs
High-Tech Talk
Looking Ahead
Making Use of the Web
Trailblazers
Web Links

Features

Chapter Forum
Install Computer
Lab Exercises
Maintain Computer
Tech News
Timeline 2008

Key Terms

You should know the Primary Terms and be familiar with the Secondary Terms. Use the list below to help focus your study. To further enhance your understanding of the Key Terms in this chapter, visit scsite.com/dc2008/ch4/terms. See an example of and a definition for each term, and access current and additional information about the term from the Web.

Primary Terms

(shown in bold-black characters in the chapter)

AC adapter (213)
access time (203)
adapter card (204)
analog (194)
arithmetic logic unit (188)
bay (212)
binary system (195)
bit (195)
Bluetooth (210)
bus (211)
byte (195)
cache (201)
Celeron (190)
central processing unit (CPU) (187)
chip (186)
clock speed (189)
complementary metal-oxide semiconductor (CMOS) (203)
connector (206)
control unit (187)
Core (190)
digital (194)
drive bays (212)
dual-core processor (190)
eSATA port (210)
expansion slot (204)
ExpressCard module (205)
ExpressCard slot (205)
FireWire hub (209)
FireWire port (209)
firmware (202)
flash memory (202)
flash memory card (205)
gigabyte (GB) (197)

gigahertz (GHz) (189)
IrDA port (210)
Itanium (190)
jack (206)
kilobyte (KB or K) (197)
megabyte (MB) (197)
memory (197)
memory cache (201)
memory module (199)
memory slots (199)
MIDI port (209)
motherboard (186)
multi-core processor (190)
nanosecond (203)
parallel port (208)
PC Card (205)
PC Card slot (205)
Pentium (190)
peripheral (204)
Plug and Play (205)
port (206)
power supply (213)
processor (187)
RAM (198)
read-only memory (ROM) (201)
SCSI port (210)
serial port (207)
sound card (204)
system clock (189)
system unit (184)
terabyte (TB) (197)
USB hub (208)
USB port (208)
video card (204)
word size (211)
Xeon (190)

Secondary Terms

(shown in italic characters in the chapter)

Accelerated Graphics Port (AGP) (212)
address (197)
address bus (211)
advanced transfer cache (ATC) (201)
ALU (188)
arithmetic operations (188)
ASCII (195)
binary digit (195)
bus width (211)
Centrino (192)
Centrino Duo (192)
chassis (184)
clock cycle (189)
COM port (207)
comparison operations (188)
daisy chain (208)
data bus (211)
decoding (188)
DDR SDRAM (199)
DIMM (dual inline memory module) (199)
dynamic RAM (DRAM) (199)
EBCDIC (195)
EEPROM chip (202)
executing (188)
expansion bus (212)
expansion card (204)
external drive bay (212)
external SATA port (210)
fast infrared port (210)
fetching (188)
FireWire 800 (209)
FireWire bus (212)
form factor (184)
front side bus (FSB) (212)
gender changer (206)
graphics card (204)
heat pipe (193)
heat sink (193)
hertz (189)
hot plugging (205)
Hyper-Threading (HT) Technology (190)
IBM processor (190)
IEEE 1394 port (209)
integrated circuit (186)
Intel-compatible processors (190)
internal drive bay (212)
IrDA (210)
L1 cache (201)
L2 cache (201)
L3 cache (201)

liquid cooling technology (193)
machine cycle (188)
magnetoresistive RAM (MRAM) (199)
main memory (198)
massively parallel processing (194)
microcode (202)
microprocessor (187)
MIPS (millions of instructions per second) (190)
Motorola processor (190)
Musical Instrument Digital Interface (209)
nonvolatile memory (197)
ns (203)
parallel processing (194)
PC Card bus (212)
PCI bus (212)
PCI Express bus (212)
Personal Computer Memory Card International Association (205)
pipelining (189)
PROM (programmable read-only memory) chip (202)
Rambus DRAM (RDRAM) (199)
random access memory (198)
registers (189)
RIMM (Rambus inline memory module) (199)
SCSI (210)
SETI@home (194)
SIMM (single inline memory module) (199)
static RAM (SRAM) (199)
stored program concept (197)
storing (188)
superscalar (189)
synchronous DRAM (SDRAM) (199)
synthesizer (209)
system board (186)
system bus (212)
system on a chip (192)
transistor (186)
U3 smart drive (205)
Unicode (195)
universal serial bus port (212)
USB 2.0 (208)
USB flash drive (205)
Viiv technology (192)
vPro technology (192)
volatile memory (197)

Checkpoint

Use the Checkpoint exercises to check your knowledge level of the chapter. The Beyond the Book exercises will help broaden your understanding of the concepts presented in this chapter. To complete the Checkpoint exercises interactively, visit scsite.com/dc2008/ch4/check.

Label the Figure

Identify these components.

a. expansion slots

b. memory slots

c. motherboard

d. processor chip in a processor slot

True/False

Mark T for True and F for False. (See page numbers in parentheses.)

_____ 1. The system unit is a case that contains electronic components of the computer used to process data. (184)

_____ 2. The processor interprets and carries out the basic instructions that operate a computer. (187)

_____ 3. The speed of the system clock is just one factor that influences a computer's performance. (189)

_____ 4. Most high-performance PCs use a processor in the Intel Core family or the Pentium family. (190)

_____ 5. Replacing a motherboard is a fairly simple process, whereas replacing a processor is much more complicated. (192)

_____ 6. The SETI@home scientific project runs a program on home users' Internet-connected computers whose purpose is to detect possible intelligent life outside Earth. (194)

_____ 7. A byte is the smallest unit of data the computer can process. (195)

_____ 8. Coding schemes make it possible for humans to interact with a digital computer that processes only bits. (196)

_____ 9. Two types of cache are keyboard cache and mouse cache. (201)

_____ 10. Read-only memory refers to memory chips storing permanent data and instructions. (201)

_____ 11. Serial ports usually connect devices that require fast data transmission rates. (207)

_____ 12. A hard disk connected via an eSATA port will operate much slower than one connected via a computer's USB or FireWire port. (210)

Checkpoint

 Multiple Choice   Select the best answer. (See page numbers in parentheses.)

1. The _____ describes the size and shape of the desktop personal computer system unit. (184)
   a. bus width
   b. form factor
   c. processor
   d. chassis

2. On _____, the display often is built into the system unit. (185)
   a. mobile computers and devices
   b. notebook computers
   c. desktop personal computers
   d. all of the above

3. The processor also is called the _____. (187)
   a. central processing unit (CPU)
   b. adapter card
   c. motherboard
   d. chip

4. The _____ is the component of the processor that directs and coordinates most of the operations in the computer. (187)
   a. control unit
   b. arithmetic logic unit
   c. register
   d. machine cycle

5. A processor contains small, high-speed storage locations, called _____, that temporarily hold data and instructions. (189)
   a. flash drives
   b. registers
   c. jacks
   d. heat sinks

6. Processors that can execute more than one instruction per clock cycle are said to be _____. (189)
   a. flash drives
   b. dual-core processors
   c. system on a chip
   d. superscalar

7. Each processor on a dual-core/multi-core chip generally runs at _____ clock speed than a single-core processor. (190)
   a. a faster
   b. the same
   c. a slower
   d. twice the

8. If you plan to purchase an entertainment desktop computer, you will want it to use Intel's _____ technology, which is designed to enhance digital entertainment through a home computer. (192)
   a. vPro
   b. Centrino Duo
   c. Viiv
   d. Itanium

9. Supercomputers use _____ for applications such as artificial intelligence and weather forecasting. (194)
   a. system on a chip technology
   b. massively parallel processing
   c. SCSI
   d. Accelerated Graphics Ports

10. _____ is a 16-bit coding scheme that is capable of representing more than 65,000 characters and symbols, enough for almost all the world's current written languages. (195)
    a. ASCII   b. Unicode
    c. Microcode   d. EBCDIC

11. A(n) _____ is a unique number that identifies the location of a byte in memory. (197)
    a. register
    b. kilobyte
    c. address
    d. bit

12. Many of today's computers support _____, which means the computer automatically can configure adapter cards and other peripherals as you install them. (205)
    a. Pack and Go
    b. Pick and Choose
    c. Plug and Play
    d. Park and Ride

13. A _____ port is an interface that connects devices by transferring more than one bit at a time. (208)
    a. serial
    b. parallel
    c. USB
    d. mouse

14. The PCI Express bus is an expansion bus that _____. (212)
    a. expands on and doubles the speed of the original PCI bus
    b. is backward compatible with PCI
    c. is used by nearly all video cards today
    d. all of the above

Checkpoint

Matching

Match the terms with their definitions. (See page numbers in parentheses.)

_____ 1. motherboard (186)

_____ 2. processor (187)

_____ 3. ALU (188)

_____ 4. vPro technology (192)

_____ 5. memory (197)

_____ 6. firmware (202)

_____ 7. flash memory (202)

_____ 8. access time (203)

_____ 9. U3 smart drive (205)

_____ 10. Bluetooth (210)

a. technology that uses radio waves to transmit data between two devices

b. provides the ability to track computer hardware and software, diagnose and resolve computer problems, and secure computers from outside threats

c. main circuit board of the system unit

d. performs arithmetic, comparison, and other operations

e. ROM chips that contain permanently written data, instructions, or information

f. amount of time it takes the processor to read data, instructions, and information from memory

g. stores frequently used instructions and data

h. nonvolatile memory that can be erased electronically and rewritten

i. USB device that includes pre-installed software accessed through a Windows-type interface

j. number of bits the processor can interpret and execute at a given time

k. electronic components that store instructions, data, and results of processed data

l. interprets and carries out the basic instructions that operate a computer

Short Answer

Write a brief answer to each of the following questions.

1. What is the motherboard? _____ What is a computer chip? _____

2. What are the four basic operations in a machine cycle? _____ What are some functions of registers? _____

3. What is the system clock? _____ What are some capabilities that processors for notebook computers may include? _____

4. What is a system on a chip? _____ What types of devices typically have them? _____

5. Describe the two basic types of buses in a computer. _____ Describe the different types of expansion buses. _____

Beyond the Book

Read the following book elements, learn more about each using the Web, and then write a brief report.

1. Ethics & Issues — Can Computers Think? (187), Discarded Computer Components: Whose Problem Is It? (193), Should Schools Supply Computers to All Students? (200), or Should Notebook Computers Be Banned on Airplanes? (214)

2. Career Corner — Computer Engineer (217)

3. Companies on the Cutting Edge — AMD or Intel (219)

4. FAQs (189, 193, 200, 202, 203, 208, 209, 210, 213, 216)

5. High-Tech Talk — Random Access Memory (RAM): The Genius of Memory (218)

6. Looking Ahead — Hybrid Technology to Power Supercomputer (190) or Healing Bodies with Nanotechnology (215)

7. Making Use of the Web — Online Social Networks and Media Sharing (120)

8. Picture Yourself Computer Shopping (182)

9. Technology Trailblazers — Jack Kilby or Gordon Moore (219)

10. Web Links (186, 190, 199, 201, 202, 204, 205, 209, 210)

Learn It Online

Use the Learn It Online exercises to reinforce your understanding of the chapter concepts. To access the Learn It Online exercises, visit scsite.com/dc2008/ch4/learn.

(1) At the Movies — The Leopard with a Time Machine

To view the The Leopard with a Time Machine movie, click the number 1 button. Locate your video and click the corresponding High-Speed or Dial-Up link, depending on your Internet connection. Watch the movie and then complete the exercise by answering the question that follows. Apple Computer's "Time Machine" software allows users to travel through time by scrolling through different windows that represent days, to help them find the files that they need. What does Time Machine do for your Mac?

(2) Video and Audio: You Review It — Bluetooth Technology

In this chapter you learned about Bluetooth technology. Click the number 2 button to view the suggested links and begin your search for videos, podcasts, or vodcasts related to Bluetooth technology. Choose a video, podcast, or vodcast that discusses Bluetooth technology and is of interest to you, and then write a description of its contents. Explain why you chose this piece, what you liked about it, what you disliked about it, and whether you would recommend it to a fellow student. Finish your review by giving the video, podcast, or vodcast a rating of 1 – 5 stars. Submit your review in the format requested by your instructor.

(3) Student Edition Labs — Understanding the Motherboard

Click the number 3 button. A new browser window will open, displaying the Student Edition Labs. Follow the on-screen instructions, and complete the Understanding the Motherboard Lab. When finished, click the Exit button. If required, submit your results to your instructor.

(4) Student Edition Labs — Binary Numbers

Click the number 4 button. A new browser window will open, displaying the Student Edition Labs. Follow the on-screen instructions, and complete the Binary Numbers Lab. When finished, click the Exit button. If required, submit your results to your instructor.

(5) Practice Test

Click the number 5 button. Answer each question. When completed, enter your name and click the Grade Test button to submit the quiz for grading. Make a note of any missed questions. If required, submit your score to your instructor.

(6) Who Wants To Be a Computer Genius²?

Click the number 6 button to find out if you are a computer genius. Directions about how to play the game will be displayed. When you are ready to play, click the Play button. Submit your score to your instructor.

(7) Wheel of Terms

Click the number 7 button to reinforce important terms you learned in this chapter by playing the Shelly Cashman Series version of this popular game. Directions about how to play the game will be displayed. When you are ready to play, click the Play button. Submit your score to your instructor.

Learn It Online

(8) DC Track and Field

Click the number 8 button to use what you have learned in this chapter to compete against other students in three track and field events. Directions about how to play the game will be displayed. When you are ready to play, click the start first event button. If required, submit your score to your instructor.

(9) You're Hired!

Click the number 9 button to use what you have learned in this chapter to embark on the path to a career in computers. Directions about how to play the game will be displayed. When you are ready to play, click the begin game button. If required, submit your score to your instructor.

(10) Crossword Puzzle Challenge

Click the number 10 button, then click the Crossword Puzzle Challenge link. Directions about how to play the game will be displayed. Complete the puzzle to reinforce skills you learned in this chapter. When you are ready to play, click the Continue button. Submit the completed puzzle to your instructor.

(11) Vista Exercises

Click the number 11 button. When the Vista Exercises menu appears, click the exercise assigned by your instructor. A new browser window will open. Follow the on-screen instructions to complete the exercise. When finished, click the Exit button. If required, submit your results to your instructor.

(12) In the News

In February 2006, the forerunner of the modern computer had its 60th anniversary. By today's standards for electronic computers, the ENIAC (Electronic Numerical Integrator And Computer) was a grotesque monster. With 30 separate units, plus a power supply and forced-air cooling, it weighed more than 30 tons. Its 19,000 vacuum tubes, 1,500 relays, and hundreds of thousands of resistors, capacitors, and inductors consumed almost 200 kilowatts of electrical power. The ENIAC performed fewer than 1,000 calculations per minute; today, personal computers can process more than 300 million instructions per second. The rapid development of computing power and capabilities is astonishing, and the rate of that development is accelerating. Click the number 12 button and read a news article about the introduction of a new or improved computer component. What is the component? Who is introducing it? Will the component change the way people use computers? If so, how?

(13) Chapter Discussion Forum

Select an objective from this chapter on page 183 about which you would like more information. Click the number 13 button, and post a short message listing a meaningful message title accompanied by one or more questions concerning the selected objective. In two days, return to the threaded discussion by clicking the number 13 button. Submit to your instructor your original message and at least one response to your message.

(14) Configuring and Pricing Computers

Click the number 14 button to learn how to configure and price a custom computer. Research at least two manufacturers' Web sites, and get a quote from each site you visit. Make sure you include any software you may require. Also, add any upgrade items that you would like to have on your system including peripheral items (printer, scanner, etc.). Print the quotes from each site and submit the results to your instructor.

Learn How To

Use the Learn How To activities to learn fundamental skills when using a computer and accompanying technology. Complete the exercises and submit them to your instructor. Visit scsite.com/dc2008/ch4/howto to obtain more information pertaining to each activity.

LEARN HOW TO 1: Purchase and Install Memory in a Computer

One of the less expensive and more effective ways to speed up a computer, make it capable of processing more programs at the same time, and enable it to handle graphics, gaming, and other high-level programs is to increase the amount of memory. The process of increasing memory is accomplished in two phases — purchasing the memory and installing the memory. To purchase memory for a computer, complete the following steps:

1. Determine the amount of memory currently in the computer. For a method to do this, see Learn How To number 3 in Chapter 1.

2. Determine the maximum amount of memory your computer can contain. This value can change for different computers, based primarily on the number of slots on the motherboard available for memory and the size of the memory modules you can place in each slot. On most computers, different size memory modules can be inserted in slots. A computer, therefore, might allow a 128 MB, 256 MB, 512 MB, or 1 GB memory module to be inserted in each slot. To determine the maximum memory for a computer, in many cases you can multiply the number of memory slots on the computer by the maximum size memory module that can be inserted in each slot.

   For example, if a computer contains four memory slots and is able to accept memory modules of 128 MB, 256 MB, 512 MB, or 1 GB in each of its memory slots, the maximum amount of memory the computer can contain is 4 GB (4 x 1 GB).

   You can find the number of slots and the allowable sizes of each memory module by contacting the computer manufacturer, looking in the computer's documentation, or contacting sellers of memory such as Kingston (www.kingston.com) or Crucial (www.crucial.com) on the Web. These sellers have documentation for most computers, and even programs you can download to run on your computer that will specify how much memory your computer currently has and how much you can add.

3. Determine how much memory you want to add, which will be somewhere between the current memory and the maximum memory allowed on the computer.

4. Determine the current configuration of memory on the computer. For example, if a computer with four memory slots contains 512 MB of memory, it could be using one memory module of 512 MB in a single slot and the other three slots would be empty; two memory modules of 256 MB each in two slots with two slots empty; one memory module of 256 MB and two memory modules of 128 MB each in three slots with one slot empty; or four memory modules of 128 MB each in four slots with no slots empty. You may be required to look inside the system unit to make this determination. The current memory configuration on a computer will determine what new memory modules you should buy to increase the memory to the amount determined in Step 3.

   You also should be aware that a few computers require memory to be installed in matching pairs. This means a computer with four slots could obtain 512 MB of memory with two memory modules of 256 MB in two slots, or four memory modules of 128 MB in four slots.

5. Determine the number of available memory slots on your computer and the number and size memory modules you must buy to fulfill your requirement. Several scenarios can occur (in the following examples, assume you can install memory one module at a time).

   a. Scenario 1: The computer has one or more open slots. In this case, you might be able to purchase a memory module that matches the amount of memory increase you desire. For example, if you want to increase memory by 256 MB, you should purchase a 256 MB memory module for insertion in the open slot. Generally, you should buy the maximum size module you can for an open slot. So, if you find two empty slots and wish to increase memory by 256 MB, it is smarter to buy one 256 MB module and leave one empty slot rather than buy two 128 MB memory modules and use both slots. This allows you to increase memory again without removing currently used modules.

Learn How To

b. Scenario 2: The computer has no open slots. For example, a computer containing 512 MB of memory could have four slots each containing 128 MB memory modules. If you want to increase the memory on the computer to 1 GB, you will have to remove some of the 128 MB memory modules and replace them with the new memory modules you purchase. In this example, you want to increase the memory by 512 MB. You would have several options: (1) You could replace all four 128 MB memory modules with 256 MB memory modules; (2) You could replace all four 128 MB memory modules with two 512 MB memory modules; (3) You could replace one 128 MB memory module with a 512 MB memory module, and replace a second 128 MB module with a 256 MB memory module. Each of these options results in a total memory of 1 GB. The best option will depend on the price of memory and whether you anticipate increasing the memory size at a later time. The least expensive option probably would be number 3.

c. Scenario 3: Many combinations can occur. You may have to perform calculations to decide the combination of modules that will work for the number of slots on the computer and the desired additional memory.

6. Determine the type of memory to buy for the computer. Computer memory has many types and configurations, and it is critical that you buy the kind of memory for which the computer was designed. It is preferable to buy the same type of memory that currently is found in the computer. That is, if the memory is DDR2 SDRAM with a certain clock speed, then that is the type of additional memory you should place in the computer. The documentation for the computer should specify the memory type. In addition, the Web sites cited on the previous page, and others as well, will present a list of memory modules that will work with your computer. Enough emphasis cannot be placed on the fact that the memory you buy must be compatible with the type of memory usable on your computer. Because there are so many types and configurations, you must be especially diligent to ensure you purchase the proper memory for your computer.

7. Once you have determined the type and size of memory to purchase, buy it from a reputable dealer. Buying poor or mismatched memory is a major reason for a computer's erratic performance and is a difficult problem to troubleshoot.

After purchasing the memory, you must install it on your computer. Complete the following steps to install memory:

1. Unplug the computer, and remove all electrical cords and device cables from the ports on the computer. Open the case of the system unit. You may want to consult the computer's documentation to determine the exact procedure.

2. Ground yourself so you do not generate static electricity that can cause memory or other components within the system unit to be damaged. To do this, wear an antistatic wristband you can purchase inexpensively in a computer or electronics store; or, before you touch any component within the system unit, touch an unpainted metal surface. If you are not wearing an antistatic wristband, periodically touch an unpainted metal surface to dissipate any static electricity.

3. Within the system unit, find the memory slots on the motherboard. The easiest way to do this is look for memory modules that are similar to those you purchased. The memory slots often are located near the processor. If you cannot find the slots, consult the documentation. A diagram often is available to help you spot the memory slots.

4. Insert the memory module in the next empty slot. Orient the memory module in the slot to match the modules currently installed. A notch or notches on the memory module will ensure you do not install the module backwards. If your memory module is a DIMM, insert the module straight down into grooves on the clips and then apply gentle pressure (see Figure 4-18 on page 199). If your memory is SIMM, insert the module at a 45 degree angle and then rotate it to a vertical position until the module snaps into place.

5. If you must remove one or more memory modules before inserting the new memory, carefully release the clips before lifting the memory module out of the memory slot.

6. Plug in the machine and replace all the device cables without replacing the cover.

7. Start the computer. In most cases, the new memory will be recognized and the computer will run normally. If an error message appears, determine the cause of the error.

8. Replace the computer cover.

Exercise

1. Assume you have a computer that contains 512 MB of memory. It contains four memory slots. Each slot can contain 128 MB, 256 MB, or 512 MB memory modules. Two of the slots contain 256 MB memory modules. What memory chip(s) would you buy to increase the memory on the computer to 1 GB? What is the maximum memory on the computer? Submit your answers to your instructor.

2. Assume you have a computer that contains 1 GB of memory. It contains four memory slots. Each slot can contain 128 MB, 256 MB, 512 MB, or 1 GB memory modules. Currently, each slot contains a 256 MB memory module. What combinations of memory modules will satisfy your memory upgrade to 2 GB? Visit a Web site to determine which of these combinations is the least expensive. Submit your answers and recommendations to your instructor.

Web Research

Use the Internet-based Web Research exercises to broaden your understanding of the concepts presented in this chapter. Visit scsite.com/dc2008/ch4/research to obtain more information pertaining to each exercise. To discuss any of the Web Research exercises in this chapter with other students, post your thoughts or questions at scsite.com/dc2008/ch4/forum.

① **Scavenger Hunt** Use one of the <u>search engines</u> listed in Figure 2-8 in Chapter 2 on page 78 or your own favorite search engine to find the answers to the questions below. Copy and paste the Web address from the Web page where you found the answer. Some questions may have more than one answer. If required, submit your answers to your instructor. (1) What is an ultracapacitator? (2) When was the Xerox Alto developed? Why is it an important step in computer development? (3) What is a daughterboard? (4) What is CAS Latency? (5) What are rune stones and their connection to Danish King Harald Blatand (Bluetooth)? (6) What is the name of the type of memory that retains its contents until it is exposed to ultraviolet light?

② **Search Sleuth** <u>Ask.com</u>, a popular search engine, uses natural language, which allows researchers to type millions of questions each day using words a human would use rather than code a computer understands. Visit this Web site and then use your word processing program to answer the following questions. Then, if required, submit your answers to your instructor. (1) Click the Search text box, type `What is a memory stick?`, and then click the Search button. Review the Narrow Your Search links on the right side of the page. Click the How Does a Memory Stick Work link, and then scroll through the links and click one to find the answer to this question. (2) Click your browser's Back button or press the BACKSPACE key to return to the Ask.com home page. Review the list of Search Tools on the right side of the page. In addition to Web and News, what are the names of the other available tools? (3) Click the Weather search tool. What city is listed in the Example Weather Result? What is the current temperature there? (4) Click the News search tool on the right side of the page. Click the Top Stories link in the News Photos column. Click one of the Top Stories Photos links and review the material. If required, submit to your instructor a 50-word summary of the information.

③ **Journaling** Respond to your readings in this chapter by writing at least one page containing your reactions, evaluations, and reflections about <u>buying a computer</u>. For example, based on your needs, would you consider buying or have you bought an Apple? What are the pros and cons of buying a notebook versus a desktop computer? How much memory should your computer have? What type of processor? How many ports? Will you need adapter cards or other hardware? You also can write about the new terms you learned by reading this chapter. If required, submit your journal to your instructor.

④ **Expanding Your Understanding** A <u>brick-and-click</u> business allows customers to conduct transactions at a physical location as well as online. Many banks and retailers, such as Citibank and Best Buy, are brick-and-click businesses. Choose a brick-and-click business and then visit the physical location and its Web site. Compare the type, availability, and cost of products or services. Write a report summarizing your findings, focusing on the advantages and disadvantages of conducting business at a physical location and online. If required, submit your report to your instructor.

⑤ **Ethics in Action** More than 50 law enforcement agencies use handheld wireless devices to access commercial databases. For example, Massachusetts state police stationed at Logan International Airport use the <u>LocatePLUS Holdings Corporation</u>'s database, which has information on 98 percent of Americans. The data is composed of motor vehicle records, credit bureau reports, property tax payments, and telephone directories. Police say accessing this information helps them perform their jobs more efficiently. Privacy experts, in contrast, say that information collected for one purpose should not be available in other contexts. View online sites that provide information about commercial databases for sale. Write a report summarizing your findings, and include a table of links to Web sites that provide additional details. If required, submit your report to your instructor.

Case Studies

Use the Case Studies to apply the concepts presented in the chapter to real-world situations. Visit scsite.com/dc2008/ch4/cases to obtain more information pertaining to each exercise. To discuss the Case Studies in this chapter with other students, visit scsite.com/dc2008/ch4/forum and post your thoughts or questions.

CASE STUDY 1 — Class Discussion   You are the purchasing manager at TechnoInk, a company that specializes in designing and producing logos for local high school and college sports teams. The company has 35 nonnetworked computers that are used throughout the company for common business applications. The computers are four years old, and you would like to replace them. The director of information technology agrees, but he has reservations. He has asked you to complete a study on the cost of new computers, comparing the major features found on <u>system units</u> at three different price levels: less than $1,000; $1,000 to $1,750; and greater than $1,750. Prepare a brief summary report on the major features of system units at the various price levels. Include recommendations on which system units would meet the company's needs most economically. Be prepared to discuss your recommendations in class.

CASE STUDY 2 — Class Discussion   Universal Computing, Inc. has decided to upgrade several hundred PCs used in their offices nationwide. The Information Technology Department has recommended that the company again purchase PCs for approximately $1,500 each. The system units would include Intel Core family processors with speeds of 2.60 GHz with 1 GB of RAM. From her days in college, the CFO has preferred Apple computers and currently uses an <u>Apple iMac</u> at home. She has hired you as a consultant to determine if the company would be better off purchasing iMacs in the same price range and with similar capabilities. Use the Web and/or print media to select a comparable iMac. Which one starts faster? Which one opens files faster? Which one loads Web pages faster? Is the iMac in the same price range as the PC? List any other advantages and disadvantages of each. Prepare a brief summary report and be prepared to discuss your findings in class.

CASE STUDY 3 — Research   Your company wants to make the transition to <u>Bluetooth technology</u>. As manager of the IT department, you have been assigned the task of researching the most economical way to make the switch. None of the portable devices the company owns is Bluetooth enabled. Use the Internet and/or print media to research Bluetooth devices. Based on your findings, would it be more economical to purchase Bluetooth ExpressCard modules and port adapters, or would it be better to purchase all new portable devices that are Bluetooth enabled? Write a brief report and share your findings with your class.

CASE STUDY 4 — Research   Many system unit manufacturers provide a toll-free telephone number that customers can call with technical problems or questions. If the <u>service technician</u> determines a difficulty is a hardware problem that the customer can fix, the technician might ask the customer to open the system unit and make some adjustments. For this reason, every computer user can benefit by being familiar with the inside of the system unit. If you own a personal computer or have access to a personal computer, unplug the power supply and take the cover off the system unit. Be careful not to touch any of the system unit components. Make a sketch of the system unit and try to identify each part. By referring to the computer's *User Guide*, list some of the computer's specifications (clock speed, memory size, and so on). Compare your sketch and list with a classmate who has done this exercise with a different computer. How are the computers similar? How are they different?

CASE STUDY 5 — Team Challenge   Computers have become an integral part of military operations. Many military research projects are done with simulators that resemble civilian computer games. Your company has been contacted by the Department of Defense for a research project. Form a four-member team, and then form two two-member groups. Assign each group one of the following topics to research: 1) How have <u>notebook computers</u> changed the combat environment, and how have these military uses impacted the design of your personal computer? 2) How can the utilization of microchips worn by soldiers, or wearable computers, be integrated into civilian use? Write a summary report or use PowerPoint to create a group presentation and share your findings with the class.

CHAPTER FIVE

Input

Picture Yourself Using Input Devices

As part of the community service requirements for your scholarship, you have volunteered to teach a brief computer literacy class to a group of middle-school students at your community center. This week, you are discussing input devices, and you have asked the children to compile a list of input devices they see being used each day. You are bringing your PDA and stylus as examples.

When class begins that evening, you are expecting rather obvious choices from their lists, such as keyboard and mouse. You are pleasantly surprised at how knowledgeable these kids are. One girl says her father uses RFID when he drives to work on the toll road. Another girl says that she uses the Click Wheel on her portable media player each day. Two boys had visited a video arcade and used several gaming input devices, including game controllers, baseball bats, golf putters, and dance pads while playing video games. Another transfers images from her parents' digital camera to the computer. One boy says his parents pay for groceries using a fingerprint scanner at the local supermarket, and another one's brother uses a Web cam to show Web site visitors his home construction business in action. They also mention handheld scanners used by delivery staff.

You had planned to use your Tablet PC and a digital pen to enter their answers so that you could illustrate another type of input device. After hearing their knowledgeable answers, you decide to connect your microphone to your notebook computer and show them voice input instead!

Read Chapter 5 to learn about the keyboard and mouse, RFID readers, game controllers, digital cameras, scanners, and Web cams, and discover many other types of input devices.

WHAT IS INPUT?

Input is any data and instructions entered into the memory of a computer. As shown in Figure 5-1, people have a variety of options for entering data or instructions into a computer.

As discussed in Chapter 1, *data* is a collection of unprocessed text, numbers, images, audio, and video. Once data is in memory, the computer interprets and executes instructions to process the data into information. Instructions entered into the computer can be in the form of programs, commands, and user responses.

• A *program* is a series of instructions that tells a computer what to do and how to do it. When a programmer writes a program, he or she enters the program into the computer by using a keyboard, mouse, or other input device. The programmer then stores the program in a file that a user can execute (run). When a user runs a program, the computer loads the program from a storage

keyboard

mouse

touch screen

stylus

digital pen

biometric input

magnetic stripe card reader

input

data collection device

MICR

FIGURE 5-1   Users can enter data and instructions into a computer in a variety of ways.

medium into memory. Thus, a program is entered into a computer's memory.

- Programs respond to commands that a user issues. A *command* is an instruction that causes a program to perform a specific action. Users issue commands by typing or pressing keys on the keyboard, clicking a mouse button, speaking into a microphone, or touching an area on a screen.

- A *user response* is an instruction a user issues by replying to a question displayed by a program. A response to the question instructs the program to perform certain actions. Assume the program asks the question, Is the time card correct? If you answer Yes, the program processes the time card. If you answer No, the program gives you the opportunity to modify the time card entries.

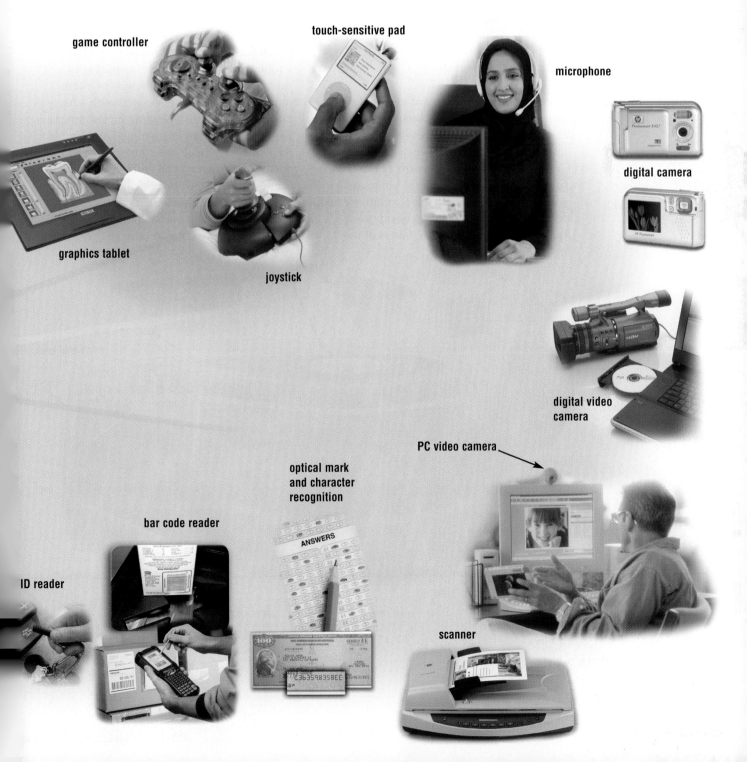

game controller

touch-sensitive pad

microphone

graphics tablet

joystick

digital camera

digital video camera

PC video camera

optical mark and character recognition

bar code reader

ID reader

scanner

WHAT ARE INPUT DEVICES?

An **input device** is any hardware component that allows users to enter data and instructions (programs, commands, and user responses) into a computer. Depending on the application and your particular requirements, the input device selected may vary. The following pages discuss a variety of input devices.

Storage devices, such as disk drives, serve as both input and output devices. Chapter 7 discusses storage devices.

THE KEYBOARD

Many people use a keyboard as one of their input devices. A **keyboard** is an input device that contains keys users press to enter data and instructions into a computer (Figure 5-2).

Desktop computer keyboards typically have from 101 to 105 keys. Keyboards for smaller computers such as notebook computers contain fewer keys. All computer keyboards have a typing area that includes the letters of the alphabet, numbers, punctuation marks, and other basic keys. Many desktop computer keyboards also have a numeric keypad on the right side of the keyboard. A keyboard also contains other keys that allow users to enter data and instructions into the computer. Read Ethics & Issues 5-1 for a related discussion.

Most of today's desktop computer keyboards are enhanced keyboards. An *enhanced keyboard* has twelve or more function keys along the top; it also has two CTRL keys, two ALT keys, and a set of arrow and additional keys between the typing area and the numeric keypad (Figure 5-2). *Function keys,* which are labeled with the letter F followed by a number, are special keys programmed to issue commands to a computer. The command associated with a function key may vary, depending on the program with which you are interacting. For example, the F3 key may issue one command to an operating system and an entirely different command to a word processing program. To issue commands, users often can press a function key in combination with other special keys (SHIFT, CTRL, ALT, and others).

FIGURE 5-2 On a desktop computer keyboard, you type using keys in the typing area and on the numeric keypad.

ETHICS & ISSUES 5-1

Keyboard Monitoring — Privacy Risk?

Do you get the feeling that someone is watching everything you type on your computer at work? Are you concerned about your teenager's conversations in Internet chat rooms? Keyboard monitoring software can dispel your doubts. When installed on a computer, *keyboard monitoring software*, also called a *keylogger*, records every keystroke in a hidden file, which later can be accessed by supplying the correct password. With keyboard monitoring software, you can see everything that was typed on the computer keyboard. Some programs also store a record of software used, Web sites visited, user logons, and periodic screen shots. The software can run completely undetected. With keyboard monitoring software, you can discover that an employee is providing sensitive information to a competitor or recognize that your teenager has made a potentially dangerous contact in a chat room. Businesses sometimes use keyboard monitoring software to analyze the efficiency of data entry personnel. Recently, courts ruled that law-enforcement agencies secretly can install keyboard monitoring software on suspects' computers if a proper search warrant is obtained. Many maintain, however, that keyboard monitoring software is an invasion of privacy, even in the workplace, and some states have outlawed the secret installation of such software. Should keyboard monitoring software ever be used? If so, when? Some marketers of keyboard monitoring software recommend computer users be informed that the software is installed. Is this a good idea? Why or why not?

Nearly all keyboards have toggle keys. A *toggle key* is a key that switches between two states each time a user presses the key. When you press the NUM LOCK key, for example, it locks the numeric keypad so you can use the keypad to type numbers. When you press the NUM LOCK key again, the numeric keypad unlocks so the same keys can serve to move the insertion point. Many keyboards have status lights that light up when you activate a toggle key.

Keyboards also often have WINDOWS key(s) and an APPLICATION key. When pressed, the WINDOWS key displays the Windows Start menu, and the APPLICATION key displays an item's shortcut menu.

Keyboards also contain keys that allow you to position the insertion point, also known as a *cursor* in some programs. The **insertion point** is a symbol on the screen, usually a blinking vertical bar, that indicates where the next character you type will be displayed (Figure 5-3). Users can move the insertion point left, right, up, or down by pressing the arrow keys and other keys on the keyboard.

Keyboards with media control buttons allow you to run and control your media player program, access the computer's CD/DVD drive, and adjust speaker volume. Internet control buttons allow you to open an e-mail program, start a Web browser, and search the Internet. Some keyboards have USB ports so you can plug a USB device directly in the keyboard instead of in the system unit. Some keyboards include a fingerprint scanner, which is discussed later in this chapter.

A *gaming keyboard* is a keyboard designed specifically for users that enjoy playing games on the computer. Gaming keyboards typically include programmable keys so gamers can customize the keyboard to the game being played.

FAQ 5-1

What is the rationale for the arrangement of keys in the typing area?

The keys originally were arranged to reduce the frequency of key jams on old mechanical typewriters. Called a *QWERTY keyboard*, the first letters on the top alphabetic line spell QWERTY. A *Dvorak keyboard*, by contrast, places frequently typed letters in the middle of the typing area. Despite the Dvorak keyboard's logical design, most people and computers use a QWERTY keyboard. For more information, visit scsite.com/dc2008/ch5/faq and then click Keyboards.

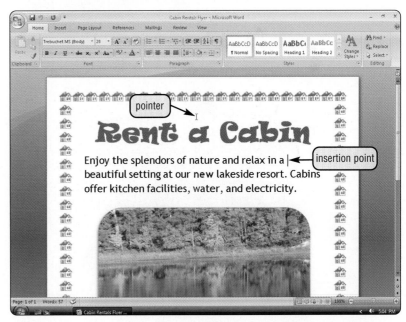

FIGURE 5-3 In most programs, such as Word, the insertion point is a blinking vertical bar. You use the keyboard or other input device to move the insertion point. The pointer, another symbol that is displayed on the screen, is controlled using a pointing device such as a mouse.

The keys on gaming keyboards light up so they are visible in all lighting conditions. Some even have small displays that show important game statistics, such as time or targets remaining.

Keyboard Connections

Desktop computer keyboards often attach via a cable to a serial port, a keyboard port, or a USB port on the system unit. Some keyboards, however, do not have any wires connecting the keyboard to the system unit. A *wireless keyboard*, or *cordless keyboard*, is a battery-powered device that transmits data using wireless technology, such as radio waves or infrared light waves. Wireless keyboards often communicate with a receiver attached to a port on the system unit. The port type varies depending on the type of wireless technology. For example, a Bluetooth-enabled keyboard communicates via radio waves with a Bluetooth receiver that typically plugs in a USB port (Figure 5-4).

On notebook computers and some handheld computers, PDAs, and smart phones, the keyboard is built in the top of the system unit. To fit in these mobile computers and devices, the keyboards usually are smaller and have fewer keys. A typical notebook computer keyboard usually has only about 85 keys. To provide all of the functionality of a desktop computer keyboard, manufacturers design many of the keys to serve two or three purposes.

Keyboard Ergonomics

Regardless of size, many keyboards have a rectangular shape with the keys aligned in straight, horizontal rows. Users who spend a lot of time typing on these keyboards sometimes experience repetitive strain injuries (RSI) of their wrists and hands. For this reason, some manufacturers offer ergonomic keyboards. An *ergonomic keyboard* has a design that reduces the chance of wrist and hand injuries. Even keyboards that are not ergonomically designed attempt to offer a user more comfort by including a wrist rest or palm rest (Figure 5-2 on page 236).

The goal of **ergonomics** is to incorporate comfort, efficiency, and safety in the design of the workplace. Employees can be injured or develop disorders of the muscles, nerves, tendons, ligaments, and joints from working in an area that is not ergonomically designed.

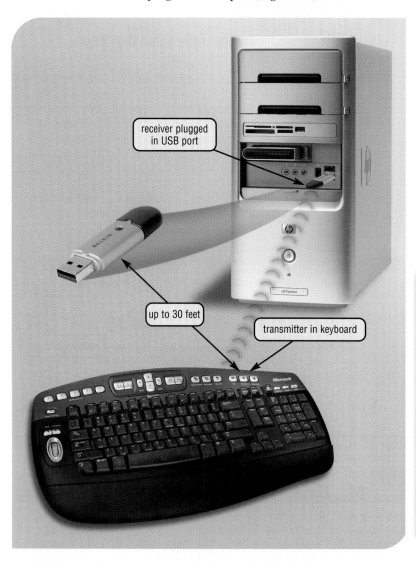

receiver plugged in USB port

up to 30 feet

transmitter in keyboard

FIGURE 5-4 Some personal computers have built-in Bluetooth technology. On computers that are not Bluetooth-enabled, you plug a Bluetooth receiver in a USB port on the system unit. A transmitter inside the keyboard communicates with the receiver, which should be within 30 feet from each other.

 FAQ 5-2

What can I do to reduce chances of experiencing repetitive strain injuries?

Do not rest your wrist on the edge of a desk; use a wrist rest. Keep your forearm and wrist level so your wrist does not bend. Take a break and do hand exercises every 15 minutes. Keep your shoulders, arms, hands, and wrists relaxed while you work. Maintain good posture. Keep feet flat on the floor, with one foot slightly in front of the other. Immediately stop using the computer if you begin to experience pain or fatigue. For more information, visit scsite.com/dc2008/ch5/faq and then click Repetitive Strain Injuries.

POINTING DEVICES

A **pointing device** is an input device that allows a user to control a pointer on the screen. In a graphical user interface, a **pointer** is a small symbol on the screen (Figure 5-3 on page 237) whose location and shape change as a user moves a pointing device. A pointing device can be used to move the insertion point; select text, graphics, and other objects; and click buttons, icons, links, and menu commands. The following sections discuss the mouse and other pointing devices.

MOUSE

A **mouse** is a pointing device that fits under the palm of your hand comfortably. The mouse is the most widely used pointing device on desktop computers.

With a mouse, users control the movement of the pointer, often called a *mouse pointer* in this case. As you move a mouse, the pointer on the screen also moves. Generally, you use the mouse to move the pointer on the screen to an object such as a button, a menu, an icon, a link, or text. Then, you press a mouse button to perform a certain action associated with that object. The top and sides of a mouse have one to four buttons; some also have a small wheel. The bottom of a mouse is flat and contains a mechanism, such as a ball or a light, that detects movement of the mouse.

A *mechanical mouse,* which was the first type of mouse used with personal computers, has a rubber or metal ball on its underside. Electronic circuits in the mouse translate the movement of the mouse into signals the computer can process. A mechanical mouse is placed on a *mouse pad,* which is a rectangular rubber or foam pad that provides better traction than the top of a desk. The mouse pad also protects the ball in the mouse from a build-up of dust and dirt, which could cause it to malfunction.

Most computer users today have some type of optical mouse, which has no moving mechanical parts inside. Instead, an *optical mouse* uses devices that emit and sense light to detect the mouse's movement. Some use optical sensors, and others use a laser. The latter type often is referred to as a *laser mouse* (Figure 5-5), which is more expensive than the former. You can place an optical mouse on nearly all types of surfaces, eliminating the need for a mouse pad. An optical mouse is more precise than a mechanical mouse and does not require cleaning as does a mechanical mouse, but it also is more expensive.

The mobile user who makes presentations may prefer a mouse that has additional buttons on the bottom for running a slide show and controlling media, similar to a remote control (Figure 5-6). An *air mouse* is a newer type of motion-sensing mouse that, in addition to the typical buttons, allows you to control objects, media players, and slide shows by moving the mouse in predetermined directions through the air. For example, raising the mouse up would increase the volume on your media player.

A mouse connects to a computer in several ways. Many types connect with a cable that attaches to a serial port, mouse port, or USB port on the system unit. A *wireless mouse,* or *cordless mouse,* is a battery-powered device that transmits data using wireless technology, such as radio waves or infrared light waves. The technology used for a wireless mouse is similar to that of a wireless keyboard discussed earlier. Some users prefer a wireless mouse because it frees up desk space and eliminates the clutter of a cord.

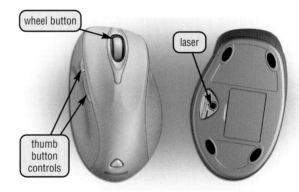

FIGURE 5-5 This mouse uses a laser to detect movement of the mouse. It also includes buttons you push with your thumb that enable forward and backward navigation through Web pages.

FIGURE 5-6 The bottom of this mouse has buttons that allow you to advance forward and backward through a slide show and also adjust media controls.

Using a Mouse

Windows users work with a mouse that has at least two buttons. For a right-handed user, the left button usually is the primary mouse button, and the right mouse button is the secondary mouse button. Left-handed people, however, can reverse the function of these buttons.

Operations you can perform with the mouse include point, click, right-click, double-click, triple-click, drag, right-drag, rotate wheel, free-spin wheel, press wheel button, and tilt wheel. The table in Figure 5-7 explains how to perform these mouse operations. Some programs also use keys in combination with the mouse to perform certain actions. The function of the mouse buttons and the wheel varies depending on the program. Read Ethics & Issues 5-2 for a related discussion.

Some programs support *mouse gestures*, where the user performs certain operations by holding a mouse button while moving the mouse in a particular pattern. For example, moving the mouse down and to the left may close all open windows. Mouse gestures minimize the amount of time users spend navigating through menus or toolbars because users can perform these tasks by simply moving (gesturing) the mouse.

WEB LINK 5-1

Mouse

For more information, visit scsite.com/dc2008/ch5/weblink and then click Mouse.

FAQ 5-3

How do I use a wheel on a mouse?

Roll it forward or backward to scroll up or down. Tilt it to the right or left to scroll horizontally. Hold down the CTRL key while rolling the wheel to make the text on the screen bigger or smaller. These scrolling and zooming functions work with most software and also on the Web. For more information, visit scsite.com/dc2008/ch5/faq and then click Using a Mouse.

MOUSE OPERATIONS

Operation	Mouse Action	Example
Point	Move the mouse across a flat surface until the pointer on the desktop is positioned on the item of choice.	Position the pointer on the screen.
Click	Press and release the primary mouse button, which usually is the left mouse button.	Select or deselect items on the screen or start a program or program feature.
Right-click	Press and release the secondary mouse button, which usually is the right mouse button.	Display a shortcut menu.
Double-click	Quickly press and release the left mouse button twice without moving the mouse.	Start a program or program feature.
Triple-click	Quickly press and release the left mouse button three times without moving the mouse.	Select a paragraph.
Drag	Point to an item, hold down the left mouse button, move the item to the desired location on the screen, and then release the left mouse button.	Move an object from one location to another or draw pictures.
Right-drag	Point to an item, hold down the right mouse button, move the item to the desired location on the screen, and then release the right mouse button.	Display a shortcut menu after moving an object from one location to another.
Rotate wheel	Roll the wheel forward or backward.	Scroll vertically.
Free-spin wheel	Whirl the wheel forward or backward so it spins freely on its own.	Scroll through hundreds of pages in seconds.
Press wheel button	Press the wheel button while moving the mouse on the desktop.	Scroll continuously.
Tilt wheel	Press the wheel toward the right or left.	Scroll horizontally.

FIGURE 5-7 The more common mouse operations.

ETHICS & ISSUES 5-2

Are Employers Responsible for Medical Problems Related to Computer Use?

When you consider the causes of workplace injuries, you might not put clicking a mouse in the same category with lifting a bag of concrete, but perhaps you should. According to the chairman of a National Academy of Sciences panel that investigated workplace injuries, every year one million Americans lose workdays because of repetitive strain injuries. Repetitive strain injuries are caused when muscle groups perform the same actions over and over again. Once, repetitive strain injuries were common among factory workers who performed the same tasks on an assembly line for hours a day. Today, these injuries, which often result from prolonged use of a computer mouse and keyboard, are the largest job-related injury and illness problem in the United States and are almost completely avoidable with proper computer use. OSHA proposed standards whereby employers would have to establish programs to prevent workplace injuries with respect to computer use. Yet, congress rejected the standards, accepting the argument that the cost to employers would be prohibitive and unfair. Some argue that it is each employee's responsibility to be aware of preventative measures against repetitive strain injuries. Should the government establish laws regarding computer use? Why or why not? Are employees, employers, or the government responsible for repetitive strain injuries? Why? Who should be responsible for the costs of prevention and medical care? Why?

WEB LINK 5-2

Repetitive Strain Injuries

For more information, visit scsite.com/dc2008/ch5/weblink and then click Repetitive Strain Injuries.

OTHER POINTING DEVICES

The mouse is the most widely used pointing device today. Some users, however, work with other pointing devices. These include the trackball, touchpad, pointing stick, light pen, touch screen, stylus, and pens. The following sections discuss each of these pointing devices.

Trackball

A **trackball** is a stationary pointing device with a ball on its top or side (Figure 5-8). The ball in most trackballs is about the size of a Ping-Pong ball.

To move the pointer using a trackball, you rotate the ball with your thumb, fingers, or the palm of your hand. In addition to the ball, a trackball usually has one or more buttons that work just like mouse buttons.

A trackball requires frequent cleaning because it picks up oils from fingers and dust from the environment. For users who have limited desk space, however, a trackball is a good alternative to a mouse because the device is stationary.

Touchpad

A **touchpad** is a small, flat, rectangular pointing device that is sensitive to pressure and motion (Figure 5-9). To move the pointer using a touchpad, slide your fingertip across the surface of the pad. Some touchpads have one or more buttons around the edge of the pad that work like mouse buttons. On most touchpads, you also can tap the pad's surface to imitate mouse operations such as clicking. Touchpads are found most often on notebook computers.

FIGURE 5-8 A trackball.

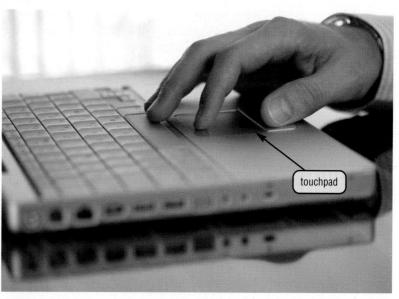

FIGURE 5-9 Most notebook computers have a touchpad that allows users to control the movement of the pointer.

Pointing Stick

A **pointing stick** is a pressure-sensitive pointing device shaped like a pencil eraser that is positioned between keys on a keyboard (Figure 5-10). To move the pointer using a pointing stick, you push the pointing stick with a finger. The pointer on the screen moves in the direction you push the pointing stick. By pressing buttons below the keyboard, users can click and perform other mouse-type operations with a pointing stick. A pointing stick does not require any additional desk space.

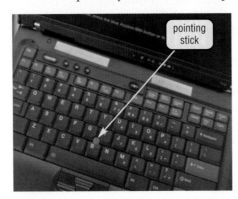

pointing stick

FIGURE 5-10   Some notebook computers include a pointing stick to allow a user to control the movement of the pointer.

Light Pen

A **light pen** is a handheld input device that can detect the presence of light. To select objects on the screen, a user presses the light pen against the surface of the screen or points the light pen at the screen and then presses a button on the pen. Light pens also are ideal for areas where employees' hands might contain food, dirt, grease, or other chemicals that could damage the computer.

Touch Screen

A **touch screen** is a touch-sensitive display device. Users can interact with these devices by touching areas of the screen. Because touch screens require a lot of arm movements, you do not enter large amounts of data using a touch screen. Instead, you touch words, pictures, numbers, letters, or locations identified on the screen.

Kiosks, which are freestanding computers, often have touch screens (Figure 5-11). For example, travelers use kiosks in airports to print tickets ordered online and in hotels for easy check in and check out. To allow easy

access of your bank account from a car, many ATMs have touch screens. Many handheld game consoles also have touch screens.

FIGURE 5-11   This user edits digital pictures using a photo kiosk.

Pen Input

Mobile users often enter data and instructions with a pen-type device. With **pen input**, users write, draw, and tap on a flat surface to enter input. The surface may be a monitor, a screen, a special type of paper, or a graphics tablet. Two devices used for pen input are the stylus and digital pen. A **stylus** is a small metal or plastic device that looks like a tiny ink pen but uses pressure instead of ink (Figure 5-12). A **digital pen**, which is slightly larger than a stylus, is available in two forms: some are pressure-sensitive; others have a tiny built-in digital camera.

stylus

FIGURE 5-12   PDAs and smart phones use a stylus.

WEB LINK 5-3

Touch Screen

For more information, visit scsite.com/dc2008/ch5/weblink and then click Touch Screen.

Some mobile computers and nearly all mobile devices have touch screens. Instead of using a finger to enter data and instructions, most of these devices include a pressure-sensitive digital pen or stylus. You write, draw, or make selections on the computer screen by touching the screen with the pen or stylus. For example, Tablet PCs use a pressure-sensitive digital pen (Figure 5-13) and PDAs use a stylus. Pressure-sensitive digital pens, often simply called pens, typically provide more functionality than a stylus, featuring electronic erasers and programmable buttons.

Computers and mobile devices often use *handwriting recognition software* that translates the handwritten letters and symbols into characters that the computer or device can process.

If you want to use pen input on a computer that does not have a touch screen, you can attach a graphics tablet to the computer. A **graphics tablet** is a flat, rectangular, electronic, plastic board. Architects, mapmakers, designers, artists, and home users create drawings and sketches by using a pressure-sensitive pen or a cursor on a graphics tablet (Figure 5-14). A *cursor* looks similar to a mouse, except it has a window with cross hairs, so the user can see through to the tablet. Each location on the graphics tablet corresponds to a specific location on the screen. When drawing on the tablet with a pen or cursor, the tablet detects and converts the movements into digital signals that are sent in the computer. Large-scale applications sometimes refer to the graphics tablet as a *digitizer*.

FIGURE 5-13 Tablet PCs use a pressure-sensitive digital pen.

Digital pens that have built-in digital cameras work differently from pressure-sensitive digital pens. These pens look much like a ballpoint pen and typically do not contain any additional buttons. In addition to the tiny digital camera, these pens contain a processor, memory, and an ink cartridge. As you write or draw on special digital paper with the pen, it captures every handwritten mark by taking more than 100 pictures per second and then stores the images in the pen's memory. You transfer the images from the pen to a computer or mobile device, such as a smart phone. Some pens have a cradle for transferring images; others communicate wirelessly using Bluetooth.

WEB LINK 5-4

Pen Input
For more information, visit scsite.com/ dc2008/ch5/weblink and then click Pen Input.

FIGURE 5-14a
(artist using a pen)

FIGURE 5-14b
(civil engineer using a cursor)

FIGURE 5-14 Graphics tablets use digital pens or cursors.

CONTROLLERS FOR GAMING AND MEDIA PLAYERS

Video games and computer games use a **game controller** as the input device that directs movements and actions of on-screen objects. Game controllers include gamepads, joysticks and wheels, light guns, dance pads, and a variety of motion-sensing controllers. Portable media players use a touch-sensitive pad as their input device. The following sections discuss a variety of game controllers (Figure 5-15) and the touch-sensitive scroll pad.

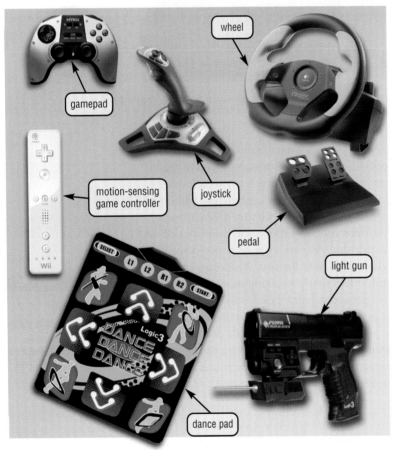

FIGURE 5-15   A variety of game controllers.

Gamepads

A **gamepad**, which is held with both hands, controls the movement and actions of players or objects in video games or computer games. On the gamepad, users press buttons with their thumbs or move sticks in various directions to trigger events. Gamepads communicate with a game console or a personal computer via wired or wireless technology.

Joysticks and Wheels

Users running game software or flight and driving simulation software often use a joystick or wheel to control an airplane, vehicle, or player. A **joystick** is a handheld vertical lever mounted on a base. You move the lever in different directions to control the actions of the simulated vehicle or player. The lever usually includes buttons, called triggers, that you press to initiate certain events. Some joysticks also have additional buttons you press to perform other actions.

A **wheel** is a steering-wheel-type input device. Users turn the wheel to simulate driving a car, truck, or other vehicle. Most wheels also include foot pedals for acceleration and braking actions. Joysticks and wheels typically attach via a cable to a personal computer or game console.

Light Guns

A **light gun** is used to shoot targets and moving objects after you pull the trigger on the weapon. Instead of emitting light, most light guns work by detecting light. When the user pulls the trigger, the screen uses one of several techniques to send light, which is received by a receptor in the barrel of the gun. Light guns typically attach via a cable to a game console or personal computer.

Dance Pads

A **dance pad** is a flat electronic device divided into panels that users press with their feet in response to instructions from a music video game. These games test the user's ability to step on the correct panel at the correct time, following a pattern that is synchronized with the rhythm or beat of a song. Dance pads communicate with a game console or a personal computer via wired or wireless technology.

Motion-Sensing Game Controllers

Motion-sensing game controllers allow the user to guide on-screen elements by moving a handheld input device in predetermined directions through the air. Some are sold with a particular type of game; others are general purpose. Sports games, for example, use motion-sensing game controllers, such as baseball bats and golf clubs, as their input device. These types of controllers communicate with a game console or a personal computer via wired or wireless technology.

WEB LINK 5-5

Wii Remote
For more information, visit scsite.com/dc2008/ch5/weblink and then click Wii Remote.

A popular general-purpose, motion-sensing game controller is Nintendo's Wii Remote. Shaped like a television remote control and operated with one hand, the *Wii Remote* is a motion-sensing input device that uses Bluetooth wireless technology to communicate with the Wii game console. Users point the Wii Remote in different directions and rotate it to control on-screen players, vehicles, and other objects.

Touch-Sensitive Pads

The *touch-sensitive pad* on a portable media player is an input device that enables users to scroll through and play music, view pictures, watch videos or movies, adjust volume, and customize settings. Touch-sensitive pads typically contain buttons and/or wheels that are operated with a thumb or finger. For example,

users rotate a *Click Wheel* to browse through its song, picture, or movie lists and press the Click Wheel's buttons to play or pause media, display a menu, and other actions (Figure 5-16).

FIGURE 5-16   You use your thumb to rotate or press buttons on a Click Wheel.

Test your knowledge of pages 234 through 245 in Quiz Yourself 5-1.

QUIZ YOURSELF 5-1

Instructions: Find the true statement below. Then, rewrite the remaining false statements so they are true.

1. A keyboard is an output device that contains keys users press to enter data in a computer.
2. A light pen is a flat, rectangular, electronic, plastic board.
3. A trackball is a small, flat, rectangular pointing device commonly found on notebook computers.
4. Input is any data or instructions entered into the memory of a computer.
5. Operations you can perform with a wheel include point, click, right-click, double-click, triple-click, drag, right-drag, rotate wheel, free-spin wheel, press wheel button, and tilt wheel.
6. PDAs use a pressure-sensitive digital pen, and Tablet PCs use a stylus.

Quiz Yourself Online: To further check your knowledge of input techniques, the keyboard, the mouse and other pointing devices, and controllers for gaming and media players, visit scsite.com/dc2008/ch5/quiz and then click Objectives 1 – 4.

VOICE INPUT

As an alternative to using a keyboard to enter data and instructions, some users talk to their computers and watch the spoken words appear on the screen as they talk. **Voice input** is the process of entering input by speaking into a microphone. The microphone may be a stand-alone peripheral that sits on top of a desk, or built in the computer or device, or in headphones or earphones. Some external microphones have a cable that attaches to a port on the sound card on the computer. Others communicate using wireless technology such as Bluetooth.

Uses of voice input include instant messaging that supports voice conversations, chat rooms

that support voice chats, Internet telephony, and voice recognition. Recall that Internet telephony, or Voice over IP, enables users to speak to other users over the Internet. **Voice recognition**, also called *speech recognition*, is the computer's capability of distinguishing spoken words. Popular voice recognition programs include IBM ViaVoice and Dragon NaturallySpeaking (Figure 5-17).

FIGURE 5-17   With voice recognition software, users can dictate text and enter instructions to the computer by speaking into a microphone.

Voice recognition programs recognize a vocabulary of preprogrammed words, which can range from two words to millions of words. The automated telephone system at your bank may ask you to answer questions by speaking the words Yes or No into the telephone. A voice recognition program on your computer, by contrast, may recognize up to two million words.

Most voice recognition programs are a combination of speaker dependent and speaker independent. With *speaker-dependent software*, the computer makes a profile of your voice, which means you have to train the computer to recognize your voice. To train the computer, you must speak words and phrases into the computer repeatedly. *Speaker-independent software* has a built-in set of word patterns so you do not have to train a computer to recognize your voice. Many products today include a built-in set of words that grows as the software learns your words. Most of today's programs allow you to speak in a flowing conversational tone, called *continuous speech.*

Keep in mind that the best voice recognition programs are 90 to 95 percent accurate, which means the software may interpret as many as one in ten words incorrectly.

WEB LINK 5-6

Voice Input

For more information, visit scsite.com/ dc2008/ch5/weblink and then click Voice Input.

Audio Input

Voice input is part of a larger category of input called audio input. **Audio input** is the process of entering any sound into the computer such as speech, music, and sound effects. To enter high-quality sound into a personal computer, the computer must have a sound card. Users enter sound into a computer via devices such as microphones, tape players, CD/DVD players, or radios, each of which plugs in a port on the sound card.

Some users also enter music and other sound effects into a computer using external MIDI devices such as an electronic piano keyboard (Figure 5-18). As discussed in the previous chapter, in addition to being a port, *MIDI (musical instrument digital interface)* is the electronic music industry's standard that defines how digital musical devices represent sounds electronically. These devices connect to the sound card on a computer. Software that conforms to the MIDI standard allows users to compose and edit music and many other sounds. For example, you can change the speed, add notes, or rearrange the score to produce an entirely new sound.

FIGURE 5-18   An electronic piano keyboard is an external MIDI device that allows users to record music, which can be stored in the computer.

INPUT FOR PDAs, SMART PHONES, AND TABLET PCs

Mobile devices, such as the PDA and smart phone, and mobile computers, such as the Tablet PC, offer convenience for the mobile user. A variety of alternatives for entering data and instructions is available for these devices and computers.

PDAs

A user enters data and instructions into a PDA in many ways (Figure 5-19). PDAs ship with a basic stylus, which is the primary input device. Users often purchase a more elaborate stylus that has a ballpoint pen at one end and a stylus at the other. With the stylus, you enter data in two ways: using an on-screen keyboard or using handwriting recognition software that

use one end of the pen/stylus to make selections on the PDA screen and the other end to write on paper

take pictures by inserting the card attached to the digital camera in the PDA's card slot

scan documents by inserting the card attached to the scanner in the PDA's card slot

enter text-based messages by pressing buttons on an on-screen keyboard

transfer data and instructions to and from computer and PDA in its cradle by connecting cradle to computer with a cable

cradle

FIGURE 5-19   Users enter data and instructions into a PDA using a variety of techniques.

is built in the PDA. For example, drawing a straight vertical line in a downward motion displays the number 1 on the PDA.

For users who prefer typing to handwriting, some PDAs have a built-in mini keyboard. Other users type on a desktop computer or notebook computer keyboard and transfer the data to the PDA. Some users prefer to enter data into a PDA using a portable keyboard. A *portable keyboard* is a full-sized keyboard you conveniently use with a PDA or other mobile device (Figure 5-20). Some portable keyboards physically attach to and remove from a PDA; others are wireless.

As an alternative to typing, some PDAs allow users to speak data and instructions into the device. Some PDAs also have cameras built in so you can take photographs and view them on a PDA. On other models, you simply attach a digital camera directly to the PDA. You also can use a PDA to scan small documents, such as business cards and product labels, by attaching a scanner to the PDA. For more information about PDAs, read the Personal Mobile Devices feature that follows this chapter.

FIGURE 5-20   This convenient portable wireless keyboard unfolds into a full-sized keyboard, to which you can attach a PDA.

Smart Phones

Users enter data and instructions into a smart phone using a variety of techniques. You can talk directly into the smart phone's microphone or into a Bluetooth headset that wirelessly communicates with the smart phone to receive audio. Some smart phones have digital cameras that take pictures and touch-sensitive pads that enable you to interact with media, such as music and pictures. Most smart phones include PDA capabilities. Thus, input devices used with PDAs typically also are available for smart phones. For example, some smart phones have a built-in

mini keyboard. For those that do not, users enter data and messages into the smart phone using its keypad (Figure 5-21). Types of messages users send with smart phones include text messages, instant messages, and picture messages.

FIGURE 5-21   Users send text messages, instant messages, and picture messages with smart phones.

TEXT MESSAGING   Instead of calling someone's smart phone or cellular telephone, users can enter and send typed messages using *text messaging*. To send a text message, you type a short message, typically less than 160 characters, to another smart phone by pressing buttons on the telephone's keypad. As with chat rooms and instant messaging, text messaging uses abbreviations and emoticons to minimize the amount of typing required. For example, instead of typing the message, I am surprised, a user can type the emoticon, :-O.

INSTANT MESSAGING   As previously discussed, instant messaging (IM) is a real-time communications service that allows you to exchange messages with other online users. Some wireless Internet service providers (WISPs) partner with IM services so you can use your smart phone to communicate with computer users of the same IM service. For example, with Cingular Wireless service, users can send and receive instant messages with AOL Instant Messenger and Yahoo! Messenger.

FAQ 5-4

How do I type text using a phone keypad?

Phone keypads often contain fewer keys than there are letters in the alphabet. For this reason, each key is responsible for typing multiple characters, which are identified on the key. For example, the "2" key displays the letters A, B, and C on its face. Pressing a key multiple times on the phone's keypad will allow you to cycle through the number, letters, and any other symbols displayed on that key. For more information, visit scsite.com/dc2008/ch5/faq and then click Phone Keypads.

PICTURE MESSAGING   With *picture messaging,* users can send graphics, pictures, video clips, and sound files, as well as short text messages to another smart phone with a compatible picture messaging service. Many smart phones today have a built-in camera so users easily can take pictures and videos and even incorporate short voice recordings in their picture messages (Figure 5-22). After taking the pictures, users can send them to another smart phone, e-mail them to any e-mail address, or post them on a Web site.

As an alternative to text messaging, some users write a message with a digital pen, transfer the message from the pen to the smart phone, and then use picture messaging to send the handwritten message. Read Ethics & Issues 5-3 for a related discussion.

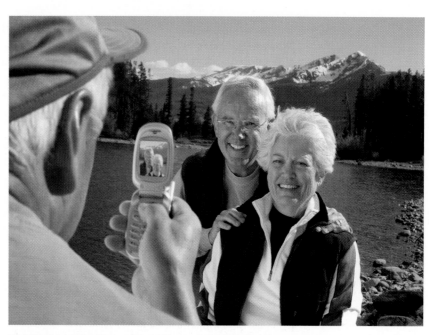

FIGURE 5-22   Many smart phones include a digital camera so users can send pictures and videos to others.

ETHICS & ISSUES 5-3

Should Talking on a Cellular Phone While Driving Be Illegal?

Cellular phone sales are soaring. In addition to talking on the phone, many drivers are using their phones to send and receive text messages, instant messages, picture messages, and e-mail, and to access and view Web pages. For drivers, however, cellular phones may be a liability. Estimates vary widely, but studies link between 800 and 8,000 fatalities on U.S. highways to phone use. Because of their additional capabilities, some experts believe cellular phones pose an even greater risk. Many countries have placed bans or restrictions on the use of phones while driving. In the United States, several states have considered or enacted similar legislation. New York and California, for example, permit vehicle operators to use only hands-free phones. Yet, some studies report that just talking on a phone can cause enough driver inattention to trigger an accident. Supporters of a cellular phone ban cite a British study that found drivers talking on phones had reaction times 50 percent slower than when not talking on a phone, and 30 percent slower than drivers who were intoxicated. Opponents of a ban note, however, that other driver activities, like tuning a radio or having a conversation, can be equally distracting and that phones are a factor in fewer than 1 percent of crashes. They also claim that the economic benefits of using a phone while driving may be greater than the costs associated with more accidents. Furthermore, drivers may have good reasons to use phones while driving, and laws may not take this into account. Should the use of phones be banned while driving? Why? What other measures, if any, could be taken to prevent drivers from endangering themselves and others while using phones?

Tablet PCs

The primary input device for a Tablet PC is a pressure-sensitive digital pen, which allows users to write on the device's screen. A Tablet PC's handwriting recognition software works similarly to that of a PDA. The computer converts the handwriting into characters it can process.

Both the slate and convertible designs of a Tablet PC provide a means for keyboard input for those users who prefer typing to handwriting.

You can attach a removable keyboard to the slate Tablet PC. The convertible Tablet PC has an attached keyboard that can be rotated 180 degrees so the computer resembles a notebook computer.

To access peripherals at their home or office, users can slide their Tablet PC in a docking station. A *docking station,* which is an external device that attaches to a mobile computer or device, contains a power connection and provides connections to peripherals.

In the docking station, Tablet PC users can work with a full-sized keyboard, mouse, CD/DVD drives, and other desktop peripherals (Figure 5-23). The design of docking stations varies, depending on the type of mobile computer or the device to which they are attached.

FAQ 5-5

What security issues affect mobile computers or devices?

Mobile computers and mobile devices are susceptible to virus threats when you download infected Web pages or open infected e-mail messages. Another risk involves wireless networks, which provide a means for others to connect to your computer or device without your knowledge. Once users connect to your computer or device, they may be able to add to, change, or remove your data. For more information, visit scsite.com/dc2008/ch5/faq and then click Security Threats and Mobile Devices.

FIGURE 5-23   To use a slate Tablet PC while working at a desk, insert the Tablet PC in a docking station. Devices such as a keyboard and CD drive can be plugged in the docking station.

DIGITAL CAMERAS

A **digital camera** allows users to take pictures and store the photographed images digitally, instead of on traditional film (Figure 5-24). While many digital cameras look like a traditional camera, some models attach to PDAs or are built in PDAs and smart phones usually via a memory card. Mobile users such as real estate agents, insurance agents, general contractors, and photojournalists use digital cameras so they immediately can view photographed images on the camera. Home and business users have digital cameras to save the expense of film developing, duplication, and postage.

Most digital cameras have some amount of internal flash memory to store images. Many also can store additional images on mobile storage media, such as a flash memory card, memory stick, and mini-disc. Chapter 7 discusses these and other storage media in depth. Generally, higher-capacity storage devices can hold more pictures.

Digital cameras typically allow users to review, and sometimes edit, images while they are in the camera. Some digital cameras can connect to or communicate wirelessly with a printer, allowing users to print or view images directly from the camera. Most cameras can connect with a cable to a computer's USB port, so you can use the computer to access the media in the camera just like you access any other drive on the computer.

FIGURE 5-24   With a digital camera, users can view photographed images immediately through a small screen on the camera to see if the picture is worth keeping.

Often users prefer to *download*, or transfer a copy of, the images from the digital camera to the computer's hard disk. With some digital cameras, images download through a cable that connects between the digital camera (or the camera's docking station) and a USB port or a FireWire port on the system unit. For cameras that store images on miniature mobile storage media, simply insert the media in a reading/writing device that communicates wirelessly or attaches to a port on the system unit. Copying images from the miniature media to the computer's hard disk is just like copying files from any other disk drive. Some cameras store images on a mini CD/DVD. In this case, insert the disc in the computer's disc drive and then copy the pictures to the computer's hard disk (or you can view the contents of the disc by inserting it in a CD or DVD player).

When you copy images to the hard disk in a computer, the images are available for editing with photo editing software, printing, faxing, sending via e-mail, including in another document, or posting to a Web site or photo community for everyone to see. Many users add pictures to greeting cards, a computerized photo album, a family newsletter, certificates, and awards.

The three basic types of digital cameras are studio cameras, field cameras, and point-and-shoot cameras. The most expensive and highest quality of the three is a *studio camera*, which is a stationary camera used for professional studio work. Often used by photojournalists, a *field camera* is a portable camera that has many lenses and other attachments. As with the studio camera, a field camera can be quite expensive. A *point-and-shoot camera* is much more affordable and lightweight and provides acceptable quality photographic images for the home or small business user. Figure 5-25 illustrates how one make of point-and-shoot digital camera works.

A point-and-shoot camera often features flash, zoom, automatic focus, and special effects. Some allow users to record short audio narrations for photographed images. Others even record short video clips in addition to still images. Point-and-shoot digital cameras often have a built-in TV out port, allowing users to

FAQ 5-6

What should I look for when shopping for a digital camera?

First, determine your price range and search for cameras within that range. Consider factors such as the physical size and weight, the type of removable storage media, the size of the display, the built-in features, and the method of zooming. An *optical zoom* changes the position of the camera lens to zoom in and out, while a *digital zoom* digitally alters the pixels at the center of the CCD (see Figure 5-25), at the expense of the image quality, to give the appearance of a zoomed image. For more information, visit scsite.com/dc2008/ch5/faq and then click Digital Cameras.

FIGURE 5-25   HOW A DIGITAL CAMERA MIGHT WORK

Step 1: Point to the image to photograph and take the picture. Light passes into the lens of the camera.

Step 2: The image is focused on a chip called a *charge-coupled device* (*CCD*).

Step 3: The CCD generates an analog signal that represents the image.

Step 4: The analog signal is converted to a digital signal by an analog-to-digital converter (ADC).

Step 5: A processor in the camera adjusts the quality of the image and usually stores the digital image on miniature mobile storage media inserted in the camera.

display photographed images or play recorded video clips directly on a television.

For additional information about digital cameras, read the Digital Imaging and Video Technology feature that follows Chapter 6.

Digital Camera Quality

One factor that affects the quality of a digital camera is its resolution. **Resolution** is the number of horizontal and vertical pixels in a display device. A *pixel* (short for picture element) is the smallest element in an electronic image (Figure 5-26). The greater the number of pixels the camera uses to capture an image, the better the quality of the image. Thus, the higher the resolution, the better the image quality, but the more expensive the camera.

Digital camera resolutions range from approximately 3 million to more than 16 million pixels (*MP*). A camera with a 5.1-megapixel (5,100,000 pixels) resolution will provide a better quality than one with a 3.2-megapixel resolution. As a general rule, a 3-megapixel camera is fine for pictures sent via e-mail or posted on the Web. For good quality printed photographs, users should have a 4-megapixel camera for 4 × 6 inch photographs, a 5-megapixel camera for 8 × 10 photographs, and 6-megapixel or greater camera for larger size prints or more professional results.

Manufacturers often use pixels per inch to represent a digital camera's resolution. *Pixels per inch* (*ppi*) is the number of pixels in one inch of screen display. For example, a 2304 × 1728

(pronounced 2304 by 1728) ppi camera has 2,304 pixels per vertical inch and 1,728 pixels per horizontal inch. Multiplying these two numbers together gives an approximate total number of pixels. For example, 2304 times 1728 equals approximately 4 million, or 4 megapixels. If just one number is stated, such as 1600 ppi, then both the vertical and horizontal numbers are the same.

Many digital cameras provide a means to adjust the ppi to the desired resolution. With a lower ppi, you can capture and store more images in the camera. For example, a camera set at 1280 × 960 ppi might capture and store 61 images, if it has sufficient storage capacity. The number of images may reduce to 24 on the same camera set at 2592 × 1944 ppi, because each image consumes more storage space.

The actual photographed resolution is known as the *optical resolution*. Some manufacturers state *enhanced resolution*, instead of, or in addition to, optical resolution. Optical resolution is different from enhanced resolution. The enhanced resolution usually is higher because it uses a special formula to add pixels between those generated by the optical resolution. Be aware that some manufacturers compute a digital camera's megapixels from the enhanced resolution, instead of optical resolution.

Another measure of a digital camera's quality is the number of bits it stores in a pixel. Each pixel consists of one or more bits of data. The more bits used to represent a pixel, the more colors and shades of gray that can be represented. One bit per pixel is enough for simple one-color images. For multiple colors and shades of gray, each pixel requires more than one bit of data. A point-and-shoot camera should be at least 24 bit.

FAQ 5-7

What is dpi?

Some advertisements incorrectly use dpi to mean the same as ppi. The acronym *dpi*, which stands for *dots per inch*, is a measure of a print resolution. For screen resolution, the proper measurement term is ppi (pixels per inch). For more information, visit scsite.com/dc2008/ch5/faq and then click Resolution.

FIGURE 5-26   A pixel is a single point in an electronic image.

> pixel

VIDEO INPUT

Video input is the process of capturing full-motion images and storing them on a computer's storage medium such as a hard disk or DVD.

Some video devices record video using analog signals. Computers, by contrast, use digital signals. To enter video from an analog device into a personal computer, the analog signal must be converted to a digital signal. To do this, plug a video camera, VCR, or other analog video device in a video capture port on the system unit. One type of adapter card that has a video capture port is a *video capture card*, which converts an analog video signal into a digital signal that a computer can process. Most new computers are not equipped with a video capture card because not all users have the need for this type of adapter card.

A **digital video (DV) camera**, by contrast, records video as digital signals instead of analog signals. Many DV cameras can capture still frames, as well as motion. To transfer recorded images to a hard disk or CD or DVD, users connect DV cameras directly to a USB port or a FireWire port on the system unit. Thus, the computer does not need a video capture card. Simply connect the video device to the computer and begin transferring images. After saving the video on a storage medium, such as a hard disk or DVD, you can play it or edit it using video editing software on a computer (Figure 5-27).

PC Video Cameras

A **PC video camera**, or **PC camera**, is a type of digital video camera that enables a home or small business user to capture video and still images, send e-mail messages with video attachments, add live images to instant messages, broadcast live images over the Internet, and make video telephone calls. During a *video telephone call*, both parties see each other as they communicate over the Internet (Figure 5-28). The cost of PC video cameras usually is less than $100.

Attached to the computer's USB port or FireWire port, a PC video camera usually sits on top of the monitor. For more flexibility, some PC video cameras are portable. That is, you can detach them from the base and use them as a stand-alone digital camera. Some notebook computers have built-in PC video cameras.

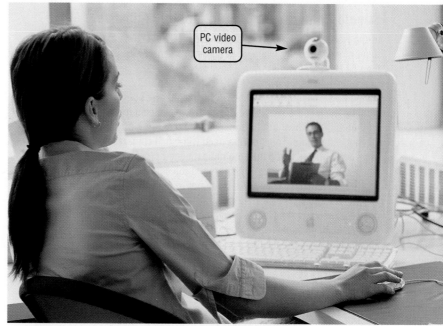

FIGURE 5-28 Using a PC video camera, home users can see each other as they communicate over the Internet.

amera

video is displayed on computer screen

FIGURE 5-27 Home users can transfer videos to their computers and then use video editing software to edit the video.

Web Cams

A **Web cam** is any video camera that displays its output on a Web page. A Web cam attracts Web site visitors by showing images that change regularly. Home or small business users might use Web cams to show a work in progress, weather and traffic information, employees at work, photographs of a vacation, and countless other images. Read Ethics & Issues 5-4 for a related discussion.

Some Web sites have live Web cams that display still pictures and update the displayed image at a specified time or time intervals, such as 15 seconds. Another type of Web cam, called a *streaming cam*, has the illusion of moving images because it sends a continual stream of still images.

WEB LINK 5-7

Web Cams

For more information, visit scsite.com/dc2008/ch5/weblink and then click Web Cams.

ETHICS & ISSUES 5-4

Should Cameras Be Able to Monitor Your Every Move?

In the world of George Orwell's classic novel *1984*, "Telescreens" constantly monitor each citizen's every word and movement. Since its publication more than 50 years ago, most people have viewed the novel as a warning against a future that should be avoided. Whether it is on a busy street corner, on a casino floor, in a subway station, in the neighborhood grocery store, in an elevator, or even in the workplace, the watchful eye continues to become more and more ubiquitous. In Chicago, cameras monitor high-crime areas and even listen for gunshots. The software used with such cameras continues to get more sophisticated, and the automatic recognition of a broad range of suspicious activities and crimes is just around the corner. Some software instantly scans images from a crowd in an attempt to match a face in the crowd to known or wanted criminals and then alerts authorities. Businesses and governments claim that advances in the technology and the low cost as compared to other options allow them to provide greater security and safety. Privacy advocates say that the cameras violate the Constitution's guarantee against unreasonable searches. Many cases of abuse of video monitoring have been noted, such as stores secretly listening in on spouses discussing a potential purchase. What are the differences between George Orwell's Telescreens and the current state of video monitoring? What are the similarities? Would you feel more secure or more paranoid living in a continuously monitored society? Why? What are the benefits of video monitoring? Should you have nothing to fear from security cameras if you have done nothing wrong?

Video Conferencing

A **video conference** is a meeting between two or more geographically separated people who use a network or the Internet to transmit audio and video data (Figure 5-29). To participate in a video conference, you need video conferencing software along with a microphone, speakers, and a video camera attached to a computer.

Examples of video conferencing software include CUworld, Live Meeting, and WebEx.

As you speak, members of the meeting hear your voice on their speakers. Any image in front of the video camera, such as a person's face, appears in a window on each participant's screen. A *whiteboard* is another window on the screen that displays notes and drawings simultaneously on all participants' screens. This window provides multiple users with an area on which they can write or draw.

As the costs of video conferencing hardware and software decrease, increasingly more business meetings, corporate training, and educational classes will be conducted as video conferences.

FAQ 5-8

Do I need a fast Internet connection to participate in a video conference?

Yes. Video conferences transfer a large amount of audio and video in a short time frame. A fast Internet connection allows you to see the video and hear the audio with minimal delay. For more information, visit scsite.com/dc2008/ch5/faq and then click Video Conferencing.

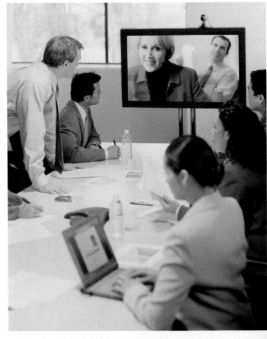

FIGURE 5-29 To save on travel expenses, many large businesses are turning to video conferencing.

Test your knowledge of pages 245 through 254 in Quiz Yourself 5-2.

QUIZ YOURSELF 5-2

Instructions: Find the true statement below. Then, rewrite the remaining false statements so they are true.

1. A digital camera allows users to take pictures and store the photographed images digitally, instead of on traditional film.

2. DV cameras record video as analog signals.

3. Instant messaging is the computer's capability of distinguishing spoken words.

4. Many smart phones today have a built-in camera so users easily can send text messages.

5. The lower the resolution of a digital camera, the better the image quality, but the more expensive the camera.

Quiz Yourself Online: To further check your knowledge of voice input; input for PDAs, smart phones, and Tablet PCs; digital cameras; and video input, visit scsite.com/dc2008/ch5/quiz and then click Objectives 5 – 8.

SCANNERS AND READING DEVICES

Some input devices save users time by eliminating manual data entry. With these devices, users do not type, speak, or write into the computer. Instead, these devices capture data from a *source document*, which is the original form of the data. Examples of source documents include time cards, order forms, invoices, paychecks, advertisements, brochures, photographs, inventory tags, or any other document that contains data to be processed.

Devices that can capture data directly from a source document include optical scanners, optical readers, bar code readers, RFID readers, magnetic stripe card readers, and magnetic-ink character recognition readers. The following pages discuss each of these devices.

Optical Scanners

An *optical scanner*, usually called a **scanner**, is a light-sensing input device that reads printed text and graphics and then translates the results into a form the computer can process. Four types of scanners are flatbed, pen, sheet-fed, and drum (Figure 5-30).

TYPES OF SCANNERS

Scanner	Method of Scanning and Use	Scannable Items
Flatbed	• Similar to a copy machine • Scanning mechanism passes under the item to be scanned, which is placed on a glass surface	• Single-sheet documents • Bound material • Photographs • Some models include trays for slides, transparencies, and negatives
Pen or Handheld	• Move pen over text to be scanned, then transfer data to computer • Ideal for mobile users, students, and researchers • Some connect to a PDA or smart phone	• Any printed text
Sheet-fed	• Item to be scanned is pulled into a stationary scanning mechanism • Smaller than a flatbed scanner • A model designed specifically for photographs is called a *photo scanner*	• Single-sheet documents • Photographs • Slides (with an adapter) • Negatives
Drum	• Item to be scanned rotates around stationary scanning mechanism • Very expensive • Used in large businesses	• Single-sheet documents • Photographs • Slides • Negatives

FIGURE 5-30 This table describes the various types of scanners.

A **flatbed scanner** works in a manner similar to a copy machine except it creates a file of the document in memory instead of a paper copy (Figure 5-31). Once you scan a document or picture, you can display the scanned object on the screen, modify its appearance, store it on a storage medium, print it, fax it, attach it to an e-mail message, include it in another document, or post it to a Web site or photo community for everyone to see.

As with a digital camera, the quality of a scanner is measured by the number of bits it stores in a pixel and the number of pixels per inch, or resolution. The higher each number, the better the quality, but the more expensive the scanner. Most of today's affordable color desktop scanners for the home or small business range from 30 to 48 bits and have an optical resolution ranging from 600 to 9600 ppi. Commercial scanners designed for power users range from 9600 to 14,000 ppi.

Many scanners include *OCR (optical character recognition) software*, which can read and convert text documents into electronic files. OCR software is useful if you need to modify a document but do not have the original word processing file. For example, if you scan a business report with a flatbed scanner and do not use OCR software, you cannot edit the report because the scanner saves the report as an image. This is because the scanner does not differentiate between text and graphics. OCR software, however, would convert the scanned image into a text file that you could edit, for example, with a word processing program. Current OCR software has a high success rate and usually can identify more than 99 percent of scanned material.

Businesses often use scanners for *image processing*, which consists of capturing, storing, analyzing, displaying, printing, and manipulating images. Image processing allows users to convert paper documents such as reports, memos, and procedure manuals into electronic images. Users distribute and publish these electronic documents on networks and the Internet.

Business users typically store and index electronic documents with an image processing system. An *image processing system* is similar to an electronic filing cabinet that provides access to exact reproductions of the original documents. Local governments, for example, use image processing systems to store property deeds and titles to provide the public and professionals, such as lawyers and loan officers, quick access to electronic documents.

FAQ 5-9

How can I improve the quality of scanned documents?

Place a blank sheet of paper behind translucent papers, newspapers, and other see-through types of paper. If the original image is crooked, draw a line on the back at the bottom of the image. Use that mark to align the original on the scanner. Use photo editing software to fix imperfections in images. For more information, visit scsite.com/dc2008/ch5/faq and then click Scanning.

FIGURE 5-31 HOW A FLATBED SCANNER WORKS

Step 1: Place the document to be scanned face down on the glass window. Using buttons on the scanner or the scanner program, start the scanning process.

Step 2: The scanner converts the document content to digital information, which is transmitted through the cable to the memory of the computer.

Step 3: Once in the memory of the computer, users can display the image, print it, e-mail it, include it in a document, or place it on a Web page.

Optical Readers

An *optical reader* is a device that uses a light source to read characters, marks, and codes and then converts them into digital data that a computer can process. Two technologies used by optical readers are optical character recognition and optical mark recognition.

OPTICAL CHARACTER RECOGNITION Optical **character recognition (OCR)** is a technology that involves reading typewritten, computer-printed, or hand-printed characters from ordinary documents and translating the images into a form that the computer can process. Most **OCR devices** include a small optical scanner for reading characters and sophisticated software to analyze what is read.

OCR devices range from large machines that can read thousands of documents per minute to handheld wands that read one document at a time. OCR devices read printed characters in an OCR font. A widely used OCR font is called OCR-A (Figure 5-32). During the scan of a document, an OCR device determines the shapes of characters by detecting patterns of light and dark. OCR software then compares these shapes with predefined shapes stored in memory and converts the shapes into characters the computer can process.

```
ABCDEFGHIJKLM
NOPQRSTUVWXYZ
1234567890
-=■;',.·/
```

FIGURE 5-32 A portion of the characters in the OCR-A font. Notice how characters such as the number 0 and the letter O are shaped differently so the reading device easily can distinguish between them.

Many companies use OCR characters on turnaround documents. A **turnaround document** is a document that you return (turn around) to the company that creates and sends it. For example, when consumers receive a bill, they often tear off a portion of the bill and send it back to the company with their payment (Figure 5-33). The portion of the bill they return usually has their payment amount, account number, and other information printed in OCR characters.

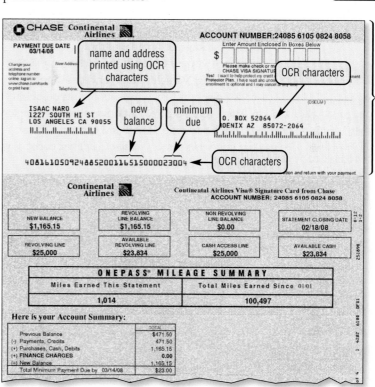

FIGURE 5-33 OCR characters frequently are used with turnaround documents. With this bill, you tear off the top portion and return it with a payment.

OPTICAL MARK RECOGNITION Optical mark **recognition (OMR)** is a technology that reads hand-drawn marks such as small circles or rectangles. A person places these marks on a form, such as a test, survey, or questionnaire answer sheet. With a test, the OMR device first scans the answer key sheet to record correct answers based on patterns of light. The OMR device then scans the remaining documents and matches their patterns of light against the answer key sheet.

Bar Code Readers

A **bar code reader**, also called a **bar code scanner**, is an optical reader that uses laser beams to read bar codes by using light patterns that pass through the bar code lines (Figure 5-34). A **bar code** is an identification code that consists either of a set of vertical lines and spaces of different widths or a two-dimensional pattern of dots, squares, and other images. A 2-D bar code can store much more data than the traditional linear bar code. The bar code represents data that identifies the manufacturer and the item.

Manufacturers print a bar code either on a product's package or on a label that is affixed to a product. A variety of products such as groceries, books, clothing, vehicles, mail, and packages have bar codes. Each industry uses its own type of bar code. The United States Postal Service (USPS) uses a POSTNET bar code. Retail and grocery stores use the *UPC* (*Universal Product Code*) bar code (Figure 5-35). Read Ethics & Issues 5-5 for a related discussion.

WEB LINK 5-8

Bar Code Readers

For more information, visit scsite.com/dc2008/ch5/weblink and then click Bar Code Readers.

ETHICS & ISSUES 5-5

Scanner Errors at the Checkout Counter?

Have you ever taken an item to a store's checkout and discovered that the price displayed when the item's bar code was scanned was different from the price shown on a shelf tag, sign, or advertisement? If you have, you are not alone. A government survey found that eight percent of the time, an item's scanned price is different from the price presented elsewhere. When an item is scanned at a store's checkout counter, a computer finds the item's price in the store's database. Store owners claim that discrepancies between the scanned price and a listed price are the result of human error — either failure to update the store's price database or incorrect shelf tags, signs, or advertisements. Yet, some consumer advocates claim that the discrepancy sometimes is intentional. They accuse stores of *scanner fraud*, insisting that some stores advertise one price and then charge another, hoping buyers will not recognize the difference. Most states have laws that protect consumers against scanner fraud. Some laws even require stores to pay consumers an immediate reward, sometimes $5 or more, if the consumer finds a scanner error. Who do you think is responsible for differences between scanned prices and posted costs? Why? Should stores be responsible for pricing errors? Why or why not? Do you think that the increased use of self-checkout registers will increase or decrease scanner fraud claims? Why or why not?

FIGURE 5-34   A bar code reader uses laser beams to read bar codes on products such as ID cards and books.

FIGURE 5-35   This UPC identifies a carton of skim milk.

RFID Readers

RFID (*radio frequency identification*) is a technology that uses radio signals to communicate with a tag placed in or attached to an object, an animal, or a person. RFID tags, which contain a memory chip and an antenna, are available in many shapes and sizes and sometimes are embedded in glass, labels, or cards. Some RFID tags are as small as a grain of sand; others are the size of a luggage tag. An **RFID reader** reads information on the tag via radio waves. RFID readers can be handheld devices or mounted in a stationary object such as a doorway.

Many retailers see RFID as an alternative to bar code identification because it does not require direct contact or line-of-site transmission. Each product in a store would contain a tag that identifies the product (Figure 5-36). As consumers remove products from the store shelves and walk through a checkout area, an RFID reader reads the tag(s) and communicates with a computer that calculates the amount due, eliminating the need for checking out each item.

Other uses of RFID include tracking times of runners in a marathon; tracking location of soldiers, employee wardrobes, and airline baggage; checking lift tickets of skiers; gauging pressure and temperature of tires on a vehicle; checking out library books; and tracking payment as vehicles pass through booths on tollway systems. Read Ethics & Issues 5-6 for a related discussion. Read Looking Ahead 5-1 for a look at the next generation of RFID.

ETHICS & ISSUES 5-6

Will RFID Track Your Every Move?

The rapid growth of RFID worries some privacy advocates. RFID (radio frequency identification) uses a tiny computer chip that can be mounted on a tag attached to a product, sewn into an article of clothing, or even attached to a document. For merchants, RFID can help to locate items in a warehouse and identify items that need to be replenished. For consumers, RFID can supply detailed product information, and someday let buyers bypass check-out lines and take purchases directly from the store, with the item's cost charged to their card. The federal government started a program to include RFID chips on all passports. Privacy advocates worry, however, that RFID could obliterate a person's anonymity. They fear that with an RFID reader, any individual or organization could track a person's movements and make that information available to marketers or government agencies. Some fear that the RFID chip in a passport could be copied by a hidden RFID reader and then used for nefarious purposes such as faking one's identity. To protect privacy, privacy advocates insist that merchants should be forced to disable RFID transmitters as soon as buyers leave a store. They also recommend that RFID-enabled documents, such as passports, be kept in special containers made of material that will not allow the chip to be read until it is removed from the container. Would you be comfortable purchasing a product that includes RFID? Why or why not? Should buyers be allowed to request that RFID transmitters be disabled after they make a purchase, or should merchants be required to render transmitters inoperative when the product leaves the store? Why? Would you feel comfortable carrying a form of identification that is RFID-enabled? Why or why not?

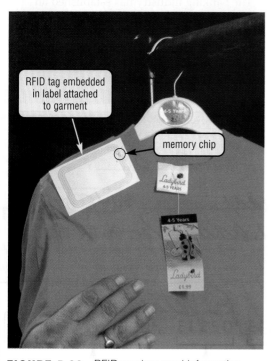

FIGURE 5-36 RFID readers read information stored on an RFID tag and then communicate this information to computers, which instantaneously compute payments and update inventory records. In this example, the RFID tag is embedded in a label attached to the garment.

RFID tag embedded in label attached to garment

memory chip

LOOKING AHEAD 5-1

Paying with Your Cellular Telephone

Your waiting time in the checkout lane may be shortened if merchants adopt new RFID technology. Cellular telephone manufacturers, including Nokia, are building the RFID chips into their products, so shoppers will be able to wave their phones one inch in front of a contactless reader to pay for merchandise. They also will need to enter a code number if the purchase is more than $25.

Similar RFID technology already is in place with 20 million Americans' credit or debit cards. Nokia says, however, shoppers can leave those cards at home and carry only their cellular phones.

Cellular telephone manufacturers currently are testing their RFID systems worldwide, and some merchants are hopeful the technology will provide faster service in line, fewer thefts, and increased profits. Some consumer advocates, however, predict some merchants will install RFID chip readers in their stores' doorways and then track customers' shopping patterns without their knowledge. For more information, visit scsite.com/dc2008/ch5/looking and then click RFID Chips.

Many POS terminals handle credit card or debit card payments and thus also include a magstripe reader. Some have fingerprint scanners (discussed in the next section) that read your fingerprint, which is linked to a payment method such as a checking account or credit card. After swiping your card through the reader or reading your fingerprint, the POS terminal connects to a system that authenticates the purchase. Once the transaction is approved, the terminal prints a receipt for the customer.

A self-service POS terminal allows consumers to perform all checkout-related activities (Figure 5-40). That is, they scan the items, bag the items, and pay for the items themselves. Consumers with small orders find the self-service POS terminals convenient because these terminals often eliminate the hassle of waiting in long lines.

touch screen with graphical user interface

bar code reader reads UPC labels

FIGURE 5-40 Many grocery stores offer self-serve checkouts, where the consumers themselves use the POS terminals to scan purchases, scan their store saver card and coupons, and then pay for the goods.

Automated Teller Machines

An **automated teller machine (ATM)** is a self-service banking machine that connects to a host computer through a network (Figure 5-41). Banks place ATMs in convenient locations, including grocery stores, convenience stores, retail outlets, shopping malls, and gas stations, so customers conveniently can access their bank accounts.

Using an ATM, people withdraw cash, deposit money, transfer funds, or inquire about an account balance. Some ATMs have a touch screen; others have special buttons or keypads for entering input. To access a bank account, you insert a plastic bankcard in the ATM's magstripe reader. The ATM asks you to enter a password,

called a *personal identification number* (*PIN*), which verifies that you are the holder of the bankcard. When your transaction is complete, the ATM prints a receipt for your records.

magstripe reader

FIGURE 5-41 An ATM is a self-service banking terminal that allows customers to access their bank accounts.

BIOMETRIC INPUT

Biometrics is the technology of authenticating a person's identity by verifying a personal characteristic. Biometric devices grant users access to programs, systems, or rooms by analyzing some biometric identifier. A *biometric identifier* is a physiological (related to physical or chemical activities in the body) or behavioral characteristic. Examples include fingerprints, hand geometry, facial features, voice, signatures, and eye patterns.

A *biometric device* translates a personal characteristic (the input) into a digital code that is compared with a digital code stored in the computer. If the digital code in the computer does not match the personal characteristic's code, the computer denies access to the individual.

The most widely used biometric device today is a fingerprint scanner. A **fingerprint scanner** captures curves and indentations of a fingerprint. With the cost of fingerprint scanners less than $100, home and small business users install fingerprint scanners to authenticate users before they can access a personal computer. External fingerprint scanners usually plug into a parallel or USB port. To save on desk space, some newer keyboards and notebook computers have a fingerprint scanner built into them, which allows users to log on to programs and Web sites via their fingerprint instead of entering a user name and password (Figure 5-42). Grocery and retail stores now use fingerprint scanners as a means of payment, where the customer's fingerprint is linked to a payment method such as a checking account or credit card. For a technical discussion about fingerprint scanners, read the High-Tech Talk article on page 268.

A *face recognition system* captures a live face image and compares it with a stored image to determine if the person is a legitimate user. Some buildings use face recognition systems to secure access to rooms. Law enforcement, surveillance systems, and airports use face recognition to protect the public. Some notebook computers use this security technique to safeguard a computer. The computer will not start unless the user is legitimate. These programs are becoming more sophisticated and can recognize people with or without glasses, makeup, or jewelry, and with new hairstyles.

Biometric devices measure the shape and size of a person's hand using a *hand geometry system* (Figure 5-43). Because their cost is more than $1,000, larger companies use these systems as time and attendance devices or as security devices. Colleges use hand geometry systems to verify students' identities. Day-care centers and hospital nurseries use them to verify parents who pick up their children.

A *voice verification system* compares a person's live speech with their stored voice pattern. Larger organizations sometimes use voice verification systems as time and attendance devices. Many companies also use this technology for access to sensitive files and networks. Some financial services use voice verification systems to secure telephone banking transactions. These systems use speaker-dependent voice recognition software. That is, users train the computer to recognize their inflection patterns.

A *signature verification system* recognizes the shape of your handwritten signature, as well as measures the pressure exerted and the motion used to write the signature. Signature verification systems use a specialized pen and tablet.

FIGURE 5-42 Keyboard with built-in fingerprint scanner.

FIGURE 5-43 A hand geometry system verifies this student's identity before he is allowed access to the school recreation center.

INPUT DEVICES FOR PHYSICALLY CHALLENGED USERS

The ever-increasing presence of computers in everyone's lives has generated an awareness of the need to address computing requirements for those who have or may develop physical limitations. The **Americans with Disabilities Act** (**ADA**) requires any company with 15 or more employees to make reasonable attempts to accommodate the needs of physically challenged workers.

Besides voice recognition, which is ideal for blind or visually impaired users, several other input devices are available. A *keyguard* is a metal or plastic plate placed over the keyboard that allows users to rest their hands on the keyboard without accidentally pressing any keys (Figure 5-47). A keyguard also guides a finger or pointing device so a user presses only one key at a time.

Keyboards with larger keys also are available. Still another option is the *on-screen keyboard*, in which a graphic of a standard keyboard is displayed on the user's screen (Figure 5-48).

FIGURE 5-47   A keyguard.

Various pointing devices are available for users with motor disabilities. Small trackballs that the user controls with a thumb or one finger can be attached to a table, mounted to a wheelchair, or held in the user's hand. Another option for people with limited hand movement is a *head-mounted pointer* to control the pointer or insertion point (Figure 5-49). To simulate the functions of a mouse button, a user works with switches that control the pointer. The switch might be a hand pad, a foot pedal, a receptor that detects facial motions, or a pneumatic instrument controlled by puffs of air.

Two exciting developments in this area are gesture recognition and computerized implant devices. Both in the prototype stage, they attempt to provide users with a natural computer interface.

With *gesture recognition*, the computer will detect human motions. Computers with gesture recognition capability have the potential to recognize sign language, read lips, track facial movements, or follow eye gazes. For paralyzed or speech impaired individuals, a doctor will implant a computerized device into the brain. This device will contain a transmitter. As the user thinks thoughts, the transmitter will send signals to the computer.

FIGURE 5-49   A camera/receiver mounted on the monitor tracks the position of the head-mounted pointer, which is reflective material that this user is wearing on the brim of her hat. As the user moves her head, the pointer on the screen also moves.

FIGURE 5-48   As you click letters on the on-screen keyboard, they appear in the document at the location of the insertion point.

Test your knowledge of pages 255 through 266 in Quiz Yourself 5-3.

QUIZ YOURSELF 5-3

Instructions: Find the true statement below. Then, rewrite the remaining false statements so they are true.

1. A fingerprint scanner captures curves and indentations of a signature.

2. After swiping a credit card through an MICR reader, a POS terminal connects to a system that authenticates the purchase.

3. ATMs ask you to enter a password, called a biometric identifier, which verifies that you are the holder of the bankcard.

4. Four types of source documents are flatbed, pen, sheet-fed, and drum.

5. Retail and grocery stores use the POSTNET bar code.

6. RFID is a technology that uses laser signals to communicate with a tag placed in an object, an animal, or a person.

7. The Americans with Disabilities Act (ADA) requires any company with 15 or more employees to make reasonable attempts to accommodate the needs of physically challenged workers.

Quiz Yourself Online: To further check your knowledge of scanners and reading devices, terminals, biometric devices, and input for physically challenged users, visit scsite.com/dc2008/ch5/quiz and then click Objectives 9 – 12.

CHAPTER SUMMARY

Input is any data and instructions you enter into the memory of a computer. This chapter described the various techniques of entering input and several commonly used input devices (read Looking Ahead 5-2 for a look at the next generation of input devices). Topics presented included the keyboard, mouse, and other pointing devices; controllers for gaming and media players; voice input; input for PDAs, smart phones, and Tablet PCs; digital cameras; video input; scanners and reading devices; terminals; biometric input; and input devices for physically challenged users.

LOOKING AHEAD 5-2

Controlling Games by Thinking

Putting on your thinking cap one day may take on a whole new meaning for gamers. A brain-machine interface being developed in Berlin could replace a joystick in traditional gaming. Scientists are envisioning a gamer wearing a baseball-cap device and then having a wireless connection with a computer. Tiny, metal sensors will detect brainwave activity without skin contact.

Using special software, the wearer must calibrate his individual brainwaves with the computer. During this five-minute process, the wearer will imagine moving his left or right hand or foot or rotating an object. Electrodes then pick up these thought signals. Once the person is in sync with the computer, he can imagine moving his hands or feet to trigger an action in the game.

The thought-controlled cap also could be used as a communication tool for people who cannot speak or sign by translating their brainwave electrical impulses into letters and words. For more information, visit scsite.com/dc2008/ch5/looking and then click Thought-Controlled Input.

CAREER CORNER — Data Entry Clerk

Data entry clerks have an essential role in today's information-producing industry. A *data entry clerk* enters data into documents, databases, and other applications using computer keyboards and visual display devices. Duties can include manipulating, editing, and maintaining data to ensure that it is accurate and up-to-date, and researching information.

Some data entry clerks telecommute. Although they generally use keyboards, they also work with other input from scanners or electronically transmitted files. Because of the nature of their job, data entry clerks often sit for hours typing in front of monitors. They can be susceptible to repetitive stress injuries and neck, back, and eye strain. To prevent these injuries, many offices use ergonomically designed input devices and incorporate regularly scheduled exercise breaks.

Data entry clerks usually are high school graduates with keyboarding skills. Some employers require an associate's degree or at least two years of post-high-school education plus two years of office experience. Data entry training, basic language skills, and familiarity with word processing, spreadsheet, and database programs are important. Data entry often serves as a stepping-stone to other administrative positions. The average annual salary for data entry clerks is around $24,000. Salaries start at about $21,500 and, with experience, can exceed $35,000. For more information, visit scsite.com/dc2008/ch5/careers and then click Data Entry Clerk.

Chapter Review

The Chapter Review section summarizes the concepts presented in this chapter. To listen to the audio version of this Chapter Review, visit scsite.com/dc2008/ch5/review. To obtain help from other students regarding any subject in this chapter, visit scsite.com/dc2008/ch5/forum and post your thoughts or questions.

① What Is Input? **Input** is any *data* or instructions entered into the memory of a computer. An **input device** is any hardware component that allows users to enter data and instructions.

② What Are the Characteristics of a Keyboard? A **keyboard** is an input device that contains keys users press to enter data into a computer. Computer keyboards have a typing area that includes letters of the alphabet, numbers, punctuation marks, and other basic keys. Most keyboards also have *function keys* programmed to issue commands; keys used to move the **insertion point**, usually a blinking vertical bar, on the screen; and *toggle keys* that switch between two states when pressed. A *gaming keyboard* is a keyboard designed specifically for users that enjoy playing games on the computer.

③ What Are Different Mouse Types, and How Do They Work? A **pointing device** is an input device that allows users to control a small graphical symbol, called a **pointer**, on the screen. A **mouse** is a pointing device that fits under the palm of your hand. As you move a mouse, the pointer on the screen also moves. A *mechanical mouse* translates the movement of a ball on its underside into signals the computer can process. An *optical mouse* uses devices that emit and sense light to detect the mouse's movement. A *laser mouse* uses a laser to detect movement. A *wireless mouse* transmits data using wireless technology.

④ How Do Pointing Devices and Controllers for Gaming and Media Players Work? A **trackball** is a stationary pointing device with a ball that you rotate to move the pointer. A **touchpad** is a flat, pressure-sensitive device that you slide your finger across to move the pointer. A **pointing stick** is a device positioned on the keyboard that you push to move the pointer. A **light pen** is a light-sensitive device that you press against or point at the screen to select objects. A **touch screen** is a touch-sensitive display device that you interact with by touching areas of the screen. A **stylus** and a **digital pen** use pressure to write or draw. A **gamepad** controls the movement and actions of players or objects in video games or computer games. A **joystick** is a vertical lever that you move to control a simulated vehicle or player. A **wheel** is a steering-wheel-type device that you turn to simulate driving a vehicle. A **light gun** is used to shoot targets as you pull the trigger on the weapon. A **dance pad** is an electronic device, divided into panels, that users press with their feet. A *motion-sensing game controller*, such as the *Wii Remote*, guides on-screen elements by moving a handheld input device through the air. A *Click Wheel* is used to browse through songs, pictures, or movie lists on a portable media player.

connect
Visit scsite.com/dc2008/ch5/ or click the Quiz Yourself button. Click Objectives 1 – 4.

⑤ How Does Voice Recognition Work? **Voice recognition** is the computer's capability of distinguishing spoken words. Voice recognition programs recognize a vocabulary of preprogrammed words. Most voice recognition programs are a combination of *speaker-dependent software*, which makes a profile of your voice, and *speaker-independent software*, which has a built-in set of word patterns.

⑥ What Are Input Devices for PDAs, Smart Phones, and Tablet PCs? A primary input device for a PDA is a basic stylus. Some PDAs have a built-in keyboard or support voice input. You can attach a full-sized *portable keyboard* to a PDA. Because most smart phones include PDA capabilities, input devices used with PDAs usually are available for smart phones. You can send typed messages using *text messaging*. Some smart phones can use IM to communicate over the Internet, and many have a camera so that users can use *picture messaging*. The primary input device for a Tablet PC is a digital pen, with which you can write on the device's screen. If you slide a Tablet PC into a *docking station*, you can use a full-sized keyboard, mouse, and other peripherals.

Chapter Review

(7) How Does a Digital Camera Work? A **digital camera** allows users to take pictures and store the photographed images digitally. When you take a picture, light passes into the camera lens, which focuses the image on a *charge-coupled device (CCD)*. The CCD generates an analog signal that represents the image. An analog-to-digital converter (ADC) converts the analog signal to a digital signal. A processor in the camera stores the digital image on the camera's storage media. The image is downloaded to a computer's hard disk via cable or copied from the camera's storage media.

(8) How Are PC Video Cameras, Web Cams, and Video Conferencing Used? A **PC video camera** is a digital video camera that enables users to capture video and still images and then send or broadcast the images over the Internet. A **Web cam** is any video camera that displays its output on a Web page. A **video conference** is a meeting between geographically separated people who use a network or the Internet to transmit audio and video data.

> Visit scsite.com/dc2008/ch5/quiz or click the Quiz Yourself button. Click Objectives 5 – 8.

(9) What Are Various Types of Scanners and Reading Devices, and How Do They Work? A **scanner** is a light-sensing input device that reads printed text and graphics and translates the results into a form the computer can process. A **flatbed scanner** works in a manner similar to a copy machine except it creates a file of the document. An *optical reader* uses a light source to read characters, marks, and codes and converts them into digital data. **Optical character recognition (OCR)** reads characters from ordinary documents. **Optical mark recognition (OMR)** reads hand-drawn marks such as small circles. A **bar code reader** is an optical reader that uses laser beams to read a **bar code**, or identification code. **RFID** (*radio frequency identification*) uses radio signals to communicate with an embedded tag. A *magstripe reader* reads the magnetic stripe on the back of credit cards and other similar cards. **MICR** (*magnetic-ink character recognition*) reads text printed with magnetized ink.

(10) What Are Types of Terminals? A *terminal* consists of a keyboard, a monitor, a video card, and memory. A *dumb terminal* has no processing power and relies on a host computer for processing. A *smart terminal* has a processor and can perform some functions independent of the host computer. POS terminals and ATMs are special-purpose terminals. A **POS** (*point-of-sale*) **terminal** records purchases, processes credit or debit cards, and updates inventory. An **automated teller machine (ATM)** is a self-service banking machine that connects to a host computer. To access a bank account, you insert a bankcard into the ATM's card reader and enter a *personal identification number (PIN)*.

(11) What Are Various Biometric Devices? A *biometric device* translates a personal characteristic into digital code that is compared with a digital code stored in the computer to identify an individual. A **fingerprint scanner** captures curves and indentations of a fingerprint. A *face recognition system* captures a live face image. A *hand geometry system* measures the shape and size of a hand. A *voice verification system* compares live speech with a stored voice pattern. A *signature verification system* recognizes the shape of a signature. An *iris recognition system* reads patterns in the iris of the eye. *Retinal scanners* scan patterns of blood vessels in the back of the retina.

(12) What Are Alternative Input Devices for Physically Challenged Users? Voice recognition is ideal for visually impaired users. A *keyguard* is a plate placed over the keyboard that allows users with limited hand mobility to rest their hands and press only one key at a time. Keyboards with larger keys or an *on-screen keyboard* displayed on a user's screen also are available. A small trackball or a *head-mounted pointer* helps users with limited hand movement to control the pointer. Two developments in the prototype stage are *gesture recognition* and computerized implant devices.

> Visit scsite.com/dc2008/ch5/quiz or click the Quiz Yourself button. Click Objectives 9 – 12.

Key Terms

You should know the Primary Terms and be familiar with the Secondary Terms. Use the list below to help focus your study. To further enhance your understanding of the Key Terms in this chapter, visit scsite.com/dc2008/ch5/terms. See an example of and a definition for each term, and access current and additional information about the term from the Web.

Primary Terms

(shown in bold-black characters in the chapter)

Americans with Disabilities Act (ADA) (266)
audio input (246)
automated teller machine (ATM) (262)
bar code (258)
bar code reader (258)
bar code scanner (258)
dance pad (244)
digital camera (250)
digital pen (242)
digital video (DV) camera (253)
ergonomics (238)
fingerprint scanner (262)
flatbed scanner (256)
game controller (244)
gamepad (244)
graphics tablet (243)
input (234)
input device (236)
insertion point (237)
joystick (244)
keyboard (236)
light gun (244)
light pen (242)
magnetic stripe card reader (260)
MICR (260)
MICR reader (260)

mouse (239)
OCR devices (257)
optical character recognition (OCR) (257)
optical mark recognition (OMR) (257)
PC camera (253)
PC video camera (253)
pen input (242)
pointer (239)
pointing device (239)
pointing stick (242)
POS terminal (261)
resolution (252)
RFID (259)
RFID reader (259)
scanner (255)
smart card (264)
stylus (242)
touch screen (242)
touchpad (241)
trackball (241)
turnaround document (257)
video conference (254)
video input (253)
voice input (245)
voice recognition (245)
Web cam (254)
wheel (244)

Secondary Terms

(shown in italic characters in the chapter)

air mouse (239)
biometric device (262)
biometric identifier (262)
biometrics (262)
charge-coupled device (CCD) (251)
Click Wheel (245)
command (235)
continuous speech (246)
cordless keyboard (238)
cordless mouse (239)
cursor (application program) (237)
cursor (graphics tablet) (243)
data (234)
data collection device (261)
digitizer (243)
docking station (249)
download (251)
dumb terminal (261)
enhanced keyboard (236)
enhanced resolution (252)
ergonomic keyboard (238)
face recognition system (263)
field camera (251)
function keys (236)
gaming keyboard (237)
gesture recognition (266)
hand geometry system (263)
handwriting recognition software (243)
head-mounted pointer (266)
image processing (256)
image processing system (256)
iris recognition system (264)
keyguard (266)
laser mouse (239)
magnetic-ink character recognition (260)
magstripe reader (260)
mechanical mouse (239)
MIDI (musical instrument digital interface) (246)
motion-sensing game controllers (244)
mouse gestures (240)
mouse pad (239)

mouse pointer (239)
MP (252)
OCR (optical character recognition) software (256)
on-screen keyboard (266)
optical mouse (239)
optical reader (257)
optical resolution (252)
optical scanner (255)
personal identification number (PIN) (262)
photo scanner (255)
picture messaging (249)
pixel (252)
pixels per inch (ppi) (252)
point-and-shoot camera (251)
point of sale (POS) (261)
portable keyboard (248)
program (234)
radio frequency identification (259)
retinal scanners (264)
signature verification system (263)
smart terminal (261)
source document (255)
speaker-dependent software (246)
speaker-independent software (246)
speech recognition (245)
streaming cam (254)
studio camera (251)
terminal (261)
text messaging (248)
toggle key (237)
touch-sensitive pad (245)
UPC (Universal Product Code) (258)
user response (235)
video capture card (253)
video telephone call (253)
voice verification system (263)
whiteboard (254)
Wii Remote (245)
wireless keyboard (238)
wireless mouse (239)

Checkpoint

Use the Checkpoint exercises to check your knowledge level of the chapter. The Beyond the Book exercises will help broaden your understanding of the concepts presented in this chapter. To complete the Checkpoint exercises interactively, visit scsite.com/dc2008/ch5/check.

Label the Figure

Identify these areas and keys on a desktop computer keyboard.

a. arrow keys
b. function keys
c. Internet controls
d. media controls
e. numeric keypad
f. typing area
g. WINDOWS key
h. wrist rest

True/False

Mark T for True and F for False. (See page numbers in parentheses.)

_____ 1. Once data is in memory, the computer interprets and executes instructions to process the data into information. (234)

_____ 2. An input device is any hardware component that allows users to enter data and instructions into a computer. (236)

_____ 3. The command associated with a function key will remain the same from program to program. (236)

_____ 4. An air mouse allows you to control objects, media players, and slide shows by moving the mouse in predetermined directions through the air. (239)

_____ 5. A touchpad is a small, flat, rectangular pointing device that is sensitive to pressure and motion. (241)

_____ 6. A light pen is a handheld input device that can detect the presence of light. (242)

_____ 7. Pressure-sensitive digital pens typically provide less functionality than a stylus. (243)

_____ 8. Speaker-dependent software has a built-in set of word patterns so you do not have to train a computer to recognize your voice. (246)

_____ 9. The primary input device for a Tablet PC is a mouse. (249)

_____ 10. Resolution is the smallest element in an electronic image. (252)

_____ 11. A whiteboard is a meeting between two or more geographically separated people who use a network or the Internet to transmit audio and video data. (254)

_____ 12. A scanner is a light-sensing input device that reads printed text and graphics and then translates the results into a form the computer can process. (255)

Checkpoint

 Multiple Choice   Select the best answer. (See page numbers in parentheses.)

1. _____ is a series of instructions that tells a computer what to do and how to do it. (234)
   a. Data
   b. A program
   c. A command
   d. A user response

2. A(n) _____ has twelve function keys along the top; it also has two CTRL keys, two ALT keys, and a set of arrow and additional keys between the typing area and the numeric keypad. (236)
   a. portable keyboard
   b. enhanced keyboard
   c. keyguard
   d. touchpad

3. A(n) _____ has a design that reduces the chance of wrist and hand injuries. (238)
   a. ergonomic keyboard
   b. cordless keyboard
   c. gaming keyboard
   d. function key

4. A(n) _____ has a rubber or metal ball on its underside. (239)
   a. air mouse
   b. laser mouse
   c. optical mouse
   d. mechanical mouse

5. Architects, mapmakers, designers, artists, and home users create drawings and sketches on a _____. (243)
   a. trackball
   b. smart terminal
   c. graphics tablet
   d. touchpad

6. A _____ controls the movement and actions of players or objects in video games or computer games. (244)
   a. control pad
   b. gamepad
   c. dance pad
   d. touchpad

7. _____ is the process of entering any sound into the computer such as speech, music, and sound effects. (246)
   a. MIDI
   b. Voice input
   c. Voice recognition
   d. Audio input

8. The most expensive and highest quality digital camera is a _____, which is a stationary camera used for professional work. (251)
   a. PC camera
   b. point-and-shoot camera
   c. studio camera
   d. field camera

9. A(n) _____ is a type of digital video camera that enables a home or small business user to capture video and still images, send e-mail messages with video attachments, add live images to instant messages, broadcast live images over the Internet, and make video telephone calls. (253)
   a. PC camera
   b. digital video camera
   c. Web cam
   d. optical scanner

10. Scanners capture data from a _____, which is the original form of the data. (255)
    a. duplicate document
    b. secondary document
    c. derivative document
    d. source document

11. RFID is a technology that uses _____ to communicate with a tag placed in or attached to an object, an animal, or a person. (259)
    a. a thin wire   b. pixels
    c. radio signals   d. light waves

12. The most widely used biometric device is the _____. (262)
    a. fingerprint scanner
    b. iris recognition system
    c. retinal scanner
    d. face recognition system

13. A smart card stores the personal data on a _____ embedded in the card. (264)
    a. biometric device
    b. thin microprocessor
    c. magnetic strip
    d. optical mark

14. With _____, the computer will detect human motion. (266)
    a. an on-screen keyboard
    b. a head-mounted pointer
    c. gesture recognition
    d. a computerized implant

Checkpoint

Matching

Match the terms with their definitions. (See page numbers in parentheses.)

_____ 1. insertion point (237)

_____ 2. gaming keyboard (237)

_____ 3. pointer (239)

_____ 4. gamepad (244)

_____ 5. game controller (244)

_____ 6. light gun (244)

_____ 7. dance pad (244)

_____ 8. video capture card (253)

_____ 9. bar code (258)

_____ 10. retinal scanner (264)

a. projects an infrared image of a keyboard on any flat surface

b. identification code that consists either of vertical lines and spaces of different widths or a two-dimensional pattern of dots, squares, and other images

c. scans patterns of blood vessels in the back of the retina

d. controls the movement and actions of players or objects in video games or computer games

e. graphical symbol whose location and shape change with the movement of a pointing device

f. symbol on the screen that indicates where the next character typed will be displayed

g. keyboard designed specifically for users that enjoy playing games on the computer

h. a flat electronic device divided into panels that users press with their feet in response to instructions from a music video game

i. used to shoot targets and moving objects after you pull the trigger on the weapon

j. converts an analog video signal to a digital signal that a computer can process

k. self-service banking machine that connects to a host computer

l. used by video games and computer games as the input device that directs movements and actions of on-screen objects

Short Answer

Write a brief answer to each of the following questions.

1. What are three different types of mouse devices? _____ What makes them different from each other? _____

2. How do motion-sensing game controllers work? _____ What is the Wii Remote and how is it used? _____

3. What is OCR (optical character recognition)? _____ What is OMR (optical mark recognition)? _____

4. What is a biometric identifier and what are some examples? _____ How does a biometric device work? _____

5. What is the Americans with Disabilities Act (ADA)? _____ How might gesture recognition and computerized implant devices help physically challenged users in the future? _____

Beyond the Book

Read the following book elements, learn more about each using the Web, and then write a brief report.

1. Ethics & Issues — Keyboard Monitoring — Privacy Risk? (237), Are Employers Responsible for Medical Problems Related to Computer Use? (241), Should Talking on a Cellular Phone While Driving Be Illegal? (249), Should Cameras Be Able to Monitor Your Every Move? (254), Scanner Errors at the Checkout Counter? (258), or Will RFID Track Your Every Move? (259)

2. Career Corner — Data Entry Clerk (267)

3. Companies on the Cutting Edge — Logitech or Palm (269)

4. FAQs (237, 238, 240, 248, 250, 251, 252, 254, 256, 264)

5. High-Tech Talk — Biometrics: Personalized Security (268)

6. Looking Ahead — Paying with Your Cellular Telephone (259) or Controlling Games by Thinking (267)

7. Making Use of the Web — Blogs (121)

8. Picture Yourself Using Input Devices (232)

9. Technology Trailblazers — Charles Walton and Douglas Engelbart (269)

10. Web Links (240, 241, 242, 243, 244, 246, 254, 258, 264)

Learn It Online

Use the Learn It Online exercises to reinforce your understanding of the chapter concepts. To access the Learn It Online exercises, visit scsite.com/dc2008/ch5/learn.

(1) At the Movies — A Digital Whiteboard to Make Presentations Roar

To view the A Digital Whiteboard to Make Presentations Roar movie, click the number 1 button. Locate your video and click the corresponding High-Speed or Dial-Up link, depending on your Internet connection. Watch the movie and then complete the exercise by answering the question that follows. Polyvision CEO Michael Dunn shares his vision of the whiteboards and meetings of the future. Why is using the digital whiteboard more effective than using a regular wipe board and markers?

(2) Video and Audio: You Review It — Voice Recognition

In this chapter you learned about voice recognition. Click the number 2 button to view the suggested links and begin your search for videos, podcasts, or vodcasts related to voice recognition. Choose a video, podcast, or vodcast that discusses voice recognition and is of interest to you, and then write a description of its contents. Explain why you chose this piece, what you liked about it, what you disliked about it, and whether you would recommend it to a fellow student. Finish your review by giving the video, podcast, or vodcast a rating of 1 – 5 stars. Submit your review in the format requested by your instructor.

(3) Student Edition Labs — Working with Audio

Click the number 3 button. A new browser window will open, displaying the Student Edition Labs. Follow the on-screen instructions to complete the Working with Audio Lab. When finished, click the Exit button. If required, submit your results to your instructor.

(4) Student Edition Labs — Working with Video

Click the number 4 button. A new browser window will open, displaying the Student Edition Labs. Follow the on-screen instructions to complete the Working with Video Lab. When finished, click the Exit button. If required, submit your results to your instructor.

(5) Practice Test

Click the number 5 button. Answer each question. When completed, enter your name and click the Grade Test button to submit the quiz for grading. Make a note of any missed questions. If required, submit your results to your instructor.

(6) Who Wants To Be a Computer Genius²?

Click the number 6 button to find out if you are a computer genius. Directions about how to play the game will be displayed. When you are ready to play, click the Play button. Submit your score to your instructor.

(7) Wheel of Terms

Click the number 7 button to reinforce important terms you learned in this chapter by playing the Shelly Cashman Series version of this popular game. Directions about how to play the game will be displayed. When you are ready to play, click the Play button. Submit your score to your instructor.

Learn It Online

(8) DC Track and Field

Click the number 8 button to use what you have learned in this chapter to compete against other students in three track and field events. Directions about how to play the game will be displayed. When you are ready to play, click the start first event button. If required, submit your score to your instructor.

(9) You're Hired!

Click the number 9 button to use what you have learned in this chapter to embark on the path to a career in computers. Directions about how to play the game will be displayed. When you are ready to play, click the begin game button. If required, submit your score to your instructor.

(10) Crossword Puzzle Challenge

Click the number 10 button, then click the Crossword Puzzle Challenge link. Directions about how to play the game will be displayed. Complete the puzzle to reinforce skills you learned in this chapter. When you are ready to play, click the Continue button. Submit the completed puzzle to your instructor.

(11) Vista Exercises

Click the number 11 button. When the Vista Exercises menu appears, click the exercise assigned by your instructor. A new browser window will open. Follow the on-screen instructions to complete the exercise. When finished, click the Exit button. If required, submit your results to your instructor.

(12) In the News

Many people spend a great deal of time jotting notes on scratch pads, napkins, or self-stick notes. This may be fine for the occasional thought; however, in a situation where you would rather concentrate on the substance of the ideas being expressed, you may need a more sophisticated method for taking notes. Tape recorders have long been the mainstay for recording lectures, interviews, or one's thoughts, but they are restricted by the fact that the tapes last only so long before they have to be flipped over or switched altogether. One new development is the voice pen, which is a flash-memory-based recording device. It records digitally, which offers higher quality over standard tapes, easy indexing, and instant erasure. It is approximately the size of a small cellular telephone or remote control unit and can record up to 500 minutes on long play settings. Click the number 12 button and read a news article about a new or improved input device, an input device being used in a new way, or an input device being made more available. What is the device? Who is promoting it? How will it be used? Will the input device change the number, or effectiveness, of potential users? If so, why?

(13) Chapter Discussion Forum

Select an objective from this chapter on page 233 about which you would like more information. Click the number 13 button and post a short message listing a meaningful message title accompanied by one or more questions concerning the selected objective. In two days, return to the threaded discussion by clicking the number 13 button. Submit to your instructor your original message and at least one response to your message.

(14) eHow.com

Click the number 14 button to learn how to use eHow.com to locate information about a project you want to learn how to complete. Read other users contributions' and then complete the project. Write a brief report about your experience and then post your report to the topic you chose so that others can learn from your experience. Print your report and submit to your instructor.

Learn How To

Use the Learn How To activities to learn fundamental skills when using a computer and accompanying technology. Complete the exercises and submit them to your instructor. To see a video of a Learn How To activity, visit scsite.com/dc2008/ch5/howto.

LEARN HOW TO 1: Install and Use a PC Video Camera

A PC video camera, sometimes called a Web cam, is a digital video camera that allows you to capture video and still images. The videos can be used in live instant messages or for live images over the Internet. Recordings of the videos can be included on Web pages or in e-mail messages as attachments. In addition, some cameras include software that enables you to establish a visual security environment where the camera can be used to detect and record movement in its general vicinity.

Using a PC video camera requires two phases: 1) purchasing and installing the PC video camera, and 2) using the video camera to transmit live video or to record video or digital images.

To purchase and install a PC video camera, complete the following steps:

1. Determine how you want to use the video camera in order to decide the quality of camera you require and the camera software you need. PC video cameras range in price from about $25 to more than $125, and vary in picture quality, features, and accompanying software. If you are not sure of all features and prices, search the Web to determine the best camera for your use.
2. After making your purchase, you will find that most cameras are accompanied by a CD-ROM containing the software that enables the camera to communicate and work with the computer. Often, the instructions with the device will specify that you should place the CD-ROM in a CD or DVD drive and follow the on-screen instructions to install the software on the computer.
3. After the software is installed, you likely will be told to connect the camera to the computer. You do so by connecting the USB cable first to the camera and then to a USB port on your computer. When the camera is connected, you will be able to start the camera software from either the All Programs list or the desktop.

Once you have started the camera software, you will be able to use the camera for any of the tasks you require. Each camera and its accompanying software will allow you to create a video, use instant messaging to send live video to your IM contacts, and other uses as well. In addition, you often will be able to control the quality of your video output by modifying brightness, contrast, and clarity. With many cameras, you will be able to zoom in and out, and, from your keyboard, enter commands to move the camera lens left, right, up, and down.

On some cameras, you even can use a feature called face tracking, where the camera will remain focused on your face even when you move. This feature allows you to be more natural and not be concerned with always making sure you are placed exactly right for the camera.

As you can see, once you have purchased and installed a PC video camera, you will open an entirely new world of communication right from your computer.

Exercise

1. Assume you have decided to purchase a PC video camera to use for instant messaging. Search the Web to find the highest rated cameras available for purchase that can be used for your purposes. What is the most expensive camera you found? The least expensive? What features distinguish the two? Based on your use of the camera for instant messaging, what camera would you choose to buy? Why? Submit your answers to your instructor.
2. Optional: Purchase a PC video camera or borrow one from a friend. Install the camera software on a computer. Warning: If you are using a computer that is not your own, complete this exercise only with the owner's permission. Connect the camera to the computer. Practice with the camera and the accompanying software. What features does the software provide? Which feature do you find the most compelling? What features could you do without? Record a video of yourself answering these questions. Submit the video to your instructor.

Learn How To

LEARN HOW TO 2: Use the On-Screen Keyboard for Physically Challenged Users

Everyone who uses a computer must enter data and instructions into the computer. For people with limited hand and arm mobility, this can prove a daunting task. Windows Vista and a variety of other applications provide a number of aids that can be useful. One of these is the on-screen keyboard.

The on-screen keyboard allows a user to view the keyboard on the screen and select characters to enter by using several different methods. To display and use the on-screen keyboard, complete the following steps:

1. Click the Start button on the Windows taskbar, click All Programs on the Start menu, click Accessories in the All Programs list, click Ease of Access in the Accessories list, and then click On-Screen Keyboard in the Ease of Access list to display the On-Screen Keyboard window.
2. In the On-Screen Keyboard window, click Settings on the menu bar. Ensure a checkmark is next to Always on Top.
3. If necessary, click Settings on the menu bar again. Click Typing Mode on the Settings menu to display the Typing Mode dialog box (Figure 5-51).
4. Ensure the Click to select option button is selected and then click the OK button in the Typing Mode dialog box.
5. Start your Web browser and click the Address bar.
6. Using the on-screen keyboard, enter the characters www.cnn.com and then click the ENT key.
7. When the cnn.com Web page appears, click the Enter Symbol box in the Market Update section of the page. Using the on-screen keyboard, enter ibm and then click the ENT key.
8. After finding the stock price for IBM, close the browser window.
9. Start the WordPad program (see Learn How To number 1 on page 48).
10. In the On-Screen Keyboard window, click Settings on the menu bar and then click Typing Mode on the Settings menu.
11. Click the Hover to select option button to select it. If necessary, click the Minimum time to hover box arrow and select 1.00 seconds in the list. Click the OK button.
12. Click in the WordPad window to position the insertion point.
13. You can cause a character to be entered in the WordPad window by placing the mouse pointer over the desired key (hovering) for one second. Type the following using the on-screen keyboard: Ease of Access tools are vital for computer users.
14. Close the WordPad window without saving changes, and then close the On-Screen Keyboard window.

Typing Mode dialog box

Click to select option button

Typing Mode

◉ Click to select

○ Hover to select

Minimum time to hover:

Hover to select option button

○ Joystick or key to select

Scan interval: Advanced...

Joystick or key to select option button   **OK button**   OK   Cancel

FIGURE 5-51

You have seen how one of the Ease of Access tools within Windows Vista functions. You are encouraged to explore all of the tools and discover how these tools can be useful to those people for whom they were designed.

Exercise

1. Start WordPad and then display the on-screen keyboard. In the On-Screen Keyboard window, click Settings on the menu bar and then click Typing Mode. In the Typing Mode dialog box, select Joystick or key to select. Click the Advanced button. Ensure the Keyboard key box contains a checkmark and then click Space in the list. Click the OK buttons to close the dialog boxes. Then, on the Keyboard menu, select Block Layout. Click in the WordPad window and then press the SPACEBAR. What happened? Keep pressing the SPACEBAR until you cause a character to be entered in the WordPad window. Use the BKSP key on the on-screen keyboard to backspace and erase the character, and then use the on-screen keyboard to type On-Screen Keyboard usage in the WordPad window. When you are done, close the WordPad window and the On-Screen Keyboard window. Which means of using the on-screen keyboard (click a key, hover, or the SPACEBAR) did you find easiest to use? Why? Why would a physically challenged person prefer one method over another? Prepare your answers using the on-screen keyboard and then submit your answers to your instructor.

Web Research

Use the Internet-based Web Research exercises to broaden your understanding of the concepts presented in this chapter. Visit scsite.com/dc2008/ch5/research to obtain more information pertaining to each exercise. To discuss any of the Web Research exercises in this chapter with other students, post your thoughts or questions at scsite.com/dc2008/ch5/forum.

① Scavenger Hunt   Use one of the search engines listed in Figure 2-10 in Chapter 2 on page 78 or your own favorite search engine to find the answers to the questions below. Copy and paste the Web address from the Web page where you found the answer. Some questions may have more than one answer. If required, submit your answers to your instructor. (1) Consumers use touch screens at bank ATMs, airport check-ins, and mall kiosks. What did Dr. Samuel C. Hurst invent in 1971 that led to the development of touch screen technology? (2) What are some of the services available from providers, such as Yahoo! Photo, to help consumers store and share digital photos online? What are the costs of some of these services? (3) Who holds patents awarded in the 1950s for automatic video scanning and inspection methods, which led to bar code technology?

② Search Sleuth   MetaCrawler (metacrawler.com) is a different type of search Web site because it returns combined results from leading search engines. Visit this Web site and then use your word processing program to answer the following questions. Then, if required, submit your answers to your instructor. (1) Click the About MetaCrawler link at the bottom of the page. Which search engines are you searching when you use MetaCrawler? (2) Click your browser's Back button or press the BACKSPACE key to return to the MetaCrawler home page. Locate the Popular Searches section. What are the six most popular searches today? (3) Click the Images link on the home page, type sunset in the search text box, and then click the Search button. How many results did your search yield? Click the Audio link above the search text box to search for audio files of sunsets. How many results did your search yield? (4) Click your browser's Back button or press the BACKSPACE key three times to return to the MetaCrawler home page. Click the Tools & Tips link at the bottom of the page. Click the FAQ link. Click several question links concerning conducting searches on this Web site and read the answers to these questions. Summarize the information you read and then write a 50-word summary that may be submitted to your instructor.

③ Journaling   Respond to your readings in this chapter by writing at least one page about your reactions, evaluations, and reflections about using input devices. For example, which pointing devices, such as a trackball, touchpad, stylus, digital pen, joystick, or gamepad, do you use? Are they wireless? Do you use text messaging or picture messaging on your cellular telephone? You also can write about the new terms you learned by reading this chapter. If required, submit your journal to your instructor.

④ Expanding Your Understanding   Journalists, attorneys, law enforcement officials, and students consider tape recorders and notepads essential components of their daily activities. An alternate means of capturing information is a voice pen, which is a flash-memory-based recording device approximately the size of a small smart phone. Visit a local electronics store or view electronics Web sites to learn more about voice pens. Compare their features, cost, recording time, and warranty. Write a report summarizing your findings, focusing on comparing and contrasting the voice pens. If required, submit your report to your instructor.

⑤ Ethics in Action   Some reports suggest that a global surveillance system is monitoring e-mail messages, telephone calls, and faxes. This organization known as Echelon attempts to intercept more than three billion satellite, microwave, cellular, and fiber-optic messages per day, according to the reports. The National Security Agency is forbidden to monitor U.S. citizens, but privacy experts contend that at least 90 percent of U.S. communication is gathered and reviewed. View online sites that provide information about Echelon, including Echelon Watch (www.echelonwatch.org). Write a report summarizing your findings, and include a table of links to Web sites that provide additional details. If required, submit your report to your instructor.

Case Studies

Use the Case Studies to apply the concepts presented in the chapter to real-world situations. Visit scsite.com/dc2008/ch5/cases to obtain more information pertaining to each exercise. To discuss the Case Studies in this chapter with other students, visit scsite.com/dc2008/ch5/forum and post your thoughts or questions.

CASE STUDY 1 — Class Discussion   You work in the Efficiency Analysis department of one of the largest retail companies in the world, with multiple stores in every state and many other countries. For the past 25 years, the company has used optical scanners at checkout counters that read the UPC bar code on products to determine from a database the price to charge customers. The company is considering replacing the optical scanners with <u>radio frequency identification</u>, or RFID. The reader receives the code identifying the product via a chip with an antenna that is part of the box or label on the outside of the product. Your manager has asked you to draft a memo outlining the impact such a change would have on the company, its suppliers, and its customers. Be prepared to discuss your findings in class.

CASE STUDY 2 — Class Discussion   Your company recently purchased several notebook computers. While the recipients of the notebook computers enjoy having the ability to work outside the office, they have found that working with the notebook computer's touchpad functioning as a <u>mouse</u> has affected their productivity. You have been asked to research purchasing mouse devices that are compatible with the new notebook computers. Your boss has recommended the MoGo Wireless Bluetooth Mouse based on an article she recently read. Research at least three other wireless mouse devices and compare with the MoGo mouse. Write a brief report summarizing your findings. Include your recommendation in the report and the reasons for that recommendation. Be prepared to share your findings with your class.

CASE STUDY 3 — Research   While attending college part-time for the past two years, you have worked as a data entry clerk for Salmon Mirror. Recently, you began to feel an unusual pain in your right wrist. Your doctor diagnosed the problem as <u>carpal tunnel syndrome</u>, which is the most well-known of a series of musculoskeletal disorders that fall under the umbrella of repetitive strain injuries (RSIs). Your doctor made several recommendations to relieve the pain, one of which was to find a new job. Before you begin job hunting, however, you want to learn more about this debilitating injury. Use the Web and/or print media to investigate carpal tunnel syndrome. Prepare a report and/or PowerPoint presentation on your findings. Include information about carpal tunnel syndrome warning signs, risk factors, suggestions about proper workstation ergonomics, and procedures for healing the injury. Share your report or presentation with your class.

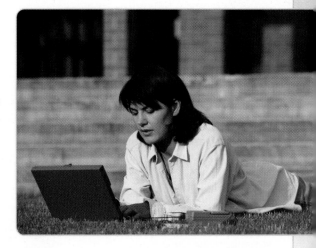

CASE STUDY 4 — Research   An electronics company where you are employed as an analyst spends hundreds of thousands of dollars each year on travel to the multiple locations where they operate around the country. In an effort to curb the ever-increasing costs of travel, the CFO has asked you to look into the feasibility of adopting <u>video conferencing</u> at all of its major locations. Use the Web and/or print media to determine the advantages and disadvantages of video conferencing. Can the technology replace all or most face-to-face meetings? What are the costs of common video conferencing systems and the recurring costs their use incurs? Compare those costs to the cost of travel for a team of three people making six trips per year between New York and Los Angeles, including hotel, airline, and food expenses. Write a brief report or use PowerPoint to create a presentation and share your findings with your class.

CASE STUDY 5 — Team Challenge   The Transportation Security Administration (TSA) is looking into ways to expedite the airport screening experience of frequent flyers without compromising security. The TSA has hired your team as consultants to investigate <u>biometric technology</u>. In particular, they want your team to review three biometric devices for screening frequent flyers — fingerprint scanner, face recognition system, and iris recognition system. Form a three-member team and have each team member choose a different biometric device. Using the Web and/or print media, have each team member determine the advantages and disadvantages of their chosen biometric device. Include in each report how frequent flyer applicants would apply, accuracy rates of the device, and whether the device would indeed enhance security or open a loophole for terrorists. As a team, merge your findings into a team report and/or PowerPoint presentation and share your recommendations with your class.

Personal Mobile Devices

Personal mobile devices usually can fit in your pocket, and include such devices as PDAs, smart phones, portable media players, ultra personal computers, handheld navigation devices, and handheld game consoles (Figure 1). Page 22 in Chapter 1 discusses PDAs and smart phones. A **PDA** provides personal organizer functions, such as calendar, appointment book, address book, calculator, and notepad. A **smart phone** is an Internet-enabled telephone that usually provides PDA functionality. Both smart phones and PDAs usually allow you to send and receive e-mail, access the Web, download and play media files, and take photos and make short video clips. A **portable media player** is a handheld device capable of video playback, audio playback, or photo display. Portable media players sometimes provide PDA functionality. An **ultra personal computer (uPC)** is a personal computer small enough to fit in one hand and allows you to run a desktop operating system. Page 21 discusses ultra personal computers. A **handheld navigation device** includes a GPS receiver and application software that assist in guiding you from one location to another. A **handheld game console** is a mobile computing device, small enough to fit in one hand, that is designed for single-player or multiplayer video games.

Because the various types of personal mobile devices usually offer similar capabilities, they often are categorized by their form factor. A device's **form factor** refers to its size, shape, and configuration. For example, Figure 1 shows a smart phone that has a PDA form factor and a smart phone that has a phone form factor. While the device with the phone form factor may include PDA functionality, its main purpose is to be used as a phone. Its smaller size may make using it as a PDA more cumbersome than the smart phone with a PDA form factor. The PDA form factor, while larger, provides a better interface for accessing the PDA functionality. An ultra personal computer includes most of the functionality of a typical personal computer or notebook computer, but its form factor is what differentiates it from those types of computers.

This special feature provides an overview of accessories and software available for personal mobile devices. The final section of the feature lists the criteria you should consider when deciding which personal mobile device is right for you.

personal computer with uPC form factor

PDA

smart phone with phone form factor

smart phone with PDA form factor

FIGURE 1   Your choice of a personal mobile device depends on the features you require, the desired form factor, the available accessories, and the available software for the device.

EXAMPLES OF PERSONAL MOBILE DEVICES

Personal mobile devices are available in many shapes and sizes and run a variety of operating systems. Figure 2 shows examples of some popular personal mobile devices. The device you choose depends on several factors. Some of the decisions you must make before you purchase a device are listed on pages 296 and 297.

PDA running Palm OS		PDAs that run the Palm OS are popular due to the tens of thousands of programs that have been written for them. The devices also run longer on a battery recharge than most other devices and are among the smallest PDAs. The device shown includes Wi-Fi and Bluetooth wireless technology and is capable of playing music and short video clips.
PDA running Windows Mobile for Pocket PC		Smart phones that run a Windows-based mobile operating system give users the same look and feel of the Windows operating system that they use on their desktop or notebook computers. The devices often run mobile versions of some Microsoft Office programs. The user interacts with the device using a stylus to touch the screen. This device includes both Wi-Fi and Bluetooth wireless technology.
smart phone running Palm OS		A smart phone that runs the Palm OS includes all the advantages of the Palm OS along with the capability to make and receive phone calls. The smart phone shown includes a QWERTY keyboard, high-speed Internet access, a camera, and Bluetooth wireless technology.
smart phone running Symbian operating system		This Nokia smart phone does not include a keyboard. Instead, the user interacts with the phone using a stylus and controls on either side of the device. This smart phone includes a camera to take pictures and video, a radio receiver, and high-speed wireless Internet connectivity. The large screen allows the user to view word processing documents and spreadsheets.
smart phone running Windows Mobile Pocket PC Phone Edition		Smart phones that run a Windows-based mobile operating system give users the same look and feel of the Windows operating system that they use on their desktop or notebook computers. This device includes a slide-out keyboard on which the user types. The device also includes high-speed Internet access.
BlackBerry		BlackBerry devices from Research in Motion (RIM) are popular with business people who are on the move. The devices handle corporate e-mail and messaging especially well, but also include the capability to make and receive phone calls.
portable media player		The iPod is the most popular portable media player. With an iPod, you listen to music, watch videos, view photos, and play games. Most portable media players synchronize media with the user's desktop or notebook computer. Some devices also can serve as secondary storage for the user's computer. Portable media players typically include only a few controls that are simple and intuitive to use.
ultra personal computer running Windows Vista		Ultra personal computers are popular with physicians, realtors, and other professionals who need a great deal of computing power wherever they go. An ultra personal computer serves as a mobile device, but is powerful enough to double as a desktop computer.
handheld navigation device		Handheld navigation devices include a GPS receiver, which receives signals from GPS satellites to determine a location and/or speed. The devices typically include programs and maps to guide you from location to location. Some devices, such as the one shown, show you a 3-D representation of any area so that you easily can navigate to your destination.
handheld game console		Handheld game consoles allow you to take your favorite games on the road. This device includes two screens — one of which is touch-sensitive, wireless Internet access, virtual surround sound, and a microphone. The wireless connectivity also can be used to play games against your friends.

FIGURE 2   Personal mobile devices are available in many shapes and sizes and run a variety of operating systems.

ACCESSORIES FOR PERSONAL MOBILE DEVICE SOFTWARE

Most personal mobile devices have the capability to take advantage of add-on accessories. For example, using an external keyboard with a device greatly enhances the ability to enter data or notes quickly. Figure 3 lists the more common accessories available for a personal mobile device.

ACCESSORIES FOR PERSONAL MOBILE DEVICES

Accessory	Description
Keyboard	External keyboards provide much faster input when taking notes as opposed to using a small, built-in keyboard on a device or relying on handwriting recognition. Keyboards may be wireless or attached to the device using a special cable.
Memory card	Memory cards provide additional storage space for a device. Some memory cards may include hardware enhancements such as wireless capability, a camera, or Bluetooth capability. Some cards contain preinstalled software or a vast amount of data, such as a dictionary.
Car kit	Car kits allow you to integrate a device with your car by providing mounting and/or hands-free operation of a device.
Camera	Add-on cameras provide picture and video taking capability to devices with no such built-in functionality.
Case	Most mobile devices can be placed in a case or holster for protection while the device is not in use. Some devices include built-in flip screens to protect the device. You may want a case that fits comfortably in your pocket, or one that includes a belt clip. A good case protects the device when it is dropped from a height of 3 or 4 feet.
Headset/earphones/ microphone	Headsets allow you to wear a combined earpiece and microphone while keeping the device in your hand, pocket, or next to you. Some headsets use Bluetooth to communicate wirelessly with the device. Earphones are used when you want to listen to sound on your device, such as when listening to music or an e-book, or when watching a video. Some portable media players allow you to add a microphone with which you record voice memos or other audio.
GPS receiver	A GPS receiver contains an antenna, radio receiver, and processor and receives signals from GPS satellites to determine a location and/or speed. GPS receivers turn a personal mobile device into a complete GPS unit. The receivers typically include software that you must install on the device.
Media transmission	Some portable media players allow you to add accessories to broadcast or transmit media to other devices, such as a television or radio. For example, you can add an FM transmitter which broadcasts audio output from the player to a nearby FM radio.

FIGURE 3 Some accessories for personal mobile devices are common to most devices, while others are specialized.

BUILT-IN PERSONAL MOBILE DEVICE SOFTWARE

Most personal mobile devices include several programs that provide basic functionality, such as an **address book** and **date book**. Figure 4 lists the types of software that usually are preinstalled on a personal mobile device.

BUILT-IN PERSONAL MOBILE DEVICE SOFTWARE

Application	Description
Address book and contacts	Maintains a list of acquaintances, including names, addresses, telephone numbers, e-mail addresses, and notes.
To-do list	Maintains a list of tasks. Tasks can be categorized and assigned a priority.
Calculator	Offers functionality of standard desktop calculators.
Datebook and calendar	Maintains appointments and important dates, such as birthdays and holidays. You also set audio or visual alarms to trigger when an appointment time arrives.
Media player	Allows you to play audio and video or display photos. A media player on a phone may pause a song automatically when a phone call is received. Some devices may allow you to watch streaming video in real-time over a wireless Internet connection.
Memos and notepad	Keeps track of notes.
Launcher	The interface that allows you to execute, or launch, programs.
Dialer	Smart phones typically include dialer software that assists you in using the telephone capabilities of a device. Some dialer software is integrated into the operating system so that you use dialing capabilities in other programs. For example, you can select a telephone number in the word processing program and request that the number be dialed.

FIGURE 4 Personal mobile devices typically contain this preinstalled software.

SYNCHRONIZATION SOFTWARE

Most personal mobile devices allow you to share data and information between a personal computer and your device. The software that enables the sharing is called **synchronization software**. A personal mobile device may synchronize, or sync (pronounced sink), with a personal computer or a server on a network. Corporations often standardize their synchronization software so that employees share data across the corporate network, and so the data is backed up properly on a server. Figure 5 lists popular synchronization software for personal mobile devices.

SYNCHRONIZATION SOFTWARE FOR PERSONAL MOBILE DEVICES

Application	Description	Samples
Built-in	Most devices include software that the user loads on a personal computer that allows the computer to communicate with the device and share data and information.	• The Palm OS includes HotSync software • Pocket PC PDAs include ActiveSync software • Blackberry devices use the Blackberry Desktop Software
iSync	Apple's iSync software allows a user to keep a calendar and contact information synchronized up to the minute between a smart phone, an Apple iPod, a Palm OS device, or multiple Macs.	• Apple iSync
Portable media player	Most portable media players sync with a personal computer through a media player on a personal computer. Some portable media players also will synchronize to a personal computer's calendar or contact list.	• Apple iTunes • Microsoft Media Player
Synching many sources	Some device users have data and information stored in many places. For example, users may want to have their address books on the Web, on their personal computers, on their cellular phones, and on their PDAs. Special synchronization software allows users to keep all of the address books up-to-date.	• Intellisync Handheld Edition • PocketMirror • Susteen DataPilot
SyncML	**SyncML** is a standard that is being adopted by many companies that create personal mobile devices. SyncML allows for common information stored on a device to be shared among many devices, such as cellular telephones, other personal mobile devices, and personal computers.	• IBM WebSphere Everyplace Access • Intellisync Handheld Edition • fusionOne MightyPhone • Symbian based devices use SyncML

FIGURE 5 Personal mobile devices use synchronization software to share data and information with a personal computer or server.

BUSINESS SOFTWARE

Most programs used on a personal mobile device have some counterpart program on a desktop computer. For example, both a personal computer and a PDA or smart phone may include a word processing program. Many business programs have counterparts on personal mobile devices. The personal mobile device versions of these programs generally have fewer features and options. For example, a word processing program on a PDA may not have a spelling checker, and a spreadsheet program may not include all of the built-in calculations of its desktop computer counterpart. A smart phone with a phone form factor may allow you only to view documents, rather than edit documents. Figure 6 lists business software for personal mobile devices. The software for an ultra personal computer usually is the same software that is used on a desktop computer and is, therefore, not listed in the figure.

BUSINESS SOFTWARE FOR PERSONAL MOBILE DEVICES

Application	Description	Samples
Word processing	Allows for simple creation, editing, and viewing of documents.	• Documents To Go • WordSmith • Pocket Word
Spreadsheet	Allows you to create, edit, and view worksheets.	• Pocket Excel • TinySheet • MiniCalc • SmartSheet
Readers	Allows read-only (view only) access to word processing documents, spreadsheets, or databases that you download to a personal mobile device from a personal computer. Readers are useful for taking large documents on the road to read them without the ability to modify them. Some readers allow you to view all of these types of documents, while others are targeted to specific desktop program counterparts, such as presentation viewers or word processing document viewers.	• Pocket SlideShow • TealDoc • iSilo • Microsoft Reader for Pocket PC • Mobipocket Reader
Database and list management	Allows creation, editing, and viewing of databases or lists. List management is a popular use of personal mobile devices. Some examples of lists that are handy to store on a device include shopping lists, to-do lists, exercise logs, and automobile maintenance logs.	• HanDBase • thinkDB • SmartList To Go • JFile • ListPro • Mobile Data Viewer
Financial	Financial software includes programs to manage a bank account, track expenses during a trip, manage a budget, or track an investment portfolio. Many personal computer financial programs include personal mobile device companion software that keeps the information on a device synchronized with the financial information on a personal computer or the Web.	• Microsoft Money for Windows Mobile-based Pocket PC • Pocket Quicken • BankBook • Ultrasoft Money • Handy Expense

FIGURE 6 Business software provides scaled-down versions of common desktop programs.

SOFTWARE AND SERVICES FOR WIRELESS DEVICES

Most of the software used to interact with the Internet using a personal computer has a counterpart on wireless mobile devices. Some devices come equipped with e-mail software or a Web browser. Often, special servers allow the device to communicate securely with corporate databases or Web sites. Many Web sites include enhanced services for mobile devices, such as the ability to make payment or purchases through the use of text messaging. For personal mobile devices that do not include wireless Internet connectivity, a special modem connects the device to the Internet. Often, a device without built-in wireless capability can be connected to a mobile phone that can connect the device to the Internet. Web content and e-mail also synchronize to the device from a personal computer, and the information may be browsed offline while using the device. Figure 7 provides a list of popular communications software for personal mobile devices.

COMMUNICATIONS SOFTWARE FOR PERSONAL MOBILE DEVICES

Application	Description	Samples
E-mail	Used for composing and reading e-mail. Many personal mobile devices include a preinstalled e-mail program.	• Pocket Outlook • riteMail • Mail+ • SnapperMail
Web browsers	Allows Web browsing. Some browsers use an **intermediate server** to make the pages smaller by removing images or making images smaller. Others attempt to display the full Web page on the personal mobile device. Many personal mobile devices include a preinstalled Web browser.	• Pocket Internet Explorer • ThunderHawk • AvantGo • Opera browser
Instant messaging	Instant messaging programs usually allow you to use the same instant messaging ID as that used on a personal computer.	• Windows Live Messenger • AIM for Palm OS • Agile Messenger
Clipping	**Web clippings** are programs that gather and display only the critical elements, or clips, of a Web page.	• Travelocity.com • The Weather Channel • Moviefone.com
Media sharing software	Used to share media, such as audio, video, and photos with other computers, Web sites, or personal mobile devices. Some software is built-in, such as software that allows users to share music or games with other users with a similar device.	• YouTube Mobile Upload • MySpace Mobile
Blogging	Many smart phones allow blogging through the use of text messaging. A **moblog** is a blog created with a personal mobile device. Some blogs provide software for personal mobile devices that allow you to blog and upload photos, podcasts, and video.	• Nokia Lifeblog • Blogger Mobile
Internet telephony	Some Internet telephony providers offer software that works with mobile devices. Using Internet telephony rather than the mobile network often is less expensive.	• Skype • Vonage Mobile

FIGURE 7 Communications software allows a mobile device to access the Internet and other data sources and share data while you are away from the classroom or office.

CORPORATE/GOVERNMENT SOFTWARE

Large organizations, such as corporations and government agencies, take advantage of some personal mobile devices' capability of keeping current information in the hands of their personnel. The organization's central employee telephone book is kept up-to-date and synchronized to each employee's device on a regular basis. Executives synchronize key corporate information. Traveling sales personnel and field technicians synchronize appointments, e-mail, notes about contact with customers, product lists, corporate podcasts, and sales information. Corporate/government software for personal mobile devices is listed in Figure 8.

CORPORATE/GOVERNMENT SOFTWARE FOR PERSONAL MOBILE DEVICES

Application	Description	Samples
Executive	Executives keep up-to-date corporate information on their personal mobile devices. Executives may keep current sales information, financial information, and inventory information available to make informed decisions.	• mySAP.com • Siebel 7 Mobile Solutions
Sales	Sales people working away from the office are perhaps the largest group of personal mobile device users. The devices are useful for keeping product information handy, keeping scheduled appointments, and maintaining customer information.	• Siebel 7 Mobile Sales • Salesforce.com • ActionNames
Field technicians and mobile workers	Field technicians visit customer locations to troubleshoot problems. Personal mobile devices help technicians keep track of customer information, maintain up-to-date information on replacement parts, and log troubleshooting information.	• UPS and FedEx use specialized devices and software for their drivers to track package pickups and drop-offs.
Military and law enforcement	The military and law enforcement agencies deploy personal mobile devices to manage the special needs of the military and law enforcement.	• Most software of this nature is custom made for the needs of particular agencies. Such programs help track cases or serve as legal references.
Connecting and synchronizing with corporate data sources	Several solutions exist for synchronizing corporate data with personal mobile devices. Special software keeps track of user permissions and makes certain that the right people get the data they require on a day-to-day basis.	• Intellisync Gold • MessageWireless
Large organization management issues	In organizations with thousands of personal mobile device users, the support of those devices becomes tedious, especially when users install unsupported software on the devices that may interfere with the corporate software and data for which the device was intended. Server software may detect these conflicts when the user synchronizes with the corporate server and deletes or reports the offending software.	• Much of the software of this nature is custom built for each enterprise, as needs and infrastructure of each organization are different.

FIGURE 8 Large organizations utilize special software to keep their employees synchronized.

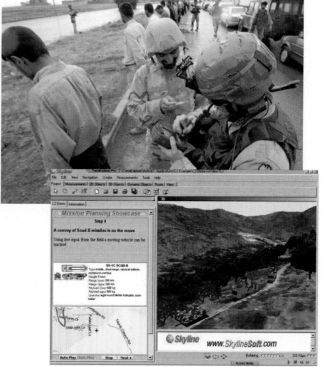

MEDICAL SOFTWARE

One of the largest communities to adopt personal mobile device software in significant numbers is the medical community. Physicians and other medical workers routinely use specialized software to track patient charts, check information on drugs, and browse electronic versions of large reference books. The end result is a savings in time and money, and an increase in the level of care for the patient. Physicians have become one of the main groups of professionals to use ultra personal computers because of the devices' power and portability. Figure 9 lists some popular medical software for personal mobile devices.

MEDICAL SOFTWARE FOR PERSONAL MOBILE DEVICES

Application	Description	Samples
Patient and case management	Patient and case management programs allow medical workers to enter data as they interact with the patient. This eliminates transcription errors or the need for the worker to find a computer to do his or her work.	• MedLogs • PatientKeeper Personal • Handy Patients • MD Coder PocketPC Edition
Drug information and drug interactions	Allows for fast access to critical drug information, such as dosages and drug interactions.	• Epocrates Rx • eDrugsDatabase • Dr. Drugs
Reference books	Medical workers often rely on a large collection of references to do their jobs. Electronic versions of many popular references, such as the *Physicians' Desk Reference*, are available in electronic format and are kept up-to-date easily through regular downloads.	• PDRDrugs • eDrugs Database • DiagnosisPro for Pocket PC • MedRules
Prescriptions	With electronic prescribing, physicians write prescriptions electronically. Physicians print legible prescriptions and hand the prescriptions to the patient. If the personal mobile device is connected to the Internet or hospital network, the physician checks the patient's medication or medical history.	• iScribe • PocketRx • Medicalis
Medical calculations	Medical workers often make quick calculations for medication dosages or patient status. Programs assist many of these calculations and target the worker's specialty.	• MedMath • MedCalc • Medical MathPad

FIGURE 9 The medical community quickly has become one of the larger users of specialized PDA software.

SCIENTIFIC SOFTWARE

The mobility of personal mobile devices makes them valuable tools for scientific use. Researchers use these devices to gather and record data in the field and later download the data to a personal computer or server. Scientists also use specialized software targeted to their specific field, such as astronomy or meteorology, as a replacement for bulky reference manuals or observation notes (Figure 10).

SCIENTIFIC SOFTWARE FOR PERSONAL MOBILE DEVICES

Application	Description	Samples
Data gathering	Scientists can enter observations quickly into a personal mobile device. These programs often are used in the field for gathering research statistics.	• iCollect
Calculations and conversions	Users can perform specialized calculations or data conversions. Many fields of science, such as astronomy, require special calculations that are useful to have available on a personal mobile device.	• ME Tools • CoolCalc for the Pocket PC • Convert It! • APCalc Converter
Reference	Scientists can look up information quickly, rather than using cumbersome manuals or textbooks.	• ChemRef Basic • Packed Periodic Table • Gene • ABC's of Science
Astronomy	Observers can follow the stars. With the large number of amateur astronomers in the world, programs specific to astronomy are some of the more popular scientific titles.	• Pocket Universe • Planetarium • Astronomist • Pocket Stars
Weather	Meteorologists' specific needs are addressed because these programs allow quick calculations or data gathering in a changing environment. Some programs are linked to add-on hardware that measure temperature, humidity, and other meteorological data.	• Weather Manager • WorldMate • Weather Calculator for Palm OS • Weather.com

FIGURE 10 Scientific programs help scientists manage complex information.

TRAVEL SOFTWARE AND SERVICES

The portable nature of personal mobile devices makes them ideal for the business or leisure traveler. Even a night on the town can be enhanced by a list of popular attractions. The user keeps his or her itinerary handy along with maps and directions while traveling to new places. A GPS-enabled mobile device tracks a user's route and keeps the user on course. Wireless connectivity allows the user to book flights and hotels from the back of a taxi cab. Figure 11 lists travel software for personal mobile devices.

TRAVEL SOFTWARE AND SERVICES FOR PERSONAL MOBILE DEVICES

Application	Description	Samples
Itinerary consolidation	Manages travel itineraries, including flights, hotels, and car rentals. The software may keep track of travel preferences and make suggestions about travel and accommodations when planning a new trip.	• Traveler (Pocket PC edition) • Time Traveler • WorldMate
Mapping	Mapping software may download maps from the Web or a personal computer. Or, the software may include maps. The software may suggest travel routes or driving directions from point to point, or simply serve as a reference.	• Yahoo! Mobile Driving Directions • Pocket Streets • Google Maps for Mobile
City guides	City guides are one of the more popular personal mobile device programs. You install city guides for specific cities or an entire country. Guides include restaurant listings and ratings, hotels, directions, popular attractions, and local customs.	• Intelliguide Professional • Vindigo for Palm OS or Pocket PC • WorldMate • Frommer's Port@ble Guide • iFodor's
Hotel and flight	You can view current hotel and flight information while planning a trip. Some of these programs require the device to connect to the Internet. Others occasionally allow downloading the information to a device from a personal computer. Some programs link to booking systems on the Internet, so you make reservations directly from a personal mobile device.	• OAG Club • SkyGuide
GPS	Usually requires additional GPS hardware connected to the device. Some software includes mapping data or only displays and saves GPS information, such as location and speed.	• GPS Port@ble Navigator — Travelers Edition • GPS Wireless Navigation System • GPS Atlas

FIGURE 11 Travel software and services act as a personal concierge for the business or leisure traveler.

EDUCATIONAL SOFTWARE

With so much to organize, students and instructors greatly benefit from mobile software geared for educational uses (Figure 12). Students load textbook chapters or entire textbooks onto media cards and use special software to read the books and highlight key material. Instructors distribute electronic versions of the class syllabus, automatically updating each student's calendar on the students' devices. Some schools even acquire PDAs for the entire student body and require their use in the classroom.

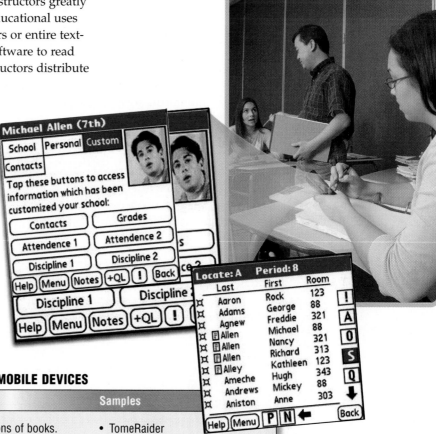

EDUCATIONAL SOFTWARE FOR PERSONAL MOBILE DEVICES

Application	Description	Samples
E-books and references	E-books are electronic versions of books. E-books are specially formatted files that may be viewed using Reader software, as noted in Figure 6 on page 287. Many e-books are available at no cost, and many authors and publishing companies make e-books available to those who have purchased a hard copy of a particular book.	• TomeRaider • PocketLingo Pro • Formulas for Palm OS • Speed Reader Plus • The collected works of William Shakespeare for Microsoft Reader • eWord for Blackberry • Mobipocket Reader Pro for Symbian OS
Class schedules and course management	Helps instructors and students manage their respective schedules. The information may include syllabus details distributed in electronic format by an instructor. The software also may link to a central data repository of a school. The software helps track grading, assignments, to-do lists, instructor office hours, and notes.	• 4.0Student by Handmark course management • Pocket ClassPro for Pocket PC • MyClasses • Hi-CE handheld software • MxWeb eTeacher
Roster	Manages grading, rosters, attendance, and contact information for students.	• Teachers PET • Teach File
Review	Includes programs for quizzing students and reviewing coursework. Students often train the application to help them review troublesome material.	• Herbert's Math Time • Mental Arithmetic • Quizzler

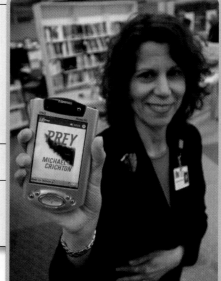

FIGURE 12 Educational software benefits both students and instructors.

MULTIMEDIA SOFTWARE

Most personal mobile devices include the capability of viewing images and video and listening to audio. Devices often contain, or allow you to attach, a camera or recording device to capture video or audio and then download the captured images and sounds to a personal computer or send them directly to an e-mail address, blog, or Web site. Some image viewers allow you to use a personal mobile device as an electronic picture frame while the device rests in its cradle on your desk. Many devices include built-in media players, and some devices allow you to install additional multimedia software. Popular multimedia software for personal mobile devices is listed in Figure 13.

MULTIMEDIA SOFTWARE FOR PERSONAL MOBILE DEVICES

Application	Description	Samples
Picture viewer	Allows you to view images uploaded to a personal mobile device using software on a personal computer or camera. Some viewers have a slide show mode that rotates through a list of images automatically.	• SplashPhoto • PocketPhoto • Palbum Picture Viewer • Resco Photo Viewer for Smartphone • Pictures
Media player	Allows you to watch video clips and listen to audio, such as music or podcasts, on a personal mobile device. Some devices are equipped with additional hardware, such as microphones, headphones, or media controls to enhance the multimedia experience.	• Windows Media Player Mobile • PocketTV for Pocket PC • ActiveSky Media Player

FIGURE 13 Multimedia software gives personal mobile device users the ability to view images, watch video, and listen to audio.

ENTERTAINMENT SOFTWARE

While on the train ride to work or waiting at the airport, a personal mobile device user can enjoy his or her favorite games. The infrared port or wireless connectivity of a device allows a user to play some games against other players. Most devices include buttons to control games. Figure 14 lists popular entertainment software for personal mobile devices.

ENTERTAINMENT SOFTWARE FOR PERSONAL MOBILE DEVICES

Application	Description	Samples
Strategy	Includes classic board games such as chess, backgammon, and Monopoly.	• PocketChess • ChessGenius • Handmark Monopoly • SimCity
Card	Includes casino games, solitaire games, and other card games.	• AcidSolitaire • BlackJack++ • Pocket Cribbage
Action	Games that require quick reflexes, including many arcade-style games.	• Tomb Raider • Breakfast • Vexed for Symbian
Puzzle	Thought-provoking puzzles to pass time and sharpen the mind, such as crossword puzzles, mazes, and word games.	• Handmark SCRABBLE • Crossword • Advanced Brain Trainer
Sports	Games that mimic real-life sports.	• Pocket Mini Golf • Smart Tennis • Bowling Master

FIGURE 14 Entertainment software allows you to relax with a personal mobile device and enjoy your favorite games.

OBTAINING AND INSTALLING PERSONAL MOBILE DEVICE SOFTWARE

Software often is available at computer or electronics stores. Ultra personal computers can run any software made for personal computers. A significant number of programs are available as shareware, freeware, or trial editions at various Web sites. Most of the software listed in the previous figures is accessible on the Web sites listed in Figure 15. Because software for personal mobile devices usually is smaller than the personal computer counterparts, downloading the software from the Web to your personal computer and then uploading it to your device often is the best alternative when you want to try something new. Software downloaded from the Web to a personal computer requires that the software be installed using the device's synchronization software. Additionally, some personal computer application software includes accompanying mobile device software that corresponds with the personal computer software. Wireless-enabled devices may allow you to download new software over the wireless connection.

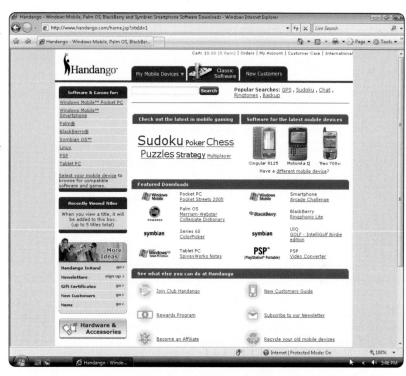

Software for personal mobile devices sold in a retail location often is supplied on a CD-ROM. The CD-ROM first installs the software on a personal computer. The device's synchronization software then is used to load the software onto the device while the device is connected to the personal computer. Depending on the type of software installed, this process may be automatic. Some software is packaged as an add-on card that you insert into the device's expansion slot. Some Web sites allow you to browse a software catalog from a wireless device's Web browser and download the software directly to the device. When synchronizing a personal mobile device on a corporate network, some companies automatically install software on the employees' devices with no interaction required from the employee.

WHERE TO OBTAIN PERSONAL MOBILE DEVICE SOFTWARE

Application	Description	Samples
Web sites	Software publishers make their products available at their Web sites. Several Web sites also exist specifically to distribute mobile device software. Tens of thousands of titles are available, and most can be downloaded on a trial basis.	palmgear.com handandgo.com pdamd.com tucows.com itunes.com
Retail	Many popular software titles can be purchased at electronics and computer stores. The most popular titles at these locations include productivity and entertainment software.	bestbuy.com compusa.com
Develop in-house	Many corporations develop their own personal mobile device software to use internally to meet specific needs. These programs usually tap into existing corporate databases of product and customer information. The companies that produce mobile device operating systems often make the development tools for such software available at no cost or a minimal cost.	palmsource.com/developers microsoft.com/windowsmobile/ developers blackberry.net/developers symbian.com/developer

For an updated list of where to obtain PDA software, visit scsite.com/dc2008/ch5/pda.

FIGURE 15 Personal mobile device software is available from a number of sources.

HOW TO PURCHASE A PERSONAL MOBILE DEVICE

Whether you choose a PDA, smart phone, ultra personal computer, or portable media player, handheld navigation device, or handheld game console depends on where, when, and how you will use the device. If you need to stay organized when you are on the go, then a PDA may be the right choice. PDAs typically are categorized by the operating system they run (Figure 2 on page 283). If you need to stay organized and in touch when on the go, then a smart phone or ultra personal computer may be the right choice. Choose a handheld navigation device if you often need directions or information about your surroundings. If you plan to relax and play games, then a handheld game console may be right for you. Busy professionals who are on the move often carry more than one personal mobile device.

This section lists guidelines you should consider when purchasing a PDA, smart phone, ultra personal computer, portable media player, handheld navigation device, or handheld game console. You also should visit the Web sites listed in Figure 16 to gather more information about the type of personal mobile device that best suits your computing needs.

1 DETERMINE THE PROGRAMS YOU PLAN TO RUN ON YOUR DEVICE.

All PDAs and most smart phones can handle basic organizer-type software such as a calendar, address book, and notepad. Portable media players and handheld navigation devices usually have the fewest programs available to run on them. Ultra personal computers usually have the most number of programs available because the devices can run almost any personal computer software. The availability of other software depends on the operating system you choose. The depth and breadth of software for the Palm OS is significant, with more than 20,000 basic programs and more than 600 wireless programs. Devices that run Windows-based operating systems, such as Windows Mobile may have fewer programs available, but the operating system and application software are similar to those with which you are familiar, such as Word and Excel. When choosing a handheld game console, consider whether your favorite games are available for the device. Consider if you want extras on the device, such as the capability of playing media files.

2 CONSIDER HOW MUCH YOU WANT TO PAY.

The price of a personal mobile device can range from $100 to more than $2,000, depending on its capabilities. Some Palm OS devices are at the lower end of the cost spectrum, and ultra personal computers often are at the higher end. A PDA will be less expensive than a smart phone with a similar configuration. For the latest prices, capabilities, and accessories, visit the Web sites listed in Figure 16.

3 DETERMINE WHETHER YOU NEED WIRELESS ACCESS TO THE INTERNET AND E-MAIL OR MOBILE TELEPHONE CAPABILITIES WITH YOUR DEVICE.

Smart phones often give you access to e-mail and other data and Internet services. Some PDAs, smart phones, ultra personal computers, and handheld game consoles include wireless networking capability to allow you to connect to the Internet wirelessly. These wireless features and services allow users to access real-time information from anywhere to help make decisions while on the go. Most portable media players do not include the capability to access Internet services.

4 FOR WIRELESS DEVICES, DETERMINE HOW AND WHERE YOU WILL USE THE SERVICE.

When purchasing a wireless device, you must subscribe to a wireless service. Determine if the wireless network (carrier) you choose has service in the area where you plan to use the device. Some networks have high-speed data networks only in certain areas, such as large cities or business districts. Also, a few carriers allow you to use your device in other countries.

When purchasing a smart phone, determine if you plan to use the device more as a phone, PDA, or wireless data device. Some smart phones, such as those based on the Pocket PC Phone edition or the Palm OS, are geared more for use as a PDA and have a PDA form factor. Other smart phones, such as those based on Microsoft Smartphone or Symbian operating systems, mainly are phone devices that include robust PDA functionality. Research in Motion Blackberry-based smart phones include robust data features that are oriented to accessing e-mail and wireless data services.

5 MAKE SURE YOUR DEVICE HAS ENOUGH MEMORY AND STORAGE.

Memory (RAM) is not a major issue with low-end devices with monochrome displays and basic organizer functions. Memory is a major issue, however, for high-end devices that have color displays and wireless features. Without enough memory, the performance level of your device will drop dramatically. If you plan to purchase a high-end device running the Palm OS operating system, the device should have at least 32 MB of RAM. If you plan to purchase a high-end device running the Windows Mobile operating system, the PDA should have at least 64 MB of RAM. An ultra personal computer can have 512 MB of RAM or more while a handheld navigation device may have over 2 GB of flash memory.

An ultra personal computer can have 512 MB of RAM or more while a handheld navigation device may have over 2 GB of flash memory.

Many personal mobile devices include a hard disk for storage. Portable media players, ultra personal computers, and some smart phones include hard disks to store media and other data. Consider how much media and other data you need to store on your device. The hard disk size may range from 4 GB to more than 80 GB.

PRACTICE WITH THE TOUCH SCREEN, HANDWRITING RECOGNITION, AND BUILT-IN KEYBOARD BEFORE DECIDING ON A MODEL.

To enter data into a PDA, smart phone, and some ultra personal computers and handheld game consoles, you use a pen-like stylus to handwrite on the screen or a keyboard. The keyboard either slides out or is mounted on the front of the device. With handwriting recognition, the device translates the handwriting into a computerized font. You also can use the stylus as a pointing device to select items on the screen and enter data by tapping on an on-screen keyboard. By practicing data entry before buying a device, you can learn if one device may be easier for you to use than another. You also can buy third-party software to improve a device's handwriting recognition.

 DECIDE WHETHER YOU WANT A COLOR DISPLAY.

PDAs, ultra personal computers, some handheld navigation devices, and some handheld game consoles usually come with a color display that supports as many as 65,536 colors. Smart phones also have the option for color displays. Having a color display does result in greater on-screen detail, but it also requires more memory and uses more power. Resolution also influences the quality of the display.

 COMPARE BATTERY LIFE.

Any mobile device is good only if it has the power required to run. For example, smart phones with monochrome screens typically have a much longer battery life than Pocket PC devices with color screens. The use of wireless networking will shorten battery time considerably. To help alleviate this problem, most devices have incorporated rechargeable batteries that can be recharged by placing the device in a cradle or connecting it to a charger.

 SERIOUSLY CONSIDER THE IMPORTANCE OF ERGONOMICS.

Will you put the device in your pocket, a carrying case, or wear it on your belt? How does it feel in your hand? Will you use it indoors or outdoors? Many screens are unreadable outdoors. Do you need extra ruggedness, such as would be required in construction, in a plant, or in a warehouse? A smart phone with a PDA form factor may be larger than a typical PDA. A smart phone with a phone form factor may be smaller, but have fewer capabilities.

 CHECK OUT THE ACCESSORIES.

Determine which accessories you want for your personal mobile device. Accessories include carrying cases, portable mini- and full-sized keyboards, removable storage, modems, synchronization cradles and cables, car chargers, wireless communications, global positioning system modules, digital camera modules, expansion cards, dashboard mounts, replacement styli, headsets, microphones, and more.

 DECIDE WHETHER YOU WANT ADDITIONAL FUNCTIONALITY.

In general, off-the-shelf Microsoft operating system-based devices have broader functionality than devices with other operating systems. For example, voice-recording capability, e-book players, and media players are standard on most Windows Mobile devices. If you are leaning towards a Palm OS device and want these additional functions, you may need to purchase additional software or expansion modules to add them later. Determine whether your employer permits devices with cameras on the premises, and if not, do not consider devices with cameras. Some handheld game consoles include the capability to access the Web. High-end handheld navigation devices may include destination information, such as information about restaurants and points of interest, an e-book reader, a media player, and currency converter.

 DETERMINE WHETHER SYNCHRONIZATION OF DATA WITH OTHER DEVICES OR PERSONAL COMPUTERS IS IMPORTANT.

Most devices include a cradle that connects to the USB or serial port on your computer so you can synchronize data on your device with your desktop or notebook computer. Increasingly more devices are Bluetooth and/or wireless networking enabled, which gives them the capability of synchronizing wirelessly. Many devices today also have an infrared port that allows you to synchronize data with any device that has a similar infrared port, including desktop and notebook computers or other personal mobile devices.

Web Site	Web Address
CNET Shopper	shopper.cnet.com
iPod	ipod.com
Palm	palm.com
Microsoft	windowsmobile.com pocketpc.com microsoft.com/smartphone
Oqo	oqo.com
MobileTechReview	pdabuyersguide.com
Nintendo	nintendo.com/channel/ds
Research in Motion	rim.com
Garmin	garmin.com
Symbian	symbian.com
Wireless Developer Network	wirelessdevnet.com
Sharp	www.myzaurus.com
For an updated list of reviews and information about personal mobile devices and their Web addresses, visit scsite.com/dc2008/ch5/pda.	

FIGURE 16 Web site reviews and information about personal mobile devices.

CHAPTER
SIX

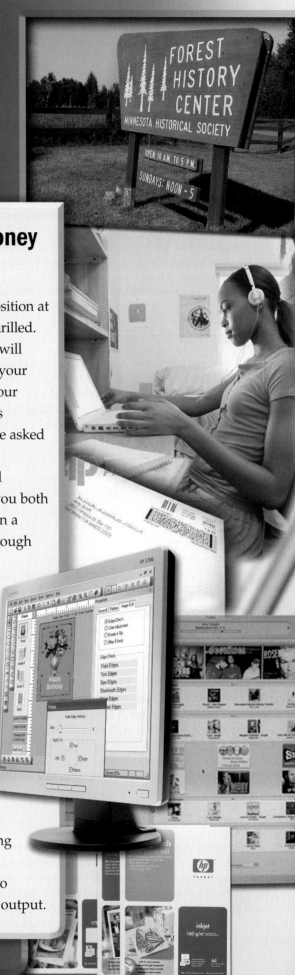

Picture Yourself Saving Time and Money Using a Computer

At last, you have landed your dream job — a part-time position at the county historical society. As a history major, you are thrilled. As a full-time student, however, you realize that working will limit your free time. You fear that you will have to curtail your volunteer work with the local youth group. In addition, your sister now is a freshman and has moved into your campus apartment. With two children in college, your parents have asked you to economize.

Your sister, a computer major, has some great time- and money-saving ideas. She sets up online banking so that you both can pay bills and balance accounts while viewing them on a computer monitor. For items that still must be mailed through the postal service, you will print the postage stamps on your printer, along with envelopes or mailing labels. Besides saving an enormous amount of time, you save money by not driving to the bank or post office.

With your sister's guidance, you use software to create and print flyers and announcements for the youth group. The time savings enable you to continue volunteering. For special occasions, your sister and you will use greeting card software to design cards on the computer screen, personalizing them with digital pictures, and then print them in color on card paper. You both plan to download music to your portable media players to save the cost of purchasing an entire CD, as well as the time spent driving to the store.

Read Chapter 6 to learn about monitors, printers, audio output, and paper, and to discover many other forms of output.

After completing this chapter, you will be able to:

1. Describe the four categories of output

2. Summarize the characteristics of LCD monitors, LCD screens, and plasma monitors

3. Describe the characteristics of a CRT monitor and factors that affect its quality

4. Explain the relationship between graphics chips and monitors

5. Describe various ways to print

6. Differentiate between a nonimpact printer and an impact printer

7. Summarize the characteristics of ink-jet printers, photo printers, laser printers, thermal printers, mobile printers, label and postage printers, and plotters and large-format printers

8. Describe the uses of speakers, headphones, and earphones

9. Identify the output characteristics of fax machines and fax modems, multifunction peripherals, data projectors, joysticks, wheels, and gamepads

10. Identify output options for physically challenged users

CONTENTS

WHAT IS OUTPUT?

Output is data that has been processed into a useful form. That is, computers process data (input) into information (output). A computer generates several types of output, depending on the hardware and software being used and the requirements of the user.

Users view or watch output on a screen, print it, or hear it through speakers, headphones, or earphones. Monitors, notebook computers, Tablet PCs, portable media players, PDAs, and smart phones have screens that allow users to view documents, Web sites, e-mail messages, pictures, videos, movies, and other types of output. Some printers produce black-and-white documents, and others produce brilliant colors, enabling users to print color documents, photographs, and transparencies. Through the computer's speakers, headphones, or earphones, users listen to sounds, music, and voice messages.

While working with a computer, a user encounters four basic categories of output: text, graphics, audio, and video (Figure 6-1). Very often, a single form of output, such as a Web page, includes more than one of these categories.

- Text — Examples of text-based output are memos, letters, press releases, reports, advertisements, newsletters, envelopes, mailing labels, and e-mail messages. On the Web, users view and print many other types of text-based output. These include blogs, newspapers, magazines, books, play or television show transcripts, stock quotes, famous speeches, and historical lectures.
- Graphics — Output often includes graphics to enhance its visual appeal and convey information. Business letters have logos. Reports include charts. Newsletters use drawings, clip art, and photographs. Users print high-quality photographs taken with a digital camera. Many Web sites use animated

FIGURE 6-1   Four categories of output are text, graphics, audio, and video.

graphics, such as blinking icons, scrolling messages, or simulations.

- Audio — Users insert their favorite music CD in a CD or DVD drive and listen to the music while working on the computer. Software such as games, encyclopedias, and simulations often have musical accompaniments for entertainment and audio clips, such as narrations and speeches, to enhance understanding. On the Web, users tune into radio and television stations and listen to audio clips, podcasts, or live broadcasts of interviews, talk shows, sporting events, news, music, and concerts. They also use the Internet to conduct real-time conversations with friends, coworkers, or family members, just as if they were speaking on the telephone.

- Video — As with audio, software and Web sites often include video clips to enhance understanding. Vodcasts and video blogs, for example, add a video component to the traditional podcast and blog. Users watch a live or prerecorded news report, view a replay while attending a live sporting event, observe weather conditions, or enjoy a live performance of their favorite musician or musical group on the computer. Instead of renting a movie, users can download movie content from a Web site for a fee and then watch the entire movie on a computer or mobile device. Attaching a video camera to the computer allows users to watch home movies on the computer. They also can attach a television's antenna or cable to the computer and watch a television program on the computer screen.

An **output device** is any type of hardware component that conveys information to one or more people. Commonly used output devices include display devices; printers; speakers, headphones, and earphones; fax machines and fax modems; multifunction peripherals; data projectors; and force-feedback joysticks, wheels, and gamepads. This chapter discusses each of these output devices.

LCD Technology

A **liquid crystal display** (**LCD**) uses a liquid compound to present information on a display device. Computer LCDs typically contain fluorescent tubes that emit light waves toward the liquid-crystal cells, which are sandwiched between two sheets of material. When an electrical charge passes through the cells, the cells twist. This twisting causes some light waves to be blocked and allows others to pass through, creating images on the display.

LCD monitors and LCD screens produce color using either passive-matrix or active-matrix technology. An *active-matrix display*, also known as a *TFT (thin-film transistor) display*, uses a separate transistor to apply charges to each liquid crystal cell and thus displays high-quality color that is viewable from all angles. A newer type of TFT technology, called *organic LED (OLED)*, uses organic molecules that produce an even brighter, easier-to-read display than standard TFT displays. OLEDs are less expensive to produce, consume less power, and can be fabricated on flexible surfaces. Read Looking Ahead 6-1 for a look at the next generation of OLEDs.

A *passive-matrix display* uses fewer transistors, requires less power, and is less expensive than an active-matrix display. The color on a passive-matrix display often is not as bright as an active-matrix display. Users view images on a passive-matrix display best when working directly in front of it.

WEB LINK 6-1

LCD Technology

For more information, visit scsite.com/ dc2008/ch6/weblink and then click LCD Technology.

LCD Quality

The quality of an LCD monitor or LCD screen depends primarily on its resolution, response time, brightness, dot pitch, and contrast ratio.

- **Resolution** is the number of horizontal and vertical pixels in a display device. For example, a monitor that has a 1600 × 1200 resolution displays up to 1600 pixels per horizontal row and 1200 pixels per vertical row, for a total of 1,920,000 pixels to create a screen image. Recall that a *pixel* (short for picture element) is a single point in an electronic image. A higher resolution uses a greater number of pixels and thus provides a smoother, sharper, and clearer image. As you increase the resolution, however, some items on the screen appear smaller (Figure 6-5).

  With LCD monitors and screens, resolution generally is proportional to the size of the device. For example, a 17-inch LCD monitor typically has a resolution of 1280 × 1024, while a 20-inch LCD monitor has a resolution of 1600 × 1200. LCDs are geared for a specific resolution, called the *native resolution*. Check the monitor's documentation for its native resolution, and for optimal results, be sure the computer uses the native resolution setting.

- *Response time* of an LCD monitor or screen is the time in milliseconds (ms) that it takes to turn a pixel on or off. LCD monitors' and screens' response times range from 5 to 16 ms. The lower the number, the faster the response time.

 LOOKING AHEAD 6-1

Rollable Displays Lock and Roll

Your newspaper arrives each morning at your front door rolled up and secured with a rubber band or in a plastic bag. Your computer monitor soon may arrive rolled up so you can transport it easily in your book bag or luggage.

Lightweight, flexible screens can be stored in pen-sized cases and then unrolled when needed. They can be connected wirelessly with various electronic devices, such as cellular telephones and CD and DVD players, so gamers could play on a moment's notice and movie buffs could watch the latest releases easily while sitting on airplanes and buses. GPS programs would allow hikers and bikers to view their locations, then slip the rugged screen back inside the case and then into their backpacks or pockets.

Engineers are developing stand-alone products with touch screens and keypads. For more information, visit scsite.com/dc2008/ch6/looking and then click Rollable Displays.

FIGURE 6-5a (screen resolution at 800 × 600)

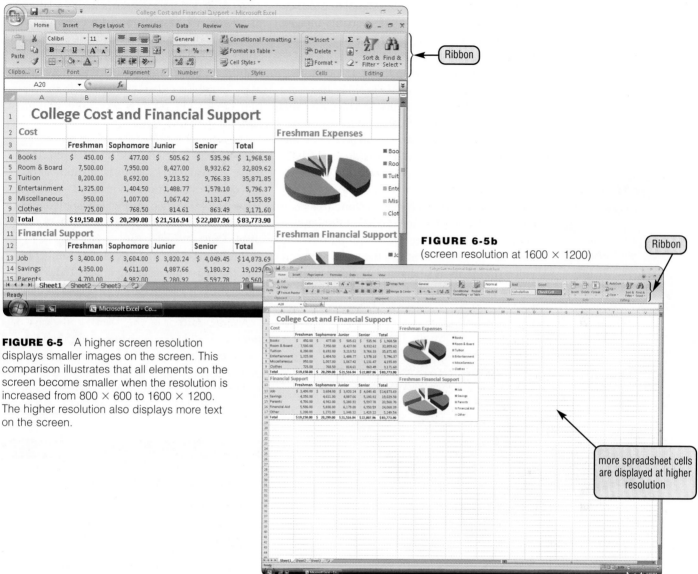

FIGURE 6-5 A higher screen resolution displays smaller images on the screen. This comparison illustrates that all elements on the screen become smaller when the resolution is increased from 800 × 600 to 1600 × 1200. The higher resolution also displays more text on the screen.

FIGURE 6-5b
(screen resolution at 1600 × 1200)

more spreadsheet cells are displayed at higher resolution

- Brightness of an LCD monitor or LCD screen is measured in nits. A *nit* is a unit of visible light intensity equal to one candela (formerly called candlepower) per square meter. The *candela* is the standard unit of luminous intensity. LCD monitors and screens today range from 250 to 550 nits. The higher the nits, the brighter the images.

- *Dot pitch,* sometimes called *pixel pitch,* is the distance in millimeters between pixels on a display device. Text created with a smaller dot pitch is easier to read. Advertisements normally specify a monitor's dot pitch or pixel pitch. Average dot pitch on LCD monitors and screens should be .28 mm or lower. The lower the number, the sharper the image.

- *Contrast ratio* describes the difference in light intensity between the brightest white and

darkest black that can be displayed on an LCD monitor. Contrast ratios today range from 400:1 to 800:1. Higher contrast ratios represent colors better.

Graphics Chips, Ports, and LCD Monitors

A cable on a monitor plugs in a port on the system unit, which enables communications from a graphics chip. This chip, called the *graphics processing unit (GPU),* controls the manipulation and display of graphics on a display device. The graphics processing unit either is integrated on the motherboard or resides on a video card (graphics card) in a slot in the motherboard. Video cards usually contain a fan or heat sink to keep this and other chips from overheating.

LCD monitors use a digital signal to produce a picture. To display the highest quality images, an LCD monitor should plug in a *DVI (Digital Video Interface) port*, which enables digital signals to transmit directly to the LCD monitor. Current models of system units either have an integrated DVI chip or contain a video card that has a DVI port. They usually also have a standard monitor port and an *S-video port*, allowing users to connect external devices such as a television, DVD player, or video recorder, to the computer (Figure 6-6).

Over the years, several video standards have been developed to define the resolution, number of colors, and other display properties. The table in Figure 6-7 identifies the more common video standards available today, along with their typical resolution and aspect ratio. The *aspect ratio* defines a display's width relative to its height. A 2:1 aspect ratio, for example, means the display is twice as wide as it is tall. Some display devices support multiple video standards. For a display device to show images as defined by a video standard, both the display device and graphics processing unit must support the same video standard.

The number of colors a graphics processing unit displays is determined by bit depth. The *bit depth*, also called *color depth*, is the number of bits used to store information about each pixel. For example, a video card with a 24-bit depth uses 24 bits to store information about each pixel. Thus, this video card can display 2^{24} or 16.7 million colors. The greater the number of bits, the better the resulting image. Today's video cards typically have a 24-bit depth or a 32-bit depth.

A video card or motherboard, in the case of integrated video, must have enough video memory to generate the resolution and number of colors you want to display. This memory, which often is 256 MB or 512 MB on current video cards, stores information about each pixel.

WEB LINK 6-2

Video Cards

For more information, visit scsite.com/ dc2008/ch6/weblink and then click Video Cards.

standard monitor port

S-video port

DVI port

FIGURE 6-6 Ports on current video cards.

 FAQ 6-3

How do I change my screen resolution?

You can change your monitor's screen resolution through your operating system's display properties. Before changing your screen resolution, you first should make sure your monitor and video card support your desired resolution. For more information, visit scsite.com/dc2008/ch6/faq and then click Screen Resolution.

Video Standard		Typical Resolution	Aspect Ratio
SVGA	Super Video Graphics Array	800 × 600	4:3
XGA	Extended Graphics Array	1024 × 768	4:3
SXGA	Super XGA	1280 × 1024	5:4
WXGA	Wide XGA	1280 × 1024 or 1366 × 768	16:10 or 16:9
UXGA	Ultra XGA	1600 × 1200	4:3
WSXGA	Wide Super XGA	1680 × 1050	16:10
WUXGA	Wide Ultra XGA	1920 × 1200	16:10
WQXGA	Wide Quad XGA	2560 × 1600	16:10

FIGURE 6-7 Wide video standard formats are preferable for users who watch movies and play video games on the computer.

Plasma Monitors

Large business or power users sometimes have plasma monitors, which often measure more than 60 inches wide (Figure 6-8). A **plasma monitor** is a display device that uses gas plasma technology, which sandwiches a layer of gas between two glass plates. When voltage is applied, the gas releases ultraviolet (UV) light. This UV light causes the pixels on the screen to glow and form an image.

Plasma monitors offer larger screen sizes and richer colors than LCD monitors but are more expensive. Like LCD monitors, plasma monitors can hang directly on a wall.

Televisions

Home users sometimes use their television as a display device. Connecting a computer to an analog television requires a converter that translates the digital signal from the computer into an analog signal that the television can display. The best analog televisions have a resolution of only 520 × 400 pixels. Thus, users are turning to *digital television* (*DTV*) for crisper, higher-quality output on their LCD or plasma televisions.

Digital television signals provide two major advantages over analog signals. First, digital signals produce a higher-quality picture. Second, many programs can be broadcast on a single digital channel, whereas only one program can be broadcast on an analog channel. Today, all broadcast stations must transmit digital signals, as mandated by the FCC.

HDTV (*high-definition television*) is the most advanced form of digital television, working with digital broadcast signals, transmitting digital sound, supporting wide screens, and providing resolutions up to 1920 × 1080 pixels. With HDTV, the broadcast signals are digitized when they are sent via over-the-air (OTA) broadcasts from local television networks, satellite, or cable. To receive the HDTV signals via OTA broadcasts, you need a VHF/UHF antenna; via satellite, you need an HDTV-compatible satellite receiver/tuner; and via cable, you need an HDTV-compatible cable box.

With game consoles, such as Microsoft's Xbox 360, Nintendo's Wii, and Sony's PlayStation 3, the output device often is a television (Figure 6-9). Users plug one end of a cable in the game console and the other end in the video port on the television. Although some game consoles include a small LCD screen (usually 5 inches or smaller), home users often prefer the larger television displays for game playing, watching movies, and browsing the Internet on a television connected to a game console.

FIGURE 6-8 Large plasma monitors can measure more than 60 inches wide.

FIGURE 6-9 Video game players often use a television as their game console's output device.

FAQ 6-4

What is the largest high-definition display to date?

Dolphin Stadium in Miami, Florida has a 1,750-inch display, measuring about 37 feet wide and 50 feet tall. For more information, visit scsite.com/dc2008/ch6/faq and then click Largest High-Definition Display.

CRT MONITORS

A **CRT monitor** is a desktop monitor that contains a cathode-ray tube (Figure 6-10). A *cathode-ray tube* (*CRT*) is a large, sealed glass tube. The front of the tube is the screen. Tiny dots of phosphor material coat the screen on a CRT. Each dot consists of a red, a green, and a blue phosphor. The three dots combine to make up each pixel. Inside the CRT, an electron beam moves back and forth across the back of the screen. This causes the dots on the front of the screen to glow, which produces an image on the screen.

CRT monitors have a much larger footprint than do LCD monitors; that is, they take up more desk space. CRT monitors for desktop computers are available in various sizes, with the more common being 15, 17, 19, 21, and 22 inches. In addition to monitor size, advertisements also list a CRT monitor's viewable size. The *viewable size* is the diagonal measurement of the actual viewing area provided by the screen in the CRT monitor. A 21-inch monitor, for example, may have a viewable size of 20 inches.

A CRT monitor usually costs less than an LCD monitor, but it also generates more heat and uses more power than an LCD monitor. To help reduce the amount of electricity used by monitors and other computer components, the United States Department of Energy (DOE) and the United States Environmental Protection Agency (EPA) developed the **ENERGY STAR program**. This program encourages manufacturers to create energy-efficient devices that require little power when they are not in use. Monitors and devices that meet ENERGY STAR guidelines display an ENERGY STAR label.

CRT monitors produce a small amount of electromagnetic radiation. *Electromagnetic radiation* (*EMR*) is a magnetic field that travels at the speed of light. Excessive amounts of EMR can pose a health risk. To be safe, all high-quality CRT monitors comply with MPR II standards. *MPR II* is a set of standards that defines acceptable levels of EMR for a monitor. To protect yourself even further, sit at arm's length from the CRT monitor because EMR travels only a short distance.

FAQ 6-5

Are CRT monitor sales decreasing?

Yes. Decreasing flat-panel display prices are enabling consumers to purchase these more attractive alternatives to CRT monitors. In addition, consumers now are able to purchase larger flat-panel displays than they previously were able to afford. For more information, visit scsite.com/dc2008/ch6/faq and then click Monitor Sales.

FIGURE 6-10   The core of a CRT monitor is a cathode-ray tube.

Quality of a CRT Monitor

The quality of a CRT monitor depends largely on its resolution, dot pitch, and refresh rate.

- Most CRT monitors support a variety of screen resolutions. Standard CRT monitors today usually display up to a maximum of 1800 × 1440 pixels, with 1280 × 1024 often the norm. High-end CRT monitors (for the power user) can display 2048 × 1536 pixels or more.

- As with LCD monitors, text created with a smaller dot pitch, or pixel pitch, is easier to read. To minimize eye fatigue, use a CRT monitor with a dot pitch of .27 millimeters or lower.

- Electron beams inside a CRT monitor "draw" an image on the entire screen many times per second so the phosphor dots, and therefore the image, do not fade. The number of times the image is drawn per second is called the *refresh rate*, or *scan rate*. A CRT monitor's refresh rate, which is expressed in hertz (Hz), should be fast enough to maintain a constant, flicker-free image. A slower refresh rate causes the image to fade and then flicker as it is redrawn. This flicker can lead to eye fatigue and cause headaches for some users.

A high-quality CRT monitor will provide a vertical refresh rate of at least 68 Hz. This means the image on the screen redraws itself vertically 68 times in a second.

Graphics Chips and CRT Monitors

Many CRT monitors use an analog signal to produce an image. As with an LCD monitor, a cable on the CRT monitor plugs in a port on the system unit, which enables communications from a graphics chip. If the graphics chip resides on a video card, for example, the video card converts digital output from the computer into an analog video signal and sends the signal through the cable to the monitor, which displays output on the screen.

As with LCD monitors, the greater the video card's bit depth, the better the resulting image. Both the video card and the monitor must support the video standard to generate the desired resolution and number of colors, and the video card must have enough memory to generate the resolution and number of colors you want to display. Some users place additional video cards in their system unit, allowing multiple monitors to display output from a single computer simultaneously.

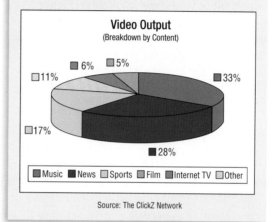

FAQ 6-6

What type of video content do users view on display devices?

Music videos and newscasts are the most widely viewed video content on display devices, as shown in the chart below. For more information, visit scsite.com/dc2008/ch6/faq and then click Video Output Content.

Video Output
(Breakdown by Content)

6% 5% 33% 11% 17% 28%

Music | News | Sports | Film | Internet TV | Other

Source: The ClickZ Network

Test your knowledge of pages 300 through 309 in Quiz Yourself 6-1.

QUIZ YOURSELF 6-1

Instructions: Find the true statement below. Then, rewrite the remaining false statements so they are true.

1. A lower resolution uses a greater number of pixels and thus provides a smoother image.

2. An output device is any type of software component that conveys information to one or more people.

3. Documents often include text to enhance their visual appeal and convey information.

4. LCD monitors have a larger footprint than CRT monitors.

5. Types of CRTs include LCD monitors, LCD screens, and plasma monitors.

6. You measure a monitor diagonally from one corner to the other.

Quiz Yourself Online: To further check your knowledge of output, flat-panel displays, and CRT monitors, visit scsite.com/dc2008/ch6/quiz and then click Objectives 1 – 4.

PRINTERS

A **printer** is an output device that produces text and graphics on a physical medium such as paper or transparency film. Printed information, called *hard copy*, exists physically and is a more permanent form of output than that presented on a display device (soft copy).

A hard copy, also called a *printout*, is either in portrait or landscape orientation (Figure 6-11). A printout in *portrait orientation* is taller than it is wide, with information printed across the shorter width of the paper. A printout in *landscape orientation* is wider than it is tall, with information printed across the widest part of the paper. Letters, reports, and books typically use portrait orientation. Spreadsheets, slide shows, and graphics often use landscape orientation.

Home computer users might print less than a hundred pages a week. Small business computer users might print several hundred pages a day. Users of mainframe computers, such as large utility companies that send printed statements to hundreds of thousands of customers each month, require printers that are capable of printing thousands of pages per hour.

To meet this range of printing needs, many different printers exist with varying speeds, capabilities, and printing methods. Figure 6-12 presents a list of questions to help you decide on the printer best suited to your needs.

The following pages discuss various ways of producing printed output, as well as many different types of printers.

FIGURE 6-11a (portrait orientation)

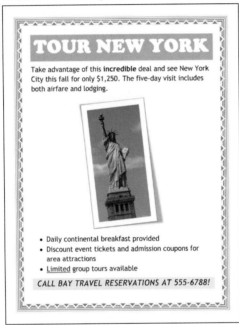

FIGURE 6-11b (landscape orientation)

DRINK PLENTY OF WATER

× At least eight 8-ounce servings
  + Drink throughout the day
    × Start and end your day with water
    × Do not wait until you are thirsty
  + Do not substitute with caffeinated beverages
  + Cool water is best for keeping hydrated

KEEP YOUR COOL ON HOT DAYS

FIGURE 6-11 Portrait orientation is taller than it is wide. Landscape orientation is wider than it is tall.

1. What is my budget?
2. How fast must my printer print?
3. Do I need a color printer?
4. What is the cost per page for printing?
5. Do I need multiple copies of documents?
6. Will I print graphics?
7. Do I want to print photographs?
8. Do I want to print directly from a memory card or other type of miniature storage media?
9. What types of paper does the printer use?
10. What sizes of paper does the printer accept?
11. Do I want to print on both sides of the paper?
12. How much paper can the printer tray hold?
13. Will the printer work with my computer and software?
14. How much do supplies such as ink and paper cost?
15. Can the printer print on envelopes and transparencies?
16. How many envelopes can the printer print at a time?
17. How much do I print now, and how much will I be printing in a year or two?
18. Will the printer be connected to a network?
19. Do I want wireless printing capability?

FIGURE 6-12 Questions to ask when purchasing a printer.

Producing Printed Output

Until a few years ago, printing a document required connecting a computer to a printer with a cable via the USB or parallel port on the computer. Although many users today continue to print using this method, a variety of printing options are available, as shown in Figure 6-13.

Today, wireless printing technology makes the task of printing from a notebook computer, Tablet PC, PDA, smart phone, or digital camera much easier. As discussed in Chapter 4, two wireless technologies for printing are Bluetooth

and infrared. With *Bluetooth printing*, a computer or other device transmits output to a printer via radio waves. The computer or other device and the printer do not have to be aligned with each other; rather, they need to be within an approximate 30-foot range. With *infrared printing*, a printer communicates with a computer or other device using infrared light waves. To print from a smart phone, for example, a user lines up the IrDA port on the smart phone with the IrDA port on the printer.

WEB LINK 6-3

Printing Digital Camera Images

For more information, visit scsite.com/dc2008/ch6/weblink and then click Printing Digital Camera Images.

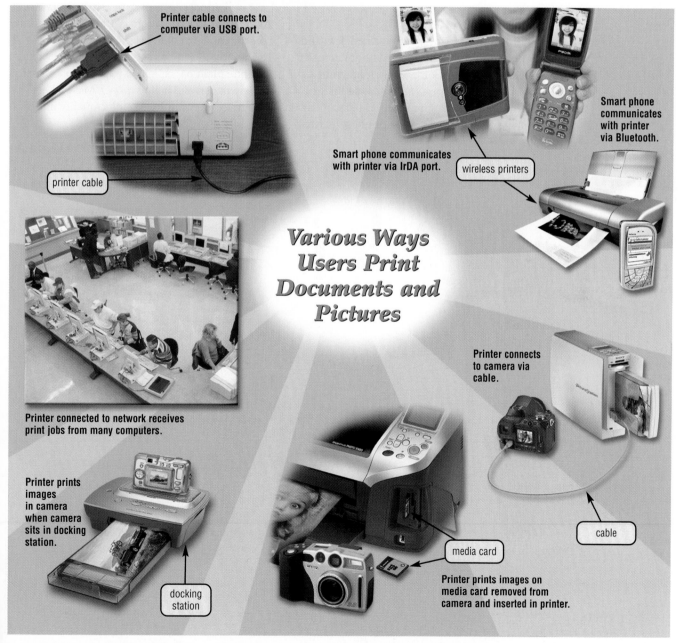

Printer cable connects to computer via USB port.

printer cable

Smart phone communicates with printer via IrDA port.

wireless printers

Smart phone communicates with printer via Bluetooth.

Various Ways Users Print Documents and Pictures

Printer connected to network receives print jobs from many computers.

Printer prints images in camera when camera sits in docking station.

docking station

Printer connects to camera via cable.

cable

media card

Printer prints images on media card removed from camera and inserted in printer.

FIGURE 6-13   Users print documents and pictures using a variety of printing methods.

Users can print images taken with a digital camera without downloading the images to the computer using a variety of techniques. Some cameras connect directly to a printer via a cable. Others store images on media cards that can be removed and inserted in the printer. Some printers have a docking station, into which the user inserts the camera to print pictures stored in the camera.

Finally, many home and business users print to a central printer on a network. Their computer may communicate with the network printer via cables or wirelessly.

Nonimpact Printers

A **nonimpact printer** forms characters and graphics on a piece of paper without actually striking the paper. Some spray ink, while others use heat or pressure to create images.

Commonly used nonimpact printers are ink-jet printers, photo printers, laser printers, thermal printers, mobile printers, label and postage printers, plotters, and large-format printers.

Ink-Jet Printers

An **ink-jet printer** is a type of nonimpact printer that forms characters and graphics by spraying tiny drops of liquid ink onto a piece of paper. Ink-jet printers have become a popular type of color printer for use in the home. A reasonable quality ink-jet printer costs less than $100.

Ink-jet printers produce text and graphics in both black-and-white and color on a variety of paper types (Figure 6-14). These printers normally use individual sheets of paper stored in one or two removable or stationary trays. Ink-jet printers accept papers in many sizes, ranging from 3 × 5 inches to 8½ × 14 inches. Available paper types include plain paper, ink-jet paper, photo paper, glossy paper, and banner paper. Most ink-jet printers can print photographic-quality images on any of these types of paper.

FIGURE 6-14 Ink-jet printers are a popular type of color printer used in the home.

Ink-jet printers also print on other materials such as envelopes, labels, index cards, greeting card paper (card stock), transparencies, and iron-on T-shirt transfers. Many ink-jet printers include software for creating greeting cards, banners, business cards, letterheads, and transparencies.

As with many other input and output devices, one factor that determines the quality of an ink-jet printer is its resolution. Printer resolution is measured by the number of *dots per inch* (*dpi*) a printer can print. With an ink-jet printer, a dot is a drop of ink. A higher dpi means the drops of ink are smaller. Most ink-jet printers can print from 1200 to 4800 dpi.

As shown in Figure 6-15, the higher the dpi, the better the print quality. The difference in quality becomes noticeable when the size of the printed image increases. That is, a wallet-sized image printed at 1200 dpi may look similar in quality to one printed at 2400 dpi. When you increase the size of the image, to 8 × 10 for example, the printout of the 1200 dpi resolution may look grainier than the one printed using a 2400 dpi resolution.

The speed of an ink-jet printer is measured by the number of pages per minute (ppm) it can print. Most ink-jet printers print from 6 to 33 ppm. Graphics and colors print at a slower rate. For example, an ink-jet printer may print 20 ppm for black text and only 15 ppm for color and/or graphics.

FIGURE 6-15 You will notice a higher quality output with printers that can print at a higher dpi.

The print head mechanism in an ink-jet printer contains ink-filled print cartridges. Each cartridge has fifty to several hundred small ink holes, or nozzles. The steps in Figure 6-16 illustrate how a drop of ink appears on a page. The ink propels through any combination of the nozzles to form a character or image on the paper.

When the print cartridge runs out of ink, you simply replace the cartridge. Most ink-jet printers have at least two print cartridges: one

FIGURE 6-16 HOW AN INK-JET PRINTER WORKS

Step 1:
A small resistor heats the ink, causing the ink to boil and form a vapor bubble.

Step 2:
The vapor bubble forces the ink through the nozzle.

Step 3:
Ink drops onto the paper.

Step 4:
As the vapor bubble collapses, fresh ink is drawn into the firing chamber.

WEB LINK 6-4

Ink-Jet Printers

For more information, visit scsite.com/dc2008/ch6/weblink and then click Ink-Jet Printers.

containing black ink and the other(s) containing colors. Cartridges with black ink cost $15 to $30 each. Color ink cartridge prices range from $20 to $35 each. The number of pages a single cartridge can print varies by manufacturer and the type of documents you print. For example, black ink cartridges typically print from 200 to 800 pages, and color ink cartridges from 125 to 450 pages. Read Ethics & Issues 6-1 for a related discussion.

ETHICS & ISSUES 6-1

Should Companies Prohibit Consumers from Refilling Ink Cartridges?

In 1903, King Camp Gillette introduced an innovative product — a safety razor with disposable blades. Gillette accompanied his product with an even more innovative idea — sell the razor, which was purchased once, at or below cost, and rely on sales of the razor blades, which were purchased repeatedly, for profit. The idea made Gillette a millionaire. Manufacturers of ink-jet printers use a similar approach. The printers are inexpensive, often less than $100. The ink cartridges the printers use, however, can cost from $30 to $50 each time they are replaced. To avoid the high cost of cartridges, some people get cartridges refilled cheaply by a third party vendor. At least one printer company, which holds approximately 4,000 patents related to ink and cartridges, legally prohibits the practice, and violators may be breaking patent and contract law if they refill a cartridge. Additionally, some printer manufacturers have inserted special chips that keep a cartridge from being refilled and, some claim, shut down a cartridge before it really is out of ink. This charge led to consumers winning a class-action lawsuit against one manufacturer. Opponents of these practices say that the printer companies are gouging customers and that no legitimate reason exists why someone should not be able to refill an ink-jet cartridge in the same way a soap dispenser can be refilled. Should manufacturers be allowed to prohibit people from refilling ink cartridges? Why? Would you use an ink refill kit? Why or why not?

WEB LINK 6-5

PictBridge

For more information, visit scsite.com/dc2008/ch6/weblink and then click PictBridge.

Photo Printers

A **photo printer** is a color printer that produces photo-lab-quality pictures (Figure 6-17). Some photo printers print just one or two sizes of images, for example, 3 × 5 inches and 4 × 6 inches. Others print up to letter size, legal size, or even larger. Some even print panoramic

photographs. Generally, the more sizes the printer prints, the more expensive the printer.

Many photo printers use ink-jet technology. With models that can print letter-sized documents, users connect the photo printer to their computer and use it for all their printing needs. For a few hundred dollars, this type of photo printer is ideal for the home or small business user. Other photo printer technologies are discussed later in the chapter. Read Ethics & Issues 6-2 for a related discussion.

Most photo printers are PictBridge enabled, so you can print pictures without a computer. *PictBridge* is a standard technology that allows you to print pictures directly from a digital camera by connecting a cable from the digital camera to a USB port on the printer.

prints only 4 × 6 size

prints 4 × 6, 5 ×
8 × 10, 8½ × 11
and panoramic size

FIGURE 6-17   Photo printers print in a range of siz

ETHICS & ISSUES 6-2

Who Is Responsible for Stopping Counterfeiting?

Some college students found a solution to their money problems: they made their own. With a scanner, personal computer, and color printer, they produced bogus bills and passed more than $1,000 in counterfeit currency before they were caught. As printer and scanner quality continues to improve, it is estimated that more than $1 million in fraudulent funds is produced every week. As one federal agent points out, counterfeiting has gone from a high-skill, low-tech job to a high-tech, low-skill job. While counterfeiters previously specialized in higher-domination bills ($20, $50, and $100), today phony $10, $5, and even $1 bills are circulated. Spotting fake money is not that difficult, but most people never look that closely. Manufacturers of printers have introduced technology to produce lines or streaks when a printed image contains too much bank-note green color. Many color laser printers and copiers print nearly undetectable information on every page that includes the machine's serial number and/or the current date and time. The information can be used to track counterfeit currency. Producers of scanners and scanning software often include technology that prevents the scanner from scanning currency. Should the manufacturers of high-quality printers and scanners take responsibility for this problem? Why or why not? It is illegal to pass counterfeit currency knowingly. Should it be illegal to offer templates knowingly online that could be used to produce counterfeit documents? Can you offer any other possible solutions?

Photo printers also usually have a built-in card slot(s) so the printer can print digital photographs directly from a media card. Simply remove the media card from the digital camera and insert it in the printer's card slot. Then, push buttons on the printer to select the desired photo, specify the number of copies, and indicate the size of the printed image. Some photo printers have built-in LCD color screens, allowing users to view and enhance the pictures before printing them.

Laser Printers

A **laser printer** is a high-speed, high-quality nonimpact printer (Figure 6-18). Laser printers are available in both black-and-white and color models. A laser printer for personal computers ordinarily uses individual $8\frac{1}{2} \times 11$-inch sheets of paper stored in one or more removable trays that slide in the printer case. Some laser printers have built-in trays that accommodate different sizes of paper, while others require separate trays for letter- and legal-sized paper. Most laser printers have a manual feed slot where you can insert individual sheets and envelopes. You also can print transparencies on a laser printer.

Laser printers print text and graphics in high-quality resolutions, usually 1200 dpi for black-and-white printers and up to 2400 dpi for color printers. While laser printers usually cost more than ink-jet printers, they also are much faster. A laser printer for the home and small office user typically prints black-and-white text at speeds of 12 to 35 ppm. Color laser printers print 8 to 30 ppm. Laser printers for large business users print more than 150 ppm.

Depending on the quality, speed, and type of laser printer, the cost ranges from a few hundred to a few thousand dollars for the home and small

FAQ 6-7

What type of paper is available for a photo printer?

Many photo papers are available in various surface finishes, brightness, and weights. Surface finishes include high gloss, soft gloss, satin, or matte. The higher the brightness rating, the more brilliant the whiteness. The greater the paper weight, which is measured in pounds, the thicker the paper. In the United States, the weight of paper is stated in pounds per 500 sheets of 17 × 22-inch paper, each sheet of which equals four letter-sized sheets. For more information, visit scsite.com/dc2008/ch6/faq and then click Photo Paper.

black-and-white laser printer

color laser printer

FIGURE 6-18
Laser printers are available in both black-and-white and color models.

office user, and several hundred thousand dollars for the large business user. Color laser printers are slightly higher priced than otherwise equivalent black-and-white laser printers.

When printing a document, laser printers process and store the entire page before they actually print it. For this reason, laser printers sometimes are called page printers. Storing a page before printing requires that the laser printer has a certain amount of memory in the device.

Depending on the amount of graphics you intend to print, a laser printer for the small business user can have up to 544 MB of memory and a 20 GB hard disk. To print a full-page 1200-dpi picture, for instance, you might need 32 MB of memory in the printer. If the printer does not have enough memory to print the picture, either it will print as much of the picture as its memory will allow, or it will display an error message and not print any of the picture.

Laser printers use software that enables them to interpret a *page description language* (*PDL*), which tells the printer how to lay out the contents of a printed page. When you purchase a laser printer, it comes with at least one of two common page description languages: PCL or PostScript. Developed by Hewlett-Packard, a leading printer manufacturer, *PCL* (*Printer Control Language*) is a standard printer language that supports the fonts and layout used in standard office documents. Professionals in the desktop publishing and graphic art fields commonly

use *PostScript* because it is designed for complex documents with intense graphics and colors.

Operating in a manner similar to a copy machine, a laser printer creates images using a laser beam and powdered ink, called *toner*. The laser beam produces an image on a special drum inside the printer. The light of the laser alters the electrical charge on the drum wherever it hits. When this occurs, the toner sticks to the drum and then transfers to the paper through a combination of pressure and heat (Figure 6-19).

When the toner runs out, you replace the toner cartridge. Toner cartridge prices range from $50 to $100 for about 5,000 printed pages.

WEB LINK 6-6

Laser Printers
For more information, visit scsite.com/dc2008/ch6/weblink and then click Laser Printers.

FAQ 6-8

How do I dispose of toner cartridges?
Do not throw them in the garbage. The housing contains iron, metal, and aluminum that is not biodegradable. The ink toner inside the cartridges contains toxic chemicals that pollute water and soil if discarded in dumps. Instead, recycle empty toner cartridges. Recycling programs in which some schools and organizations participate offer discounts or cash to customers who bring in depleted cartridges. If you are unable to find a recycling program in your area, contact your printer manufacturer to see if it has a recycling program. For more information, visit scsite.com/dc2008/ch6/faq and then click Recycling Toner Cartridges.

FIGURE 6-19 HOW A BLACK-AND-WHITE LASER PRINTER WORKS

Step 1: After the user sends an instruction to print a document, the drum rotates as gears and rollers feed a sheet of paper into the printer.

Step 2: A rotating mirror deflects a low-powered laser beam across the surface of a drum.

Step 3: The laser beam creates a charge that causes toner to stick to the drum.

Step 4: As the drum continues to rotate and press against the paper, the toner transfers from the drum to the paper.

Step 5: A set of rollers uses heat and pressure to fuse the toner permanently to the paper.

Thermal Printers

A **thermal printer** generates images by pushing electrically heated pins against heat-sensitive paper. Basic thermal printers are inexpensive, but the print quality is low and the images tend to fade over time. Self-service gas pumps often print gas receipts using a built-in lower-quality thermal printer.

Two special types of thermal printers have high print quality. A *thermal wax-transfer printer* generates rich, nonsmearing images by using heat to melt colored wax onto heat-sensitive paper. Thermal wax-transfer printers are more expensive than ink-jet printers, but less expensive than many color laser printers.

A *dye-sublimation printer*, sometimes called a *digital photo printer*, uses heat to transfer colored dye to specially coated paper. Most dye-sublimation printers create images that are of photographic quality (Figure 6-20). Professional applications requiring high image quality, such as photography studios, medical labs, and security identification systems, use dye-sublimation printers. These high-end printers cost thousands of dollars and print images in a wide range of sizes. Most dye-sublimation printers for the home or small business user, by contrast, typically print images in only one or two sizes and are much slower than their professional counterparts. These lower-end dye-sublimation printers are comparable in cost to a photo printer based on ink-jet technology. Some are small enough for the mobile user to carry the printer in a briefcase.

Mobile Printers

A **mobile printer** is a small, lightweight, battery-powered printer that allows a mobile user to print from a notebook computer, Tablet PC, PDA, or smart phone while traveling (Figure 6-21). Barely wider than the paper on which they print, mobile printers fit easily in a briefcase alongside a notebook computer.

Mobile printers mainly use ink-jet, thermal, thermal wax-transfer, or dye-sublimation technology. Many of these printers connect to a USB port. Others have a built-in wireless port through which they communicate with the computer wirelessly.

FIGURE 6-20a (dye-sublimation printer for the professional)

FIGURE 6-20b (dye-sublimation printer for the home or small office user)

FIGURE 6-20 The printers shown in this figure use dye-sublimation technology to create photographic-quality output.

FIGURE 6-21 A mobile printer is a compact printer that allows the mobile user to print from a notebook computer or mobile device.

Label and Postage Printers

A **label printer** is a small printer that prints on an adhesive-type material (Figure 6-22) that can be placed on a variety of items such as envelopes, packages, CDs, DVDs, audio-cassettes, photographs, file folders, and toys. Most label printers also print bar codes. Label printers typically use thermal technology.

A *postage printer* is a special type of label printer that has a built-in digital scale and prints postage stamps. Postage printers allow users to buy and print digital postage, called *Internet postage*, right from their computer. That is, you purchase an amount of postage from an authorized postal service Web site. As you need a stamp, you print it on the postage printer. Each time a postage stamp prints, your postage account is updated.

FIGURE 6-22
A label printer.

Plotters and Large-Format Printers

Plotters are sophisticated printers used to produce high-quality drawings such as blueprints, maps, and circuit diagrams. These printers are used in specialized fields such as engineering and drafting and usually are very costly. Current plotters use a row of charged wires (called styli) to draw an electrostatic pattern on specially coated paper and then fuse toner to the pattern. The printed image consists of a series of very small dots, which provides high-quality output.

Using ink-jet printer technology, but on a much larger scale, a **large-format printer** creates photo-realistic-quality color prints. Graphic artists use these high-cost, high-performance printers for signs, posters, and other professional quality displays (Figure 6-23).

Plotters and large-format printers can accommodate paper with widths up to 60 inches because blueprints, maps, signs, posters and other such drawings and displays can be quite large. Some plotters and large-format printers use individual sheets of paper, while others take large rolls.

Impact Printers

An **impact printer** forms characters and graphics on a piece of paper by striking a mechanism against an inked ribbon that physically contacts the paper. Impact printers characteristically are noisy because of this striking activity. These printers commonly produce *near letter quality* (*NLQ*) output, which is print quality slightly less clear than what is acceptable for business letters. Companies may use impact printers for routine jobs such as printing mailing labels, envelopes, and invoices. Impact printers also are ideal for printing multipart forms because they easily print through many layers of paper. Factories and retail counters use impact printers because these printers withstand dusty environments, vibrations, and extreme temperatures.

Two commonly used types of impact printers are dot-matrix printers and line printers.

FIGURE 6-23 Graphic artists use large-format printers to print signs, posters, and other professional quality displays.

DOT-MATRIX PRINTERS   A **dot-matrix printer** is an impact printer that produces printed images when tiny wire pins on a print head mechanism strike an inked ribbon (Figure 6-24). When the ribbon presses against the paper, it creates dots that form characters and graphics.

Most dot-matrix printers use *continuous-form paper*, in which thousands of sheets of paper are connected together end to end. The pages have holes along the sides to help feed the paper through the printer.

The print head mechanism on a dot-matrix printer contains 9 to 24 pins, depending on the manufacturer and the printer model. A higher number of pins means the printer prints more dots per character, which results in higher print quality.

The speed of a dot-matrix printer is measured by the number of characters per second (cps) it can print. The speed of most dot-matrix printers ranges from 300 to 1100 characters per second (cps), depending on the desired print quality.

LINE PRINTERS   A **line printer** is a high-speed impact printer that prints an entire line at a time (Figure 6-25). The speed of a line printer is measured by the number of lines per minute (lpm) it can print. Some line printers print as many as 3,000 lpm. Mainframes, servers, or networked applications, such as manufacturing, distribution, or shipping, often use line printers. These printers typically use 11 × 17-inch continuous-form paper.

Two popular types of line printers used for high-volume output are band and shuttle-matrix. A *band printer* prints fully formed characters when hammers strike a horizontal, rotating band that contains shapes of numbers, letters of the alphabet, and other characters. A *shuttle-matrix printer* functions more like a dot-matrix printer. The difference is the shuttle-matrix printer moves a series of print hammers back and forth horizontally at incredibly high speeds, as compared with standard line printers. Unlike a band printer, a shuttle-matrix printer prints characters in various fonts and font sizes.

FIGURE 6-25   A line printer is a high-speed printer often connected to a mainframe, server, or network.

continuous-form paper

FIGURE 6-24   A dot-matrix printer produces printed images when tiny pins strike an inked ribbon.

Test your knowledge of pages 310 through 319 in Quiz Yourself 6-2.

QUIZ YOURSELF 6-2

Instructions: Find the true statement below. Then, rewrite the remaining false statements so they are true.

1. A laser printer generates images by pushing electrically heated pins against heat-sensitive paper.
2. A photo printer creates images using a laser beam and powdered ink, called toner.
3. An ink-jet printer is a type of impact printer that forms characters and graphics by spraying tiny drops of liquid nitrogen onto a piece of paper.
4. Printed information is called soft copy.
5. Two commonly used types of impact printers are ink-jet printers and line printers.
6. With Bluetooth printing, a computer or other device transmits output to a printer via radio waves.

Quiz Yourself Online: To further check your knowledge of ways to print and various types of printers, visit scsite.com/dc2008/ch6/quiz and then click Objectives 5 – 7.

SPEAKERS, HEADPHONES, AND EARPHONES

An **audio output device** is a component of a computer that produces music, speech, or other sounds, such as beeps. Three commonly used audio output devices are speakers, headphones, and earphones.

Most personal computers have a small internal speaker that usually emits only low-quality sound. Thus, many personal computer users add surround sound **speakers** to their computers to generate a higher-quality sound for playing games, interacting with multimedia presentations, listening to music CDs, and viewing DVDs (Figure 6-26).

Most surround sound computer speaker systems include one or two center speakers and two or more *satellite speakers* that are positioned so sound emits from all directions. Speakers typically have tone and volume controls, allowing users to adjust settings. To boost the low bass sounds, surround sound speaker systems also include a *subwoofer*.

Surround sound systems are available in a variety of configurations. For example, a 2.1 speaker system contains two speakers and a subwoofer. A 5.1 speaker system has four satellite speakers, a center speaker, and a subwoofer. A 6.1 speaker system has four satellite speakers, a front center speaker, a rear center speaker, and a subwoofer. A 7.1 speaker system has four satellite speakers, two side speakers, a center speaker, and a subwoofer.

In many cases, users connect the speakers and subwoofer to ports on the sound card. With wireless speakers, however, a transmitter connects to the sound card, which wirelessly communicates with the speakers. To take full advantage of high-end surround sound speaker systems, be sure the sound card in the computer is compatible with the speaker system. For a more technical discussion about how sound cards produce sound, read the High-Tech Talk article on page 328.

Many users opt for a wireless music system, which includes a USB transmitter that plugs into a computer, a receiver that connects to a television or stereo system, and a remote control.

satellite speakers

subwoofer

center speaker

satellite speakers

FIGURE 6-26 Most personal computer users add high-quality surround sound speaker systems to their computers.

With this system, you can play any CD, DVD, or media file on your computer and transmit the audio to a home or office stereo or television at a distance of up to 330 feet. You also can plug a portable media player, such as an iPod, into the computer to hear its songs on the stereo or television speakers.

When using speakers, anyone in listening distance can hear the output. In a computer laboratory or other crowded environment, speakers might not be practical. Instead, users can plug headphones or earphones in a port on the sound card, in a speaker, or on the front of the system unit. With headphones or earphones, only the individual wearing the headphones or earphones hears the sound from the computer. The difference is that **headphones** cover or are placed outside of the ear (Figure 6-27), whereas

earphones, or *earbuds* (shown in Figure 6-1 on page 300), rest inside the ear canal.

Electronically produced voice output is growing in popularity. **Voice output** occurs when you hear a person's voice or when the computer talks to you through the speakers on the computer. In some programs, the computer can speak the contents of a document through voice output. On the Web, you can listen to (or download and then listen to) interviews, talk shows, sporting events, news, recorded music, and live concerts from many radio and television stations. Some Web sites dedicate themselves to providing voice output, where you can hear songs, quotes, historical lectures, speeches, and books (Figure 6-28). Read Ethics & Issues 6-3 for a related discussion.

WEB LINK 6-7

Wireless Music System
For more information, visit scsite.com/dc2008/ch6/weblink and then click Wireless Music System.

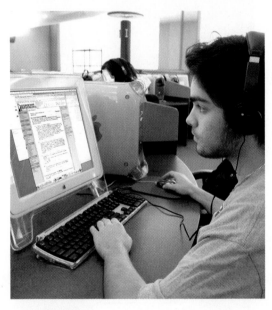

FIGURE 6-27 In a crowded environment where speakers are not practical, users wear headphones or earphones to hear audio output.

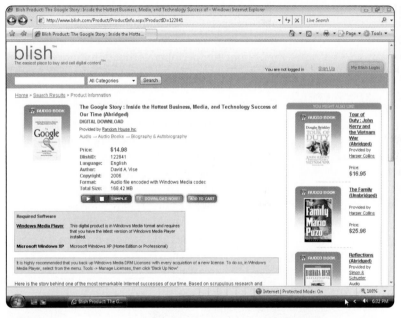

FIGURE 6-28 Through this Web site, users can purchase and then download a book in digital audio format and then listen to the book's contents via their computer's speakers or a portable media player such as an iPod.

ETHICS & ISSUES 6-3

Should Colleges Provide Free Access to Music for Students?

In recent years, many college administrators discovered that their computer networks had become completely saturated with the illegal sharing of copyrighted music files. At peak usage times during the day, the networks quickly were becoming unusable for legitimate purposes as students shared large music files. At the same time, the music industry began threatening colleges with legal action, claiming that the colleges are responsible for the illegal file sharing done by students on the school's network. College administrators and some music companies decided that a good solution is to allow a school to purchase licenses for music and then set up a shared music service for all students to access. While the university pays a fee for the service, the music is made available for free to students. The music files include, however, some restrictions. For example, in some agreements students are not allowed to use the files after they leave the school. In other arrangements, the files cannot be shared with others or burned on a CD. Some services include technology that helps the school identify illegal file sharing. Students have had a mixed reaction to the services due to the number of restrictions placed on the music. Some college administrators feel that the services amount to legalized blackmail because of the threat of legal action if the schools do not stop illegal file sharing. Should colleges provide free access to music for students? Why or why not? How could colleges make their free music services more attractive to students? What restrictions would you be comfortable with if you were able to obtain free music files at your school? Why?

Very often, voice output works with voice input. For example, when you call an airline to check the status of gates, terminals, and arrival times, your voice interacts with a computer-generated voice output. Another example is *Internet telephony*, which allows users to speak to other users over the Internet using their desktop computer, mobile computer, or mobile device.

Sophisticated programs enable the computer to converse with you. Talk into the microphone and say, "I'd like today's weather report." The computer replies, "For which city?" You reply, "Chicago." The computer says, "Sunny and 80 degrees."

OTHER OUTPUT DEVICES

In addition to display devices, printers, and speakers, many other output devices are available for specific uses and applications. These devices include fax machines and fax modems, multifunction peripherals, data projectors, and force-feedback joysticks, wheels, and gamepads.

Fax Machines and Fax Modems

A **fax machine** is a device that codes and encodes documents so they can be transmitted over telephone lines. The documents can contain text, drawings, or photographs, or can be handwritten. The term *fax* refers to a document that you send or receive via a fax machine.

A stand-alone fax machine scans an original document, converts the image into digitized data, and transmits the digitized image (Figure 6-29). A fax machine at the receiving end reads the incoming data, converts the digitized data back into an image, and prints or stores a copy of the original image.

Many computers include fax capability by using a fax modem. A *fax modem* is a modem that also allows you to send (and sometimes receive) electronic documents as faxes (Figure 6-30). A fax modem transmits computer-prepared documents, such as a word processing letter, or documents that have been digitized with a scanner or digital camera. A fax modem transmits these faxes to a fax machine or to another fax modem.

WEB LINK 6-8

Fax Modems

For more information, visit scsite.com/ dc2008/ch6/weblink and then click Fax Modems.

FIGURE 6-29 A stand-alone fax machine.

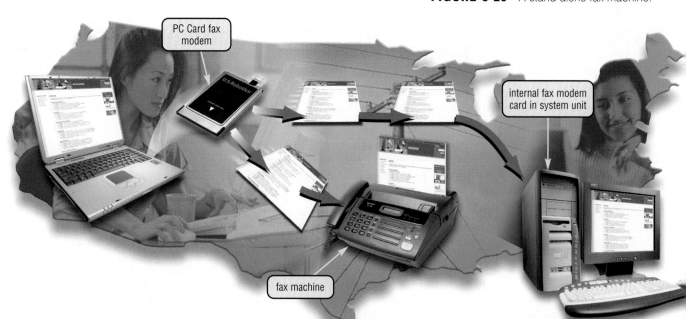

PC Card fax modem

internal fax modem card in system unit

fax machine

FIGURE 6-30 A fax modem allows users to send (and sometimes receive) electronic documents as faxes to a fax machine or another computer.

When a computer (instead of a fax machine) receives a fax, users can view the fax on the screen, saving the time and expense of printing it. If necessary, you also can print the fax. The quality of a viewed or printed fax is less than that of a word processing document because the fax actually is an image. Optical character recognition (OCR) software, which was discussed in Chapter 5, enables you to convert the image to text and then edit it.

A fax modem can be an external device that plugs in a port on the system unit, an internal adapter card inserted in an expansion slot on the motherboard, a chip integrated on the motherboard, or a PC Card that inserts in a PC Card slot.

Multifunction Peripherals

A **multifunction peripheral** is a single device that looks like a copy machine but provides the functionality of a printer, scanner, copy machine, and perhaps a fax machine (Figure 6-31). The features of these devices, which sometimes are called *all-in-one devices*, vary. For example, some use color ink-jet printer technology, while others include a black-and-white laser printer.

Small offices and home office (SOHO) users have multifunction peripherals because these devices require less space than having a separate printer, scanner, copy machine, and fax machine. Another advantage of these devices is they are significantly less expensive than if you purchase each device separately. If the device breaks down, however, you lose all four functions, which is the primary disadvantage.

Data Projectors

A **data projector** is a device that takes the text and images displaying on a computer screen and projects them on a larger screen so an audience can see the image clearly (Figure 6-32). For example, many classrooms use data projectors so all students easily can see an instructor's presentation on the screen.

Some data projectors are large devices that attach to a ceiling or wall in an auditorium. Others, designed for the mobile user, are small portable devices that can be transported easily. Two types of smaller, lower-cost units are LCD projectors and DLP projectors.

An *LCD projector*, which uses liquid crystal display technology, attaches directly to a computer, and uses its own light source to display the information shown on the computer screen. Because LCD projectors tend to produce lower-quality images, users often prefer DLP projectors for their sharper, brighter images.

WEB LINK 6-9

Multifunction Peripherals

For more information, visit scsite.com/dc2008/ch6/weblink and then click Multifunction Peripherals.

FIGURE 6-31 This multifunction peripheral is a color printer, scanner, copy machine, and fax machine all-in-one device.

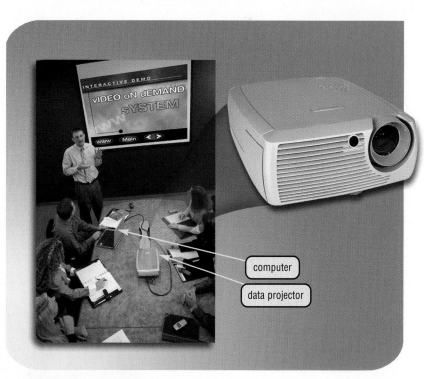

FIGURE 6-32 A data projector projects an image from a computer screen on a larger screen so an audience easily can see the image.

A *digital light processing (DLP) projector* uses tiny mirrors to reflect light, which produces crisp, bright, colorful images that remain in focus and can be seen clearly even in a well-lit room. Some newer televisions use DLP instead of LCD or plasma technology. Read Looking Ahead 6-2 for a look at the next generation of picture technology.

LOOKING AHEAD 6-2

Ultra HDTV Puts Viewers in the Picture

Vibrant colors and pictures so detailed television viewers feel like they actually are courtside at a basketball game or squishing wet sand between their toes at the beach are the promise of *Ultra High Definition TV (U-HDTV)*.

Using dramatically enhanced picture quality and sound, U-HDTV moves

television viewers from merely watching real objects to feeling like they are part of the scenes they are viewing. U-HDTV, demonstrated by researchers from Japanese state broadcaster NHK at the 2006 International Broadcasting Convention, featured 16 times the resolution of current HDTV and incorporated advanced surround sound utilizing 24 speakers.

With no currently available LCD or plasma screens with resolution high enough to display U-HDTV pictures, commercial development is still years away; however, the technology may have more immediate applications for movie studios or museum archives. For more information, visit scsite.com/dc2008/ch6/looking and then click U-HDTV.

Force-Feedback Joysticks, Wheels, and Gamepads

As discussed in Chapter 5, joysticks, wheels, and gamepads are input devices used to control movement and actions of a player or object in computer games, simulations, and video games. Today's joysticks, wheels, and gamepads also include *force feedback*, which is a technology that sends resistance to the device in response to actions of the user (Figure 6-33).

For example, as you use the simulation software to drive from a smooth road onto a gravel alley, the steering wheel trembles or vibrates, making the driving experience as realistic as possible. In addition to games, these devices are used in practical training applications such as in the military and aviation.

FAQ 6-9

Who plays video games?

Studies have shown that people between 18 and 34 years of age spend the most time playing video games. This age group spends more money on video games than in movie theaters. For more information, visit scsite.com/dc2008/ch6/faq and then click Video Gaming.

WEB LINK 6-10

Force Feedback Devices

For more information, visit scsite.com/dc2008/ch6/weblink and then click Force Feedback Devices.

FIGURE 6-33 Gaming devices often provide force feedback, giving the user realistic experience.

PUTTING IT ALL TOGETHER

Many factors influence the type of output devices you should use: the type of output desired, the hardware and software in use, and the anticipated cost. Figure 6-34 outlines several suggested monitors, printers, and other output devices for various types of computer users.

SUGGESTED OUTPUT DEVICES BY USER

User	Monitor	Printer	Other
HOME	• 17- or 19-inch LCD monitor	• Ink-jet color printer; or • Photo printer	• Speakers • Headphones or earphones • Force-feedback joystick, wheel, and/or gamepad
SMALL OFFICE/ HOME OFFICE	• 19- or 21-inch LCD monitor • LCD screen on Tablet PC, PDA, or smart phone	• Multifunction peripheral; or • Ink-jet color printer; or • Laser printer (black-and-white or color) • Label printer • Postage printer	• Fax machine • Speakers
MOBILE	• 17-inch LCD screen on notebook computer • LCD screen on Tablet PC, PDA, or smart phone	• Mobile color printer • Ink-jet color printer; or • Laser printer for in-office use (black-and-white or color) • Photo printer	• Fax modem • Headphones or earphones • DLP data projector
POWER	• 23-inch LCD monitor	• Laser printer (black-and-white or color) • Plotter or large-format printer; or • Photo printer; or • Dye-sublimation printer	• Fax machine or fax modem • Speakers • Headphones or earphones
LARGE BUSINESS	• 19- or 21-inch LCD monitor • LCD screen on Tablet PC, PDA, or smart phone	• High-speed laser printer • Laser printer, color • Line printer (for large reports from a mainframe) • Label printer	• Fax machine or fax modem • Speakers • Headphones or earphones • DLP data projector

FIGURE 6-34 This table recommends suggested output devices for various types of users.

OUTPUT DEVICES FOR PHYSICALLY CHALLENGED USERS

As Chapter 5 discussed, the growing presence of computers has generated an awareness of the need to address computing requirements for those with physical limitations. Read Ethics & Issues 6-4 for a related discussion.

For users with mobility, hearing, or vision disabilities, many different types of output devices are available. Hearing-impaired users, for example, can instruct programs to display words instead of sounds. With the Windows Vista operating system, users also can set options to make programs easier to use. The Magnifier, for example, enlarges text and other items in a window on the screen (Figure 6-35).

Visually impaired users can change Windows Vista settings, such as increasing the size or changing the color of the text to make the words easier to read. Instead of using a monitor, blind users can work with voice output via Windows Vista's Narrator. That is, the computer reads the information that is displayed on the screen. Another alternative is a *Braille printer*, which prints information on paper in Braille (Figure 6-36).

FIGURE 6-36
A Braille printer.

location of line that contains mouse pointer is magnified at top of screen

FIGURE 6-35 The Magnifier in Windows Vista enlarges text and other on-screen items for visually impaired users.

ETHICS & ISSUES 6-4

Should Web Sites Be Held Accountable for Accessibility Levels for Physically Challenged People?

The World Wide Web Consortium (W3C) has published accessibility guidelines for Web sites. The guidelines specify measures that Web site designers can take to increase accessibility for physically challenged users. Among its guidelines, the W3C urges Web site designers to provide equivalent text for audio or visual content, include features that allow elements to be activated and understood using a variety of input and output devices, and make the user interface follow principles of accessible design. A recent report found that most Web sites do not meet all of the W3C guidelines. This failure is disappointing, because many physically challenged users could benefit from the Web's capability to bring products and services into the home. Ironically, a survey discovered that more than 50 percent of the Web sites run by disability organizations also fail to meet the W3C guidelines. Critics contend that these Web sites neglect the needs of their users and fail to lead by example. The Web site supporters contend, however, that many sponsoring organizations lack the funding necessary to comply with the guidelines. Should the government require that all Web sites meet the W3C accessibility guidelines? Why or why not? Do Web sites run by disability organizations have a moral obligation to meet the guidelines? Why? What can be done to encourage people and organizations to make their Web sites more accessible?

Test your knowledge of pages 320 through 327 in Quiz Yourself 6-3.

QUIZ YOURSELF 6-3

Instructions: Find the true statement below. Then, rewrite the remaining false statements so they are true.

1. A digital light processing (DLP) projector uses tiny lightbulbs to reflect light.
2. A stand-alone fax machine scans an original document, converts the image into digitized data, and transmits the digitized image.
3. Many personal computer users add surround sound printer systems to their computers to generate a higher-quality sound.
4. Multifunction peripherals require more space than having a separate printer, scanner, copy machine, and fax machine.
5. Some joysticks, wheels, and gamepads include real-time action, which is a technology that sends resistance to the device in response to actions of the user.

Quiz Yourself Online: To further check your knowledge of speakers, headphones, and earphones; other output devices; and output for physically challenged users, visit scsite.com/dc2008/ch6/quiz and then click Objectives 8 – 10.

CHAPTER SUMMARY

Computers process and organize data (input) into information (output). This chapter described the various methods of output and several commonly used output devices. Output devices presented were flat-panel displays; CRT monitors; printers; speakers, headphones, and earphones; fax machines and fax modems; multifunction peripherals; data projectors; and force-feedback joysticks, wheels, and gamepads.

CAREER CORNER

Graphic Designer/Illustrator

Graphic designers and *graphic illustrators* are artists, but many do not create original works. Instead, they portray visually the ideas of their clients. Illustrators create pictures for books and other publications and sometimes for commercial products, such as greeting cards. They work in fields such as fashion, technology, medicine, animation, or even cartoons. Illustrators often prepare their images on a computer. Designers combine practical skills with artistic talent to convert abstract concepts into designs for products and advertisements. Many use computer-aided design (CAD) tools to create, visualize, and modify designs. Designer careers usually are specialized in particular areas, such as:

- Graphic designers — book covers, stationery, and CD covers
- Commercial and industrial designers — products and equipment
- Costume and theater designers — costumes and settings for theater and television
- Interior designers — layout, decor, and furnishings of homes and buildings
- Merchandise displayers — commercial displays
- Fashion designers — clothing, shoes, and other fashion accessories

Certificate, two-year, four-year, and masters-level educational programs are available within design areas. About 30 percent of graphic designers/illustrators choose to freelance, while others work with advertising agencies, publishing companies, design studios, or specialized departments within large companies. Salaries range from $35,000 to $100,000-plus, based on experience and educational background. For more information, visit scsite.com/dc2008/ch6/careers and then click Graphic Designer/Illustrator.

High-Tech Talk

SOUND CARDS: BRINGING YOUR COMPUTER TO LIFE

Speakers, headphones, earphones, and other audio output devices rely on sound cards or integrated sound card functionality to produce sounds such as music, voice, beeps, and chimes. Sound cards contain the chips and circuitry to record and play back a wide range of sounds using analog-to-digital conversion and digital-to-analog conversion, as described in the Chapter 1 High-Tech Talk on page 38.

To record a sound, the sound card must be connected to an input device, such as a microphone or audio CD player. The input device sends the sound to the sound card as an analog signal. The analog signal flows to the sound card's analog-to-digital-converter (ADC). The ADC converts the signal into digital (binary) data of 1s and 0s by sampling the signal at set intervals.

The analog sound is a continuous waveform, with a range of frequencies and volumes. To represent the waveform in a recording, the computer would have to store the waveform's value at every instant in time. Because this is not possible, the sound is recorded using a sampling process. *Sampling* involves breaking up the waveform into set intervals and representing all values during that interval with a single value.

Several factors in the sampling process — sampling rate, audio resolution, and mono or stereo recording — affect the quality of the recorded sound during playback.

- *Sampling rate*, also called sampling frequency, refers to the number of times per second the sound is recorded. The more frequently a sound is recorded, the smaller the intervals and the better the quality. The sampling frequency used for audio CDs, for example, is 44,100 times per second, which is expressed in hertz (Hz) as 44,100 Hz. Cassette-tape-quality multimedia files use a sampling rate of 22,050 Hz; and basic Windows sounds use a sampling rate of 11,025 Hz.

- *Audio resolution* — defined as a bit rate such as 8-bit, 16-bit, or 24-bit — refers to the number of bytes used to represent the sound at any one interval. A sound card using 8-bit resolution, for example, represents a sound with any 1 of 256 values (2^8). A 16-bit sound card uses any 1 of 65,536 values (2^{16}) for each interval. Using a higher resolution provides a finer measurement scale, which results in a more accurate representation of the value of each sample and better sound quality. With 8-bit resolution, the sound quality is like that of an AM radio; 16-bit resolution gives CD-quality sound, and a 24-bit resolution is used for high-quality digital audio editing.

- Mono or stereo recording refers to the number of channels used during recording. *Mono* means that the same sound emits from both the left and right speaker during playback; *stereo* means that two separate channels exist in the recording: one each for the left and right speakers. Most sound cards support stereo recording for better playback.

After the ADC converts the analog sound through sampling, the digital data flows to the digital signal processor (DSP) on the sound card. The DSP then requests instructions from the sound card's memory chip on how to process the digital data. Typically, the DSP then compresses the digital data to save space. Finally, the DSP sends the compressed data to the computer's main processor, which stores the data in .WAV, .MP3, or other audio file format.

To play a recorded sound, such as a WAV, an MP3, or a CD track, the main processor retrieves the sound file from a hard disk, CD, or other storage device (Figure 6-37). The processor then sends the digital data to the DSP, which decompresses the data and looks to the memory chip to determine how to recreate the sound.

The DSP then sends the digital signals to the sound card's digital-to-analog converter (DAC), which converts the sound in digital format back to an analog electrical voltage. An output device, such as a speaker, uses an amplifier to strengthen the electrical voltage. This causes the speaker's cone to vibrate, recreating the sound.

All of this happens in an instant. The next time your computer beeps or chirps, consider the complex process required to make that simple sound. Then, insert your favorite CD and hear your computer come to life with the sweet music provided courtesy of the sound card. For more information, visit scsite.com/dc2008/ch6/tech and then click Sound Cards.

FIGURE 6-37
The path of sound from media to speakers.

Companies on the Cutting Edge

HEWLETT-PACKARD
TECHNOLOGY FOR BUSINESS AND LIFE

If you have printed a document recently, chances are the printer manufacturer was *Hewlett-Packard (HP)*. Market analysts estimate that 60 percent of printers sold today bear the HP logo, and HP says it ships one million printers each week.

HP is noted for a range of high-quality printers, disk storage systems, UNIX and Windows servers, and notebook, desktop, and handheld computers. The company grew to become the world's number one personal computer vendor in 2006.

William Hewlett and David Packard started the company in a one-car garage in 1939 with the goal of manufacturing test and measurement equipment. HP has been developing personal information devices, including calculators and computers, for more than 30 years. For more information, visit scsite.com/dc2008/ch6/companies and then click Hewlett-Packard.

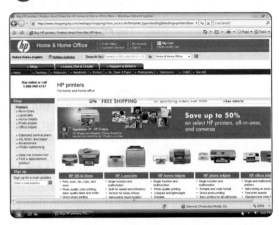

VIEWSONIC
VISUAL TECHNOLOGY LEADER

We live in a "display-centric world" according to industry leaders at *ViewSonic*. ViewSonic's products focus on visual technology, including CRT and LCD monitors, data projectors, plasma screens, and high-definition television. The company also designs mobile products, such as Tablet PCs and wireless monitors. The company's logo consisting of three colorful Gouldian finches represent outstanding quality and value, radiant color, and crisp resolution.

President and CEO James Chu founded ViewSonic in 1987 with the goal of increasing workers' productivity while creating an ergonomically comfortable workspace. A 2006 study, commissioned by ViewSonic, found that at least 40 percent of European office workers are suffering from health, productivity, and motivation ailments from using old and poor computer equipment. For more information, visit scsite.com/dc2008/ch6/companies and then click ViewSonic.

Technology Trailblazers

STEVE JOBS
APPLE COMPUTER AND PIXAR COFOUNDER

Steve Jobs has an uncompromising drive for perfection. He helped build the first desktop personal computer, cofounded Apple Computer Corporation, marketed a revolutionary operating system, and became a millionaire all before his 35th birthday. He is a brilliant motivator and charismatic corporate leader.

Under his direction, Apple took advantage of advances in both memory and battery technology to develop the iPod, the world's most popular portable media player.

Jobs has led Pixar's award-winning animators to create some of the most beloved animated films, such as *Toy Story*, *Cars*, *A Bug's Life*, *Monsters, Inc.*, and *Finding Nemo*. Pixar merged with The Walt Disney Company in 2006, and Jobs now serves on Disney's board of directors. For more information, visit scsite.com/dc2008/ch6/people and then click Steve Jobs.

DONNA DUBINSKY
Palm Cofounder

PDAs are ubiquitous, partly due to the efforts of *Donna Dubinsky*. In the mid-1990s, she sensed that people wanted to own an electronic version of their paper appointment books. She and Jeff Hawkins introduced the original Palm Pilot at Palm Computing in 1996. Sales of more than two million units made the Palm Pilot the most rapidly adopted new computing product ever manufactured.

Dubinsky and Hawkins left Palm in 1998 to cofound Handspring, where they introduced several successful products, including the Treo smart phone. In 2003, Handspring merged with the Palm hardware group to create palmOne, now called Palm.

Dubinsky currently serves as CEO and chairman of Numenta, Inc., which develops computer memory. She was appointed trustee of her alma mater, Yale University, in 2006. For more information, visit scsite.com/dc2008/ch6/people and then click Donna Dubinsky.

Quizzes and Learning Games

Computer Genius
Crossword Puzzle
DC Track and Field
Practice Test
Quiz Yourself
Wheel of Terms
You're Hired!

Exercises

Case Studies
Chapter Review
Checkpoint
▶ Key Terms
Learn How To
Learn It Online
Web Research

Beyond the Book

Career Corner
Companies
FAQs
High-Tech Talk
Looking Ahead
Making Use of the Web
Trailblazers
Web Links

Features

Chapter Forum
Install Computer
Lab Exercises
Maintain Computer
Tech News
Timeline 2008

Key Terms

You should know the Primary Terms and be familiar with the Secondary Terms. Use the list below to help focus your study. To further enhance your understanding of the Key Terms in this chapter, visit scsite.com/dc2008/ch6/terms. See an example of and a definition for each term, and access current and additional information about the term from the Web.

Primary Terms

(shown in bold-black characters in the chapter)

audio output device (320)
CRT monitor (308)
data projector (323)
display device (302)
dot-matrix printer (319)
earphones (321)
ENERGY STAR program (308)
fax machine (322)
HDTV (307)
headphones (321)
impact printer (318)
ink-jet printer (312)
label printer (318)
large-format printer (318)
laser printer (315)
LCD monitor (302)
line printer (319)
liquid crystal display (LCD) (304)
mobile printer (317)
monitor (302)
multifunction peripheral (323)
nonimpact printer (312)
output (300)
output device (301)
photo printer (314)
plasma monitor (307)
plotters (318)
printer (310)
resolution (304)
speakers (320)
thermal printer (317)
voice output (321)

Secondary Terms

(shown in italic characters in the chapter)

active-matrix display (304)
all-in-one devices (323)
aspect ratio (306)
band printer (319)
bit depth (306)
Bluetooth printing (311)
Braille printer (326)
candela (305)
cathode-ray tube (CRT) (308)
color depth (306)
continuous-form paper (319)
contrast ratio (305)
digital light processing (DLP) projector (324)
digital photo printer (317)
digital television (DTV) (307)
display (302)
dot pitch (305)
dots per inch (dpi) (313)
DVI (Digital Video Interface) port (306)
dye-sublimation printer (317)
earbuds (321)
electromagnetic radiation (EMR) (308)
fax (322)
fax modem (322)
flat-panel monitor (302)
flat-panel display (302)
footprint (302)
force feedback (324)
graphics processing unit (GPU) (305)
hard copy (310)
high-definition television (307)
infrared printing (311)
Internet postage (318)
Internet telephony (322)
landscape orientation (310)

LCD projector (323)
monochrome (302)
MPR II (308)
native resolution (304)
near letter quality (NLQ) (318)
nit (305)
organic LED (OLED) (304)
page description language (PDL) (316)
passive-matrix display (304)
PCL (Printer Control Language) (316)
PictBridge (314)
pixel (304)
pixel pitch (305)
portrait orientation (310)
postage printer (318)
PostScript (316)
printout (310)
refresh rate (309)
response time (304)
satellite speakers (320)
scan rate (309)
shuttle-matrix printer (319)
soft copy (302)
subwoofer (320)
S-video port (306)
SVGA (306)
SXGA (306)
TFT (thin-film transistor) display (304)
thermal wax-transfer printer (317)
toner (316)
UXGA (306)
viewable size (308)
WQXGA (306)
WSXGA (306)
WUXGA (306)
WXGA (306)
XGA (306)

Checkpoint

Use the Checkpoint exercises to check your knowledge level of the chapter. The Beyond the Book exercises will help broaden your understanding of the concepts presented in this chapter. To complete the Checkpoint exercises interactively, visit scsite.com/dc2008/ch6/check.

Label the Figure

Identify the ports on this video card.

a. DVI port

b. standard monitor port

c. S-video port

True/False

Mark T for True and F for False. (See page numbers in parentheses.)

_____ 1. A computer generates several types of output, depending on the hardware and software being used and the requirements of the user. (300)

_____ 2. Information on a display device sometimes is called soft copy. (302)

_____ 3. Most mobile computers and devices do not integrate the display and other components into the same physical case. (302)

_____ 4. The color on an active-matrix display often is not as bright as a passive-matrix display. (304)

_____ 5. LCD monitors use an analog signal to produce a picture. (306)

_____ 6. The WUXGA video standard has a higher typical resolution than the WXGA video standard. (306)

_____ 7. With game consoles, the output device often is a television. (307)

_____ 8. A printout in portrait orientation is taller than it is wide. (310)

_____ 9. With Bluetooth printing, a computer or other device transmits output to a printer via infrared light waves. (311)

_____ 10. Most photo printers are PictBridge enabled, which requires the use of a computer to print pictures. (314)

_____ 11. A laser printer is a high-speed, low-quality nonimpact printer. (315)

_____ 12. Mobile printers mainly use ink-jet, thermal, thermal wax-transfer, or dye-sublimation technology. (317)

Checkpoint

Multiple Choice Select the best answer. (See page numbers in parentheses.)

1. Examples of text-based documents are _____. (300)
   a. drawings, clip art, and photographs
   b. home movies and live performances
   c. letters, reports, and e-mail messages
   d. music, narrations, and speeches

2. _____ uses organic molecules that produce an even brighter, easier-to-read display than standard TFT displays. (304)
   a. HDTV   b. OLED
   c. LCD   d. LED

3. The _____ defines a display's width relative to its height. (306)
   a. bit depth
   b. nit
   c. aspect ratio
   d. resolution

4. For a display device to show images as defined by a video standard, both the display device and the graphics processing unit must _____. (306)
   a. be the same size
   b. contain a heat sink or fan
   c. use an analog signal
   d. support the same video standard

5. Plasma monitors offer larger screens _____. (307)
   a. but poorer color than LCD monitors and are less expensive
   b. but poorer color than LCD monitors and are more expensive
   c. and richer colors than LCD monitors but are less expensive
   d. and richer colors than LCD monitors but are more expensive

6. The viewable size of a monitor is the _____ measurement of the actual viewing area provided by the screen in the monitor. (308)
   a. horizontal
   b. vertical
   c. three-dimensional
   d. diagonal

7. On a CRT monitor, the number of times the image is drawn per second is called the _____. (309)
   a. contrast ratio
   b. refresh rate
   c. bit rate
   d. response time

8. Printer resolution is measured by the number of _____ a printer can print. (313)
   a. pages per minute (ppm)
   b. pixels per inch (ppi)
   c. lines per minute (lpm)
   d. dots per inch (dpi)

9. Laser printers usually cost _____. (315)
   a. more than ink-jet printers and are faster
   b. less than ink-jet printers and are faster
   c. more than ink-jet printers and are slower
   d. less than ink-jet printers and are slower

10. The speed of a(n) _____ is measured by the number of characters per second (cps) it can print. (319)
    a. dot-matrix printer
    b. laser printer
    c. ink-jet printer
    d. thermal printer

11. Most surround sound computer speaker systems include one or two center speakers and two or more _____ that are positioned so sound emits from all directions. (320)
    a. satellite speakers
    b. subwoofers
    c. headphones
    d. none of the above

12. A(n) _____ is a device that takes the text and images displaying on a computer screen and projects them on a larger screen so an audience can see the image clearly. (323)
    a. DLP projector
    b. LCD projector
    c. data projector
    d. all of the above

13. The disadvantage of multifunction peripherals is that _____. (323)
    a. if the multifunction peripheral breaks down, all functions are lost
    b. they require more space than having separate devices
    c. they are significantly more expensive than purchasing each device separately
    d. all of the above

14. A(n) _____ uses tiny mirrors to reflect light, which produces crisp, bright, colorful images that remain in focus and can be seen clearly even in a well-lit room. (324)
    a. plasma monitor
    b. LCD projector
    c. CRT
    d. digital light processing projector

Checkpoint

Matching

Match the terms with their definitions. (See page numbers in parentheses.)

_____ 1. soft copy (302)
_____ 2. LCD monitor (302)
_____ 3. nit (305)
_____ 4. candela (305)
_____ 5. dot pitch (305)
_____ 6. ENERGY STAR program (308)
_____ 7. hard copy (310)
_____ 8. nonimpact printer (312)
_____ 9. LCD projector (323)
_____ 10. force feedback (324)

a. information on a display device that exists electronically and appears for a temporary period
b. technology that sends resistance to a device in response to actions of the user
c. distance in millimeters between pixels on a display device
d. unit of visible light intensity equal to one candela per square meter
e. forms characters and graphics on a piece of paper without actually striking the paper
f. standard unit of luminous intensity
g. attaches directly to a computer and uses its own light source to display information
h. changes the brightness and contrast of pixels surrounding each letter
i. encourages manufacturers to create energy-efficient devices that require little power when they are not in use
j. a desktop monitor that uses a liquid crystal display to produce images
k. uses many shades of gray from white to black to enhance the quality of graphics
l. printed information that exists physically and is a more permanent form of output

Short Answer

Write a brief answer to each of the following questions.

1. What determines the quality of an LCD monitor or LCD screen? _____ What are the differences between active-matrix and passive-matrix displays? _____

2. What type of monitor emits electromagnetic radiation? _____ What can you do to protect yourself from electromagnetic radiation from a monitor? _____

3. How is portrait orientation different from landscape orientation? _____ What is continuous-form paper? _____

4. What are two types of wireless printing technology? _____ How do they differ in how they communicate with a computer or other device? _____

5. How does an ink-jet printer work? _____ What are the differences between dye-sublimation printers used by professionals as compared to home or small business users? _____

Beyond the Book

Read the following book elements, learn more about each using the Web, and then write a brief report.

1. Ethics & Issues — Should Companies Prohibit Consumers from Refilling Ink Cartridges? (314), Who Is Responsible for Stopping Counterfeiting? (315), Should Colleges Provide Free Access to Music for Students? (321), or Should Web Sites Be Held Accountable for Accessibility Levels for Physically Challenged People? (327)

2. Career Corner — Graphic Designer/Illustrator (327)

3. Companies on the Cutting Edge — Hewlett-Packard or ViewSonic (329)

4. FAQs (302, 303, 306, 308, 309, 315, 316, 324)

5. High-Tech Talk — Sound Cards: Bringing Your Computer to Life (328)

6. Looking Ahead — Rollable Displays Lock and Roll (304), or Ultra HDTV Puts Viewers in the Picture (324)

7. Making Use of the Web — Government (122)

8. Picture Yourself Saving Time and Money Using a Computer (298)

9. Technology Trailblazers — Steve Jobs and Donna Dubinsky (329)

10. Web Links (304, 306, 311, 314, 316, 321, 322, 323, 324)

Learn It Online

Use the Learn It Online exercises to reinforce your understanding of the chapter concepts. To access the Learn It Online exercises, visit scsite.com/dc2008/ch6/learn.

(1) At the Movies — Plasma vs. LCD

To view the SID: Size Matters movie, click the number 1 button. Locate your video and click the corresponding High-Speed or Dial-Up link, depending on your Internet connection. Watch the movie and then complete the exercise by answering the question that follows. A 100-inch HD screen and a dual-image screen are displayed at a technology trade show exhibit showing the use of two-way viewing. What is two-way viewing? List one possible application and one drawback to this new technology.

(2) Video and Audio: You Review It — HDTV

In this chapter you learned about HDTV. Click the number 2 button to view the suggested links and begin your search for videos, podcasts, or vodcasts related to HDTV. Choose a video, podcast, or vodcast that discusses HDTV and is of interest to you, and then write a description of its contents. Explain why you chose this piece, what you liked about it, what you disliked about it, and whether you would recommend it to a fellow student. Finish your review by giving the video, podcast, or vodcast a rating of 1 – 5 stars. Submit your review in the format requested by your instructor.

(3) Student Edition Labs — Peripheral Devices

Click the number 3 button. A new browser window will open, displaying the Student Edition Labs. Follow the on-screen instructions to complete the Peripheral Devices Lab. When finished, click the Exit button. If required, submit your results to your instructor.

(4) Student Edition Labs — Working with Graphics

Click the number 4 button. A new browser window will open, displaying the Student Edition Labs. Follow the on-screen instructions to complete the Working with Graphics Lab. When finished, click the Exit button. If required, submit your results to your instructor.

(5) Practice Test

Click the number 5 button. Answer each question. When completed, enter your name and click the Grade Test button to submit the quiz for grading. Make a note of any missed questions. If required, submit your results to your instructor.

(6) Who Wants To Be a Computer Genius²?

Click the number 6 button to find out if you are a computer genius. Directions about how to play the game will be displayed. When you are ready to play, click the Play button. Submit your score to your instructor.

(7) Wheel of Terms

Click the number 7 button to reinforce important terms you learned in this chapter by playing the Shelly Cashman Series version of this popular game. Directions about how to play the game will be displayed. When you are ready to play, click the Play button. Submit your score to your instructor.

Learn It Online

(8) DC Track and Field

Click the number 8 button to use what you have learned in this chapter to compete against other students in three track and field events. Directions about how to play the game will be displayed. When you are ready to play, click the start first event button. If required, submit your score to your instructor.

(9) You're Hired!

Click the number 9 button to use what you have learned in this chapter to embark on the path to a career in computers. Directions about how to play the game will be displayed. When you are ready to play, click the begin game button. If required, submit your score to your instructor.

(10) Crossword Puzzle Challenge

Click the number 10 button, then click the Crossword Puzzle Challenge link. Directions about how to play the game will be displayed. Complete the puzzle to reinforce skills you learned in this chapter. When you are ready to play, click the Continue button. Submit the completed puzzle to your instructor.

(11) Vista Exercises

Click the number 11 button. When the Vista Exercises menu appears, click the exercise assigned by your instructor. A new browser window will open. Follow the on-screen instructions to complete the exercise. When finished, click the Exit button. If required, submit your results to your instructor.

(12) Choosing a Printer

The printer is a key component of any new personal computer that you purchase. Whether you are printing black-and-white reports or producing photo-lab-quality pictures, determining which printer is best for your individual needs requires some research. Printers are available in a range of speeds and capabilities. Click the number 12 button for a tutorial about how to select the printer that is best for your particular requirements.

(13) In the News

Display device technology continues to advance. Not long ago, computer users would have considered connecting their $1,000 computers to a color television instead of paying outrageous prices for a color monitor. Today, you can purchase a 20-inch monitor that is faster and sharper than that color television for less than $300. Yet, as prices fall, consumers surely will purchase the display devices for HDTV and crystal-clear Internet access. Click the number 13 button and then read a news article about a new or improved output device. What is the device? Who manufactures it? How is the output device better than, or different from, earlier devices? Who do you think is most likely to use the device? Why?

(14) Chapter Discussion Forum

Select an objective from this chapter on page 299 about which you would like more information. Click the number 14 button and post a short message listing a meaningful message title accompanied by one or more questions concerning the selected objective. In two days, return to the threaded discussion by clicking the number 14 button. Submit to your instructor your original message and at least one response to your message.

(15) Howstuffworks.com

Click the number 15 button to learn how to use Howstuffworks.com to discover how a laser printer works in comparison to an ink-jet printer. Follow the instructions to display the computer peripherals page. Read the articles about how both types of printers work. Write a report listing the major differences between the printers. Which type of printer would you recommend to your fellow students? Why? Print your report and submit it to your instructor.

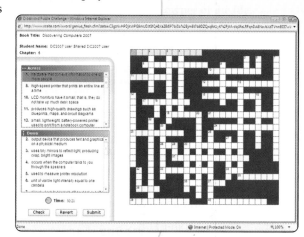

Web Research

Use the Internet-based Web Research exercises to broaden your understanding of the concepts presented in this chapter. Visit scsite.com/dc2008/ch6/research to obtain more information pertaining to each exercise. To discuss any of the Web Research exercises in this chapter with other students, post your thoughts or questions at scsite.com/dc2008/ch6/forum.

(1) Scavenger Hunt Use one of the <u>search engines</u> listed in Figure 2-10 in Chapter 2 on page 78 or your own favorite search engine to find the answers to the questions below. Copy and paste the Web address from the Web page where you found the answer. Some questions may have more than one answer. If required, submit your answers to your instructor. (1) Who invented the liquid crystal display? (2) What company introduced acoustic waveguide technology? What problem did it solve? (3) What is the current cost of a surround sound computer speaker system? (4) What is an ambient light sensor on a monitor? (5) What company introduced the first laser printer?

(2) Search Sleuth Some search engines use computers to index the World Wide Web automatically, so they generally find more Web sites than human indexers can catalog. One of the most aggressive automatic, or robot, search engines is <u>AltaVista</u> (altavista.com), which attempts to catalog the entire World Wide Web. AltaVista also developed Babel Fish, the Web's first Internet machine translation service. Visit this Web site and then use your word processing program to answer the following questions. Then, if required, submit your answers to your instructor. (1) Click the About AltaVista link and then click the Search link. Scroll down and then read the information about innovations. What languages are translated by Babel Fish? (2) Click your browser's Back button or press the BACKSPACE key twice to return to the AltaVista home page. Click the Babel Fish Translation link. In addition to a block of text, what else can Babel Fish translate? (3) Click the Tools link at the top of the page. Click the Converter link. Read the information about AltaVista short-cuts. Click the Temperature link. Click the example. How many degrees Celsius does 32 degrees Fahrenheit equal? (4) Click the Advanced Search link. Click the Help link and read the information on using the Query Builder and the Free-form Boolean query. Summarize the information you read and then write a 50-word summary that may be submitted to your instructor.

(3) Journaling Respond to your readings in this chapter by writing at least one page about your reactions, evaluations, and reflections about using <u>output devices</u>. For example, what is most important to you when buying a printer? Do you use more than one printer for different purposes, such as printing photos taken with a digital camera, or do you use a multifunction peripheral that combines output devices in one unit? Do you use headphones or earphones for listening to music or other voice output? Where would you dispose of old monitors? You also can write about the new terms you learned by reading this chapter. If required, submit your journal to your instructor.

(4) Expanding Your Understanding If you are using a Tablet PC and your coworker is using a PDA, it is cumbersome to transfer files from one device to the other. Engineers are developing <u>digital pens</u> that might ease the file exchange process. Using this special pen, one user can select a file on his computer and then place the pen on the other user's computer to transfer the file. Other digital pens allow users to write or draw and then retrieve all the handwritten information on a computer. Visit a local electronics store or Web site to learn more about digital pens. Compare their features, cost, file transfer process, and warranty. Write a report summarizing your findings, focusing on comparing and contrasting the digital pens. If required, submit your report to your instructor.

(5) Ethics in Action <u>Internet addiction disorder</u> (IAD) may be affecting some Internet users. People claim to be addicted when they spend up to 10 hours a day online, they occasionally binge for extended Internet sessions, and they suffer withdrawal symptoms when they have not been online for some time. "Netomania" is not a recognized disorder, however, and some researchers believe the Internet problem is just a symptom of other psychiatric disorders, such as manic-depression. View online sites that provide information about IAD, including the Center for Online and Internet Addiction (netaddiction.com). Write a report summarizing your findings and include a table of links to Web sites that provide additional details. If required, submit your report to your instructor.

Case Studies

Use the Case Studies to apply the concepts presented in the chapter to real-world situations. Visit scsite.com/dc2008/ch6/cases to obtain more information pertaining to each exercise. To discuss the Case Studies in this chapter with other students, visit scsite.com/dc2008/ch6/forum and post your thoughts or questions.

Case Study 1 — Class Discussion   Several of the administrative assistants in your company say they need larger monitors. They claim the small monitors they use now are hard on their eyes and that larger, clearer monitors would help with their efficiency. Your boss wants you to explore the use of <u>widescreen monitors</u> versus side-by-side monitors. Use the Web and/or print media to compare the costs associated with each setup. What would be the advantages of having side-by-side monitors? Write a brief report to your boss summarizing your recommendations. Be prepared to discuss your recommendations in class.

Case Study 2 — Class Discussion   Your company currently uses ink-jet printers for printing color documents and photos. Your manager is tired of frequently ordering replacement ink cartridges and thinks that it may be time to upgrade to <u>color laser printers</u>. He knows the initial costs of the laser printers will be high, but he thinks the quality of the printout and the longevity of the printer cartridges will offset that initial cost. He wants you to submit a report summarizing the long-term costs associated with both types of printers. Be sure to include the average number of copies each printer can produce before changing cartridges. Be prepared to discuss your findings in class.

Case Study 3 — Research   Printing requirements vary greatly among users. The local insurance agency where you are employed part time is shopping for a <u>printer</u>. The owner is aware that you are taking a computer class and has asked you to assist her in making a decision on what printer to buy. Figure 6-12 on page 310 lists several questions that should be considered when choosing a printer. Use what you learned in class to answer the questions posed in Figure 6-12. Answer each question according to what you believe to be your employer's needs. Then, use the Web and/or print media to find at least two printers that fit the requirements. List the name of each printer and note their advantages and disadvantages. Which of the two printers would you buy? Why? Prepare a report and/or PowerPoint presentation and share your findings with your class.

Case Study 4 — Research   While printers produce an image on a page from top to bottom, <u>plotters</u> can draw on any part of a page at random, and then move on to any other part. This capability, coupled with their capacity to use large sheets of paper, makes plotters particularly valuable to people who produce maps or blueprints. A local engineering firm that has used hand drawings for the past 50 years has hired you to assist them in purchasing three 42-inch plotters with a maximum print length of 300 feet and at least 1200 × 600 dpi. What is the advantage or disadvantage of using a plotter compared to simply creating a drawing by hand? Use the Web and/or print media to research both the initial and recurring costs of plotters that meet the stated requirements from three different manufacturers. Include in your research how long each plotter takes to produce an image and other noteworthy information. Prepare a report and/or PowerPoint presentation summarizing your findings.

Case Study 5 — Team Challenge   Three accountants at the company you work for want to go off on their own and set up a small accounting office with approximately 20 to 25 employees. They have hired your group as consultants to help with the setup. The goal is to determine the type of output devices you think they will need within the office. Consider the types and number of printers, types and number of display devices, <u>audio devices</u>, microphones, LCD projectors, considerations for the physically challenged, and whether fax machines, fax modems, and/or multifunction peripherals are needed. Form a three-member team and assign each team member one or more categories of output devices. Have the team members use the Web and/or print media to research their assignments. Combine your findings in a table listing the advantages and disadvantages of the various devices, your team's recommendations, and a short explanation of why the team selected each device. Share your findings with your class.

Digital Imaging and Video Technology

Everywhere you look, people are capturing moments they want to remember. They take pictures or make movies of their vacations, birthday parties, activities, accomplishments, sporting events, weddings, and more. Because of the popularity of digital cameras and digital video cameras, increasingly more people desire to capture their memories digitally, instead of on film. With digital technology, photographers have the ability to modify and share the digital images and videos they create.

When you use special hardware and/or software, you can copy, manipulate, print, and distribute digital images and videos using your personal computer and the Internet. Amateurs can achieve professional quality results by using more sophisticated hardware and software.

digital camera (input)

digital video camera (input)

FireWire or USB 2.0

television (output)

FIGURE 1 The top portion of the figure shows a typical home digital imaging setup, and the lower portion of the figure shows a typical home setup for editing personal video.

Digital photography and recordings deliver significant benefits over film-based photography and movie making. With digital cameras, no developing is needed. Instead, the images reside on storage media such as a hard disk, DVD, or flash memory card. Unlike film, storage media can be reused, which reduces costs, saves time, and provides immediate results. Digital technology allows greater control over the creative process, both while taking pictures and video and in the editing process. You can check results immediately after capturing a picture or video to determine whether it meets your expectations. If you are dissatisfied with a picture or video, you can erase it and recapture it, again and again.

As shown in the top portion of Figure 1, a digital camera functions as an input device when it transmits pictures through a cable to a personal computer via a USB port or FireWire port. Using a digital camera in this way allows you to edit the pictures, save them on storage media, and print them on a photographic-quality printer via a USB port or FireWire port.

The lower portion of Figure 1 illustrates how you might use a digital video camera with a personal computer. The process typically is the same for most digital video cameras. You capture the images or video with the video camera. Next, you connect the video camera to your personal computer using a FireWire or USB 2.0 port, or you place the storage media used on the camera in the computer. The video then is copied or downloaded to the computer's hard disk. Then, you can edit the video using video editing software. If desired, you can preview the video during the editing process on a television. Finally, you save the finished result to the desired media, such as a DVD+RW or, perhaps, e-mail the edited video or post it to a media sharing Web site. In this example, a DVD player also can be used to input video from a DVD.

USB

photographic-quality printer (output)

personal computer

ideo

DVD recorder (input, output, storage)

DIGITAL IMAGING TECHNOLOGY

Digital imaging technology involves capturing and manipulating still photographic images in an electronic format. The following sections outline the steps involved in the process of using digital imaging technology.

① Select a Digital Camera

A **digital camera** is a type of camera that stores photographed images electronically instead of on traditional film. Digital cameras are divided into three categories (Figure 2) based mainly on image resolution, features, and of course, price. The image resolution is measured in pixels (short for picture element). The image quality increases with the number of pixels. The image resolution usually is measured in **megapixels** (million of pixels), often abbreviated as **MP**. Features of digital cameras include red-eye reduction, zoom, autofocus, flash, self-timer, and manual mode for fine-tuning settings. Figure 3 summarizes the three categories of digital cameras.

TYPES OF DIGITAL CAMERAS

Type	Resolution Range	Features	Price
Point-and-shoot cameras	Less than 6 MP	Fully automatic; fits in your pocket; easy to use; ideal for average consumer usage.	Less than $450
Field cameras	Greater than 7 MP	Used by photojournalists; portable but flexible; provides ability to change lenses and use other attachments; great deal of control over exposure and other photo settings.	$450 to $2,000
Studio cameras	Greater than 8 MP	Stationary camera used for professional studio work; flexible; widest range of lenses and settings.	$1,500 and up

FIGURE 3 Digital cameras often are categorized by image resolution, features, and price.

(a) point-and-shoot

(b) field

(c) studio

FIGURE 2 The point-and-shoot digital camera (a) requires no adjustments before shooting. The field digital camera (b) offers improved quality and features that allow you to make manual adjustments before shooting and use a variety of lenses. The studio digital camera (c) offers better color and resolution and greater control over exposure and lenses.

② Take Pictures

Digital cameras provide you with several options that are set before a picture is taken. Three of the more important options are the resolution, compression, and image file format in which the camera should save the picture. While a camera may allow for a very high resolution for a large print, you may choose to take a picture at a lower resolution if the image does not require great detail or must be a small size. For example, you may want to use the image on a Web page where smaller image file sizes are beneficial.

Compression results in smaller image file sizes. Figure 4 illustrates the image file sizes for varying resolutions and compressions under standard photographic conditions using a 6-megapixel digital camera. Figure 4 also shows the average picture size for a given resolution. The camera may take more time to save an image at lower compression, resulting in a longer delay before the camera is ready to take another picture. A higher compression, however, may result in some loss of image quality. If a camera has a 16 MB flash memory card, you can determine the number of pictures the card can hold by dividing 16 MB by the file size. Flash memory cards are available in sizes from 16 MB to 16 GB or more.

Most digital cameras also allow you to choose an image file format. Two popular file formats are TIFF and JPEG. The **TIFF** file format saves the image uncompressed. All of the image detail is captured and stored, but the file sizes can be large. The **JPEG** file format is compressed. The resolution of the image may be the same as a TIFF file, but some detail may be lost in the image.

Finally, before you take the photograph, you should choose the type of media on which to store the resulting image file. Some cameras allow for a choice of media to which you can store the image, such as a CompactFlash card or Memory Stick, while others allow for only one type of storage media. One major advantage of a digital camera is that you easily can erase pictures from its media, freeing up space for new pictures.

IMAGE FILE SIZE WITH A SIX MEGAPIXEL DIGITAL CAMERA

Resolution in Pixels	COMPRESSION			Picture Size in Inches
	Low	Medium	High	
	Resulting Image File Size			
3000 × 2000	8.9 MB	3.3 MB	780 KB	16 × 20
2272 × 1704	2 MB	1.1 MB	556 KB	11 × 17
1600 × 1200	1 MB	558 KB	278 KB	8 × 10
1024 × 768	570 KB	320 KB	170 KB	4 × 6

FIGURE 4 Image file sizes for varying resolutions and compressions under standard photographic conditions using a 6-megapixel digital camera.

③ Transfer and Manage Image Files

The method of transferring images from the camera to the personal computer differs greatly depending on the capabilities of both. Digital cameras use a variety of storage media (Figure 5). If your camera uses a flash memory card such as CompactFlash, Memory Stick, SmartMedia, xD Picture card, or Secure Digital (SD), you can remove the media from the camera and place it in a slot on the personal computer or in a device, such as a card reader, connected to the personal computer. Your camera or card reader also may connect to the personal computer using a USB, USB 2.0, or FireWire (Figure 6) port. Some personal computers include an internal card reader. When you insert the memory card or connect the camera, software on the personal computer guides you through the process of transferring the images to the hard disk. Some operating systems and software recognize a memory card or camera as though it is another hard disk on the computer. This feature allows you to access the files, navigate them, and then copy, delete, or rename the files while the media still is in the camera.

After you transfer the files to the hard disk on your personal computer, you should organize the files by sorting them or renaming them so that information, such as the subject, date, time, and purpose, is saved along with the image. Finally, before altering the images digitally or using the images for other purposes, you should back up the images to another location, such as a CD or DVD, so the original image is recoverable.

FIGURE 5 SD Cards, CompactFlash Cards, and xD Picture Cards are popular storage devices for digital cameras.

FIGURE 6 Using a USB or FireWire connection, you can add a card reader to your personal computer.

④ Edit Images

Image editing software allows you to edit digital images. You should edit a copy, not the original image file, so that you always have the original file to use as a backup or for other editing projects. The following list summarizes the more common image enhancements or alterations:

- Adjust the contrast and brightness; correct lighting problems; or help give the photograph a particular feeling, such as warm or stark.
- Remove red-eye.
- Crop an image to remove unnecessary elements and resize it.
- Rotate the image to change its orientation.
- Add elements to the image, such as descriptive text, a date, a logo, or decorative items; create collages or add missing elements.
- Replace individual colors with a new color.
- Add special effects, such as texture, motion blurring or reflections to enhance the image.
- Add aging to make the image appear as it was taken a long time ago.

Some popular image editing programs are Adobe Photoshop, Microsoft Digital Image Suite, and Corel Paint Shop Pro Photo. Figure 7 shows some of the effects available in Corel Paint Shop Pro X on the Artistic Effects submenu.

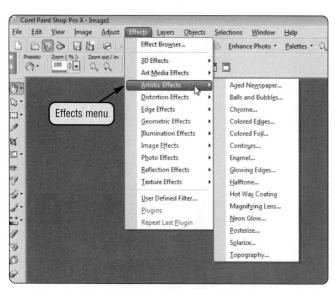

FIGURE 7 The capability of applying effects separates digital photography from film photography.

⑤ Print Images

Once an image is altered digitally, it is ready to be printed. You can print images on a personal color printer or send them to a professional service that specializes in digital photo printing.

When printing the images yourself, make sure that the resolution used to create the image was high enough for the size of the print you want to create. For example, if the camera used a resolution of 640 × 480 pixels, then the ideal print size is a wallet size. If you print such an image at a size of 8 × 10 inches, then the image will appear **pixilated**, or blurry. Use high-quality photo paper for the best results. A photo printer gives the best results when printing digital photography.

Many services print digital images, either over the Internet or through traditional photo developing locations and kiosks (Figure 8), such as those found in drug stores or shopping marts. Some services allow you to e-mail or upload the files to the service, specify the size, quality, and quantity of print; and then receive the finished prints via the postal service. Other services allow you to drop off flash memory cards or CD-ROMs at a photo shop and later pick up the prints, just as you do with traditional photo developing shops.

FIGURE 8 A kiosk allows you to print digital images in high resolution on photo paper.

6 Distribute Images Electronically

Rather than printing images, you often need to use the images electronically. Depending on the electronic use of the image, the image may require additional processing. If you use the images on a Web site or want to e-mail a photo, you probably want to send a lower-resolution image. Image editing software allows you to lower the resolution of the image, resulting in a smaller file size. Some photo sharing Web sites automatically will change the resolution of your photos for you. You also should use standard file formats when distributing an electronic photo. The JPEG format is viewable using most personal computers or Web browsers. Some online services allow you to upload and share your photos free of charge and will automatically change your photos to a lower resolution and JPEG format.

You can store very high resolution photos on a DVD or a CD. **DVD and CD mastering software** allows you to create slide show presentations on a recordable DVD or CD that can play in many home DVD players or personal computer DVD drives. Photo sharing Web sites, such as Fotki and Flickr (Figure 9), allow you to share your photos with acquaintances or with the whole world. You also can search for and view photos of others.

Finally, you should back up and store images that you distribute electronically with the same care as you store your traditional film negatives.

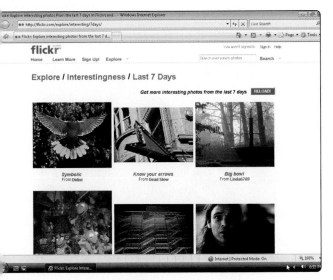

FIGURE 9 The Flickr photo sharing Web site allows you to share your photos, organize your photos, and search for photos.

DIGITAL VIDEO TECHNOLOGY

Digital video technology allows you to input, edit, manage, publish, and share your videos using a personal computer. With digital video technology, you can transform home videos into Hollywood-style movies by enhancing the videos with scrolling titles and transitions, cutting out or adding scenes, and adding background music and voice-over narration. The following sections outline the steps involved in the process of using digital video technology.

1 Select a Video Camera

Video cameras record in either analog or digital format. **Analog formats** include 8mm, Hi8, VHS-C, and Super VHS-C. **Digital formats** include Mini-DV, MICROMV, Digital8, DVD, and HDV (high-definition video format). Digital video cameras fall into three general categories: high-end consumer, consumer, and webcasting and monitoring (Figure 10). Consumer digital video cameras are by far the most popular type among consumers. High-end consumer models may support the HDV high-definition standard. Others may allow you to record directly on a DVD disc. A video recorded in high-definition can be played back on a high-definition display. Digital video cameras provide more features than analog video cameras, such as a higher level of zoom, better sound, or greater control over color and lighting.

(a) high-end consumer

(b) consumer

(c) webcasting and monitoring

FIGURE 10 The high-end consumer digital video camera (a) can produce professional-grade results. The consumer digital video camera (b) produces amateur-grade results. The webcasting and monitoring digital video camera (c) is appropriate for webcasting and security monitoring.

2 Record a Video

Most video cameras provide you with a choice of recording programs, which sometimes are called automatic settings. Each recording program includes a different combination of camera settings, so you can adjust the exposure and other functions to match the recording environment. Usually, several different programs are available, such as point-and-shoot, point-and-shoot with manual adjustment, sports, portrait, spotlit scenes, and low light. You also have the ability to select special digital effects, such as fade, wipe, and black and white. If you are recording outside on a windy day, then you can enable the wind screen to prevent wind noise. If you are recording home videos or video meant for a Web site, then the point-and-shoot recording program is sufficient.

3 Transfer and Manage Videos

After recording the video, the next step is to transfer the video to your personal computer. Most video cameras connect directly to a USB 2.0 or FireWire port on your personal computer (Figure 11). Transferring video with a digital camera is easy, because the video already is in a digital format that the computer can recognize.

An analog camcorder or VCR requires additional hardware to convert the analog signals to a digital format before the video can be manipulated on a personal computer. The additional hardware includes a special video capture card using a standard RCA video cable or an S-video cable (Figure 12). *S-video* cables provide sharper images and greater overall quality. When you use video capture hardware with an analog video, be sure to close all open programs on your computer because capturing video requires a great deal of processing power.

FIGURE 11 A digital video camera is connected to the personal computer via a FireWire or USB 2.0 port. No additional hardware is needed.

FIGURE 12 An analog camcorder or VCR is connected to the personal computer via an S-video port on a video capture card.

When transferring video, plan to use approximately 15 to 30 gigabytes of hard disk storage space per hour of digital video. A typical video project requires about four times the amount of raw footage as the final product. Therefore, at the high end, a video that lasts an hour may require up to 120 gigabytes of storage for the raw footage, editing process, and final video. This storage requirement can vary depending on the software you use to copy the video from the video camera to the hard disk and the format you select to save the video. For example, Microsoft's Windows Movie Maker can save 15 hours of video in 10 gigabytes when creating video for playback on a computer, but saves only 1 hour of video in 10 gigabytes when creating video for playback on a DVD. A high-definition video file may require over 10 gigabytes per hour.

The video transfer requires application software on the personal computer (Figure 13). Windows Vista includes the Windows Movie Maker software that allows you to transfer the video from your video camera. Depending on the length of video and the type of connection used, the video may take a long time to download. Make certain that no other programs are running on your personal computer while transferring the video.

The frame rate of a video refers to the number of frames per second (fps) that are captured in the video. The most widely used frame rate is 30 fps. A smaller frame rate results in a smaller file size for the video, but playback of the video will not be as smooth as one recorded with a higher frame rate.

When transferring video, the software may allow you to choose a file format and a codec to store the video. A video

file format holds the video information in a manner specified by a vendor, such as Apple or Microsoft. Four of the more popular file formats are listed in Figure 14.

File formats support codecs to encode the audio and video into the file formats. A particular file format may be able to store audio and video in a number of different codecs. A **codec** specifies how the audio and video is compressed and stored within the file. Figure 15 shows some options available for specifying a file format and codec in a video capture program. The dialog box in Figure 15 allows the user to determine whether the video is smoother in playback or if the video is more crisp, meaning that it includes more detail. The file format and codec you choose often is based on what you plan to do with the movie. For example, if you plan to upload your video to the YouTube video sharing Web site, the best choices are DivX and Xvid MPEG-4 file formats.

After transferring the video to a personal computer, and before manipulating the video, you should store the video files in appropriate folders, named correctly, and backed up. Most video transfer application software helps manage these tasks.

POPULAR VIDEO FILE FORMATS

File Format	File Extensions
Apple QuickTime	.MOV or .QT
DivX	.DIVX
Microsoft Windows Media Video	.WMV or .ASF
Real RealMedia	.RM or .RAM

FIGURE 14 Apple, DivX, Microsoft, and Real offer the more popular video file formats.

FIGURE 13 Some video editing software allows you to transfer your video from any video source to a hard disk.

FIGURE 15 Video editing software allows you to specify a combination of file format and codec when saving a video.

4 Edit a Video

Once the video is stored on your hard disk, the next step is to edit, or manipulate, the video. If you used a video capture card to transfer analog video to your computer (Figure 12 on page 348), the files may require extra initial processing. When you use a video capture card, some of the video frames may be lost in the transfer process. Some video editing programs allow you to fix this problem with **frame rate correction** tools.

The first step in the editing process is to split the video into smaller pieces, or *scenes*, that you can manipulate more easily. This process is called *splitting*. Most video software automatically splits the video into scenes, thus sparing you the task. After splitting, you should cut out unwanted scenes or portions of scenes. This process is called *pruning*.

After you create the scenes you want to use in your final production, you edit each individual scene. You can *crop*, or change the size of, scenes. That is, you may want to cut out the top or a side of a scene that is irrelevant. You also can resize the scene. For example, you may be creating a video that will be displayed in a Web browser. Making a smaller video, such as 320 × 200 pixels instead of 640 × 480 pixels, results in a smaller file that transmits faster over the Internet. Some video sharing Web sites recommend smaller video resolutions, such as 320 × 200 pixels.

If video has been recorded over a long period, using different cameras or under different lighting conditions, the video may need color correction. *Color correction tools* (Figure 16) analyze your video and match brightness, colors, and other attributes of video clips to ensure a smooth look to the video.

You can add logos, special effects, or titles to scenes. You can place a company logo or personal logo in a video to identify yourself or the company producing the video. Logos often are added on the lower-right corner of a video and remain for the duration of the video. Special effects include warping, changing from color to black and white, morphing, or zoom motion. *Morphing* is a special effect in which one video image is transformed into another image over the course of several frames of video, creating the illusion of metamorphosis. You usually add titles at the beginning and end of a video to give the video context. A training video may have titles throughout the video to label a particular scene, or each scene may begin with a title.

FIGURE 16 Color correction tools in video editing software allow a great deal of control over the mood of your video creation.

The next step in editing a video is to add audio effects, including voice-over narration and background music. Many video editing programs allow you to add additional tracks, or *layers*, of sound to a video in addition to the sound that was recorded on the video camera. You also can add special audio effects.

The final step in editing a video is to combine the scenes into a complete video (Figure 17). This process involves ordering scenes and adding transition effects between scenes (Figure 18). Video editing software allows you to combine scenes and separate each scene with a transition. *Transitions* include fading, wiping, blurry, bursts, ruptures, erosions, and more.

FIGURE 17 In Ulead VideoStudio, scenes, shown on the top, are combined into a sequence on the bottom of the screen.

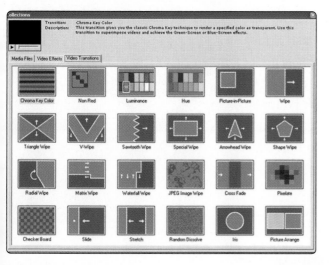

FIGURE 18 Smooth and dynamic transitions eliminate the hard cuts between scenes typically found in raw footage.

⑤ Distribute the Video

After editing the video, the final step is to distribute it or save it on an appropriate medium. You can save video in a variety of formats. Using special hardware, you can save the video on standard video tape. *A digital-to-analog converter* is necessary to allow your personal computer to transmit video to a VCR. A digital-to-analog converter may be an external device that connects to both the computer and input device, or may be a video capture card inside the computer.

Video also can be stored in digital formats in any of several DVD formats, on CD-R, on a video sharing Web site, or on video CD (VCD). *DVD* or *CD creation software*, which often is packaged with video editing software, allows you to create, or *master*, DVDs and CDs. You can add interactivity to your DVDs. For example, you can allow viewers to jump to certain scenes using a menu. A *video CD (VCD)* is a CD format that stores video on a CD-R that can be played in many DVD players.

You also can save your video creation in electronic format for distribution over the Web or via e-mail. Popular video sharing Web sites, such as YouTube (Figure 19), have recommendations for the best file format and codecs to use for video that you upload to them. Your video editing software must support the file format and codec you want to use. For example, Apple's iMovie software typically saves files in the QuickTime file format.

Professionals use hardware and software that allow them to create a film version of digital video that can be played in movie theaters. This technology is becoming increasingly popular. The cost of professional video editing software ranges from thousands to hundreds of thousands of dollars. Video editing software for the home user is available for a few hundred dollars or less. Some Hollywood directors believe that eventually, all movies will be recorded and edited digitally.

After creating your final video for distribution or your personal video collection, you should back up the final video file. You can save your scenes for inclusion in other video creations or create new masters using different effects, transitions, and ordering of scenes.

FIGURE 19 Video sharing Web sites allow you to share your videos with acquaintances or the entire world.

CHAPTER SEVEN

Storage

Picture Yourself Working with Mobile Storage Media

Your friend, Kara, announces excitedly, "I did it! I'm going to Spain! But I need a favor." She explains that she is going to study abroad for a semester and needs you to fill in for her at the student newspaper, where she is photo editor. You are a journalism major, so this is a good opportunity for you, but you are not sure what her job entails. You decide to meet at the newspaper office on campus, where she will walk you through the process.

Kara explains that you will be working with the student photographers — more precisely, with their mobile media. The photographers take many pictures while on various assignments. All of them use digital cameras. Part of your job is to print pictures taken by the student photographers. Because each student uses a different make and model of camera, the digital pictures are stored on a variety of mobile media. Some of the cameras use flash memory cards such as CompactFlash cards, xD Picture cards, and Memory Sticks. One student transfers his pictures to a pocket hard drive. Some copy their pictures on a CD, and another submits a USB flash drive containing all her pictures.

After you receive the media, you will insert it in the appropriate card reader, card slot, drive, or port. You then will begin the process of storing the images on a hard disk and finally printing the images.

To learn about these various types of mobile media, read Chapter 7 and discover many other types of storage devices.

OBJECTIVES

After completing this chapter, you will be able to:

1. Differentiate between storage devices and storage media
2. Describe the characteristics of magnetic disks
3. Describe the characteristics of a hard disk
4. Discuss various types of miniature, external, and removable hard disks
5. Describe the characteristics of optical discs
6. Differentiate among CD-ROMs, recordable CDs, rewritable CDs, DVD-ROMs, BD-ROMs, HD DVD-ROMs, recordable DVDs, and rewritable DVDs
7. Identify the uses of tape
8. Discuss PC Cards, ExpressCard modules, and the various types of miniature mobile storage media
9. Identify uses of microfilm and microfiche

CONTENTS

STORAGE

Storage holds data, instructions, and information for future use. Every computer stores system software and application software. To start up, a computer locates an operating system (system software) in storage, usually a hard disk, and loads it into memory (RAM). When a user issues a command to start application software, such as a word processing program or a Web browser, the operating system locates the program in storage, such as on a hard disk, CD, or DVD, and loads it into memory (RAM).

In addition to programs, users store a variety of data and information on mainframe computers, servers, desktop computers, notebook computers, Tablet PCs, handheld computers, PDAs,

and smart phones. For example, all types of users store digital photographs; appointments, schedules, and contact/address information; and correspondence, such as letters and e-mail messages. Other items stored by specific types of users include the following:

- The home user might also store budgets, bank statements, a household inventory, records of stock purchases, tax data, homework assignments, recipes, music, and videos.
- The small office/home office user also often stores faxes, business reports, financial records, tax data, travel records, customer orders, payroll records, inventory records, and Web pages.
- The mobile user usually also stores faxes, presentations, travel records, homework assignments, and quotations.

internal hard disk

miniature hard disk

external hard disks

microfilm

Storage

smart card

USB fla

FIGURE 7-1 A variety of storage media.

- The power user also stores diagrams, drawings, blueprints, designs, marketing literature, corporate newsletters, product catalogs, audio recordings, multimedia presentations, videos, and Web pages.
- The large business user also accesses many stored items such as tax data, inventory records, presentations, contracts, marketing literature, and Web pages. The large business user accesses hundreds or thousands of employee, customer, and vendor records, including data and information about orders, invoices, payments, and payroll.

Storage requirements among these users vary greatly. Home users, small office/home office users, and mobile users typically have much smaller storage requirements than the large business user or power user. For example, a home user may need 160 billion bytes of storage, while large businesses may require 50 quadrillion bytes of storage.

A **storage medium** (media is the plural), also called *secondary storage*, is the physical material on which a computer keeps data, instructions, and information. Examples of storage media are hard disks, floppy disks, CDs and DVDs, tape, PC Cards and ExpressCard modules, flash memory cards, USB flash drives, smart cards, and microfilm (Figure 7-1). Memory (RAM), by contrast, typically consists of one or more chips on the motherboard or some other circuit board in the computer.

floppy disk

CD or DVD

tape

flash memory cards

PC Card

ExpressCard module

Capacity is the number of bytes (characters) a storage medium can hold. Figure 7-2 identifies the terms manufacturers use to define the capacity of storage media. For example, a reasonably priced USB flash drive can store up to 512 MB of data (approximately 512 million bytes) and a typical hard disk has 250 GB (approximately 250 billion bytes) of storage capacity.

STORAGE TERMS

Storage Term	Approximate Number of Bytes	Exact Number of Bytes
Kilobyte (KB)	1 thousand	2^{10} or 1,024
Megabyte (MB)	1 million	2^{20} or 1,048,576
Gigabyte (GB)	1 billion	2^{30} or 1,073,741,824
Terabyte (TB)	1 trillion	2^{40} or 1,099,511,627,776
Petabyte (PB)	1 quadrillion	2^{50} or 1,125,899,906,842,624
Exabyte (EB)	1 quintillion	2^{60} or 1,152,921,504,606,846,976
Zettabyte (ZB)	1 sextillion	2^{70} or 1,180,591,620,717,411,303,424
Yottabyte (YB)	1 septillion	2^{80} or 1,208,925,819,614,629,174,706,176

FIGURE 7-2   The capacity of a storage medium is measured by the number of bytes it can hold.

Items on a storage medium remain intact even when power is removed from the computer. Thus, a storage medium is nonvolatile. Most memory (i.e., RAM), by contrast, holds data and instructions temporarily and thus is volatile. Figure 7-3 illustrates the concept of volatility. For an analogy, think of a filing cabinet that holds file folders as a storage medium, and the top of your desk as memory. When you want to work with a file, you remove it from the filing cabinet (storage medium) and place it on your desk (memory). When you are finished with the file, you remove it from your desk (memory) and return it to the filing cabinet (storage medium).

A **storage device** is the computer hardware that records and/or retrieves items to and from storage media. **Writing** is the process of transferring data, instructions, and information from memory to a storage medium. **Reading** is the process of transferring these items from a storage medium into memory. When storage devices write data on storage media, they are creating output. Similarly, when storage devices read from storage media, they function as a source of input. Nevertheless, they are categorized as storage devices, not as input or output devices.

AN ILLUSTRATION OF VOLATILITY

State of Computer	Screen Display Volatile	Contents of Memory (most RAM) Volatile	Contents of Storage Nonvolatile

FIGURE 7-3   A screen display is considered volatile because its contents disappear when power is removed. Likewise, most RAM chips are volatile. That is, their contents are erased when power is removed from the computer. Storage, by contrast, is nonvolatile. Its contents remain when power is off.

screen displays and contents of most RAM (memory) erased when power is off

contents of storage retained when power is off

The speed of storage devices and memory is defined by access time. **Access time** measures (1) the amount of time it takes a storage device to locate an item on a storage medium or (2) the time required to deliver an item from memory to the processor. The access time of storage devices is slow, compared with the access time of memory. Memory (chips) accesses items in billionths of a second (nanoseconds). Storage devices, by contrast, access items in thousandths of a second (milliseconds) or millionths of a second (microseconds).

Instead of, or in addition to access time, some manufacturers state a storage device's transfer rate because it affects access time. *Transfer rate* is the speed with which data, instructions, and information transfer to and from a device. Transfer rates for storage are stated in *KBps* (kilobytes per second) and *MBps* (megabytes per second).

Numerous types of storage media and storage devices exist to meet a variety of users' needs. Figure 7-4 shows how different types of storage media and memory compare in terms of transfer rates and uses. This chapter discusses these and other storage media.

MAGNETIC DISKS

Magnetic disks use magnetic particles to store items such as data, instructions, and information on a disk's surface. Depending on how the magnetic particles are aligned, they represent either a 0 bit or a 1 bit. Recall from Chapter 4 that a bit (binary digit) is the smallest unit of data a computer can process. Thus, the alignment of the magnetic particles represents the data.

Before any data can be read from or written on a magnetic disk, the disk must be formatted. **Formatting** is the process of dividing the disk into tracks and sectors (Figure 7-5), so the operating system can store and locate data and information on the disk. A *track* is a narrow recording band that forms a full circle on the surface of the disk. The disk's storage locations consist of pie-shaped sections, which break the tracks into small arcs called *sectors*. On a magnetic disk, a sector typically stores up to 512 bytes of data.

For reading and writing purposes, sectors are grouped into clusters. A *cluster* is the smallest unit of disk space that stores data and information. Each cluster, also called an *allocation unit*, consists of two to eight sectors (the number varies depending on the operating system). Even if a file consists of only a few bytes, it uses an entire cluster. Each cluster holds data from only one file. One file, however, can span many clusters.

		Stores...
Memory	Memory (most RAM)	Items waiting to be interpreted and executed by the processor
Storage	Hard Disk	Operating system, application software, user data and information, including pictures, music, and videos
	Flash Memory Cards and USB Flash Drives	Digital pictures or files to be transported
	CDs and DVDs	Software, backups, movies, music
	Tape	Backups
	Floppy Disk	Small files to be transported

faster transfer rates ↑

slower transfer rates ↓

FIGURE 7-4 A comparison of different types of storage media and memory in terms of relative speed and uses. Memory is faster than storage but is expensive and not practical for all storage requirements. Storage is less expensive but is slower than memory.

FIGURE 7-5 Tracks form circles on the surface of a magnetic disk. The disk's storage locations are divided into pie-shaped sections, which break the tracks into small arcs called sectors.

Sometimes, a sector has a flaw and cannot store data. When you format a disk, the operating system marks these bad sectors as unusable. For a technical discussion about formatting, read the High-Tech Talk article on page 382.

Two types of magnetic disks are hard disks and floppy disks. Some disks are portable; others are not. With respect to a storage medium, the term *portable* means you can remove the medium from one computer and carry it to another computer.

Hard Disks

A **hard disk**, also called a *hard disk drive* or hard drive, is a storage device that contains one or more inflexible, circular platters that magnetically store data, instructions, and information. Home users store documents, spreadsheets, presentations, databases, e-mail messages, Web pages, digital photographs, music, videos, and software on hard disks. Businesses use hard disks to store correspondence, reports, financial records, e-mail messages, customer orders and invoices, payroll records, inventory records, presentations, contracts, marketing literature, schedules, and Web sites.

The system unit on most desktop and notebook computers contains at least one hard disk. The entire device is enclosed in an airtight, sealed case to protect it from contamination. A hard disk that is mounted inside the system unit sometimes is called a *fixed disk* because it is not portable (Figure 7-6). Portable hard disks are discussed later in this chapter.

Current personal computer hard disks have storage capacities from 80 to 750 GB and more. Traditionally, hard disks stored data using *longitudinal recording*, which aligned the magnetic particles horizontally around the surface of the disk. With *perpendicular recording*, by contrast, hard disks align the magnetic particles vertically, or perpendicular to the disk's surface, making much greater storage capacities possible. Experts estimate that hard disks using perpendicular recording will provide storage capacities about 10 times greater than disks that use longitudinal recording. Read Looking Ahead 7-1 for a look at the next generation of hard disk storage capacities.

Hard disks are read/write storage media. That is, you can read from and write on a hard disk any number of times. If the computer contains only one hard disk, the operating system designates it as drive C. Additional hard disks are assigned the next available drive letter.

WEB LINK 7-1

Perpendicular Recording

For more information, visit scsite.com/ dc2008/ch7/weblink and then click Perpendicular Recording.

FIGURE 7-6 The hard disk in a desktop personal computer is enclosed inside an airtight, sealed case inside the system unit.

FAQ 7-1

Have personal computer hard disk capacities grown much since their inception?

Yes, hard disk capacities have grown phenomenally over the past several years, as shown in the chart to the right. This trend is expected to continue at a rate of 60 percent annually. For more information, visit scsite.com/dc2008/ch7/faq and then click Hard Disk Capacities.

Personal Computer Hard Disk Growth
(Historical and Projected)

LOOKING AHEAD 7-1

Heat Increases Disk Capacity

Things are heating up in the data storage industry. Engineers at IBM Research are testing the use of heat to record data inexpensively on magnetic media, such as hard disks.

Within the next ten years, the researchers predict that this new technique will allow storage of more than one terabit per square inch, which is the equivalent of 25 DVDs on an area the size of a postage stamp. With this capacity, a hard disk that can store seven terabits will be commonplace.

IBM calls this new storage system *Millipede*. It uses heated tips mounted on the ends of cantilevers, in a fashion similar to the way the stylus on an old phonograph sat on the grooves of vinyl records. For more information, visit scsite.com/dc2008/ch7/looking and then click Heated Storage.

ARACTERISTICS OF A HARD DISK Characteristics a hard disk include its capacity, platters, read/ te heads, cylinders, sectors and tracks, revolu-ns per minute, transfer rate, and access time. ure 7-7 shows characteristics of a sample 500 GB d disk. The following paragraphs discuss each hese characteristics.

The capacity of a hard disk is determined from the number of platters it contains, together with composition of the magnetic coating on the platters. A *platter* is made of aluminum, glass, or ceramic and is coated with an alloy material that allows items to be recorded magnetically on its surface. The coating usually is three millionths of an inch thick.

SAMPLE HARD DISK CHARACTERISTICS

Advertised capacity	500 GB
Platters	4
Read/write heads	8
Cylinders	16,383
Bytes per sector	512
Sectors per track	63
Sectors per drive	976,773,168
Revolutions per minute	7,200
Transfer rate	300 MB per second
Access time	8.5 ms

FIGURE 7-7 Characteristics of a sample 500 GB hard disk. The actual disk's capacity sometimes is different from the advertised capacity because of bad sectors on the disk.

On desktop computers, platters most often have a *form factor*, or size, of approximately 3.5 inches in diameter; on notebook computers and mobile devices, the form factor is 2.5 inches or less. A typical hard disk has multiple platters stacked on top of one another. Each platter has two read/write heads, one for each side. The hard disk has arms that move the read/write heads to the proper location on the platter (Figure 7-8). A *read/write head* is the mechanism that reads items and writes items in the drive as it barely touches the disk's recording surface.

The location of the read/write heads often is referred to by its cylinder. A *cylinder* is the vertical section of a track that passes through all platters (Figure 7-9). A single movement of the read/write head arms accesses all the platters in a cylinder. If a hard disk has two platters (four sides), each with 1,000 tracks, then it will have 1,000

FIGURE 7-9 A cylinder is the vertical section of track through all platters on a hard disk.

FIGURE 7-8 HOW A HARD DISK WORKS

Step 2:
A small motor spins the platters while the computer is running.

Step 3:
When software requests a disk access, the read/write heads determine the current or new location of the data.

Step 1:
The circuit board controls the movement of the head actuator and a small motor.

Step 4:
The head actuator positions the read/write head arms over the correct location on the platters to read or write data.

cylinders with each cylinder consisting of 4 tracks (2 tracks for each platter).

While the computer is running, the platters in the hard disk rotate at a high rate of speed. This spinning, which usually is 5,400 to 15,000 *revolutions per minute (rpm)*, allows nearly instant access to all tracks and sectors on the platters. The platters typically continue to spin until power is removed from the computer. (On many computers, the hard disk stops spinning or slows down after a specified time to save power.) The spinning motion creates a cushion of air between the platter and its read/write head. This cushion ensures that the read/write head floats above the platter instead of making direct contact with the platter surface. The distance between the read/write head and the platter is about two millionths of one inch.

As shown in Figure 7-10, this close clearance leaves no room for any type of contamination. Dirt, hair, dust, smoke, and other particles could cause the hard disk to have a head crash. A *head crash* occurs when a read/write head touches the surface of a platter, usually resulting in a loss of data or sometimes loss of the entire drive.

FIGURE 7-10 The clearance between a disk read/write head and the platter is about two millionths of an inch. A smoke particle, dust particle, human hair, or other contaminant could render the drive unusable.

Although current internal hard disks are built to withstand shocks and are sealed tightly to keep out contaminants, head crashes do occasionally still occur. Thus, it is crucial that you back up your hard disk regularly. A **backup** is a duplicate of a file, program, or disk placed on a separate storage medium that you can use in case the original is lost, damaged, or destroyed. Chapter 8 discusses backup techniques.

Depending on the type of hard disk, transfer rates range from 15 MBps to 320 MBps. Access time for today's hard disks ranges from about 3 to 12 ms (milliseconds).

Hard disks improve their access time by using disk caching. *Disk cache* (pronounced *cash*), sometimes called a buffer, consists of a memory chip(s) on a hard disk that stores frequently accessed items such as data, instructions, and information (Figure 7-11). Disk cache and memory cache work in a similar fashion. When a processor requests data, instructions, or information from the hard disk, the hard disk first checks its disk cache — before moving any mechanical parts to access the platters. If the requested item is in disk cache, the hard disk sends it to the processor. If the hard disk does not find the requested item in the disk cache, then the processor must wait for the hard disk to locate and transfer the item from the disk to the processor. Hard disks today contain between

FIGURE 7-11 HOW DISK CACHE WORKS

Step 1:
A special-purpose chip on the hard disk, called a controller, receives a request for data, instructions, or information from the processor.

Step 2a:
The controller first checks disk cache for the requested item.

Step 2b:
If the controller does not find the requested item in disk cache, it locates the requested item on the hard disk's platters.

Step 3:
The controller transfers the requested item to the processor.

- *SATA* (*Serial Advanced Technology Attachment*), the newest type of hard disk interface, uses serial signals to transfer data, instructions, and information. The primary advantage of SATA interfaces is their cables are thinner, longer, more flexible, and less susceptible to interference than cables used by hard disks that use parallel signals. SATA interfaces have data transfer rates of up to 300 MBps. In addition to hard disks, SATA interfaces support connections to CD and DVD drives.

- *EIDE* (*Enhanced Integrated Drive Electronics*) is a hard disk interface that uses parallel signals to transfer data, instructions, and information. EIDE interfaces can support up to four hard disks at 137 GB per disk. These interfaces have data transfer rates up to 100 MBps. EIDE interfaces also provide connections for CD and DVD drives and tape drives. Some manufacturers market their EIDE interfaces as Fast ATA or Ultra ATA.

- *SCSI* interfaces, which also use parallel signals, can support up to eight or fifteen peripheral devices. Supported devices include hard disks, CD and DVD drives, tape drives, printers, scanners, network cards, and much more. Recall from Chapter 4 that SCSI is an acronym for Small Computer System Interface. Some computers have a built-in SCSI interface, while others use an adapter card to add a SCSI interface. SCSI interfaces provide up to 320 MBps data transfer rates.

FAQ 7-3

What are the transfer rates of USB 2.0 and FireWire 800?

USB 2.0, also called *Hi-Speed USB*, has transfer rates up to 480 *Mbps* (megabits per second). FireWire 800 has transfer rates up to 800 Mbps. For more information, visit scsite.com/dc2008/ ch7/faq and then click USB 2.0 and FireWire 800.

MAINTAINING DATA STORED ON A HARD DISK
Most manufacturers guarantee their hard disks to last approximately three to five years. Many last much longer with proper care. To prevent the loss of items stored on a hard disk, you regularly should perform preventive maintenance such as defragmenting or scanning the disk for errors. Chapter 8 discusses these and other utilities in depth.

ONLINE STORAGE Some users choose online storage instead of storing data locally on a hard disk. **Online storage** is a service on the Web that provides hard disk storage to computer users, for free or for a minimal monthly fee (Figure 7-15). Fee arrangements for use of these Internet hard disks vary. For example, one online storage service provides 5 GB of storage free to registered users; another charges $10 per month for 5 GB of storage.

WEB LINK 7-4

Online Storage
For more information, visit scsite.com/ dc2008/ch7/weblink and then click Online Storage.

FIGURE 7-15   An example of one Web site advertising its online storage service.

Users subscribe to an online storage service for a variety of reasons:

- To access files on the Internet hard disk from any computer or device that has Internet access
- To store large audio, video, and graphics files on an Internet hard disk instantaneously, instead of spending time downloading to a local hard disk
- To allow others to access files on their Internet hard disk so others can listen to an audio file, watch a video clip, or view a picture — instead of e-mailing the file to them
- To view time-critical data and images immediately while away from the main office or location; for example, doctors can view x-ray images from another hospital, home, or office, or while on vacation
- To store offsite backups of data (Chapter 8 presents this and other backup strategies)

Once users subscribe to the online storage service, they can save on the Internet hard disk in the same manner they save on their local hard disk or any other drive.

Floppy Disks

A **floppy disk**, also called a *diskette*, is a portable, inexpensive storage medium that consists of a thin, circular, flexible plastic Mylar film with a magnetic coating enclosed in a square-shaped plastic shell. Although the exterior of current floppy disks is not bendable, users refer to this storage medium as a floppy disk because of the flexible film inside the rigid plastic 3.5-inch outer cover.

A standard floppy disk has storage capacities up to 1.44 MB. Floppy disks are not as widely used as they were 15 years ago because of their low storage capacity.

A **floppy disk drive** is a device that reads from and writes on a floppy disk. A user inserts a floppy disk in and removes it from a floppy disk drive. In the past, desktop personal computers and notebook computers had a

floppy disk drive installed inside the system unit. Most computers today do not include a floppy disk drive as standard equipment. On these computers, you can use an *external floppy disk drive*, in which the drive is a separate device with a cable that plugs in a port on the system unit (Figure 7-16). These external drives are attached to the computer only when the user needs to access items on a floppy disk. If a personal computer has one floppy disk drive, it is named drive A.

Floppy disk drive access times are about 84 milliseconds, or approximately 1/12 of a second. The transfer rates range from 250 to 500 KBps.

You can read from and write on a floppy disk any number of times. A typical floppy disk stores data on both sides of the disk, has 80 tracks on each side of the recording surface, and has 18 sectors per track.

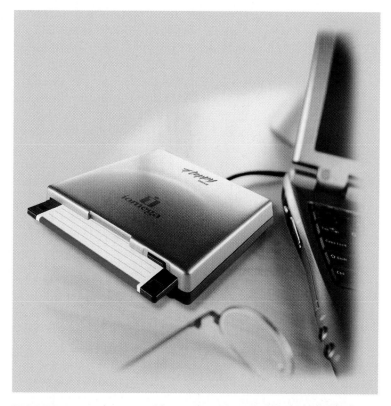

FIGURE 7-16 An external floppy disk drive attached to a computer with a cable.

Test your knowledge of pages 354 through 365 in Quiz Yourself 7-1.

QUIZ YOURSELF 7-1

Instructions: Find the true statement below. Then, rewrite the remaining false statements so they are true.

1. Miniature hard disks are a type of optical disc.
2. Hard disks contain one or more inflexible, circular platters that magnetically store data, instructions, and information.
3. SATA is a hard disk interface that uses parallel signals to transfer data, instructions, and information.
4. Storage media is the computer hardware that records and/or retrieves items to and from a storage device.
5. Two types of manual disks are hard disks and floppy disks.
6. Users can move an internal hard disk from computer to computer as needed by connecting the disk to a USB port or FireWire port on the system unit.

Quiz Yourself Online: To further check your knowledge of storage devices and storage media, hard disks, and floppy disks, visit scsite.com/dc2008/ch7/quiz and then click Objectives 1 – 4.

OPTICAL DISCS

An *optical disc* is a type of storage media that consists of a flat, round, portable disc made of metal, plastic, and lacquer that is written and read by a laser. (The spelling, disk, is used for magnetic media, and disc is used for optical media.) Optical discs used in personal computers are 4.75 inches in diameter and less than one-twentieth of an inch thick. Smaller computers and devices, however, use *mini discs* that have a diameter of 3 inches or less.

Optical discs primarily store software, data, digital photographs, movies, and music. Some optical disc formats are read only, meaning users cannot write (save) on the media. Others are read/write, which allows users to save on the disc just as they save on a hard disk.

Nearly every personal computer today has some type of optical disc drive installed in a drive bay. On these drives, you push a button to slide out a tray, insert the disc, and then push the same button to close the tray (Figure 7-17). Other convenient features on most of these drives include a volume control button and a headphone port (or jack) so you can use headphones to listen to audio without disturbing others nearby.

With some discs, you can read and/or write on one side only. Manufacturers usually place a silk-screened label on the top layer of these single-sided discs. You insert a single-sided disc in the drive with the label side up. Other discs are double-sided. Simply remove the disc from the drive, flip it over, and reinsert it in the drive to use the other side of the disc. Double-sided discs often have no label; instead each side of the disc is identified with small writing

Push the button to slide out the tray.

Insert the disc, label side up.

Push the same button to close the tray.

FIGURE 7-17 On optical disc drives, you push a button to slide out a tray, insert the disc, and then push the same button to close the tray.

around the center of the disc. Some drives use *LightScribe technology,* which works with specially coated optical discs, to etch labels directly on the disc (as opposed to placing an adhesive label on the disc).

The drive designation of an optical disc drive usually follows alphabetically after that of all the hard disks and portable disks. For example, if the computer has one internal hard disk (drive C) and an external hard disk (drive D), then the first optical disc drive is drive E. A second optical disc drive would be drive F.

Optical discs store items by using microscopic pits (indentations) and lands (flat areas) that are in the middle layer of the disc (Figure 7-18). A high-powered laser light creates the pits. A lower-powered laser light reads items from the disc by reflecting light through the bottom of the disc, which usually is either solid gold or silver in color. The reflected light is converted into a series of bits the computer can process. A land causes light to reflect, which is read as binary digit 1. Pits absorb the light; this absence of light is read as binary digit 0.

Optical discs commonly store items in a single track that spirals from the center of the disc to the edge of the disc. As with a hard disk, this single track is divided into evenly sized sectors on which items are stored (Figure 7-19).

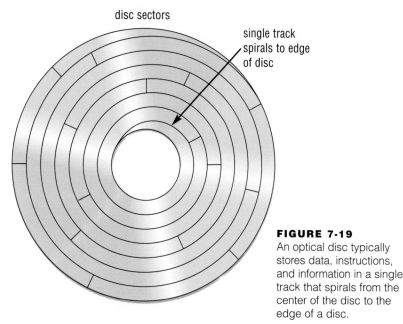

FIGURE 7-19
An optical disc typically stores data, instructions, and information in a single track that spirals from the center of the disc to the edge of a disc.

FIGURE 7-18   HOW A LASER READS DATA ON AN OPTICAL DISC

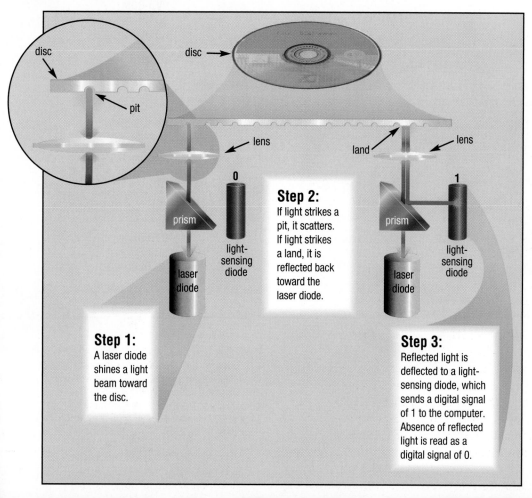

Care of Optical Discs

Manufacturers claim that a properly cared for high-quality optical disc will last 5 years but could last up to 100 years. Figure 7-20 offers some guidelines for the proper care of optical discs. Never bend a disc; it may break. Do not expose discs to extreme temperatures or humidity. The ideal temperature range for disc storage is 50 to 70 degrees Fahrenheit. Stacking discs, touching the underside of discs, or exposing them to any type of contaminant may scratch a disc. Place an optical disc in its protective case, called a *jewel box*, when you are finished using it and store in an upright (vertical) position.

FAQ 7-4

Can I clean a disc?

Yes, you can remove dust, dirt, smudges, and fingerprints from the surface of an optical disc. Moisten a nonabrasive cloth with warm water or rubbing alcohol and then wipe the disc in straight lines from the center outward. You also can repair scratches on the surface with a specialized disc repair kit. For more information, visit scsite.com/dc2008/ch7/faq and then click Cleaning and Repairing Discs.

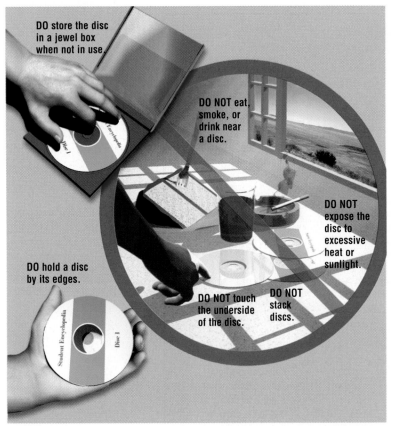

FIGURE 7-20   Some guidelines for the proper care of optical discs.

Types of Optical Discs

Many different formats of optical discs exist toda[y] Figure 7-21 identifies a variety of optical disc form[ats] and specifies whether a user can read from the disc[,] write to the disc, and/or erase the disc. The followi[ng] sections describe characteristics unique to each of t[he] disc formats.

OPTICAL DISC FORMATS

Optical Disc	Read	Write	Erase
CD-ROM	Y	N	N
CD-R	Y	Y	N
CD-RW	Y	Y	Y
DVD-ROM BD-ROM HD DVD-ROM	Y	N	N
DVD-R DVD+R BD-R HD DVD-R	Y	Y	N
DVD-RW DVD+RW DVD-RAM BD-RE HD DVD-RW	Y	Y	Y

FIGURE 7-21   Manufacturers sell CD-ROM and DVD-ROM media prerecorded (written) with audio, vide[o] and software. Users cannot change the contents of the[se] discs. Users, however, can purchase the other formats [of] CDs and DVDs as blank media and record (write) their own data, instructions, and information on these discs.

CD-ROMs

A **CD-ROM** (pronounced SEE-DEE-rom), or *compact disc read-only memory*, is a type of optical disc that users can read but not write (record) or erase — hence, the name read-only. Manufacturers write the contents of standard CD-ROMs. A standard CD-ROM is called a *single-session disc* because manufacturers write all items on the disc at one time. Software manufacturers often distribute their programs using CD-ROMs (Figure 7-22).

A typical CD-ROM holds from 650 MB to 1 GB of data, instructions, and information. To read a CD-ROM, insert the disc in a **CD-ROM drive** or a CD-ROM player. Because audio CDs and CD-ROMs use the same laser technology, you may be able to use a CD-ROM drive to listen to an audio CD while working on the computer. Some music companies, however, configure their CDs so the music will not play on a computer. They do this to protect themselves from customers illegally copying and sharing the music.

The speed of a CD-ROM drive determines how fast it installs programs and accesses the disc. Original CD-ROM drives were single-speed drives with transfer rates of 150 KBps (kilobytes per second). Manufacturers measure all optical disc drives relative to this original CD-ROM drive. They use an X to denote the original transfer rate of 150 KBps. For example, a 48X CD-ROM drive has a data transfer rate of 7,200 (48 × 150) KBps, or 7.2 MBps.

Current CD-ROM drives have transfer rates, or speeds, ranging from 48X to 75X or faster. The higher the number, the faster the CD-ROM drive. Faster CD-ROM drives are more expensive than slower drives. Read Looking Ahead 7-2 for a look at the future of storage.

WEB LINK 7-5

CD-ROMs

For more information, visit scsite.com/dc2008/ch7/weblink and then click CD-ROMs.

LOOKING AHEAD 7-2

Bookshelf Design Streamlines Entertainment Storage

Imagine tossing bulky collections of CDs, movies, and video games and replacing them with a streamlined storage system that turns a personal computer into a digital bookshelf.

Two Purdue University industrial designers created *Bookshelf*, a personal computer design featuring a 7-inch cube-shaped central processing unit with add-on hard disk attachments arranged on a shelf and held in place with latched bookends. By adding hardware attachments containing multiple movies, magazines, or games, users easily can create their own custom-designed multimedia libraries at their computers. The attachments, supplied by digital service providers through subscription payments, feature a universal design, so they can be arranged side by side on the computer shelf.

Content categories are viewed much like looking at book titles. The design protects entertainment copyrights while also increasing convenience and portability for users. For more information, visit scsite.com/dc2008/ch7/looking and then click Bookshelf.

FIGURE 7-22 Encyclopedias, games, simulations, and many other programs are distributed on CD-ROM.

PICTURE CDs A Kodak **Picture CD** is a single-session CD-ROM that stores digital versions of film using a jpg file format. Many film developers offer Picture CD service for consumers when they drop off film to be developed. The resolution of images stored on a Picture CD usually is 1024 × 1536 pixels. The average cost for a Picture CD is about $3 per roll of film.

Most optical disc drives can read a Picture CD. Using photo editing software and photographs on the Picture CD, you can remove red eye, crop the photograph, enhance colors, trim away edges, adjust the lighting, and edit just about any aspect of a photograph. In addition, a Picture CD allows you to print copies of the photographs on glossy paper with an ink-jet

printer. If you do not have a printer to print the images, many stores have kiosks at which you can print pictures from a Picture CD or other media (Figure 7-23).

CD-Rs and CD-RWs

A **CD-R** (*compact disc-recordable*) is a multisession optical disc on which users can write, but not erase, their own items such as text, graphics, and audio. *Multisession* means you can write on part of the disc at one time and another part at a later time. Each part of a CD-R, however, can be written on only one time, and the disc's contents cannot be erased.

Writing on the CD-R requires a *CD recorder* or a **CD-R drive**. A CD-R drive usually can read both audio CDs and standard CD-ROMs. These

WEB LINK 7-6

Picture CDs

For more information, visit scsite.com/ dc2008/ch7/weblink and then click Picture CDs.

FIGURE 7-23 HOW A PICTURE CD WORKS

Step 1: Drop off the film to be developed. Mark the Picture CD box on the film-processing envelope.

Step 2: When you pick up prints and negatives, a Picture CD contains digital images of each photograph.

Step 3: At home, print images from the Picture CD on your ink-jet or photo printer. At a store, print images from the Picture CD at a kiosk.

drives read at speeds of 48X or more and write at speeds of 40X or more. Manufacturers often list the write speed first, for example, as 40/48.

A **CD-RW** (*compact disc-rewritable*) is an erasable multisession disc you can write on multiple times. CD-RW overcomes the major disadvantage of CD-R because it allows users to write and rewrite data, instructions, and information on the CD-RW disc multiple times — instead of just once. Reliability of the disc tends to drop, however, with each successive rewrite.

To write on a CD-RW disc, you must have CD-RW software and a **CD-RW drive**. These drives have write speeds of 52X or more, rewrite speeds of 24X or more, and read speeds of 52X or more. Manufacturers state the speeds in this order; that is, write speed, rewrite speed, and read speed is stated as 52/24/52. Most CD-RW drives can read audio CDs, CD-ROMs, CD-Rs, and CD-RWs.

Many personal computers today include a CD-RW drive as a standard feature so users can burn their own discs. The process of writing on an optical disc is called *burning*. Some operating systems, such as Windows Vista, include the capability of burning discs.

Using a CD-RW disc, users easily back up large files from a hard disk. Another popular use of CD-RW and CD-R discs is to create audio CDs. For example, users can record their own music and save it on a CD, purchase and download MP3 songs from the Web, or rearrange tracks on a purchased music CD. The process of copying audio and/or video data from a purchased disc and saving it on digital media is called *ripping*. Read Ethics & Issues 7-1 for a related discussion.

FAQ 7-5

Is it legal to copy songs or movies to a disc or other media?

It is legal to copy songs or movies from a disc that you obtained legally, if you use the copied music or movie for your own personal use. If you share the copy with a friend, however, you are violating copyright law. It is legal to download copyrighted material if the copyright holder has granted permission to do so. In most cases, you pay a fee. For more information, visit scsite.com/dc2008/ch7/faq and then click Copying Songs and Movies.

VIDEO CDS A *video CD (VCD)* is a CD format that stores video on a CD-R that can be played in CD or DVD drives, many DVD players, and some game consoles. Standard VCDs can hold from 74 to 80 minutes of video. Although the quality is not as high as DVD, some users opt to burn video CDs with their existing CD-R drive because it saves the expense of purchasing a DVD burner.

FAQ 7-6

How do I share my digital videos online?

Web sites such as Yahoo! Video and YouTube allow you to share videos online. Before sharing a video, you must first create an account on the site and agree to the terms of service. Once your account is created, you may upload your video and specify characteristics such as its title, description, and category. Do not post any videos that are protected by copyright laws. For more information, visit scsite.com/dc2008/ch7/faq and then click Video Sharing.

ETHICS & ISSUES 7-1

Does Music and Movie Downloading Harm CD and DVD Sales?

With millions of songs and movies both legally and illegally available on the Internet, the entertainment industry claims that sharing music is harming CD and DVD sales, which results in less money in the artists' and studios' pockets. When Apple Computer announced that the company would sell movies through its iTunes online service, large retailer chains complained that their DVD movie sales would suffer. Both retailers and the entertainment companies make far more money when someone purchases a CD or DVD instead of buying the media online. A study by researchers showed that the availability and sharing of recent CD releases did not have an effect on the sales of the CDs. While music publishing companies have seen a modest decline in sales since the advent of illegal music sharing, they have released significantly fewer titles, and some claim that the quality of music has declined. Also, CD and DVD sales may have been exceptionally high in the 1990s as people replaced older media, such as cassette tapes and VHS tapes, with the newer CD and DVD formats. Do readily available online music and movies harm CD and DVD sales? Why? Are there any situations in which the availability can increase sales? How? Are the entertainment industry and retail chain complaints justified? Why?

WEB LINK 7-7

CD-Rs and CD-RWs

For more information, visit scsite.com/ dc2008/ch7/weblink and then click CD-Rs and CD-RWs.

DVD-ROMs, BD-ROMs, and HD DVD-ROMs

A **DVD-ROM** (*digital versatile disc-read-only memory* or *digital video disc-read-only memory*) is a high-capacity optical disc on which users can read but not write or erase. Manufacturers write the contents of DVD-ROMs and distribute them to consumers. DVD-ROMs store movies, music, music videos, huge databases, and complex software (Figure 7-24).

The storage capacity of a DVD-ROM is more than enough to hold a telephone book containing every resident in the United States. Not only is the storage capacity of a DVD-ROM greater than that of a CD, a DVD-ROM's quality also far surpasses that of CDs because images are stored at higher resolution.

To read a DVD-ROM, you must have a **DVD-ROM drive** or DVD player. Most DVD-ROM drives also can read audio CDs, CD-ROMs, CD-Rs, and CD-RWs. DVD-ROM drives can read DVDs at speeds of 16X or more and CDs at speeds of 52X or more.

Although the size and shape of a CD-ROM and DVD-ROM are similar, a DVD-ROM stores data, instructions, and information in a slightly different manner and thus achieves a higher storage capacity. Widely used DVD-ROMs are capable of storing 4.7 GB to 17 GB, depending on the storage techniques used. The first storage technique involves making the disc denser by packing the pits closer together. The second involves using two layers of pits. For this technique to work, the lower layer of pits is semitransparent so the laser can read through it to the upper layer. This technique doubles the capacity of the disc. Finally, some DVD-ROMs are double-sided.

Two newer, more expensive competing DVD formats are Blu-ray and HD DVD, both of which are higher capacity and better quality than standard DVDs. A *Blu-ray Disc-ROM (BD-ROM)* has storage capacities of 100 GB, with expectations of exceeding 200 GB in the future. Blu-ray drives and players are backward compatible with DVD and CD formats. Some game consoles include a Blu-ray drive. The *HD DVD-ROM disc*, which stands for high-density DVD-ROM, has storage capacities up to 60 GB with future projections of 90 GB capacities. HD DVD drives and players are backward compatible with DVD formats. Some game consoles work with an HD DVD drive. Figure 7-25 compares the current storage capacities of DVD-ROM, BD-ROM, and HD DVD-ROM media. Read Ethics & Issues 7-2 for a related discussion.

A mini-DVD that has grown in popularity is the UMD, which works specifically with the PlayStation Portable handheld game console. The *UMD* (Universal Media Disc), which has a diameter of about 2.4 inches, can store up to 1.8 GB of games, movies, or music (Figure 7-26).

FAQ 7-7

What is a DVD/CD-RW drive?

It is a combination drive that reads DVD and CD media; it also writes on CD-RW media. This drive allows you to watch a DVD or burn a CD. For more information, visit scsite.com/dc2008/ch7/faq and then click DVD/CD-RW Drives.

DVD, BD, AND HD DVD STORAGE CAPACITIES

Sides	Layers	DVD-ROM	BD-ROM	HD DVD-ROM
1	1	4.7 GB	25 GB	15 GB
1	2	8.5 GB	50 GB	30 GB
2	1	9.4 GB	50 GB	30 GB
2	2	17 GB	100 GB	60 GB

FIGURE 7-25   Storage capacities of DVDs, BDs, and HD DVDs.

FIGURE 7-24   A DVD-ROM is a high-capacity optical disc.

FIGURE 7-26
This UMD contains the game, Gran Turismo.

ETHICS & ISSUES 7-2

Is the Blu-ray and HD DVD Competition Good for Consumers?

In the early 1980s, a battle raged over the VHS and Betamax video tape formats. Eventually, the VHS format won over the hearts and dollars of consumers despite experts' claims of the superiority of the Betamax format, and the Betamax format remains a footnote in the history of consumer electronics. Today, a similar rivalry exists between the Blu-ray and HD DVD formats as two competing groups of consumer electronic corporate giants vie to get their players and discs in your home.

Some differences exist between the standards. While a Blu-ray Disc (BD) can hold more data than an HD DVD disc, the HD DVD players are much less expensive and still include enough capacity to hold a high-definition movie. HD DVD discs are less expensive to make, though more movie studios have announced support for Blu-ray. Some consumer advocates claim that the competition between the standards will benefit consumers as each side tries to win through lower prices and more features. Others claim that two standards hurt consumers because some movie studios, computer companies, and software providers will choose to support only one format. If this happens, consumers may choose to purchase both types of devices or, in frustration, not purchase a player at all. Some predict that high-definition DVD players eventually will support both formats. Is the availability of two high-definition DVD formats good for consumers? Why or why not? Do you think that prices will go up if one format eventually wins over the other? Why or why not? With limited shelf space, how should video rental and retail stores cope with keeping both formats for a movie in stock?

Recordable and Rewritable DVDs

Many types of recordable and rewritable DVD formats are available. *DVD-R* and *DVD+R* are competing DVD-recordable formats, each with up to 4.7 GB storage capacity. Similarly, *BD-R* and *HD DVD-R* are competing high-capacity DVD-recordable formats. Each of these formats allows users to write on the disc once and read (play) it many times. In concept, DVD-R, DVD+R, BD-R, and HD DVD-R are similar to CD-R.

Instead of recordable DVDs, however, most users work with rewritable DVDs because these discs can be written on multiple times and also erased. Three competing rewritable DVD formats, each with storage capacities up to 4.7 GB per side are **DVD-RW**, **DVD+RW**, and **DVD+RAM**. Likewise, *BD-RE* and *HD DVD-RW* are competing high-capacity rewritable DVD formats. These rewritable DVDs are similar in concept to CD-RW. To write on these discs, you must have a compatible drive or recorder. Rewritable drives usually can read a variety of DVD and CD media. Before investing in equipment, check to be sure it is compatible with the media on which you intend to record.

As the cost of DVD technologies becomes more reasonable, many industry professionals expect that DVD eventually will replace all CD media.

FAQ 7-8

Are DVD drives and recorders compatible with both the + and – DVD formats?

When you purchase recordable or rewritable DVDs, you will notice that they are available in either the + (plus) or – (minus) format. You first should check your DVD drive or recorder to identify the DVD formats it will accept. Many new DVD drives and recorders accept both + and – formats, while some still accept only one or the other. For more information, visit scsite.com/dc2008/ch7/faq and then click DVD Formats.

WEB LINK 7-8

Blu-ray and HD DVD

For more information, visit scsite.com/dc2008/ch7/weblink and then click Blu-ray and HD DVD.

Test your knowledge of pages 366 through 373 in Quiz Yourself 7-2.

QUIZ YOURSELF 7-2

Instructions: Find the true statement below. Then, rewrite the remaining false statements so they are true.

1. A CD-RW is a type of optical disc on which users can read but not write (record) or erase.

2. A DVD-RAM is a single-session disc that stores digital versions of film using a jpg file format.

3. DVDs have the same storage capacities as CDs.

4. Optical discs are written and read by mirrors.

5. Single session means you can write on part of the disc at one time and another part at a later time.

6. Three competing rewritable DVD formats are DVD-RW, DVD+RW, and DVD+RAM.

Quiz Yourself Online: To further check your knowledge of optical discs and various optical disc formats, visit scsite.com/dc2008/ch7/quiz and then click Objectives 5 – 6.

TAPE

One of the first storage media used with mainframe computers was tape. **Tape** is a magnetically coated ribbon of plastic capable of storing large amounts of data and information at a low cost. Tape no longer is used as a primary method of storage. Instead, business users utilize tape most often for long-term storage and backup.

Comparable to a tape recorder, a **tape drive** reads and writes data and information on a tape. Although older computers used reel-to-reel tape drives, today's tape drives use tape cartridges. A *tape cartridge* is a small, rectangular, plastic housing for tape (Figure 7-27). Tape cartridges that contain quarter-inch-wide tape are slightly larger than audiocassette tapes. Business users sometimes back up personal computer hard disks to tape, often using an external tape drive. On larger computers, tape cartridges are mounted in a separate cabinet called a *tape library*. Transfer rates of tape drives range from 1.25 MBps to 6 MBps.

Tape storage requires *sequential access*, which refers to reading or writing data consecutively. As with a music tape, you must forward or rewind the tape to a specific point to access a specific piece of data. For example, to access item W requires passing through points A through V sequentially.

Hard disks, CDs, and DVDs all use direct access. *Direct access*, also called *random access*, means that the device can locate a particular data item or file immediately, without having to move consecutively through items stored in front of the desired data item or file. When writing or reading specific data, direct access is much faster than sequential access.

FIGURE 7-27   A tape drive and a tape cartridge.

PC CARDS AND EXPRESSCARD MODULES

As discussed in Chapter 4, a **PC Card** is a thin, credit-card-sized removable flash memory device that fits into a PC Card slot. An **ExpressCard module** is a removable device, smaller than a PC Card, that fits in an ExpressCard slot. PC Cards and ExpressCard modules can be used to add memory, storage, communications, multimedia, and security capabilities to a computer. Both developed by the PCMCIA (Personal Computer Memory Card International Association), PC Cards and ExpressCard modules commonly are used in notebook computers.

PC Cards are about 86 mm long and 54 mm wide. ExpressCard modules, by contrast, are either rectangular at 75 mm long and 34 mm wide or L-shaped with a width of 54 mm (Figure 7-28).

FIGURE 7-28   Comparison of PC Card and ExpressCard module form factors.

MINIATURE MOBILE STORAGE MEDIA

Miniature mobile storage media allow mobile users easily to transport digital images, music, or documents to and from computers and other devices (Figure 7-29). Many desktop computers, notebook computers, Tablet PCs, PDAs, smart phones, digital cameras, and portable media players have built-in slots or ports to read from and write on miniature mobile storage media. For computers or devices without built-in slots, users insert the media in separate peripherals such as a card reader/writer, which typically plugs in a USB port. The following sections discuss the widely used miniature storage media: flash memory cards, USB flash drives, and smart cards.

FIGURE 7-29 Many types of computers and devices use miniature mobile storage media.

Flash Memory Cards

Previously, this chapter discussed miniature hard disks (magnetic media) and mini discs such as the UMD (optical media). Flash memory cards, by contrast, are a type of *solid-state media*, which means they consist entirely of electronic components and contain no moving parts. Common types of flash memory cards include *CompactFlash* (*CF*), *Secure Digital* (*SD*), *xD Picture Card*, and *Memory Stick*. The table in Figure 7-30 compares storage capacities and uses of these media.

Depending on the device, manufacturers claim miniature mobile storage media can last from 10 to 100 years. Transfer rates range from about 1 MBps to 10 MBps or more, depending on the device. Flash memory cards are quite expensive compared to other storage media.

For example, the cost of a 4 GB CompactFlash card is the same as a 500 GB SATA hard disk.

To view, edit, or print images and information stored on miniature mobile storage media, you transfer the contents to your desktop computer or other device. Some printers have slots to read flash memory cards. If your computer or printer does not have a built-in slot, you can purchase a *card reader/writer*, which is a device that reads and writes data, instructions, and information stored on flash memory cards. Card reader/writers usually connect to the USB port or FireWire port on the system unit. The type of card you have will determine the type of card reader/writer needed. Figure 7-31 shows how one type of flash memory card works with a card reader/writer.

VARIOUS FLASH MEMORY CARDS

Media Name	Storage Capacity	Use
CompactFlash	64 MB to 16 GB	Digital cameras, PDAs, smart phones, photo printers, portable media players, notebook computers, desktop computers
Secure Digital	64 MB to 4 GB	Digital cameras, digital video cameras, PDAs, smart phones, photo printers, portable media players
xD Picture Card	64 MB to 2 GB	Digital cameras, photo printers
Memory Stick	256 MB to 4 GB	Digital cameras, digital video cameras, PDAs, photo printers, smart phones, handheld game consoles, notebook computers
Memory Stick PRO Duo	128 MB to 4 GB	Digital cameras, smart phones, handheld game consoles

FIGURE 7-30 A variety of flash memory cards.

FIGURE 7-31 HOW ONE TYPE OF FLASH MEMORY CARD WORKS

Step 1:
When you insert a memory card in a card reader/writer or card slot, the memory card's metallic conductors make contact with connectors in the card reader/writer or card slot, allowing the transfer of pictures and other items between the card and the reading/writing device.

metallic conductors

write-protect switch

Step 4:
Some memory cards contain write-protect switches, which prevent users from accidentally erasing pictures and other items stored on the flash memory chips.

controller chip

flash memory chips

card reader/writer

memory card

notch

Step 2:
A notch on the side of the memory card prevents the card from accidentally slipping out of the card reader/writer or card slot.

registers

Step 3:
Flash memory chips store pictures and other types of data and information. When requested, the controller transfers items stored on the flash memory chips to the metallic conductors, using registers for temporary storage, as needed.

WEB LINK 7-9

Flash Memory Cards
For more information, visit scsite.com/dc2008/ch7/weblink and then click Flash Memory Cards.

FAQ 7-7

Why do drive letters for removable media sometimes change?
When you connect a removable storage device, such as a USB flash drive or pocket hard drive, to your computer, Windows assigns the device the next available drive letter. If the last drive letter used on your computer is D, your removable storage device will be assigned the letter E. Because the number of drives in a computer will vary from computer to computer, the next available drive letter also will vary. For more information, visit scsite.com/dc2008/ch7/faq and then click Drive Letters.

USB Flash Drives

A **USB flash drive**, sometimes called a *pen drive* or *thumb drive*, is a flash memory storage device that plugs in a USB port on a computer or mobile device (Figure 7-32). USB flash drives are convenient for mobile users because they are small and lightweight enough to be transported on a keychain or in a pocket. With a USB flash drive, users easily transfer documents, pictures, music, and videos from one computer to another. Current USB flash drives have data transfer rates of about 12 MBps and storage capacities ranging from 32 MB to 64 GB, with the latter being extremely expensive.

USB flash drives have become the mobile user's primary portable storage device, making the floppy disk nearly obsolete because they have much greater storage capacities and are much more convenient to carry. A special type of USB flash drive, called a *U3 smart drive*, offers even more convenience because it includes pre-installed software accessed through a Windows-type interface.

The drive designation of a USB flash drive usually follows alphabetically after all other disks. For example, if the computer has one internal hard disk (drive C) and a DVD drive (drive D) and no other disk drives, then the USB flash drive probably will be drive E.

FIGURE 7-32 A USB flash drive.

WEB LINK 7-10

USB Flash Drives
For more information, visit scsite.com/dc2008/ch7/weblink and then click USB Flash Drives.

Smart Cards

A **smart card**, which is similar in size to a credit card or ATM card, stores data on a thin microprocessor embedded in the card. Smart cards contain a processor and have input, process, output, and storage capabilities. When you insert the smart card in a specialized card reader, the information on the smart card is read and, if necessary, updated (Figure 7-33).

Uses of smart cards include storing medical records, vaccination data, and other health-care and identification information; tracking information such as employee attendance or customer purchases; storing a prepaid amount of money, such as for student purchases on campus; and authenticating users such as for Internet purchases or building access. In addition, smart cards can double as an ID card. Read Ethics & Issues 7-3 for a related discussion.

FAQ 7-10

Are some credit cards smart cards?

Yes. More than 200 million smart Visa cards, which contain a microchip filled with their personal information, currently are in use around the world. Credit card smart cards offer the consumer the convenience of using the card to make purchases in stores and online. For more information, visit scsite.com/dc2008/ch7/faq and then click Credit Card Smart Cards.

ETHICS & ISSUES 7-3

Should the World Become a Cashless Society?

Do you toss your loose change in a jar with the hopes of making a special purchase with the savings someday? This habit may become futile if the world goes cashless. Some forecasters say that the world is moving toward a cashless society. One form of payment that could end the need for cash is the smart card, which can store a dollar amount on a thin microprocessor and update the amount whenever a transaction is made. Advocates claim that smart cards would eliminate muggings and robberies, make it difficult to purchase illegal goods, and reduce taxes by identifying tax cheats. Also, payment using biometrics, such as fingerprints, is becoming more common. Several high-profile security breaches at credit reporting and credit card companies, however, have heightened concerns over privacy. In a recent survey, most Americans said that they would not use a smart card even if privacy was guaranteed. Another survey shows that most Americans believe that fingerprints are a trustworthy form of identification. A cash purchase usually is anonymous. Yet, a smart card purchase preserves a record of the transaction that could become available to other merchants, advertisers, government agencies, or hackers. Considering the advantages and disadvantages, should the world become a cashless society? Why or why not? Would you be comfortable using a smart card or fingerprint instead of cash for all transactions? Why?

WEB LINK 7-11

Smart Cards

For more information, visit scsite.com/ dc2008/ch7/weblink and then click Smart Cards.

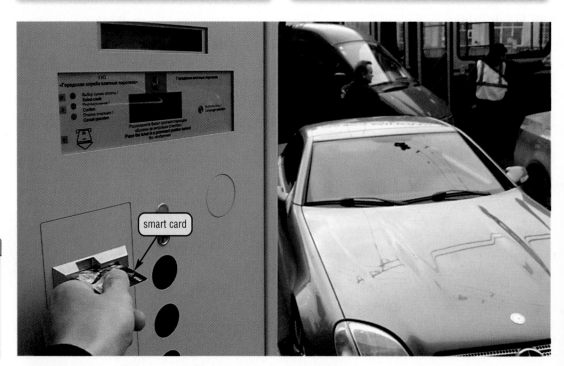

smart card

FIGURE 7-33 Motorists use their smart cards to pay parking fees.

MICROFILM AND MICROFICHE

Microfilm and microfiche store microscopic images of documents on roll or sheet film. **Microfilm** is a 100- to 215-foot roll of film. **Microfiche** is a small sheet of film, usually about 4 × 6 inches. A *computer output microfilm recorder* is the device that records the images on the film. The stored images are so small that you can read them only with a microfilm or microfiche reader (Figure 7-34).

Applications of microfilm and microfiche are widespread. Libraries use these media to store back issues of newspapers, magazines, and genealogy records. Some large organizations use microfilm and microfiche to archive inactive files. Some banks use them to store transactions and canceled checks. The U.S. Army uses them to store personnel records.

The use of microfilm and microfiche provides a number of advantages. They greatly reduce the amount of paper firms must handle. They are inexpensive and have the longest life of any storage media (Figure 7-35).

ENTERPRISE STORAGE

A large business, commonly referred to as an enterprise, has hundreds or thousands of employees in offices across the country or around the world. Enterprises use computers and computer networks to manage and store huge volumes of data and information about customers, suppliers, and employees (Figure 7-36).

To meet their large-scale needs, enterprises use special hardware geared for heavy use, maximum availability, and maximum efficiency. One or more servers on the network have the sole purpose of providing storage to connected users. For high-speed storage access, entire networks are dedicated exclusively to connecting devices that provide storage to other servers. In an enterprise, some storage systems can provide more than 185 terabytes (trillion bytes) of storage capacity. CD-ROM servers and DVD-ROM servers hold hundreds of CD-ROMs or DVD-ROMs.

An enterprise's storage needs usually grow daily. Thus, the storage solutions an enterprise chooses must be able to store its data and information requirements today and tomorrow.

FIGURE 7-34   Images on microfilm can be read only with a microfilm reader.

MEDIA LIFE EXPECTANCIES* (when using high-quality media)

Media Type	Guaranteed Life Expectancy	Potential Life Expectancy
Magnetic disks	3 to 5 years	20 to 30 years
Optical discs	5 to 10 years	50 to 100 years
Microfilm	100 years	500 years

* according to manufacturers of the media

FIGURE 7-35   Microfilm is the medium with the longest life.

FIGURE 7-36   An enterprise uses computers and high-capacity storage devices.

PUTTING IT ALL TOGETHER

Many factors influence the type of storage devices you should use: the amount of data, instructions, and information to be stored; the hardware and software in use; and the desired cost. The table in Figure 7-37 outlines several suggested storage devices for various types of computer users.

CATEGORIES OF USERS

User	Typical Storage Devices
HOME	• 250 GB hard disk • Online storage • CD or DVD drive • Card reader/writer • USB flash drive
SMALL OFFICE/ HOME OFFICE	• 500 GB hard disk • Online storage • CD or DVD drive • External hard disk for backup • USB flash drive
MOBILE	• 100 GB hard disk • Online storage • CD or DVD drive • Card reader/writer • Portable hard disk for backup • USB flash drive
POWER	• 1.5 TB hard disk • Online storage • CD or DVD drive • Portable hard disk for backup • USB flash drive

LARGE BUSINESS	• Desktop Computer
	  - 500 GB hard disk
	  - CD or DVD drive
	  - Smart card reader
	  - Tape drive
	  - USB flash drive
	• Server or Mainframe
	  - Network storage server
	  - 40 TB hard disk system
	  - CD-ROM or DVD-ROM server
	  - Microfilm or microfiche

FIGURE 7-37   Recommended storage devices for various users.

st your knowledge of pages 374 through 380 in Quiz Yourself 7-3.

QUIZ YOURSELF 7-3

Instructions: Find the true statement below. Then, rewrite the remaining false statements so they are true.

1. A smart card stores data on a thin magnetic stripe embedded in the card.

2. A USB flash drive is a flash memory storage device that plugs in a parallel port on a computer or mobile device.

3. Flash memory cards are a type of magnetic media, which means they consist entirely of electronic components and contain no moving parts.

4. Microfilm and microfiche have the shortest life of any storage media.

5. Tape storage requires direct access, which refers to reading or writing data consecutively.

6. An ExpressCard module is a removable smart card device that fits in an ExpressCard slot.

Quiz Yourself Online: To further check your knowledge of tape, PC Cards and ExpressCard modules, miniature mobile storage media, and microfilm and microfiche, visit scsite.com/dc2008/ch7/quiz and then click Objectives 7 – 9.

HAPTER SUMMARY

orage holds data, instructions, and formation, which includes pictures, usic, and videos, for future use. Users pend on storage devices to provide cess to their storage media for years and cades to come. Read Ethics & Issues 7-4 r a discussion about the future of storage. This chapter identified and discussed rious storage media and storage devices. orage media covered included internal rd disks, external and removable hard sks, floppy disks, CD-ROMs, recordable Ds, rewritable CDs, DVD-ROMs, Blu-ray scs (BDs), HD DVD discs, recordable VDs, rewritable DVDs, tape, PC Cards and xpressCard modules, flash memory cards, SB flash drives, smart cards, and microfilm d microfiche.

ETHICS & ISSUES 7-4

Who Should Be Looking at Your Medical Records?

A medical transcriber based in a foreign country and hired by a U.S. medical center threatened to post private medical records to the Internet if she was not paid more. With the widespread use of computers and an explosion in data storage capacity around the world, private information, such as medical records, requires increased diligence by companies, governments, and individuals to maintain this privacy. The government would like most Americans' health care records available in privacy-protected electronic format by 2014. Although these records will be stored by a corporation or the government, individuals will have complete control, or ownership, of these electronic records. Updates to the Health Insurance Portability and Accountability Act (HIPAA) effective in 2003 set rigorous standards for medical record privacy. The law, however, still leaves much of your medical information at risk. The law does not cover financial records, education records, or employment records — each of which may contain medical information about you. Your medical information also may be examined by insurance companies, government agencies, the Medical Information Bureau (MIB), employers, and the courts. You also inadvertently may pass on medical information to direct marketers when you participate in informal health screenings or surveys. Some people have found that discussing medical conditions via Internet chat rooms or newsgroups has resulted in unwanted attention, and they later regret the disclosures. Proponents of greater electronic access to medical records claim that more access means that physicians can be better prepared when they see patients, physicians will make fewer errors, and insurance companies can better root out fraud. Should more limits be placed on what other people can do with your medical information? Why or why not? What are the advantages of increased access to medical records? What are the disadvantages?

CAREER CORNER

Computer Technician

The demand for computer technicians is growing in every organization and industry. For many, this is the entry point for a career in the computer/information technology field. The responsibilities of a *computer technician*, also called a computer service technician, include a variety of duties. Most companies that employ someone with this title expect the technician to have basic across-the-board knowledge of concepts in the computer electronics field. Some of the tasks are hardware repair and installation; software installation, upgrade, and configuration; and troubleshooting client and/or server problems. Because the computer field is changing rapidly, technicians must work to remain abreast of current technology and become aware of future developments. Computer technicians generally work with a variety of users, which requires expert people skills, especially the ability to work with groups of nontechnical users.

Most entry-level computer technicians possess the *A+ certification*. This certification attests that a computer technician has demonstrated knowledge of core hardware and operating system technology including installation, configuration, diagnosing, preventive maintenance and basic networking that meets industry standards and has at least six months of experience in the field. The Electronics Technicians Association also provides a Computer Service Technician (CST) certification program.

Because this is an entry-level position, the pay scale is not as high as other more demanding and skilled positions. Individuals can expect an average annual starting salary of around $36,000 to $45,000. Companies pay more for computer technicians with experience and certification. For more information, visit scsite.com/dc2008/ch7/careers and then click Computer Technician.

High-Tech Talk

DISK FORMATTING AND FILE SYSTEMS

Formatting a disk can be compared to starting a library. Before any books can be put in place, you must install the bookshelves and a catalog system. Similarly, a disk must have a file system set up to make it ready to receive data. This is true of many different storage media — including hard disks, removable hard disks, and CDs and DVDs — all of which must be formatted, to allow a way to organize and find files saved on the disk.

This discussion focuses on the formatting process required to take a hard disk from its newly manufactured state to a fully functional storage medium. Three main steps are involved in the process of formatting a hard disk: (1) low-level (physical) formatting, (2) partitioning, and (3) high-level (logical) formatting.

A hard disk must be formatted physically before it can be formatted logically. The hard disk manufacturer usually performs a hard disk's physical formatting, or *low-level formatting*. The hard disk manufacturer physically formats a hard disk by writing a pattern of 1s and 0s on the surface of the disk. The 1s and 0s act as small electronic markers, which divide the hard disk platter into its basic physical elements: tracks, sectors, and cylinders.

These elements define the way data is written on and read from the disk physically. As the read/write head moves over the spinning disks, it reads the electronic markers that define the tracks, sectors, and cylinders to determine where it is in relation to the data on the disk's surface.

Once a hard disk has been formatted physically, it can be partitioned. *Partitioning* is the process of dividing the hard disk into regions called partitions. Each partition occupies a group of adjacent cylinders. Partitioning allows you to organize a hard disk into segments and lets you run multiple operating systems on a single computer. You also can keep the entire hard disk as one partition. After a disk partition has been formatted, it is referred to as a *volume*.

After a hard disk has been formatted physically and partitioned, it must be formatted logically. Logical formatting, known as *high-level formatting*, places a file system on the disk. A *file system* allows an operating system to use the space available on a hard disk to store and retrieve files. The operating system uses the file system to store information about the disk's directory, or folder, structure.

The file system also defines the size of the clusters used to store data on the hard disk. A cluster, or *block*, is made up of two or more sectors on a single track on a hard disk. Even if a file has a size of 1 byte, a cluster as large as 64 KB might be used to store the file on large drives. The number of sectors and tracks and, therefore, the number of clusters that a drive can create on a disk's surface determine the capacity of the disk.

While creating the file system during logical formatting, the drive creates a special table in the disk's first sector, sector 0. This table stores entries that the operating system uses to locate files on a disk. Each entry in the table takes up a certain number of bits, which is why file systems often are referred to as 12-bit, 16-bit, or 32-bit. The content of each entry consists of a whole number, which identifies one or more clusters where the file is stored.

Depending on the operating system used to format the disk, the file system can be one of several types, as shown in the table in Figure 7-38. Whatever file system is used, the file system is the interface between the operating system and drives. For more information, visit scsite.com/dc2008/ch7/tech and then click Disk Formatting.

File System	Description	Key Features
FAT (also called FAT12 and FAT16)	The standard file system for DOS and Windows. Because of its widespread use, FAT also is accessible by most other operating systems.	• FAT12 is used for floppy disk drives and very small hard disks (up to 16 MB) • FAT16 is used for small to medium-sized hard disk volumes (up to 2 GB)
VFAT (Virtual FAT)	A newer protected-mode version of the FAT file system, introduced with Windows 95.	• Supports long file names up to 255 characters • Faster than FAT because the computer can read files at least 32 bits at a time
FAT32	A 32-bit version of FAT, introduced with Windows 95.	• Same key features as VFAT • Used for medium-sized to large hard disk volumes (up to 2 terabytes)
NTFS (NT File System)	The 32-bit file system currently used for Windows NT, Windows 2000, Windows XP, and Windows Vista.	• 32- or 64-bit entries in file system table • Fully recoverable file system, designed to restore consistency after a system crash • Used for medium-sized to very large hard disk volumes (up to 256 terabytes)
WinFS (Windows Future Storage)	Originally planned as a file storage subsystem meant to be used with Windows XP and Windows Vista, technologies from this file storage subsystem instead will be used in future versions of other Microsoft products, such as ADO.NET and Microsoft SQL Server.	• Uses database technology; allows users to query for data items • Works in conjunction with the NTFS file system

FIGURE 7-38   Comparison of various file systems.

Companies on the Cutting Edge

SEAGATE TECHNOLOGY
INFORMATION STORAGE SUPPLIER

Consumers understand the need to back up their data, but fewer than 25 percent of computer users back up their data on a weekly basis. Hard-disk manufacturer *Seagate* has been persuading people to save copies of their important documents so they will suffer less data loss in the event of a fire or natural disaster.

Seagate is a leading manufacturer of hard disks and storage solutions for desktop computers, high-performance servers, and consumer electronics, including digital video recorders and game consoles. *Forbes Magazine* named Seagate the "2006 Company of the Year" for operational excellence, market leadership, innovation, and efficiency.

Seagate completed its acquisition of rival Maxtor Corporation in 2006. For more information, visit scsite.com/dc2008/ch7/companies and then click Seagate.

SANDISK CORPORATION
WORLD'S LARGEST FLASH MEMORY CARD SUPPLIER

The next time you buy milk at the grocery store or shampoo at the drug store, you might want to purchase a flash memory card for your digital camera, too. *SanDisk Corporation* products can be found in more than 100,000 retail stores across the United States. Best Buy teamed with SanDisk and RealNetworks' Rhapsody in 2006 to launch the Best Buy Digital Music Store.

With retail sales of flash memory cards soaring, SanDisk executives believe consumers buy multiple flash memory cards to store their digital photographs in much the same manner as they formerly stored film negatives in shoe boxes. They also prefer to take a separate flash memory card to digital photo processing centers, which produce high-quality prints.

SanDisk is the only company with the rights to manufacture and sell every flash card format. For more information, visit scsite.com/dc2008/ch7/companies and then click SanDisk.

Technology Trailblazers

AL SHUGART
STORAGE EXPERT

Al Shugart enjoyed fixing broken items and developing new technology. The day after receiving his bachelor's degree in 1951, he went to work at IBM to repair broken machines. IBM then promoted him to supervisor of the product development team that developed the first removable rigid read/write disk drive.

He left IBM in 1969 and went to work as vice president of product development for Memorex. In 1973, he started Shugart Associates, a pioneer in the manufacture of floppy disks. Six years later, he and some associates founded Seagate Technology, Inc., which is a leader in designing and manufacturing storage products.

He served as president and CEO of Al Shugart International, a venture capital firm in California, until his death in 2006. For more information, visit scsite.com/dc2008/ch7/people and then click Al Shugart.

MARK DEAN
IBM INVENTOR

The next generation of IBM's hardware and software might be the work of *Mark Dean*. As vice president of IBM's Almaden Research Center lab in California, Dean is responsible for developing innovative products.

His designs are used in more than 40 million personal computers manufactured each year. He has more than 40 patents or patents pending, including four of the original seven for the architecture of the original personal computer.

Dean joined IBM in 1979 after graduating at the top of his class at the University of Tennessee. Dean earned his Ph.D. degree at Stanford, and he headed a team at IBM that invented the first CMOS microprocessor to operate at 1 gigahertz (1,000 MHz). For more information, visit scsite.com/dc2008/ch7/people and then click Mark Dean.

Chapter Review

The Chapter Review section summarizes the concepts presented in this chapter. To listen to the audio version of this Chapter Review, visit scsite.com/dc2008/ch7/review. To obtain help from other students regarding any subject in this chapter, visit scsite.com/dc2008/ch7/forum and post your thoughts or questions.

(1) How Are Storage Devices Different from Storage Medium? A **storage medium** is the physical material on which a computer keeps data, instructions, and information, which includes pictures, music, and videos. The number of bytes (characters) a storage medium can hold is its **capacity**. A **storage device** is the computer hardware that records and/or retrieves items to and from storage media. **Writing** is the process of transferring items from memory to a storage medium, and **reading** is the process of transferring these items from a storage medium into memory.

(2) What Are the Characteristics of Magnetic Disks? *Magnetic disks* use magnetic particles to store data, instructions, and information on a disk's surface. Before any data can be read from or written on a magnetic disk, the disk must be formatted. **Formatting** is the process of dividing the disk into *tracks* and *sectors*. Two types of magnetic disks are hard disks and floppy disks.

(3) What Are the Characteristics of a Hard Disk? A **hard disk**, also called a *hard disk drive* or hard drive, is a storage device that contains one or more inflexible, circular platters that store data, instructions, and information. A *platter* is made of aluminum, glass, or ceramic and is coated with a material that allows items to be recorded magnetically on its surface. Each platter has two read/write heads, one for each side. The location of a *read/write head* often is referred to by its *cylinder,* which is the vertical section of a track that passes through all platters. While the computer is running, the platters rotate at 5,400 to 15,000 *revolutions per minute* (*rpm*), which allows nearly instant access to all tracks and sectors on the platters. The spinning creates a cushion of air between the platters and the read/write heads. A *head crash* occurs when a read/write head touches the surface of a platter, usually resulting in a loss of data. A **backup** is a duplicate of a file, program, or disk placed on a separate storage medium that you can use in case the original is lost, damaged, or destroyed.

(4) What Are the Various Types of Miniature, External, and Removable Hard Disks? Many mobile devices include miniature hard disks. A type of miniature hard disk called a **pocket hard drive** is a self-contained unit that you insert in or remove from a slot in a device or computer or plug in a USB port on a computer. Miniature hard disks have storage capacities that range from 4 GB to 160 GB. An **external hard disk** is a separate free-standing hard disk that connects with a cable to a USB or FireWire port. External hard disks have storage capacities up to 750 GB. A **removable hard disk** can be inserted or removed from a built-in or external drive. Removable hard disks have storage capacities up to 500 GB.

connect Visit scsite.com/dc2008/ch7/quiz or click the Quiz Yourself button. Click Objectives 1 – 4.

(5) What Are the Characteristics of Optical Discs? An *optical disc* is a type of storage media that consists of a flat, round, portable disc made of metal, plastic, and lacquer that is written and read by a laser. Optical discs, which primarily store software, data, digital photographs, movies, and music, contain microscopic pits (indentations) and lands (flat areas) in their middle layer. Optical discs commonly store items in a single track that spirals from the center of the disc to its edge. Like a hard disk, the single track is divided into evenly sized sectors. Common optical discs used today are CD-ROM, CD-R, CD-RW, DVD-ROM, BD-ROM, HD DVD-ROM, UMD, DVD-R, DVD+R, BD-R, HD DVD-R, DVD-RW, DVD+RW, DVD+RAM, BD-RE, and HD DVD-RW.

Chapter Review

6 **How Are CD-ROMs, Recordable CDs, Rewritable CDs, DVD-ROMs, Recordable DVDs, and Rewritable DVDs Different?** A **CD-ROM**, or *compact disc read-only memory*, is a type of optical disc that uses laser technology to store items. A typical CD-ROM holds from 650 MB to 1 GB of data, instructions, and information. Users can read the contents of standard CD-ROMs but cannot erase or modify their contents. A **CD-R** (*compact disc-recordable*) is a *multisession* disc on which users can record their own items. Each part of a CD-R can be written on only one time, and the disc's contents cannot be erased. A **CD-RW** (*compact disc-rewritable*) is an erasable disc that can be written on multiple times. A **DVD-ROM** (*digital versatile disc-ROM* or *digital video disc-ROM*) is a high capacity optical disc that you can read but not write on or erase. Not only is the storage capacity of a DVD-ROM greater than that of a CD-ROM, a DVD-ROM's quality also far surpasses that of a CD-ROM. Two newer, competing DVD formats are *Blu-ray Disc* and *HD DVD*, both with higher capacity and better quality than standard DVDs. **DVD-RW**, **DVD+RW**, and **DVD+RAM** discs are a recordable version of DVD that allows users to erase and record multiple times.

connect Visit scsite.com/dc2008/ch7/quiz or click the Quiz Yourself button. Click Objectives 5 – 6.

7 **How Is Tape Used?** **Tape** is a magnetically coated ribbon of plastic capable of storing large amounts of data and information at a low cost. A **tape drive** reads and writes data and information on tape. Businesses sometimes back up personal computer hard disks on tape.

8 **What Are PC Cards, ExpressCard Modules, and Other Types of Miniature Mobile Storage Media?** A **PC Card** is a thin, credit-card-sized removable flash memory device that fits into a PC Card slot. An **ExpressCard module** is a removable device, smaller than a PC Card, that fits in an ExpressCard slot. Both PC Cards and ExpressCard modules can add memory, storage, communications, or other capabilities to a computer. Many desktop and notebook computers, Tablet PCs, PDAs, smart phones, digital cameras, and portable media players have built-in slots or ports for miniature mobile storage media. Common types of miniature mobile storage media include flash memory cards, USB flash drives, and smart cards. Common flash memory cards include *CompactFlash* (*CF*), *Secure Digital* (*SD*), *xD Picture Card*, and *Memory Stick*. A **USB flash drive** is a flash memory storage device that plugs in a port on a computer or mobile device. A **smart card**, which is similar in size to a credit or ATM card, stores data on a thin microprocessor embedded in the card.

9 **How Are Microfilm and Microfiche Used?** **Microfilm** is a 100- to 215-foot roll of film. **Microfiche** is a small sheet of film, usually about 4 × 6 inches. Libraries use microfilm and microfiche to store back issues of newspapers, magazines, and records; some large organizations use them to archive inactive files; some banks use them to store transactions and canceled checks; and the U.S. Army uses them to store personnel records.

connect Visit scsite.com/dc2008/ch7/quiz or click the Quiz Yourself button. Click Objectives 7 – 9.

Key Terms

You should know the Primary Terms and be familiar with the Secondary Terms. Use the list below to help focus your study. To further enhance your understanding of the Key Terms in this chapter, visit scsite.com/dc2008/ch7/terms. See an example of and a definition for each term, and access current and additional information about the term from the Web.

Primary Terms

(shown in bold-black characters in the chapter)

access time (357)
backup (361)
capacity (356)
CD-R (370)
CD-R drive (370)
CD-ROM (369)
CD-ROM drive (369)
CD-RW (371)
CD-RW drive (371)
DVD+RAM (373)
DVD+RW (373)
DVD-ROM (372)
DVD-ROM drive (372)
DVD-RW (373)
ExpressCard module (374)
external hard disk (363)
floppy disk (365)
floppy disk drive (365)
formatting (357)
hard disk (358)
microfiche (379)
microfilm (379)
online storage (364)
PC Card (374)
Picture CD (370)
pocket hard drive (362)
RAID (362)
reading (356)
removable hard disk (363)
smart card (378)
storage device (356)
storage medium (355)
tape (374)
tape drive (374)
USB flash drive (377)
writing (356)

Secondary Terms

(shown in italic characters in the chapter)

allocation unit (357)
BD-R (373)
BD-RE (373)
Blu-ray Disc-ROM (BD-ROM) (372)
burning (371)
card reader/writer (376)
CD recorder (370)
cluster (357)
compact disc read-only memory (369)
compact disc-recordable (370)
compact disc-rewritable (371)
CompactFlash (CF) (376)
computer output microfilm recorder (379)
cylinder (360)
density (362)
digital versatile disc-read-only memory (372)
digital video disc-read-only memory (372)
direct access (374)
disk cache (361)
disk controller (363)
diskette (365)
DVD+R (373)
DVD-R (373)
EIDE (Enhanced Integrated Drive Electronics) (364)
external floppy disk drive (365)
fixed disk (358)
form factor (360)
hard disk drive (358)
head crash (360)
HD DVD-R (373)
HD DVD-RW (373)
HD DVD-ROM disc (372)
jewel box (368)
KBps (357)
LightScribe technology (367)
longitudinal recording (358)
magnetic disks (357)
MBps (357)
Memory Stick (376)
mini discs (366)
multisession (370)
optical disc (366)
pen drive (377)
perpendicular recording (358)
platter (359)
portable (358)
random access (374)
read/write head (360)
revolutions per minute (rpm) (360)
ripping (371)
SATA (Serial Advanced Technology Attachment) (364)
SCSI (364)
secondary storage (355)
sectors (357)
Secure Digital (SD) (376)
sequential access (374)
single-session disc (369)
solid-state media (376)
storage (354)
tape cartridge (374)
tape library (374)
thumb drive (377)
track (357)
transfer rate (357)
U3 smart drive (377)
UMD (372)
video CD (VCD) (371)
xD Picture Card (376)

Checkpoint

Use the Checkpoint exercises to check your knowledge level of the chapter. The Beyond the Book exercises will help broaden your understanding of the concepts presented in this chapter. To complete the Checkpoint exercises interactively, visit scsite.com/dc2008/ch7/check.

Label the Figure

Identify the storage media.

a. flash memory card
b. internal hard disk
c. tape
d. CD or DVD
e. external hard disk
f. miniature hard disk
g. floppy disk
h. USB flash drive

1.

2.

3.

5.

7.

6.

4.

True/False

Mark T for True and F for False. (See page numbers in parentheses.)

_____ 1. Every computer stores system software and application software. (354)

_____ 2. A storage medium is the physical material on which a computer keeps data, instructions, and information. (355)

_____ 3. Reading is the process of transferring data, instructions, and information from memory to a storage medium. (356)

_____ 4. Formatting is the process of dividing the disk into clusters and cylinders. (357)

_____ 5. A cluster can hold data from only one file. (357)

_____ 6. A typical hard disk contains multiple platters. (360)

_____ 7. A removable hard disk is a separate, free-standing hard disk that connects with a cable to a port on the system unit. (363)

_____ 8. SCSI interfaces can support up to eight or fifteen peripheral devices. (364)

_____ 9. BD-R is an older low-capacity DVD-recordable format. (373)

_____ 10. BD-RE and HD DVD-RW are competing high-capacity rewritable DVD formats. (373)

_____ 11. Unlike PC Cards, ExpressCard modules can be used to add memory, storage, communications, multimedia, and security capabilities to a computer. (374)

_____ 12. A U3 smart drive includes preinstalled software accessed through a Windows-type interface. (377)

Checkpoint

 Multiple Choice Select the best answer. (See page numbers in parentheses.)

1. Examples of storage media include all of the following, except _____. (355)
   a. CDs and DVDs
   b. monitors and printers
   c. floppy disks and hard disks
   d. tape and PC Cards

2. _____ is the speed with which data, instructions, and information transfer to and from a device. (357)
   a. Formatting
   b. Access time
   c. Transfer rate
   d. Reading

3. A group of two or more integrated hard disks is called a _____. (362)
   a. backup
   b. disk cache
   c. RAID
   d. portable hard disk

4. A(n) _____ is a self-contained unit that you insert in and remove from a slot or USB port in a device or a computer. (362)
   a. RAID
   b. pocket hard drive
   c. online storage unit
   d. hard disk controller

5. Users store data and information on online storage to _____. (365)
   a. save time by storing large files instantaneously
   b. allow others to access files
   c. store offsite backups of data
   d. all of the above

6. Floppy disks are not as widely used as they were 15 years ago because _____. (365)
   a. they are expensive
   b. they are not portable
   c. of their low storage capacity
   d. they would bend too easily

7. A(n) _____ is a type of storage media that consists of a flat, round, portable disc made of metal, plastic, and lacquer that is written and read by a laser. (366)
   a. optical disc
   b. hard disk
   c. floppy disk
   d. pen drive

8. _____ technology works with specially coated optical discs to etch labels directly on the disc. (367)
   a. SCSI
   b. SATA
   c. LightSaber
   d. LightScribe

9. All of the following are guidelines for the proper care of optical discs except _____. (368)
   a. do not expose the disc to extreme temperatures
   b. do not stack discs
   c. do not hold a disc by its edges
   d. do not eat, smoke, or drink near a disc

10. The process of copying audio and/or video data from a purchased disc and saving it on digital media is called _____. (371)
    a. formatting
    b. ripping
    c. burning
    d. reading

11. _____ are competing high-capacity DVD-recordable formats. (373)
    a. DVD-R and DVD+R
    b. BD-R and HD DVD-R
    c. DVD-RAM and DVD-ROM
    d. BD-RE and BM-W

12. _____ storage requires sequential access. (374)
    a. Hard disk
    b. Tape
    c. UMD
    d. CD

13. A thumb drive is a(n) _____ storage device that plugs in a USB port on a computer or mobile device. (377)
    a. flash memory
    b. optical
    c. magnetic
    d. tape

14. Microfilm and microfiche _____. (379)
    a. greatly increase the amount of paper firms must handle
    b. are expensive
    c. have the longest life of any storage media
    d. all of the above

Checkpoint

Matching

Match the terms with their definitions. (See page numbers in parentheses.)

_____ 1. capacity (356)

_____ 2. cluster (357)

_____ 3. form factor (360)

_____ 4. head crash (360)

_____ 5. disk cache (361)

_____ 6. disk controller (363)

_____ 7. Picture CD (370)

_____ 8. burning (371)

_____ 9. tape drive (374)

_____ 10. pen drive (377)

a. special-purpose chip and electronic circuits that control the transfer of items to and from the system bus

b. the number of bytes (characters) a storage medium can hold

c. size of hard disk platters on computers

d. flash memory storage device that plugs in a USB port

e. memory chips that the processor uses to store frequently accessed items

f. smallest unit of disk space that stores data and information

g. occurs when a read/write head touches the surface of a platter on a hard disk

h. the process of writing on an optical disc

i. piece of metal on a floppy disk that slides to expose the surface of the disk

j. single-session CD-ROM that stores digital versions of film using a jpg file format

k. reads and writes data and information on a tape

Short Answer

Write a brief answer to each of the following questions.

1. What is access time? _____ What is the difference between a sector and a track? _____

2. Why is a hard disk inside the system unit sometimes called a fixed disk? _____ What are some advantages of external and removable hard disks over internal hard disks? _____

3. How is a single-session disc different from a multisession disc? _____ What is a VCD? _____

4. Why might you use miniature mobile storage? _____ What types of devices might include miniature mobile storage? _____

5. What are the common types of flash memory cards? _____ How might you transfer the contents of a miniature mobile storage device to your computer or printer? _____

Beyond the Book

Read the following book elements, learn more about each using the Web, and then write a brief report.

1. Ethics & Issues — Does Music and Movie Downloading Harm CD and DVD Sales? (371), Is the Blu-ray and HD DVD Competition Good for Consumers? (373), Should the World Become a Cashless Society? (378), or Who Should Be Looking at Your Medical Records? (381)

2. Career Corner — Computer Technician (381)

3. Companies on the Cutting Edge — Seagate Technology or SanDisk Corporation (383)

4. FAQs (359, 362, 364, 368, 371, 372, 373, 377, 378)

5. High-Tech Talk — Disk Formatting and File Systems (382)

6. Looking Ahead — Heat Increases Disk Capacity (359) or Bookshelf Design Streamlines Entertainment Storage (369)

7. Making Use of the Web — Shopping and Auctions (123)

8. Picture Yourself Working with Mobile Storage Media (352)

9. Technology Trailblazers — Al Shugart or Mark Dean (383)

10. Web Links (358, 362, 364, 369, 370, 371, 373, 377, 378)

Learn It Online

Use the Learn It Online exercises to reinforce your understanding of the chapter concepts. To access the Learn It Online exercises, visit scsite.com/dc2008/ch7/learn.

(1) At the Movies — Got Your Video Right Here

To view the Got Your Video Right Here movie, click the number 1 button. Locate your video and click the corresponding High-Speed or Dial-Up link, depending on your Internet connection. Watch the movie and then complete the exercise by answering the questions that follow. The Sling Media Slingbox is the best way to beam your favorite shows to any broadband-connected computer or Windows Mobile device in the world. How does the Slingbox work? What is one function that it currently is not able to support?

(2) At the Movies — Blu-ray Disc

In this chapter, you learned about BD-ROM. Click the number 2 button to view the suggested links and begin your search for videos, podcasts, or vodcasts related to BD-ROM. Choose a video, podcast, or vodcast that discusses BD-ROM and is of interest to you, and then write a description of its contents. Explain why you chose this piece, what you liked about it, what you disliked about it, and whether you would recommend it to a fellow student. Finish your review by giving the video, podcast, or vodcast a rating of 1 – 5 stars. Submit your review in the format requested by your instructor.

(3) Student Edition Labs — Maintaining a Hard Drive

Click the number 3 button. A new browser window will open, displaying the Student Edition Labs. Follow the on-screen instructions to complete the Maintaining a Hard Drive Lab. When finished, click the Exit button. If required, submit your results to your instructor.

(4) Student Edition Labs — Managing Files and Folders

Click the number 4 button. A new browser window will open, displaying the Student Edition Labs. Follow the on-screen instructions to complete the Managing Files and Folders Lab. When finished, click the Exit button. If required, submit your results to your instructor.

(5) Practice Test

Click the number 5 button. Answer each question. When completed, enter your name and click the Grade Test button to submit the quiz for grading. Make a note of any missed questions. If required, submit your results to your instructor.

(6) Who Wants To Be a Computer Genius[2]?

Click the number 6 button to find out if you are a computer genius. Directions about how to play the game will be displayed. When you are ready to play, click the Play button. Submit your score to your instructor.

(7) Wheel of Terms

Click the number 7 button to reinforce important terms you learned in this chapter by playing the Shelly Cashman Series version of this popular game. Directions about how to play the game will be displayed. When you are ready to play, click the Play button. Submit your score to your instructor.

Learn It Online

8 DC Track and Field

Click the number 8 button to use what you have learned in this chapter to compete against other students in three track and field events. Directions about how to play the game will be displayed. When you are ready to play, click the start first event button. If required, submit your score to your instructor.

9 You're Hired!

Click the number 9 button to use what you have learned in this chapter to embark on the path to a career in computers. Directions about how to play the game will be displayed. When you are ready to play, click the begin game button. If required, submit your score to your instructor.

10 Crossword Puzzle Challenge

Click the number 10 button, then click the Crossword Puzzle Challenge link. Directions about how to play the game will be displayed. Complete the puzzle to reinforce skills you learned in this chapter. When you are ready to play, click the Continue button. Submit the completed puzzle to your instructor.

11 Vista Exercises

Click the number 11 button. When the Vista Exercises menu appears, click the exercise assigned by your instructor. A new browser window will open. Follow the on-screen instructions to complete the exercise. When finished, click the Exit button. If required, submit your results to your instructor.

12 In the News

Hitachi sells a small disk drive, about the size of a quarter, which is capable of storing up to 4 GB of information, as much as 50 CDs. The drive is used in devices such as PDAs or digital cameras. What other storage devices are on the horizon? Click the number 12 button and read a news article about a new or improved storage device. What is the device? Who manufactures it? How is the storage device better than, or different from, earlier devices? How will the device be used? Why?

13 Chapter Discussion Forum

Select an objective from this chapter on page 353 about which you would like more information. Click the number 13 button and post a short message listing a meaningful message title accompanied by one or more questions concerning the selected objective. In two days, return to the threaded discussion by clicking the number 13 button. Submit to your instructor your original message and at least one response to your message.

14 Blogs

Click the number 14 button to learn how to use blogs to find information about a topic. Follow the instructions to use MSNBC.com's Blogs Etc. to find a blog about a popular topic, such as the hottest national news story or another topic of national interest. Write a report comparing opinions of two different people about the selected topic. Print your report and submit to your instructor.

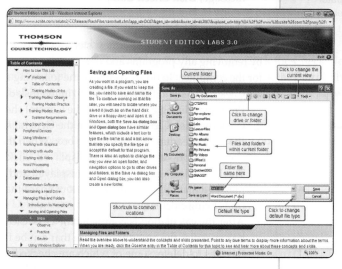

Web Research

Use the Internet-based Web Research exercises to broaden your understanding of the concepts presented in this chapter. Visit scsite.com/dc2008/ch7/research to obtain more information pertaining to each exercise. To discuss any of the Web Research exercises in this chapter with other students, post your thoughts or questions at scsite.com/dc2008/ch7/forum.

(1) Scavenger Hunt   Use one of the <u>search engines</u> listed in Figure 2-10 in Chapter 2 on page 78 or your own favorite search engine to find the answers to the questions that follow. Copy and paste the Web address from the Web page where you found the answer. Some questions may have more than one answer. If required, submit your answers to your instructor. (1) Who invented and patented smart cards? How many smart cards are expected to be produced this year? (2) What companies are sponsor members of the USB Flash Drive Alliance? (3) What is the Red Book standard? (4) During which decade were optical discs introduced? (5) What is areal density? What unit of measurement is used to describe this density? (6) What is IBM's Millipede project?

(2) Search Sleuth   Many computer users search the World Wide Web by typing words in the search text box, and often they are overwhelmed when the search engine returns thousands of possible Web sites. You can narrow your search by typing quotation marks around phrases and by adding words that give details about the phrase. <u>Go.com</u> is a Web portal developed by the Walt Disney Internet Group. It features a search engine, the latest news and entertainment information, stock market quotes, weather forecasts, maps, and games. Visit this Web site and then use your word processing program to answer the following questions. Then, if required, submit your answers to your instructor. (1) Locate the Movie Finder link. Type your postal code in the Search text box. What movies are playing in your area today? (2) Click your browser's Back button or press the BACKSPACE key to return to the Go.com home page. (3) Click the Search for text box at the top of the page. Type "USB flash drive" in the box. How many pages of search results are returned that are not Sponsored links? What are Sponsored results? (4) Click the Search for text box after the words, "USB flash drive". Add +"8 GB" and +"data reliability" as the search terms. How many pages of search results are returned that are not Sponsored links? (5) Review your search results and then write a 50-word summary of your findings.

(3) Journaling   Respond to your readings in this chapter by writing at least one page about your reactions, evaluations, and reflections about using <u>storage devices</u>. For example, which of these storage devices do you currently use: CDs, DVDs, USB flash drives? How do you care for your mobile storage media? Do you use a Picture CD or a credit card smart card? What is the storage capacity of your school, office, or home computer's hard disk? Have you attempted to repair a scratched CD or DVD? You also can write about the new terms you learned by reading this chapter. If required, submit your journal to your instructor.

(4) Expanding Your Understanding   Bill Gates, Microsoft's founder, considers <u>holographic storage</u> an impressive new storage system. The holographic process can store more than 100 movie, photo, and music files on one disc holding one terabyte of data. View Web sites to learn more about holographic storage. What factors are driving the rush to develop this system? How are images stored? What companies are researching and developing this technology? Write a report summarizing your findings, focusing on the possible uses of this storage medium and current engineering efforts to commercialize the technology. If required, submit your report to your instructor.

(5) Ethics in Action   The United States Federal Bureau of Investigation used a controversial program until January 2005 to monitor and store the e-mail and Internet activity of suspected criminals. Originally called Carnivore, the surveillance program was renamed <u>DCS1000</u>. The program was designed to track the activities of potential terrorists, spies, drug traffickers, and organized crime ring members. FBI agents needed to obtain a court order to monitor an individual, but privacy advocates claim the software tracked people not covered under the court order. View online sites that provide information about DCS1000 or Carnivore, including HowStuffWorks (computer.howstuffworks.com/carnivore.htm). Write a report summarizing your findings, and include a table of links to Web sites that provide additional details. If required, submit your report to your instructor.

Case Studies

Use the Case Studies to apply the concepts presented in the chapter to real-world situations. Visit scsite.com/dc2008/ch7/cases to obtain more information pertaining to each exercise. To discuss the Case Studies in this chapter with other students, visit scsite.com/dc2008/ch7/forum and post your thoughts or questions.

CASE STUDY 1 — Class Discussion The owner of the motorcycle repair shop where you are employed as a part-time office manager is tired of continually upgrading the company's computer system. After attending a seminar on how small businesses can make use of the Internet, she asked you to look into the feasibility of using <u>online storage</u> (also called an Internet hard disk), rather than purchasing additional storage for the company's computer. Write a brief report outlining the advantages and disadvantages of using online storage. Compare Yahoo! Briefcase and Google's Gmail online storage offerings. Which company offers the best arrangement? Why? Be prepared to discuss your recommendations in class.

CASE STUDY 2 — Class Discussion Paul's Trucking Company has hired you as an IT consultant. The company plans to purchase 15 computers for use in the accounting department. The first task assigned to you by the president of the company is to recommend the number and types of <u>CD and DVD drives</u> to include with the computers they plan to purchase. They want to use CDs and/or DVDs to share data and information among employees and to back up critical files. Create a brief memo that includes a table summarizing the advantages and disadvantages of using CD-ROM, recordable CD, rewritable CD, DVD-ROM, recordable DVD, and rewritable DVD. Include in the table both the approximate cost of the drive and the media. Be prepared to discuss your findings in class.

CASE STUDY 3 — Research An old aphorism claims, "You never can have too much money." Many computer users support a similar maxim, "You never can have too much storage." Your manager at MJ National Bank where you are employed as an analyst, however, is tired of buying more hardware to meet the bank's storage needs. She wants you to investigate alternative ways to improve <u>storage capacity</u>. Use the Web and/or print media to find out more about hard disk partitions and data compression as a means of increasing storage capacity. How do partitions increase the capacity of hard disks? What kind of data compression is most suitable for communications devices? What are the most well known data compression algorithms? How can compression ratios of different algorithms be compared? What are some formats for data compression archives? Prepare a report and/or PowerPoint presentation and share your findings with your class.

CASE STUDY 4 — Research Data and information backup is as important for people with personal computers as it is for companies. If data is not backed up regularly, a company could suffer a setback of weeks or months trying to get current after a crash. Having had a recent data loss scare, a local health club has hired your firm to recommend a <u>backup system</u>. The club uses ten computers through a server. They store all member information, such as name, address, membership type, and payment information. They constantly are updating their database, but have never backed up the data. Using the Web and/or print media, prepare a report or PowerPoint presentation detailing what you would consider the ideal system for the club. Include in your report the devices you would require and information that supports your choices.

CASE STUDY 5 — Team Challenge Your team has been assigned to do IT research for a new local magazine-subscription telemarketing company that is about to open for business. The company's business plan calls for 150 telemarketers to make a minimum of 100 calls a day. If a telemarketer does not meet the minimum number of calls, then he or she is required to finish the calls from home. The company plans to buy used computers for each telemarketer to use at home. The company also has to decide on the type of <u>storage device</u> to provide the telemarketers so that when they have to make calls from home, they have a way to take the necessary data home with them. Senior management has narrowed down their choice to three storage devices — rewritable CDs, rewritable DVDs, or USB flash drives. Form a three-member team and have each team member choose a different storage device. Using the Web and/or print media, have each team member determine the advantages and disadvantages of their chosen device. Include such features as capacity, access time, durability of media, and cost. As a team, merge your findings into a team report and/or PowerPoint presentation and share your recommendations with your class.

CHAPTER EIGHT

Operating Systems and Utility Programs

Picture Yourself Getting a Virus through E-Mail

Arriving home after class, you eagerly check your e-mail. You have been looking for a new job and have submitted your resume online to several places. You are delighted when you see an e-mail with "Your job search" as the subject line. You open the e-mail and realize too late that you have made an enormous mistake. Your computer freezes. The mouse and keyboard are unresponsive. You restart the computer, but the Windows Vista desktop never appears. You know that you unwittingly caused your computer to get a virus by opening the e-mail.

In your computer literacy course, you learned how to keep a computer safe from viruses and other infections. You installed antivirus software, enabled a firewall, and backed up your hard disk. Unfortunately, many weeks have elapsed since then. You did not keep the antivirus software updated. You temporarily disabled the firewall so that you could access one of your favorite Web sites more easily. Your last hard disk backup was two months ago. Furthermore, you broke the cardinal rule: never open an e-mail from someone you do not know.

After an hour on the telephone with a technical support specialist, your computer is functional again, and you are much wiser. You mentally resolve to be scrupulous about keeping your computer safe with regular updates and backups. Needless to say, you never will open an e-mail message from someone you do not know, no matter how enticing the subject line.

Read Chapter 8 to learn about antivirus software, firewall settings, backups, and recovery discs, and discover features of most operating systems and utility programs.

After completing this chapter, you will be able to:

1. Identify the types of system software

2. Summarize the startup process on a personal computer

3. Describe the functions of an operating system

4. Discuss ways that some operating systems help administrators control a network and administer security

5. Explain the purpose of the utilities included with most operating systems

6. Summarize the features of several stand-alone operating systems

7. Identify various network operating systems

8. Identify devices that use several embedded operating systems

9. Explain the purpose of several stand-alone utility programs

CONTENTS

SYSTEM SOFTWARE

When you purchase a personal computer, it usually has system software installed on its hard disk. **System software** consists of the programs that control or maintain the operations of the computer and its devices. System software serves as the interface between the user, the application software, and the computer's hardware.

Two types of system software are operating systems and utility programs. Several types of utility programs are provided with an operating system. Other utility programs are available stand-alone, that is, as programs separate from the operating system. This chapter discusses the operating system and its functions, as well as several types of utility programs for personal computers.

OPERATING SYSTEMS

An **operating system** (**OS**) is a set of programs containing instructions that coordinate all the activities among computer hardware resources. Most operating systems perform similar functions that include starting a computer, providing a user interface, managing programs, managing memory, scheduling jobs, configuring devices,

start the computer

administer security

control a network

provide file management and other utilities

functions of an operating system

FIGURE 8-1   Most operating systems perform similar functions, which are illustrated with Windows Vista in this figure.

establishing an Internet connection, monitoring performance, and providing file management utilities. Some operating systems also allow users to control a network and administer security (Figure 8-1).

In most cases, the operating system is installed and resides on the computer's hard disk. On handheld computers and many mobile devices such as PDAs and smart phones, however, the operating system may reside on a ROM chip.

Different sizes of computers typically use different operating systems. For example, a mainframe computer does not use the same operating system as a personal computer. Even the same types of computers, such as desktop computers, may not use the same operating system. Some, however, can run multiple operating systems. When purchasing application software, you must ensure that it works with the operating system installed on your computer.

The operating system that a computer uses sometimes is called the *platform*. On purchased application software, the package identifies the required platform (operating system). A *cross-platform* program is one that runs the same on multiple operating systems.

provide a user interface

manage programs

manage memory

schedule jobs and configure devices

establish an Internet connection

monitor performance

OPERATING SYSTEM FUNCTIONS

Many different operating systems exist, designed for all types of computers. Regardless of the size of the computer, however, most operating systems provide similar functions. The following sections discuss functions common to most operating systems. The operating system handles many of these functions automatically, without requiring any instructions from a user.

Starting a Computer

The process of starting or restarting a computer is called **booting**. When turning on a computer that has been powered off completely, you are performing a **cold boot**. A **warm boot**, by contrast, is the process of using the operating system to restart a computer. A warm boot properly closes any running processes and programs; however, it does not save any unsaved work. Thus, always remember to save your work before rebooting (restarting) a computer.

With Windows Vista, you can perform a warm boot by clicking the Start button on the taskbar, clicking the Lock button arrow on the Start menu, and then clicking Restart on the Lock button menu (Figure 8-2). Some computers have a reset button that when pressed restarts a computer as if it had been powered off. A reset button does not properly close running processes and programs.

When you install new software or update existing software, often an on-screen prompt instructs you to restart the computer. In this case, a warm boot is appropriate. If your computer stops responding, try to restart it with a warm boot first. If it does not respond to the warm boot, then try pushing the reset button on the computer, if the computer has a reset button. As a last resort, restart the computer with a cold boot; that is, push the power button. Pushing the power button does not properly close running processes and programs.

Each time you boot a computer, the kernel and other frequently used operating system instructions are loaded, or copied, from the hard disk (storage) into the computer's memory (RAM). The *kernel* is the core of an operating system

that manages memory and devices, maintains the computer's clock, starts applications, and assigns the computer's resources, such as devices, programs, data, and information. The kernel is *memory resident*, which means it remains in memory while the computer is running. Other parts of the operating system are *nonresident*, that is, these instructions remain on the hard disk until they are needed.

When you boot a computer, a series of messages may be displayed on the screen. The actual information displayed varies depending on the make and type of the computer and the equipment installed. The boot process, however, is similar for large and small computers.

The steps in the following paragraphs explain what occurs during a cold boot on a personal computer using the Windows Vista operating system. The steps in Figure 8-3 illustrate and correspond to the steps discussed in the following paragraphs.

Step 1: When you turn on the computer, the power supply sends an electrical signal to the components in the system unit.

Step 2: The charge of electricity causes the processor chip to reset itself and find the ROM chip(s) that contains the BIOS. The **BIOS** (pronounced BYE-ose), which stands for *basic input/output system*, is firmware that contains the computer's startup instructions.

Step 3: The BIOS executes a series of tests to make sure the computer hardware is connected properly and operating correctly. The tests, collectively called the *power-on self test* (*POST*), check the various system components including the buses, system clock, adapter cards, RAM chips, mouse, keyboard, and drives. As the POST executes, LEDs (tiny lights) flicker on devices such as the disk drives and keyboard. Beeps also may sound, and messages may be displayed on the screen.

Step 4: The POST results are compared with data in a CMOS chip. As discussed in Chapter 4, CMOS is a technology that uses battery power to retain information when the computer is off. The CMOS chip stores configuration information about the computer, such as the amount of memory; type of disk drives, keyboard, and monitor; the current date and time; and other startup information. It also detects any new devices connected to the computer. If any problems are identified, the computer may beep, display error messages, or cease operating — depending on the severity of the problem.

FIGURE 8-2   To reboot a running computer, click Restart on the Lock button menu.

Step 5: If the POST completes successfully, the BIOS searches for specific operating system files called *system files*. The BIOS may look first to see if a USB flash drive plugged in a USB port or a disc in a CD or DVD drive contains the system files. If these ports or drives do not contain media or if the system files are not on media in the port or drive, the BIOS looks in drive C (the designation usually given to the first hard disk) for the system files.

Step 6: Once located, the system files load into memory (RAM) from storage (usually the hard disk) and execute. Next, the kernel of the operating system loads into memory. Then, the operating system in memory takes control of the computer.

Step 7: The operating system loads system configuration information. In Windows Vista, the *registry* consists of several files that contain the system configuration information. Windows Vista constantly accesses the registry during the computer's operation for information such as installed hardware and software devices and individual user preferences for mouse speed, passwords, and other information. The Windows Vista registry also constantly checks user credentials to verify they have the necessary privileges to run programs.

Necessary operating system files are loaded into memory. On some computers, the operating system verifies that the person attempting to use the computer is a legitimate user. Finally, the Windows Vista desktop and icons are displayed on the screen. The operating system executes programs in the *Startup folder*, which contains a list of programs that open automatically when you boot the computer.

WEB LINK 8-1

Windows Registry
For more information, visit scsite.com/dc2008/ch8/weblink and then click Windows Registry.

FIGURE 8-3 HOW A PC BOOTS UP

Step 1:
The power supply sends a signal to the components in the system unit.

Step 2:
The processor finds the ROM chip(s) that contains the BIOS (basic input/output system).

Step 3:
The BIOS performs the POST (power-on self test), which checks components, such as the mouse, keyboard, and adapter cards.

Step 4:
The results of the POST are compared with data in a CMOS chip.

Step 5:
The BIOS sometimes looks for the system files on a USB flash drive or on a CD or DVD drive and then drive C (hard disk).

Step 6:
The system files and the kernel of the operating system load into memory (RAM) from storage (hard disk).

Step 7:
The operating system loads configuration information, may request user information, and displays the desktop on the screen.

system unit

CD drive

DVD drive

Core 2 Duo processor

CMOS

(RAM) memory modules

ROM BIOS

ROM BIOS

hard disk

sound card

video card

USB flash drive

BOOT DISK A **boot drive** is the drive from which your personal computer boots (starts). In most cases, drive C (the hard disk) is the boot drive. Sometimes a hard disk becomes damaged and the computer cannot boot from the hard disk. In this case, you can boot from a special disk, called a **boot disk** or a **recovery disk**, that contains a few system files that will start the computer. When you purchase a computer, it usually includes a boot disk in the form of a CD. If you do not have a boot disk, the operating system may provide a means to create one. The Windows Vista installation disc is itself a boot disk, which you can use to start Windows Vista in the event you cannot boot from the hard disk.

FAQ 8-1

How do I shut down a computer that uses Windows Vista?

The Start menu in Windows Vista provides many options from which to choose when you are finished using your computer. Clicking the Power button on the Start menu will place your computer in *sleep mode*, which is a low-power state that allows you to resume your work quickly when you return to your computer. If you click the Lock button arrow, you can select commands that allow you to switch users, log off, lock the computer, restart the computer, put the computer to sleep, and shut down (power off) the computer. For more information, visit scsite.com/dc2008/ch8/faq and then click Shut-Down Options.

Providing a User Interface

You interact with software through its user interface. That is, a **user interface** controls how you enter data and instructions and how information is displayed on the screen. Two types of user interfaces are command-line and graphical. Operating systems often use a combination of these interfaces to define how a user interacts with a computer.

COMMAND-LINE INTERFACE To configure devices, manage system resources, and troubleshoot network connections, network administrators and other advanced users work with a command-line interface. In a *command-line interface*, a user types commands or presses special keys on the keyboard (such as function keys or key combinations) to enter data and instructions (Figure 8-4). Command-line interfaces often are difficult to use because they require exact spelling, grammar, and punctuation. Minor errors, such as a missing period, generate an error message. Command-line interfaces, however, give a user more control to manage detailed settings. When working with a command-line interface, the set of commands entered into the computer is called the *command language*.

FIGURE 8-4 A command-line interface is difficult to use because it requires you enter exact spelling, grammar, and punctuation.

GRAPHICAL USER INTERFACE Most users today work with a graphical user interface. With a *graphical user interface* (*GUI*), you interact with menus and visual images such as buttons and other graphical objects to issue commands. Many current GUI operating systems incorporate features similar to those of a Web browser, such as links and navigation buttons (i.e., Back button and Forward button). Windows Vista offers two different GUIs, depending on your hardware configuration. Computers with less than 1 GB of RAM work with the *Windows Vista Basic* interface (Figure 8-5a). Computers with more than 1 GB of RAM work with the *Windows Aero* interface (Figure 8-5b), which provides an enhanced visual look, additional navigation options, and animation.

Managing Programs

Some operating systems support a single user and only one running program at a time. Others support thousands of users running multiple programs. How an operating system handles programs directly affects your productivity.

A *single user/single tasking* operating system allows only one user to run one program at a time. For example, if you are working in a graphics program and want to check e-mail messages, you must quit the graphics program before you can run the e-mail program. Early systems were single user/single tasking. Most of today's operating systems are multitasking. PDAs, smart phones, and other small computing devices, however, often use a single user/single tasking operating system.

A *single user/multitasking* operating system allows a single user to work on two or more programs that reside in memory at the same time. Using the example just cited, if you are

FIGURE 8-5a (Windows Vista Basic interface)

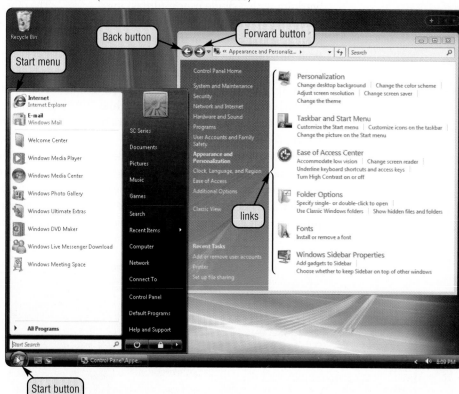

FIGURE 8-5b (Windows Aero interface)

FIGURE 8-5 Windows Vista offers two different graphical user interfaces, depending on your hardware configuration.

working with a single user/multitasking operating system, you do not have to quit the graphics program to run the e-mail program. Both programs can run concurrently. Users today typically run multiple programs concurrently. It is common to have an e-mail program and Web browser open at all times, while working with application programs such as word processing or graphics.

When a computer is running multiple programs concurrently, one program is in the foreground and the others are in the background. The one in the *foreground* is the active program, that is, the one you currently are using.

The other programs running but not in use are in the *background*. In Figure 8-6, the PowerPoint program, which is showing a slide show, is in the foreground, and three other programs are running in the background (Windows Media Player, Microsoft Excel, and Chess Titans). For example, Windows Media Player can be playing music while you are modifying the slide show.

The foreground program typically displays on the desktop, and the background programs are partially or completely hidden behind the foreground program. You easily can switch between foreground and background programs. To make a program active (in the foreground) in

FIGURE 8-6 The foreground program, PowerPoint, is displayed on the desktop. The other programs (Windows Media Player, Microsoft Excel, and Chess Titans) are in the background.

Windows Vista, click its program button on the taskbar. This causes the operating system to place all other programs in the background.

In addition to application programs, an operating system manages other processes. These processes include utilities or routines that provide support to other programs or hardware. Some are memory resident. Others run as they are required. Figure 8-7 shows a list of all processes running on a Windows Vista computer. The list contains the applications programs running, as well as other programs and processes.

Some operating systems use preemptive multitasking to prevent any one process from monopolizing the computer's resources. With *preemptive multitasking*, the operating system interrupts a program that is executing and passes control to another program waiting to be executed. An advantage of preemptive multitasking is the operating system regains control if one program stops operating properly.

A *multiuser* operating system enables two or more users to run programs simultaneously. Networks, servers, mainframes, and supercomputers allow hundreds to thousands of users to connect at the same time, and thus are multiuser.

A *multiprocessing* operating system supports two or more processors running programs at the same time. Multiprocessing involves the coordinated processing of programs by more than one processor. Multiprocessing increases a computer's processing speed.

A computer with separate processors also can serve as a fault-tolerant computer. A *fault-tolerant computer* continues to operate when one of its components fails, ensuring that no data is lost. Fault-tolerant computers have duplicate components such as processors, memory, and disk drives. If any one of these components fails, the computer switches to the duplicate component and continues to operate. Airline reservation systems, communications networks, automated teller machines, and other systems that must be operational at all times use fault-tolerant computers.

Managing Memory

The purpose of **memory management** is to optimize the use of random access memory (RAM). As Chapter 4 discussed, RAM consists of one or more chips on the motherboard that

FIGURE 8-7 An operating system manages multiple programs and processes while you use the computer.

hold items such as data and instructions while the processor interprets and executes them. The operating system allocates, or assigns, data and instructions to an area of memory while they are being processed. Then, it carefully monitors the contents of memory. Finally, the operating system releases these items from being monitored in memory when the processor no longer requires them.

If you have multiple programs running simultaneously, it is possible to run out of RAM. For example, assume an operating system requires 512 MB of RAM, an antivirus program — 256 MB of RAM, a Web browser — 128 MB of RAM, a business software suite — 512 MB of RAM, and a photo editing program — 256 MB of RAM. With all these programs running simultaneously, the total RAM required would be 1664 MB of RAM (512 + 256 + 128 + 512 + 256). If the computer has only 512 MB of RAM, the operating system may have to use virtual memory to solve the problem.

With **virtual memory**, the operating system allocates a portion of a storage medium, usually the hard disk, to function as additional RAM (Figure 8-8). As you interact with a program, part of it may be in physical RAM, while the rest of the program is on the hard disk as virtual memory. Because virtual memory is slower than RAM, users may notice the computer slowing down while it uses virtual memory.

The area of the hard disk used for virtual memory is called a *swap file* because it swaps (exchanges) data, information, and instructions between memory and storage. A *page* is the amount of data and program instructions that can swap at a given time. The technique of swapping items between memory and storage, called *paging*, is a time-consuming process for the computer.

When an operating system spends much of its time paging, instead of executing application software, it is said to be *thrashing*. If application software, such as a Web browser, has stopped responding and the hard disk's LED blinks repeatedly, the operating system probably is thrashing.

FAQ 8-2

How can I stop a computer from thrashing?

Try to quit the program that stopped responding. If the computer does not respond and continues to thrash, do a warm boot. When the computer reboots, check whether the available hard disk space is less than 200 MB. If it is, remove unnecessary files from the hard disk and if possible uninstall seldom used programs. Defragment the hard disk (discussed later in this chapter). If thrashing continues to occur, you may need to install more RAM in the computer. For more information, visit scsite.com/dc2008/ch8/faq and then click Optimizing Memory.

Scheduling Jobs

The operating system determines the order in which jobs are processed. A **job** is an operation the processor manages. Jobs include receiving data from an input device, processing instructions, sending information to an output device, and transferring items from storage to memory and from memory to storage.

FIGURE 8-8   HOW A COMPUTER MIGHT USE VIRTUAL MEMORY

page swapped out

RAM (physical memory)

disk (virtual memory)

swap file

Step 1:
The operating system transfers the least recently used data and program instructions from RAM to the hard disk because RAM is needed for other functions.

Step 2:
The operating system transfers data and program instructions from the hard disk to RAM when they are needed.

page swapped in

A mulituser operating system does not always process jobs on a first-come, first-served basis. Sometimes, one user may have a higher priority than other users. In this case, the operating system adjusts the schedule of jobs.

Sometimes, a device already may be busy processing one job when it receives a second job. This occurs because the processor operates at a much faster rate of speed than peripheral devices. For example, if the processor sends five print jobs to a printer, the printer can print only one document at a time and store as many documents as its memory can handle.

While waiting for devices to become idle, the operating system places items in buffers. A **buffer** is a segment of memory or storage in which items are placed while waiting to be transferred from an input device or to an output device.

The operating system commonly uses buffers with print jobs. This process, called **spooling**, sends print jobs to a buffer instead of sending them immediately to the printer. The buffer holds the information waiting to print while the printer prints from the buffer at its own rate of speed. By spooling print jobs to a buffer, the processor can continue interpreting and executing instructions while the printer prints. This allows users to work on the computer for other tasks while a printer is printing. Multiple print jobs line up in a **queue** (pronounced Q)

in the buffer. A program, called a *print spooler*, intercepts print jobs from the operating system and places them in the queue (Figure 8-9).

Configuring Devices

A **driver**, short for *device driver*, is a small program that tells the operating system how to communicate with a specific device. Each device on a computer, such as the mouse, keyboard, monitor, printer, card reader/writer, and scanner, has its own specialized set of commands and thus requires its own specific driver. When you boot a computer, the operating system loads each device's driver. These devices will not function without their correct drivers.

If you attach a new device to a computer, such as a printer or scanner, its driver must be installed before you can use the device. Today, many devices and operating systems support Plug and Play. As discussed in Chapter 4, **Plug and Play** means the operating system automatically configures new devices as you install them. Specifically, it assists you in the device's installation by loading the necessary drivers automatically and checking for conflicts with other devices. With Plug and Play, a user plugs in a device, turns on the computer, and then uses the device without having to configure the system manually. Devices that connect to a USB port on the system unit typically are Plug and Play.

WEB LINK 8-2

Plug and Play

For more information, visit scsite.com/ dc2008/ch8/weblink and then click Plug and Play.

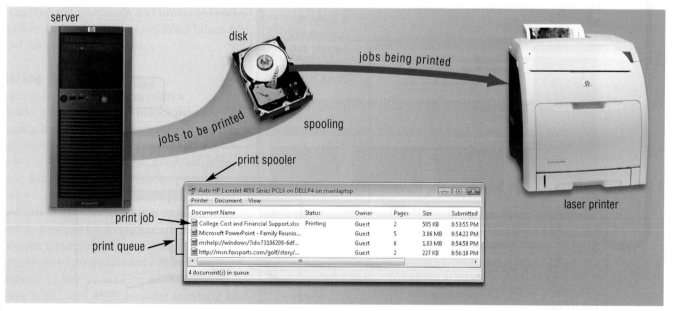

FIGURE 8-9   Spooling increases both processor and printer efficiency by placing print jobs in a buffer on disk before they are printed. This figure illustrates three jobs in the queue with one job printing.

Utility programs included with most operating systems provide the following functions: managing files, searching for files, viewing images, securing a computer from unauthorized access, uninstalling programs, scanning disks, defragmenting disks, diagnosing problems, backing up files and disks, and setting up screen savers. The following sections briefly discuss each of these utilities.

File Manager

A **file manager** is a utility that performs functions related to file management. Windows Vista includes file managers called *Explorers:* the Document Explorer, Picture Explorer, and Music Explorer. Some of the file management functions that a file manager performs are displaying a list of files on a storage medium (Figure 8-15); organizing files in folders; copying, renaming, deleting, moving, and sorting files and folders; and creating shortcuts. A **folder** is a specific named location on a storage medium that contains related documents. A **shortcut** is an icon on the desktop that provides a user with immediate access to a program or file.

Search Utility

A **search utility** is a program that attempts to locate a file on your computer based on criteria you specify. The criteria could be a word or words contained in a file, date the file was created or modified, size of the file, location of the file, file name, author/artist, and other similar properties. Search utilities can look through documents, pictures, music, and other files.

Search utilities typically use an index to assist with locating files quickly. An *index* stores a variety of information about a file, including its name, date created, date modified, author name, and so on. When you enter search criteria, instead of looking through every file and folder on the storage medium, the search utility looks through the index first to find a match. Each entry in the index contains a link to the actual file on the disk for easy retrieval. Windows Vista has a built-in search utility. All the Explorer windows, as well as the Start menu, contain a Search box where you enter the search criteria.

Image Viewer

An **image viewer** is a utility that allows users to display, copy, and print the contents of a graphics file, such as a picture. With an image viewer, users can see images without having to open them in a paint or image editing program. Windows Vista includes an image viewer called *Windows Photo Gallery,* which also allows you to manage and edit pictures (Figure 8-16). To display a file in this image viewer, simply double-click the thumbnail of the image in the file manager. For example, double-clicking a thumbnail in the Picture Explorer (Figure 8-15) displays the image in a Windows Photo Gallery window.

FIGURE 8-15 Windows Vista includes file managers that allow you to view documents, pictures, and music. In this case, thumbnails of pictures are displayed.

FIGURE 8-16 Windows Photo Gallery allows users to see the contents of a picture file.

Personal Firewall

A **personal firewall** is a utility that detects and protects a personal computer from unauthorized intrusions. Personal firewalls constantly monitor all transmissions to and from a computer.

When connected to the Internet, your computer is vulnerable to attacks from a hacker. A *hacker* is someone who tries to access a computer or network illegally. Users with broadband Internet connections, such as through DSL and Internet cable television service, are even more susceptible than those with dial-up access because the Internet connection is always on.

Windows Vista automatically enables its built-in personal firewall upon installation. This firewall, called Windows Firewall, is easy to access and configure (Figure 8-17). If your operating system does not include a personal firewall or you want additional protection, you can purchase a stand-alone personal firewall utility or a hardware firewall, which is a device such as a router that has a built-in firewall.

Uninstaller

An **uninstaller** is a utility that removes a program, as well as any associated entries in the system files. In Windows Vista, the uninstaller is available through the Uninstall a program command in the Control Panel.

When you install a program, the operating system records the information it uses to run the software in the system files. The uninstaller deletes files and folders from the hard disk, as well as removes program entries from the system files.

Personal Firewalls
For more information, visit scsite.com/ dc2008/ch8/weblink and then click Personal Firewalls.

FIGURE 8-17 Through the Security Center in the Control Panel of Windows Vista, users can configure Windows Firewall, which is a personal firewall utility built into Windows Vista.

FAQ 8-5

Should I use Document Explorer to delete a program?

No! If you remove software from a computer by deleting the files and folders associated with the program without running the uninstaller, the system file entries are not updated. This may cause the operating system to display error messages when you start the computer. If the program has an uninstaller, always use it to remove software. For more information, visit scsite.com/dc2008/ch8/faq and then click Uninstalling Programs.

Disk Scanner

A **disk scanner** is a utility that searches for and removes unnecessary files. Windows Vista includes a disk scanner utility, called *Disk Cleanup*, which searches for and removes unnecessary files such as temporary files (Figure 8-18).

FIGURE 8-18 Disk Cleanup searches for and removes unnecessary files.

Disk Defragmenter

A **disk defragmenter** is a utility that reorganizes the files and unused space on a computer's hard disk so the operating system accesses data more quickly and programs run faster. When an operating system stores data on a disk, it places the data in the first available sector on the disk. It attempts to place data in sectors that are contiguous (next to each other), but this is not always possible. When the contents of a file are scattered across two or more noncontiguous sectors, the file is *fragmented*.

Fragmentation slows down disk access and thus the performance of the entire computer. **Defragmenting** the disk, or reorganizing it so the files are stored in contiguous sectors, solves this problem (Figure 8-19). Windows Vista includes a disk defragmenter available in the System Tools list.

FIGURE 8-19 A fragmented disk has many files stored in noncontiguous sectors. Defragmenting reorganizes the files so they are located in contiguous sectors, which speeds access time.

Diagnostic Utility

A **diagnostic utility** compiles technical information about your computer's hardware and certain system software programs and then prepares a report outlining any identified problems. For example, Windows Vista includes the diagnostic utility, *Problem Reports and Solutions*, which diagnoses problems as well as suggests courses of action. Information in the report assists technical support staff in remedying any problems.

Backup Utility

A **backup utility** allows users to copy, or *back up*, selected files or an entire hard disk to another storage medium such as CD, DVD, external hard disk, tape, or USB flash drive. During the backup process, the backup utility monitors progress and alerts you if it needs additional discs or tapes. Many backup programs *compress*, or shrink the size of, files during the backup process. By compressing the files, the backup program requires less storage space for the backup files than for the original files.

Because they are compressed, you usually cannot use backup files in their backed up form. In the event you need to use a backup file, a **restore program** reverses the process and returns backed up files to their original form. Backup utilities include restore programs.

You should back up files and disks regularly in the event your originals are lost, damaged, or destroyed. Windows Vista includes a backup utility (Figure 8-20). Instead of backing up to a local disk storage device, some users opt to use online storage to back up their files. As described in Chapter 7, online storage is a service on the Web that provides hard disk storage to computer users, usually for free or for a minimal monthly fee.

FIGURE 8-20 A backup utility allows users to copy files or an entire hard disk to another storage medium.

Screen Saver

A **screen saver** is a utility that causes a display device's screen to show a moving image or blank screen if no keyboard or mouse activity occurs for a specified time (Figure 8-21). When you press a key on the keyboard or move the mouse, the screen saver disappears and the screen returns to the previous state.

Screen savers originally were developed to prevent a problem called *ghosting*, in which images could be permanently etched on a monitor's screen. Although ghosting is not as severe of a problem with today's displays, manufacturers continue to recommend that users install screen savers for this reason. Screen savers also are popular for security, business, and entertainment purposes. To secure a computer, users configure their screen saver to require a password to deactivate. Many of the Windows Vista screen savers require the Windows Aero interface. In addition to those included with the operating system, many screen savers are available in stores and on the Web for free or a minimal fee.

WEB LINK 8-4

Screen Savers
For more information, visit scsite.com/dc2008/ch8/weblink and then click Screen Savers.

FIGURE 8-21 Windows Vista has built-in screen savers.

TYPES OF OPERATING SYSTEMS

Many of the first operating systems were device dependent and proprietary. A *device-dependent* program is one that runs only on a specific type or make of computer. *Proprietary software* is privately owned and limited to a specific vendor or computer model. Some operating systems still are device dependent. The trend today, however, is toward *device-independent* operating systems that run on computers provided by a variety of manufacturers. The advantage of device-independent operating systems is you can retain existing application software and data files even if you change computer models or vendors.

When you purchase a new computer, it typically has an operating system preinstalled. As new versions of the operating system are released, users upgrade their existing computers to incorporate features of the new version. An upgrade usually costs less than purchasing the entire operating system.

Some software manufacturers, such as Microsoft and IBM, release free downloadable updates to their software, often called a *service pack*. Users also can order service packs on CD for a minimal shipping fee. Service packs provide enhancements to the original software and fix bugs (errors) in the software. Read Ethics & Issues 8-3 for a related discussion.

New versions of an operating system usually are downward compatible. That is, they recognize and work with application software written for an earlier version of the operating system (or platform). The application software, by contrast, is said to be upward compatible, meaning it will run on new versions of the operating system.

The three basic categories of operating systems that exist today are stand-alone, network, and embedded. The table in Figure 8-22 lists specific names of operating systems in each category. The following pages discuss the operating systems listed in the table.

WEB LINK 8-5

Windows Vista

For more information, visit scsite.com/ dc2008/ch8/weblink and then click Windows Vista.

CATEGORIES OF OPERATING SYSTEMS

Category	Operating System Name
Stand-alone	• DOS • Early Windows versions (Windows 3.x, Windows 95, Windows NT Workstation, Windows 98, Windows 2000 Professional, Windows Millennium Edition) • Windows XP • Windows Vista • Mac OS X • UNIX • Linux
Network	• Early Windows Server versions (Windows NT Server, Windows 2000 Server) • Windows Server 2003 • UNIX • Linux • Solaris • NetWare
Embedded	• Windows CE • Windows Mobile • Palm OS • Embedded Linux • Symbian OS

FIGURE 8-22 Examples of stand-alone, network, and embedded operating systems. Some stand-alone operating systems include the capability of configuring small home or office networks.

ETHICS & ISSUES 8-3

Does Windows Genuine Advantage Give an Advantage to Hackers?

When Microsoft releases new software updates for a Windows operating system, the *Windows Genuine Advantage* program that is built into the operating system determines whether the operating system is a fully licensed, legitimate copy and is not a pirated copy. If the computer does not pass the test, then the updates are not installed and the computer user is notified of the potential infraction. Microsoft claims that users are being protected from potentially dangerous pirated versions of the operating system. The company also has no obligation to provide security updates or software patches to those who obtain the operating system illegally, and Microsoft has the right to protect its operating system from being pirated. Critics of the Windows Genuine Advantage program, however, want the updates available to all. Even if a user owns a pirated version of the operating system, a computer that does not receive the updates may be more susceptible to viruses and other malware. For example, the computer may become a zombie for a hacker, which means that a hacker secretly can use the computer over the Internet to spread more malware or to send spam e-mail. Furthermore, in some cases a computer owner is not aware that an unscrupulous computer seller has sold them a pirated copy of the operating system. In such cases, experts claim that the user should not suffer the consequences of the computer seller's actions. Do you think that Microsoft has legitimate reasons for the Windows Genuine Advantage program? Why or why not? Should users of pirated copies of an operating system be allowed to receive security updates and software patches? Why or why not? If a computer user is unaware that they have purchased a pirated copy of the operating system, should Microsoft have the ability to remotely disable the computer? Why?

STAND-ALONE OPERATING SYSTEMS

A **stand-alone operating system** is a complete operating system that works on a desktop computer, notebook computer, or mobile computing device. Some stand-alone operating systems are called *client operating systems* because they also work in conjunction with a network operating system. Client operating systems can operate with or without a network. Other stand-alone operating systems include networking capabilities, allowing the home and small business user to set up a small network.

Examples of currently used stand-alone operating systems are Windows XP, Windows Vista, Mac OS X, UNIX, and Linux. The following paragraphs briefly discuss these operating systems.

FAQ 8-6

What was Microsoft's first operating system?

In the early 1980s, Microsoft introduced *DOS* (Disk Operating System) as its first operating system. The two more widely used versions of DOS were PC-DOS and MS-DOS. At first, DOS used a command-line interface, but later versions introduced a menu-driven interface. DOS once was used on an estimated 70 million computers, but hardly is used today because it lacks a graphical user interface and does not take full advantage of modern personal computer processors. For more information, visit scsite.com/dc2008/ch8/faq and then click DOS.

Windows XP

In the mid-1980s, Microsoft developed its first version of Windows, which provided a graphical user interface (GUI). Since then, Microsoft continually has updated its Windows operating system, incorporating innovative features and functions with each subsequent version (Figure 8-23). **Windows XP** is a fast, reliable Windows operating system, providing quicker startup, better performance, increased security, and a simpler visual look than previous Windows versions. Using Windows XP, home and small office users easily can set up a network and secure it from hackers with Windows Firewall. Windows Messenger, included with Windows XP, enables users to send instant messages. Windows XP

HIGHLIGHTS OF STAND-ALONE WINDOWS VERSIONS

Windows Version	Year Released	Highlights
Windows 3.x	1990	• Provided a GUI • An operating environment only — worked in combination with DOS
Windows NT 3.1	1993	• Client OS that connected to a Windows NT Advanced Server • Interface similar to Windows 3.x
Windows 95	1995	• True multitasking operating system • Improved GUI • Included support for networking, Plug and Play technology, longer file names, and e-mail
Windows NT Workstation 4.0	1996	• Client OS that connected to a Windows NT Server • Interface similar to Windows 95 • Network integration
Windows 98	1998	• Upgrade to Windows 95 • More integrated with the Internet; included *Internet Explorer* (a Web browser) • Faster system startup and shutdown, better file management, support for multimedia technologies (e.g., DVDs), and USB connectivity
Windows Millennium Edition	2000	• Upgrade to Windows 98 • Designed for the home user who wanted music playing, video editing, and networking capabilities
Windows 2000 Professional	2000	• Upgrade to Windows NT Workstation 4.0 • Complete multitasking client OS designed for business personal computers • Certified device drivers, faster performance, adaptive Start menu, image viewer, enhanced for mobile users
Windows XP	2001	• Upgrade to Windows Millennium Edition called Windows XP Home Edition • Upgrade to Windows 2000 Professional called Windows XP Professional • Windows XP Tablet PC Edition designed for Tablet PC users • Windows XP Media Center Edition designed for PCs used for home entertainment • Windows XP Professional x64 Edition designed for workstations that use 64-bit processors • Improved interface and increased performance in all editions
Windows XP SP2 (Service Pack 2)	2004	• Enhancement to Windows XP that offers more built-in security technologies • Improved firewall utility • Automatic blocking of Internet pop-up advertisements
Windows Vista	2006	• Upgrade to Windows XP • Easier to navigate user interface • Enhanced administration of user accounts • Improved firewall • Simplified customization techniques • New Instant Search improves searching capabilities • New Document Explorer, Picture Explorer, and Music Explorer improve organizing capabilities • Improved performance and reliability

FIGURE 8-23 Microsoft has released many versions of Windows.

also includes Windows Media Player, which allows users to listen to Internet radio stations, play MP3 and other music formats, copy music and data to CDs, and watch DVD movies.

Windows XP is available in five editions: Home Edition, Professional (Figure 8-24), Media Center Edition, Tablet PC Edition, and Professional x64 Edition. With Windows XP Home Edition, users easily can organize and share digital pictures, download and listen to music, create and edit videos, network home computers, send and receive instant messages, and recover from problems with easy-to-use tools. Windows XP Professional includes all the capabilities of Windows XP Home Edition and also offers greater data security, remote access to a computer, simpler administration of groups of users, multiple language user interface, and support for a wireless network.

Windows XP Media Center Edition includes all features of Windows XP Professional and is designed for Media Center PCs. A *Media Center PC* is a home entertainment personal computer that includes a mid- to high-end processor, large-capacity hard disk, CD and DVD drives, a remote control, and advanced graphics and audio capabilities.

Windows XP Tablet PC Edition includes all features of Windows XP Professional and provides additional features designed to make users more productive while working on their Tablet PC. Windows XP Professional x64 Edition is designed for power users with workstations that use 64-bit processors.

Windows Vista

Windows Vista, the successor to Windows XP, Microsoft's fastest, most reliable and efficient operating system to date, offering quicker application start up, built-in diagnostics, automatic recovery, improved security, and enhanced searching and organizing capabilities (Figure 8-25).

Windows Vista is available in five editions: Windows Vista Home Basic, Windows Vista Home Premium, Windows Vista Ultimate, Windows Vista Business, and Windows Vista Enterprise.

- *Windows Vista Home Basic*, designed for the basic home user, includes the Windows Vista Basic interface and allows users easily to search for files, protect their computer from unauthorized intruders and unwanted programs, and set parental controls to monitor the use of games, the Internet, instant messaging, and other communications programs.

- *Windows Vista Home Premium* includes all the capabilities of Windows Vista Home Basic and also offers the Windows Aero interface with its Flip 3D feature (Figure 8-26). It also provides tools to create DVDs and edit movies, record and watch television shows, connect to a game console, securely connect to Wi-Fi networks, work with a Tablet PC, and quickly view messages on a powered-off, specially equipped notebook computer.

- *Windows Vista Ultimate* includes all features of Windows Vista Home Premium and provides additional features designed to make mobile users' computers more secure and easier to network. Windows Vista features are summarized in Figure 8-27.

FIGURE 8-24 Windows XP, with its simplified look, is a fast, reliable Windows operating system.

FIGURE 8-25 Windows Vista has a new interface, easier navigation and searching techniques, and improved security.

- With *Windows Vista Business*, users in all sizes of businesses are provided a secure operating environment that uses the Windows Aero interface where they easily can search for files, protect their computers from unauthorized intruders and unwanted programs, use improved backup technologies, securely connect to Wi-Fi networks, quickly view messages on a powered-off, specially equipped notebook computer, and easily share documents and collaborate with other users.
- *Windows Vista Enterprise* includes all the features of Windows Vista Business and also offers greater levels of data protection and a multi-language interface.

To run Windows Vista Basic, your computer must have at least 512 MB of RAM. For all other editions, your computer must have at least 1 GB of RAM and at least 128 MB of video (graphics) memory. Windows Vista adapts to the hardware configuration on which it is installed. Thus, two users with the same edition of Windows Vista may experience different functionality and interfaces.

FIGURE 8-26 With Windows Vista Flip 3D, users flip through open windows by rolling the wheel on their mouse.

 FAQ 8-7

How do I know that my hardware and software will work with Windows Vista?

Hardware and software compatible with Windows Vista may display either the Certified for Windows Vista or Works with Windows Vista logo on the packaging. If neither of these logos appears, check the manufacturer's Web site for compatibility information. For more information, visit scsite.com/dc2008/ch8/faq and then click Windows Vista Compatibility.

WINDOWS VISTA FEATURES

Reliability and Performance	• New Sleep state combines the resume to your work speed of Windows XP Standby mode and low power consumption of Hibernate mode • Programs start faster with Windows SuperFetch technology • Automatically detects and fine tunes performance problems • Built-in hardware diagnostics detect and repair problems automatically • Automatically recovers from failures, including restoring an unbootable computer to a usable state
Security	• User Account Control allows administrators to restrict permissions • Improved firewall • Protects users from dangerous Web sites • *Windows Defender* protects your computer from spyware
Information Management	• *Document Explorer, Picture Explorer*, and *Music Explorer* help users locate documents by showing thumbnails that preview documents' content and allowing users to adjust thumbnail size to view a document without opening it • Use Instant Search to locate files based on file name or any other property saved with the file • Easily share files with other users
Appearance and Navigation	• Easy-to-navigate user interface with translucent windows to minimize distraction, customizes itself based on the hardware capabilities of the computer on which it is installed • *Flip 3D* works with the mouse to flip through open windows arranged in a stack • *Windows Sidebar* connects to personalized mini-applications, called gadgets, such as weather, photos, or headline news • Display a preview of the current window when you point to a program button on the taskbar • *Windows SideShow* allows viewing of messages on a powered-off notebook computer equipped with a secondary display • Common dialog boxes shared by all applications
Communications and the Internet	• Enhanced Internet Explorer • Improved e-mail program with built-in spam filter • Consistent and secure wireless network connections • Speech recognition allows you to interact with the computer by voice

FIGURE 8-27 Some features of Windows Vista.

Mac OS X

Since it was released in 1984 with Macintosh computers, Apple's **Macintosh operating system** has set the standard for operating system ease of use and has been the model for most of the new GUIs developed for non-Macintosh systems. The latest version, **Mac OS X**, is a multitasking operating system available only for computers manufactured by Apple (Figure 8-28). Read Looking Ahead 8-1 for a look at the future of Apple and Mac OS X.

Mac OS X includes features from previous versions of the Macintosh operating system such as large photo-quality icons, built-in networking support, e-mail, online shopping, enhanced speech recognition, CD burning, and enhanced multimedia capabilities. In addition, Mac OS X includes these features:

- New desktop search technology
- Dashboard, a desktop area for mini-applications
- Built-in, fast Web browser
- Parental controls
- Accessibility interface reads e-mail messages
- 3-D personal video and audio conferencing
- Filter to eliminate junk e-mail messages
- Contact lists synchronized with PDA or Bluetooth-enabled smart phone
- Latest version of QuickTime to listen to music and view videos on the Internet
- Easy networking of computers and devices
- Windows network connection and shared Windows documents

WEB LINK 8-6

Mac OS X

For more information, visit scsite.com/dc2008/ch8/weblink and then click Mac OS X.

FIGURE 8-28 Mac OS X is the operating system used with Apple Macintosh computers.

 LOOKING AHEAD 8-1

Apple Marching to Its Own Tune

When the iPod hit the marketplace in 2001, few people expected that it would become one of the most successful products of the young century. More than 60 million people, including England's Queen Elizabeth and Pope Benedict, own one of these units. Five years later, Apple CEO Steve Jobs acknowledged that although the iPod and iTunes account for more than 40 percent of the company's revenues, the entire line will be entirely overhauled and become a significant part of wearable technology.

At Apple's annual Worldwide Developers Conference in 2006, Jobs and other company executives announced key future updates. Among them are improvements to Mac OS X, including effortless backups, the capability for Intel-based Macs to run more Windows applications, and an expanded search engine.

Photographs, music, movies, and downloaded videos will be accessed from a single interface, and users with physical disabilities will have improved universal access. For more information, visit scsite.com/dc2008/ch8/looking and then click Apple Future.

UNIX

UNIX (pronounced YOU-nix) is a multitasking operating system developed in the early 1970s by scientists at Bell Laboratories. Bell Labs (a subsidiary of AT&T) was prohibited from actively promoting UNIX in the commercial marketplace because of federal regulations. Bell Labs instead licensed UNIX for a low fee to numerous colleges and universities, where UNIX obtained a wide following. UNIX was implemented on many different types of computers. After deregulation of the telephone companies in the 1980s, UNIX was licensed to many hardware and software companies.

Several versions of this operating system exist, each slightly different. When programmers move application software from one UNIX version to another, they sometimes have to rewrite some of the programs. Although some versions of UNIX have a command-line interface, most versions of UNIX offer a graphical user interface (Figure 8-29).

Today, a version of UNIX is available for most computers of all sizes.

 WEB LINK 8-7

UNIX

For more information, visit scsite.com/dc2008/ch8/weblink and then click UNIX.

Power users often work with UNIX because of its flexibility and power. Manufacturers such as Sun and IBM sell personal computers and workstations with a UNIX operating system.

GURE 8-29 Some versions of UNIX have a graphical er interface.

Linux

Linux is one of the faster growing operating systems. **Linux** (pronounced LINN-uks) is a popular, multitasking UNIX-type operating system. In addition to the basic operating system, Linux also includes many free programming languages and utility programs.

Linux is not proprietary software like the operating systems discussed thus far. Instead, Linux is *open source software*, which means its code is provided for use, modification, and redistribution. It has no restrictions from the copyright holder regarding modification of the software's internal instructions and redistribution of the software. Many programmers have donated time to modify and redistribute Linux to make it the best possible version of UNIX. Promoters of open source software state two main advantages: users who modify the software share their improvements with others, and customers can personalize the software to meet their needs. Read Ethics & Issues 8-4 for a related discussion.

Some versions of Linux are command-line. Others are GUI. The two most popular GUIs available for Linux are GNOME and KDE. Some companies such as Red Hat market software applications that run on their own version of Linux (Figure 8-30). Many application programs, utilities, and plug-ins have Linux versions, including OpenOffice.org, StarOffice, Mozilla, Netscape, Yahoo! Messenger, RealPlayer, QuickTime, and Acrobat Reader.

Users obtain Linux in a variety of ways. Some download it free from the Web. Others purchase it from vendors such as Red Hat or IBM, who bundle their own software with the operating system. Linux CD-ROMs are included in many Linux books and also are available for purchase from vendors. Another option is *Live CD* or *Live USB*, where the CD or USB flash drive is bootable. In this case, the CD or USB drive contains files necessary to boot and work with the Linux operating system, which allows users to preview the operating system without installing it. Some retailers such as Dell will preinstall Linux on a new computer's hard disk on request.

ETHICS & ISSUES 8-4

Closed Source vs. Open Source Operating Systems

Linux is a fast-growing, innovative operating system. One of the features that make it different from other operating systems is that Linux is open source and its source code, along with any changes, remains public. Since its introduction in 1991, Linux has been altered, adapted, and improved by thousands of programmers. Unlike Linux, most operating systems are proprietary, and their program code often is a zealously guarded secret. At one large software developer, an employee reported that application programmers had little opportunity to contribute to operating system programs because they had no access to the operating system program source code. Supporters of open source maintain that source code should be open to the public so that it can be scrutinized, corrected, and enhanced. In light of concerns about security and fears of possible virus problems, however, some people are not sure open source software is a good idea. Besides, they argue, companies and programmers should be able to control, and profit from, the operating systems they create. On the other hand, open source software can be scrutinized for errors by a much larger group of people and changes can be made immediately. Are open source operating systems a good idea? Why or why not? How can the concerns about open source operating systems be addressed? What are the advantages and disadvantages of open versus closed source operating systems? Does the open source model lead to better software?

FIGURE 8-30 Red Hat provides a version of Linux called Red Hat Enterprise Linux.

Test your knowledge of pages 410 through 421 in Quiz Yourself 8-2.

QUIZ YOURSELF 8-2

Instructions: Find the true statement below. Then, rewrite the remaining false statements so they are true.

1. A file manager is a utility that detects and protects a personal computer from unauthorized intrusions.
2. Fragmenting a disk is the process of reorganizing it so the files are stored in contiguous sectors.
3. Windows Vista Home Basic uses the Windows Aero interface.
4. Mac OS X is a multitasking operating system available only for computers manufactured by Apple.
5. Flip 3D is a UNIX-type operating system that is open source software.
6. You should uninstall files and disks regularly in the event your originals are lost, damaged, or destroyed.

Quiz Yourself Online: To further check your knowledge of utilities included with most operating systems and stand-alone operating systems, visit scsite.com/dc2008/ch8/quiz and then click Objectives 5 – 6.

NETWORK OPERATING SYSTEMS

As discussed earlier in this chapter, a network operating system is an operating system that is designed specifically to support a network. A network operating system typically resides on a server. The client computers on the network rely on the server(s) for resources. Many of the client operating systems discussed in the previous section work in conjunction with a network operating system.

Some of the stand-alone operating systems discussed in the previous section include networking capability; however, network operating systems are designed specifically to support all sizes of networks, including medium to large-sized businesses and Web servers. Examples of network operating systems include Windows Server 2003, UNIX, Linux, Solaris, and NetWare.

Windows Server 2003

Windows Server 2003 is an upgrade to Windows 2000 Server, which was an upgrade to Windows NT Server. Windows Server 2003, which includes features of previous server versions, offers the following capabilities:
- Web site management and hosting
- Delivery and management of multimedia across intranets and the Internet
- Document storage in Web folders
- Central information repository about network users and resources with *Active Directory*
- Client support using Windows, Mac OS X, UNIX, and Linux

To meet the needs of all sizes of businesses, the **Windows Server 2003 family** includes five products:
- *Windows Small Business Server 2003* designed for businesses with fewer than 75 users and limited networking expertise
- *Windows Server 2003, Standard Edition* for the typical small- to medium-sized business network
- *Windows Server 2003, Enterprise Edition* for medium- to large-sized businesses, including those with e-commerce operations; available in 64-bit version
- *Windows Server 2003, Datacenter Edition* for businesses with huge volumes of transactions and large-scale databases; available in 64-bit version
- *Windows Server 2003, Web Edition* for Web server and Web hosting businesses

Windows Server 2003 is part of Windows Server System. In addition to Windows Server 2003, *Windows Server System* provides developers with dynamic development tools that allow businesses and customers to connect and communicate easily via the Internet. Through Windows Server System, programmers have the ability to use *Web services*, which are Web applications created with any programming language or any operating system to communicate and share data seamlessly.

UNIX

In addition to being a stand-alone operating system, UNIX also is a network operating system. That is, UNIX is capable of handling a high volume of transactions in a multiuser environment and working with multiple processors using multiprocessing. For this reason, some computer professionals call UNIX a *multipurpose operating system* because it is both a stand-alone and network operating system. Many Web servers use UNIX as their operating system.

Linux

Some network servers use Linux as their operating system. Thus, Linux also is a multi-purpose operating system. With Linux, a net-work administrator can configure the network, administer security, run a Web server, and process e-mail. Clients on the network can run Linux, UNIX, or Windows. Versions of Linux include both the Netscape and Mozilla Web browsers.

FAQ 8-8

How widespread is Linux usage?

Forecasters predict that Linux will command more than one-third of the server market by 2009. Desktop personal computers, however, have a much lower Linux usage — only six percent worldwide. For more information, visit scsite.com/dc2008/ch8/faq and then click Linux Users.

Solaris

Solaris, a version of UNIX developed by Sun Microsystems, is a network operating system designed specifically for e-commerce applications. Solaris manages high-traffic accounts and incorporates security necessary for Web transactions. Client computers often use a desk-top program, such as GNOME desktop, that communicates with the Solaris operating system.

NetWare

Novell's *NetWare* is a network operating system designed for client/server networks. NetWare has a server portion that resides on the network server and a client portion that resides on each client computer connected to the net-work. NetWare supports open source software and runs on all types of computers from mainframes to personal computers.

The server portion of NetWare allows users to share hardware devices attached to the server (such as a printer), as well as e-mail, databases, or any other files and software stored on the server. The client portion of NetWare communicates with the server. Client computers also can have their own stand-alone operating system such as Windows Vista, Windows XP, Mac OS X, or a Linux-based client.

WEB LINK 8-8

Solaris
For more information, visit scsite.com/dc2008/ch8/weblink and then click Solaris.

EMBEDDED OPERATING SYSTEMS

The operating system on most PDAs and small devices, called an **embedded operating system**, resides on a ROM chip. Popular embedded operating systems today include Windows CE, Windows Mobile, Palm OS, Blackberry, embed-ded Linux, and Symbian OS. The following sections discuss these operating systems.

Windows CE

Windows CE is a scaled-down Windows operating system designed for use on com-munications, entertainment, and computing devices with limited functionality. Examples of devices that use Windows CE include Voice over IP devices, industrial control devices, point-of-sale terminals, security robots, navi-gation systems, media players, ticket machines, and computerized sewing machines (Figure 8-31).

FIGURE 8-31 This sewing machine uses Windows CE to assist with stitching quilts, garments, crafts, decorations, and embroidery.

Windows CE is a GUI that supports color, sound, multitasking, multimedia, e-mail, Internet access, and Web browsing. A built-in file viewer allows users to view files created in popular applications such as Word, Excel, and PowerPoint.

Devices equipped with Windows CE can communicate wirelessly with computers and other devices using Bluetooth or other wireless technologies, as long as the device is equipped with the necessary communications hardware.

Windows Mobile

Windows Mobile, an operating system based on Windows CE, includes functionality, applications, and a user interface designed for specific types of devices. Windows Mobile-based devices include PDAs, called the **Pocket PC**, and smart phones (Figure 8-32). With the Windows Mobile operating system and a Pocket PC or smart phone, users have access to all the basic PIM (personal information manager) functions such as contact lists, schedules, tasks, calendars, and notes. Information on the PDA or smart phone easily synchronizes with a personal computer or prints on a printer using a cable or a wireless technology.

Windows Mobile also provides numerous additional features that allow users to check e-mail, browse the Web, listen to music, take pictures or record video, watch a video, send and receive instant messages, record a voice message, manage finances, or read an e-book. Many applications, such as Word, Excel, Outlook, and Internet Explorer, have scaled-down versions that run with Windows Mobile. Some devices with Windows Mobile also support handwriting and voice input. With the Pocket PC Phone devices, users can make telephone calls and send text messages using the PDA.

WEB LINK 8-9

Windows Mobile
For more information, visit scsite.com/dc2008/ch8/weblink and then click Windows Mobile.

smart phone

FIGURE 8-32 Windows Mobile runs on Pocket PCs and many smart phones.

Palm OS

A competing operating system to Windows Mobile is *Palm OS*, which runs on PDAs and smart phones (Figure 8-33). With Palm OS devices, users manage schedules and contacts, telephone messages, project notes, reminders, task and address lists, and important dates and appointments. Information on the PDA or smart phone easily synchronizes with a personal computer or prints on a printer using a cable or a wireless technology. Palm users also can exchange information with other Palm users wirelessly through IrDA technology.

Palm OS includes handwriting recognition software, called Graffiti. Many Palm OS devices allow users to connect wirelessly to the Internet, browse the Web, send and receive e-mail messages and instant messages, listen to music, record voice messages, and view digital photos. The latest version of Palm OS includes improved security for data transmission, allows for biometric identification, and supports the use of smart cards.

Palm OS PDA

FIGURE 8-33 Palm OS runs on PDAs and smart phones.

BlackBerry

The *BlackBerry* operating system runs on handheld devices supplied by RIM (Research in Motion). BlackBerry devices provide PDA capabilities such as managing schedules and contacts, as well as telephone capabilities (Figure 8-34). They also provide wireless functionality that includes sending e-mail messages, text messages, and instant messages; connecting to the Internet; and accessing Bluetooth devices. Some BlackBerry devices allow users to take pictures, play music, and access maps and directions.

BlackBerry device

FIGURE 8-34 A handheld device that uses the BlackBerry operating system.

Embedded Linux

Embedded Linux is a scaled-down Linux operating system designed for PDAs, smart phones, smart watches, set-top boxes, Internet telephones, and many other types of devices and computers requiring an embedded operating system. PDAs and smart phones with embedded Linux offer calendar and address book and other PIM functions, touch screens, and handwriting recognition. Many also allow you to connect to the Internet, take pictures, play videos, listen to music, and send e-mail and instant messages. Devices that use embedded Linux synchronize with desktop computers using a variety of technologies including Bluetooth.

Symbian OS

Symbian OS is an open source multitasking operating system designed for smart phones (Figure 8-35). In addition to making telephone calls, users of Symbian OS can maintain contact lists; save appointments;

FIGURE 8-35 This smart phone uses the Symbian OS.

browse the Web; and send and receive text and picture messages, e-mail messages, and faxes using a smart phone. Users enter data by pressing keys on the keypad or keyboard, touching the screen, writing on the screen with a stylus, or speaking into the smart phone. Symbian OS allows users to communicate wirelessly using a variety of technologies including Bluetooth and IrDA.

STAND-ALONE UTILITY PROGRAMS

Although operating systems typically include some built-in utilities, many stand-alone utility programs are available for purchase. For example, you can purchase personal firewall, backup utilities, and screen savers. These stand-alone utilities typically offer improvements over those features built into the operating system or provide features not included in an operating system.

Other functions provided by stand-alone utilities include protecting against viruses, removing spyware and adware, filtering Internet content, converting files, compressing files, playing media files, burning CDs and DVDs, and maintaining a personal computer. The following sections discuss each of these utilities.

Antivirus Programs

The term, computer **virus**, describes a potentially damaging computer program that affects, or infects, a computer negatively by altering the way the computer works without the user's knowledge or permission. More specifically, a computer virus is a segment of program code from some outside source that implants itself in a computer. Once the virus is in a computer, it can spread throughout and may damage your files and operating system.

Computer viruses do not generate by chance. The programmer of a virus, known as a *virus author*, intentionally writes a virus program. Some virus authors find writing viruses a challenge. Others write virus programs to cause destruction. Writing a virus program usually requires significant programming skills.

Some viruses are harmless pranks that simply freeze a computer temporarily or display sounds or messages. The Music Bug virus, for

WEB LINK 8-10

BlackBerry

For more information, visit scsite.com/dc2008/ch8/weblink and then click BlackBerry.

example, instructs the computer to play a few chords of music. Other viruses destroy or corrupt data stored on the hard disk of the infected computer. If you notice any unusual changes in your computer's performance, it may be infected with a virus. Figure 8-36 outlines some common symptoms of virus infection.

Viruses are just one type of malicious software. *Malware* (short for malicious software) is software that acts without a user's knowledge and deliberately alters the computer's operations. In addition to viruses, worms and Trojan horses are malware.

A **worm**, such as Sasser or Klez, copies itself repeatedly, for example, in memory or over a network, using up system resources and possibly shutting the system down. A **Trojan horse** (named after the Greek myth) hides within or looks like a legitimate program such as a screen saver. A certain condition or action usually triggers the Trojan horse. Unlike a virus or worm, a Trojan horse does not replicate itself to other computers. Currently, more than 180,000 known viruses, worms, Trojan horses, and other malware exist. For a more technical discussion about computer viruses, read the High-Tech Talk article in Chapter 3 on page 168.

To protect a computer from virus attacks, users should install an antivirus program and update it frequently. An **antivirus program** protects a computer against viruses by identifying and

removing any computer viruses found in memory, on storage media, or on incoming files (Figure 8-37). Most antivirus programs also protect against worms and Trojan horses. When you purchase a new computer, it often includes antivirus software.

Three more popular antivirus programs are McAfee VirusScan, Norton AntiVirus, and Windows Live OneCare, the latter of which also contains spyware removers, Internet filters, PC maintenance, and backup utilities. As an alternative to purchasing these products on CD, both McAfee and Norton offer Web-based antivirus programs.

FAQ 8-9

What steps should I take to prevent virus infections on my computer?

Set up the antivirus software to scan on a regular basis. Update your virus definitions regularly. Never open an e-mail attachment unless you are expecting the attachment and it is from a trusted source. If you use Windows, install the latest Microsoft updates. Set macro security in programs such as word processing and spreadsheet so you can enable or disable macros. Back up files regularly. For more information, visit scsite.com/dc2008/ch8/faq and then click Preventing Virus Infections.

SIGNS OF VIRUS INFECTION

- An unusual message or image is displayed on the computer screen
- An unusual sound or music plays randomly
- The available memory is less than what should be available
- A program or file suddenly is missing
- An unknown program or file mysteriously appears
- The size of a file changes without explanation
- A file becomes corrupted
- A program or file does not work properly
- System properties change

FIGURE 8-36 Viruses attack computers in a variety of ways. This list indicates some of the more common signs of virus infection.

FIGURE 8-37 An antivirus program scans memory, disks, and incoming e-mail messages and attachments for viruses and attempts to remove any viruses it finds.

Spyware Removers

Spyware is a program placed on a computer without the user's knowledge that secretly collects information about the user, often related to Web browsing habits. Spyware often enters a computer when a user installs a new program. The spyware program communicates information it collects to an outside source while you are online.

Adware is a program that displays an online advertisement in a banner or pop-up window on Web pages, e-mail, or other Internet services. Sometimes, spyware is hidden in adware. A **spyware remover** is a program that detects and deletes spyware, adware, and other similar programs. Most spyware removers cost less than $50; some are available on the Web at no cost. Some operating systems include spyware removers and adware blockers. Popular spyware and adware removers include Ad-Aware, Spy Sweeper, Spybot - Search and Destroy, and Windows Defender.

Internet Filters

Filters are programs that remove or block certain items from being displayed. Three widely used Internet filters are anti-spam programs, Web filters, and pop-up blockers.

ANTI-SPAM PROGRAMS *Spam* is an unsolicited e-mail message or newsgroup posting sent to many recipients or newsgroups at once. Spam is Internet junk mail. The content of spam ranges from selling a product or service, to promoting a business opportunity, to advertising offensive material. An **anti-spam program** is a filtering program that attempts to remove spam before it reaches your inbox. If your e-mail program does not filter spam, many anti-spam programs are available at no cost on the Web. Internet access providers often filter spam as a service for their subscribers.

WEB FILTERS **Web filtering software** is a program that restricts access to certain material on the Web. Some restrict access to specific Web sites; others filter sites that use certain words or phrases. Many businesses use Web filtering software to limit employee's Web access. Some schools, libraries, and parents use this software to restrict access to minors.

POP-UP BLOCKERS A *pop-up ad* is an Internet advertisement that appears in a new window in the foreground of a Web page displayed in your browser. A **pop-up blocker** is a filtering program that stops pop-up ads from displaying on Web pages. If your Web browser does not block pop-up

ads, many pop-up blockers can be downloaded from the Web at no cost.

FAQ 8-10

Should anti-spam programs be installed on home computers?

Yes. Reports indicate that spam originated as early as 1978, when an e-mail was sent to several ARPANET addresses. As shown in the chart below, spam now accounts for approximately 90 percent of e-mail traffic, with that number increasing daily. Fortunately, anti-spam programs installed on your computer, combined with your Internet access provider's anti-spam measures, greatly reduce the amount of spam you receive. For more information, visit scsite.com/dc2008/ch8/faq and then click Spam.

Source: The ClickZ Network

File Conversion

A *file conversion utility* transforms the contents of a file or data from one format to another. When a business develops a new information system, often the data in the current system is not in the correct format for the new system. Thus, part of the system development process is to convert data — instead of having users reenter all the existing data in the new system. On a smaller scale, when home users purchase new software, they may need to convert files so the files will be displayed properly in the new software.

File Compression

A **file compression utility** shrinks the size of a file(s). A compressed file takes up less storage space than the original file. Compressing files frees up room on the storage media and improves system performance. Attaching a compressed file to an e-mail message, for example, reduces the time needed for file transmission. Uploading and downloading compressed files to and from the Internet reduces the file transmission time.

Compressed files, sometimes called **zipped files**, usually have a .zip extension. When you receive or download a compressed file, you must uncompress it. To **uncompress**, or *unzip*, a file, you restore it to its original form. Some operating systems such as Windows Vista include file compression and uncompression capabilities. Two popular stand-alone file compression utilities are PKZIP and WinZip.

Media Player

A **media player** is a program that allows you to view images and animation, listen to audio, and watch video files on your computer (Figure 8-38). Media players may also include the capability to organize media files, convert them to different formats, connect to and purchase media from an online media store, download podcasts and vodcasts, burn audio CDs, and transfer media to portable media players such as an iPod. Windows Vista includes Windows Media Player. Two other popular media players are iTunes and RealPlayer.

WEB LINK 8-11

Media Players

For more information, visit scsite.com/ dc2008/ch8/weblink and then click Media Players.

FIGURE 8-38   iTunes is a popular media player.

CD/DVD Burning

CD/DVD burning software writes text, graphics, audio, and video files on a recordable or rewritable CD or DVD, including Blu-ray and HD DVD. This software enables the home user easily to back up contents of their hard disk on a CD/DVD and make duplicates of uncopyrighted music or movies. CD/DVD burning software usually also includes photo editing, audio editing, and video editing capabilities (Figure 8-39).

When you buy a recordable or rewritable CD or DVD, it typically includes CD/DVD burning software. You also can buy CD/DVD burning software for a cost of less than $100.

FIGURE 8-39   Using CD/DVD burning software, you can copy text, graphics, audio, and video files on CD or DVD, provided you have the correct type of CD/DVD drive and media.

Personal Computer Maintenance

Operating systems typically include a diagnostic utility that diagnoses computer problems but does not repair them. A **personal computer maintenance utility** identifies and fixes operating system problems, detects and repairs disk problems, and includes the capability of improving a computer's performance. Additionally, some personal computer maintenance utilities continuously monitor a computer while you use it to identify and repair problems before they occur. Norton SystemWorks is a popular personal computer maintenance utility designed for Windows operating systems (Figure 8-40).

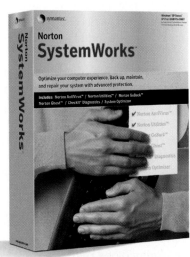

FIGURE 8-40   A popular maintenance program for Windows users.

Test your knowledge of pages 422 through 428 in Quiz Yourself 8-3.

QUIZ YOURSELF 8-3

Instructions: Find the true statement below. Then, rewrite the remaining false statements so they are true.

1. A pop-up blocker shrinks the size of a file(s).

2. An anti-spam program protects a computer against viruses by identifying and removing any computer viruses found in memory, on storage media, or on incoming files.

3. Examples of network operating systems include Windows Server 2003, UNIX, Linux, Solaris, and Netware.

4. Pocket PCs use Palm OS as their operating system.

5. Web filtering software writes text, graphics, audio, and video files to a recordable or rewritable CD or DVD.

Quiz Yourself Online: To further check your knowledge of network operating systems, embedded operating systems, and stand-alone utility programs, visit scsite.com/dc2008/ch8/quiz and then click Objectives 7 – 9.

LOOKING AHEAD 8-2

Online Operating Systems Proposed

Microsoft Windows' dominance in the operating system world is being challenged by proposed Web operating systems. Experts predict that within a few years computer users will see Google, Yahoo!, and Mozilla release Internet-enabled products. Independent programmers are developing their own online operating systems, such as YouOS and XIN.

If these operating systems come to fruition, computer users will access content and manage data using a Web browser. Applications will be written for this Web browser and will not be dependent upon a specific machine or cellular phone.

Proposed applications include reading e-mail, blogs, and news offline; backing up files to an online service; and managing audio and video files. For more information, visit scsite.com/dc2008/ch8/looking and then click Operating Systems.

CHAPTER SUMMARY

This chapter defined an operating system and then discussed the functions common to most operating systems. Next, it introduced several utility programs commonly found in operating systems. The chapter discussed a variety of stand-alone operating systems, network operating systems, and embedded operating systems (read Looking Ahead 8-2 for a look at the next generation of operating systems). Finally, the chapter described several stand-alone utility programs.

CAREER CORNER

Systems Programmer

System software is a key component in any computer. A *systems programmer* evaluates, installs, and maintains system software and provides technical support to the programming staff.

Systems programmers work with the programs that control computers, such as operating systems, network operating systems, and database systems. They identify current and future processing needs and then recommend the software and hardware necessary to meet those needs. In addition to selecting and installing system software, systems programmers must be able to adapt system software to the requirements of an organization, provide regular maintenance, measure system performance, determine the impact of new or updated software on the system, design and implement special software, and provide documentation. Because they are familiar with the entire system, systems programmers often help application programmers to diagnose technical problems.

Systems programmers must be acquainted thoroughly with a variety of operating systems. They must be able to think logically, pay attention to detail, work with abstract concepts, and devise solutions to complex problems. Systems programmers often work in teams and interact with programmers and nontechnical users, so communications skills are important.

Most systems programmers have a four-year B.S. degree in Computer Science or Information Technology. Depending on responsibilities and experience, salaries range from $60,000 to more than $115,000. For more information, visit scsite.com/dc2008/ch8/careers and then click Systems Programmer.

High-Tech Talk

LOSSY VS. LOSSLESS DATA COMPRESSION: USING COMPRESSION ALGORITHMS TO REDUCE FILE SIZE

As discussed earlier in this chapter, compression is the process of shrinking the size of a file. Text, graphics, audio, and video are the four types of files that can be compressed. Whether you are backing up data, transferring media to or from a portable media player, recording video with a digital video camera, or taking pictures with a digital camera, you usually will need to choose a file compression type. Take, for example, a digital video camera. If you want to share the videos electronically, you first must transfer it from the camera to your computer. Before or after the transfer process completes, you will choose how to save the video. At this point, you can choose a compression type. A digital video camera also may allow you to specify what type of compression to use while it records the video. Each option for saving or recording the video corresponds with a different type, or level, of compression. Depending on the type of compression you apply, you may or may not be able to view or modify the file before it is uncompressed, or restored to its original form.

Before you can make an informed decision about a compression type, you first should understand the differences between lossy and lossless compression. When *lossy* data compression is applied to a file, the quality of the file will decrease slightly each time you compress the file, and you will be unable to restore the file to its exact original state. Degradations in quality resulting from lossy compression sometimes are unrecognizable; however, these degradations, also known as the *compression artifacts*, will become more apparent if a higher rate of compression is applied to a file, or if the file has been compressed and uncompressed multiple times. The extent to which a file is compressed is known as the *data compression ratio*. Figure 8-41 displays three versions of the same image, each saved with a different compression ratio. Audio files can be compressed up to one-tenth of their original size before you may notice a decrease in quality. Video files can retain the same noticeable visible quality with a much higher data compression ratio, but graphics often can afford only a small compression ratio before sacrificing quality. You can calculate the compression ratio by dividing the compressed file size by the original file size. For example, if a 20 MB file has been compressed to 5 MB, the data compression ratio would be 5/20, or 25 percent. Files that are compressed using lossy compression usually are smaller files than those compressed using lossless compression.

Lossless data compression is used when you must compress a file, but also must be able to return that file to its exact original state. For example, if you want to compress a series of word processing files before e-mailing them to a colleague, your colleague must be able to return those files to their original state without a reduction in quality. If a word processing file is affected by a reduction in quality, letters, words, or entire paragraphs may be lost or otherwise unreadable when the file is uncompressed. For this reason, lossless compression is more appropriate for text files.

Programs use a *compression algorithm*, which is a set of steps that are used to compress a file. Multiple compression algorithms currently exist and determine the extent to which you can compress a file. Backup programs, such as Windows Vista's Backup and Restore Center, often use a lossless compression algorithm so that backed up files can be restored to their original state. Programs, such as iTunes, that are used to play media, as well as transfer media to and from portable media players can apply lossy or lossless compression. If you prefer high-quality audio, you should use lossless compression. For low-quality audio, lossy compression is sufficient. Similarly, digital cameras and digital video cameras also allow you select from lossy and lossless compression. Once again, lossless compression algorithms should be used to maintain high-quality files, and lossy compression algorithms should be used when lower quality is acceptable. For more information, visit scsite.com/dc2008/ch8/tech and then click Compression.

FIGURE 8-41 Each of these three photos was saved with a different compression ratio. Notice that the photo on the left, which was compressed the most, has the lowest quality, and the photo on the right, which was compressed the least, has the highest quality.

Companies on the Cutting Edge

RED HAT
OPEN SOURCE SOFTWARE DISTRIBUTOR

When you were young, you were taught to share. University professors share their research with colleagues throughout the world; and *Red Hat* shares software code, or instructions, with computer users.

Red Hat is the largest supplier of open source software, which allows buyers to view, modify, and perhaps improve, the software. The company delivers the software improvements to customers through the Red Hat Network, the company's Internet service.

Bob Young and Marc Ewing founded Red Hat in 1994 and started distributing a version of the Red Hat Linux operating system complete with documentation and support. Today, Linux is Red Hat's most well-known product. Subscriptions to the company's premium Linux software have helped boost the company to profitability. The company expanded its global presence in 2006 when it announced its participation in the next-generation telecommunication service used across the European Union. For more information, visit scsite.com/dc2008/ch8/companies and then click Red Hat.

RESEARCH IN MOTION (RIM)
WIRELESS MOBILE COMMUNICATIONS DEVICES MANUFACTURER

In today's mobile world, people often need to access their e-mail wirelessly. Chances are they find *Research in Motion (RIM)*'s products valuable. More than 4 million people are using RIM's popular BlackBerry models, which combine e-mail, telephone, Internet browsing, and organizer features. The built-in keyboards allow users to send and receive text messages.

Mike Lazaridis, the current co-CEO, founded RIM in 1984 in Waterloo, Ontario. His passion for wireless technology emerged in high school as a member of the local amateur radio and television club. He developed RIM's first major product, the Inter@ctive Pager, in 1996. Two years later, the same hardware was used in the first BlackBerry; this product's success was due to its capability to combine a wireless mailbox with a corporate mailbox so that users could access e-mail continuously.

In 2006, RIM settled a long-time patent dispute, which allowed its wireless service to continue to its more than 3 million customers. For more information, visit scsite.com/dc2008/ch8/companies and then click RIM.

Technology Trailblazers

ALAN KAY
COMPUTER PIONEER

Chances are that every time you use your computer you use one of *Alan Kay*'s ideas. More than 35 years ago — long before the personal computer became ubiquitous — he was developing a notebook computer complete with a flat screen, wireless network, and storage. More than 20 years ago, he engineered a graphical user interface, object-oriented languages, and personal computer networks.

Kay did much of his early work at the U.S. Defense Department's Advance Research Project Agency (DARPA) and Xerox's Palo Alto Research Center (PARC). Today he is a computer science professor at UCLA and president of the Viewpoints Research Institute, a nonprofit organization dedicated to helping children develop fluency in critical thinking, math, and science. For more information, visit scsite.com/dc2008/ch8/people and then click Alan Kay.

LINUS TORVALDS
LINUX CREATOR

When *Linus Torvalds* developed a new operating system in 1991, he announced his project in an Internet newsgroup, made the source code available, and asked for suggestions. Computer users responded by reviewing the system and offering enhancements. Three years later, Torvalds released a much-enhanced version of an open source operating system he called Linux.

Torvalds developed the innovative operating system when he was a 21-year-old computer science student in Finland. Today, Linux is estimated to be running on at least 10 percent of computers and is Microsoft's main competitor. Torvalds leads the development of Linux as a fellow at OSDL (Open Source Development Labs), a not-for-profit consortium of companies dedicated to developing and promoting the operating system. In 2006, he took fifth place in *Computer Weekly*'s list of the Top 10 greatest IT people. For more information, visit scsite.com/dc2008/ch8/people and then click Linus Torvalds.

Chapter Review

The Chapter Review section summarizes the concepts presented in this chapter. To listen to the audio version of this Chapter Review, visit scsite.com/dc2008/ch8/review. To obtain help from other students regarding any subject in this chapter, visit scsite.com/dc2008/ch8/forum and post your thoughts or questions.

① What Are the Types of System Software? **System software** consists of the programs that control or maintain the operations of a computer and its devices. Two types of system software are operating systems and utility programs. An **operating system (OS)** contains instructions that coordinate all the activities among computer hardware resources. A **utility program** performs maintenance-type tasks, usually related to managing a computer, its devices, or its programs.

② What Is the Startup Process on a Personal Computer? **Booting** is the process of starting or restarting a computer. When a user turns on a computer, the power supply sends a signal to the system unit. The processor chip finds the ROM chip(s) that contains the **BIOS**, which is firmware with the computer's startup instructions. The BIOS performs the *power-on self test* (*POST*) to check system components and compares the results with data in a CMOS chip. If the POST completes successfully, the BIOS searches for the *system files* and the *kernel* of the operating system, which manages memory and devices, and loads them into memory from storage. Finally, the operating system loads configuration information, requests any necessary user information, and displays the desktop on the screen.

③ What Are the Functions of an Operating System? The operating system provides a user interface, manages programs, manages memory, schedules jobs, configures devices, establishes an Internet connection, and monitors performance. The **user interface** controls how data and instructions are entered and how information is displayed. Two types of user interfaces are a *command-line interface* and a *graphical user interface (GUI)*. Managing programs refers to how many users, and how many programs, an operating system can support at one time. An operating system can be *single user/single tasking*, *single user/multitasking*, *multiuser*, or *multiprocessing*. **Memory management** optimizes the use of random access memory (RAM). If memory is insufficient, the operating system may use **virtual memory**, which allocates a portion of a storage medium to function as additional RAM. Scheduling jobs determines the order in which jobs are processed. A **job** is an operation the processor manages. Configuring devices involves loading each device's driver when a user boots the computer. A **driver** is a program that tells the operating system how to communicate with a specific device. Establishing an Internet connection sets up a connection between a computer and an Internet service provider. A **performance monitor** is an operating system program that assesses and reports information about computer resources and devices.

④ How Can Operating Systems Help Administrators Control a Network and Manage Security? A **network operating system**, or *network OS*, is an operating system that organizes and coordinates how multiple users access and share network resources. A *network administrator* uses the network OS to add and remove users, computers, and other devices to and from the network. A network administrator also uses the network OS to administer network security. For each user, the network administrator establishes a user account that enables the user to **log on**, or access, the network by supplying the correct **user name** and **password**.

connect

Visit scsite.com/dc2008/ch8/• or click the Quiz Yourself button. Click Objectives 1 – 4.

⑤ What Is the Purpose of the Utilities Included with Most Operating Systems? Most operating systems include several built-in utility programs. A **file manager** performs functions related to file management. A **search utility** attempts to locate a file on your computer based on criteria you specify. An **image viewer** displays, copies, and prints the contents of a graphics file, such as a picture. A **personal firewall** detects and protects a computer from unauthorized intrusions. An **uninstaller** removes a program and any associated entries in the system files. A **disk scanner** searches for and removes unnecessary files. A **disk defragmenter** reorganizes the

Chapter Review

files and unused space on a computer's hard disk. A **diagnostic utility** compiles and reports technical information about a computer's hardware and certain system software programs. A **backup utility** is used to copy, or *back up*, selected files or an entire hard disk. A **screen saver** displays a moving image or blank screen if no keyboard or mouse activity occurs for a specified time.

(6) **What Are Features of Several Stand-Alone Operating Systems?**   A **stand-alone operating system** is a complete operating system that works on a desktop computer, notebook computer, or mobile computing device. Stand-alone operating systems include DOS, Windows XP, Windows Vista, Mac OS X, UNIX, and Linux. **Windows XP** is a fast, reliable Windows operating system, providing better performance, increased security, and a simpler look. **Windows Vista**, successor to Windows XP, is Microsoft's fastest, most reliable and efficient operating system to date, offering quicker application start up, built-in diagnostics, automatic recovery, improved security, and enhanced searching and organizing capabilities. **Mac OS X** is a multitasking operating system available only for Apple computers. **UNIX** is a multitasking operating system developed at Bell Laboratories. **Linux** is a popular, multitasking UNIX-type operating system that is *open source software*, which means its code is available to the public.

> connect
> Visit scsite.com/dc2008/ch8/quiz or click the Quiz Yourself button. Click Objectives 5 – 6.

(7) **What Are Various Network Operating Systems?**   Network operating systems include Windows Server 2003, UNIX, Linux, and Netware. **Windows Server 2003** is an upgrade to Windows 2000 Server and includes features of previous server versions. Linux, like UNIX, is a *multipurpose operating system* because it is both a stand-alone and network operating system. *Solaris*, a version of UNIX developed by Sun Microsystems, is a network OS designed for e-commerce applications. Novell's *NetWare* is a network OS designed for client/server networks.

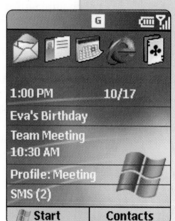

(8) **What Devices Use Embedded Operating Systems?**   Most PDAs and small devices have an **embedded operating system** that resides on a ROM chip. Popular embedded operating systems include Windows CE, Windows Mobile, Palm OS, BlackBerry, embedded Linux, and Symbian OS. **Windows CE** is a scaled-down Windows operating system designed for use on communications, entertainment, and computing devices with limited functionality. **Windows Mobile**, an operating system based on Windows CE, provides a user interface designed for a specific type of devices, such as PDAs, called the **Pocket PC**. *Palm OS* is an operating system used on PDAs and smart phones. The *BlackBerry* operating system runs on handheld devices supplied by RIM. *Embedded Linux* is a scaled-down Linux operating system for PDAs, smart phones, and other devices. *Symbian OS* is an open source multitasking operating system designed for smart phones.

(9) **What Is the Purpose of Several Stand-Alone Utility Programs?**   Stand-alone utility programs offer improvements over features built into the operating system or provide features not included in the operating system. An **antivirus program** protects computers against a **virus**, or potentially damaging computer program, by identifying and removing any computer viruses. A **spyware remover** detects and deletes *spyware*, *adware*, and other similar programs. Internet filter programs can include an **anti-spam** program, **Web filtering software**, and a **pop-up blocker**. A *file conversion utility* transforms the contents of a file from one format to another. A **file compression utility** shrinks the size of a file so that it takes up less storage space. A **media player** allows you to view images and animation, listen to audio, and watch video files on a computer. **CD/DVD burning software** writes on a recordable or rewritable CD or DVD. A **personal computer maintenance utility** identifies and fixes operating system problems and improves a computer's performance.

> connect
> Visit scsite.com/dc2008/ch8/quiz or click the Quiz Yourself button. Click Objectives 7 – 9.

Quizzes and
Learning Games

Computer Genius
Crossword Puzzle
DC Track and Field
Practice Test
Quiz Yourself
Wheel of Terms
You're Hired!

Exercises

Case Studies
Chapter Review
Checkpoint
▶ Key Terms
Learn How To
Learn It Online
Web Research

Beyond the Book

Career Corner
Companies
FAQs
High-Tech Talk
Looking Ahead
Making Use of
the Web
Trailblazers
Web Links

Features

Chapter Forum
Install Computer
Lab Exercises
Maintain Computer
Tech News
Timeline 2008

Key Terms

You should know the Primary Terms and be familiar with the Secondary Terms. Use the list below to help focus your study. To further enhance your understanding of the Key Terms in this chapter, visit scsite.com/dc2008/ch8/terms. See an example of and a definition for each term, and access current and additional information about the term from the Web.

Primary Terms

(shown in bold-black characters in the chapter)

anti-spam program (427)
antivirus program (426)
backup utility (415)
BIOS (400)
boot disk (402)
boot drive (402)
booting (400)
buffer (407)
CD/DVD burning software (428)
cold boot (400)
defragmenting (414)
diagnostic utility (414)
disk defragmenter (414)
disk scanner (414)
driver (407)
embedded operating system (423)
file compression utility (427)
file manager (412)
folder (412)
image viewer (412)
job (406)
Linux (421)
log on (410)
Mac OS X (420)
Macintosh operating system (420)
media player (428)
memory management (405)
network operating system (410)
operating system (OS) (398)
password (410)
performance monitor (409)

personal computer maintenance utility (428)
personal firewall (413)
Plug and Play (407)
Pocket PC (424)
pop-up blocker (427)
queue (407)
recovery disk (402)
restore program (415)
screen saver (415)
search utility (412)
shortcut (412)
spooling (407)
spyware remover (427)
stand-alone operating system (416)
system software (398)
Trojan horse (426)
uncompress (427)
uninstaller (413)
UNIX (420)
user ID (410)
user interface (402)
user name (410)
utility (411)
utility program (411)
virtual memory (405)
virus (425)
warm boot (400)
Web filtering software (427)
Windows CE (423)
Windows Mobile (424)
Windows Server 2003 (422)
Windows Server 2003 family (422)
Windows Vista (418)
Windows XP (417)
worm (426)
zipped files (427)

Secondary Terms

(shown in italic characters in the chapter)

Active Directory (422)
adware (427)
back up (415)
background (404)
basic input/output system (400)
BlackBerry (424)
client operating systems (416)
command language (402)
command-line interface (402)
compress (415)
cross-platform (399)
device driver (407)
device-dependent (415)
device-independent (415)
Disk Cleanup (414)
Document Explorer (419)
embedded Linux (425)
encryption (410)
Explorers (412)
fault-tolerant computer (405)
file conversion utility (427)
Flip 3D (419)
foreground (404)
fragmented (414)
ghosting (415)
graphical user interface (GUI) (403)
hacker (413)
index (412)
Internet Explorer (417)
IRQ (interrupt request line) (409)
kernel (400)
Live CD (421)
Live USB (421)
malware (426)
Media Center PC (418)
memory resident (400)
multiprocessing (405)
multipurpose operating system (423)
multiuser (405)
Music Explorer (419)
NetWare (423)
network administrator (410)
network OS (410)
nonresident (400)
open source software (421)
page (406)

paging (406)
Palm OS (424)
Picture Explorer (419)
platform (399)
pop-up ad (427)
power-on self test (POST) (400)
preemptive multitasking (405)
print spooler (407)
Problem Reports and Solution (414)
proprietary software (415)
registry (401)
service pack (416)
single user/multitasking (403)
single user/single tasking (403)
Solaris (423)
spam (427)
spyware (427)
Startup folder (401)
swap file (406)
Symbian OS (425)
system files (401)
thrashing (406)
unzip (427)
virus author (425)
Web services (422)
Windows Aero (403)
Windows Defender (419)
Windows Photo Gallery (412)
Windows Server 2003, Datacenter Edition (422)
Windows Server 2003, Enterprise Edition (422)
Windows Server 2003, Standard Edition (422)
Windows Server 2003, Web Edition (422)
Windows Server System (422)
Windows Sidebar (419)
Windows SideShow (419)
Windows Small Business Serv 2003 (422)
Windows Vista Basic (403)
Windows Vista Business (419)
Windows Vista Enterprise (419)
Windows Vista Home Basic (419)
Windows Vista Home Premiur (419)
Windows Vista Ultimate (418)

Checkpoint

Use the Checkpoint exercises to check your knowledge level of the chapter. The Beyond the Book exercises will help broaden your understanding of the concepts presented in this chapter. To complete the Checkpoint exercises interactively, visit scsite.com/dc2008/ch8/check.

Label the Figure

Identify the various elements of these user interfaces.

a. Forward button

b. links

c. Back button

d. Start menu

e. command prompt

f. command entered by user

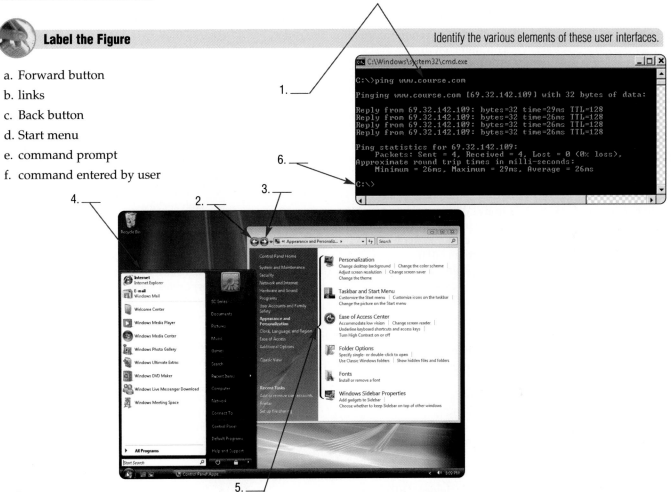

True/False

Mark T for True and F for False. (See page numbers in parentheses.)

_____ 1. All sizes of computers typically use the same operating system. (399)

_____ 2. Booting is the process of permanently removing a computer from operation. (400)

_____ 3. A user interface controls how you enter data and instructions and how information is displayed on the screen. (402)

_____ 4. When spooling print jobs to a buffer, multiple print jobs line up in a queue in the buffer. (407)

_____ 5. Encryption is the process of encoding data and information into an unreadable form. (410)

_____ 6. A disk scanner is a utility that reorganizes the files and unused space on a computer's hard disk so the operating system accesses data more quickly and programs run faster. (414)

_____ 7. Windows Defender protects your computer from theft. (419)

_____ 8. Linux is open source software, which means its code cannot be modified or redistributed. (421)

_____ 9. BlackBerry devices provide PDA capabilities such as managing schedules and contacts, as well as telephone capabilities. (424)

_____ 10. A pop-up blocker is a filtering program that stops pop-up ads from displaying on Web pages. (427)

Checkpoint

 Multiple Choice

Select the best answer. (See page numbers in parentheses.)

1. The _____ chip, which uses battery power, stores configuration information about the computer. (400)
   a. CMOS
   b. BIOS
   c. POST
   d. RAM

2. _____ often are difficult to use because they require exact spelling, grammar, and punctuation. (402)
   a. Graphical user interfaces
   b. Command-line interfaces
   c. Menu-driven interfaces
   d. All of the above

3. In the Windows Vista operating system, the _____ interface provides an enhanced visual look, additional navigation options, and animation. (403)
   a. Plug and Play
   b. Windows Vista Basic
   c. Mac OS X
   d. Windows Aero

4. When an operating system spends much of its time paging, instead of executing application software, it is said to be _____. (406)
   a. booting
   b. thrashing
   c. spooling
   d. formatting

5. A _____ is a small program that tells the operating system how to communicate with a specific device. (407)
   a. buffer
   b. driver
   c. performance monitor
   d. device

6. When you enter search criteria, instead of looking through every file and folder on the storage medium, a search utility looks through the _____ first to find a match. (412)
   a. file manager
   b. buffer
   c. index
   d. driver

7. A _____ is a program that attempts to locate a file on your computer based on criteria you specify. (412)
   a. file manager
   b. search utility
   c. Startup folder
   d. kernel

8. Defragmenting reorganizes the files on a disk so they are located in _____ access time. (414)
   a. noncontiguous sectors, which slows
   b. noncontiguous sectors, which speeds
   c. contiguous sectors, which speeds
   d. contiguous sectors, which slows

9. A _____ contains files necessary to boot and work with the Linux operating system, which allows users to preview the operating system without installing it. (421)
   a. UNIX
   b. Web service
   c. Live CD
   d. BIOS

10. _____, developed by Sun Microsystems, manages high-traffic accounts and incorporates security necessary for Web transactions. (423)
    a. Solaris
    b. Linux
    c. Windows Server 2003
    d. Netware

11. _____ is an open source multitasking operating system designed for smart phones. (425)
    a. Symbian OS
    b. Linux
    c. Palm OS
    d. Solaris

12. A _____ is malware that does not replicate itself to other computers. (426)
    a. virus
    b. Trojan horse
    c. worm
    d. all of the above

13. _____ is a program that displays an online advertisement in a banner or pop-up window on Web pages, e-mail, or other Internet services. (427)
    a. Spyware
    b. A Trojan horse
    c. Adware
    d. A pop-up ad

14. A _____ is a program that allows you to view images and animation, listen to audio, and watch video files on your computer. (428)
    a. file manager
    b. media player
    c. service pack
    d. Media Center PC

Checkpoint

Matching

Match the terms with their definitions. (See page numbers in parentheses.)

_____ 1. boot disk (402)

_____ 2. fault-tolerant computer (405)

_____ 3. page (406)

_____ 4. spooling (407)

_____ 5. IRQ (409)

_____ 6. user name (410)

_____ 7. image viewer (412)

_____ 8. Flip 3D (419)

_____ 9. Live USB (421)

_____ 10. spam (427)

a. a utility that allows users to display, copy, and print the contents of a graphics file

b. communications line between a device and the processor

c. continues to operate when one of its components fails

d. a bootable USB flash drive

e. works with the mouse to flip through open windows arranged in a stack in Windows Vista

f. program that tells the operating system how to communicate with a device

g. unsolicited e-mail message or newsgroup posting sent to many recipients or newsgroups at once

h. disk that contains a few system files that will start the computer

i. with virtual memory, the amount of data and program instructions that can be swapped at a given time

j. hides within or looks like a legitimate program such as a screen saver

k. process that sends print jobs to a buffer instead of sending them immediately to the printer

l. unique combination of characters that identifies one specific user

Short Answer

Write a brief answer to each of the following questions.

1. How is a cold boot different from a warm boot? _____ How is a memory-resident part of an operating system different from a nonresident part of an operating system? _____

2. What is a user interface? _____ How are a command-line interface and a graphical user interface different? _____

3. What is the purpose of memory management? _____ What is the purpose of virtual memory, and where is virtual memory stored? _____

4. What Explorers are included in the Windows Vista operating system? _____ What is the purpose of each Explorer? _____

5. What is the difference between Windows Vista Home Basic and Windows Vista Home Premium? _____ What is the difference between Windows Vista Business and Windows Vista Enterprise? _____

Beyond the Book

Read the following book elements, learn more about each using the Web, and then write a brief report.

1. Ethics & Issues — What Should Be in an Operating System? (409), Who Should Be Responsible for Notebook Computer Security? (411), Does Windows Genuine Advantage Give an Advantage to Hackers? (416), or Closed Source vs. Open Source Operating Systems (421)

2. Career Corner — Systems Programmer (429)

3. Companies on the Cutting Edge – Red Hat or Research in Motion (RIM) (431)

4. FAQs (402, 406, 409, 411, 414, 417, 419, 423, 426, 427)

5. High-Tech Talk — Lossy vs. Lossless Data Compression: Using Compression Algorithms to Reduce File Size (430)

6. Looking Ahead — Apple Marching to Its Own Tune (420) or Online Operating Systems Proposed (429)

7. Making Use of the Web — Weather, Sports, and News (124)

8. Picture Yourself Getting a Virus through E-Mail (396)

9. Technology Trailblazers — Alan Kay or Linus Torvalds (431)

10. Web Links (401, 407, 413, 415, 416, 420, 423, 424, 425, 428)

Learn It Online

Use the Learn It Online exercises to reinforce your understanding of the chapter concepts. To access the Learn It Online exercises, visit scsite.com/dc2008/ch8/learn.

① At the Movies — New View of Vista

To view the New View of Vista movie, click the number 1 button. Locate your video and click the corresponding High-Speed or Dial-Up link, depending on your Internet connection. Watch the movie and then complete the exercise by answering the questions that follow. Take a look at some of the key features in Microsoft's new Windows Vista operating system. What are some of the new features Microsoft has made available in their new Windows Vista operating system?

② Video and Audio: You Review It — Spyware

In this chapter you learned about spyware. Click the number 2 button to view the suggested links and begin your search for videos, podcasts, or vodcasts related to spyware. Choose a video, podcast, or vodcast that discusses spyware and is of interest to you, and then write a description of its contents. Explain why you chose this piece, what you liked about it, what you disliked about it, and whether you would recommend it to a fellow student. Finish your review by giving the video, podcast, or vodcast a rating of 1 – 5 stars. Submit your review in the format requested by your instructor.

③ Student Edition Labs — Installing and Uninstalling Software

Click the number 3 button. A new browser window will open, displaying the Student Edition Labs. Follow the on-screen instructions to complete the Installing and Uninstalling Software Lab. When finished, click the Exit button. If required, submit your results to your instructor.

④ Student Edition Labs — Keeping Your Computer Virus Free

Click the number 4 button. A new browser window will open, displaying the Student Edition Labs. Follow the on-screen instructions to complete the Keeping Your Computer Virus Free Lab. When finished, click the Exit button. If required, submit your results to your instructor.

⑤ Practice Test

Click the number 5 button. Answer each question. When completed, enter your name and click the Grade Test button to submit the quiz for grading. Make a note of any missed questions. If required, submit your results to your instructor.

⑥ Who Wants To Be a Computer Genius²?

Click the number 6 button to find out if you are a computer genius. Directions about how to play the game will be displayed. When you are ready to play, click the Play button. Submit your score to your instructor.

⑦ Wheel of Terms

Click the number 7 button to reinforce important terms you learned in this chapter by playing the Shelly Cashman Series version of this popular game. Directions about how to play the game will be displayed. When you are ready to play, click the Play button. Submit your score to your instructor.

Learn It Online

(8) DC Track and Field

Click the number 8 button to use what you have learned in this chapter to compete against other students in three track and field events. Directions about how to play the game will be displayed. When you are ready to play, click the start first event button. If required, submit your score to your instructor.

(9) You're Hired!

Click the number 9 button to use what you have learned in this chapter to embark on the path to a career in computers. Directions about how to play the game will be displayed. When you are ready to play, click the begin game button. If required, submit your score to your instructor.

(10) Crossword Puzzle Challenge

Click the number 10 button, then click the Crossword Puzzle Challenge link. Directions about how to play the game will be displayed. Complete the puzzle to reinforce skills you learned in this chapter. When you are ready to play, click the Continue button. Submit the completed puzzle to your instructor.

(11) Vista Exercises

Click the number 11 button. When the Vista Exercises menu appears, click the exercise assigned by your instructor. A new browser window will open. Follow the on-screen instructions to complete the exercise. When finished, click the Exit button. If required, submit your results to your instructor.

(12) In the News

When Windows XP was introduced in October 2001, hundreds queued up at computer outlets. It is unclear, however, whether the anticipation was caused by the new operating system or by the promotions many dealers offered. Click the number 12 button and read a news article about the impact, quality, or promotion of an operating system. What operating system was it? What was done to sell the operating system? Is the operating system recommended? Why or why not?

(13) Chapter Discussion Forum

Select an objective from this chapter on page 397 about which you would like more information. Click the number 13 button and post a short message listing a meaningful message title accompanied by one or more questions concerning the selected objective. In two days, return to the threaded discussion by clicking the number 13 button. Submit to your instructor your original message and at least one response to your message.

(14) Airline Schedules

Click the number 14 button to learn how to use the Internet to price, reserve, and track airline flights. Follow the instructions to use Southwest Airlines' Web site to price a flight from Chicago to Las Vegas. Using the Schedules link, check for available flights for the dates you select. Once you have selected a flight, use the Reservations link to price the flight. Print a copy of the pricing for your selected flight. Check the status of a current flight comparable to the flight you priced. Write a report comparing the different fares available and summarizing what information is available when you check the status of a flight. Include in your report what the circumstances would have to be for you to choose a more expensive flight. Print your report and submit it to your instructor.

Learn How To

Use the Learn How To activities to learn fundamental skills when using a computer and accompanying technology. Complete the exercises and submit them to your instructor. To see a video of a Learn How To activity, visit scsite.com/dc2008/ch8/howto.

LEARN HOW TO 1: Install a Computer

Once you have purchased a computer, you must install it for use. Based on years of experience, a set of guidelines for installing and using your computer has been developed. To examine these guidelines, complete the following steps:

1. Start the browser on your computer.
2. Type the Web address `scsite.com/dc2008` in the Address box and then press the ENTER key.
3. Click the Chapter 8 link in the top navigation bar.
4. Click Install Computer in the left sidebar below the heading, Beyond the Book.
5. Read the material presented about how to install a computer.

Exercise

1. Using your Web search skills, research the latest recommendations with respect to proper ergonomics for using a computer. What information did you find that you did not know before? What changes would you make to your current computer setup that might make you more productive? Submit your answers to your instructor.
2. Many people report illnesses or injuries from using computers. Perform research in a library or on the Web to discover the five most common ailments associated with using a computer. Determine the actions people can take to minimize or eliminate these ailments. Submit a report to your instructor describing your findings.
3. Your computer lab at school contains multiple computers for student use. Using the knowledge you have obtained from this Learn How To activity, evaluate the computer installation in your school lab. In a report to your instructor, specify those items you think can be improved in the lab.

LEARN HOW TO 2: Maintain a Computer

While computers are amazingly resilient and reliable, you still should perform certain activities to ensure they maintain peak performance. To learn about these activities, complete the following steps:

1. Start the browser on your computer.
2. Type the Web address `scsite.com/dc2008` in the Address box and then press the ENTER key
3. Click the Chapter 8 link in the top navigation bar.
4. Click Maintain Computer in the left sidebar below the heading, Beyond the Book.
5. Read the material presented about how to maintain a computer.

Exercise

1. On either your computer or the computer on which you are working, perform a hardware and software inventory of at least five hardware devices and five application programs on the computer. List the vendor, product, vendor Web address, vendor e-mail address, and vendor support telephone number. Submit your inventory to your instructor.
2. Record the serial number of the computer on which you are working. Then, record the serial number for seven different application programs on the computer. Submit this information to your instructor.

Learn How To

LEARN HOW TO 3: Keep Windows Vista Up-to-Date

Keeping Windows Vista up-to-date is a critical part of keeping your computer in good working order. The updates made available by Microsoft for no charge over the Internet will keep errors from occurring on your computer and will ensure that all security safeguards are in place. To update Windows, complete the following steps:

1. Click the Start button on the Windows taskbar, click All Programs, and then click Windows Update in the All Programs list (Figure 8-42) to display the Windows Update window.
2. Click the Check for updates link to list the updates that are available for your computer.
3. If necessary, select those updates you wish to install and then click the Install button. Be aware that some updates might take 20 minutes or more to download and install, based primarily on your Internet access speed.
4. Often, after installation of updates, you must restart your computer to allow those updates to take effect. Be sure to save any open files before restarting your computer.

FIGURE 8-42

You also can schedule automatic updates for your computer. To do so, complete the following steps:

1. Click the Start button on the Windows taskbar and then click Control Panel on the Start menu.
2. In the Control Panel window, click System and Maintenance to display the System and Maintenance window.
3. In the System and Maintenance window, click Turn automatic updating on or off to display the Change settings window (Figure 8-43).
4. Select the option you want to use for Windows updates. Microsoft, together with all security and operating system experts, strongly recommends you select Install updates automatically so updates will be installed on your computer automatically. Notice that if you select Install updates automatically, you also should select a time when your computer will be on and be connected to the Internet. A secondary choice is to download the suggested updates and then choose when you want to install them, and a third choice allows you to check for updates and then choose when you want to download and install them.
5. When you have made your selection, click the OK button in the Change settings window.

Updating Windows on your computer is vital to maintain security and operational integrity.

Exercise

1. Open the Windows Update window. Make a list of the important updates to Windows Vista on the computer you are using. Add to the list the optional updates that are available. If you are using your own computer, install the updates of your choice on your computer. Submit the list of updates to your instructor.

FIGURE 8-43

2. Optional: If you are not using your own computer, do not complete this exercise. Open the Control Panel, click System and Maintenance, and then click Turn automatic updating on or off. Select the level of automatic updates you want to use. Write a report justifying your choice of automatic updates and then submit the report to your instructor.

Web Research

Use the Internet-based Web Research exercises to broaden your understanding of the concepts presented in this chapter. Visit scsite.com/dc2008/ch8/research to obtain more information pertaining to each exercise. To discuss any of the Web Research exercises in this chapter with other students, post your thoughts or questions at scsite.com/dc2008/ch8/forum.

(1) Scavenger Hunt   Use one of the search engines listed in Figure 2-10 in Chapter 2 on page 7 or your own favorite search engine to find the answers to the questions that follow. Copy and paste the Web address from the Web page where you found the answer. Some questions may have more than one answer. If required, submit your answers to your instructor. (1) What is the UNIX billennium? (2) The term, spool, is an acronym for what words? What company invented the term? (3) What is the origin of the term, booting? (4) What are three applications that use a real-time operating system (RTOS)? (5) What is Larry the cow's relationship to Linux?

(2) Search Sleuth   A search engine using a concept-based search system seeks Web sites containing a search term along with related concepts. Google Book Search (books.google.com) has been created to help individuals locate books on a broad range of topics. Links to book previews, book reviews, and book purchasing information are available at this site, and visitors also can obtain information from the site's library partners to borrow books. Visit this Web site and then use your word processing program to answer the following questions. Then, if required, submit your answers to your instructor. (1) Type Linux in the search text box. How many search results are returned that are not sponsored links? (2) Click one of these book titles and review the information. Click the Find this book in a library link on the right side of the page. Type your postal code in the Enter Location Information text box and then click the Go button. How many libraries within a 25-mile radius carry this book? (3) Click your browser's Back button or press the BACKSPACE key several times to return to the Google Book Search home page. Click the Google Book Search Help link. Read the information and then write a 50-word summary of your findings.

(3) Journaling   Respond to your readings in this chapter by writing at least one page about your reactions, evaluations, and reflections about using stand-alone utility programs. For example, do you back up your hard disk? If not, why not? Do you use a spyware remover, anti-spam program, or pop-up blocker? Do you use a disk defragmenter or file compression utility? What CD/DVD burning software is installed on your computer? Do you have a recovery disk? Do you have a personal firewall? You also can write about the new terms you learned by reading this chapter. If required, submit your journal to your instructor.

(4) Expanding Your Understanding   Instant messaging (IM) is moving into the workplace. According to America Online, 59 percent of Internet users use IM, and 27 percent of these people use IM at work. Computer industry analysts predict this method of electronic communication will overtake e-mail during the next few years. With IM's popularity comes spim, a junk message. Yahoo! reports that 2 percent of the instant messages sent over its network are spim. View Web sites to learn more about IM's popularity and spim. What programs allow you to filter instant messages? Write a report summarizing your findings, focusing on the possible uses of this method of communication in the workplace. If required, submit your report to your instructor.

(5) Ethics in Action   Several automobile insurers, including Progressive Casualty Insurance Company, are promising drivers insurance premium discounts if they install a data recorder in their cars to track their driving and then exercise good driving behavior. Progressive customers voluntarily taking part in this TripSense program upload the data from their monitors monthly and hope to decrease their insurance bills by a maximum of 25 percent. Privacy experts predict more insurance companies will offer this monitoring system and that it eventually will become mandatory. These critics fear that negative data will be used against poor drivers and possibly be subpoenaed in litigation. View online sites that provide information about vehicle monitoring devices. Write a report summarizing your findings and include a table of links to Web sites that provide additional details. If required, submit your report to your instructor.

Case Studies

Use the Case Studies to apply the concepts presented in the chapter to real-world situations. Visit scsite.com/dc2008/ch8/cases to obtain more information pertaining to each exercise. To discuss the Case Studies in this chapter with other students, visit scsite.com/dc2008/ch8/forum and post your thoughts or questions.

CASE STUDY 1 — Class Discussion   Many students at the local college have been using the college's computers to download music from the Internet. You have been asked to serve on a student committee to draft a policy addressing this questionable use of the college's computers. Is it the college's responsibility to block music downloads? Why or why not? How would the college prevent students from **downloading music**? What is the difference between taping a song heard on the radio and downloading music from the Internet? Should violators be expelled, fined, required to attend a seminar on the ethical use of computers, or given a verbal warning? What recommendations would you give to the committee regarding the downloading of music? Draft a memo addressed to all students regarding this matter. Be prepared to discuss your recommendations in class.

CASE STUDY 2 — Class Discussion   Many application programs are designed to be used with specific operating systems. To determine if software is compatible with your operating system, you should read the packaging or research the software's Web site prior to purchasing the software. Select four **application programs** that interest you. Use the Web and/or print media to answer the following questions: What operating system is required for each application? What is the earliest version of the operating system that can be used? What operating system would you choose? Write a brief report, and be prepared to discuss your recommendations in class.

CASE STUDY 3 — Research   Your cousin is buying a new computer both for personal use and to operate his consulting business, which he runs out of his home. He is undecided on the Windows operating system to purchase with his new computer. **Windows Vista** Business is intended for business users. Windows Vista Home Premium is designed for home computing. He has asked you to help him decide if he should buy one or the other. Use the Web and/or print media to develop a report that lists the differences. Which Windows Vista Business features are not available in Windows Vista Home Premium? Submit your report or use PowerPoint to create a presentation and share your findings with your class.

CASE STUDY 4 — Research   Many programs are available for users of personal computers. The owner of the party supply store, Crazy Pete's Party Palace, where you work part time is interested in purchasing an **antivirus program**. Because you are taking a computer class, he has asked you to help him choose the best program. Choose at least two competing manufacturers of antivirus programs. Use the Web and/or print media and compare the programs. For each program, answer the following questions: What is the program's function? What are the system requirements? How easy is the program to use? Does it include a firewall? Does it protect against spam, spyware, and adware? How do you obtain updates to the program? How much does the program cost? In your opinion, is the program worth the price? Why or why not? Which one would you buy? Why? Write a brief report or use PowerPoint to create a presentation and share your findings with your class.

CASE STUDY 5 — Team Challenge   Your team members are employed as analysts at Soap-n-Suds, an international manufacturer of laundry soaps. The company currently uses an early version of the Windows operating system on its 5,000 desktop computers. Next year, the company plans to upgrade the operating system and, if necessary, its desktop computers. The vice-president of information technology has asked your team to compare the latest desktop versions of the Windows operating system, the **Mac operating system**, and the Linux operating system. Assign each member of your team an operating system. Have each member use the Web and/or print media to develop a feature/benefit report. What is the initial cost of the operating system per computer? What are the memory and storage requirements? Will the operating system require the company to purchase new computers? Are training costs involved? Which one is best at avoiding viruses, spam, and spyware? Which operating system is easier to use? Why? Can Microsoft Office 2007 run under the operating system? As a team, merge your findings into a team report and/or PowerPoint presentation and share your findings with your class.

Buyer's Guide 2008:
How to Purchase a Personal Computer

(a) desktop computer

(b) mobile computer (notebook computer or Tablet PC)

At some point, perhaps while you are taking this cours you may decide to buy a personal computer. The deci sion is an important one and will require an investme of both time and money. Like many buyers, you may have l tle computer experience and find yourself unsure of how t proceed. You can get started by talking to your friends, coworkers, and instructors about their computers. What ty of computers did they buy? Why? For what purposes do t use their computers? You also should answer the followin three questions to help narrow your choices to a specific computer type, before reading this Buyer's Guide.

Should I buy a desktop or mobile computer?

For what purposes will I use the computer?

Should the computer I buy be compatible with the computers at school or work?

1 **Do you want a desktop computer or mobile computer?** A desktop computer (Figure 1a) is designed as a stationary device that sits on or below a desk table in a location such as a home, office, or do mitory room. A desktop computer must be plugged in an electrical outlet to operate. A mobile computer, such as a notebook compute or Tablet PC (Figure 1b), is smaller than a desk top computer, more portable, and has a battery that allows you to operate it for a period witho an electrical outlet.

Desktop computers are a good option if yo work mostly in one place and have plenty of sp in your work area. Desktop computers generall give you more performance for your money.

Increasingly, more corporations are buying mobile computers to take advantage of their po bility to work while traveling and at home. The past disadvantages of mobile computers, such a lower processor speeds, poor-quality monitors, weight, short battery life, and significantly high prices, have all but disappeared. Today, hard dr speed, capacity, processor speed, and graphics capability in notebook computers are equal to, i not better than, desktop computers.

If you are thinking of using a mobile com puter to take notes in class or in business meet ings, then consider a Tablet PC with handwritin

FIGURE 1

and drawing capabilities. Typically, note-taking involves writing text notes and drawing charts, schematics, and other illustrations. By allowing you to write and draw directly on the screen with a digital pen, a Tablet PC eliminates the distracting sound of the notebook keyboard tapping and allows you to capture drawings. Some notebook computers can convert to Tablet PCs.

Mobile computers used to have several drawbacks, including the lack of high-end capabilities. Today's high-end notebook computers include most of the capabilities of a good desktop computer. Manufacturers have made great strides in improving durability and battery life. Most notebook computers are 1.5 to 2 inches thick and weigh less than 10 pounds, making them very portable and easy to carry.

2 **For what purposes will you use the computer?**   Having a general idea of the purposes for which you want to use your computer will help you decide on the type of computer to buy. At this point in your research, it is not necessary to know the exact application software titles or version numbers you might want to use. Knowing that you plan to use the computer primarily to create word processing, spreadsheet, database, and presentation documents, however, will point you in the direction of a desktop or notebook computer. If you want the portability of a smart phone or PDA, but you need more computing power, then a Tablet PC may be the best alternative. You also must consider that some application software runs only on a Mac, while others run only on a PC with the Windows operating system. Still other software may run only on a PC running the UNIX or Linux operating system.

3 **Should the computer be compatible with the computers at school or work?**   If you plan to bring work home, telecommute, or take distance education courses, then you should purchase a computer that is compatible with those at school or work.

Compatibility is primarily a software issue. If your computer runs the same operating system version, such as Microsoft Windows Vista, and the same application software, such as Microsoft Office, then your computer will be able to read documents created at school or work and vice versa. Incompatible hardware can become an issue if you plan to connect directly to a school or office network using a cable or wireless technology. You usually can obtain the minimum system requirements from the Information Technology department at your school or workplace.

After evaluating the answers to these three questions, you should have a general idea of how you plan to use your computer and the type of computer you want to buy. Once you have decided on the type of computer you want, you can follow the guidelines presented in this Buyer's Guide to help you purchase a specific computer, along with software, peripherals, and other accessories.

Many of the desktop computer guidelines presented also apply to the purchase of a notebook computer and a Tablet PC. Later in this Buyer's Guide, sections on purchasing a notebook computer or Tablet PC address additional considerations specific to those computer types.

This Buyer's Guide concentrates on recommendations for purchasing a desktop computer or mobile computer.

HOW TO PURCHASE A DESKTOP COMPUTER

Once you have decided that a desktop computer is most suited to your computing needs, the next step is to determine specific software, hardware, peripheral devices, and services to purchase, as well as where to buy the computer.

1 **Determine the specific software you want to use on your computer.**   Before deciding to purchase software, be sure it contains the features necessary for the tasks you want to perform. Rely on the computer users in whom you have confidence to help you decide on the software to use. The minimum requirements of the software you select may determine the operating system (Microsoft Windows Vista, Linux, UNIX, Mac OS X) you need. If you have decided to use a particular operating system that does not support software you want to use, you may be able to purchase similar software from other manufacturers.

Many Web sites and trade magazines, such as those listed in Figure 2, provide reviews of software products. These Web sites frequently have articles that rate computers and software on cost, performance, and support.

Your hardware requirements depend on the minimum requirements of the software you will run on your computer.

Type of Computer	Web Site	Web Address
PC	CNET Shopper	shopper.cnet.com
	PC World Magazine	pcworld.com
	BYTE Magazine	byte.com
	PC Magazine	pcmag.com
	Yahoo! Computers	computers.yahoo.com
	MSN Shopping	shopping.msn.com
	Dave's Guide to Buying a Home Computer	css.msu.edu/PC-Guide
Mac	Macworld Magazine	macworld.com
	Apple	apple.com
	Switch to Mac Campaign	apple.com/switch

For an updated list of hardware and software reviews and their Web site addresses, visit scsite.com/dc2008/ch8/buyers.

FIGURE 2   Hardware and software reviews.

Some software requires more memory and disk space than others, as well as additional input, output, and storage devices. For example, suppose you want to run software that can copy one CD's or DVD's contents directly to another CD or DVD, without first copying the data to your hard disk. To support that, you should consider a desktop computer or a high-end notebook computer, because the computer will need two CD or DVD drives: one that reads from a CD or DVD, and one that reads from and writes on a CD or DVD. If you plan to run software that allows your computer to work as an entertainment system, then you will need a CD or DVD drive, quality speakers, and an upgraded sound card.

2 **Know the System Requirements of the Operating System.** After deciding the software you want to run on your new computer, you need to determine the operating system you want to use. If, however, you purchase a new computer, chances are it will have the latest version of your preferred operating system (Windows Vista, Linux, UNIX, Mac OS X). Figure 3 lists the minimum computer requirements of Windows Vista versions.

Windows Vista Versions	Minimum Computer Requirements
Windows Vista Home Basic	• 800 MHz processor • 512 MB of RAM • DirectX 9 capable graphics processor
Windows Vista Home Premium **Windows Vista Ultimate** **Windows Vista Business** **Windows Vista Enterprise**	• 1 GHz processor • 1 GB of RAM • DirectX 9 capable graphics processor with WDDM driver and 128 MB of graphics memory • 40 GB of hard disk capacity (15 GB free space) • DVD-ROM drive • Audio output capability • Internet access capability

FIGURE 3 Hardware requirements for Windows Vista.

3 **Look for bundled software.** When you purchase a computer, it may come bundled with software. Some sellers even let you choose which software you want. Remember, however, that bundled software has value only if you would have purchased the software even if it had not come with the computer. At the very least, you probably will want word processing software and a browser to access the Internet. If you need additional applications, such as a spreadsheet, a database,

or presentation graphics, consider purchasing Microsoft Works, Microsoft Office, OpenOffice.org, or Sun StarOffice, which include several programs at a reduced price.

4 **Avoid buying the least powerful computer available.** Once you know the application software you want to use, you then can consider the following important criteria about the computer's components: (1) processor speed, (2) size and types of memory (RAM) and storage, (3) types of input/output devices, (4) types of ports and adapter cards, and (5) types of communications devices. You also need to consider if the computer is upgradeable and to what extent you are able to upgrade. For example, all manufacturers limit the amount of memory you can add. The information in Figures 4 and 5 can help you determine what system components are best for you. Figure 4 outlines considerations for specific hardware components. Figure 5 (on page 449) provides a Base Components worksheet that lists PC recommendations for each category of user discussed in this book: Home User, Small Office/Home Office User, Mobile User, Power User, and Large Business User. In the worksheet, the Home User category is divided into two groups: Application Home User and Game Home User. The Mobile User recommendations list criteria for a notebook computer, but do not include the PDA or Tablet PC options.

Computer technology changes rapidly, meaning a computer that seems powerful enough today may not serve your computing needs in a few years. In fact, studies show that many users regret not buying a more powerful computer. To avoid this, plan to buy a computer that will last you for two to three years. You can help delay obsolescence by purchasing the fastest processor, the most memory, and the largest hard disk you can afford. If you must buy a less powerful computer, be sure you can upgrade it with additional memory, components, and peripheral devices as your computer requirements grow.

5 **Consider upgrades to the mouse, keyboard, monitor, printer, microphone, and speakers.** You use these peripheral devices to interact with your computer, so you should make sure they are up to your standards. Review the peripheral devices listed in Figure 4 on pages 447 and 448 and then visit both local computer dealers and large retail stores to test the computers on display. Ask the salesperson what input and output devices would be best for you and whether you should upgrade beyond what comes standard. Consider purchasing a wireless keyboard and wireless mouse to eliminate bothersome wires on your desktop. A few extra dollars spent on these components when you initially purchase a computer can extend its usefulness by years.

CD/DVD Drives: Most computers come with a CD-RW drive. A CD-RW drive allows you to create your own custom data CDs for data backup or data transfer purposes. It also will allow you to store and share video files, digital photos, and other large files with other people who have access to a CD-ROM drive. An even better alternative is to upgrade to a DVD±RW combination drive. It allows you to read DVDs and CDs and to write data on (burn) a DVD or CD. A DVD has a capacity of at least 4.7 GB versus the 650 MB capacity of a CD. An HD DVD has a minimum capacity of 45 GB.

Card Reader/Writer: A card reader/writer is useful for transferring data directly to and from a removable flash memory card, such as the ones used in your camera or audio player. Make sure the card reader/writer can read from and write on the flash memory cards that you use.

Digital Camera: Consider an inexpensive point-and-shoot digital camera. They are small enough to carry around, usually operate automatically in terms of lighting and focus, and contain storage cards for storing photographs. A 5-megapixel camera with a 512 MB storage card is fine for creating images for use on the Web or to send via e-mail.

Digital Video Capture Device: A digital video capture device allows you to connect your computer to a camcorder or VCR and record, edit, manage, and then write video back on a VCR tape, a CD, or a DVD. To create quality video (true 30 frames per second, full-sized TV), the digital video capture device should have a USB 2.0 or FireWire port. You also will need sufficient storage: an hour of data on a VCR tape takes up about 5 GB of disk storage.

External Hard Disk: An external hard disk can serve many purposes: it can serve as extra storage for your computer, provide a way to store and transport large files or large quantities of files, and provide security by allowing you to keep all of your data on the external disk without leaving any data on the computer. External hard disks can be purchased with the same amount of capacity as any internal disk. If you are going to use it as a backup to your internal hard disk, you should purchase an external hard drive with at least as much capacity as your internal hard disk.

Hard Disk: It is recommended that you buy a computer with 60 to 80 GB if your primary interests are browsing the Web and using e-mail and Office suite-type applications; 80 to 100 GB if you also want to edit digital photographs; 100 to 200 GB if you plan to edit digital video or manipulate large audio files even occasionally; and 200 to 500 GB if you will edit digital video, movies, or photography often; store audio files and music; or consider yourself to be a power user. It also is recommended that you use Serial ATA (SATA) as opposed to Parallel ATA (PATA). SATA has many advantages over PATA, including support for Plug and Play devices.

Joystick/Wheel: If you use your computer to play games, then you will want to purchase a joystick or a wheel. These devices, especially the more expensive ones, provide for realistic game play with force feedback, programmable buttons, and specialized levers and wheels.

Keyboard: The keyboard is one of the more important devices used to communicate with the computer. For this reason, make sure the keyboard you purchase has 101 to 105 keys, is comfortable and easy to use, and has a USB connection. A wireless keyboard should be considered, especially if you have a small desk area.

Microphone: If you plan to record audio or use speech recognition to enter text and commands, then purchase a close-talk headset with gain adjustment support.

Modem: Most computers come with a modem so that you can use your telephone line to access the Internet. Some modems also have fax capabilities. Your modem should be rated at 56 Kbps.

Monitor: The monitor is where you will view documents, read e-mail messages, and view pictures. A minimum of a 17" screen is recommended, but if you are planning to use your computer for graphic design or game playing, then you may want to purchase a 19" or 21" monitor. The LCD flat panel monitor should be considered, especially if space is an issue.

Mouse: As you work with your computer, you use the mouse constantly. For this reason, spend a few extra dollars, if necessary, and purchase a mouse with an optical sensor and USB connection. The optical sensor replaces the need for a mouse ball, which means you do not need a mouse pad. For a PC, make sure your mouse has a wheel, which acts as a third button in addition to the top two buttons on the left and right. An ergonomic design is also important because your hand is on the mouse most of the time when you are using your computer. A wireless mouse should be considered to eliminate the cord and allow you to work at short distances from your computer.

FIGURE 4   Hardware guidelines.

Ports: Depending on how you are using your computer, you may need anywhere from 4 to 10 USB 2.0 ports. USB 2.0 ports have become the connection of choice in the computer industry. They offer an easy way to connect peripheral devices such as printers, digital cameras, portable media players, etc. Many computers intended for home or professional audio/video use have built-in FireWire ports. Most personal computers come with a minimum of six USB 2.0 ports and two FireWire ports.

Port Hub Expander: If you plan to connect several peripheral devices to your computer at the same time, then you need to be concerned with the number of ports available on your computer. If your computer does not have enough ports, then you should purchase a port hub expander. A port hub expander plugs into a single FireWire port or USB port and gives several additional ports.

Printer: Your two basic printer choices are ink-jet and laser. Color ink-jet printers cost on average between $50 and $300. Laser printers cost from $200 to $2,000. In general, the cheaper the printer, the lower the resolution and speed, and the more often you are required to change the ink cartridge or toner. Laser printers print faster and with a higher quality than an ink-jet, and their toner on average costs less. If you want color, then go with a high-end ink-jet printer to ensure quality of print. Duty cycle (the number of pages you expect to print each month) also should be a determining factor. If your duty cycle is on the low end — hundreds of pages per month — then stay with a high-end ink-jet printer, rather than purchasing a laser printer. If you plan to print photographs taken with a digital camera, then you should purchase a photo printer. A photo printer is a dye-sublimation printer or an ink-jet printer with higher resolution and features that allow you to print quality photographs.

Processor: For a PC, an Intel Core 2 Duo processor at 2.66 GHz is more than enough processor power for application home and small office/home office users. Game home, large business, and power users should upgrade to faster processors.

RAM: RAM plays a vital role in the speed of your computer. Make sure the computer you purchase has at least 512 MB of RAM. If you have extra money to invest in your computer, then consider increasing the RAM to 1 GB or more. The extra money for RAM will be well spent.

Scanner: The most popular scanner purchased with a computer today is the flatbed scanner. When evaluating a flatbed scanner, check the color depth and resolution. Do not buy anything less than a color depth of 48 bits and a resolution of 1200 x 2400 dpi. The higher the color depth, the more accurate the color. A higher resolution picks up the more subtle gradations of color.

Sound Card: Many computers come with a standard sound card that supports Dolby 5.1 surround and are capable of recording and playing digital audio. Make sure they are suitable in the event you decide to use your computer as an entertainment or gaming system.

Speakers: Once you have a good sound card, quality speakers and a separate subwoofer that amplifies the bass frequencies of the speakers can turn your computer into a premium stereo system.

PC Video Camera: A PC video camera is a small camera used to capture and display live video (in some cases with sound), primarily on a Web page. You also can capture, edit, and share video and still photos. The camera sits on your monitor or desk. Recommended minimum specifications include 640 x 480 resolution, a video with a rate of 30 frames per second, and a USB 2.0 or FireWire port.

USB Flash Drive: If you work on different computers and need access to the same data and information, then this portable miniature mobile storage device is ideal. USB flash drive capacity varies from 16 MB to 4 GB.

Video Card: Most standard video cards satisfy the monitor display needs of application home and small office users. If you are a game home user or a graphic designer, you will want to upgrade to a higher quality video card. The higher refresh rates will further enhance the display of games, graphics, and movies.

Wireless LAN Access Point: A wireless LAN access point allows you to network several computers, so they can share files and access the Internet through a single cable modem or DSL connection. Each device that you connect requires a wireless card. A wireless LAN access point can offer a range of operations up to several hundred feet, so be sure the device has a high-powered antenna.

ASE COMPONENTS

	Application Home User	Game Home User	Small Office/Home Office User	Mobile User	Large Business User	Power User
HARDWARE						
essor	Intel Core 2 Duo at 2.66 GHz	Intel Core 2 Duo at 2.93 GHz	Intel Core 2 Duo at 2.93 GHz	Intel Core 2 Duo at 2.33 GHz	Intel Core 2 Duo at 2.66 GHz	Intel Core 2 Extreme
	512 MB	4 GB	1 GB	1 GB	1 GB	2 GB
e	512 KB L2	512 KB L2	512 KB L2	512 KB L2	512 KB L2	2 MB L3
Disk	250 GB	300 GB	500 GB	100 GB	500 GB	1.5 TB
Flat Panel	17" or 19"	21"	19" or 21"	17" Wide Display	19" of 21"	23"
Card	256 MB	512 MB	256 MB	256 MB	256 MB	256 MB
VD Bay 1	CD-RW	Blue-ray or HD DVD reader/writer	CD-RW	CD-RW/DVD	CD-RW	Blue-ray or HD DVD reader/writer
VD Bay 2	DVD±RW	DVD±RW	DVD±RW	DVD±RW	DVD±RW	DVD±RW
er	Color Ink-Jet	Color Ink-Jet	18 ppm Laser	Portable Ink-Jet	50 ppm Laser	10 ppm Color Laser
ideo Camera	Yes	Yes	Yes	Yes	Yes	Yes
Modem	Yes	Yes	Yes	Yes	Yes	Yes
ophone	Close-Talk Headset With Gain Adjustment	Close-Talk Headset With Gain Adjustment	Close-Talk Headset With Gain Adjustment	Close-Talk Headset With Gain Adjustment	Close-Talk Headset With Gain Adjustment	Close-Talk Headset With Gain Adjustment
akers	5.1 Dolby Surround	5.1 Dolby Surround	5.1 Dolby Surround	Stereo	5.1 Dolby Surround	5.1 Dolby Surround
ting Device	IntelliMouse or Optical Mouse	Laser Mouse and Joystick	IntelliMouse or Optical Mouse	Touchpad or Pointing Stick and Laser Mouse	IntelliMouse or Optical Mouse	IntelliMouse or Laser Mouse and Joystick
oard	Yes	Yes	Yes	Built-In	Yes	Yes
kup Disk/Tape Drive	External or Removable Hard Disk	External or Removable Hard Disk	External or Removable Hard Disk	External or Removable Hard Disk	Tape Drive	External or Removable Hard Disk
Flash Drive	256 MB	512 MB	512 MB	512 MB	4 GB	2 GB
d Card	Sound Blaster Compatible	Sound Blaster Audigy 2	Sound Blaster Compatible	Built-In	Sound Blaster Compatible	Sound Blaster Audigy 2
ork Card	Yes	Yes	Yes	Yes	Yes	Yes
ut Connector	Yes	Yes	Yes	Yes	Yes	Yes
2.0 Port	6	8	6	4	9	10
Vire Port	2	2	2	1	2	2
SOFTWARE						
ating System	Windows Vista Home Basic	Windows Vista Home Premium	Windows Vista Business	Windows Vista Business	Windows Vista Enterprise	Windows Vista Ultimate
ication Suite	Office Standard 2007	Office Standard 2007	Office Small Business 2007	Office Small Business 2007	Office Professional 2007	Office Professional 2007
virus	Yes, 12-Mo. Subscription	Yes, 12-Mo. Subscription	Yes, 12-Mo. Subscription	Yes, 12-Mo. Subscription	Yes, 12-Mo. Subscription	Yes, 12-Mo. Subscription
net Access	Cable, DSL, or Dial-up	Cable or DSL	Cable or DSL	Wireless or Dial-up	LAN/WAN (T1/T3)	Cable or DSL
OTHER						
e Protector	Yes	Yes	Yes	Portable	Yes	Yes
anty	3-Year Limited, 1-Year Next Business Day On-Site Service	3-Year Limited, 1-Year Next Business Day On-Site Service	3-year On-Site Service	3-Year Limited, 1-Year Next Business Day On-Site Service	3-year On-Site Service	3-year On-Site Service
r		Wheel	Postage Printer	Docking Station Carrying Case Fingerprint Scanner Portable Data Projector		Graphics Tablet Plotter or Large-Format Printer

Optional Components for all Categories	
2.11g Wireless Card	Graphics Tablet
uetooth Enabled	Portable Media Player
ometric Input Device	IrDA Port
rd Reader/Writer	Multifunction Peripheral
gital Camera	Photo Printer
gital Video Capture Device	Port Hub Expander
gital Video Camera	Portable Data Projector
al-Monitor Support with cond Monitor	Scanner
gonomic Keyboard	TV/FM Tuner
ternal Hard Disk	Uninterruptible Power Supply

E 5 Base desktop and mobile computer components and optional components. A copy of the Base Components worksheet is part of Files for Students. To obtain a copy of the Data Files for Students, see the inside back cover of this book for instructions.

6 Determine whether you want to use telephone lines or broadband (cable or DSL) to access the Internet. If your computer has a modem, then you can access the Internet using a standard telephone line. Ordinarily, you call a local or toll-free 800 number to connect to an ISP (see Guideline 7 on the next page). Using a dial-up Internet connection is relatively inexpensive but slow.

DSL and cable connections provide much faster Internet connections, which are ideal if you want faster file download speeds for software, digital photos, and music. As you would expect, they also are more expensive. DSL, which is available through local telephone companies, also may require that you subscribe to an ISP. Cable is available through your local cable television provider and some online service providers (OSPs). If you get cable, then you would not use a separate Internet service provider or online service provider.

7 **If you are using a dial-up or wireless connection to connect to the Internet, then select an ISP or OSP.** You can access the Internet via telephone lines in one of two ways: an ISP or an OSP. Both provide Internet access for a monthly fee that ranges from $6 to $25. Local ISPs offer Internet access to users in a limited geographic region, through local telephone numbers. National ISPs provide access for users nationwide (including mobile users), through local and toll-free telephone numbers and cable. Because of their size, national ISPs generally offer more services and have a larger technical support staff than local ISPs. OSPs furnish Internet access as well as members-only features for users nationwide. Figure 6 lists several national ISPs and OSPs. Before you choose an ISP or OSP, compare such features as the number of access hours, monthly fees, available services (e-mail, Web page hosting, chat), and reliability.

Company	Service	Web Address
America Online	OSP	aol.com
AT&T Worldnet	ISP	www.att.net
Comcast	OSP	comcast.net
CompuServe	OSP	compuserve.com
EarthLink	ISP	earthlink.net
Juno	OSP	juno.com
NetZero	OSP	netzero.com
MSN	OSP	msn.com
Prodigy	ISP/OSP	myhome.prodigy.net

For an updated list of national ISPs and OSPs and their Web site addresses, visit scsite.com/dc2008/ch8/buyers.

FIGURE 6 National ISPs and OSPs.

8 **Use a worksheet to compare computers, services, and other considerations.** You can use a separate sheet of paper to take notes on each vendor's computer and then summarize the information on a worksheet, such as the one shown in Figure 7. You can use Figure 7 to compare prices for either a PC or a Mac. Most companies advertise a price for a base computer that includes components housed in the system unit (processor, RAM, sound card, video card), disk drives (hard disk, CD-ROM, CD-RW, DVD-ROM, and DVD±RW), a keyboard, mouse, monitor, printer, speakers, and modem. Be aware, however, that some advertisements list prices for computers with only some of these components. Monitors and printers, for example, often are not included in a base computer's price. Depending on how you plan to use the computer, you may want to invest in additional or more powerful components. When you are comparing the prices of computers, make sure you are comparing identical or similar configurations.

PC or MAC Cost Comparison Worksheet

Dealers list prices for computers with most of these components (instead of listing individual component costs). Some dealers do not supply a monitor. Some dealers offer significant discounts, but you must subscribe to an Internet service for a specified period to receive the discounted price. To compare computers, enter overall system price at top and enter a 0 (zero) for components included in the system cost. For any additional components not covered in the system price, enter the cost in the appropriate cells.

Items to Purchase	Desired System (PC)	Desired System (Mac)	Local Dealer #1	Local Dealer #2	Online Dealer #1	Online Dealer #2	Comment
OVERALL SYSTEM							
Overall System Price	< $2,000	< $2,000					
HARDWARE							
Processor	Intel Core 2 Duo	Intel Core 2 Duo					
RAM	1 GB	1 GB					
Cache	256 KB L2	256 KB L2					
Hard Disk	250 GB	250 GB					
Monitor/LCD Flat Panel	20 Inch	20 Inch					
Video Card	256 MB	256 MB					
USB Flash Drive	1 GB	1 GB					
CD/DVD Bay 1	CD-RW	DVD±RW					
CD/DVD Bay 2	DVD±RW	NA					
Speakers	Dolby 5.1 Surround	Dolby 5.1 Surround					
Sound Card	Sound Blaster Compatible	Sound Blaster Compatible					
USB 2.0 Port	6	6					
FireWire Port	2	2					
Network Card	Yes	Yes					
Fax/Modem	56 Kbps	56 Kbps					
Keyboard	Standard	Apple Pro Keyboard					
Pointing Device	IntelliMouse	Intellimouse or Apple Pro Mouse					
Microphone	Close-Talk Headset with Gain Adjustment	Close-Talk Headset with Gain Adjustment					
Printer	Color Ink-Jet	Color Ink-Jet					
SOFTWARE							
Operating System	Windows Vista Ultimate	Mac OS X					
Application Software	Office 2007 Small Business	Office 2007 for Mac					
Antivirus	Yes - 12 Mo. Subscription	Yes - 12 Mo. Subscription					
OTHER							
Card Reader							
Digital Camera	5-Megapixel	5-Megapixel					
Internet Connection	1-Year Subscription	1-Year Subscription					
Joystick	Yes	Yes					
PC Video Camera	With Microphone	With Microphone					
Port Hub Expander							
Scanner							
Surge Protector							
Warranty	3-Year On-Site Service	3-Year On-Site Service					
Wireless Card	Internal	Internal					
Wireless LAN Access Point	LinkSys	Apple AirPort					
Total Cost			$.	$.	$.	$.	

FIGURE 7 A worksheet is an effective tool for summarizing and comparing components and prices of different computer vendors. A copy of the Computer Cost Comparison Worksheet is part of the Data Files for Students. To obtain a copy of the Data Files for Students, see the inside back cover of this book for instructions.

9 If you are buying a new computer, you have several purchasing options: buying from your school bookstore, a local computer dealer, a local large retail store, or ordering by mail via telephone or the Web. Each purchasing option has certain advantages. Many college bookstores, for example, sign exclusive pricing agreements with computer manufacturers and, thus, can offer student discounts. Local dealers and local large retail stores, however, more easily can provide hands-on support. Mail-order companies that sell computers by telephone or online via the Web (Figure 8) often provide the lowest prices, but extend less personal service. Some major mail-order companies, however, have started to provide next-business-day, on-site services. A credit card usually is required to buy from a mail-order company. Figure 9 lists some of the more popular mail-order companies and their Web site addresses.

10 If you are buying a used computer, stay with name brands such as Dell, Gateway, Hewlett-Packard, and Apple. Although brand-name equipment can cost more, most brand-name computers have longer, more comprehensive warranties, are better supported, and have more authorized centers for repair services. As with new computers, you can purchase a used computer from local computer dealers, local large retail stores, or mail order via the telephone or the Web. Classified ads and used computer sellers offer additional outlets for purchasing used computers. Figure 10 lists several major used computer brokers and their Web site addresses.

11 If you have a computer and are upgrading to a new one, then consider selling or trading in the old one. If you are a replacement buyer, your older computer still may have value. If you cannot sell the computer through the classified ads, via a Web site, or to a friend, then ask if the computer dealer will buy your old computer. An increasing number of companies are taking trade-ins, but do not expect too much money for your old computer. Other companies offer free disposal of your old PC.

12 Be aware of hidden costs. Before purchasing, be sure to consider any additional costs associated with buying a computer, such as an additional telephone line, a cable or DSL modem, an uninterruptible power supply (UPS), computer furniture, a USB flash drive, paper, and computer training classes you may want to take. Depending on where you buy your computer, the seller may be willing to include some or all of these in the computer purchase price.

Type of Computer	Company	Web Address
PC	CNET Shopper	shopper.cnet.com
	Hewlett-Packard	hp.com
	CompUSA	compusa.com
	TigerDirect	tigerdirect.com
	Dell	dell.com
	Gateway	gateway.com
Macintosh	Apple Computer	store.apple.com
	ClubMac	clubmac.com
	MacConnection	macconnection.com
	PC & MacExchange	macx.com

For an updated list of mail-order computer companies and their Web site addresses, visit scsite.com/dc2008/ch8/buyers.

FIGURE 9 Computer mail-order companies.

Company	Web Address
Amazon.com	amazon.com
TigerDirect.com	tigerdirect.com
American Computer Express	americancomputerex.com
U.S. Computer Exchange	usce.org
eBay	ebay.com

For an updated list of used computer mail-order companies and their Web site addresses, visit scsite.com/dc2008/ch8/buyers.

FIGURE 10 Used computer mail-order companies.

FIGURE 8 Mail-order companies, such as Dell, sell computers online.

13 **Consider more than just price.** The lowest-cost computer may not be the best long-term buy. Consider such intangibles as the vendor's time in business, the vendor's regard for quality, and the vendor's reputation for support. If you need to upgrade your computer often, you may want to consider a leasing arrangement, in which you pay monthly lease fees, but can upgrade or add on to your computer as your equipment needs change. No matter what type of buyer you are, insist on a 30-day, no-questions-asked return policy on your computer.

14 **Avoid restocking fees.** Some companies charge a restocking fee of 10 to 20 percent as part of their money-back return policy. In some cases, no restocking fee for hardware is applied, but it is applied for software. Ask about the existence and terms of any restocking policies before you buy.

15 **Use a credit card to purchase your new computer.** Many credit cards offer purchase protection and extended warranty benefits that cover you in case of loss of or damage to purchased goods. Paying by credit card also gives you time to install and use the computer before you have to pay for it. Finally, if you are dissatisfied with the computer and are unable to reach an agreement with the seller, paying by credit card gives you certain rights regarding withholding payment until the dispute is resolved. Check your credit card terms for specific details.

16 **Consider purchasing an extended warranty or service plan.** If you use your computer for business or require fast resolution to major computer problems, consider purchasing an extended warranty or a service plan through a local dealer or third-party company. Most extended warranties cover the repair and replacement of computer components beyond the standard warranty. Most service plans ensure that your technical support calls receive priority response from technicians. You also can purchase an on-site service plan that states that a technician will come to your home, work, or school within 24 hours. If your computer includes a warranty and service agreement for a year or less, think about extending the service for two or three years when you buy the computer.

CENTURY COMPUTERS
Performance Guarantee
(See reverse for terms & conditions of this contract)

Invoice #: 1984409   Effective Date: 10/12/08
Invoice Date: 10/12/08   Expiration Date: 10/12/11

Customer Name: Leon, Richard   System & Serial Numbers
Date: 10/12/08   IMB computer
Address: 1123 Roxbury   S/N: US759290C
         Sycamore, IL 60178
Day phone: (815) 555-0303
Evening Phone: (728) 555-0203

John Smith   _10/12/08_
Print Name of Century's Authorized Signature   Date

HOW TO PURCHASE A NOTEBOOK COMPUTER

If you need computing capability when you travel or to use in lecture or meetings, you may find a notebook computer to be an appropriate choice. The guidelines mentioned in the previous section also apply to the purchase of a notebook computer. The following are additional considerations unique to notebook computers.

1 **Purchase a notebook computer with a sufficiently large active-matrix screen.**
Active-matrix screens display high-quality color that is viewable from all angles. Less expensive, passive-matrix screens sometimes are difficult to see in low-light conditions and cannot be viewed from an angle. Notebook computers typically come with a 12.1-inch, 13.3-inch, 14.1-inch, 15.4-inch, or 17-inch display. For most users, a 14.1-inch display is satisfactory. If you intend to use your notebook computer as a desktop computer replacement, however, you may opt for a 15.7-inch or 17-inch display. Dell offers a notebook computer with a 20.1-inch display that looks like a briefcase when closed. Notebook computers with these larger displays weigh seven to ten pounds, however, so if you travel a lot and portability is essential, you might want a lighter computer with a smaller display. The lightest notebook computers, which weigh less than 3 pounds, are equipped with a 12.1-inch display. Regardless of size, the resolution of the display should be at least 1024 × 768 pixels. To compare the monitor size on various notebook computers, visit the company Web sites in Figure 11.

Type of Notebook	Company	Web Address
PC	Acer	global.acer.com
	Dell	dell.com
	Fujitsu	fujitsu.com
	Gateway	gateway.com
	Hewlett-Packard	hp.com
	Lenovo	lenovo.com/us/en/
	NEC	nec.com
	Sony	sony.com
	Toshiba	toshiba.com
Mac	Apple	apple.com

For an updated list of companies and their Web site addresses, visit scsite.com/dc2008/ch8/buyers.

FIGURE 11 Companies that sell notebook computers.

2 **Experiment with different keyboards and pointing devices.** Notebook computer keyboards are far less standardized than those for desktop computers. Some notebook computers, for example, have wide wrist rests, while others have none, and keyboard layouts on notebook computers often vary. Notebook computers also use a range of pointing devices, including pointing sticks, touchpads, and trackballs. Before you purchase a notebook computer, try various types of keyboard and pointing devices to determine which is easiest for you to use. Regardless of the pointing device you select, you also may want to purchase a regular mouse to use when you are working at a desk or other large surface.

3 **Make sure the notebook computer you purchase has a CD and/or DVD drive.** Most notebook computers come with a CD and/or a DVD drive. Although DVD drives are slightly more expensive, they allow you to play CDs and DVD movies using your notebook computer and a headset.

4 **If necessary, upgrade the processor, memory, and disk storage at the time of purchase.** As with a desktop computer, upgrading your notebook computer's memory and disk storage usually is less expensive at the time of initial purchase. Some disk storage is custom designed for notebook computer manufacturers, meaning an upgrade might not be available in the future. If you are purchasing a light-weight notebook computer, then it should include at least an Intel Core Duo processor, 512 MB RAM, and 80 GB of storage.

5 **The availability of built-in ports and a port extender on a notebook computer is important.** A notebook computer does not have a lot of room to add adapter cards. If you know the purpose for which you plan to use your notebook computer, then you can determine the ports you will need. Most notebooks come with common ports, such as a mouse port, IrDA port, serial port, parallel port, video port, a FireWire port, and multiple USB ports. If you plan to connect your notebook computer to a TV, however, then you will need a PCtoTV port. If you want to connect to networks at school or in various offices via a network cable, make sure the notebook computer you purchase has a network port. If your notebook computer does not come with a network port, then you will have to purchase an external network card that slides into an expansion slot in your notebook computer, as well as a network cable. While newer portable media players connect to a USB port, older ones require a FireWire port.

6 **If you plan to use your notebook computer for note-taking at school or in meetings, consider a notebook computer that converts to a Tablet PC.** Some computer manufacturers have developed convertible notebook computers that allow the screen to rotate 180 degrees on a central hinge and then fold down to cover the keyboard and become a Tablet PC (Figure 12). You then can use a stylus to enter text or drawings into the computer by writing on the screen. Some notebook computers have wide screens for better viewing and editing, and some even have a screen on top of the unit in addition to the regular screen.

FIGURE 12
The HP Compaq tc4200 Tablet PC converts to a notebook computer.

7 **Purchase a notebook computer with a built-in wireless network connection.** A wireless network connection (Bluetooth, Wi-Fi a/b/g, WiMAX, etc.) can be useful when you travel or as part of a home network. Increasingly more airports, hotels, and cafes have wireless networks that allow you to connect to the Internet. Many users today are setting up wireless home networks. With a wireless home network, the desktop computer functions as the server, and your notebook computer can access the desktop computer from any location in the house to share files and hardware, such as a printer, and browse the Web. Most home wireless networks allow connections from distances of 150 to 800 feet.

8 **If you are going to use your notebook computer for long periods without access to an electrical outlet, purchase a second battery.** The trend among notebook computer users today is power and size over battery life, and notebook computer manufacturers have picked up on this. Many notebook computer users today are willing to give up longer battery life for a larger screen, faster processor, and more storage. In addition, some manufacturers typically sell the notebook with the lowest capacity battery. For this reason, you need to be careful in choosing a notebook computer if you plan to use it without access to electrical outlets for long periods, such as an airplane flight. You also might want to purchase a second battery as a backup. If you anticipate running your notebook computer on batteries frequently, choose a computer that uses lithium-ion batteries, which last longer than nickel cadmium or nickel hydride batteries.

9 **Purchase a well-padded and well-designed carrying case.** An amply padded carrying case will protect your notebook computer from the bumps it will receive while traveling. A well-designed carrying case will have room for accessories such as spare CDs and DVDs, a user manual, pens, and paperwork (Figure 13).

FIGURE 13 A well-designed notebook computer carrying case.

10 **If you travel overseas, obtain a set of electrical and telephone adapters.** Different countries use different outlets for electrical and telephone connections. Several manufacturers sell sets of adapters that will work in most countries.

11 **If you plan to connect your notebook computer to a video projector, make sure the notebook computer is compatible with the video projector.** You should check, for example, to be sure that your notebook computer will allow you to display an image on the computer screen and projection device at the same time (Figure 14). Also, ensure that your notebook computer has the ports required to connect to the video projector. You also may consider purchasing a notebook computer with a built-in video camera for videoconferencing purposes.

12 **For improved security, consider a fingerprint scanner.** More than half a million notebook computers are stolen or lost each year. If you have critical information stored on your notebook computer, then consider purchasing one with a fingerprint scanner (Figure 15) to protect the data if your computer is stolen or lost. Fingerprint security offers a level of protection that extends well beyond the standard password protection. If your notebook computer is stolen, the odds of recovering it improve dramatically with anti-theft tracking software. Manufacturers claim recovery rates of 90 percent or more for notebook computers using their product.

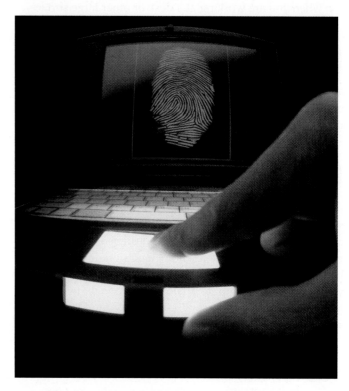

FIGURE 15 Fingerprint scanner technology offers greater security than passwords.

FIGURE 14
A notebook computer connected to a video projector projects the image displayed on the screen.

HOW TO PURCHASE A TABLET PC

The Tablet PC (Figure 16) combines the mobility features of a traditional notebook computer with the simplicity of pencil and paper, because you can create and save Office-type documents by writing and drawing directly on the screen with a digital pen. Tablet PCs use the Windows Tablet Technology in Windows Vista operating system. A notebook computer and a Tablet PC have many similarities. For this reason, if you are considering purchasing a Tablet PC, review the guidelines for purchasing a notebook computer, as well as the guidelines below.

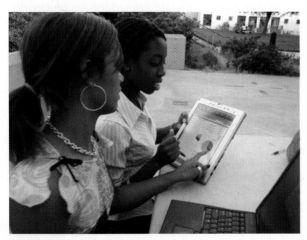

FIGURE 16 The lightweight Tablet PC, with its handwriting capabilities, is the latest addition to the family of mobile computers.

1 **Make sure the Tablet PC fits your mobile computing needs.** The Tablet PC is not for every mobile user. If you find yourself in need of a computer in class or you are spending more time in meetings than in your office, then the Tablet PC may be the answer. Before you invest money in a Tablet PC, however, determine the programs you plan to use on it. You should not buy a Tablet PC simply because it is an interesting type of computer. For additional information on the Tablet PC, visit the Web sites listed in Figure 17. You may have to use the search capabilities on the home page of the companies listed to locate information about the Tablet PC.

Company	Web Address
Fujitsu	fujitsu.com
Hewlett-Packard	hp.com
Microsoft	microsoft.com/windowsxp/tabletpc
ViewSonic	viewsonic.com

For an updated list of companies and their Web site addresses, visit scsite.com/dc2008/ch8/buyers.

FIGURE 17 Companies involved with Tablet PCs and their Web sites.

2 **Decide whether you want a convertible or pure Tablet PC.** Convertible Tablet PCs have an attached keyboard and look like a notebook computer. You rotate the screen and lay it flat against the computer for note-taking. The pure Tablet PCs are slim and lightweight, weighing less than four pounds. They have the capability of easily docking at a desktop to gain access to a large monitor, keyboard, and mouse. If you spend a lot of time attending lectures or meetings, then the pure Tablet PC is ideal. Acceptable specifications for a Tablet PC are shown in Figure 18.

TABLET PC SPECIFICATIONS

Dimensions	12" × 9" × 1.2"
Weight	Less than 5 Pounds
Processor	Pentium M Processor at 2 GHz
RAM	1 GB
Hard Disk	60 GB
Display	12.1" TFT
Digitizer	Electromagnetic Digitizer
Battery	6-Cell High Capacity Lithium-Ion
USB	3
FireWire	1
Docking Station	Grab and Go with CD-ROM, Keyboard, and Mouse
Bluetooth Port	Yes
Wireless	802.11a/b/g Card
Network Card	10/100 Ethernet
Modem	56 Kbps
Speakers	Internal
Microphone	Internal
Operating System	Windows Vista
Application Software	Office Small Business Edition
Antivirus Software	Yes – 12 Month Subscription
Warranty	1-Year Limited Warranty Parts and Labor

FIGURE 18 Tablet PC specifications.

3 **Be sure the weight and dimensions are conducive to portability.** The weight and dimensions of the Tablet PC are important because you carry it around like a notepad. The Tablet PC you buy should weigh four pounds or less. Its dimensions should be approximately 12 inches by 9 inches by 1.2 inches.

Port availability, battery life, and durability are even more important with a Tablet PC than they are with a notebook computer.
Make sure the Tablet PC you purchase has the ports required for the applications you plan to run. As with any mobile computer, battery life is important especially if you plan to use your Tablet PC for long periods without access to an electrical outlet. A Tablet PC must be durable because if you use it the way it was designed to be used, then you will be handling it much like you handle a pad of paper.

 Experiment with different models of the Tablet PC to find the digital pen that works best for you. The key to making use of the Tablet PC is to be comfortable with its handwriting capabilities and on-screen keyboard. Not only is the digital pen used to write on the screen (Figure 19), you also use it to make gestures to complete tasks, in a manner similar to the way you use a mouse. Figure 20 compares the standard point-and-click of a mouse with the gestures made with a digital pen. Other gestures with the digital pen replicate some of the commonly used keys on a keyboard.

FIGURE 19 A Tablet PC lets you handwrite notes and draw on the screen using a digital pen.

Mouse	Digital Pen
Point	Point
Click	Tap
Double-click	Double-tap
Right-click	Tap and hold
Click and drag	Drag

FIGURE 20 Standard point-and-click of a mouse compared with the gestures made with a digital pen.

 Check out the comfort level of handwriting in different positions. You should be able to handwrite on a Tablet PC with your hand resting on the screen. You also should be able to handwrite holding the Tablet PC in one hand, as well as with it sitting in your lap.

Make sure the LCD display device has a resolution high enough to take advantage of Microsoft's ClearType technologies.
Tablet PCs use a digitizer under a standard 10.4-inch motion-sensitive LCD display to make the digital ink on the screen look like real ink on paper. To ensure you get the maximum benefits from the new ClearType technology, make sure the LCD display has a resolution of 800 × 600 in landscape mode and a 600 × 800 in portrait mode.

Test the built-in Tablet PC microphone and speakers. Although most application software, including Microsoft Office, recognizes human speech, it is important that the Tablet PC's built-in microphone operates at an acceptable level. If the microphone is not to your liking, you may want to purchase a close-talk headset with your Tablet PC. Increasingly more users are sending information as audio files, rather than relying solely on text. For this reason, you also should check the speakers on the Tablet PC to make sure they meet your standards.

Consider a Tablet PC with a built-in PC video camera. A PC video camera adds streaming video and still photography capabilities to your Tablet PC, while still allowing you to take notes in lectures or meetings.

Review the docking capabilities of the Tablet PC. The Tablet Technology in Windows Vista operating system supports a grab-and-go form of docking, so you can pick up and take a docked Tablet PC with you, just as you would pick up a notepad on your way to a meeting (Figure 21).

FIGURE 21
A Tablet PC docked to create desktop computer with the Tab as the monitor.

Wireless access to the Internet and your e-mail is essential with a Tablet PC. Make sure the Tablet PC has wireless networking (Bluetooth, Wi-Fi a/b/g, WiMAX, etc.), so you can access the Internet and your e-mail anytime and anywhere. Your Tablet PC also should include standard network connections, such as dial-up and Ethernet connections.

Review available accessories to purchase with your Tablet PC. Tablet PC accessories include docking stations, mouse units, keyboards, security cables, additional memory and storage, protective handgrips, screen protectors, and various types of digital pens.

CHAPTER NINE

Communications and Networks

Picture Yourself Communicating Wirelessly

Much to your delight, you have been accepted to graduate school at a university near San Francisco. You are en route to the airport for a campus visit. In the taxi, you receive a text message from the airline notifying you that your flight has been delayed. Once you arrive at the airport, you use your BlackBerry to check San Francisco's weather and then text message some friends.

On the plane, you use your notebook computer to review your itinerary and decide which campus highlights you want to see. In the rental car after leaving the airport, you use GPS to locate your hotel and the campus. Using your Bluetooth headset, you call home to let everyone know you have arrived safely. At the hotel, you enter the next day's itinerary in your BlackBerry. You want to stretch your legs after the flight, so you stroll to a park. Taking full advantage of San Francisco's city-wide Wi-Fi, you bring your notebook computer along to check and respond to your e-mail.

On campus the next day, you use your camera phone to take pictures of the three dorms you are considering to help you remember your choices when you get home. Before leaving campus, you use your BlackBerry again to make some final notes about your visit.

Read Chapter 9 to learn about wireless communications with a notebook computer, PDA, and smart phone to discover other uses of communications.

OBJECTIVES

After completing this chapter, you will be able to:

1. Discuss the components required for successful communications
2. Identify various sending and receiving devices
3. Describe uses of computer communications
4. List advantages of using a network
5. Differentiate among client/server, peer-to-peer, and P2P networks
6. Describe the various network communications standards
7. Explain the purpose of communications software
8. Describe various types of lines for communications over the telephone network
9. Describe commonly used communications devices
10. Discuss different ways to set up a home network
11. Identify various physical and wireless transmission media

CONTENTS

COMMUNICATIONS

Computer **communications** describes a process in which two or more computers or devices transfer data, instructions, and information. Today, even the smallest computers and devices communicate directly with one another, with hundreds of computers on a company network, or with millions of other computers around the globe — often via the Internet.

Figure 9-1 shows a sample communications system. Some communications involve cables and wires; others are sent wirelessly through the air. For successful communications, you need the following:

- A **sending device** that initiates an instruction to transmit data, instructions, or information.
- A communications device that connects the sending device to a communications channel.
- A **communications channel**, or transmission media on which the data, instructions, or information travel.

FIGURE 9-1   An example of a communications system. Some devices that serve as sending devices and receiving devices are (a) mainframe computers, (b) servers, (c) desktop computers, (d) notebook computers, (e) Tablet PCs, (f) smart phones, (g) Internet-enabled PDAs, and (h) GPS receivers. The communications channel consists of telephone and power lines, cable television and other underground lines, microwave stations, and satellites.

- A communications device that connects the communications channel to a receiving device.
- A **receiving device** that accepts the transmission of data, instructions, or information.

As shown in Figure 9-1, all types of computers and mobile devices serve as sending and receiving devices in a communications system. This includes mainframe computers, servers, desktop computers, notebook computers,

Tablet PCs, smart phones, PDAs, and GPS receivers. One type of communications device that connects a communications channel to a sending or receiving device such as a computer is a modem. Two examples of communications channels are cable television lines and telephone lines.

This chapter presents various uses of communications, discusses different types of networks, and then examines several types of communications devices and communications channels.

USES OF COMPUTER COMMUNICATIONS

Computer communications are everywhere. Many require that users subscribe to an Internet access provider. With other computer communications, an organization such as a business or school provides communications services to employees, students, or customers. The following pages discuss a variety of computer communications.

Internet, Web, E-Mail, Instant Messaging, Chat Rooms, Newsgroups, Internet Telephony, FTP, Web Folders, Video Conferencing, and Fax

Previous chapters discussed many uses of computer communications as they related to a particular topic. In the course of a day, it is likely you use, or use information generated by, one or more of these previously discussed communications technologies. The table in Figure 9-2 reviews the features of these modes of communications.

The following pages discuss a variety of other uses of communications that have not been discussed previously. These include wireless messaging services, wireless Internet access points, cybercafés, global positioning systems, collaboration, groupware, voice mail, and Web services.

Wireless Messaging Services

Users can send and receive wireless messages to and from smart phones, cellular telephones, or PDAs using three techniques: text messaging, wireless instant messaging, and picture/video messaging (Figure 9-3). The type of messaging you use depends primarily on the services offered by the wireless Internet service provider (WISP) that works with the cellular phone or PDA you select. In most cases, you can receive these messages at no cost but pay a per use or monthly fee to send messages to others. Read Ethics & Issues 9-1 for a related discussion.

ETHICS & ISSUES 9-1

Should Cell Phones Be Banned in the Workplace?

Most people would never consider cutting in line at the company cafeteria or stealing somebody else's personal parking space in the company parking lot. This courtesy seems to elude many people when it comes to cellular phone etiquette. While most consider cellular phones to be essential business tools, some people have taken the use of the phones in the workplace to extremes, spending hours a day in loud cell phone conversations. Many people take calls during meetings or other inappropriate times. Often people feel entitled to use the phones for personal calls because they may be paying for the service themselves. Psychologists have found that it may not be the cell phone users' speech volume that annoys us, but rather that the person is having a seemingly one-way conversation with no one, which is a much more difficult background noise for the brain to filter out. Some businesses have declared one day of the week to be cell-phone free in the workplace. Others have designated that cell phones only should be used when working outside of the workplace. These workplaces, however, are very much in the minority. Should cell phone use be banned or limited in the workplace? Why or why not? Should simple rules of etiquette for cell phone use be more publicized or enforced? Why or why not? If so, by whom?

PREVIOUSLY DISCUSSED USES OF COMMUNICATIONS

Internet — Worldwide collection of networks that links millions of businesses, government agencies, educational institutions, and individuals

Web — Worldwide collection of electronic documents on the Internet that users access through a Web browser

E-Mail — Transmission of messages and files via a computer network

Instant Messaging — Real-time one-on-one Internet communications service that notifies you when one or more people are online and then allows you to exchange messages, pictures, files, audio, and video

Chat Rooms — Real-time typed conversation among two or more people that takes place on a computer connected to a network that also may allow the exchange of messages, pictures, files, audio, and video

Newsgroups — Online areas in which users have written discussions about a particular subject

Internet Telephony — Conversation that takes place over the Internet using a telephone connected to a computer or mobile device

FTP — Internet standard that permits users to upload and download files to and from FTP servers on the Internet

Web Folders — Location on a Web server (also known as an HTTP server) to which users publish documents and other files

Video Conferencing — Real-time meeting between two or more geographically separated people who use a network to transmit audio and video data

Fax Machine or Computer Fax/Modem — Transmits and receives documents over telephone lines

FIGURE 9-2 Uses of communications discussed in earlier chapters.

FIGURE 9-3 Users can send and receive text messages, wireless instant messages, and picture/video messages to and from their smart phones and other computers and devices.

TEXT MESSAGING A mobile device with **text messaging**, also called **SMS** (*short message service*), capability allows users to send and receive short text messages on a phone or PDA. Most text messaging services limit messages to a specific number of characters, usually fewer than 300 characters. Text messaging services typically provide users with several options for sending and receiving messages:
- Mobile to Mobile: send a message from your mobile device to another mobile device
- Mobile to E-Mail: send a message from your mobile device to an e-mail address anywhere in the world
- Web to Mobile: send a message from a text messaging Web site to a mobile device or request that a Web site alert a mobile device with messages of breaking news and other updates, such as sports scores, stock prices, and weather forecasts

- Mobile to Provider: send a message by entering a *common short code (CSC)*, which is a four- or five-digit number assigned to a specific content or wireless service provider, followed by the message, such as a vote for a television program contestant or an entry for a sweepstakes

Most services store incoming text messages for about 72 hours. After that time, the WISP deletes any unread messages from its server.

WIRELESS INSTANT MESSAGING Wireless instant messaging (IM) is a real-time Internet communications service that allows wireless mobile devices to exchange messages with one or more mobile devices or online users. Some WISPs partner with IM services so you can use your smart phone or PDA to send and receive wireless instant messages. Cingular Wireless service, for example, allows communications through various instant messengers such as AOL Instant Messenger (AIM) and Yahoo! Messenger. With a compatible IM service, users have these IM options:

- Mobile to Mobile: use a wireless instant messenger to communicate between two mobile devices
- Mobile to Personal Computer: use a wireless instant messenger to communicate between a mobile device and a personal computer
- Web to Mobile: send or forward messages from a personal computer's instant messenger to a mobile device

PICTURE/VIDEO MESSAGING With **picture messaging**, users can send pictures and sound files, as well as short text messages, to a phone, PDA, or computer. With **video messaging**, users can send short video clips, usually about 15 seconds, in addition to all picture messaging services. Smart phones and PDAs with picture/video messaging, also called *MMS (multimedia message service)*, capability typically have a digital camera built into the device. A phone with picture messaging capability often is called a *camera phone* or *picture phone*. Similarly, a phone with video messaging capability often is called a *video phone*. Read Ethics & Issues 9-2 for a related discussion.

Picture/video messaging services typically provide users these options for sending and receiving messages:

- Mobile to Mobile: send the picture/video from your mobile device to another mobile device

- Mobile to E-Mail: send the picture/video from your mobile device to an e-mail address anywhere in the world

If you send a picture message to a phone that does not have picture/video messaging capability, the phone usually displays a text message directing the user to a Web page that contains the picture/video message.

Wireless Internet Access Points

At home, work, school, and in many public locations, people connect wirelessly to the Internet through a **wireless Internet access point** using mobile computers or other devices. Two types of wireless Internet access points are hot spots and 3G networks.

A *hot spot* is a wireless network that provides Internet connections to mobile computers and other devices. Through the hot spot, mobile users check e-mail, browse the Web, and access any service on the Internet — as long as their computers or devices have built-in wireless capability or the appropriate wireless network card, PC Card, ExpressCard module, or USB network adapter (Figure 9-4). Two popular hot spot technologies are Wi-Fi and WiMAX. In general, Wi-Fi hot spots have an indoor range of 100 feet and an outdoor range of 300 feet. Wi-Fi hot spots provide wireless network connections to users in public locations such as airports, train stations, hotels, convention centers, schools, campgrounds, marinas, shopping malls, bookstores, libraries, restaurants, and coffee shops. The coverage range for WiMAX hot spots, by contrast, can extend to more than 30 miles and cover entire cities. Sections later in this chapter discuss Wi-Fi and WiMAX in more detail.

Some hot spots provide free Internet access, some charge a per-use fee, and others require users to subscribe to a WISP, to which they pay per access fees, daily fees, or a monthly fee. Per access fees average $3, daily fees range from $5 to $20, and monthly fees range from $20 to $60 for unlimited access, with the higher monthly fee providing greater coverage areas.

Instead of hot spots, some users access the Internet wirelessly through 3G networks. A *3G network* uses cellular radio technology to provide users with high-speed wireless Internet connections, as long as they are in the network's range. A 3G network usually includes most major cities and airports. Users access the 3G network through a cellular phone or notebook computer equipped with the appropriate wireless PC Card or ExpressCard module.

WEB LINK 9-1

Video Messaging

For more information, visit scsite.com/ dc2008/ch9/weblink and then click Video Messaging.

ETHICS & ISSUES 9-2

High-Tech Cheating via Wireless Messaging Services

Several schools have banned student smart phones claiming that they disrupt classes and sometimes are used for illegal activities, such as drug sales. Now, schools may have another reason to prohibit smart phones and other wireless devices among students.

Once, teachers only had to watch test-takers to make sure that no one was copying from a neighbor's paper or secretly referring to notes concealed under a desk. Recently, however, some students have been caught using their smart phones' messaging service to send each other answers to test questions. Others have been caught using camera-enabled smart phones to take pictures of tests and forwarding the images to other students who were scheduled to take the test at a later time. Some teachers fear that more students soon may be using wireless devices, such as gaming devices, to communicate covertly with classmates during a test, or even to receive messages from sources outside the classroom. Some schools have gone as far as installing electronic jamming equipment to stop wireless communications. To eliminate this high-tech method of cheating, should smart phones, digital cameras, notebook computers, Tablet PCs, PDAs, and other wireless devices be banned during lectures and exams? Why or why not? Short of banning these devices, what, if anything, can schools do to prevent students from using them to cheat? Is it possible for schools to seek a point of compromise so that they can both embrace the new technology and control it?

FIGURE 9-4 Mobile users in this hot spot access the Internet through their notebook computers. One computer uses a wireless USB network adapter; another uses a wireless network PC Card. Others have Intel's built-in wireless Centrino or Centrino Duo technology.

Subscription fees for unlimited monthly Internet access through a cellular phone range from $30 to $50. Fees for notebook computer access are higher, ranging from $60 to $80 per month. A section later in this chapter discusses 3G technology in more depth.

Cybercafés

When mobile users travel without their notebook computer or Internet-enabled mobile device, they can visit a cybercafé to access e-mail, the Web, and other Internet services. A **cybercafé**, or Internet cafe, is a coffeehouse, restaurant, or other location that provides personal computers with Internet access to its customers (Figure 9-5). More than 4,200 cybercafés exist in cities around the world. Although some provide free Internet access, most charge a per-hour or per-minute fee. Some cybercafés also are hot spots, providing wireless Internet connections to users with mobile computers and devices.

FIGURE 9-5 People using Internet-connected computers in a cybercafé.

Global Positioning System

A **global positioning system** (**GPS**) is a navigation system that consists of one or more earth-based receivers that accept and analyze signals sent by satellites in order to determine the receiver's geographic location (Figure 9-6). A *GPS receiver* is a handheld, mountable, or embedded device that contains an antenna, a radio receiver, and a processor. Many include a screen display that shows an individual's location on a map.

Many mobile devices such as PDAs and smart phones have GPS capability built into the device or as an add-on feature. Some users carry a handheld GPS receiver; others mount a receiver to an object such as an automobile, boat, airplane, farm and construction equipment, or computer.

The first and most used application of GPS technology is to assist people with determining where they are located. The data obtained from a GPS, however, can be applied to a variety of other uses: creating a map, ascertaining the best route between two points, locating a lost person or stolen object, monitoring the movement of a person or object, determining altitude, and calculating speed. Many vehicles use GPSs to provide drivers with directions or other information, automatically call for help if the airbag is deployed, dispatch roadside assistance, unlock the driver's side door if keys are locked in the car, and track the vehicle if it is stolen. Hikers and remote campers may carry GPS receivers in case they need emergency help or directions.

WEB LINK 9-2

GPS

For more information, visit scsite.com/dc2008/ch9/weblink and then click GPS.

FIGURE 9-6   HOW A GPS WORKS

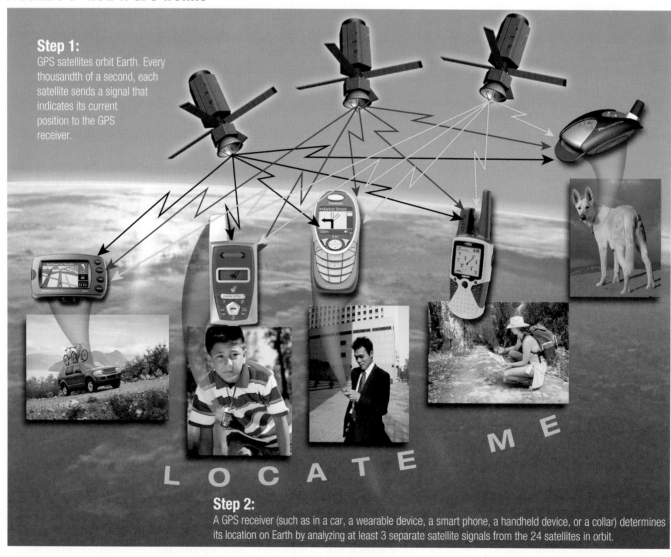

Step 1:
GPS satellites orbit Earth. Every thousandth of a second, each satellite sends a signal that indicates its current position to the GPS receiver.

Step 2:
A GPS receiver (such as in a car, a wearable device, a smart phone, a handheld device, or a collar) determines its location on Earth by analyzing at least 3 separate satellite signals from the 24 satellites in orbit.

For applications that locate or track people, the GPS receiver typically works in conjunction with a cellular wireless network. When a user presses a button on the GPS receiver or at regularly scheduled times, the GPS receiver captures data from the satellite and sends location information to a cellular wireless network. Once the cellular wireless network receives the data, its computer calculates the exact location of a person or object.

Collaboration

Many programs provide a means to **collaborate**, or work online, with other users connected to a server. Three methods of collaboration include collaborative software, reviewing via e-mail, and document management systems.

Collaborative software includes tools that enable users to share documents via online meetings and communicate with other connected users. An *online meeting* allows users to share documents with others in real time (Figure 9-7). That is, all participants see the document at the same time. As someone changes the document, everyone in the meeting sees the changes being made. During the online meeting, participants have the ability to open a chat window and type messages to one another. Collaborative software often has whiteboard and video/audio conferencing capabilities. Examples of collaborative software include Acrobat Connect, GoToMeeting, Microsoft Groove, Microsoft Live Meeting, and WebEx. Microsoft Office SharePoint Server 2007 contains a suite of programs, one of which is collaborative software.

Instead of interacting in a live meeting, users often collaborate via e-mail. For example, if users want others to review a document, they can e-mail the document for review. When the recipients (reviewers) receive the document, they may add comments to the document. As they make changes to the document, both the original text and the changes are displayed. When the originator receives the document back from all reviewers, he or she can merge all comments and changes into a single document.

Some companies use document management systems to make collaboration possible among employees. A *document management system* provides for storage and management of a company's documents, such as word processing documents, presentations, and spreadsheets. Users then access these documents, depending on their needs. A document management system can track all changes made to a document. It also can store additional information such as the document's creation date, the user who created the document, a summary of the document, and any keywords associated with the document.

Groupware

Groupware is software that helps groups of people work together on projects and share information over a network. Groupware is a component of a broad concept called *workgroup computing*, which includes network hardware and software that enables group members to communicate, manage projects, schedule meetings, and make group decisions. To assist with these activities, most groupware provides personal information manager (PIM) functions, such as an electronic appointment calendar, an address book, and a notepad. A major feature of groupware is group scheduling, in which a group calendar tracks the schedules of multiple users and helps coordinate appointments and meeting times.

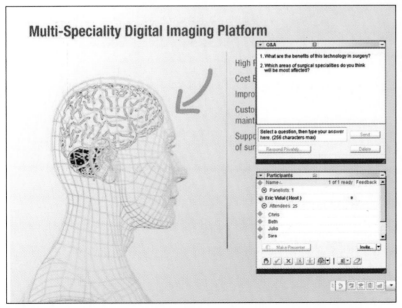

FIGURE 9-7 Through an online meeting, all participants see the document at the same time.

Voice Mail

Voice mail, which functions much like an answering machine, allows someone to leave a voice message for one or more people. Unlike answering machines, however, a computer in the voice mail system converts an analog voice message into digital form. Once digitized, the message is stored in a voice mailbox. A *voice mailbox* is a storage location on a hard disk in the voice mail system. Some voice mail systems can send digital voice mail files to e-mail addresses.

Web Services

Web services describe standardized software that enables programmers to create applications that communicate with other remote computers over the Internet or on an internal business network (Figure 9-8). Businesses are the primary users of Web services because this technology provides a means for departments to communicate with each other, suppliers, vendors, and with clients. For example, third-party vendors can use Web services to communicate with their online retailer's Web site to manage their inventory levels.

Web services do not require a specific programming language, operating system, or Web browser. Different applications from different platforms can communicate with each other by sending properly formatted *XML* (eXtensible Markup Language) files to the Web services. A Windows application, for example, can communicate with a UNIX application. Web services do not have a user interface because the application's user interface interacts with the Web service.

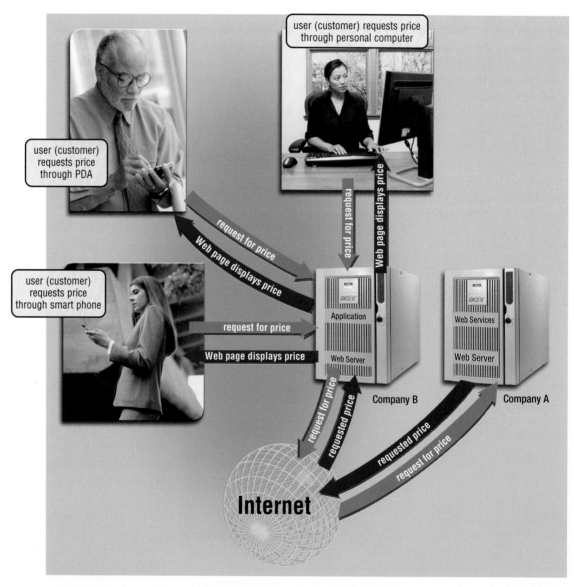

FIGURE 9-8 An example of Web services.

Test your knowledge of pages 460 through 468 in Quiz Yourself 9-1.

QUIZ YOURSELF 9-1

Instructions: Find the true statement below. Then, rewrite the remaining false statements so they are true.

1. A cybercafé is a wireless network that provides Internet connections to mobile computers and other devices.

2. A Web folder is a navigation system that consists of one or more earth-based receivers that accept and analyze signals sent by satellites in order to determine the receiver's geographic location.

3. Web services describe standardized software that enables programmers to create applications that communicate with other remote computers over the Internet or on an internal business network.

4. Receiving devices initiate an instruction to transmit data, instructions, or information.

5. Users can send pictures and sound files, as well as short text messages, with text messaging.

Quiz Yourself Online: To further check your knowledge of required components for communications, sending and receiving devices, and uses of computer communications, visit scsite.com/dc2008/ch9/quiz and then click Objectives 1 – 3.

NETWORKS

As discussed in Chapter 1, a **network** is a collection of computers and devices connected together via communications devices and transmission media. Many businesses network their computers together to facilitate communications, share hardware, share data and information, share software, and transfer funds (Figure 9-9). The next page elaborates on how businesses use networks.

Reasons Businesses Use a Network

new message

message sent

facilitate communications

transfer funds

share software

share hardware

share data and information

FIGURE 9-9 Businesses use networks to facilitate communications, share hardware, share data and information, share software, and transfer funds.

A network can be internal to an organization or span the world by connecting to the Internet. Networks facilitate communications among users and allow users to share resources, such as data, information, hardware, and software. The following paragraphs explain the advantages of using a network.

- Facilitating communications — Using a network, people communicate efficiently and easily via e-mail, instant messaging, chat rooms, blogs, online social networks, video telephone calls, online meetings, video conferencing, Internet telephony, wireless messaging services, and groupware. Some of these communications, such as e-mail, occur within a business's internal network. Other times, they occur globally over the Internet.

- Sharing hardware — In a networked environment, each computer on the network has access to hardware on the network. Business and home users network their hardware to save money. That is, it may be too costly to provide each user with the same piece of hardware such as a printer. If the computers and a laser printer are connected to a network, the computer users each access the laser printer on the network, as they need it.

- Sharing data and information — In a networked environment, any authorized computer user can access data and information stored on other computers on the network. A large company, for example, might have a database of customer information. Any authorized person, including a mobile user with a PDA or smart phone connected to the network, has access to the database.

  Most businesses use a standard, such as EDI (*electronic data interchange*), that defines how data transmits across telephone lines or other means. For example, companies use EDI to handle product catalog distribution, bids, requests for quotations, proposals, order placement, shipping notifications, invoicing, and payment processing. EDI enables businesses to operate with a minimum amount of paperwork.

  Another popular data sharing standard is XML, described earlier in this chapter. Using XML, Web programmers can create one version of a Web page that then can be displayed in a form appropriate for a variety of display devices. XML also is used in RSS, which is used to distribute content, such as news, to subscribers.

- Sharing software — Users connected to a network have access to software on the network. To support multiple users' access of software, most vendors sell network versions or site licenses of their software, which usually cost less than buying individual copies of the software for each computer. A *network license* is a legal agreement that allows multiple users to access the software on a server simultaneously. The network license fee usually is based on the number of users or the number of computers attached to the network. A *site license* is a legal agreement that permits users to install the software on multiple computers — usually at a volume discount.

- Transferring funds — Called *electronic funds transfer* (*EFT*), it allows users connected to a network to transfer money from one bank account to another via transmission media. Both businesses and consumers use EFT. Consumers use an ATM to access their bank account. Businesses deposit payroll checks directly in employees' bank accounts. Consumers use credit cards to make purchases from a retail Web site. Businesses use EFT to purchase and pay for goods purchased from vendors. Both businesses and consumers pay bills online, with which they instruct a bank to use EFT to pay creditors.

Instead of using the Internet or investing in and administering an internal network, some companies hire a value-added network provider for network functions. A *value-added network* (*VAN*) is a third-party business that provides networking services such as secure data and information transfer, storage, e-mail, and management reports. Some VANs charge an annual or monthly fee; others charge by service used.

For a technical discussion about networks, read the High-Tech Talk article on page 498.

LANs, MANs, and WANs

Networks usually are classified as a local area network, metropolitan area network, or wide area network. The main differentiation among these classifications is their area of coverage, as described in the following paragraphs.

LAN   A **local area network (LAN)** is a network that connects computers and devices in a limited geographical area such as a home, school computer laboratory, office building (Figure 9-10), or closely positioned group of buildings. Each computer or device on the network, called a *node*, often shares resources such as printers, large hard disks, and programs. Often, the nodes are connected via cables.

A **wireless LAN (WLAN)** is a LAN that uses no physical wires. Computers and devices that access a wireless LAN must have built-in wireless capability or the appropriate wireless network card, PC Card, ExpressCard module, USB network adapter, or flash card. Very often, a WLAN communicates with a wired LAN for access to its resources, such as software, hardware, and the Internet (Figure 9-11).

WEB LINK 9-3

WLANs

For more information, visit scsite.com/ dc2008/ch9/weblink and then click Wireless Local Area Networks.

customer service offices

marketing department offices

servers for local area network

FIGURE 9-10   Computers on different floors access the same local area network (LAN) in an office building.

Internet

high-speed Internet connection

wired network

wireless access point

wireless network

FIGURE 9-11   Computers on a wireless LAN often communicate via an access point with a wired LAN to access its software, printer, the Internet, and other resources.

MAN A *metropolitan area network* (*MAN*) is a high-speed network that connects local area networks in a metropolitan area such as a city or town and handles the bulk of communications activity across that region. A MAN typically includes one or more LANs, but covers a smaller geographic area than a WAN. The state of Pennsylvania, for example, has a MAN that connects state agencies and individual users in the region around the state capital.

A MAN usually is managed by a consortium of users or by a single network provider that sells the service to the users. Local and state governments, for example, regulate some MANs. Telephone companies, cable television operators, and other organizations provide users with connections to the MAN.

WAN A **wide area network** (**WAN**) is a network that covers a large geographic area (such as a city, country, or the world) using a communications channel that combines many types of media such as telephone lines, cables, and radio waves (Figure 9-12). A WAN can be one large network or can consist of two or more LANs connected together. The Internet is the world's largest WAN.

Network Architectures

The design of computers, devices, and media in a network, sometimes called the *network architecture*, is categorized as either client/server or peer-to-peer. The following paragraphs discuss these network architectures.

CLIENT/SERVER On a **client/server network**, one or more computers act as a server, and the other computers on the network request services from the server (Figure 9-13). A **server**, sometimes called a *host computer*, controls access to the hardware, software, and other resources on the network and provides a centralized storage area for programs, data, and information. The **clients** are other computers and mobile devices on the network that rely on the server for its resources. For example, a server might store a database of customers. Clients on the network (company employees) access the customer database on the server.

FIGURE 9-13 On a client/server network, one or more computers act as a server, and the clients access the server(s).

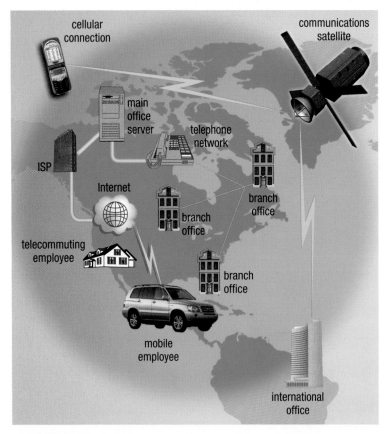

FIGURE 9-12 An example of a WAN.

Some servers, called *dedicated servers*, perform a specific task and can be placed with other dedicated servers to perform multiple tasks. For example, a *file server* stores and manages files. A *print server* manages printers and print jobs. A *database server* stores and provides access to a database. A *network server* manages network traffic (activity).

Although it can connect a smaller number of computers, a client/server network typically provides an efficient means to connect 10 or more computers. Most client/server networks require a person to serve as a network administrator because of the large size of the network.

PEER-TO-PEER One type of *peer-to-peer network* is a simple, inexpensive network that typically connects fewer than 10 computers. Each computer, called a *peer*, has equal responsibilities and capabilities, sharing hardware (such as a printer), data, or information with other computers on the peer-to-peer network (Figure 9-14). Each computer stores files on its own storage devices. Thus, each computer on the network contains both the network operating system and application software. All computers on the network share any peripheral device(s) attached to any computer. For example, one computer may have a laser printer and a scanner, while another has an ink-jet printer and an external hard disk.

Peer-to-peer networks are ideal for very small businesses and home users. Some operating systems, such as Windows, include a peer-to-peer networking utility that allows users to set up a peer-to-peer network.

INTERNET PEER-TO-PEER Another type of peer-to-peer, called *P2P*, describes an Internet network on which users access each other's hard disks and exchange files directly over the Internet (Figure 9-15). This type of peer-to-peer network sometimes is called a *file sharing network* because users with compatible software and an Internet connection copy files from someone else's hard disk to their hard disks. As more users connect to the network, each user has access to shared files on other users' hard disks. When users log off the network, others no longer have access to their hard disks. To maintain an acceptable speed for communications, some implementations of P2P limit the number of users.

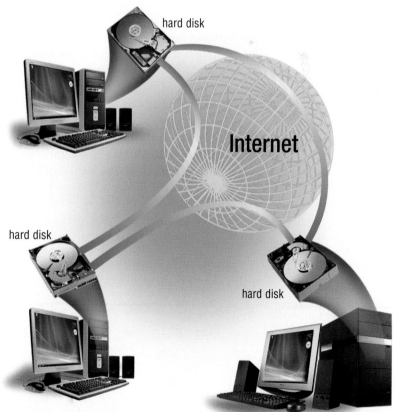

FIGURE 9-14 Each computer on a peer-to-peer network shares its hardware and software with other computers on the network.

FIGURE 9-15 P2P describes an Internet network on which users connect to each other's hard disks and exchange files directly.

WEB LINK 9-4

BitTorrent

For more information, visit scsite.com/dc2008/ ch9/weblink and then click BitTorrent.

Examples of networking software that support P2P are BitTorrent, Gnutella, and Kazaa, which allow users to swap music and other files via the Web. For example, when one user requests a song, the program searches through lists of shared files — which are stored on one or more connected computers, called supernodes. If a match is found, the music file is copied from the computer on which it resides to the requesting computer. These programs initially stirred much controversy with respect to copyright infringement of music because they allowed users easily to copy music and movie files free from one computer to another. To help reduce copyright infringement, today's music and movie sharing services typically are fee based, and music and movie files often are encrypted as they travel across the Internet.

Many businesses also see an advantage to using P2P. That is, companies and employees can exchange files using P2P, freeing the company from maintaining a network server for this purpose. Business-to-business e-commerce Web sites find that P2P easily allows buyers and sellers to share company information such as product databases.

Network Topologies

A **network topology** refers to the layout of the computers and devices in a communications network. Three commonly used network topologies are bus, ring, and star. Networks usually use combinations of these topologies.

Bus Network A *bus network* consists of a single central cable, to which all computers and other devices connect (Figure 9-16). The *bus* is the physical cable that connects the computers and other devices. The bus in a bus network

transmits data, instructions, and information in both directions. When a sending device transmits data, the address of the receiving device is included with the transmission so the data is routed to the appropriate receiving device.

Bus networks are popular on LANs because they are inexpensive and easy to install. One advantage of the bus network is that computers and other devices can be attached and detached at any point on the bus without disturbing the rest of the network. Another advantage is that failure of one device usually does not affect the rest of the bus network. The greatest risk to a bus network is that the bus itself might become inoperable. If that happens, the network remains inoperative until the bus is back in working order.

Ring Network On a *ring network*, a cable forms a closed loop (ring) with all computers and devices arranged along the ring (Figure 9-17). Data transmitted on a ring network travels from device to device around the entire ring, in one direction. When a computer or device sends data, the data travels to each computer on the ring until it reaches its destination.

FIGURE 9-17 On a ring network, all connected devices form a continuous loop.

FIGURE 9-16 Devices in a bus network share a single data path.

If a computer or device on a ring network fails, all devices before the failed device are unaffected, but those after the failed device cannot function. A ring network can span a larger distance than a bus network, but it is more difficult to install. The ring topology primarily is used for LANs, but also is used in WANs.

STAR NETWORK On a *star network*, all of the computers and devices (nodes) on the network connect to a central device, thus forming a star (Figure 9-18). Two types of devices that provide a common central connection point for nodes on the network are a *hub* and a *switch*. All data that transfers from one node to another passes through the hub/switch.

Star networks are fairly easy to install and maintain. Nodes can be added to and removed from the network with little or no disruption to the network.

On a star network, if one node fails, only that node is affected. The other nodes continue to operate normally. If the hub/switch fails, however, the entire network is inoperable until the device is repaired. Most large star networks, therefore, keep backup hubs/switches available in case the primary one fails.

Intranets

Recognizing the efficiency and power of the Internet, many organizations apply Internet and Web technologies to their own internal networks. An *intranet* (intra means within) is an internal network that uses Internet technologies. Intranets generally make company information accessible to employees and facilitate working in groups.

Simple intranet applications include electronic publishing of organizational materials such as telephone directories, event calendars, procedure manuals, employee benefits information, and job postings. Additionally, an intranet typically includes a connection to the Internet. More sophisticated uses of intranets include groupware applications such as project management, chat rooms, newsgroups, group scheduling, and video conferencing.

An intranet essentially is a small version of the Internet that exists within an organization. It has a Web server, supports multimedia Web pages coded in HTML, and is accessible via a Web browser such as Internet Explorer, Firefox, Netscape, Opera, and Safari. Users update information on the intranet by creating and posting a Web page, using a method similar to that used on the Internet.

Sometimes a company uses an *extranet*, which allows customers or suppliers to access part of its intranet. Package shipping companies, for example, allow customers to access their intranet to print air bills, schedule pickups, and even track shipped packages as the packages travel to their destinations.

FIGURE 9-18 A star network contains a single, centralized hub or switch through which all the devices in the network communicate.

NETWORK COMMUNICATIONS STANDARDS

Today's networks connect terminals, devices, and computers from many different manufacturers across many types of networks, such as wide area, local area, and wireless. For the different devices on various types of networks to be able to communicate, the network must use similar techniques of moving data through the network from one application to another. For example, an IBM mainframe computer cannot communicate directly with an Apple Macintosh network — some form of translation must occur for devices on these two types of networks to communicate.

To alleviate the problems of incompatibility and ensure that hardware and software components can be integrated into any network, various organizations such as ANSI and IEEE (pronounced I triple E) propose, develop, and approve network standards. A *network standard* defines guidelines that specify the way computers access the medium to which they are attached, the type(s) of medium used, the speeds used on different types of networks, and the type(s) of physical cable and/or the wireless technology used. A standard that outlines characteristics of how two network devices communicate is called a *protocol*. Specifically, a protocol may define data format, coding schemes, error handling, and sequencing techniques. Hardware and software manufacturers design their products to meet the guidelines specified in a particular standard, so their devices can communicate with the network.

The following sections discuss some of the more widely used network communications standards and protocols for both wired and wireless networks including Ethernet, token ring, TCP/IP, 802.11 (Wi-Fi), Bluetooth, UWB, IrDA, RFID, WiMAX, and WAP. Oftentimes, these network standards and protocols work together to move data through a network. Some of these standards define how a network is arranged physically; others specify how messages travel along the network, and so on. Thus, as data moves through the network from one application to another, it may use one or more of these standards.

WEB LINK 9-5

Ethernet

For more information, visit scsite.com/ dc2008/ch9/weblink and then click Ethernet.

Ethernet

Ethernet is a network standard that specifies no central computer or device on the network (nodes) should control when data can be transmitted; that is, each node attempts to transmit data when it determines the network is available to receive communications. If two computers on an Ethernet network attempt to send data at the same time, a collision will occur, and the computers must attempt to send their messages again.

Ethernet is based on a bus topology, but Ethernet networks can be wired in a star pattern. The Ethernet standard defines guidelines for the physical configuration of a network, e.g., cabling, network cards, and nodes. Today, Ethernet is the most popular network standard for LANs because it is relatively inexpensive and easy to install and maintain.

Ethernet networks often use cables to transmit data. At a 10 Mbps (million bits per second) data transfer rate, the original Ethernet standard is not very fast by today's standards. A more recent Ethernet standard, called *Fast Ethernet*, has a data transfer rate of 100 Mbps, ten times faster than the original standard. *Gigabit Ethernet* provides an even higher speed of transmission, with transfer rates of 1 Gbps (1 billion bits per second). The *10-Gigabit Ethernet* standard supports transfer rates up to 10 Gbps.

Token Ring

The **token ring** standard specifies that computers and devices on the network share or pass a special signal, called a token, in a unidirectional manner and in a preset order. A *token* is a special series of bits that function like a ticket. The device with the token can transmit data over the network. Only one token exists per network. This ensures that only one computer transmits data at a time.

Token ring is based on a ring topology (although it can use a star topology). The token ring standard defines guidelines for the physical configuration of a network, e.g., cabling, network cards, and devices. Some token ring networks connect up to 72 devices. Others use a special type of wiring that allows up to 260 connections. The data transfer rate on a token ring network can be 4 Mbps, 16 Mbps, 100 Mbps, or 1 Gbps.

TCP/IP

Short for *Transmission Control Protocol/Internet Protocol*, **TCP/IP** is a network standard, specifically a protocol, that defines how messages (data) are routed from one end of a network to the other, ensuring the data arrives correctly. TCP/IP describes rules for dividing messages into small pieces, called *packets*; providing addresses for each packet; checking for and detecting errors; sequencing packets; and regulating the flow of messages along the network.

TCP/IP has been adopted as a network standard for Internet communications. Thus, all hosts on the Internet follow the rules defined in this standard. As shown in Figure 9-19, Internet communications also use other standards, such as the Ethernet standard, as data is routed to its destination.

When a computer sends data over the Internet, the data is divided into packets. Each packet contains the data, as well as the recipient (destination), the origin (sender), and the sequence information used to reassemble the data at the destination. Each packet travels along the fastest individual available path to the recipient's computer via communications devices called routers.

This technique of breaking a message into individual packets, sending the packets along the best route available, and then reassembling the data is called *packet switching*.

FAQ 9-1

Do HTTP, SMTP, and POP work with TCP/IP?

Yes. HTTP (Hypertext Transfer Protocol), SMTP (Simple Mail Transfer Protocol), and POP (Post Office Protocol) are standards that define the format of data as it transmits over networks that use the TCP/IP standard. HTTP works with Web browsers, and SMTP and POP work with e-mail programs. For more information, visit scsite.com/dc2008/ch9/faq and then click HTTP, SMTP, and POP.

EXAMPLE OF HOW COMMUNICATIONS STANDARDS WORK TOGETHER

client (your computer)

COMMUNICATIONS SOFTWARE:
Using a Web browser program, you request a Web page on a Web server be displayed on your computer screen.

Web server

TCP/IP:
Your computer uses the TCP/IP standard to establish a connection with the Web server that stores the requested Web page, divide the Web page into packets, provide an address for each packet, and reassemble the Web page once it arrives at your computer. Routers send the packets over the Internet from the Web server to your computer.

ETHERNET:
The Ethernet standard controls how devices (adapter cards, routers, modems, etc.) share access to the media (cables and lines) and how devices transmit data over the communications channel.

FIGURE 9-19   Network communications use a variety of standards to ensure that data travels correctly to its destination. Some standards used in Internet communications include the TCP/IP and Ethernet standards, as shown in this figure.

802.11 (Wi-Fi)

Developed by IEEE, **802.11** is a series of network standards that specifies how two wireless devices communicate over the air with each other. Using the 802.11 standard, computers or devices that have the appropriate wireless capability communicate via radio waves with other computers or devices. The table in Figure 9-20 outlines various 802.11 standards and their data transfer rates. A designation of 802.11 a/b/g on a computer or device indicates it supports all three standards. The newest standard, 802.11n, uses multiple transmitters and receivers, known as *MIMO* (multiple-input multiple-output), to reach speeds from 2 to 10 times faster than 802.11g.

The 802.11 standard often is called the *wireless Ethernet standard* because it uses techniques similar to the Ethernet standard to specify how physically to configure a wireless network. Thus, 802.11 networks easily can be integrated with wired Ethernet networks. When an 802.11 network accesses the Internet, it works in conjunction with the TCP/IP network standard.

The term **Wi-Fi** (*wireless fidelity*) identifies any network based on the 802.11 series of standards. Wi-Fi Certified products are guaranteed to be able to communicate with each other. Windows Vista and Windows Mobile include support for Wi-Fi.

One popular use of the Wi-Fi network standard is in hot spots (discussed earlier in this chapter) that offer mobile users the ability to connect to the Internet with their wireless computers and devices. Many homes and small businesses also use Wi-Fi to network computers and devices wirelessly. In open or outdoor areas free from interference, the computers or devices should be within 300 feet of each other. In closed areas, the wireless network range is about 100 feet. To obtain communications at the maximum distances, you may need to install extra hardware.

Some entire cities are set up as a *Wi-Fi mesh network*, in which each mesh node routes its data to the next available node until the data reaches its destination — usually an Internet connection. A Wi-Fi mesh network is more flexible than a hot spot because each node in a mesh network does not have to be directly connected to the Internet.

802.11 SERIES OF STANDARDS

Standard	Transfer Rates
802.11	1 or 2 Mbps
802.11a	Up to 54 Mbps
802.11b	Up to 11 Mbps
802.11g	54 Mbps and higher
802.11n	108 Mbps and higher

FIGURE 9-20
A comparison of standards in the 802.11 series.

FAQ 9-2

How do I know where hot spots exist?

If your computer has wireless capability that is enabled, Windows automatically will search for hot spots. If a hot spot exists, Windows will display a message. New notebook computers also may have a switch that allows you to determine if a hot spot exists, without turning on the computer. For more information, visit scsite.com/dc2008/ch9/faq and then click Hot Spots.

Bluetooth

Bluetooth is a network standard, specifically a protocol, that defines how two Bluetooth devices use short-range radio waves to transmit data. The data transfers between devices at a rate of up to ? Mbps. To communicate with each other, Bluetooth devices often must be within about 10 meters (about 33 feet) but can be extended to 100 meters with additional equipment.

A Bluetooth device contains a small chip that allows it to communicate with other Bluetooth devices. Examples of Bluetooth-enabled devices can include desktop computers, notebook computers, handheld computers, PDAs, smart phones, headsets, keyboards, mouse devices, microphones, digital cameras, fax machines, and printers. For computers and devices not Bluetooth-enabled, you can purchase a Bluetooth wireless port adapter that will convert an existing USB port or serial port into a Bluetooth port. Windows Vista has built-in Bluetooth support.

UWB

UWB, which stands for **ultra-wideband**, is a network standard that specifies how two UWB devices use short-range radio waves to communicate at high speeds with each other. At distances of 10 meters (about 33 feet), the data transfer rate is 110 Mbps. At closer distances, such as 2 meters (about 6.5 feet), the transfer rate is at least 480 Mbps. UWB can transmit signals through doors and other obstacles. Because of its high transfer rates, UWB is best suited for transmission of large files such as video, graphics, and audio. Examples of UWB uses include wirelessly transferring video from a digital video camera, printing pictures from a digital camera, downloading media to a portable media player, or displaying a slide show on a projector.

IrDA

As discussed in Chapter 4, some computers and devices use the **IrDA** standard to transmit data wirelessly to each other via infrared (IR) light waves. The devices transfer data at rates from 115 Kbps (thousand bits per second) to 4 Mbps between their IrDA ports.

Infrared requires a *line-of-sight transmission*; that is, the sending device and the receiving device must be in line with each other so that nothing obstructs the path of the infrared light wave. Because Bluetooth and UWB do not require line-of-sight transmission, some industry experts predict that these technologies will replace infrared.

RFID

RFID (*radio frequency identification*) is a standard, specifically a protocol, that defines how a network uses radio signals to communicate with a tag placed in or attached to an object, an animal, or a person. The tag, called a transponder, consists of an antenna and a memory chip that contains the information to be transmitted via radio waves. Through an antenna, an RFID reader, also called a transceiver, reads the radio signals and transfers the information to a computer or computing device.

RFID tags are passive or active. An active RFID tag contains a battery that runs the chip's circuitry and broadcasts a signal to the RFID reader. A passive RFID tag does not contain a battery and thus cannot send a signal until the reader activates the tag's antenna by sending out electromagnetic waves. Because passive RFID tags contain no battery, these can be small enough to be embedded in skin.

Depending on the type of RFID reader, the distance between the tag and the reader ranges from 5 inches to 15 feet. Readers can be handheld or embedded in an object such as the tollbooth shown in Figure 9-21.

WiMAX

WiMAX (Worldwide Interoperability for Microwave Access), also known as **802.16**, is a newer network standard developed by IEEE that specifies how wireless devices communicate over the air in a wide area. Using the WiMAX standard, computers or devices with the appropriate WiMAX wireless capability communicate via radio waves with other computers or devices via a WiMAX tower. The WiMAX tower, which can cover up to a 30-mile radius, connects to the Internet or to another WiMAX tower.

The WiMAX Forum is a wireless industry association of more than 350 suppliers and service providers dedicated to developing specifications and testing equipment. Current WiMAX standards have data transfer rates from 15 Mbps to 40 Mbps.

The WiMAX standard provides wireless broadband Internet access at a reasonable cost over long distances to business and home users. Experts predict that WiMAX service eventually could surpass other broadband Internet access services such as DSL and cable because it can reach rural and remote areas easily and inexpensively. The WiMAX standard, similar to the Wi-Fi standard, connects mobile users to the Internet via hot spots. The next generation of game consoles also plans to support the WiMAX standard.

WEB LINK 9-6

WiMAX

For more information, visit scsite.com/dc2008/ch9/weblink and then click WiMAX.

IGURE 9-21 HOW ELECTRONIC RFID TOLL COLLECTION WORKS

Step 1:
Motorist purchases an RFID transponder or RFID tag and attaches it to the vehicle's windshield.

Step 2:
As vehicle approaches the tollbooth, the RFID reader in the tollbooth sends a radio wave that activates the windshield-mounted RFID tag. The activated tag sends vehicle information to the RFID reader.

video camera

Step 3:
The RFID reader sends the vehicle information to the lane controller. The lane controller, which is part of a local area network, transmits the vehicle information to a central computer that subtracts the toll from the motorist's account. If the vehicle does not have an RFID tag, the video camera takes a picture of the license plate and the computer prints a violation notice, which is mailed to the motorist.

RFID reader

RFID tag

WAP

The **Wireless Application Protocol** (**WAP**) is a standard, specifically a protocol, that specifies how some wireless mobile devices such as smart phones and PDAs can display the content of Internet services such as the Web, e-mail, chat rooms, and newsgroups. For example, users can check weather, sports scores, and headline news from their WAP-enabled smart phone or PDA. To display a Web page on a smart phone, the phone should contain a microbrowser (Figure 9-22). WAP works in conjunction with the TCP/IP network standard.

WAP uses a client/server network. The wireless device contains the client software, which connects to the Internet service provider's server. On WAP-enabled devices, data transfer rates range from 9.6 to 153 Kbps depending on the type of service. Read Ethics & Issues 9-3 for a discussion related to wireless mobile devices.

FIGURE 9-22
A WAP-enabled smart phone.

COMMUNICATIONS SOFTWARE

Communications software consists of programs that (1) help users establish a connection to another computer or network; (2) manage the transmission of data, instructions, and information; and (3) provide an interface for users to communicate with one another. The first two are system software and the third is application software. Chapter 3 presented a variety of examples of application software for communications: e-mail, FTP, Web browser, newsgroup/message boards, chat rooms, instant messaging, video conferencing, and Internet telephony.

Sometimes, communications devices are preprogrammed to accomplish communications tasks. Other communications devices require separate communications software to ensure proper transmission of data. Communications software works with the network standards and protocols just discussed to ensure data moves through the network or the Internet correctly. Communications software usually is bundled with the operating system or purchased network devices.

Often, a computer has various types of communications software, each serving a different purpose. One type of communications software, for example, helps users establish an Internet connection using wizards, dialog boxes, and other on-screen messages. Another allows home and small office users to configure wired and wireless networks and connect devices to an existing network.

ETHICS & ISSUES 9-3

Should You Worry about Cellular Phone and Cellular Antenna Radiation?

Well over two billion people use cellular phones, and more than 80 percent of the world's population has access to cellular phone service from cellular antennas. These numbers are expected to rise sharply in coming years, and many are concerned about potential health effects from cellular phones and cellular antennas. Some cellular phone users who suffered rare illnesses have filed lawsuits against cellular phone companies, but the cases usually are lost due to lack of scientific evidence linking the use of the phones to the illnesses. While debates rage in communities over placement of cellular antennas, the consideration of health effects on residents is muted because the federal government's Telecommunications Act of 1996 prohibits local governments from considering health effects when making decisions about antenna placement. As cellular providers begin offering faster Internet services, they estimate that they may need to more than double the current number of antennas in the United States. It is generally agreed that no studies conclusively demonstrate negative health effects from cellular phones and cellular antennas, but skeptics claim that digital cellular technology is too new to have endured long-term studies on humans. Long-term studies that are underway may not provide results for decades. Are you concerned about cellular phone and cellular antenna radiation? Why or why not? Should more studies be done on potential health effects, and if so, who should pay for the studies? Why? Would you live next to a cellular antenna? Why or why not?

COMMUNICATIONS OVER THE TELEPHONE NETWORK

The *public switched telephone network* (*PSTN*) is the worldwide telephone system that handles voice-oriented telephone calls (Figure 9-23). Nearly the entire telephone network today uses digital technology, with the exception of the final link from the local telephone company to a home, which often is analog.

The telephone network is an integral part of computer communications. Data, instructions, and information are transmitted over the telephone network using dial-up lines or dedicated lines. The following sections discuss dial-up lines and the various types of dedicated lines that use the telephone network for data communications.

Dial-Up Lines

A **dial-up line** is a temporary connection that uses one or more analog telephone lines for communications. A dial-up connection is not permanent. Using a dial-up line to transmit data is similar to using the telephone to make a call. A modem at the sending end dials the telephone number of a modem at the receiving end. When the modem at the receiving end answers the call, a connection is established and data can be transmitted. When either modem hangs up, the communications end.

Using a dial-up line to connect computers costs no more than making a regular telephone call. Computers at any two locations establish an Internet or network connection using modems and the telephone network. Mobile users, for example, can use dial-up lines in hotels to connect to their main office network to read e-mail messages, access the Internet, and upload files.

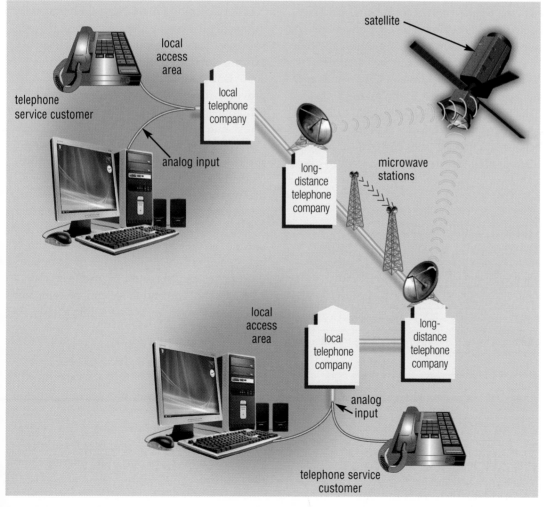

FIGURE 9-23 A sample telephone network configuration.

Dedicated Lines

A **dedicated line** is a type of always-on connection that is established between two communications devices (unlike a dial-up line where the connection is reestablished each time it is used). The quality and consistency of the connection on a dedicated line are better than a dial-up line because dedicated lines provide a constant connection.

Businesses often use dedicated lines to connect geographically distant offices. Dedicated lines can be either analog or digital. Digital lines increasingly are connecting home and business users to networks around the globe because they transmit data and information at faster rates than analog lines.

Five types of digital dedicated lines are ISDN lines, DSL, FTTH and FTTB, T-carrier lines, and ATM. Although cable television (CATV) lines and fixed wireless are not a type of standard telephone line, they are very popular ways for the home user to connect to the Internet. Fixed wireless Internet connections use an antenna on your house or business to communicate with a tower location via radio signals. Later sections in this chapter discuss the use of CATV lines and radio signals to connect to the Internet.

The table in Figure 9-24 lists the approximate monthly costs of various types of Internet connections and transfer rates (speeds), as compared with dial-up lines. The following sections discuss ISDN lines, DSL, FTTH and FTTB, T-carrier lines, and ATM.

ISDN Lines

For the small business and home user, an ISDN line provides faster transfer rates than dial-up telephone lines. Not as widely used today as in the past, *ISDN (Integrated Services Digital Network)* is a set of standards for digital transmission of data over standard copper telephone lines. With ISDN, the same telephone line that could carry only one computer signal now can carry three or more signals at once through the same line, using a technique called *multiplexing*.

ISDN requires that both ends of the connection have an ISDN modem. This type of modem is different from the type used in dial-up connections. The ISDN modem at your location must be within about 3.5 miles of the telephone company's ISDN modem. Thus, ISDN may not be an option for rural residents.

DSL

DSL is a popular digital line alternative for the small business or home user. **DSL** (*Digital Subscriber Line*) transmits at fast speeds on existing standard copper telephone wiring. Some DSL installations include a dial tone, providing users with both voice and data communications. Others share services with an existing telephone line.

To connect to DSL, a customer must have a special network card and a DSL modem. A DSL modem is different from the modem used for dial-up connections.

Not all areas offer DSL service because the local telephone company or the lines in the area may not be capable of supporting DSL technology. As with ISDN, DSL may not be an option for rural residents because the user's location (and DSL modem) and the telephone company's DSL modem must be located within about 3.5 miles of each other.

ADSL is one of the more popular types of DSLs. As shown in Figure 9-25, *ADSL (asymmetric digital subscriber line)* is a type of DSL that supports faster transfer rates when receiving data (the *downstream rate*) than when sending data (the *upstream rate*). ADSL is ideal for Internet access because most users download more information from the Internet than they upload.

SPEEDS OF VARIOUS INTERNET CONNECTIONS

Type of Line	Approximate Monthly Cost	Transfer Rates
Dial-up	Local or long-distance rates	Up to 56 Kbps
ISDN	$10 to $40	Up to 144 Kbps
DSL	$13 to $70	128 Kbps to 8.45 Mbps
Cable TV (CATV)	$20 to $50	128 Kbps to 36 Mbps
FTTH and FTTB	$35 to $180	5 Mbps to 30 Mbps
Fixed Wireless	$35 to $80	256 Kbps to 10 Mbps
Fractional T1	$200 to $700	128 Kbps to 768 Kbps
T1	$400 to $1,600	1.544 Mbps
T3	$5,000 to $15,000	44.736 Mbps
ATM	$3,000 or more	155 Mbps to 622 Mbps, can reach 10 Gbps

FIGURE 9-24   The speeds of various lines that can be used to connect to the Internet.

FIGURE 9-25 ADSL connections transmit data downstream (receiving) at a much faster rate than upstream (sending).

FTTH and FTTB

FTTH, which stands for **Fiber to the Home**, uses fiber-optic cable to provide extremely high-speed Internet access to home users. Similarly, *Fiber to the Building (FTTB)* refers to small businesses that use fiber-optic cables to access the Internet. With FTTH or FTTB service, an optical terminal at your house or business receives the signals and transfers them to a router connected to your computer. As the cost of installing fiber decreases, increasingly more homes and businesses will opt for this high-speed Internet access.

T-Carrier Lines

A **T-carrier line** is any of several types of long-distance digital telephone lines that carry multiple signals over a single communications line. Whereas a standard dial-up telephone line carries only one signal, digital T-carrier lines use multiplexing so that multiple signals share the line. T-carrier lines provide very fast data transfer rates. Only medium to large companies usually can afford the investment in T-carrier lines because these lines are so expensive.

The most popular T-carrier line is the *T1 line*. Businesses often use T1 lines to connect to the Internet. Many Internet access providers use T1 lines to connect to the Internet backbone. Home and small business users purchase *fractional T1*, in which they share a connection to the T1 line with other users. Fractional T1 is slower than a dedicated T1 line, but it also is less expensive. Users who do not have other high-speed Internet access in their areas can opt for fractional T1.

A *T3 line* is equal in speed to 28 T1 lines. T3 lines are quite expensive. Main users of T3 lines include large companies, telephone companies, and Internet access providers connecting to the Internet backbone. The Internet backbone itself also uses T3 lines.

ATM

ATM (*Asynchronous Transfer Mode*) is a service that carries voice, data, video, and multimedia at very high speeds. Telephone networks, the Internet, and other networks with large amounts of traffic use ATM. Some experts predict that ATM eventually will become the Internet standard for data transmission, replacing T3 lines.

Test your knowledge of pages 469 through 483 in Quiz Yourself 9-2.

WEB LINK 9-7

FTTH

For more information, visit scsite.com/dc2008/ch9/weblink and then click FTTH.

QUIZ YOURSELF 9-2

Instructions: Find the true statement below. Then, rewrite the remaining false statements so they are true.

1. A wireless LAN is a LAN that uses physical wires.

2. An intranet is an internal network that uses video conferencing technologies.

3. Five types of digital dial-up lines are ISDN lines, DSL, FTTH/FTTB, T-carrier lines, and ATM.

4. In a client/server network, servers on the network access resources on the client.

5. In a networked environment, any unauthorized computer user can access data and information stored on other computers on the network.

6. P2P describes an Internet network on which users access each other's hard disks and exchange files directly over the Internet.

Quiz Yourself Online: To further check your knowledge of networks, network communications standards, communications software, and communications over the telephone network, visit scsite.com/dc2008/ch9/quiz and then click Objectives 4 – 8.

COMMUNICATIONS DEVICES

A **communications device** is any type of hardware capable of transmitting data, instructions, and information between a sending device and a receiving device. At the sending end, a communications device sends the data, instructions, or information from the sending device to a communications channel. At the receiving end, a communications device receives the signals from the communications channel.

One type of communications device that connects a communications channel to a sending or receiving device such as a computer is a modem. Computers process data as digital signals. Data, instructions, and information travel along a communications channel in either analog or digital form, depending on the

communications channel. An *analog signal* consists of a continuous electrical wave. A *digital signal* consists of individual electrical pulses that represent bits grouped together into bytes.

For communications channels that use digital signals (such as cable television lines), the modem transfers the digital signals between the computer and the communications channel (Figure 9-26a). If a communications channel uses analog signals (such as some telephone lines), however, the modem first converts between analog and digital signals (Figure 9-26b).

The following pages describe these types of communications devices: dial-up modems, ISDN and DSL modems, cable modems, wireless modems, network cards, wireless access points, routers, and hubs.

FIGURE 9-26a   (all digital communications channel)

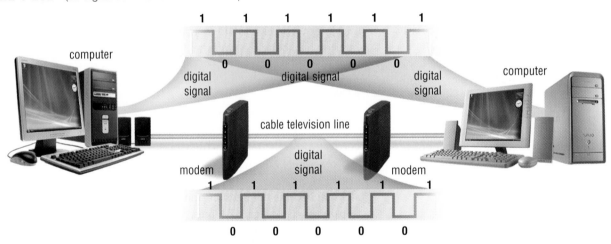

FIGURE 9-26b   (digital to analog to digital communications channel)

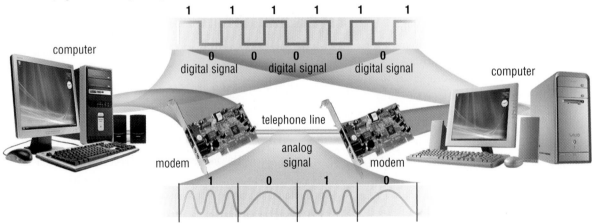

FIGURE 9-26   A modem connects a communications channel, such as a cable television line or a telephone line, to a sending or receiving device such as a computer. Depending on the type of communications channel, a modem may need to convert digital signals to analog signals (and vice versa) before transferring data, instructions, and information to or from a sending or receiving device.

Dial-Up Modems

As previously discussed, a computer's digital signals must be converted to analog signals before they are transmitted over standard telephone lines. The communications device that performs this conversion is a **modem**, sometimes called a *dial-up modem*. The word, modem, is derived from the combination of the words, *modulate*, to change into an analog signal, and *demodulate*, to convert an analog signal into a digital signal.

Both the sending and receiving ends of a standard telephone line (communications channel) must have a dial-up modem for data transmission to occur. For example, a dial-up modem connected to a sending computer converts the computer's digital signals into analog signals. The analog signals then can travel over a standard telephone line. At the receiving end, if necessary, another dial-up modem converts the analog signals back into digital signals that a receiving computer can process.

A dial-up modem usually is in the form of an adapter card that you insert in an expansion slot on a computer's motherboard. One end of a standard telephone cord attaches to a port on the modem card and the other end plugs into a telephone outlet. Devices other than computers also use modems. A stand-alone fax machine, for example, has a modem that converts a scanned digitized image into an analog signal that is sent to a recipient's fax machine.

ISDN and DSL Modems

If you access the Internet using ISDN or DSL, you need a communications device to send and receive the digital ISDN or DSL signals. A *digital modem* is a modem that sends and receives data and information to and from a digital telephone line such as ISDN or DSL. An *ISDN modem* sends digital data and information from a computer to an ISDN line and receives digital data and information from an ISDN line. A **DSL modem** sends digital data and information from a computer to a DSL line and receives digital data and information from a DSL line. ISDN and DSL modems usually are external devices, in which one end connects to the telephone line and the other end connects to a port on the system unit.

FAQ 9-3

Are digital modems really modems?

According to the definition of a modem (to convert from analog to digital signals and vice versa), the use of the term modem in this context is not correct. Although the original term for these devices was terminal adapter, the industry refers to ISDN, DSL, and cable modems as digital modems. For more information, visit scsite.com/dc2008/ch9/faq and then click Digital Modems.

Cable Modems

A **cable modem**, sometimes called a *broadband modem*, is a digital modem that sends and receives digital data over the cable television (CATV) network (Figure 9-27). With more than 100 million homes wired for cable television, cable modems provide a faster Internet access alternative to dial-up for the home user and have speeds similar to DSL. Cable modems currently can transmit data at speeds that are much faster than either a dial-up modem or ISDN (Figure 9-24 on page 482).

FIGURE 9-27   A cable modem.

As shown in Figure 9-28, CATV service enters your home through a single line. To access the Internet using the CATV service, the CATV company installs a splitter inside your house. From the splitter, one part of the cable runs to your televisions and the other part connects to the cable modem. Many CATV operators provide a cable modem as part of the installation; some offer a rental plan; and others require that you purchase one separately. A cable modem usually is an external (separate) device, in which one end of a cable connects to a CATV wall outlet and the other end plugs in a port, such as on an Ethernet card, in the system unit. An Ethernet card is a type of network card. A later section discusses network cards.

WEB LINK 9-8

Cable Modems

For more information, visit scsite.com/ dc2008/ch9/weblink and then click Cable Modems.

FAQ 9-4

Which is better, DSL or cable Internet service?

Each has its own advantages. DSL uses a line that is not shared with other users in the neighborhood. With cable Internet service, by contrast, users share the node with up to 500 other cable Internet users. Simultaneous access by many users can cause the cable Internet service to slow down. Cable Internet service, however, has widespread availability. For more information, visit scsite.com/dc2008/ ch9/faq and then click DSL and Cable Internet Service.

Wireless Modems

Some mobile users have a **wireless modem** that allows access to the Web wirelessly from a notebook computer, a PDA, a smart phone, or other mobile device (Figure 9-29). Wireless modems, which have an external or built-in antenna, typically use the same waves used by cellular telephones. These modems are available as PC Cards, ExpressCard modules, and flash cards.

antenna on wireless PC Card modem communicates with wireless Internet service provider

wireless PC Card modem inserted PC slot on notebook computer

FIGURE 9-29 Wireless modems, in the form of a PC Card, ExpressCard module, or flash card, allow users to access the Internet wirelessly using their mobile computers and devices.

Network Cards

A **network card**, sometimes called a *network interface card* (*NIC* pronounced nick), is an adapter card, PC Card, ExpressCard module, USB network adapter, or flash card that enables the computer or device that does not have built-in networking capability to access a network. The network card coordinates the transmission and receipt of data, instructions, and information to and from the computer or device containing the network card.

Network cards are available in a variety of styles (Figure 9-30). A network card for a desktop computer is an adapter card that has a port to which a cable connects. A network card for mobile computers and devices is in the form of a PC Card, ExpressCard module, USB network adapter, or a flash card. Many of these network cards have more than one type of port, which enable different types of cables to attach to the card. For example, some cable modems and DSL modems require that one end of a cable plug in

cable company

television

cable splitter

personal computer

cable modem

FIGURE 9-28 A typical cable modem installation.

the modem and the other end in a network card. (If your computer does not have a network card, these modems often allow connections to a USB port also.)

Network cards that provide wireless data transmission also are available. This type of card, called a *wireless network card*, often has an antenna. Sometimes the antenna is detachable, allowing the user to position it in a location with the best signal strength. Some network cards include support for both wired and wireless networks.

A network card follows the guidelines of a particular network communications standard, such as Ethernet or token ring. An Ethernet card is the most common type of network card. Depending on the type of wiring used, the transfer rate on an Ethernet network is 10 Mbps, 100 Mbps, or 1,000 Mbps (1 Gbps). Ethernet cards typically support one or more of these speeds. For example, some are called 10/100 because they support both 10 Mbps and 100 Mbps. Some network cards also are a combination Ethernet and dial-up modem card.

FAQ 9-5

What types of wireless connectivity are built into today's notebook computers?

Most new notebook computers now come with many integrated wireless features, including 802.11 (Wi-Fi), Bluetooth, IrDA, UWB, and WiMAX. Older notebook computers may not have any or all of these features but can be upgraded by using a PC Card, ExpressCard module, or USB network adapter. Check your computer's documentation to determine what wireless features are available, or how to upgrade your computer to obtain these features. For more information, visit scsite.com/dc2008/ch9/faq and then click Wireless Mobile Computers.

Wireless Access Points

A *wireless access point* is a central communications device that allows computers and devices to transfer data wirelessly among themselves or to transfer data wirelessly to a wired network (Figure 9-31). Wireless access points have high-quality antennas for optimal signals. For the best signal, some manufacturers suggest positioning the wireless access point at the highest possible location.

FIGURE 9-30 Network cards are available for both desktop and notebook computers.

FIGURE 9-31 Wireless access points around campus allow students to access the school network wirelessly from their classrooms, the library, dorms, and other campus locations. To access the network, the notebook computer or mobile device must have built-in wireless capability or a wireless network card.

Routers

A *router* is a communications device that connects multiple computers or other routers together and transmits data to its correct destination on the network. A router can be used on any size of network. On the largest scale, routers along the Internet backbone forward data packets to their destination using the fastest available path. For smaller business and home networks, a router allows multiple computers to share a single high-speed Internet connection such as through a cable modem or DSL modem (Figure 9-32). These routers connect from 2 to 250 computers.

To prevent unauthorized users from accessing files and computers, many routers are protected by a built-in firewall, called a *hardware firewall*. Some also have built-in antivirus protection. Routers also support wireless communications, eliminating the need for a separate wireless access point in a wireless network. If the network has a separate wireless access point, it connects to the router via a cable. Some routers also include additional functionality such as including a built-in print server.

Connecting Networks

Today, thousands of computer networks exist, ranging from small networks operated by home users to global networks operated by numerous telecommunications firms. Interconnecting these many types of networks requires various types of communications devices. For example, as shown in Figure 9-33, a hub is a device that provides a central point for cables in a network. Some hubs include routers. That is, the hub receives data from many directions and then forwards it to one or more destinations.

FAQ 9-6

What is the difference between a hub and a switch and a router?

Although hubs, switches, and routers all are used to connect networks, they differ in how they send and receive data among connected computers. When a computer connected to a hub sends and receives data, all other computers connected to the hub also can receive the data sent to and from the computer. When a computer connected to a switch sends and receives data, the switch only will transfer the data to and from that computer. A router is used to send data between two networks, and not directly between two computers. For more information, visit scsite.com/dc2008/ch9/faq and then click Hubs, Switches, and Routers.

WEB LINK 9-9

Hardware Firewalls

For more information, visit scsite.com/ dc2008/ch9/weblink and then click Hardware Firewalls.

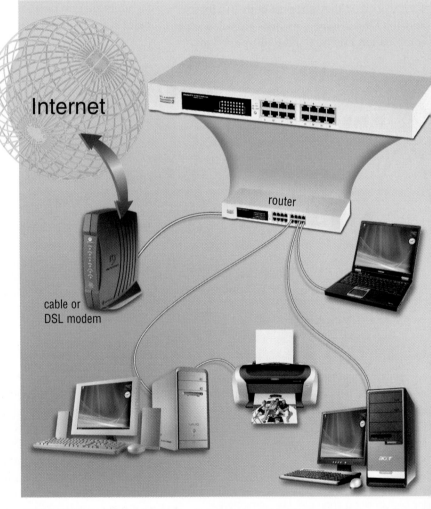

FIGURE 9-32   Through a router, home and small business networks can share access to a high-speed Internet connection such as through a cable or DSL modem.

- Play multiplayer games with players on other computers in the house
- Connect game consoles to the Internet
- Subscribe to and use Internet telephony

Many vendors offer home networking packages that include all the necessary hardware and software to network your home using wired or wireless techniques. Some of these packages also offer intelligent networking capabilities. An *intelligent home network* extends the basic home network to include features such as lighting control, thermostat adjustment, and a security system.

Wired Home Networks

As with other networks, a home network can use wires, be wireless, or use a combination of wired and wireless. Three types of wired home networks are Ethernet, powerline cable, and phoneline.

ETHERNET Some home users have an Ethernet network. As discussed earlier in this chapter, traditional Ethernet networks require that each computer have built-in network capabilities or contain a network card, which connects to a central network hub or similar device with a physical cable. This may involve running cable through walls, ceilings, and floors in the house. For the average home user, the hardware and software of an Ethernet network can be difficult to configure.

POWERLINE CABLE NETWORK A home *powerline cable network* is a network that uses the same lines that bring electricity into the house. This network requires no additional wiring. One end of a cable plugs in the computer's parallel or USB port and the other end of the cable plugs in a wall outlet. The data transmits through the existing power lines in the house.

PHONELINE NETWORK A *phoneline network* is an easy-to-install and inexpensive network that uses existing telephone lines in the home. With this network, one end of a cable connects to an adapter card or PC Card in the computer and the other end plugs in a wall telephone jack. The phoneline network does not interfere with voice and data transmissions on the telephone lines. That is, you can talk on the telephone and use the same line to connect to the Internet. One slight disadvantage is that the room with the computer must have a wall telephone jack.

hub or switch

hub or switch

FIGURE 9-33 A hub or switch is a central point that connects several devices in a network together.

HOME NETWORKS

Many home users are connecting multiple computers and devices together in a **home network**. Home networking saves the home user money and provides many conveniences. Each networked computer in the house has the following capabilities:

- Connect to the Internet at the same time
- Share a single high-speed Internet connection
- Access files and programs on the other computers in the house
- Share peripherals such as a printer, scanner, external hard disk, or DVD drive

WEB LINK 9-10

Home Networks
For more information, visit scsite.com/ dc2008/ch9/weblink and then click Home Networks.

Wireless Home Networks

To network computers and devices that span multiple rooms or floors in a home, it may be more convenient to use a wireless strategy. One advantage of wireless networks is that you can take a mobile computer outside, for example in the backyard, and connect to the Internet through the home network, as long as you are in the network's range. Two types of wireless home networks are HomeRF and Wi-Fi.

A *HomeRF (radio frequency) network* uses radio waves, instead of cables, to transmit data. A HomeRF network sends signals through the air over distances up to 150 feet. A HomeRF network usually can connect up to 10 computers.

Another home network that uses radio waves is a Wi-Fi network, which sends signals over a wider distance than the HomeRF network — up to 1,500 feet in some configurations. A Wi-Fi home network is more expensive than a HomeRF network. Despite the higher costs, increasingly more home users set up Wi-Fi networks in their homes because they are fairly easy to configure. Each computer that accesses the network needs built-in wireless networking capabilities (such as Intel's Centrino Duo technology) or a wireless network card, which communicates either with a wireless access point or a combination router/wireless access point (Figure 9-34). Even in a wireless home network,

FIGURE 9-34   HOW TO SET UP HARDWARE FOR A WI-FI HOME NETWORK

Step 1:
Sign up for high-speed Internet service, such as through a cable or DSL modem.

Step 2:
Using a cable, connect the network card in a desktop computer to the combination router/wireless access point.

Step 3:
Using a cable, connect the combination router/wireless access point to the cable modem.

Step 4:
Install a wireless network card or network adapter in other desktop computers in the home network.

Step 5:
Insert a wireless PC Card, ExpressCard module, or USB network adapter in each notebook computer that will access the home network or purchase a notebook computer with built-in wireless networking capabilities.

Step 6:
Insert a wireless compact flash card in each PDA that will access the home network or purchase a PDA with built-in wireless capabilities.

INTERNET

cable/DSL modem

wireless PDA

desktop computer

router/wireless access point

wireless desktop computer

wireless notebook computer

one desktop computer usually connects to the router/wireless access point using a cable.

Wireless networks do have the disadvantage of interference. Walls, ceilings, and electrical devices such as cordless telephones and microwave ovens can disrupt wireless communications.

COMMUNICATIONS CHANNEL

As described at the beginning of the chapter, a communications channel is the transmission media on which data, instructions, or information travel in a communications system. The amount of data, instructions, and information that can travel over a communications channel sometimes is called the **bandwidth**. The higher the bandwidth, the more the channel transmits. For example, a cable modem has more bandwidth than a dial-up modem.

For transmission of text only, a lower bandwidth is acceptable. For transmission of music, graphics, photographs, virtual reality images, or 3-D games, however, you need a higher bandwidth. When the bandwidth is too low for the application, you will notice a considerable slowdown in system performance.

Latency is the time it takes a signal to travel from one location to another on a network. Several factors that negatively can affect latency include the distance between the two points, the type of transmission media, and the number of nodes through which the data must travel over the communications channel. For best performance, bandwidth should be high and latency low.

A communications channel consists of one or more transmission media. **Transmission media** consist of materials or substances capable of carrying one or more signals. When you send data from a computer, the signal that carries the data may travel over various transmission media. This is especially true when the transmission spans a long distance.

Figure 9-35 illustrates a typical communications channel and shows the variety of transmission media used to complete the connection. Although many media and devices are involved, the entire communications process could take less than one second.

FIGURE 9-35 AN EXAMPLE OF SENDING A REQUEST OVER THE INTERNET USING A COMMUNICATIONS CHANNEL

Step 1:
The sending device requests information using either physical transmission media or wireless transmission media.

sending device

modem

microwave station

Step 2:
When the request leaves the ISP, it travels over T1 lines, and possibly microwave stations, earth-based stations, and communications satellites, until it reaches the Internet backbone.

mainframe

ISP

T1 lines

Step 3:
The request travels over T3 lines along the Internet backbone.

T3 lines

Internet backbone

Step 4:
The request travels over T1 lines until it reaches the destination network server.

destination network server

T1 lines

mainframe

Baseband media transmit only one signal at a time. By contrast, **broadband** media transmit multiple signals simultaneously. Broadband media transmit signals at a much faster speed than baseband media. In many cases, download transfer rates of broadband are faster than its upload transfer rates. Home and business users today opt for broadband Internet access because of the much faster transfer rates. Two previously discussed services that offer broadband transmission are DSL and the cable television Internet service. Satellites also offer broadband transmission. Read Looking Ahead 9-1 for a look at the future of communications systems.

Transmission media are one of two types: physical or wireless. *Physical transmission media* use wire, cable, and other tangible materials to send communications signals. *Wireless transmission media* send communications signals through the air or space using radio, microwave, and infrared signals. The following sections discuss these types of media.

PHYSICAL TRANSMISSION MEDIA

Physical transmission media used in communications include twisted-pair cable, coaxial cable, and fiber-optic cable. These cables typically are used within or underground between buildings. Ethernet and token ring LANs often use physical transmission media. The table in Figure 9-36 lists the transfer rates of LANs using various physical transmission media. The following sections discuss each of these types of cables.

TRANSFER RATES FOR VARIOUS TYPES OF LANS USING PHYSICAL TRANSMISSION MEDIA

Type of Cable and LAN	Maximum Transfer Rate
Twisted-Pair Cable	
• 10Base-T (Ethernet)	10 Mbps
• 100Base-T (Fast Ethernet)	100 Mbps
• 1000Base-T (Gigabit Ethernet)	1 Gbps
• Token ring	4 Mbps to 16 Mbps
Coaxial Cable	
• 10Base2 (ThinWire Ethernet)	10 Mbps
• 10Base5 (ThickWire Ethernet)	10 Mbps
Fiber-Optic Cable	
• 10Base-F (Ethernet)	10 Mbps
• 100Base-FX (Fast Ethernet)	100 Mbps
• FDDI (Fiber Distributed Data Interface) token ring	100 Mbps
• Gigabit Ethernet	1 Gbps
• 10-Gigabit Ethernet	10 Gbps

FIGURE 9-36 The speeds of various physical communications media when they are used in LANs.

FAQ 9-7

Do many home users have a broadband Internet connection?

As shown in the chart below, the number of home users with a broadband Internet connection has grown to more than 80 percent. For more information, visit scsite.com/dc2008/ch9/faq and then click Broadband Usage.

Broadband Growth Trend - US Home Users

Source: WebSiteOptimization.com

LOOKING AHEAD 9-1

Telepresence Expands Face-to-Face Communications

Being everywhere at once can become a reality with *telepresence* systems, which bring people together to interact and collaborate whether they are physically across the street or across the globe.

These two-way video communications systems use broadband connections to combine high-quality audio, ultra high-definition video, and interactive elements and bring them into a conference room or office. Life-size images on plasma television screens, spatial audio, and advanced cameras help create the dynamics of having voices that seem to come directly from the remote participants. Possible scenarios include job interviews, sales presentations and demonstrations, and staff meetings with personnel at remote offices.

Cisco Systems has developed telepresence systems that make possible meetings with four people at a virtual conference table, two of whom are physically at a remote site, and with twelve people, six of whom are remote participants. For more information, visit scsite.com/dc2008/ch9/looking and then click Telepresence.

Twisted-Pair Cable

One of the more widely used transmission media for network cabling and telephone systems is twisted-pair cable. **Twisted-pair cable** consists of one or more twisted-pair wires bundled together (Figure 9-37). Each *twisted-pair wire* consists of two separate insulated copper wires that are twisted together. The wires are twisted together to reduce noise. **Noise** is an electrical disturbance that can degrade communications.

Coaxial Cable

Coaxial cable, often referred to as *coax* (pronounced KO-ax), consists of a single copper wire surrounded by at least three layers: (1) an insulating material, (2) a woven or braided metal, and (3) a plastic outer coating (Figure 9-38).

Cable television (CATV) network wiring often uses coaxial cable because it can be cabled over longer distances than twisted-pair cable. Most of today's computer networks, however, do not use coaxial cable because other transmission media such as fiber-optic cable transmit signals at faster rates.

Fiber-Optic Cable

The core of a **fiber-optic cable** consists of dozens or hundreds of thin strands of glass or plastic that use light to transmit signals. Each strand, called an *optical fiber*, is as thin as a human hair. Inside the fiber-optic cable, an insulating glass cladding and a protective coating surround each optical fiber (Figure 9-39).

Fiber-optic cables have the following advantages over cables that use wire, such as twisted-pair and coaxial cables:

- Capability of carrying significantly more signals than wire cables
- Faster data transmission
- Less susceptible to noise (interference) from other devices such as a copy machine
- Better security for signals during transmission because they are less susceptible to noise
- Smaller size (much thinner and lighter weight)

Disadvantages of fiber-optic cable are it costs more than twisted-pair or coaxial cable and can be difficult to install and modify. Despite these limitations, many local and long-distance telephone companies are replacing existing telephone lines with fiber-optic cables, enabling them to offer fiber Internet access to home and business users. Businesses also are using fiber-optic cables in high-traffic networks or as the backbone in a network.

FIGURE 9-37 A twisted-pair cable consists of one or more twisted-pair wires. Each twisted-pair wire usually is color coded for identification. Telephone networks and LANs often use twisted-pair cable.

FIGURE 9-38 On a coaxial cable, data travels through a copper wire. This illustration shows computers networked together with coaxial cable.

FIGURE 9-39 A fiber-optic cable consists of hair-thin strands of glass or plastic that carry data as pulses of light.

WIRELESS TRANSMISSION MEDIA

Many users opt for wireless transmission media because it is more convenient than installing cables. In addition to convenience, businesses use wireless transmission media in locations where it is impossible to install cables. Read Ethics & Issues 9-4 for a related discussion.

Types of wireless transmission media used in communications include infrared, broadcast radio, cellular radio, microwaves, and communications satellites. The table in Figure 9-40 lists transfer rates of various wireless transmission media. The following sections discuss these types of wireless transmission media.

ETHICS & ISSUES 9-4

Is It Ethical to Steal Wireless Internet Service?

If you knew that your neighbor often left her door unlocked while she went to work, you probably never would consider walking in and watching her premium cable channels during the day without her permission. But, if you turn on your wireless notebook computer only to see that you can connect to a nearby business's wireless network and access the Internet for free, you may find yourself in an ethical quandary. Because of a lack of knowledge about how to secure wireless home networks, many people have accidentally left their networks open to use by anybody in the area or driving or walking past. One study found that 14 percent of wireless network owners have accessed their neighbor's wireless connection. In some cases, people drive around town until they find an area with an open wireless connection and then park in front of the house or business for hours at a time while surfing the Internet. Many are canceling their own costly service and secretly using the stolen connection full-time. In most areas, the law is unclear or nonexistent regarding such unauthorized use. Some lawmakers even support punishing those who leave their networks unsecured. Would you borrow your neighbor's wireless home network? Why or why not? What would you do if you found out that someone was using your wireless home network? How should the law handle such abuse, and how should violators be punished? Should those leaving their networks vulnerable be punished as well? Why?

TRANSFER RATES FOR VARIOUS TYPES OF WIRELESS TRANSMISSION MEDIA

Transmission Medium	Maximum Transfer Rate
Infrared	115 Kbps to 4 Mbps
Broadcast radio	
• Bluetooth	1 Mbps to 2 Mbps
• HomeRF	1.6 Mbps to 10 Mbps
• 802.11b	11 Mbps
• 802.11g	54 Mbps
• 802.11a	54 Mbps
• UWB	110 Mbps to 480 Mbps
Cellular radio	
• 2G	9.6 Kbps to 19.2 Kbps
• 3G	144 Kbps to 2.4 Mbps
Microwave radio	150 Mbps
Communications satellite	1 Gbps

FIGURE 9-40 The transfer rates of various wireless transmission media.

Infrared

As discussed earlier in the chapter, *infrared* (*IR*) is a wireless transmission medium that sends signals using infrared light waves. Mobile computers and devices, such as a mouse, printer, and smart phone, often have an IrDA port that enables the transfer of data from one device to another using infrared light waves. If your notebook computer has an IrDA port, simply position the port in front of the IrDA port on a printer to print a document wirelessly. Many PDAs also have IrDA ports that allow users to transfer data to another PDA or a network wirelessly.

Broadcast Radio

Broadcast radio is a wireless transmission medium that distributes radio signals through the air over long distances such as between cities, regions, and countries and short distances such as within an office or home.

For radio transmissions, you need a transmitter to send the broadcast radio signal and a receiver to accept it. To receive the broadcast radio signal, the receiver has an antenna that is located in the range of the signal. Some networks use a transceiver, which both sends and receives signals from wireless devices. Broadcast radio is slower and more susceptible to noise than physical transmission media but it provides flexibility and portability.

Bluetooth, UWB, HomeRF, Wi-Fi, and WiMAX communications technologies discussed earlier in this chapter use broadcast radio signals. Bluetooth and UWB are alternatives to infrared communications, with the latter designed for high bandwidth transmissions. HomeRF and Wi-Fi are competing technologies for home and small business networks, with Wi-Fi more predominantly used. Hot spots use Wi-Fi and WiMAX networks.

Cellular Radio

Cellular radio is a form of broadcast radio that is used widely for mobile communications, specifically wireless modems and cellular telephones (Figure 9-41). A cellular telephone is a telephone device that uses high-frequency radio waves to transmit voice and digital data messages. Because only a limited number of radio frequencies exist, cellular network providers reuse frequencies so they can accommodate the large number of users.

Some mobile users connect their notebook computer or other mobile computer to a cellular telephone to access the Web, send and receive e-mail, enter a chat room, or connect to an office or school network while away from a standard telephone line.

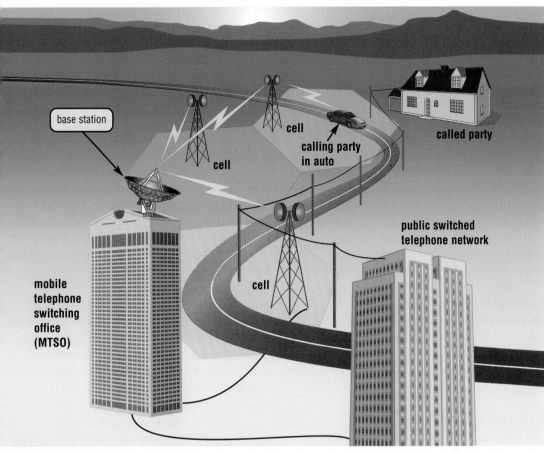

Several categories of cellular transmissions exist, defining the development of cellular networks:

- 1G (first generation) transmitted analog data
- 2G (second generation) transmit digital data at speeds from 9.6 Kbps to 19.2 Kbps
- 3G (third generation) transmit digital data at speeds from 144 Kbps to 2.4 Mbps

Examples of 3G standards include *GSM* (Global System for Mobile Communications), *UMTS* (Universal Mobile Telecommunications System), *GPRS* (General Packet Radio Service), *CDMA* (Code Division Multiple Access), *EDGE* (Enhanced Data GSM Environment), and *EVDO* (Evolution Data Optimized). These 3G standards allow users quickly to display multimedia and graphics, browse the Web, watch television or a video, have a video conference, and transfer data to a cellular device. Providers that offer 3G services include Sprint, Verizon, Cingular, Motorola, Ericsson, and Nokia.

Personal Communications Services (PCS) is the term used by the U.S. Federal Communications Commission (FCC) to identify all wireless digital communications. Devices that use PCS include

cellular telephones, PDAs, pagers, and fax machines. These devices have voice mail, call forwarding, fax capability, caller ID, and wireless modems for Internet and e-mail access.

Microwaves

Microwaves are radio waves that provide a high-speed signal transmission. Microwave transmission, often called *fixed wireless*, involves sending signals from one microwave station to another (Figure 9-42). Microwaves can transmit data at rates up to 4,500 times faster than a dial-up modem.

WEB LINK 9-11

Cellular Communications

For more information, visit scsite.com/dc2008/ch9/weblink and then click Cellular Communications.

microwave stations

FIGURE 9-42 A microwave station is a ground-based reflective dish that contains the antenna, transceivers, and other equipment necessary for microwave communications.

A *microwave station* is an earth-based reflective dish that contains the antenna, transceivers, and other equipment necessary for microwave communications. As with infrared, microwaves use line-of-sight transmission. To avoid possible obstructions, such as buildings or mountains, microwave stations often sit on the tops of buildings, towers, or mountains.

Microwave transmission typically is used in environments where installing physical transmission media is difficult or impossible and where line-of-sight transmission is available. For example, microwave transmission is used in wide-open areas such as deserts or lakes; between buildings in a close geographic area; or to communicate with a satellite. Current users of microwave transmission include universities, hospitals, city governments, cable television providers, and telephone companies. Homes and small businesses that do not have other high-speed Internet connections available in their area also opt for lower-cost fixed wireless plans.

Communications Satellite

A **communications satellite** is a space station that receives microwave signals from an earth-based station, amplifies (strengthens) the signals, and broadcasts the signals back over a wide area to any number of earth-based stations (Figure 9-43).

These earth-based stations often are microwave stations. Other devices, such as smart phones and GPS receivers, also can function as earth-based stations. Transmission from an earth-based station to a satellite is an *uplink*. Transmission from a satellite to an earth-based station is a *downlink*.

Applications such as air navigation, television and radio broadcasts, weather forecasting, video conferencing, paging, global positioning systems, and Internet connections use communications satellites. With the proper satellite dish and a satellite modem card, consumers can access the Internet using satellite technology. With satellite Internet connections, however, uplink transmissions usually are slower than downlink transmissions. This difference in speeds usually is acceptable to most Internet satellite users because they download much more data than they upload. Although a satellite Internet connection is more expensive than cable Internet or DSL connections, sometimes it is the only high-speed Internet option in remote areas. Read Looking Ahead 9-2 for a look at the future of satellite communications.

FIGURE 9-43 Communications satellites are placed about 22,300 miles above the Earth's equator.

LOOKING AHEAD 9-2

Fighting Fires, Staying Healthy with Satellites

Firefighters and healthcare providers are among the professionals who should improve their efficiency with some help from satellite communications.

The *REMSAT* (Real Time Emergency Management Via Satellite) system has proven an invaluable tool in combating and containing forest fires, and emergency personnel are hoping the system will be expanded to other disaster situations, such as earthquakes and floods. The REMSAT system is composed of a mobile communications unit equipped with a big blue box and satellite dish. The box is in constant communication with three satellites, and firefighters have handheld terminals that allow them to send and receive text messages detailing their locations and where help is needed.

The Telemedicine Working Group, which was organized by the European Space Agency, has identified two scenarios where high bandwidth communications linked via satellite to field laboratories could have a major impact: earthquakes and terrorist attacks. For more information, visit scsite.com/dc2008/ch9/looking and then click Satellites.

Test your knowledge of pages 484 through 496 in Quiz Yourself 9-3.

QUIZ YOURSELF 9-3

Instructions: Find the true statement below. Then, rewrite the remaining false statements so they are true.

1. A cable modem converts a computer's digital signals to analog signals before they are transmitted over standard telephone lines.

2. A hardware firewall is a communications device that allows computers and devices to transfer data wirelessly among themselves or to transfer data wirelessly to a wired network.

3. A network card is an adapter card, PC Card, ExpressCard module, USB network adapter, or flash card that enables the computer or device to access a network.

4. Analog signals consist of individual electrical pulses that represent bits grouped together into bytes.

5. Physical transmission media send communications signals through the air or space using radio, microwave, and infrared signals.

6. The lower the bandwidth, the more data, instructions, and information the channel transmits.

7. Two types of wireless home networks are HomeRF and powerline cable.

Quiz Yourself Online: To further check your knowledge of communications devices, home networks, and transmission media, visit scsite.com/dc2008/ch9/quiz and then click Objectives 9 – 11.

CHAPTER SUMMARY

This chapter provided an overview of communications terminology and applications. It also discussed how to join computers into a network, allowing them to communicate and share resources such as hardware, software, data, and information. It also explained various communications devices, media, and procedures as they relate to computers.

CAREER CORNER

Network Specialist

As more companies rely on networks, the demand for network specialists will continue to grow. A *network specialist* must have a working knowledge of local area networks and their application within wide area networks. A network specialist also must be familiar with the Internet, its connectivity to LANs and WANs, and Web server management. Responsibilities of a network specialist include installing, configuring, and troubleshooting network systems. Other responsibilities may include managing system and client software, Web page integration and creation, network security measures, user accounting, and monitoring network event logs for problem resolution. A network specialist must possess good problem-solving skills and the ability to work independently. They also must have the ability to concentrate on detailed projects for long periods of time. Good oral, written, and team-oriented interpersonal skills also are beneficial.

Many institutions offer two-year network specialist programs. In addition to a college degree, industry certifications are available for further career enhancement. Two of the more notable certifications are the Novell CNA (Certified Novell Administrator) and the Cisco CCNA (Certified Cisco Networking Associate). Network specialist salaries will vary depending on education, certifications, and experience. Individuals with certifications can expect an approximate starting salary between $50,000 and $70,000. For more information, visit scsite.com/dc2008/ch9/careers and then click Network Specialist.

High-Tech Talk

OSI REFERENCE MODEL: THE DRIVING FORCE BEHIND NETWORK COMMUNICATIONS

Every message sent over a network — even the simplest e-mail message — must be divided into discrete packages of data and routed via transmission media such as telephone lines. While traveling from the sending computer to the receiving computer, each data package can take a different path over the network. How do these messages get to their destination, intact and accurate?

The *Open Systems Interconnection (OSI) reference model*, a communications standard developed by the International Organization for Standardization (ISO), offers an answer. The OSI reference model describes the flow of data in a network through seven layers, from the user's application to the physical transmission media.

A simple way to understand the OSI reference model is to think of it as an elevator (Figure 9-44). On the sending end, data enters at the top floor (the application layer) and travels to the bottom floor (the physical layer). Each layer communicates with the layers immediately above and below it. When a layer receives data, it performs specific functions, adds control information to the data, and passes it to the next layer. The control information contains error-checking, routing, and other information needed to ensure proper transmission along the network.

The top layer, the *application layer*, serves as the interface between the user and the network. Using application software, such as an e-mail program, a user can type a message and specify a recipient. The application then prepares the message for delivery by converting the message data into bits and attaching a header identifying the sending and receiving computers.

The *presentation layer* translates the converted message data into a language the receiving computer can process (from ASCII to EBCDIC, for example) and also may compress or encrypt the data. Finally, the layer attaches another header specifying the language, compression, and encryption schemes.

The next layer, called the *session layer*, establishes and maintains communications sessions. A *session* is the period between establishment of a connection, transmission of the data, and termination of the connection.

The *transport layer*, also called the end-to-end layer, ensures that data arrives correctly and in proper sequence. The transport layer divides the data into segments and creates a *checksum*, a mathematical sum based on the data, and puts this information in the transport header. The checksum later is used to determine if the data was scrambled during transmission.

The *network layer* routes the message from sender to receiver. This layer splits the data segments from the transport layer into smaller groups of bits called *packets*. Next, it adds a header containing the packet sequence, the receiving computer address, and routing information. The network layer also manages network problems by rerouting packets to avoid network congestion.

The *data link layer* supervises the transmission of the message to the next network node by specifying the network technology (such as Ethernet or token ring) and grouping data accordingly. The data link layer also calculates the checksum and keeps a copy of each packet until it receives confirmation that the packet arrived undamaged at the next node.

Finally, the *physical layer* encodes the packets into a signal recognized by the medium that will carry them — such as an analog signal to be sent over a telephone line — and sends the packets along that medium to the receiving computer.

At the receiving computer, the process is reversed and the data moves back through the seven layers from the physical layer to the application layer, which identifies the recipient, converts the bits into readable data, removes some of the error-checking and control information from the data, and directs it to the appropriate application. A modified 5-layer model is used for data sent using the Transmission Control Protocol (TCP) and/or the Internet Protocol (IP). This model includes the physical, data link, network, transport, and application layers. The next time you send an e-mail message to a friend, consider the network communications processes described by the OSI reference model, which ensure that your message travels safely over many networks to your friend's computer. For more information, visit scsite.com/dc2008/ch9/tech and then click OSI Reference Model.

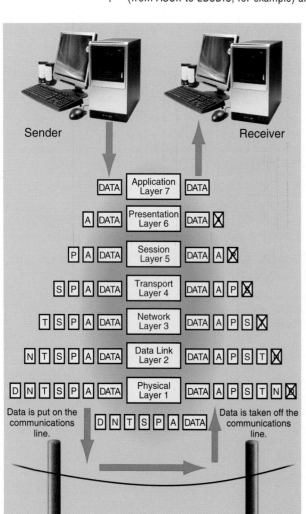

FIGURE 9-44 The seven layers of the OSI model.

Companies on the Cutting Edge

CISCO SYSTEMS
NETWORKING THE INTERNET

As the world leader in networking equipment, *Cisco Systems* strives to empower the Internet generation by connecting people and networks regardless of differences in locations, time, or types of computers. The company offers a broad line of networking equipment for transporting data within a building, across a campus, or across the globe.

A group of computer scientists from Stanford University founded Cisco in 1984. From the start, the company focused on communicating over networks. Today, Cisco's Internet Protocol-based (IP) networking equipment is the basis of the Internet and most networks.

Its key products focus on the areas of home and wireless networking, network security, and communications. The company's double-digit sales increases in 2006 were helped by its acquisition of Scientific-Atlanta, whose equipment allows cable providers to offer high-speed Internet service. For more information, visit scsite.com/dc2008/ch9/companies and then click Cisco.

QUALCOMM
WIRELESS COMMUNICATIONS LEADER

When you speak into your cellular telephone, your voice is converted into digital information that is transmitted as a radio signal with a unique code. This wireless communications process is based on Code Division Multiple Access (CDMA), which *QUALCOMM* engineers first conceptualized in 1988.

Commercial CDMA networks were unveiled in 1995, and they provided about 10 times the capacity of analog networks. Today, QUALCOMM is the world's largest provider of 3G technology and has shipped more than 1 million chips to the 125 telecommunications equipment manufacturers using the CDMA standard.

In 2006, QUALCOMM announced its OmniVision System, which allows transportation companies to better manage their fleet logistics and enhance driver productivity. For more information, visit scsite.com/dc2008/ch9/companies and then click QUALCOMM.

Technology Trailblazers

ROBERT METCALFE
ETHERNET INVENTOR

The Internet will be filled with video within 20 years, according to *Robert Metcalfe*. His prediction is likely to be correct based on his visionary track record. While studying for his doctorate degree at Harvard and working at Xerox's Palo Alto Research Center (PARC), he combined hardware with a high-speed network interface and envisioned that his invention would be used widely. This network technology developed into Ethernet, today's most popular LAN technology that links millions of computers worldwide.

In 1979, Metcalfe left Xerox to found 3Com Corporation and make Ethernet the standard for computer communications. After he retired from that company, he became a general partner in the venture capital firm, Polaris Ventures. He also is chairman of SiCortex, a Boston-based business that launched an innovative supercomputer design in 2006 emphasizing low power consumption and a compact size. For more information, visit scsite.com/dc2008/ch9/people and then click Robert Metcalfe.

PATRICIA RUSSO
LUCENT TECHNOLOGIES CHAIRMAN AND CEO

As captain of her high school cheerleading squad, *Patricia Russo* had to project a spirit of optimism, build teamwork, and solve problems. She uses these same skills in her current job as chairman and chief executive officer of Lucent Technologies, which designs and delivers communications hardware, software, and services to communications service providers worldwide.

Russo helped found Lucent in 1996 and oversaw various critical corporate functions, including global sales, strategy and business development, human resources, and public relations. She left Lucent to serve as CEO for Eastman Kodak, but nine months later Lucent asked her to return and appointed her CEO in 2002 and chairman the following year. Forbes.com listed Russo as the twenty-fifth most powerful woman in the world in its 2006 rankings. For more information, visit scsite.com/dc2008/ch9/people and then click Patricia Russo.

Chapter Review

The Chapter Review section summarizes the concepts presented in this chapter. To listen to the audio version of this Chapter Review, visit scsite.com/dc2008/ch9/review. To obtain help from other students regarding any subject in this chapter, visit scsite.com/dc2008/ch9/forum and post your thoughts or questions.

① What Components Are Required for Successful Communications? Computer **communications** describes a process in which two or more computers or devices transfer data, instructions, and information. Successful communications requires a **sending device** that initiates a transmission instruction, a communications device that connects the sending device to a communications channel, a **communications channel** on which the data travels, a communications device that connects the communications channel to a receiving device, and a **receiving device** that accepts the transmission.

② What Are Various Sending and Receiving Devices? All types of computers and mobile devices serve as sending and receiving devices. This includes mainframe computers, servers, desktop computers, notebook computers, Tablet PCs, smart phones, PDAs, and GPS receivers.

③ How Are Computer Communications Used? Communications technologies include the Internet, Web, e-mail, instant messaging, chat rooms, newsgroups, Internet telephony, FTP, Web folders, video conferencing, and fax machine or computer fax/modem. Users can send and receive wireless messages to and from smart phones, cellular telephones, or PDAs using **text messaging**, wireless instant messaging, **picture messaging** and **video messaging**. A **wireless Internet access point** lets people connect wirelessly to the Internet. A *hot spot* is a wireless network that provides Internet connections to mobile computers and devices. A *3G network* uses cellular radio technology to provide users with high-speed wireless Internet connections. A **cybercafé** is a coffeehouse, restaurant, or other location that provides computers with Internet access. A **global positioning system** (**GPS**) analyzes signals sent by satellites to determine an earth-based receiver's geographic location. Many software products provide a means to **collaborate**, or work online with other users. A *document management system* provides for storage and management of a company's documents, such as word processing documents, presentations, and spreadsheets. **Groupware** is software that helps people share information over a network. **Voice mail** allows someone to leave a voice message for one or more people.

Visit scsite.com/dc2008/ch9/quiz or click the Quiz Yourself button. Click Objectives 1 – 3.

④ What Are Advantages of Using a Network? A **network** is a collection of computers and devices connected together via communications devices and transmission media. Advantages of using a network include facilitating communications, sharing hardware, sharing data and information, sharing software, and transferring funds.

⑤ How Are Client/Server, Peer-to-Peer, and P2P Networks Different? On a **client/server network**, one or more computers acts as a **server**, which controls access to network resources and provides a centralized storage area, while the other computers on the network are **clients** that rely on the server for resources. A *peer-to-peer network* is a simple network that typically connects fewer than 10 computers, each called a *peer*, that have equal responsibilities and capabilities. *P2P* is an Internet peer-to-peer network on which users connect directly to each other's hard disks and exchange files over the Internet.

⑥ What Are Various Network Communications Standards? A *network standard* defines guidelines that specify the way computers access a medium, the type(s) of medium, the speeds on different types of networks, and the type of physical cable or wireless technology used. Network communications standards include Ethernet, token ring, TCP/IP, 802.11 (Wi-Fi), Bluetooth, UWB, IrDA, RFID, WiMAX, and WAP. **Ethernet** allows nodes to contend for access to the network. **Token ring** requires devices to share or pass a special signal, called a *token*. **TCP/IP** divides data into *packets*.

Chapter Review

802.11 is a series of standards for wireless devices. **Bluetooth** uses short-range radio waves to transmit data. **UWB**, which stands for **ultra-wideband**, specifies how two USB devices use short range radio waves to communicate at high speeds. **IrDA** transmits data wirelessly via infrared light waves. **RFID** uses radio signals for communications. **WiMAX** is a newer network standard developed by IEEE that specifies how wireless devices communicate over the air in a wide area. The **Wireless Application Protocol** (**WAP**) allows wireless mobile devices to access the Internet.

(7) What Is the Purpose of Communications Software? **Communications software** helps users establish a connection to another computer or network, manages the transmission of data, and provides an interface for users to communicate with one another.

(8) What Are Various Types of Lines for Communications Over the Telephone Network? The telephone network uses dial-up lines or dedicated lines. A **dial-up line** is a temporary connection that uses one or more analog telephone lines for communications. A **dedicated line** is an always-on connection established between two communications devices. Dedicated lines include ISDN lines, DSL, FTTH and FTTB, T-carrier lines, and ATM. *ISDN* is a set of standards for digital transmission over standard copper telephone lines. **DSL** transmits at fast speeds on existing standard copper telephone wiring. **FTTH**, or **Fiber to the Home**, uses fiber-optic cable to provide extremely high-speed Internet access to home users. *Fiber to the Building* (*FTTB*) refers to small businesses that use fiber-optic cables for Internet access. A **T-carrier line** is a long-distance digital telephone line that carries multiple signals over a single communications line. **ATM** (*Asynchronous Transfer Mode*) is a service that carries voice, data, video, and multimedia at extremely high speeds.

connect
Visit scsite.com/dc2008/ch9/quiz or click the Quiz Yourself button. Click Objectives 4 – 8.

(9) What Are Commonly Used Communications Devices? A **communications device** is hardware capable of transmitting data between a sending device and a receiving device. A **modem** converts a computer's digital signals to analog signals for transmission over standard telephone lines. An *ISDN modem* transmits digital data to and from an ISDN line, while a **DSL modem** transmits digital data to and from a DSL line. A **cable modem** is a digital modem that sends and receives digital data over the cable television network. A **wireless modem** allows wireless access to the Web. A **network card** is an adapter card, PC Card, ExpressCard module, USB network adapter, or flash card that enables a computer or device that does not have built-in networking capability to access a network. A *wireless access point* allows computers and devices to transfer data wirelessly. A *router* connects multiple computers together and transmits data to its destination on the network.

(10) How Can a Home Network Be Set Up? A **home network** connects multiple computers and devices in a home. An Ethernet network connects each computer to a hub with a physical cable. A home *powerline cable network* uses the same lines that bring electricity into the house. A *phoneline network* uses existing telephone lines in a home. A *HomeRF* (*radio frequency*) *network* and **Wi-Fi** network use radio waves, instead of cable, to transmit data.

(11) What Are Various Physical and Wireless Transmission Media? **Transmission media** consist of materials or substances capable of carrying one or more signals. *Physical transmission media* use tangible materials to send communications signals. **Twisted-pair cable** consists of one or more twisted-pair wires bundled together. **Coaxial cable** consists of a single copper wire surrounded by at least three layers: an insulating material, a woven or braided metal, and a plastic outer coating. **Fiber-optic cable** consists of thin strands of glass or plastic that use light to transmit signals. *Wireless transmission media* send communications signals through the air or space. *Infrared* (*IR*) sends signals using infrared light waves. **Broadcast radio** distributes radio signals through the air over long and short distances. **Cellular radio** is a form of broadcast radio that is used widely for mobile communications. **Microwaves** are radio waves that provide a high-speed signal transmission. A **communications satellite** is a space station that receives microwave signals from an earth-based station, amplifies the signals, and broadcasts the signals back over a wide area.

connect
Visit scsite.com/dc2008/ch9/quiz or click the Quiz Yourself button. Click Objectives 9 – 11.

Key Terms

You should know the Primary Terms and be familiar with the Secondary Terms. Use the list below to help focus your study. To further enhance your understanding of the Key Terms in this chapter, visit scsite.com/dc2008/ch9/terms. See an example of and a definition for each term, and access current and additional information about the term from the Web.

Primary Terms

(shown in bold-black characters in the chapter)

802.11 (478)
802.16 (479)
ATM (483)
bandwidth (491)
Bluetooth (478)
broadband (492)
broadcast radio (494)
cable modem (485)
cellular radio (494)
client/server network (472)
clients (472)
coaxial cable (493)
collaborate (467)
communications (460)
communications channel (460)
communications device (484)
communications satellite (496)
communications software (480)
cybercafé (465)
dedicated line (482)
dial-up line (481)
DSL (482)
DSL modem (485)
Ethernet (476)
fiber-optic cable (493)
FTTH (Fiber to the Home) (483)
global positioning system (GPS) (466)
groupware (467)
home network (489)
IrDA (478)
latency (491)

local area network (LAN) (471)
microwaves (495)
modem (485)
network (469)
network card (486)
network topology (474)
noise (493)
picture messaging (464)
receiving device (461)
RFID (479)
sending device (460)
server (472)
SMS (463)
text messaging (463)
T-carrier line (483)
TCP/IP (477)
token ring (476)
transmission media (491)
twisted-pair cable (493)
UWB (ultra-wideband) (478)
video messaging (464)
voice mail (468)
wide area network (WAN) (472)
WiMAX (479)
Wi-Fi (478)
Wireless Application Protocol (WAP) (480)
wireless Internet access point (464)
wireless LAN (WLAN) (471)
wireless modem (486)

Secondary Terms

(shown in italic characters in the chapter)

3G network (464)
10-Gigabit Ethernet (476)
1G (495)
2G (495)
3G (495)
ADSL (asymmetric digital subscriber line) (482)
analog signal (484)
Asynchronous Transfer Mode (483)
baseband (492)
broadband modem (485)
bus (474)
bus network (474)
camera phone (464)
CDMA (495)
coax (493)
collaborative software (467)
common short code (CSC) (463)
database server (473)
dedicated servers (473)
demodulate (485)
dial-up modem (485)
digital modem (485)
digital signal (484)
Digital Subscriber Line (482)
document management system (467)
downlink (496)
downstream rate (482)
EDGE (495)
EDI (electronic data interchange) (470)
electronic funds transfer (EFT) (470)
EVDO (495)
extranet (475)
Fast Ethernet (476)
Fiber to the Building (FTTB) (483)
file server (473)
file sharing network (473)
fixed wireless (495)
fractional T1 (483)
Gigabit Ethernet (476)
GPRS (495)
GPS receiver (466)
GSM (495)
hardware firewall (488)
HomeRF (radio frequency) network (490)
host computer (472)
hot spot (464)
hub (475)
infrared (IR) (494)
intelligent home network (489)
intranet (475)
ISDN (Integrated Services Digital Network) (482)
ISDN modem (485)
line-of-sight transmission (478)
metropolitan area network (MAN) (472)

microwave station (496)
MIMO (478)
MMS (multimedia message service) (464)
modulate (485)
multiplexing (482)
network architecture (472)
network interface card (NIC) (486)
network license (470)
network server (473)
network standard (476)
node (471)
online meeting (467)
optical fiber (493)
P2P (473)
packet switching (477)
packets (477)
peer (473)
peer-to-peer network (473)
Personal Communications Service (PCS) (495)
phoneline network (489)
physical transmission media (492)
picture phone (464)
powerline cable network (489)
print server (473)
protocol (476)
public switched telephone network (PSTN) (481)
radio frequency identification (479)
ring network (474)
router (488)
short message service (463)
site license (470)
star network (475)
switch (475)
T1 line (483)
T3 line (483)
token (476)
Transmission Control Protocol/ Internet Protocol (477)
twisted-pair wire (493)
UMTS (495)
uplink (496)
upstream rate (482)
value-added network (VAN) (470)
video phone (464)
voice mailbox (468)
Web services (468)
Wi-Fi mesh network (478)
wireless access point (487)
wireless Ethernet standard (478)
wireless fidelity (478)
wireless network card (487)
wireless transmission media (492)
workgroup computing (467)
XML (468)

Checkpoint

Use the Checkpoint exercises to check your knowledge level of the chapter. The Beyond the Book exercises will help broaden your understanding of the concepts presented in this chapter. To complete the Checkpoint exercises interactively, visit scsite.com/dc2008/ch9/check.

Label the Figure

Identify the elements in this sample communications system.

a. servers

b. GPS receivers

c. Internet-enabled PDAs

d. desktop computers

e. Tablet PCs

f. smart phones

g. mainframe computers

h. notebook computers

True/False

Mark T for True and F for False. (See page numbers in parentheses.)

_____ 1. A communications channel is the media on which data, instructions, or information travel. (460)

_____ 2 With video messaging, users can send short video clips, usually about 15 minutes, in addition to all picture messaging services. (464)

_____ 3. A phone with video messaging capability often is called a video phone. (464)

_____ 4. The first and most used application of GPS technology is to locate a lost person or stolen object. (466)

_____ 5. A network is a collection of computers and devices connected together via communications devices and transmission media. (469)

_____ 6. A local area network (LAN) is a network that covers a large geographic area using a communications channel that combines many types of media such as telephone lines, cables, and radio waves. (472)

_____ 7. An intranet is an internal network that uses Internet technologies. (475)

_____ 8. Bluetooth does not require line-of-sight transmission. (478)

_____ 9. Fiber to the Home (FTTH) refers to small businesses that use fiber-optic cables to access the Internet. (483)

_____ 10. Latency is the time it takes a signal to travel from one location to another on a network. (491)

_____ 11. Broadcast radio is media that sends signals using infrared light waves. (494)

Checkpoint

 Multiple Choice

Select the best answer. (See page numbers in parentheses.)

1. _____ is a four- or five-digit number assigned to a specific content or wireless service provider, followed by the message, such as a vote for a television program contestant or an entry for a sweepstakes. (463)
   a. Common short code
   b. SMS
   c. RFID
   d. None of the above

2. _____ includes tools that enable users to share documents via online meetings and communicate with other connected users. (467)
   a. A document management system
   b. Electronic data exchange
   c. Collaborative software
   d. A file sharing network

3. A document management system _____. (467)
   a. provides personal information manager functions
   b. provides for storage and management of a company's documents
   c. allows users to share documents with other users in real time
   d. prints to a Web address associated with a particular printer

4. Different applications can communicate with each other by sending XML files to the _____. (468)
   a. Internet telephony
   b. Web services
   c. instant messenger
   d. global positioning system

5. Many businesses network their computers together to _____. (469)
   a. facilitate communications
   b. share hardware, software, data, and information
   c. transfer funds
   d. all of the above

6. A _____ network is a third-party business that provides networking services such as secure data and information transfer, storage, e-mail, and management reports. (470)
   a. value-added
   b. client/server
   c. star
   d. file sharing

7. A(n) _____ is a legal agreement that allows multiple users to access the software on a server simultaneously. (470)
   a. site license
   b. EDI
   c. value-added network
   d. network license

8. _____ are devices that provide a common central connection point for nodes on the network. (475)
   a. Packets and tokens
   b. Routers and modems
   c. T1 and T3 lines
   d. Switches and hubs

9. Today, _____ is the most popular network standard for LANs because it is relatively inexpensive and easy to install and maintain. (476)
   a. token ring
   b. Ethernet
   c. TCP/IP
   d. Bluetooth

10. Communications software consists of programs that do all of the following except _____. (480)
    a. help users establish a connection to another computer or network
    b. manage the transmission of data, instructions, and information
    c. provide an interface for users to communicate with one another
    d. convert a computer's analog signals into digital signals for transmission

11. With ISDN, a telephone line can carry three or more signals at once using a technique called _____. (482)
    a. packet switching   b. file sharing
    c. multiplexing   d. collaborating

12. The most popular T-carrier line is the _____. (483)
    a. T3 line   b. ATM
    c. T1 line   d. DSL

13. A(n) _____ allows access to the Web wirelessly from a notebook computer, a PDA, a smart phone, or other mobile device. (486)
    a. wireless modem   b. ISDN modem
    c. network card   d. DSL modem

14. _____ consists of a single copper wire surrounded by at least three layers. (493)
    a. Fiber-optic cable
    b. Infrared
    c. Twisted-pair cable
    d. Coaxial cable

Checkpoint

Matching

Match the terms with their definitions. (See page numbers in parentheses.)

_____ 1. picture messaging (464)

_____ 2. camera phone (464)

_____ 3. groupware (467)

_____ 4. extranet (475)

_____ 5. network standard (476)

_____ 6. IrDA (478)

_____ 7. FTTH (483)

_____ 8. ATM (483)

_____ 9. bandwidth (491)

_____ 10. latency (491)

a. allows users to send pictures and sound files, as well as short text messages to a phone, PDA, or computer

b. specification to transmit data wirelessly among computers and devices via infrared light waves

c. service that carries voice, data, video, and multimedia at very high speeds

d. allows customers or suppliers to access part of a company's intranet

e. online area in which users have written discussions about a subject

f. amount of data, instructions, and information that can travel over a communications channel

g. guidelines that specify the way computers access a medium, type of medium, speed, and physical technology used

h. time it takes a signal to travel from one network location to another

i. software that helps groups of people share information over a network

j. type of media that transmits only one signal at a time

k. uses fiber-optic cable to provide extremely high-speed Internet access to home users

l. a phone with picture messaging capability

Short Answer

Write a brief answer to each of the following questions.

1. What is a wireless Internet access point? _____ What is a hot spot? _____

2. How are a local area network (LAN), a metropolitan area network (MAN), and a wide area network (WAN) different? _____ What is a wireless LAN? _____

3. What is a dedicated server? _____ What are some types of dedicated servers and what are their functions? _____

4. What is a network topology? _____ How are a bus network, a ring network, and a star network different? _____

5. What is UWB and what are its benefits? _____ What are some uses of UWB? _____

Beyond the Book

Read the following book elements, learn more about each using the Web, and then write a brief report.

1. Ethics & Issues — Should Cell Phones Be Banned in the Workplace? (462), High-Tech Cheating via Wireless Messaging Services (464), Should You Worry about Cellular Phone and Cellular Antenna Radiation? (480), and Is It Ethical to Steal Wireless Internet Service? (494)

2. Career Corner — Network Specialist (497)

3. Companies on the Cutting Edge — Cisco Systems or QUALCOMM (499)

4. FAQs (477, 478, 485, 486, 487, 488, 492)

5. High-Tech Talk — OSI Reference Model: The Driving Force Behind Network Communications (498)

6. Looking Ahead — Telepresence Expands Face-to-Face Communications (492) and Fighting Fires, Staying Healthy with Satellites (496)

7. Making Use of the Web — Learning (125)

8. Picture Yourself Communicating Wirelessly (458)

9. Technology Trailblazers — Robert Metcalfe or Patricia Russo (499)

10. Web Links (464, 466, 471, 474, 476, 479, 483, 486, 488, 489, 495)

Learn It Online

Use the Learn It Online exercises to reinforce your understanding of the chapter concepts. To access the Learn It Online exercises, visit scsite.com/dc2008/ch9/learn.

(1) At the Movies — A First Look at Yahoo! Messenger with Voice 8

To view the A First Look at Yahoo! Messenger with Voice 8 movie, click the number 1 button. Locate your video and click the corresponding High-Speed or Dial-Up link, depending on your Internet connection. Watch the movie and then complete the exercise by answering the question that follows. Yahoo! Messenger with Voice 8 offers paid outbound and inbound telephone calls, free voice and video chat, avatars, creative third-party plug-ins, and the ability to chat with Windows Live users. What does Yahoo! Messenger's plug-ins offer to users?

(2) Video and Audio: You Review It — Wi-Fi

In this chapter, you learned about Wi-Fi. Click the number 2 button to view the suggested links and begin your search for videos, podcasts, or vodcasts related to Wi-Fi. Choose a video, podcast, or vodcast that discusses Wi-Fi and is of interest to you, and then write a description of its contents. Explain why you chose this piece, what you liked about it, what you disliked about it, and whether you would recommend it to a fellow student. Finish your review by giving the video, podcast, or vodcast a rating of 1 – 5 stars. Submit your review in the format requested by your instructor.

(3) Student Edition Labs — Networking Basics

Click the number 3 button. A new browser window will open, displaying the Student Edition Labs. Follow the on-screen instructions to complete the Networking Basics Lab. When finished, click the Exit button. If required, submit your results to your instructor.

(4) Student Edition Labs — Wireless Networking

Click the number 4 button. A new browser window will open, displaying the Student Edition Labs. Follow the on-screen instructions to complete the Wireless Networking Lab. When finished, click the Exit button. If required, submit your results to your instructor.

(5) Practice Test

Click the number 5 button. Answer each question. When completed, enter your name and click the Grade Test button to submit the quiz for grading. Make a note of any missed questions. If required, submit your results to your instructor.

(6) Who Wants To Be a Computer Genius²?

Click the number 6 button to find out if you are a computer genius. Directions about how to play the game will be displayed. When you are ready to play, click the Play button. Submit your score to your instructor.

(7) Wheel of Terms

Click the number 7 button to reinforce important terms you learned in this chapter by playing the Shelly Cashman Series version of this popular game. Directions about how to play the game will be displayed. When you are ready to play, click the Play button. Submit your score to your instructor.

Learn It Online

(8) DC Track and Field

Click the number 8 button to use what you have learned in this chapter to compete against other students in three track and field events. Directions about how to play the game will be displayed. When you are ready to play, click the start first event button. If required, submit your score to your instructor.

(9) You're Hired!

Click the number 9 button to use what you have learned in this chapter to embark on the path to a career in computers. Directions about how to play the game will be displayed. When you are ready to play, click the begin game button. If required, submit your score to your instructor.

(10) Crossword Puzzle Challenge

Click the number 10 button, and then click the Crossword Puzzle Challenge link. Directions about how to play the game will be displayed. Complete the puzzle to reinforce skills you learned in this chapter. When you are ready to play, click the Continue button. Submit the completed puzzle to your instructor.

(11) Vista Exercises

Click the number 11 button. When the Vista Exercises menu appears, click the exercise assigned by your instructor. A new browser window will open. Follow the on-screen instructions to complete the exercise. When finished, click the Exit button. If required, submit your results to your instructor.

(12) In the News

Theoretically, business travelers can access e-mail, fax documents, and transmit data from anywhere in the world. In practice, however, incompatible telephone standards and mismatched telephone jacks can frustrate even experienced globetrotters. The 3Com Megahertz LAN PC Card addresses this problem. The modem and accompanying software allow travelers to use computer communications with more than 250 telephone systems worldwide simply by

selecting the appropriate country from a menu and attaching a suitable adapter plug. Click the number 12 button and read a news article about a product that is changing computer communications. What is the product? What does it do? Who is likely to use this product?

(13) Chapter Discussion Forum

Select an objective from this chapter on page 459 about which you would like more information. Click the number 13 button and post a short message listing a meaningful message title accompanied by one or more questions concerning the selected objective. In two days, return to the threaded discussion by clicking the number 13 button. Submit to your instructor your original message and at least one response to your message.

(14) Online Radio

Click the number 14 button to learn how to use the Internet to find and listen to various radio stations. Follow the instructions to use Windows Media Player to find and listen to a radio station of your choice. Once you have selected a genre, use the Zip Code search text box to display a list of Internet radio stations within your area. Listen to at least three different radio stations. Write a report comparing the quality of sound of each station. Include in your report any difficulties you may have encountered as well as any features you found interesting. Print your report, and submit it to your instructor.

Learn How To

Use the Learn How To activities to learn fundamental skills when using a computer and accompanying technology. Complete the exercises and submit them to your instructor. To see a video of a Learn How To activity, visit scsite.com/dc2008/ch9/howto.

LEARN HOW TO 1: Set Up and Install a Wi-Fi Home Network

In this chapter you learned about home networks and their advantages (see page 489, Home Networks). Creating a Wi-Fi home network consists of four phases: 1) subscribe to a high-speed Internet connection; 2) purchase the Wi-Fi equipment; 3) connect the physical devices; and 4) create the network through the use of software.

SUBSCRIBE TO A HIGH-SPEED INTERNET CONNECTION   A high-speed Internet connection is advisable to connect all computers on the home network to the Internet. The three primary ways for home users to obtain a fast connection to the Internet are DSL, cable, and satellite. DSL is provided by telephone companies, cable is provided by cable TV companies, and satellite connections are provided by satellite TV providers. Each has its advantages and disadvantages, including the minimum and maximum speed of Internet access, cost, and availability.

Determining the optimal high-speed Internet connection depends largely on where the network will be located, local costs, and service availability. The way to obtain the best high-speed Internet connection is to research the options available in your area.

Exercise

1. Assume you live near Coeur d'Alene, Idaho. You have decided that high-speed Internet access and a Wi-Fi network would be advantageous for your at-home business. Find answers to the following questions for this Idaho town or a town specified by your instructor: What methods of high-speed Internet access are available? Which provides the best service? Which is the cheapest? Based on the information you gather, write a plan for subscribing to a high-speed Internet connection service. Submit the answers to the questions and your plan to your instructor.

PURCHASE THE WI-FI EQUIPMENT   As part of the service when you subscribe to fast access on the Internet, you receive a modem that is capable of connecting to the Internet. In most cases, the modem is not a wireless transmitter. So, in order to establish a wireless connection between the Internet and the home network, you will need a wireless router that establishes the wireless access point.

You can visit any retail electronics store and find a wide variety of wireless routers. A key to purchasing the correct router is to ensure it will work with your modem and Internet access service. Some Internet service providers support only certain brands of routers and, while it is true that other routers may work, you might be taking a risk if you purchase an unsupported router. With the popularity of wireless home networks, though, some Internet service providers now provide a wireless router as part of the subscription service, often for an additional fee. You should investigate closely the needs for the Wi-Fi router to ensure compatibility with your Internet access service.

In addition to the router, each computer that is to be part of the Wi-Fi network needs a wireless network adapter. This device allows the computers to communicate with one another. Most external wireless network adapters plug in either a PC Card slot, ExpressCard slot, or a USB connection. Many notebook computers have a built-in wireless network adapter.

Finally, some home networks have a combination of wired and wireless devices. In these networks, the modem connects to the wireless router, and computers on the network connect to the wireless router using either a wireless or wired connection.

Once the Wi-Fi equipment is assembled, you are ready to connect your home network.

Learn How To

Exercise

1. Using your Web research skills, determine the type of IEEE 802.11 standard used by modems available from Internet service providers. What percentage use 802.11b? What percentage use 802.11g? If your modem uses 802.11b but your wireless network router is 802.11g, what happens? Based on your research, which router do you recommend? Submit your answers to your instructor.

CONNECT THE PHYSICAL DEVICES　Once you have assembled your equipment, you can connect the devices in the network. Usually, the modem will be connected to the source of the Internet transmission (DSL, cable, or satellite). Then the modem is connected to the wireless router, which in turn is connected to the computers on your network.

After these connections are completed, each of the computers that will be used in the network that do not have a built-in wireless network adapter must have the adapter attached, often by using a USB connection. Once these connections are made, the network can be created.

CREATE THE NETWORK　To establish a network, operating system software must be configured based on the design of your network. To begin the process on a Windows Vista computer, you should run the Set up a wireless router or access point Wizard by completing the following steps:

1. Click the Start button on the Windows taskbar and then click Control Panel on the Start menu.
2. In Classic View, double-click Network and Sharing Center to open the Network and Sharing Center window, and then click the Set up a connection or network link below the Tasks heading to display the Set up a connection or network dialog box.
3. Click Set up a wireless router or access point, and then click the Next button.
4. Click the Next button to start the wizard. If the User Account Control dialog box appears, click the Continue button. After Windows detects your network hardware and settings, click Create wireless network settings and save to USB drive.
5. In the Network name (SSID) text box (Figure 9-45), type a name for the wireless network you are creating. Use a name that you will recognize as the name for the network, and then click the Next button.
6. In the Passphrase text box (Figure 9-46), type a passphrase you would like others to provide, who wish to connect to your wireless network. Use a passphrase that is easy for you to remember, but hard for others to guess. Click the Next button. If the User Account Control dialog box appears, click the Continue button.
7. If necessary, click Allow sharing with anyone with a user account and password for this computer, and then click the Next button.
8. If you have not already done so, insert your USB flash drive in a USB port and wait for your computer to recognize the drive.
9. Follow the remaining instructions in the wizard to finish creating the network configuration.
10. The network has been created. Your USB flash drive now can be used to configure additional computers you wish to add to your wireless network.

FIGURE 9-45

FIGURE 9-46

Exercise

1. Form a three-person team whose responsibility is to create a Wi-Fi network for a small business in your local area. Assign tasks to each member of the team. Write a detailed plan for creating the Wi-Fi network, including the brand and type of equipment to be purchased, costs, and a schedule for completing the work. Explain why your team made each choice, and be prepared to defend your choices. Submit the plan to your instructor.

Web Research

Use the Internet-based Web Research exercises to broaden your understanding of the concepts presented in this chapter. Visit scsite.com/dc2008/ch9/research to obtain more information pertaining to each exercise. To discuss any of the Web Research exercises in this chapter with other students, post your thoughts or questions at scsite.com/dc2008/ch9/forum.

① **Scavenger Hunt**   Use one of the <u>search engines</u> listed in Figure 2-10 in Chapter 2 on page 78 or your own favorite search engine to find the answers to the questions that follow. Copy and paste the Web address from the Web page where you found the answer. Some questions may have more than one answer. If required, submit your answers to your instructor. (1) How is Boeing using RFID in its aircraft? (2) What is geocaching? (3) Who were the co-inventors of global positioning systems technology? For what initial use were GPS devices developed? (4) Who invented the concept and name of cybercafé? What is the location of the first American cybercafé? (5) What is the purpose of the Bluetooth Special Interest Group? Where is the headquarters of this organization?

② **Search Sleuth**   <u>Subject directories</u> are used to find specialized topics, such as information about automobiles, travel, and real estate. Most subject directories are arranged by topic and then displayed in a series of menus. Yahoo! is one of the more popular directories. Visit this Web site (yahoo.com) and then use your word processing program to answer the following questions. Then, if required, submit your answers to your instructor. (1) Click the Tech link in the Yahoo! Services area at the top of the page. Click the PDAs link. What are the top three products listed? Click the Compare Products button to view the prices of these products and to read reviews by Yahoo! users. (2) Click your browser's Back button or press the BACKSPACE key to return to the Yahoo! Tech page. Click the Search Yahoo! Tech text box and type "digital camera" and "9 megapixels" in the box. Sort the cameras by lowest price by clicking the Lowest Price link near the top of the page. Which camera is the least expensive? (3) Scroll down to the bottom of the page and then click one of the links in the Wi-Fi & Networking Product Categories area. Read one of the How-To articles, and then write a 50-word summary of your findings.

③ **Journaling**   Respond to your readings in this chapter by writing at least one page about your reactions, evaluations, and reflections on computer communications. For example, have you visited a <u>cybercafé</u> or a business with a hot spot where you can connect to the Internet using your notebook computer? Is your car equipped with a global positioning system? Does your pet have an RFID tag? You also can write about the new terms you learned by reading this chapter. If required, submit your journal to your instructor.

④ **Expanding Your Understanding**   More than a million drivers are finding their commutes more enjoyable with the advent of <u>satellite radio</u>. The two major providers, XM Radio and Sirius, offer hundreds of channels of specific music, talk shows, news, and sports programming. Traditional broadcasters have complained to the Federal Communication Commission, stating that the satellite companies have violated their original licenses because they have expanded their channels to include local weather and traffic advisories and plan to introduce video channels to air on back seat video screens. View Web sites to learn more about satellite radio's popularity. What is the monthly subscription fee for both services? What programming is available in your area? Write a report summarizing your findings, focusing on the broadcasters' objections. If required, submit your report to your instructor.

⑤ **Ethics in Action**   Products such as cell phones with global positioning system tracking capabilities certainly can be beneficial. The tracking information, however, could be used in detrimental ways if your electronic device always is turned on, according to privacy experts. If, for example, you regularly eat at fast-food establishments, your health insurance company could obtain the data regarding your whereabouts and then increase your premiums. Your automobile insurance company could drop your coverage if it learns you drive farther to work than you stated on your application. View online sites that provide arguments about trading <u>privacy</u> for information. Write a report summarizing your findings, and include a table of links to Web sites that provide additional details. If required, submit your report to your instructor.

Case Studies

Use the Case Studies to apply the concepts presented in the chapter to real-world situations. Visit scsite.com/dc2008/ch9/cases to obtain more information pertaining to each exercise. To discuss the Case Studies in this chapter with other students, visit scsite.com/dc2008/ch9/forum and post your thoughts or questions.

CASE STUDY 1 — Class Discussion   Your aunt owns a major development firm in the southeast. The company specializes in designing and constructing retirement communities throughout the United States. One of her biggest expenses is the cost of her project management team traveling to meetings with on-site personnel. She recently learned about the collaboration features of Microsoft Office. She is aware that you are studying about computers and has asked you to examine <u>online collaboration</u> as an alternative to some or all of the face-to-face meetings with on-site personnel. What are the advantages and disadvantages of collaborating online? What is a whiteboard? How are online meetings set up? What is NetMeeting? Does collaboration require additional hardware? Write a brief report and be prepared to discuss your findings in class.

CASE STUDY 2 — Class Discussion   You work as an intern in the Information Technology department for the *Star Journal*, a local newspaper. The newspaper's board of directors recently approved a budget for redesigning the interior of its century-old building as part of an inner-city rehabilitation project. Your manager has been asked to recommend the type of <u>transmission media</u> (hardwire or wireless) to use for the newspaper's local area network. He has asked you to submit a feature/benefit report that summarizes the advantages of wired versus wireless transmission media for the building. Which transmission media would have a greater startup cost? Which transmission media do you think is the most secure? Do the walls in the building present a problem for a wireless network? Does a wireless network present any health hazards? Be prepared to discuss your findings in class.

CASE STUDY 3 — Research   You are employed as a communications advisor at Telemark, a telemarketing firm with over 1,500 telemarketers. The president of the company recently attended the annual Internet Telephony Conference & Expo and came away with the idea that the company can save hundreds of thousands of dollars annually on local, long distance, and international calls by using <u>Internet Telephony,</u> rather than the conventional public switched telephone network (PSTN). She has asked you to look into the feasibility of making the switch. Use the Web and/or print media to research the advantages and disadvantages of Internet telephony. How does Internet telephony work? What type of hardware and software must the company purchase to make calls over the Internet? Submit your report or use PowerPoint to create a presentation and share your findings with your class.

CASE STUDY 4 — Research   You are the manager of a popular coffeehouse. The CEO recently decided to offer free wireless Internet access, or <u>free WLAN</u> to customers. He wants you to determine what is required to set it up and get it in service. During the course of your research, you discover that some providers look upon this service as stealing, because their intent is to have one user per Internet connection. The CEO suggests that he merely is sharing the signal, not selling it for profit. Use the Web and/or print media to answer the following questions: What actions are broadband providers taking to eliminate free WLAN? What are some of the drawbacks of widespread distribution of free WLAN? Do you know of any free WLAN operators in your area? Write a brief report or use PowerPoint to create a presentation and share your findings with your class.

CASE STUDY 5 — Team Challenge   Your school offers free student-intern assistance to the county government. The county in turn assigns a manager to each team of students, who is responsible for defining the project assigned to the student team and ensuring that dates are met. Your team has been assigned to the manager of communications in the information technology department. Next year, he plans to select an <u>ISP — DSL, cable, or wireless</u> — to handle all Internet communications in the county buildings. Form a three-member team and have each team member choose a different type of ISP. Using the Web and/or print media, have each team member determine the advantages and disadvantages of their chosen ISP. Include such features as start-up costs, e-mail disk storage, speed, online protection, and recurring costs. As a team, merge your findings into a team report and/or PowerPoint presentation and share your recommendations with your class.

Database Management

Picture Yourself Using Databases

Bright and early Saturday morning, you spring out of bed. You are officially on vacation! Booked on a cruise that leaves on Tuesday, today you plan to finish your last minute errands. These tasks are on your to-do list: help Aunt Lyn shop for a new car, buy a shower gift and a birthday gift, and buy cat food so the neighbor can feed your cat while you are gone.

First, you visit an online car dealership. After finding a few likely prospects, you print the information for Aunt Lyn. Still online, you visit the cruise line's Web site and review the excursions and activities available during your cruise. Deciding that snorkeling and an island tour would be fun, you reserve a spot for each excursion while online. Now, it is time to shop.

At the department store, you access and print your friend's bridal registry. After selecting a gift, you make sure the cashier updates the registry so that your friend will not receive a duplicate gift. Next stop, the grocery store. Conveniently, your grocer is a ticket agent for events at local venues. You purchase concert tickets for your sister's birthday, then proceed to the store's food section. Using an in-store price scanner, you check the price for the cat food and find that it is on sale. After paying at the self-service POS terminal, you stop at an ATM to withdraw cash for your trip. Errands complete, you are ready for your cruise!

All the above tasks involved the use of databases: car dealership database, cruise line database, gift registry database, concert ticket database, and store databases. Read Chapter 10 to learn about databases and the many features and functions of databases and database software.

After completing this chapter, you will be able to:

1. Define the term, database

2. Identify the qualities of valuable information

3. Explain why data is important to an organization

4. Discuss the terms character, field, record, and file

5. Identify file maintenance techniques

6. Differentiate between a file processing system approach and the database approach

7. Discuss the functions common to most DBMSs

8. Describe characteristics of relational, object-oriented, and multidimensional databases

9. Explain how to interact with Web databases

10. Discuss the responsibilities of database analysts and administrators

CONTENTS

DATABASES, DATA, AND INFORMATION

As presented in Chapter 3, a **database** is a collection of data organized in a manner that allows access, retrieval, and use of that data. *Data* is a collection of unprocessed items, which can include text, numbers, images, audio, and video. For example, you can type text on a keyboard, talk into a computer's microphone, transfer photographs taken with a digital camera to a computer, and capture motion and sounds with a video camera and store the recordings on a computer.

Information is processed data; that is, it is organized, meaningful, and useful. In addition

to documents, information can be in the form of audio, images, and video. For example, voice communications can be sent in an e-mail message for a family member, friend, or coworker to hear. You can post photographs taken with a digital camera on a Web page for others to view. With a PC video camera, others can see you in real time during a conference call.

Computers process data in a database into information. A database at a members-only discount warehouse, for example, contains data about its club members, e.g., member data, purchases data, etc. When someone wishes to become a warehouse club member, a membership services associate enters several data items into a computer. The associate also

FIGURE 10-1   HOW A MEMBERS-ONLY DISCOUNT WAREHOUSE MIGHT PROCESS DATA INTO INFORMATION

Step 1:
A membership services associate uses a digital camera to take a photograph of the new member and uses a keyboard to enter other member data into the computer.

uses a digital camera to photograph the new member. This picture, along with the other entered data, is stored in a database on a server's hard disk. A computer at the discount warehouse then processes the new member data and sends receipt information to a laser printer and member ID card information to an ID card printer (Figure 10-1).

With **database software**, often called a **database management system** (**DBMS**), users create a computerized database; add, change, and delete data in the database; sort and retrieve data from the database; and create forms and reports from the data in the database. A discount warehouse might use Microsoft Office Access 2007 as its database software. Database software includes many powerful features, as you will discover later in this chapter.

Most companies realize that data is one of their more valuable assets — because data is used to generate information. Many business transactions take less time when employees have instant access to information. For example, if membership services associates at a discount warehouse have instant access to member records, they can determine when a membership is due for renewal upon member request. When employees are more productive, customers (members, in this case) usually are more satisfied. When customers are happy, typically they become loyal to that business. Loyal customers can lead to referrals and an increase in profits.

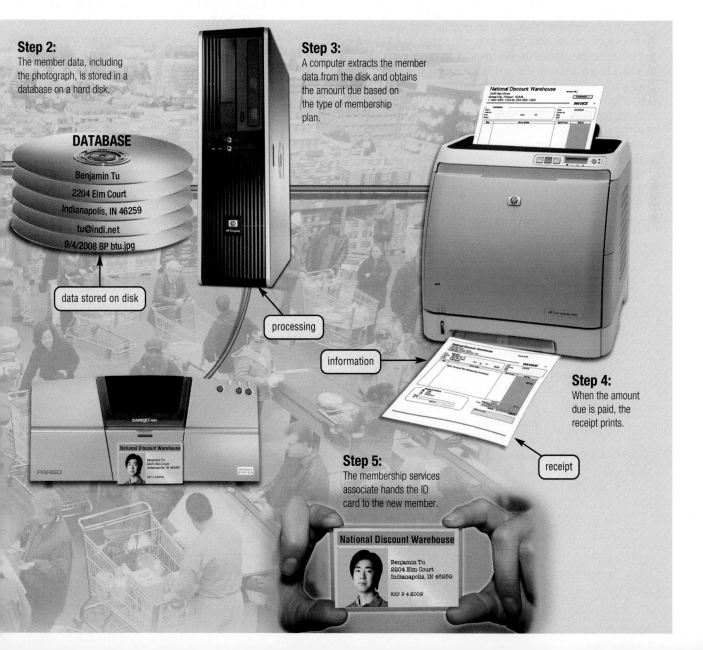

Step 2:
The member data, including the photograph, is stored in a database on a hard disk.

DATABASE

Benjamin Tu

2204 Elm Court

Indianapolis, IN 46259

tu@indi.net

9/4/2008 BP btu.jpg

data stored on disk

processing

Step 3:
A computer extracts the member data from the disk and obtains the amount due based on the type of membership plan.

information

Step 4:
When the amount due is paid, the receipt prints.

receipt

Step 5:
The membership services associate hands the ID card to the new member.

National Discount Warehouse

Benjamin Tu
2204 Elm Court
Indianapolis, IN 46259

EXP. 9 4 2009

WEB LINK 10-1

Data Security

For more information, visit scsite.com/dc2008/ch10/weblink and then click Data Security.

To ensure that data is accessible on demand, a company must manage and protect its data just as it would any other resource. Thus, it is vital that the data has integrity and is kept secure. For example, data in a database often is encrypted, or encoded in an unreadable form, to prevent unauthorized users from reading its contents. Chapter 11 discusses encryption and other forms of data security. Read Ethics & Issues 10-1 for a related discussion.

ETHICS & ISSUES 10-1

Are Portable Storage Devices a Threat to Businesses?

For years, and to the dismay of many companies, workers have carted portable storage devices loaded with valuable company information. Today's USB flash drives, portable media players, smart phones, and external hard disks allow employees to pack volumes of valuable information in their pockets. Companies now must be concerned with disgruntled employees walking off with complete customer lists, employee databases, or secret product designs and strategies. Some companies have gone as far as banning some portable media players and other portable storage devices from the company premises. Other companies have begun disabling USB and FireWire ports on employee computers, thereby preventing the devices from being used at all.

How can companies control employee use of portable storage devices to copy company information? Should companies be allowed to dictate the types of personal devices that employees bring to work? Why or why not? Is the problem solvable, just manageable, or should the company find other ways to secure its information? Why? Is it ethical for employees to take corporate information home if only for work purposes? Why or why not?

Data Integrity

For a computer to produce correct information, the data that is entered into a database must have integrity. *Data integrity* identifies the quality of the data. An erroneous member address in a member database is an example of incorrect data. When a database contains this type of error, it loses integrity. The more errors the data contains, the lower its integrity.

Garbage in, garbage out (*GIGO*) is a computing phrase that points out the accuracy of a computer's output depends on the accuracy of the input. If you enter incorrect data into a computer (garbage in), the computer will produce incorrect information (garbage out).

Data integrity is important because computers and people use information to make decisions and take actions. When you sign up for a warehouse club membership and pay with a credit card, a process begins that charges an amount to your credit card. If the membership price is not correct in the discount warehouse's database, an incorrect amount will be billed to your credit card. This type of error causes both

you and the membership services associate extra time and effort to remedy.

Qualities of Valuable Information

The information that data generates also is an important asset. People make decisions daily using all types of information such as receipts, bank statements, pension plan summaries, stock analyses, and credit reports. At school, students use grade reports and degree audits to make decisions. In a business, managers make decisions based on sales trends, competitors' products and services, production processes, and even employee skills.

To assist with sound decision making, the information must have value. For it to be valuable, information should be accurate, verifiable, timely, organized, accessible, useful, and cost-effective.

- *Accurate information* is error free. Inaccurate information can lead to incorrect decisions. For example, consumers assume their credit report is accurate. If your credit report incorrectly shows past due payments, a bank may not lend you money for a car or house.

- *Verifiable information* can be proven as correct or incorrect. For example, security personnel at an airport usually request some type of photo identification to verify that you are the person named on the ticket.

- *Timely information* has an age suited to its use. A decision to build additional schools in a particular district should be based on the most recent census report — not on one that is 20 years old. Most information loses value with time. Some information, such as information about trends, gains value as time passes and more information is obtained. For example, your transcript gains value as you take more classes.

- *Organized information* is arranged to suit the needs and requirements of the decision maker. Two different people may need the same information presented in a different manner. For example, an inventory manager may want an inventory report to list out-of-stock items first. The purchasing agent, instead, wants the report alphabetized by vendor.

- *Accessible information* is available when the decision maker needs it. Having to wait for information may delay an important decision. For example, a sales manager cannot decide which sales representative deserves the award for highest annual sales if the final sales have not yet been placed in the database.

- *Useful information* has meaning to the person who receives it. Most information is important only to certain people or groups of people. Always consider the audience when collecting and reporting information. Avoid distributing useless information. For example, an announcement of an alumni association meeting is not useful to students not yet graduated.

- *Cost-effective information* should give more value than it costs to produce. A company occasionally should review the information it produces to determine if it still is cost-effective to produce. Sometimes, it is not easy to place a value on information. For this reason, some companies create information only on demand, that is, as people request it, instead of on a regular basis. Many companies make information available online. Users then can access and print online information as they need it. For example, sending a printed benefits manual to each employee in a company could be quite costly. Instead, employees can access an online benefits manual, when they need to review it.

FAQ 10-1

How can I verify the accuracy of my credit report?

The three credit reporting companies (Equifax, Experian, and TransUnion) developed a central Web site at annualcreditreport.com. Through this Web site, you can request a free copy of your credit report from each credit reporting company every 12 months. You also can request the reports by mailing a form or calling a toll-free number. If you would like constant monitoring of the activity on your credit report, you can subscribe to a credit monitoring service for a minimal fee. The service will contact you if any unusual or suspicious activity occurs on your credit report. For more information, visit scsite.com/dc2008/ch10/faq and then click Verifying Credit Report Accuracy.

THE HIERARCHY OF DATA

Data is organized in layers. In the computer profession, data is classified in a hierarchy. Each higher level of data consists of one or more items from the lower level. For example, a member has an address, and an address consists of letters and numbers. Depending on the application and the user, different terms describe the various levels of the hierarchy.

As shown in Figure 10-2, a database contains files, a file contains records, a record contains fields, and a field is made up of one or more characters. The Discount Warehouse database contains four files: Member, Membership Plans, Member Purchases, and Products. The Member file contains records about current members. The Membership Plans file contains records identifying a type of membership and its annual fee. The Member Purchases file contains records about members' purchases at the discount warehouse, and the Products file contains records about items for sale. Each field in a record contains many characteristics, one of which is the field size.

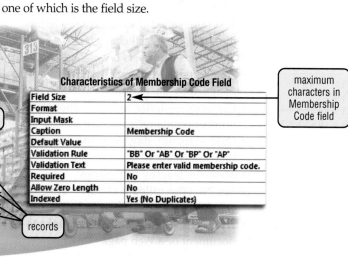

Characteristics of Membership Code Field

Field Size	2
Format	
Input Mask	
Caption	Membership Code
Default Value	
Validation Rule	"BB" Or "AB" Or "BP" Or "AP"
Validation Text	Please enter valid membership code.
Required	No
Allow Zero Length	No
Indexed	Yes (No Duplicates)

maximum characters in Membership Code field

Membership Plans File

Membership Code	Membership Name	Annual Fee
AB	Advantage Business	$90.00
AP	Advantage Personal	$40.00
BB	Basic Business	$55.00
BP	Basic Personal	$25.00

field names

characters

records

fields

FIGURE 10-2   A sample discount warehouse database with four files: Member, Membership Plans, Member Purchases, and Products. The sample Membership Plans file contains four records. Each record contains three fields. The Membership Code field can contain a maximum of two characters (bytes).

MAINTAINING DATA

File maintenance refers to the procedures that keep data current. File maintenance procedures include adding records to, changing records in, and deleting records from a file.

Adding Records

Users add new records to a file when they obtain new data. If a new member wants to join the discount warehouse club, a membership services associate adds a new record to the Member file at the discount warehouse. The process required to add this record to the file might include the following steps:

1. A membership services associate uses the database management system (DBMS) to display a Member Maintenance form that gives him or her access to the Member file. The associate then clicks the New button, which begins the process of adding a record to the Member file.

2. The associate fills in the fields of the member record with data (except for the Member ID, which automatically is assigned by the DBMS). In this example, the data entered is kept to a minimum.

3. The associate takes a picture of the member using a digital camera. The DBMS stores this picture in the Member file and prints it on a member ID card.

4. The membership services associate verifies the data on the screen and then presses a key on the keyboard or clicks a button on the screen to add the new member record to the Member file. The system software determines where to write the record on the disk, depending on the location of enough free space on the disk. In some cases, it writes the new record at the end of the file. In other cases, such as illustrated in Figure 10-5, it writes the new record for Benjamin Tu between existing records in the file.

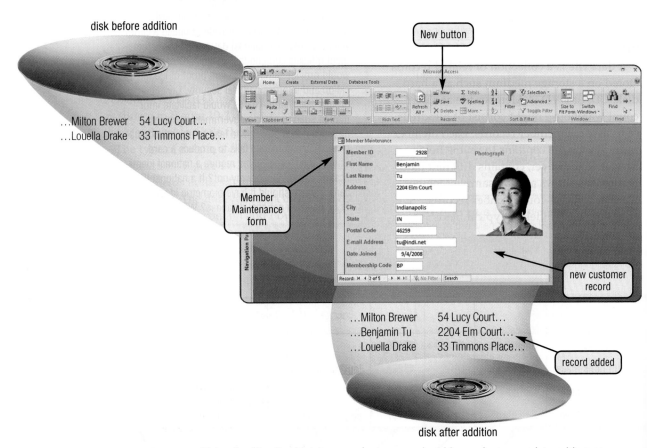

FIGURE 10-5   Using the Member Maintenance form, a membership services associate adds a new member record for Benjamin Tu. After the associate takes the photograph with the digital camera and confirms the data is correct, he or she adds the record to the database file.

Changing Records

Generally, users change a record in a file for two reasons: (1) to correct inaccurate data or (2) to update old data with new data.

As an example of the first type of change, assume that a membership services associate enters a member's e-mail address as ut@indi.net, instead of tu@indi.net. The member notices the error when he reviews his membership agreement at home. The next time he visits the discount warehouse, he requests that a membership services associate correct his e-mail address.

A more common reason to change a record is to update old data with new data. Suppose, for example, that Benjamin Tu moves from 2204 Elm Court to 76 Ash Street. The process to change the address and update Benjamin Tu's record might include the following steps:

1. The membership services associate displays the Member Maintenance form.

2. Assuming Benjamin Tu is present, the associate inserts Benjamin's member ID card in a card reader to display his member record on the screen. If Benjamin did not have his ID card or was not present, the associate could enter Benjamin's member ID — if Benjamin knew it. Otherwise, the associate could enter Tu in the Last Name field, which would retrieve all members with that same last name. The associate then would scroll through all of the retrieved records to determine which one is Benjamin's.

3. The DBMS displays data about Benjamin Tu so that the associate can confirm the correct member record is displayed.

4. The associate enters the new street address, 76 Ash Street.

5. The membership services associate verifies the data on the screen and then, if required, clicks the Save button to change the record in the Member file. The DBMS changes the record on the disk (Figure 10-6).

FIGURE 10-6 The membership services associate scans the membership ID card to display the member's record. After looking at the photograph on the screen to confirm that the correct member record is displayed, the associate changes the member's address.

Deleting Records

When a record no longer is needed, a user deletes it from a file. Assume a member named Elena Gupta is moving out of the country. The process required to delete a record from a file includes the following steps:

1. The membership services associate displays the Member Maintenance form.
2. The associate displays Elena Gupta's member record on the screen.
3. The associate confirms the correct member record is displayed. Then, the associate clicks the Delete Record command to delete the record from the Member file and then, if required, clicks the Save button to save the modified file.

DBMSs use a variety of techniques to manage deleted records. Sometimes, the DBMS removes the record from the file immediately. Other times, the record is flagged, or marked, so the DBMS will not process it again. In this case, the DBMS places an asterisk (*) or some other character at the beginning of the record (Figure 10-7).

DBMSs that maintain inactive data for an extended period commonly flag records. For example, a discount warehouse might flag canceled memberships. When a DBMS flags a deleted record, the record remains physically on the disk. The record, however, is deleted logically because the DBMS will not process it. DBMSs will ignore flagged records unless an instruction is issued to process them.

From time to time, users should run a utility program that removes flagged records and reorganizes current records. For example, the discount warehouse may remove from disk any accounts that have been canceled for more than one year. Deleting unneeded records reduces the size of files and frees up storage space.

Validating Data

Validation is the process of comparing data with a set of rules or values to find out if the data is correct. Many programs perform a *validity check* that analyzes entered data to help ensure that it is correct. For instance, when a membership services associate adds or changes data in a member record, the DBMS tests the entered data.

With an annual membership fee, you would expect to see numbers before and after a decimal point. For example, a valid annual membership fee is 30.00. An entry of XR.WP clearly is not correct. If the entered data fails a validity check, the computer should display an error message that instructs the user to enter the data again. Validity checks, sometimes called *validation rules*, reduce data entry errors and thus enhance the data's integrity.

Various types of validity checks include alphabetic checks, numeric checks, range checks, consistency checks, and completeness checks. Check digits also validate data accuracy. The following paragraphs describe the purpose of these validity checks. The table in Figure 10-8 illustrates several of these validity checks and shows valid data that passes the check and invalid data that fails the check.

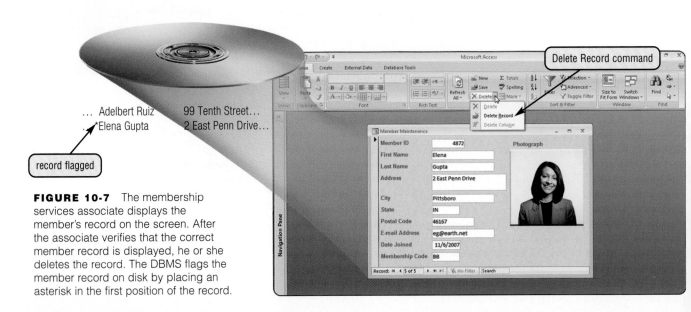

FIGURE 10-7 The membership services associate displays the member's record on the screen. After the associate verifies that the correct member record is displayed, he or she deletes the record. The DBMS flags the member record on disk by placing an asterisk in the first position of the record.

SAMPLE VALID AND INVALID DATA

Validity Check	Field(s) Being Checked	Valid Data	Invalid Data
Alphabetic Check	First Name	Karen	Ka24n
Numeric Check	Postal Code	46322	4tr22
Range Check	Annual Fee	$30.00	$120.00
Consistency Check	Date Joined and Birth Date	9/20/2007 8/27/1983	9/20/2007 8/27/2008
Completeness Check	Last Name	Tu	

FIGURE 10-8 In this table of sample valid and invalid data, the first column lists commonly used validity checks. The second column lists the name of the field that contains data being checked. The third column shows valid data that passes the validity checks. The fourth column shows invalid data that fails the validity checks.

ALPHABETIC/NUMERIC CHECK An *alphabetic check* ensures that users enter only alphabetic data into a field. A *numeric check* ensures that users enter only numeric data into a field. For example, data in a First Name field should contain only characters from the alphabet. Data in a postal code field should contain numbers (with the exception of the special characters such as a hyphen).

RANGE CHECK A *range check* determines whether a number is within a specified range. Assume the lowest annual membership fee at the discount warehouse is $25.00 and the highest is $90.00. A range check on the Annual Fee field ensures it is a value between $25.00 and $90.00.

CONSISTENCY CHECK A *consistency check* tests the data in two or more associated fields to ensure that the relationship is logical. For example, the value in a Date Joined field cannot occur earlier in time than a value in a Birth Date field.

COMPLETENESS CHECK A *completeness check* verifies that a required field contains data. For example, some fields cannot be left blank; others require a minimum number of characters. One completeness check can ensure that data exists in a Last Name field. Another can ensure that a day, month, and year are included in a Birth Date field.

CHECK DIGIT A *check digit* is a number(s) or character(s) that is appended to or inserted in a primary key value. A check digit often confirms the accuracy of a primary key value. Bank account, credit card, and other identification numbers often include one or more check digits.

A program determines the check digit by applying a formula to the numbers in the primary key value. An oversimplified illustration of a check digit formula is to add the numbers in the primary key. For example, if the primary key is 1367, this formula would add these numbers (1 + 3 + 6 + 7) for a sum of 17. Next,

the formula would add the numbers in the result (1 + 7) to generate a check digit of 8. The primary key then is 13678. This example began with the original primary key value, 1367, then the check digit, 8, was appended.

When a data entry clerk enters the primary key of 13678, for example, to look up an existing record, the program determines whether the check digit is valid. The program applies the check digit formula to the first four digits of the primary key. If the calculated check digit matches the entered check digit (8, in this example), the program assumes the entered primary key is valid. If the clerk enters an incorrect primary key, such as 13778, the check digit entered (8) will not match the computed check digit (9). In this case, the program displays an error message that instructs the user to enter the primary key value again.

Test your knowledge of pages 514 through 523 in Quiz Yourself 10-1.

QUIZ YOURSELF 10-1

Instructions: Find the true statement below. Then, rewrite the remaining false statements so they are true.

1. A coding scheme is a number(s) or character(s) that is appended to or inserted in a primary key value.
2. A database is a combination of one or more related characters or bytes and is the smallest unit of data a user accesses.
3. A record is a collection of data organized in a manner that allows access, retrieval, and use of that data.
4. Data is processed information.
5. Hierarchy of data procedures include adding records to, changing records in, and deleting records from a file.
6. To be valuable, information should be accurate, verifiable, timely, organized, accessible, useful, and cost-effective.

Quiz Yourself Online: To further check your knowledge of databases, qualities of valuable information, the hierarchy of data, and file maintenance techniques, visit scsite.com/dc2008/ch10/quiz and then click Objectives 1 – 5.

FILE PROCESSING VERSUS DATABASES

Almost all application programs use the file processing approach, the database approach, or a combination of both approaches to store and manage data. The next sections discuss these two approaches.

File Processing Systems

In the past, many organizations exclusively used file processing systems to store and manage data. In a typical **file processing system**, each department or area within an organization has its own set of files. The records in one file may not relate to the records in any other file.

Companies have used file processing systems for many years. A lot of these systems, however, have two major weaknesses: they have redundant data and they isolate data.

- Data Redundancy — Each department or area in a company has its own files in a file processing system. Thus, the same fields are stored in multiple files. If a file processing system is used at the discount warehouse, for example, the Member file and the Member Purchases file store the same members' names and addresses.

  Duplicating data in this manner wastes resources such as storage space and people's time. When new members are added or member data is changed, file maintenance tasks consume additional time because people must update multiple files that contain the same data.

  Data redundancy also can increase the chance of errors. If a member changes his or her address, for example, the discount warehouse must update the address wherever it appears. In this example, the Address field is in the Member file and also in the Member Purchases file. If the Address field is not changed in all the files where it is stored, then discrepancies among the files exist.

- Isolated Data — Often it is difficult to access data stored in separate files in different departments. Assume that the member e-mail addresses exist in the Member files, and items on sale are in the Products files. To send an e-mail message informing members about items on sale, data is needed from both the Member file and the Products file. Sharing data from multiple, separate files to generate such a list in a file processing system often is a complicated procedure and usually requires the experience of a computer programmer.

The Database Approach

When a company uses the **database approach**, many programs and users share the data in the database. A discount warehouse's database most likely contains data about members, membership plans, member purchases, and products. As shown in Figure 10-9, various areas within the discount warehouse share and

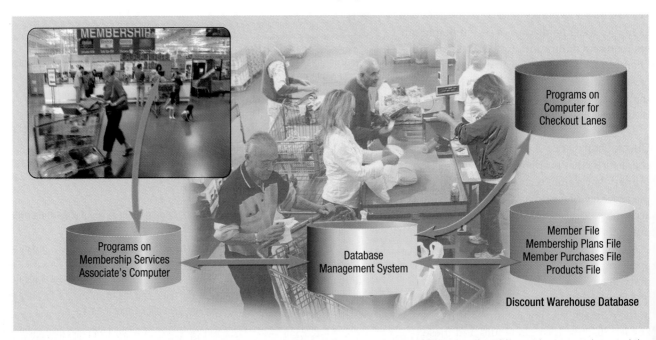

Programs on Computer for Checkout Lanes

Programs on Membership Services Associate's Computer

Database Management System

Member File
Membership Plans File
Member Purchases File
Products File

Discount Warehouse Database

FIGURE 10-9   In a discount warehouse that uses a database, the computer used by a membership services associate and the computer used in a checkout lane access data in a single database through the DBMS.

interact with the data in this database. The database does secure its data, however, so only authorized users can access certain data items.

While a user is working with the database, the DBMS resides in the memory of the computer. Instead of working directly with the DBMS, some users interact with a front end. A *front end* is a program that generally has a more user-friendly interface than the DBMS. For example, a membership services associate interacts with the Membership program. This front-end program interacts with the DBMS, which in turn, interacts with the database. Many programs today have a Web page as their front end. An application that supports a front-end program sometimes is called the *back end*. In this case, the DBMS is the back end.

The database approach addresses many of the weaknesses associated with file processing systems. The following paragraphs present some strengths of the database approach.

- Reduced Data Redundancy — Most data items are stored in only one file, which greatly reduces duplicate data. For example, a discount warehouse's database would record a member's name and address only once. When member data is entered or changed, one employee makes the change once. Figure 10-10 demonstrates the differences between how a database application and a file processing application might store data.

- Improved Data Integrity — When users modify data in the database, they make changes to one file instead of multiple files. Thus, the database approach increases the data's integrity by reducing the possibility of introducing inconsistencies.

- Shared Data — The data in a database environment belongs to and is shared, usually over a network, by the entire organization. This data is independent of, or separate from, the programs that access the data. Companies that use databases typically have security settings to define who can access, add, change, and delete the data in a database. Read Ethics & Issues 10-3 for a related discussion.

- Easier Access — The database approach allows nontechnical users to access and maintain data, providing they have the necessary privileges. Many computer users also can develop smaller databases themselves, without professional assistance.

- Reduced Development Time — It often is easier and faster to develop programs that use the database approach. Many DBMSs include several tools to assist in developing programs, which further reduces the development time. The next section discusses these tools and other DBMS features.

File Processing Example

Database Example

FIGURE 10-10 In the file processing environment, both files contain all three membership plans data fields. In a database environment, only the Membership Plans file contains the Membership Name and Annual Fee fields. Other files, however, such as the Member file, contain the Membership Code, which links to the Membership Plans file when membership plans data is needed.

ETHICS & ISSUES 10-3

Should States Share Criminal Databases?

California was the first state to employ a controversial database. Based on Megan's Law — the statute named for a seven-year-old girl who was violated and killed by a paroled felon — the database listed the names and addresses of people convicted of crimes against children. Today, all states employ similar databases and are required to share the information with a national database. Most states now allow you to use these databases to find out if these felons live near you. In some communities, when a paroled offender moves in, the police inform the local school system, which in turn sends parents a notification that includes a history, address, and picture of the wrongdoer. Some states share information with each other regarding almost all criminals, and some allow citizens to search for these offenders by name. Touted as a valuable tool in crime prevention, some feel that publishing this information makes it impossible for an offender to lead a normal life and can result in vigilantism — one paroled lawbreaker's car was firebombed only days after his name was released. Should a database of people paroled or released for crimes be made public? Why or why not? What about those who have committed other types of crimes? Who should have access to the database? Why?

Databases have many advantages as well as some disadvantages. A database can be more complex than a file processing system. People with special training usually develop larger databases and their associated applications. Databases also require more memory, storage, and processing power than file processing systems.

Data in a database is more vulnerable than data in file processing systems. A database stores most data in a single file. Many users and programs share and depend on this data. If the database is not operating properly or is damaged or destroyed, users may not be able to perform their jobs. In some cases, certain programs may stop working. To protect their valuable database resource, individuals and companies should establish and follow security procedures. Chapter 11 discusses a variety of security methods.

Despite these limitations, many business and home users work with databases because of their tremendous advantages. Although the hardware and software costs to set up a database may seem expensive, long-term benefits exceed the initial costs.

FAQ 10-3

Can a database eliminate redundant data completely?

No, a database reduces redundant data — it does not eliminate it. Key fields link data together in a database. For example, the Member ID field will exist in any database file that requires access to member data. Thus, the Member ID is duplicated (exists in many database files) in the database. For more information, visit scsite.com/dc2008/ch10/faq and then click Database Relationships.

DATABASE MANAGEMENT SYSTEMS

As previously discussed, a database management system (DBMS), or database program, is software that allows you to create, access, and manage a database. DBMSs are available for many sizes and types of computers (Figure 10-11). Whether designed for a small or large computer, most DBMSs perform common functions. The following pages discuss functions common to most DBMSs.

POPULAR DATABASE MANAGEMENT SYSTEMS

Database	Manufacturer	Computer Type
Access	Microsoft Corporation	Personal computer, server, mobile devices
Adabas	Software AG	Server, mainframe
D³	Raining Data	Personal computer, server
DB2	IBM Corporation	Personal computer, server, mainframe
Essbase	Hyperion Solutions Corporation	Personal computer, server, mobile devices
FastObjects	Versant Corporation	Personal computer, server
GemFire	GemStone Systems, Inc.	Server
Informix	IBM Corporation	Personal computer, server, mainframe
Ingres	Ingres Corporation	Personal computer, server, mainframe
InterBase	Borland Software Corporation	Personal computer, server
JDataStore	Borland Software Corporation	Personal computer, server, mobile devices
KE Texpress	KE Software, Inc.	Personal computer, server
MySQL	MySQL AB	Personal computer, server
ObjectStore	Progress Software Corporation	Personal computer, server
Oracle Database	Oracle Corporation	Personal computer, server, mainframe, mobile devices
SQL Server	Microsoft Corporation	Server, personal computer, PDA
SQL Server Compact Edition	Microsoft Corporation	Mobile devices
Sybase	Sybase Inc.	Personal computer, server, mobile devices
Teradata Database	Teradata	Server
Versant	Versant Corporation	Personal computer, server
Visual FoxPro	Microsoft Corporation	Personal computer, server

WEB LINK 10-2

MySQL

For more information, visit scsite.com/dc2008/ch10/weblink and then click MySQL.

FIGURE 10-11   Many database management systems run on multiple types of computers.

FAQ 10-4

Which database vendors have the largest revenue market share?

As shown in the chart below, Oracle has the largest market share in terms of revenue, followed by IBM and Microsoft. For more information, visit scsite.com/dc2008/ch10/faq and then click Database Market Share.

Database Vendor Market Share

- Oracle ☐ IBM ■ Microsoft
- Teradata ☐ Sybase ■ Others

3% 3% 8%

15%

49%

22%

Source: Gartner Dataquest

Data Dictionary

A **data dictionary**, sometimes called a *repository*, contains data about each file in the database and each field in those files. For each file, it stores details such as the file name, description, the file's relationship to other files, and the number of records in the file. For each field, it stores details such as the field name, description, field type, field size, default value, validation rules, and the field's relationship to other fields. Figure 10-12 shows how a data dictionary might list data for a Member file.

Because the data dictionary contains details about data, some call it *metadata* (meta means more comprehensive). Sometimes, a data dictionary also contains data about programs and users. It might keep track of who accessed data and when they accessed it. The data dictionary is a crucial backbone to a DBMS. Thus, only skilled professionals should update the contents of a data dictionary.

A DBMS uses the data dictionary to perform validation checks. When users enter data, the data dictionary verifies that the entered data matches the field's data type. For example, the data dictionary allows only dates to be entered in a Date Joined field. The data dictionary also can limit the type of data that can be entered, often allowing a user to select from a list. For example, the data dictionary ensures that the State field contains a valid two-letter state code, such as IN, by presenting a list of valid state codes to the user. By validating data, the data dictionary helps to maintain the integrity of the data.

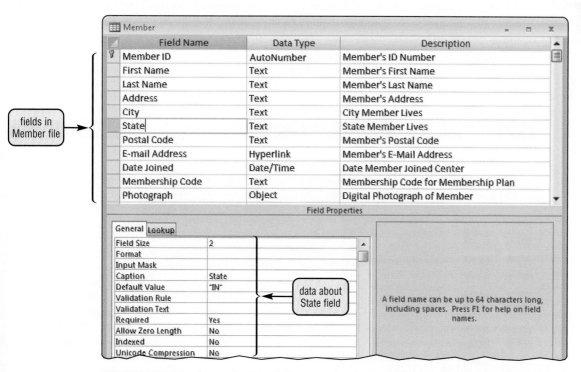

fields in Member file

Field Name	Data Type	Description
Member ID	AutoNumber	Member's ID Number
First Name	Text	Member's First Name
Last Name	Text	Member's Last Name
Address	Text	Member's Address
City	Text	City Member Lives
State	Text	State Member Lives
Postal Code	Text	Member's Postal Code
E-mail Address	Hyperlink	Member's E-Mail Address
Date Joined	Date/Time	Date Member Joined Center
Membership Code	Text	Membership Code for Membership Plan
Photograph	Object	Digital Photograph of Member

Field Properties

General Lookup

Field Size	2
Format	
Input Mask	
Caption	State
Default Value	"IN"
Validation Rule	
Validation Text	
Required	Yes
Allow Zero Length	No
Indexed	No
Unicode Compression	No

data about State field

A field name can be up to 64 characters long, including spaces. Press F1 for help on field names.

FIGURE 10-12 A sample data dictionary entry shows the fields in the Member file and the properties of the State field.

A data dictionary allows users to specify a default value for a field. A *default value* is a value that the DBMS initially displays in a field. If most members who join the warehouse club live in Indiana, then the DBMS initially could display IN in the State field. The user does not have to type in a default value. Displaying a default value reduces the possibility of errors. A user typically can override a default value if it does not apply for a certain record. For example, you can change the value from IN to OH if the member lives in Ohio.

File Retrieval and Maintenance

A DBMS provides several tools that allow users and programs to retrieve and maintain data in the database. As discussed earlier in this chapter, file maintenance involves adding new records, changing data in existing records, and removing unwanted records from the database.

To retrieve or select data in a database, you query it. A **query** is a request for specific data from the database. Users can instruct the DBMS to display, print, or store the results of a query. The capability of querying a database is one of the more powerful database features.

To meet the needs of a wide variety of database users, from trained experts to non-technical staff, a DBMS offers several methods to retrieve and maintain its data. The four more commonly used are query languages, query by example, forms, and report generators. The following paragraphs describe each of these methods. Read Looking Ahead 10-1 for a look at a future use of queries.

QUERY LANGUAGE A **query language** consists of simple, English-like statements that allow users to specify the data to display, print, or store. Each query language has its own grammar and vocabulary. A person without a programming background usually can learn a query language in a short time.

Although a query language can be used to maintain (add, change, and delete) data, most users only retrieve (query) data with a query language. To simplify the query process, many DBMSs provide wizards to guide users through the steps of creating a query. Figure 10-13 shows how to use the Simple Query Wizard in Microsoft Office Access 2007 to display the First Name, Last Name, and E-mail Address fields from the Member file.

Instead of using the Simple Query Wizard, you could enter the query language statement shown in Figure 10-13 directly in the DBMS to display the results shown in Step 3. Later in the chapter, specific query languages are presented in more depth.

QUERY BY EXAMPLE Most DBMSs include **query by example** (**QBE**), a feature that has a graphical user interface to assist users with retrieving data. Figure 10-14 shows a sample QBE screen for a query that searches for and lists members on the Basic Personal plan; that is, their Membership Code field value is equal to BP.

WEB LINK 10-3

Query

For more information, visit scsite.com/dc2008/ch10/weblink and then click Query.

LOOKING AHEAD 10-1

Archive an Entire Lifetime

Photo albums, memory boxes, and notebooks are relics of the past for Microsoft researcher Gordon Bell, and they may be for you, too. Bell is recording practically everything in his entire life and storing these memories in a searchable SQL Server-based database.

Bell's *MyLifeBits* project is composed of two parts: one that digitizes all aspects of his life experiences, such as telephone calls, faxes, photographs, cards, and music files; the second that allows anyone to create a lifetime library on a home computer.

Bell can organize, query, comment on, and use the database content. The data items can be linked together, such as matching a person in a photograph with a telephone voice mail message and tying those items to a calendar, so the calendar becomes a photo diary of one of the day's events. For more information, visit scsite.com/dc2008/ch10/looking and then click MyLifeBits.

FIGURE 10-13 HOW TO USE THE SIMPLE QUERY WIZARD

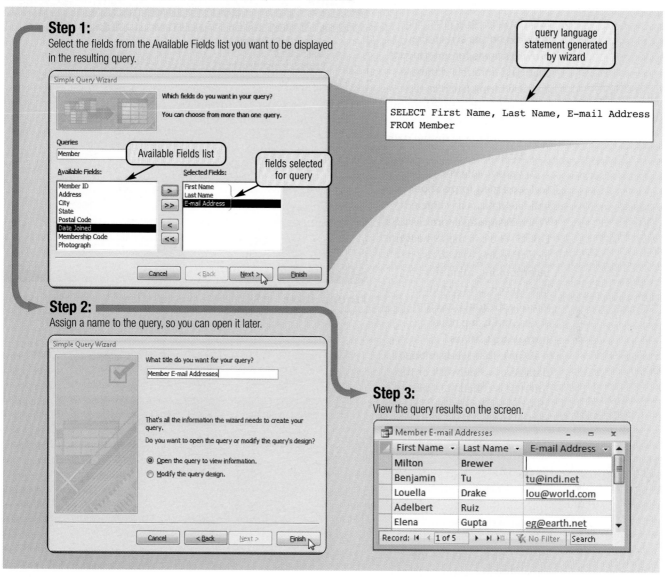

Step 1:
Select the fields from the Available Fields list you want to be displayed in the resulting query.

query language statement generated by wizard

```
SELECT First Name, Last Name, E-mail Address
FROM Member
```

Available Fields list

fields selected for query

Step 2:
Assign a name to the query, so you can open it later.

Step 3:
View the query results on the screen.

FIGURE 10-14a (query by example screen)

Last Name	Address	City	State	Postal Code	E-mail Address	Date Joined	Membership Code
							BP

criteria

FIGURE 10-14b (query results)

Last Name	Address	City	State	Postal Code	E-mail Address	Date Joined	Membership Code
Tu	76 Ash Street	Indianapolis	IN	46259	tu@indi.net	9/4/2008	BP
Ruiz	99 Tenth Street	Carmel	IN	46033		10/8/2007	BP

FIGURE 10-14 Access has many QBE capabilities. One QBE technique is Filter by Form, which uses a form to show available fields. The database program retrieves records that match criteria you enter in the form fields. This example searches for members whose Membership Code is equal to BP.

FORM   A **form**, sometimes called a *data entry form*, is a window on the screen that provides areas for entering or changing data in a database. You use forms (such as the Member Maintenance form in Figure 10-5 on page 520) to retrieve and maintain the data in a database.

To reduce data entry errors, well-designed forms should validate data as it is entered. When designing a form using a DBMS, you can make the form attractive and easy to use by incorporating color, shading, lines, boxes, and graphics; varying the fonts and font styles; and using other formatting features.

A form that sends entered data across a network or the Internet is called an *e-form*, short for *electronic form* (Figure 10-15). E-forms generally use a means to secure the data while it is transported across the network. Often, the data in the e-form automatically enters in, or updates existing data in, a database on the network or the Internet. Thus, many DBMSs include the capability of creating e-forms.

REPORT GENERATOR   A **report generator**, also called a *report writer*, allows users to design a report on the screen, retrieve data into the report design, and then display or print the report (Figure 10-16). Unlike a form, you use a report generator only to retrieve data. Report generators usually allow you to format page numbers and dates; titles and column headings; subtotals and totals; and fonts, font sizes, color, and shading. Some report generators allow you to create a report as a Web page, which can be interactive.

Data Security

A DBMS provides means to ensure that only authorized users access data at permitted times. In addition, most DBMSs allow different levels of

FIGURE 10-15   Through this e-form, users register in an online membership database.

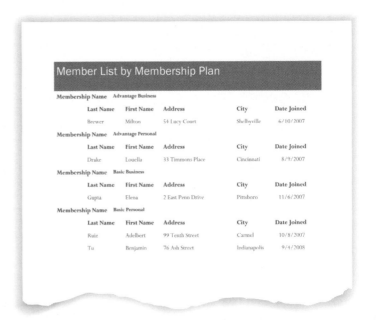

FIGURE 10-16   This report, created in Access 2007, displays member information by the type of membership in which members are enrolled.

access privileges to be identified for each field in the database. These access privileges define the actions that a specific user or group of users can perform.

Access privileges for data involve establishing who can enter new data, change existing data, delete unwanted data, and view data. In the Products file, a checkout clerk might have read-only privileges for product prices. That is, the clerk could view the prices, but cannot change them. An inventory manager, by contrast, would have full-update privileges to product data, meaning he or she can view and change the data. Finally, some users have no access privileges to the data; that is, they cannot view or change any data in the database. Chapter 11 discusses access privileges and other security techniques in more depth. Read Ethics & Issues 10-4 for a related discussion.

ETHICS & ISSUES 10-4

Would You Carry a Contactless Smart Card?

To speed up purchases and increase convenience, many credit card companies now issue *contactless smart cards*. When waved within a couple of inches of a card reader while making a purchase, an RFID chip embedded in the card sends credit card information to the reader. In many cases, a signature is not required to complete the purchase. Proponents of the cards claim that the convenience and simplicity of the cards will lead to less need for cash transactions, resulting in less theft. They state that the cards are secure and safe to use. But, some privacy advocates and security experts are wary of the security of the cards. To prove the point, one researcher hid a card reader in a briefcase and then read information from a card in another person's back pocket. Having read the card, the researcher potentially then could make a duplicate card and use it to make purchases, or use the account information in other ways. Some privacy advocates recommend using a shield around the card, such as tinfoil, when the card is not in use. Also, card readers are widely available, possibly allowing would-be thieves to steal information from any card they could get their hands on. Would you carry a contactless smart card? Why or why not? Would you be willing to carry a specially made wallet or purse that would shield the cards from hidden card readers? Why or why not? Are card issuers or card users responsible for the security of the cards? Why? Is carrying a contactless smart card more secure than carrying a great deal of cash? Why or why not?

Backup and Recovery

Occasionally a database is damaged or destroyed because of hardware failure, a problem with the software, human error, or a catastrophe such as fire or flood. A DBMS provides a variety of techniques to restore the database to a usable form in case it is damaged or destroyed.

- A **backup**, or copy, of the entire database should be made on a regular basis. Some DBMSs have their own built-in backup utilities. Others require users to purchase a separate backup utility, or use one included with the operating system.
- More complex DBMSs maintain a **log**, which is a listing of activities that change the contents of

the database. If a membership services associate modifies a member's address, for example, the change appears in the log. The DBMS places the following in the log: (1) a copy of the member record prior to the change, called the *before image* (Figure 10-17a); (2) the actual change of address data (Figure 10-17b); and (3) a copy of the member record after the change, called the *after image* (Figure 10-17c). The log also might store who made the change, when it was made, and from which computer it was made.

- A DBMS that creates a log usually provides a recovery utility. A **recovery utility** uses the logs and/or backups to restore a database when it becomes damaged or destroyed. The recovery utility restores the database using

FIGURE 10-17a (before image)

FIGURE 10-17b (change)

FIGURE 10-17c (after image)

FIGURE 10-17 When the contents of a record are changed, the DBMS places three items in the log: the before image of the record, the actual change, and the after image of the record.

rollforward and rollback techniques. In a *rollforward*, also called *forward recovery*, the DBMS uses the log to reenter changes made to the database since the last save or backup. In a *rollback*, also called *backward recovery*, the DBMS uses the log to undo any changes made to the database during a certain period. The rollback restores the database to its condition prior to the failure. Depending on the type of failure, the DBMS determines which type of recovery technique to use. For example, if the database is destroyed by a lightning strike, the DBMS would rollforward from the last backup. Assume, however, that a power failure happens at 3:15 p.m. and shuts down all computers, but does not destroy any data. Because some users may have been in the middle of entering transactions, the DBMS would rollback the database to 3:00 p.m. and send a message to all users that they need to reenter any transactions made after that time.

- *Continuous backup* is a backup plan in which all data is backed up whenever a change is made. This backup technique is costly but is growing in popularity because of its benefits. Continuous backup provides recovery of damaged data in a matter of seconds.

WEB LINK 10-4

Continuous Backup

For more information, visit scsite.com/dc2008/ch10/weblink and then click Continuous Backup.

Test your knowledge of pages 524 through 532 in Quiz Yourself 10-2.

QUIZ YOURSELF 10-2

Instructions: Find the true statement below. Then, rewrite the remaining false statements so they are true.

1. A DBMS is hardware that allows you to create, access, and manage an operating system.

2. A query contains data about files and fields in the database.

3. Backup and recovery procedures for data involve establishing who can enter new data, change existing data, delete unwanted data, and view data.

4. To reduce data entry errors, well-designed forms should rollback data as it is entered.

5. Two major weaknesses of file processing systems are data redundancy and isolated data.

Quiz Yourself Online: To further check your knowledge of file processing systems versus databases and functions of a DBMS, visit scsite.com/dc2008/ch10/quiz and then click Objectives 6 – 7.

RELATIONAL, OBJECT-ORIENTED, AND MULTIDIMENSIONAL DATABASES

Every database and DBMS is based on a specific data model. A **data model** consists of rules and standards that define how the database organizes data. A data model defines how users view the organization of the data. It does not define how the operating system actually arranges the data on the disk.

Three popular data models in use today are relational, object-oriented, and multidimensional. A database typically is based on one data model. For example, when using a relational database, users work with the relational data model. Some databases are called *object-relational databases* because they combine features of the relational and object-oriented data models.

The table in Figure 10-18 lists some popular DBMSs and the data model on which they are based. The following sections discuss the features of relational, object-oriented, and multidimensional databases.

DATA MODELS FOR POPULAR DBMSs

Data Model	Popular DBMSs
Relational	Access Adabas Informix Ingres InterBase MySQL SQL Server Sybase Teradata
Object-oriented	FastObjects GemFire KE Texpress ObjectStore Versant
Object-relational	DB2 JDataStore Oracle Polyhedra PostgreSQL Visual FoxPro Teradata
Multidimensional	D^3 Essbase Oracle Express

FIGURE 10-18 Four popular data models are relational, object-oriented, object-relational, and multidimensional. Most DBMSs are based on one of these models.

FAQ 10-5

How big is the largest commercial database?

The world's largest commercial database stores more than 100 TB (trillion bytes) of data for Yahoo! Incorporated. This database uses Oracle database software and runs on a UNIX platform. For more information, visit scsite.com/dc2008/ch10/faq and then click World's Largest Database.

DATA TERMINOLOGY

File Processing Environment	Relational Database Developer	Relational Database User
File	Relation	Table
Record	Tuple	Row
Field	Attribute	Column

FIGURE 10-19 In this data terminology table, the first column identifies the terms used in a file processing environment. The second column presents the terms used by developers of a relational database. The third column indicates terms to which the users of a relational database refer.

Relational Databases

Today, a relational database is a widely used type of database. A **relational database** is a database that stores data in tables that consist of rows and columns. Each row has a primary key and each column has a unique name.

As discussed earlier in this chapter, a file processing environment uses the terms file, record, and field to represent data. A relational database uses terms different from a file processing system. A developer of a relational database refers to a file as a *relation*, a record as a *tuple*, and a field as an *attribute*. A user of a relational database, by contrast, refers to a file as a **table**, a record as a **row**, and a field as a **column**. Figure 10-19 summarizes this varied terminology.

In addition to storing data, a relational database also stores data relationships. A **relationship** is a connection within the data. In a relational database, you can set up a relationship between tables at any time. The tables must have a common column (field). For example, you would relate the Member table and the Membership Plans table using the Membership Code column. Figure 10-20 illustrates these relational database concepts. In a relational database, the only data redundancy (duplication) exists in the common columns (fields). The database uses these common columns for relationships.

Applications best suited for relational databases are those whose data can be organized into a two-dimensional table. Many businesses use relational databases for payroll, accounts receivable, accounts payable, general ledger, inventory, order entry, invoicing, and other business-related functions.

FIGURE 10-20 The Member table is linked to the Membership Plans table through the Membership Code column. The Member table is linked to the Member Purchases table through the Member ID column. The Products table is linked to the Member Purchases table through the Product ID column.

WEB LINK 10-5

Relational Databases

For more information, visit scsite.com/ dc2008/ch10/weblink and then click Relational Databases.

A developer of relational databases uses normalization to organize the data. *Normalization* is a process designed to ensure the data within the relations (tables) contains the least amount of duplication. For a technical discussion about normalization, read the High-Tech Talk article on page 540.

SQL   Structured Query Language (SQL) is a query language that allows users to manage, update, and retrieve data. SQL has special keywords and rules that users include in SQL statements. For example, the SQL statement in Figure 10-21a shows how to write the join operation that creates the results shown in Figure 10-21b. The statement displays the First Name, Last Name, and Annual Fee fields in alphabetical order by last name for all records in the Member table.

Most relational database products for servers and mainframes include SQL. Many personal computer databases also include SQL. The structure and wording in SQL statements may differ slightly among database management systems.

WEB LINK 10-6

SQL

For more information, visit scsite.com/ dc2008/ch10/weblink and then click SQL.

FIGURE 10-21a   (SQL statement)

```
SELECT FIRST NAME, LAST NAME, ANNUAL FEE
FROM MEMBER, MEMBERSHIP PLANS
WHERE MEMBER.MEMBERSHIP CODE =
  MEMBERSHIP PLANS.MEMBERSHIP CODE
ORDER BY LAST NAME
```

FIGURE 10-21b   (SQL statement results)

First Name	Last Name	Annual Fee
Milton	Brewer	$90.00
Louella	Drake	$40.00
Elena	Gupta	$55.00
Adelbert	Ruiz	$25.00
Benjamin	Tu	$25.00

FIGURE 10-21   A sample SQL statement and its results.

Object-Oriented Databases

An **object-oriented database (OODB)** stores data in objects. An **object** is an item that contains data, as well as the actions that read or process the data. A Member object, for example, might contain data about a member such as Member ID, First Name, Last Name, Address, and so on. It also could contain instructions about how to print the member record or the formula required to calculate a member's balance due. A record in a relational database, by contrast, would contain only data about a member.

WEB LINK 10-7

Object-Oriented Databases

For more information, visit scsite.com/ dc2008/ch10/weblink and then click Object-Oriented Databases.

Object-oriented databases have several advantages compared with relational databases: they can store more types of data, access this data faster, and allow programmers to reuse objects. An object-oriented database stores unstructured data more efficiently than a relational database. Unstructured data can include photographs, video clips, audio clips, and documents. When users query an object-oriented database, the results often are displayed more quickly than the same query of a relational database. If an object already exists, programmers can reuse it instead of recreating a new object — saving on program development time.

Examples of applications appropriate for an object-oriented database include the following:

- A *multimedia database* stores images, audio clips, and/or video clips. For example, a *GIS* (geographic information system) database stores maps and other geographic data (Figure 10-22). A voice mail system database stores audio messages. A television news station database stores audio and video clips.

- A *groupware database* stores documents such as schedules, calendars, manuals, memos, and reports. Users perform queries to search the document contents. For example, you can search people's schedules for available meeting times.

- A *computer-aided design (CAD) database* stores data about engineering, architectural, and scientific designs. Data in the database includes a list of components of the item being designed, the relationship among the components, and previous versions of the design drafts.

- A *hypertext database* contains text links to other types of documents. A *hypermedia database* contains text, graphics, video, and sound. The Web contains a variety of hypertext and hypermedia databases. You can search these databases for items such as documents, graphics, audio and video clips, and links to Web pages.

- A *Web database* links to an e-form on a Web page. The Web browser sends and receives data between the form and the database. A later section in this chapter discusses Web databases in more depth.

FAQ 10-6

How is the data in GIS databases obtained?

GIS database data is created mostly from hard copy maps that are digitized using special software. Satellite imagery also can be used to collect data from locations worldwide. Some computer databases developed by government and nongovernment agencies are able to feed data directly into a GIS database. For more information, visit scsite.com/dc2008/ch10/faq and then click GIS Databases.

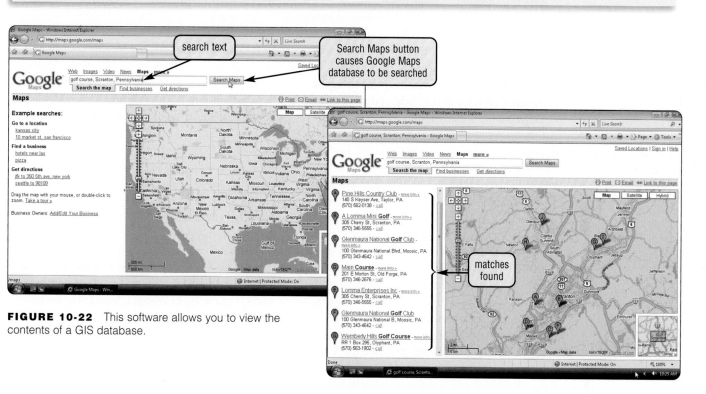

FIGURE 10-22 This software allows you to view the contents of a GIS database.

OBJECT QUERY LANGUAGE Object-oriented and object-relational databases often use a query language called *object query language* (*OQL*) to manipulate and retrieve data. OQL is similar to SQL. OQL and SQL use many of the same rules, grammar, and keywords. Because OQL is a relatively new query language, not all object databases support it.

Multidimensional Databases

A **multidimensional database** stores data in dimensions. Whereas a relational database is a two-dimensional table, a multidimensional database can store more than two dimensions of data. These multiple dimensions, sometimes known as a *hypercube*, allow users to access and analyze any view of the database data.

A Webmaster at a retailing business may want information about product sales and customer sales for each region spanning a given time. A manager at the same business may want information about product sales by department for each sales representative spanning a given time. A multidimensional database can consolidate this type of data from multiple dimensions at very high rates of speed.

The number of dimensions in a multidimensional database varies. A retail business might have four dimensions: products, customers, regions, and time. A multidimensional database for a hospital procedure could have six dimensions: time, procedure type, patient, hospital, physician, and diagnosis. A multidimensional database for an insurance policy may include five dimensions: time, policy type, agent, customer, and coverage. Nearly every multidimensional database has a dimension of time. The content of other dimensions varies depending on the subject.

The key advantage of the multidimensional database is that it can consolidate data much faster than a relational database. A relational database typically does not process and summarize large numbers of records efficiently. With a multidimensional database, users obtain summarized results very quickly. For example, a query that takes minutes or hours to execute in a relational database will take only seconds to execute in a multidimensional database.

WEB LINK 10-8

Multidimensional Databases

For more information, visit scsite.com/dc2008/ch10/weblink and then click Multidimensional Databases.

No standard query language exists for multidimensional databases. Each database uses its own language. Most are similar to SQL.

DATA WAREHOUSES One application that uses multidimensional databases is a data warehouse. A **data warehouse** is a huge database that stores and manages the data required to analyze historical and current transactions. Through a data warehouse, managers and other users access transactions and summaries of transactions quickly and efficiently. Some major credit card companies monitor and manage customers' credit card transactions using a data warehouse. Additionally, consumers can access their own transactions in the data warehouse via the Web. A data warehouse typically has a user-friendly interface, so users easily can interact with its data.

The databases in a data warehouse usually are quite large. Often, the database is distributed. The data in a *distributed database* exists in many separate locations throughout a network or the Internet. The data is accessible through a single server. The data's location is transparent to the user, who usually is unaware that the data is stored in multiple servers.

Data warehouses often use a process called *data mining* to find patterns and relationships among data. A state government could mine through data to check if the number of births has a relationship to income level. Many e-commerce sites use data mining to determine customer preferences.

A smaller version of a data warehouse is the *data mart*. A data mart contains a database that helps a specific group or department make decisions. Marketing and sales departments may have their own separate data marts. Individual groups or departments often extract data from the data warehouse to create their data marts.

WEB DATABASES

One of the more profound features of the Web is the vast amount of information it provides. The Web offers information about jobs, travel destinations, television programming, pictures, movies, videos, local and national weather, sporting events, and legislative information. You can shop for just about any product or service, buy or sell stocks, search for a job, and make airline reservations. Much of this and other information on the Web exists in databases. Some Web databases are *collaborative databases*, where users store and share photos, videos, recordings, and other personal media with other registered users (Figure 10-23). Read Ethics & Issues 10-5 for a related discussion.

To access data in a Web database, you fill in a form or enter search text on a Web page. The Web page is the front end to the database. Many search engines such as Yahoo! use databases to store Web site descriptions. Thus, the search engine's home page is the front end to the database. To

WEB LINK 10-9

Collaborative Databases

For more information, visit scsite.com/dc2008/ch10/weblink and then click Collaborative Databases.

FIGURE 10-23 Media sharing Web sites store users' digital videos, photos, and other media in a collaborative database, the contents of which are shared with other registered users.

ETHICS & ISSUES 10-5

Can the Government Be Trusted with Personal Data?

Despite laws, policies, and procedures to the contrary, a database of 1.5 million voters was found to be open to attack, and hackers could modify voter registration information. The database remained on the Web until a voter advocacy group brought the situation to the attention of authorities. In another case of government mishandling data, a judge ordered all of the Web sites of the Interior Department to be shut down for 10 weeks because a database system handling billions of dollars of payments to Native Americans was found to be vulnerable to hackers. In a recent survey, concern over many well-publicized security lapses and computer crime incidents resulted in 63 percent of adults being less likely to provide personal information to the government. In addition, 81 percent worried about the government misusing the information. Because of the volumes of information kept by the government in massive databases, the lack of resources, and an increase in outsourcing work to subcontractors, information is increasingly unsecured in many government agencies. Who should be held accountable for lapses in security, privacy, and ethics with regards to government data? Why? Should governments be limited in any way in the amount of information they store, types of information they store, or the duration for which they store the information? Why or why not? Can you think of any good reasons why so much personal information should be made available on government Web sites?

access the database, you enter search text into the search engine.

A Web database usually resides on a database server. A *database server* is a computer that stores and provides access to a database. One type of program that manages the sending and receiving of data between the front end and the database server is a *CGI* (*Common Gateway Interface*) script. CGI scripts run automatically — as soon as you click the button to send or receive information. Writing a CGI script requires computer programming skills.

In addition to accessing information, users provide information to Web databases. Many Web sites request that users enter personal information, such as name, address, telephone number, and preferences, into an e-form. The database then stores this personal information for future use. A company, for example, may send e-mail messages to certain groups of customers. If you are a frequent flyer, you may receive travel information.

For smaller databases, many personal computer database programs provide a variety of Web publishing tools that enable users without computer programming experience to create a home or small office database.

FAQ 10-7

How popular is YouTube?

YouTube originated in February 2005 and since has grown to become a major video sharing Web site. YouTube now estimates that people watch more than 70 million videos on the site everyday. Because of YouTube's popularity, Google purchased YouTube for $1.65 billion. To date, this is the most expensive purchase Google has made. For more information, visit scsite.com/dc2008/ch10/faq and then click YouTube.

DATABASE ADMINISTRATION

Managing a company's database requires a great deal of coordination. The role of coordinating the use of the database belongs to the database analysts and administrators. To carry out their responsibilities, these IT (information technology) professionals follow database design guidelines and need cooperation from all database users.

Database Design Guidelines

A carefully designed database makes it easier for a user to query the database, modify the data, and create reports. The guidelines shown in Figure 10-24 apply to databases of all sizes.

DATABASE DESIGN GUIDELINES

1. Determine the purpose of the database.

2. Design the tables or files.
   - Design tables or files on paper first.
   - Each table or file should contain data about one subject. The Member table, for example, contains data about members.

3. Design the records and fields for each table or file.
   - Be sure every record has a unique primary key.
   - Use separate fields for logically distinct items. For example, a name could be stored in six fields: Title (Mr., Mrs., Dr., etc.), First Name, Middle Name, Last Name, Suffix (Jr., Sr., etc.), and Nickname.
   - Do not create fields for information that can be derived from entries in other fields. For example, do not include a field for Age. Instead, store the birthdate and compute the age.
   - Allow enough space for each field.
   - Set default values for frequently entered data.

4. Determine the relationships among the tables or files.

FIGURE 10-24 Guidelines for developing a database.

Role of the Database Analysts and Administrators

The database analysts and administrators are responsible for managing and coordinating all database activities. The **database analyst (DA)**, or *data modeler*, focuses on the meaning and usage of data. The DA decides on the proper placement of fields, defines the relationships among data, and identifies users' access privileges. The **database administrator (DBA)** requires a more technical inside view of the data. The DBA creates and maintains the data dictionary, manages security of the database, monitors the performance of the database, and checks backup and recovery procedures.

In small companies, one person often is both the DA and DBA. In larger companies, the responsibilities of the DA and DBA are split among two or more people.

FAQ 10-8

Does DBA have two meanings?

Yes; DBA stands for either database administration or database administrator. The first, database administration, is the act of managing a database. The second, database administrator, is the person who manages the database. For more information, visit scsite.com/dc2008/ch10/faq and then click DBA.

WEB LINK 10-10

Database Administrators

For more information, visit scsite.com/dc2008/ch10/weblink and then click Database Administrators.

Role of the Employee as a User

Employees should learn how to use the data in the database effectively. The amount of information available often amazes first-time database users. Instant access to this information helps employees perform their jobs more effectively. For example, assume a car backed into your parked car. You call your insurance agent to find out where to repair your car. The agent reads to you a list of authorized car repair shops in your area. Today, employees access databases from their office desktop computers, notebook computers, or even smart phones, PDAs, and other mobile devices (Figure 10-25).

Employees also must take an active role in identifying new data for the database. For example, maybe the insurance agent does not have access to the list of car repair shops on the computer. Instead, the agent looks them up in the telephone book. The agent's job would be much easier if this information was available on the computer.

The maintenance of a database is an ongoing task that companies measure constantly against their overall goals. Users can take part in designing the database that will help them achieve those goals.

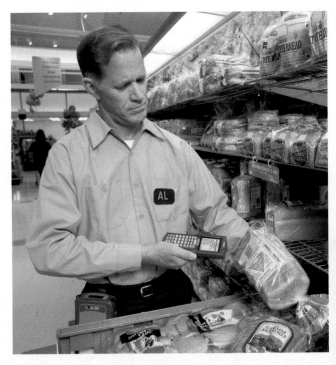

FIGURE 10-25 This grocery store employee scans the labels before placing the products on the shelf, so that the inventory accurately reflects product availability.

Test your knowledge of pages 532 through 538 in Quiz Yourself 10-3.

QUIZ YOURSELF 10-3

Instructions: Find the true statement below. Then, rewrite the remaining false statements so they are true.

1. Data warehouses often use a process called OQL to find patterns and relationships among data.

2. Object-oriented databases store data in tables.

3. One type of program that manages the sending and receiving of data between the front end and the database server is a CGI script.

4. Relational database users refer to a file as a table, a record as a column, and a field as a row.

5. SQL is a data modeling language that allows users to manage, update, and retrieve data.

6. The database analyst requires a more technical inside view of the data than does the database administrator.

Quiz Yourself Online: To further check your knowledge of relational, object-oriented, and multidimensional databases; Web databases; and database administration, visit scsite.com/dc2008/ch10/quiz and then click Objectives 8 – 10.

CHAPTER SUMMARY

This chapter discussed how data and information are valuable assets to an organization (read Looking Ahead 10-2 for a look at the next generation of preserving data and information). The chapter also presented methods for maintaining high-quality data and assessing the quality of valuable information. It then discussed the advantages of organizing data in a database and described various types of databases. It also presented the roles of the database analysts and administrators.

 LOOKING AHEAD 10-2

Preserving Electronic Files for Future Generations

Historians and researchers are concerned that Web content and rare and unique electronic works may be lost forever because they exist only in digital form.

In an attempt to gather, organize, and preserve digital files, the United States Congress approved the *National Digital Information Infrastructure & Preservation Program* and commissioned The Library of Congress to supervise the project. Six digital formats have been identified: large Web sites, electronic journals, electronic books, digitally recorded sound, digital moving images, and digital television. The Library began a "Preserving Creative America" initiative in 2006 focusing on preserving television, radio, music, film, photography, pictorial art, and video games.

Library officials have partnered with industry and educational experts to discuss how to create and maintain the database. For more information, visit scsite.com/dc2008/ch10/looking and then click Preservation.

CAREER CORNER   Database Administrator

Most businesses and organizations are built around databases. Access to timely, accurate, and relevant information is a company's lifeline. A database administrator (DBA) creates, applies, supports, and administers the policies and procedures for maintaining a company's database. Database administrators construct logical and physical descriptions of the database, establish database parameters, develop data models characterizing data elements, ensure database integrity, and coordinate database security measures including developing and implementing disaster recovery and archiving procedures. They also use query languages to obtain reports of the information in the database. With the large amounts of sensitive data generated, data integrity, backup, and security have become increasingly important aspects of the administrator's responsibilities.

Administering a database requires a great deal of mental work and the ability to focus on finite details. Database administrators must be able to read and comprehend business related information, organize data in a logical manner, apply general rules to specific problems, identify business principles and practices, and communicate clearly with database users. Being proficient with a particular database such as Oracle, Informix, or SQL Server is an added advantage. The real key, however, is learning, understanding, and becoming an expert in database design.

Database administrators usually have a bachelor or associate degree and experience with computer programming, relational databases, query languages, and online analytical processing. Typical salaries for database administrators are between $74,000 and $96,000, depending on experience. For more information, visit scsite.com/dc2008/ch10/careers and then click Database Administrator.

High-Tech Talk

ENSURE CONSISTENCY OF YOUR DATA WITH NORMALIZATION

Normalization organizes a database into one of several normal forms to remove ambiguous relationships between data and minimize data redundancy. In *zero normal form* (*ONF*), the database is completely nonnormalized, and all of the data fields are included in one relation or table. Repeating groups are listed within parentheses (Figure 10-26a). The table has large rows due to the repeating groups and wastes disk space when an order has only one item.

To normalize the data from ONF to *1NF* (*first normal form*), you remove the repeating groups (fields 3 through 7 and 8 through 12) and place them in a second table (Figure 10-26b). You then assign a primary key to the second table (Line Item), by combining the primary key of the nonrepeating group (Order #) with the primary key of the repeating group (Product #). Primary keys are underlined to distinguish them from other fields.

To further normalize the database from 1NF to *2NF* (*second normal form*), you remove partial dependencies. A *partial dependency* exists when fields in the table depend on only part of the primary key. In the Line Item table (Figure 10-26b), Product Name is dependent on Product #, which is only part of the primary key. Second normal form requires you to place the product information in a separate Product table to remove the partial dependency (Figure 10-26c).

To move from 2NF to *3NF* (*third normal form*), you move transitive dependencies. A *transitive dependency* exists when a nonprimary key field depends on another nonprimary key field. As shown in Figure 10-26c, Vendor Name is dependent on Vendor #, both of which are nonprimary key fields. If Vendor Name is left in the Order table, the database will store redundant data each time a product is ordered from the same vendor.

Third normal form requires Vendor Name to be placed in a separate Vendor table, with Vendor # as the primary key. The field that is the primary key in the new table — in this case, Vendor # — also remains in the original table as a *foreign key* and is identified by a dotted underline (Figure 10-26d). In 3NF, the database now is logically organized in four separate tables and is easier to maintain. For instance, to add, delete, or change a Vendor or Product Name, you make the change in just one table. For more information, visit scsite.com/dc2008/ch10/tech and then click Normalization.

FIGURE 10-26
The process of normalizing a database.

Order Table

repeating group I · repeating group II

Order #	Order Date	Product #	Product Name	Qty Ordered	Vendor #	Vendor Name	Product #	Product Name	Qty Ordered	Vendor #	Vendor Name
1001	6/8/2008	605	8.5" x 11" White Copy Paper	2	321	Hammermill	203	CD Jewel Cases	5	110	Fellowes
1002	6/10/2008	751	Ballpoint Pens	6	166	Pilot					
1003	6/10/2008	321	1" Ring Binder, Blue	12	450	Globe					
1004	6/11/2008	605	8.5" x 11" White Copy Paper	2	321	Hammermill	102	Interior File Folders	2	450	Globe

(a) Zero Normal Form (ONF)
(Order #, Order Date, (Product #, Product Name, Quantity Ordered, Vendor #, Vendor Name))

(b) First Normal Form (1NF)
Order (Order #, Order Date)
Line Item (Order # + Product #, Product Name, Quantity Ordered, Vendor #, Vendor Name)

(c) Second Normal Form (2NF)
Order (Order #, Order Date)
Line Item (Order # + Product #, Quantity Ordered, Vendor #, Vendor Name)
Product (Product #, Product Name)

(d) Third Normal Form (3NF)
Order (Order #, Order Date)
Line Item (Order # + Product #, Quantity Ordered, Vendor #)
Product (Product #, Product Name)
Vendor (Vendor #, Vendor Name)

Order

Order #	Order Date
1001	6/8/2008
1002	6/10/2008
1003	6/10/2008
1004	6/11/2008

Line Item

Order # + Product #	Qty Ordered	Vendor #
1001605	2	321
1001203	5	110
1002751	6	166
1003321	12	450
1004605	2	321
1004102	2	450

Product

Product #	Product Name
102	Interior File Folders
203	CD Jewel Cases
321	1" Ring Binder, Blue
605	8.5" x 11" White Copy Paper
751	Ballpoint Pens

Vendor

Vendor #	Vendor Name
110	Fellowes
166	Pilot
321	Hammermill
450	Globe

Companies on the Cutting Edge

ORACLE
DATABASE SOFTWARE DEVELOPER

More than half of the FORTUNE 100 companies use an *Oracle* product as their primary database, but Oracle's quest, according to CEO Larry Ellison, is to have its customers convert all their database applications to Oracle's software.

Ellison and two partners founded the company in 1977 with the intent of developing a commercially viable relational database. When their Oracle database was released, it was an immediate success and changed the way companies stored and managed information. For the first time, separate data tables could be connected by a common field.

The company is the world's second largest independent software company behind Microsoft. Its announcement in 2006 to offer full support for Red Hat Linux customers is expected to broaden the success of Linux in the database community. For more information, visit scsite.com/dc2008/ch10/companies and then click Oracle.

SYBASE
MANAGING DATA FOR THE UNWIRED ENTERPRISE

Researchers at the University of California, Berkeley, estimate that 95 percent of the data produced by major corporations never is used after it is stored in a database because it is disorganized and inaccessible.

Sybase helps companies unlock and use this data whenever and wherever needed through its unwired enterprise. This data access solution helps mobile database users tap into corporate networks, often wirelessly. The company focuses especially on Enterprise Portal (EP) solutions, which convert stored data into information that can be used by customers, partners, and suppliers.

For more than 20 years, Sybase has produced software that links platforms, servers, databases, applications, and mobile devices. The company's acquisition of Mobile 365 in 2006 made Sybase the world's largest provider of mobile enterprise software and services. For more information, visit scsite.com/dc2008/ch10/companies and then click Sybase.

Technology Trailblazers

E. F. CODD
RELATIONAL DATABASE MODEL INVENTOR

The majority of large and small databases are structured on the relational model, which is considered one of the greatest technological inventions of the 20th Century. *E. F. Codd* single-handedly is credited with developing and promoting that model in a series of research papers beginning with his 1969 IBM Research Report, "Derivability, Redundancy, and Consistency of Relations Stored in Large Data Banks."

Edgar F. Codd began his career in 1949 when he joined IBM as a programming mathematician after graduating from Oxford University. Throughout the 1950s he helped develop several IBM computers and then turned his attention to database management. Among his achievements is earning the prestigious A. M. Turing Award, which is the Association for Computing Machinery's highest technical achievement honor given to an individual, for his relational database theory. For more information, visit scsite.com/dc2008/ch10/people and then click E. F. Codd.

LARRY ELLISON
ORACLE CEO

On a visit to Kyoto, Japan, *Larry Ellison* became intrigued with the country's culture and the citizens' combination of confidence and humility. He says he applies these philosophical principles to his work at Oracle, where he serves as CEO.

As a young man, Ellison was interested in science and mathematics. He was inspired by E. F. Codd's relational database model and founded Oracle in 1977 under the name Software Development Laboratories with a $1,200 investment.

Under Ellison's leadership, the company doubled its sales in 11 of its first 12 years. He is known for his uncanny ability to motivate his employees and business partners toward a common goal. He received the CRM (Customer Relationship Management) Market Award in 2006 for his successes in shaping and driving industry performance at the highest level. For more information, visit scsite.com/dc2008/ch10/people and then click Larry Ellison.

Chapter Review

The Chapter Review section summarizes the concepts presented in this chapter. To listen to the audio version of this Chapter Review, visit scsite.com/dc2008/ch10/review. To obtain help from other students regarding any subject in this chapter, visit scsite.com/dc2008/ch10/forum and post your thoughts or questions.

① What Is a Database? A **database** is a collection of data organized in a manner that allows access, retrieval, and use of that data. **Database software**, often called a **database management system** (**DBMS**), allows users to create a computerized database; add, change, and delete the data; sort and retrieve the data; and create forms and reports from the data.

② What Are the Qualities of Valuable Information? *Data* is a collection of unprocessed items, which can include text, numbers, images, audio, and video. Computers process data into information. *Information* is processed data; that is, it is organized, meaningful, and useful. For information to be valuable, it should be accurate, verifiable, timely, organized, accessible, useful, and cost-effective.

③ Why Is Data Important to an Organization? Because data is used to generate information, many companies realize that data is one of their more valuable assets. *Data integrity* identifies the quality of data. Data integrity is important because computers and people use information to make decisions and take actions. For a computer to produce correct information, the data that is entered in a database must have integrity.

④ What Is Meant by Character, Field, Record, and File? Data is classified in a hierarchy, with each level of data consisting of one or more items from the lower level. A bit is the smallest unit of data a computer can process. Eight bits grouped together in a unit form a byte, and each byte represents a single **character**. A **field** is a combination of one or more related characters and is the smallest unit of data a user accesses. A **record** is a group of related fields. A **data file** is a collection of related records stored on a storage medium such as a hard disk, CD, or DVD.

⑤ How Are Files Maintained? **File maintenance** refers to the procedures that keep data current. File maintenance procedures include adding records when new data is obtained, changing records to correct inaccurate data or to update old data with new data, and deleting records when they no longer are needed. **Validation** is the process of comparing data with a set of rules or values to find out if the data is correct. Many programs perform a *validity check* that analyzes entered data to help ensure that it is correct. Types of validity checks include an *alphabetic check*, a *numeric check*, a *range check*, a *consistency check*, a *completeness check*, and a *check digit*.

connect Visit scsite.com/dc2008/ch10/c or click the Quiz Yourself button. Click Objectives 1 – 5.

⑥ How Is a File Processing System Approach Different from the Database Approach? In a **file processing system**, each department or area within an organization has its own set of data files. Two major weaknesses of file processing systems are redundant data (duplicated data) and isolated data. With a **database approach**, many programs and users share the data in a database. The database approach reduces data redundancy, improves data integrity, shares data, permits easier access, and reduces development time. A database, however, can be more complex than a file processing system, requiring special training and more computer memory, storage, and processing power. Data in a database also is more vulnerable than data in file processing systems.

⑦ What Functions Are Common to Most DBMSs? Most DBMSs perform common functions. A **data dictionary** contains data about each file in the database and each field within those files. A DBMS offers several methods to maintain and retrieve data, such as query languages, query by example, forms, and report generators. A **query language** consists of simple, English-like

Chapter Review

statements that allow users to specify the data to display, print, or store. **Query by example (QBE)** has a graphical user interface that assists users with retrieving data. A **form** is a window on the screen that provides areas for entering or changing data. A **report generator** allows users to design a report on the screen, retrieve data into the report design, and then display or print the report. To supply security, most DBMSs can identify different levels of *access privileges* that define the actions a specific user or group of users can perform for each field in a database. If a database is damaged or destroyed, a DBMS provides techniques to return the database to a usable form. A **backup** is a copy of the database. A **log** is a listing of activities that change the contents of the database. A **recovery utility** uses the logs and/or backups to restore the database. *Continuous backup* is a backup plan in which all data is backed up whenever a change is made.

connect
Visit scsite.com/dc2008/ch10/quiz or click the Quiz Yourself button. Click Objectives 6 – 7.

(8) What Are Characteristics of Relational, Object-Oriented, and Multidimensional Databases?

A **data model** consists of rules and standards that define how the database organizes data. Three popular data models are relational, object-oriented, and multidimensional. A **relational database** stores data in tables that consist of rows and columns. A relational database developer refers to a file as a *relation*, a record as a *tuple*, and a field as an *attribute*. A relational database user refers to a file as a **table**, a record as a **row**, and a field as a **column**. A **relationship** is a connection within the data in a relational database. **Structured Query Language (SQL)** allows users to manage, update, and retrieve data. An **object-oriented database (OODB)** stores data in objects. An **object** is an item that contains data, as well as the actions that read or process the data. Applications appropriate for an object-oriented database include a *multimedia database*, a *groupware database*, a *computer-aided design (CAD) database*, a *hypertext database*, a *hypermedia database*, and a *Web database*. Object-oriented databases often use an *object query language (OQL)* to manipulate and retrieve data. A **multidimensional database** stores data in dimensions. These multiple dimensions, sometimes known as a *hypercube*, allow users to access and analyze any view of the database data. One application that uses multidimensional databases is a **data warehouse**, which is a huge database that stores and manages the data required to analyze historical and current transactions. No standard query language exists for multidimensional databases.

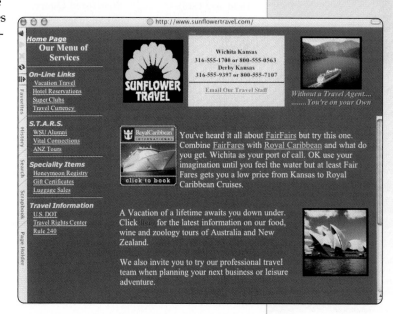

(9) How Do Web Databases Work?

To access data in a *Web database*, you fill in a form or enter search text on a Web page, which is the *front end* to the database. A Web database usually resides on a *database server*, which is a computer that stores and provides access to a database. One type of program that manages the sending and receiving of data between the front end and the database is a *CGI (Common Gateway Interface) script*.

(10) What Are the Responsibilities of Database Analysts and Administrators?

A **database analyst (DA)**, or *data modeler*, focuses on the meaning and usage of data. The DA decides on the placement of fields, defines data relationships, and identifies access privileges. A **database administrator (DBA)** requires a more technical view of the data. The DBA creates and maintains the data dictionary, manages database security, monitors database performance, and checks backup and recovery procedures.

connect
Visit scsite.com/dc2008/ch10/quiz or click the Quiz Yourself button. Click Objectives 8 – 10.

Key Terms

You should know the Primary Terms and be familiar with the Secondary Terms. Use the list below to help focus your study. To further enhance your understanding of the Key Terms in this chapter, visit scsite.com/dc2008/ch10/terms. See an example of and a definition for each term, and access current and additional information about the term from the Web.

Primary Terms

(shown in bold-black characters in the chapter)

backup (531)
character (518)
column (533)
data dictionary (527)
data file (519)
data model (532)
data type (518)
data warehouse (536)
database (514)
database administrator (DBA) (538)
database analyst (DA) (538)
database approach (524)
database management system (DBMS) (515)
database software (515)
field (518)
field name (518)
field size (518)
file maintenance (520)
file processing system (524)
form (530)

key field (519)
log (531)
multidimensional database (535)
object (534)
object-oriented database (OODB) (534)
primary key (519)
query (528)
query by example (QBE) (528)
query language (528)
record (519)
recovery utility (531)
relational database (533)
relationship (533)
report generator (530)
row (533)
Structured Query Language (SQL) (534)
table (533)
validation (522)

Secondary Terms

(shown in italic characters in the chapter)

access privileges (530)
accessible information (516)
accurate information (516)
after image (531)
alphabetic check (523)
alphanumeric (518)
attribute (533)
back end (525)
backward recovery (532)
before image (531)
BLOB (518)
Boolean (518)
CGI (Common Gateway Interface) script (537)
check digit (523)
collaborative databases (536)
completeness check (523)
computer-aided design (CAD) database (534)
consistency check (523)
continuous backup (532)
cost-effective information (517)
data (514)
data entry form (530)
data integrity (516)
data mart (536)
data mining (536)
data modeler (538)
database server (537)
default value (528)
distributed database (536)
e-form (530)
electronic form (530)

forward recovery (532)
front end (525)
garbage in, garbage out (GIGO) (516)
GIS (534)
groupware database (534)
hypercube (535)
hypermedia database (534)
hypertext database (534)
information (514)
metadata (527)
multimedia database (534)
normalization (534)
numeric check (523)
object query language (OQL) (535)
object-relational databases (532)
organized information (516)
range check (523)
relation (533)
report writer (530)
repository (527)
rollback (532)
rollforward (532)
timely information (516)
tuple (533)
useful information (517)
validation rules (522)
validity check (522)
verifiable information (516)
Web database (534)

Checkpoint

Use the Checkpoint exercises to check your knowledge level of the chapter. The Beyond the Book exercises will help broaden your understanding of the concepts presented in this chapter. To complete the Checkpoint exercises interactively, visit scsite.com/dc2008/ch10/check.

Label the Figure

Identify the database elements.

a. form

b. column

c. relationships

d. table

e. row

True/False

Mark T for True and F for False. (See page numbers in parentheses.)

_____ 1. Data is a collection of unprocessed items, which can include text, numbers, images, audio, and video. (514)

_____ 2. A database management system allows users to create forms and reports from the data in the database. (515)

_____ 3. A character is the smallest unit of data a computer can process. (518)

_____ 4. The data in a key field is the same for every record in a file. (519)

_____ 5. Validation is the process of comparing data with a set of rules or values to find out if the data is correct. (522)

_____ 6. A check digit often confirms the accuracy of a primary key value. (523)

_____ 7. Databases require less memory, storage, and processing power than a file processing system. (526)

_____ 8. To retrieve or select data in a database, you normalize it. (528)

_____ 9. A relationship is a connection within the data in a database. (533)

_____ 10. The data in a distributed database exists in many separate locations throughout a network or the Internet. (536)

Checkpoint

Multiple Choice Select the best answer. (See page numbers in parentheses.)

1. Data _____ identifies the quality of data. (516)
   a. security
   b. modeling
   c. integrity
   d. mining

2. _____ information has an age suited to its use. (516)
   a. Timely
   b. Organized
   c. Cost-effective
   d. Verifiable

3. Accessible information _____. (516)
   a. is error free
   b. has an age suited to its use
   c. has meaning to the person who receives it
   d. is available when the decision maker needs it

4. The _____ data type is used for lengthy text entries. (518)
   a. memo
   b. numeric
   c. hyperlink
   d. data

5. A _____ is a field that uniquely identifies each record in a file. (519)
   a. primary key
   b. data file
   c. data type
   d. data character

6. A range check _____. (523)
   a. ensures that users enter only alphabetic data into a field
   b. determines whether a number is within a specified range
   c. ensures that users enter only numeric data into a field
   d. verifies that a required field contains data

7. All of the following are strengths of the database approach, except _____. (525)
   a. less complexity
   b. improved data integrity
   c. easier access
   d. reduced development time

8. Because the _____ contains details about data, some call it metadata (meta means more comprehensive). (527)
   a. data mart
   b. data warehouse
   c. data modeler
   d. data dictionary

9. _____ has a graphical user interface that assists users with retrieving data. (528)
   a. A query language
   b. Query by example (QBE)
   c. A report generator
   d. A form

10. A _____ is a window on the screen that provides areas for entering or changing data in a database. (530)
    a. repository
    b. query
    c. report
    d. form

11. A developer of a database refers to a field as a(n) _____. (533)
    a. tuple
    b. record
    c. attribute
    d. relation

12. A file in a relational database is sometimes referred to as a(n) _____. (533)
    a. tuple
    b. after image
    c. object
    d. relation

13. A developer of a database sometimes refers to a record as a(n) _____. (533)
    a. tuple
    b. collaborative database
    c. DBMS
    d. relational database

14. The database analyst (DA) _____. (538)
    a. decides on the proper placement of fields
    b. creates and maintains the data dictionary
    c. monitors the performance of the database
    d. checks backup and recovery procedures

Checkpoint

Matching

Match the terms with their definitions. (See page numbers in parentheses.)

____ 1. database (514)

____ 2. field name (518)

____ 3. field size (518)

____ 4. data type (518)

____ 5. default value (528)

____ 6. backup (531)

____ 7. GIS (534)

____ 8. hypertext database (534)

____ 9. data modeler (538)

____ 10. database administrator (538)

a. a database that contains text links to other types of documents

b. smaller version of a data warehouse

c. defines the maximum number of characters a field can contain

d. database that stores maps and other geographic data

e. person who focuses on the meaning and usage of data

f. collection of data organized in a manner that allows access, retrieval, and use of that data

g. value that a DBMS initially displays in a field

h. uniquely identifies each field

i. specifies the kind of data a field can contain and how the field is used

j. an entire copy of the database

k. creates and maintains the data dictionary, manages security of the database, monitors the performance of the database, and checks backup and recovery procedures

Short Answer

Write a brief answer to each of the following questions.

1. How is a field different from a record? _____ What is a data file? _____

2. What is validation? _____ What are five types of validity checks? _____

3. Why is data redundancy a weakness of file processing systems? _____ How does the database approach reduce data redundancy? _____

4. What is contained in a data dictionary? _____ How does a query language differ from query by example (QBE)? _____

5. Describe multidimensional databases and their uses. _____ What is a data warehouse and how is it used? _____

Beyond the Book

Read the following book elements, learn more about each using the Web, and then write a brief report.

1. Ethics & Issues — Are Portable Storage Devices a Threat to Businesses? (516), Is a National Identification Card Necessary for the Security of the Nation? (519), Should States Share Criminal Databases? (525), Would You Carry a Contactless Smart Card? (531), or Can the Government Be Trusted with Personal Data? (537)

2. Career Corner — Database Administrator (539)

3. Companies on the Cutting Edge — Oracle or Sybase (541)

4. FAQs (517, 519, 526, 527, 533, 535, 537, 538)

5. High-Tech Talk — Ensure Consistency of Your Data with Normalization (540)

6. Looking Ahead — Archive an Entire Lifetime (528) or Preserving Electronic Files for Future Generations (539)

7. Making Use of the Web — Science (126)

8. Picture Yourself Using Databases (512)

9. Technology Trailblazers — E. F. Codd or Larry Ellison (541)

10. Web Links (516, 526, 528, 532, 534, 535, 536, 538)

Learn It Online

Use the Learn It Online exercises to reinforce your understanding of the chapter concepts. To access the Learn It Online exercises, visit scsite.com/dc2008/ch10/learn.

① At the Movies — How a Photo Sharing Site Keeps Its Data

To view the How a Photo Sharing Site Keeps Its Data movie, click the number 1 button. Locate your video and click the corresponding High-Speed or Dial-Up link, depending on your Internet connection. Watch the movie and then complete the exercise by answering the question that follows. Visit Equinix, the data storage site for Smugmug.com, and learn how photos are uploaded and shared on the Web. How does the photo sharing community Smugmug.com store and allow users to share photos?

② Video and Audio: You Review It — Web Databases

In this chapter you learned about Web databases. Click the number 2 button to view the suggested links and begin your search for videos, podcasts, or vodcasts related to Web databases. Choose a video, podcast, or vodcast that discusses Web databases and is of interest to you, and then write a description of its contents. Explain why you chose this piece, what you liked about it, what you disliked about it, and whether you would recommend it to a fellow student. Finish your review by giving the video, podcast, or vodcast a rating of 1 – 5 stars. Submit your review in the format requested by your instructor.

③ Student Edition Labs — Advanced Databases

Click the number 3 button. A new browser window will open, displaying the Student Edition Labs. Follow the on-screen instructions to complete the Advanced Databases Lab. When finished, click the Exit button. If required, submit your results to your instructor.

④ Student Edition Labs — Advanced Spreadsheets

Click the number 4 button. A new browser window will open, displaying the Student Edition Labs. Follow the on-screen instructions to complete the Advanced Spreadsheets Lab. When finished, click the Exit button. If required, submit your results to your instructor.

⑤ Practice Test

Click the number 5 button. Answer each question. When completed, enter your name and click the Grade Test button to submit the quiz for grading. Make a note of any missed questions. If required, submit your results to your instructor.

⑥ Who Wants To Be a Computer Genius²?

Click the number 6 button to find out if you are a computer genius. Directions about how to play the game will be displayed. When you are ready to play, click the Play button. Submit your score to your instructor.

Learn It Online

Wheel of Terms

Click the number 7 button to reinforce important terms you learned in this chapter by playing the Shelly Cashman Series version of this popular game. Directions about how to play the game will be displayed. When you are ready to play, click the Play button. Submit your score to your instructor.

8 DC Track and Field

Click the number 8 button to use what you have learned in this chapter to compete against other students in three track and field events. Directions about how to play the game will be displayed. When you are ready to play, click the start first event button. If required, submit your score to your instructor.

You're Hired!

Click the number 9 button to use what you have learned in this chapter to embark on the path to a career in computers. Directions about how to play the game will be displayed. When you are ready to play, click the begin game button. If required, submit your score to your instructor.

10 Crossword Puzzle Challenge

Click the number 10 button, then click the Crossword Puzzle Challenge link. Directions about how to play the game will be displayed. Complete the puzzle to reinforce skills you learned in this chapter. When you are ready to play, click the Continue button. Submit the completed puzzle to your instructor.

Vista Exercises

Click the number 11 button. When the Vista Exercises menu appears, click the exercise assigned by your instructor. A new browser window will open. Follow the on-screen instructions to complete the exercise. When finished, click the Exit button. If required, submit your results to your instructor.

12 In the News

To spare harried dispatchers, police officers used to request suspect information only when it was urgent. Now, IBM's eNetwork Law Enforcement Express lets officers directly access real-time databases of stolen cars, mug shots, and warrants. With a few taps on a notebook computer keyboard, police officers can search a database to see if a suspect in custody has a past criminal record. They also can find out if a suspect stopped for speeding is wanted for any more serious infractions. Click the number 12 button and read a news article about a database that is being used in a new way. Who is using the database? How is it being used? How will the database benefit the user?

13 Chapter Discussion Forum

Select an objective from this chapter on page 513 about which you would like more information. Click the number 13 button and post a short message listing a meaningful message title accompanied by one or more questions concerning the selected objective. In two days, return to the threaded discussion by clicking the number 13 button. Submit to your instructor your original message and at least one response to your message.

Financial Calculators

Click the number 14 button to learn how to use the Internet to calculate a mortgage payment, car payment, or retirement savings. Follow the instructions to use USA Today's Mortgaged calculator to determine what your monthly payment would be on a $150,000 mortgage calculated over 30 years using an interest rate of 5.5%. Use the Autos calculator to figure your monthly payment on a $20,000 auto loan calculated over 60 months using an interest rate of 7.75%. Use the Retirement calculator to determine what type of retirement savings plan will provide you with the most income. Print each calculation result and then submit it to your instructor.

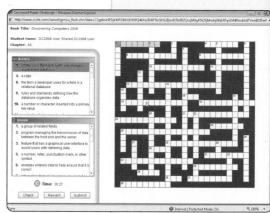

Discovering Computers 2008

Learn How To

Use the Learn How To activities to learn fundamental skills when using a computer and accompanying technology. Complete the exercises and submit them to your instructor. To see a video of a Learn How To activity, visit scsite.com/dc2008/ch10/howto.

LEARN HOW TO 1: Organize and Manage Files on a Computer

Introduction In Learn How To 1 in Chapter 3 (page 178), you learned the procedure for saving a file. In this Learn How To activity, you will learn how to manage files using folders and how to find a file if you cannot remember where you saved it.

Folders A folder is a virtual container where you can store a file on media. When you store any file, the file must be stored in a folder. The folder symbol, together with the folder name, identifies a folder.

You can create folders in a variety of ways. To create a folder on the desktop, complete the following steps:
1. Right-click the desktop in a location that does not contain an icon or toolbar.
2. Point to New on the shortcut menu that is displayed (Figure 10-27).
3. Click Folder on the New submenu.
4. When the folder icon is displayed on the desktop, type the name you want to assign to the folder and then press the ENTER key. You should choose a name that identifies the contents of the folder.

FIGURE 10-27

A folder can contain other folders. This allows you to organize your files in a hierarchical manner so that the highest-level folder contains all the folders for a given subject, and lower-level folders contain more specific files and folders. For example, your highest-level folder could be named Fall Semester. For each class, such as Computer Information Systems 110, you could define a folder within the Fall Semester folder. Within each class folder, you could define folders for each week of the class, or for each project or assignment within the class. In this manner, you would have a set of folders, each designated for a specific use. You then would save your files in the appropriate folder.

To create a folder within a folder, complete the following steps:
1. Double-click the folder name either on the desktop or in the window or dialog box in which the folder name appears.
2. Right-click a blank space in the window that is displayed.
3. Point to New on the shortcut menu that is displayed and then click Folder on the New submenu.
4. When the folder icon is displayed, type the name you want to assign to the folder, and then press the ENTER key.

To delete a folder, complete the following steps:
1. Right-click the folder.
2. On the shortcut menu that is displayed (Figure 10-28), click Delete.
3. In the Delete Folder dialog box, click the Yes button.

FIGURE 10-28

Learn How To

When you delete a folder, all the files and folders contained in the folder you are deleting, together with all files and folders on the lower hierarchical levels, are deleted. If you accidentally delete a folder, complete the following steps:

1. Double-click the Recycle Bin icon on the desktop.
2. In the Recycle Bin window, select the folder you wish to restore.
3. Click the Restore this item button.

Using folders effectively will aid you in keeping track of files you create for your classes.

Exercise

1. Assume you are taking the following courses: Computer Information Systems 120, History 210, English 145, Marketing 221, and Business Law 120. Define the hierarchy of folders you would create for these classes. In which folder would you store an assignment from English 145 that was assigned in the sixth week of class? Submit your answers to your instructor.

LEARN HOW TO 2: Search for Files and Folders

At times, you might store a file in a folder and then forget where you stored the file. The Search feature of Windows Vista enables you to search storage media on a computer to find the file. To use the Search feature, complete the following steps:

1. Click the Start button on the Windows taskbar.
2. Click Search on the Start menu.
3. If necessary, click the All filter button.
4. In the Search box, type the name of the file for which you are searching. If you do not know the entire file name, enter as much of the file name as you can remember. If you do not know any portion of the file name, click the Advanced Search button to help narrow the search.
5. If you are performing an Advanced Search, click the Search button to begin the search. Otherwise, Windows will search as you type your search criteria into the Search box (Figure 10-29).
6. All items containing the file name or partial file name will be displayed in the Search Results in Indexed Locations window to open the file with the appropriate program.
7. Double-click the file name in the list to open the file with the appropriate program.
8. Before you close the Search Results in Indexed Locations window, make a note of the location of the file. If this is not the location where you want the file to be stored, store the file in the correct location.

FIGURE 10-29

Exercise

1. Using the Windows Vista Search feature, locate the file named Green Sea Turtle. How many file names were returned? Which folder contains the Green Sea Turtle file? Submit your answers to your instructor.

2. On the computer you are using, create a hierarchy of folders for your classes. Create a WordPad file that contains the following text: This file will be found using the Search feature. Save the file in one of the folders using a file name of your choice. Using the Search feature, search for the file you just created. How many files were returned from your search? Delete all folders and files you created in this exercise. Write a paragraph describing the steps you will take to organize your files for the coming semester. Submit your responses to your instructor.

Web Research

Use the Internet-based Web Research exercises to broaden your understanding of the concepts presented in this chapter. Visit scsite.com/dc2008/ch10/research to obtain more information pertaining to each exercise. To discuss any of the Web Research exercises in this chapter with other students, post your thoughts or questions at scsite.com/dc2008/ch10/forum.

(1) Scavenger Hunt Use one of the <u>search engines</u> listed in Figure 2-10 in Chapter 2 on page 78 or your own favorite search engine to find the answers to the questions that follow. Copy and paste the Web address from the Web page where you found the answer. Some questions may have more than one answer. If required, submit your answers to your instructor. (1) Who is Michael Stonebraker? What is the name of the relational database system he helped to create in the 1970s? (2) What geographic information system (GIS) functions does ArcExplorer perform? (3) What company that was incorporated in 1911 developed the relational database? (4) What is Globalis? What organization supplies the statistics for the database? (5) What is the purpose of the European Union (EU) directive?

(2) Search Sleuth Major United States newspapers helped design <u>Clusty</u> the Clustering Engine (clusty.com). One of its unique features is returning search results for Web sites, news stories, images, and shopping sites in clusters, which are categories of folders, along with a list of links. Visit this Web site and then use your word processing program to answer the following questions. Then, if required, submit your answers to your instructor. (1) Click the About link at the bottom of the page, then click the FAQ link. What search engines does Clusty include in its metasearches? (2) Click your browser's Back button or press the BACKSPACE key to return to the Clusty home page. Type `multidimensional database` in the box and then click the Search button. Review the listing of clusters on the left side of the page and then click the Database Systems link. How many results are listed? (3) Click the News link at the top of the page and then click the Top News link. What are two stories listed for today? (4) Click the Business link and review the articles. Write a 50-word summary of your findings.

(3) Journaling Respond to your readings in this chapter by writing at least one page about your reactions, evaluations, and reflections on databases. For example, what experiences have you had completing online forms? Do you use any database management systems, such as Microsoft Access? If so, for what purposes? Have you worked in a job that required you to retrieve or select information from a database? Should Americans have a <u>national identification card</u>? You also can write about the new terms you learned by reading this chapter. If required, submit your journal to your instructor.

(4) Expanding Your Understanding Public records contain details about professional licenses, civil court filings, adoptions, foreclosures, driving records, and much other personal data. The Internet makes searching for this data quite easy, and many of the databases can be browsed for free. One of the more comprehensive free public records databases is the <u>Search Systems Public Records Directories</u>. View Web sites to learn more about searching public records. Which databases are free, and which require a subscription fee? What state records are available where you live? Write a report summarizing your findings, focusing on searching the public records databases. If required, submit your report to your instructor.

(5) Ethics in Action When you shop online, enter contests, and complete warranty registration cards, businesses automatically store data about you and your transactions in a marketing database. They often use this data to analyze sales and develop advertising campaigns. Unbeknownst to many consumers, some companies also sell this data to third parties for financial gain. Consumers can refuse to receive targeted e-mail messages and marketing materials, but they actively must search the Web sites or paper forms for check boxes to indicate these opt-out preferences. Some privacy experts, however, view this practice as unethical and urge businesses to default to not adding consumers' information to databases unless the consumer opts in to receive additional materials. View online sites that include <u>opt-in</u> or <u>opt-out</u> provisions. Write a report summarizing your findings, and include a table of links to Web sites that provide additional details about protecting consumers' data. If required, submit your report to your instructor.

Case Studies

Use the Case Studies to apply the concepts presented in the chapter to real-world situations. Visit scsite.com/dc2008/ch10/cases to obtain more information pertaining to each exercise. To discuss the Case Studies in this chapter with other students, visit scsite.com/dc2008/ch10/forum and post your thoughts or questions.

CASE STUDY 1 — Class Discussion   While attending college, you work 20 hours a week as an instructor's assistant. You earn $8.00 an hour and are paid every two weeks. You recently received a payroll check that was $160.00 less than you expected for 40 hours of work. What error do you think the data entry clerk made that resulted in the wrong check being generated? Errors such as the one illustrated here show why **data integrity** is as important to a successful information management system as the hardware and software being used. The phrase garbage in, garbage out (GIGO) has been used to explain that you cannot create correct information from incorrect data. Write a brief report that includes your suggestion regarding the error made by the data entry clerk, and summarize the various data validation techniques described in this chapter. Be prepared to discuss your findings in class.

CASE STUDY 2 — Class Discussion   Reviews of movies on a video store's new release shelf are fairly easy to find, but critiques of other movies in stock may be less accessible. To help film buffs, information on more than 100,000 movie titles is available from a database on the World Wide Web. The Internet Movie Database Ltd. can be searched using a movie's title, cast members, year produced, characters, genre, awards, or other criteria. Each movie's page offers a brief description and rating and includes links to such items as stars, summary, trivia, reviews, quotes, goofs, and recommendations. Visit the movie database and write a brief report outlining how visitors can **query** the movie database. Search for several movies. How complete was the information provided? Who would benefit most from using the movie database? Why? Be prepared to discuss your findings in class.

CASE STUDY 3 — Research   The ability to create intelligent machines has intrigued humans since ancient times. Many see the computer as the answer and the means to create artificial intelligence (AI). AI consists of two schools of thought; Conventional AI and Computational Intelligence (CI). Conventional AI has several categories. These include **expert systems**, case-based reasoning, Bayesian networks, and behavior-based AI. CI categories include neural networks, fuzzy systems, and evolutionary computation. Select one of these categories to research. What is the relationship of AI to databases? Write a brief report or use PowerPoint to create a presentation and share your findings with your class.

CASE STUDY 4 — Research   You recently were hired as a student intern to assist a local insurance agency in reorganizing their customer files. The agency employs a file processing system to maintain three distinct customer files — billing, claims, and promotion. The manager indicates that data entry has become unwieldy because of unclear relationships between data and data redundancy. Furthermore, customers are complaining about inconsistencies in the information they receive. The problem is beginning to affect business in a negative way. As a first step, she has asked you to prepare a report summarizing the benefits of **normalizing** the data in the three files. Use the Web and/or print media and High-Tech Talk on page 540 to gain an understanding of the normalization process. What is zero normal form? First normal form? Second normal form? Third normal form? Define and give an example of each of the following terms: data redundancy, primary key, and repeating group. Write a brief report or use PowerPoint to create a presentation and share your findings with your class.

CASE STUDY 5 — Team Challenge   When deciding on which database management system to use, companies have a choice of three **data models** — relational, object-oriented, and multidimensional. A major retail company has hired your team as database specialists to determine the data model best suited for their applications. Form a three-member team and have each team member choose a different data model. Have each member use the Web and/or print media to develop a feature/benefit report for each data model. Does the data model allow for query by example? How does the data model allow users to manage, update, and retrieve data? As a team, merge your findings into a team report and/or PowerPoint presentation and share your findings with your class.

COMPUTER SECURITY RISKS

Today, people rely on computers to create, store, and manage critical information. Thus, it is important that the computers and the data they store are accessible and available when needed. It also is crucial that users take measures to protect their computers and data from loss, damage, and misuse. For example, businesses must ensure that information such as credit records, employee and customer data, and purchase information is secure and confidential. Home users must ensure that their credit card number is secure when they use it to purchase goods and services from Web-based businesses.

A **computer security risk** is any event or action that could cause a loss of or damage to computer hardware, software, data, information, or processing capability. Some breaches to computer security are accidental. Others are planned intrusions. Some intruders do no damage; they merely access data, information, or programs on the computer before logging off. Other intruders indicate some evidence of their presence either by leaving a message or by deliberately altering or damaging data.

An intentional breach of computer security often involves a deliberate act that is against the law. Any illegal act involving a computer generally is referred to as a **computer crime**. The term **cybercrime** refers to online or Internet-based illegal acts. Today, cybercrime is one of the FBI's top three priorities.

Perpetrators of cybercrime and other intrusions fall into seven basic categories: hacker, cracker, script kiddie, corporate spy, unethical employee, cyberextortionist, and cyberterrorist.

- The term **hacker**, although originally a complimentary word for a computer enthusiast, now has a derogatory meaning and refers to someone who accesses a computer or network illegally. Hackers often claim the intent of their security breaches is to improve security.
- A **cracker** also is someone who accesses a computer or network illegally but has the intent of destroying data, stealing information, or other malicious action. Both hackers and crackers have advanced computer and network skills.
- A **script kiddie** has the same intent as a cracker but does not have the technical skills and knowledge. Script kiddies often are teenagers that use prewritten hacking and cracking programs to break into computers.
- Some **corporate spies** have excellent computer and network skills and are hired to break into a specific computer and steal its proprietary data and information. Unscrupulous companies hire corporate spies, a practice known as corporate espionage, to gain a competitive advantage.
- Unethical employees break into their employers' computers for a variety of reasons. Some simply want to exploit a security weakness. Others seek financial gains from selling confidential information. Disgruntled employees may want revenge.

Internet and network attacks

VIRUS ATTACK

system failure

LIGHTNING STRIKE

STOLEN IDENTITY

information theft

- A **cyberextortionist** is someone who uses e-mail as a vehicle for extortion. These perpetrators send a company a threatening e-mail message indicating they will expose confidential information, exploit a security flaw, or launch an attack that will compromise the company's network — if they are not paid a sum of money.
- A **cyberterrorist** is someone who uses the Internet or network to destroy or damage computers for political reasons. The extensive damage might destroy the nation's air traffic control system, electricity-generating companies, or a telecommunications infrastructure. Cyberterrorism usually requires a team of highly skilled individuals, millions of dollars, and several years of planning.

Business and home users must protect, or safeguard, their computers from breaches of security and other computer security risks. The more common computer security risks include Internet and network attacks, unauthorized access and use, hardware theft, software theft, information theft, and system failure (Figure 11-1). The following pages describe these computer security risks and also discuss safeguards users might take to minimize or prevent their consequences.

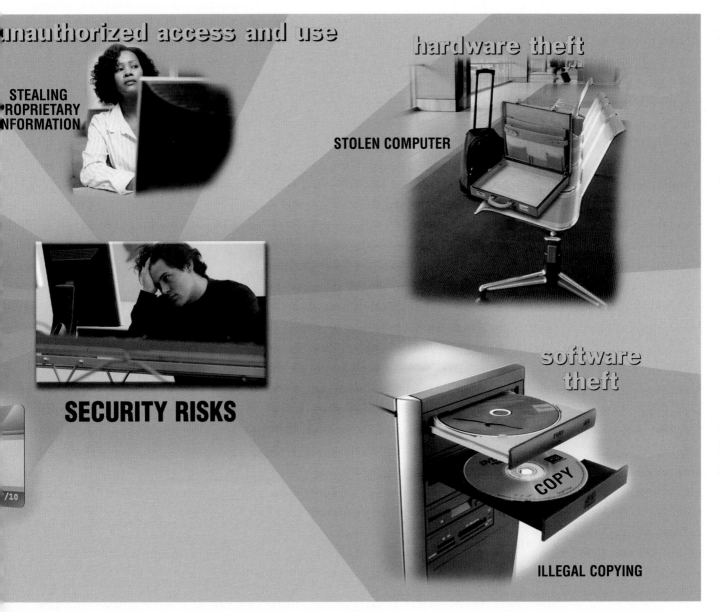

FIGURE 11-1 Computers are exposed to several types of security risks.

INTERNET AND NETWORK ATTACKS

Information transmitted over networks has a higher degree of security risk than information kept on a company's premises. In a business, network administrators usually take measures to protect a network from security risks. On the Internet, where no central administrator is present, the security risk is greater.

To determine if your computer is vulnerable to an Internet or network attack, you could use an online security service. An **online security service** is a Web site that evaluates your computer to check for Internet and e-mail vulnerabilities. The service then provides recommendations of how to address the vulnerabilities.

Companies and individuals requiring assistance or information about Internet security breaches can contact or visit the Web site for the *Computer Emergency Response Team Coordination Center,* or *CERT/CC,* which is a federally funded Internet security research and development center.

Internet and network attacks that jeopardize security include computer viruses, worms, and Trojan horses; botnets; denial of service attacks; back doors; and spoofing. The following pages address these computer security risks and suggest measures businesses and individuals can take to protect their computers while on the Internet or connected to a network.

Computer Viruses, Worms, and Trojan Horses

Every unprotected computer is susceptible to the first type of computer security risk — a computer virus, worm, and/or Trojan horse.

- A computer **virus** is a potentially damaging computer program that affects, or infects, a computer negatively by altering the way the computer works without the user's knowledge or permission. Once the virus infects the computer, it can spread throughout and may damage files and system software, including the operating system.
- A **worm** is a program that copies itself repeatedly, for example in memory or on a network, using up resources and possibly shutting down the computer or network.
- A **Trojan horse** (named after the Greek myth) is a program that hides within or looks like a legitimate program. A certain condition or action usually triggers the Trojan horse. Unlike a virus or worm, a Trojan horse does not replicate itself to other computers.

Computer viruses, worms, and Trojan horses are classified as *malware* (short for *malicious software*), which are programs that act without a user's knowledge and deliberately alter the computer's operations. Other classes of malware include back doors and spyware, which are discussed later in this chapter. Although malware often falls in one of these classes (virus, worm, Trojan horse, back door, or spyware), some malware has characteristics of two or more classes. For example, MyDoom and Blaster are worms; Melissa has elements of a virus, worm, and Trojan horse.

Unscrupulous programmers write malware and then test it to ensure it can deliver its payload (read Ethics & Issues 11-1 for a related discussion). The *payload* is the destructive event or prank the program is intended to deliver. A computer infected by a virus, worm, or Trojan horse often has one or more of the following symptoms:

- Screen displays unusual message or image
- Music or unusual sound plays randomly
- Available memory is less than expected
- Existing programs and files disappear
- Files become corrupted

WEB LINK 11-1

Computer Emergency Response Team Coordination Center

For more information, visit scsite.com/dc2008/ch11/weblink and then click Computer Emergency Response Team Coordination Center.

ETHICS & ISSUES 11-1

How Should Virus Authors Be Punished?

Recently, the author of an Internet virus that caused millions or billions of dollars in alleged damages pleaded guilty to the crime and faced 18 to 37 months in prison — about the same as that for auto theft. The author of the Sasser worm, which shut down an airline, hospitals, and government agencies, was sentenced to 21 months of probation after causing a similar amount of damage. Many experts and computer administrators claim that the punishment for the crime is out of proportion with the damages caused by the crime. Some legal experts claim that lax security on the part of Internet users is to blame, and perhaps those who help to spread the viruses via lax security should be punished as well. Others claim that some companies provide exorbitant estimates of true damages that viruses cause and that these alleged damages provoke an emotional overreaction to the crimes. The types of crimes and international extent of possible damages is relatively new territory in criminal law. Should the government create new laws specifically aimed at punishing those who spread viruses and worms? Why or why not? Should virus authors be punished in proportion to the alleged damages that they cause? Why or why not? Because the Internet is an international medium, how should countries coordinate law enforcement and punishment for virus authors?

- Programs or files do not work properly
- Unknown programs or files mysteriously appear
- System properties change

Computer viruses, worms, and Trojan horses deliver their payload on a computer in four basic ways: when a user (1) opens an infected file, (2) runs an infected program, (3) boots the computer with infected removable media inserted in a drive or plugged in a port, or (4) connects an unprotected computer to a network. Today, a common way computers become infected with viruses, worms, and Trojan horses is through users opening infected e-mail attachments. Figure 11-2 shows how a virus can spread from one computer to another through an infected e-mail attachment.

Currently, more than 180,000 known viruses, worms, and Trojan horse programs exist. Many Web sites maintain lists of all known viruses, worms, and Trojan horses. For a technical discussion about viruses, worms, and Trojan horses, read the High-Tech Talk article on page 168 in Chapter 3.

 FAQ 11-1

How long is an unprotected computer safe from intruders?

One security expert maintains that unprotected computers are compromised by an intruder within 12 minutes, on average. It is possible, however, for an unprotected computer to become infected within seconds of connecting it to a network. Slammer and Nimda, two devastating worms, wreaked worldwide havoc in 10 and 30 minutes, respectively. For more information, visit scsite.com/dc2008/ch11/faq and then click Viruses and Worms.

FIGURE 11-2 HOW A VIRUS CAN SPREAD THROUGH AN E-MAIL MESSAGE

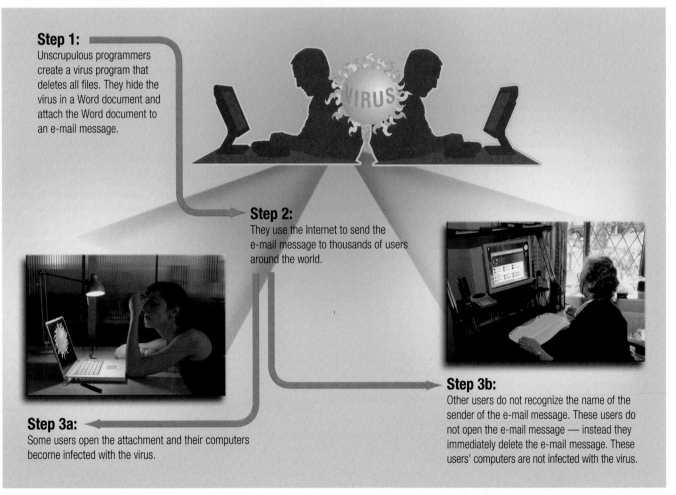

Step 1:
Unscrupulous programmers create a virus program that deletes all files. They hide the virus in a Word document and attach the Word document to an e-mail message.

Step 2:
They use the Internet to send the e-mail message to thousands of users around the world.

Step 3a:
Some users open the attachment and their computers become infected with the virus.

Step 3b:
Other users do not recognize the name of the sender of the e-mail message. These users do not open the e-mail message — instead they immediately delete the e-mail message. These users' computers are not infected with the virus.

Safeguards against Computer Viruses, Worms, and Trojan Horses

Methods that guarantee a computer or network is safe from computer viruses, worms, and Trojan horses simply do not exist. Users can take several precautions, however, to protect their home and work computers from these malicious infections. The following paragraphs discuss these precautionary measures.

Do not start a computer with removable media inserted in the drives or plugged in the ports. That is, CD and DVD drives should be empty, a USB port should not contain a USB flash drive, etc. During the startup process, a computer may attempt to execute the boot sector on media in certain drives and ports. Even if the attempt is unsuccessful, any virus on the boot sector of removable media can infect the computer's hard disk. If you must start the computer with media in a drive or port, be certain the media are uninfected.

Never open an e-mail attachment unless you are expecting the attachment *and* it is from a trusted source. A **trusted source** is a company or person you believe will not send a virus-infected file knowingly. If the e-mail message is from an unknown source or untrusted source, delete the e-mail message immediately — without opening or executing any attachments. If the e-mail message is from a trusted source, but you were not expecting an attachment, verify with the source that they intended to send you an attachment — before opening it.

Many e-mail programs allow users to preview an e-mail message before or without opening it. Some viruses and worms can deliver their payload when a user simply previews the message. Thus, you should turn off message preview in your e-mail program.

Some viruses are hidden in *macros*, which are instructions saved in software such as a word processing or spreadsheet program. In programs that allow users to write macros, you should set the macro security level (Figure 11-3a) so the application software warns users that a document they are attempting to open contains a macro (Figure 11-3b). From this warning, a user chooses to disable or enable the macro. If the document is from a trusted source, the user can enable the macro. Otherwise, it should be disabled.

Users should install an antivirus program and update it frequently. As discussed in Chapter 8, an **antivirus program** protects a computer against viruses by identifying and removing any computer viruses found in memory, on storage media, or on incoming files. Most antivirus programs also protect against worms, Trojan horses, and spyware. When you purchase a new computer, it often includes antivirus software. The table in Figure 11-4 lists popular antivirus programs.

An antivirus program scans for programs that attempt to modify the boot program, the operating system, and other programs that normally are read from but not modified. In addition, many antivirus programs automatically scan files downloaded from the Web, e-mail attachments, opened files, and all types of removable media inserted in the computer.

FIGURE 11-3a (set macro security)

FIGURE 11-3 Many application programs, such as Microsoft Word, allow users to set security levels for macros.

FIGURE 11-3b (warning is displayed because of macro security level)

POPULAR ANTIVIRUS PROGRAMS

- AVG Anti-Virus
- avast! antivirus
- CA Anti-Virus
- F-Secure Anti-Virus
- Kaspersky Anti-Virus
- McAfee VirusScan
- Norton AntiVirus
- Trend Micro Antivirus
- Vexira Antivirus

FIGURE 11-4 Popular antivirus programs.

One technique that antivirus programs use to identify a virus is to look for virus signatures. A **virus signature**, also called a **virus definition**, is a known specific pattern of virus code. Computer users should update their antivirus program's signature files regularly. Updating signature files downloads any new virus definitions that have been added since the last update. This extremely important activity allows the antivirus program to protect against viruses written since the antivirus program was released. Most antivirus programs contain an automatic update feature that regularly prompts users to download the virus signature. The vendor usually provides this service to registered users at no cost for a specified time.

Another technique that antivirus programs use to detect viruses is to inoculate existing program files. To **inoculate** a program file, the antivirus program records information such as the file size and file creation date in a separate inoculation file. The antivirus program then uses this information to detect if a virus tampers with the data describing the inoculated program file.

If an antivirus program identifies an infected file, it attempts to remove its virus, worm, or Trojan horse. If the antivirus program cannot remove the infection, it often quarantines the infected file. A **quarantine** is a separate area of a hard disk that holds the infected file until the infection can be removed. This step ensures other files will not become infected. Users also can quarantine suspicious files themselves (Figure 11-5).

In extreme cases, you may need to reformat the hard disk to remove a virus. Having uninfected, or clean, backups of all files is important. A later section in this chapter covers backup and restore techniques in detail.

In addition to an antivirus program, users often install a personal firewall program to protect a computer and its data from unauthorized intrusions. A later section discusses firewalls.

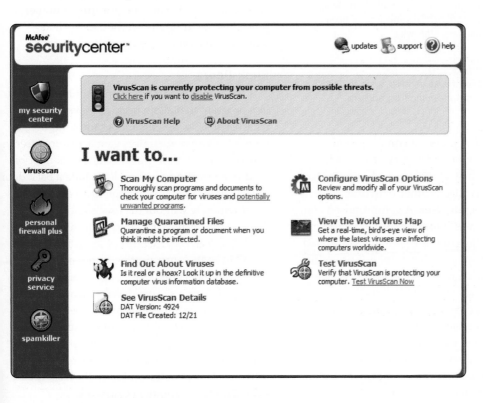

FIGURE 11-5 Most antivirus programs allow users to quarantine files, as well as scan for viruses.

Finally, stay informed about new virus alerts and virus hoaxes. A **virus hoax** is an e-mail message that warns users of a nonexistent virus, worm, or Trojan horse. Often, these virus hoaxes are in the form of a chain letter that requests the user to send a copy of the e-mail message to as many people as possible. Instead of forwarding the message, visit a Web site that publishes a list of virus alerts and virus hoaxes.

The list in Figure 11-6 summarizes important tips for protecting your computer from virus, worm, and Trojan horse infections.

Virus Hoaxes

For more information, visit scsite.com/ dc2008/ch11/weblink and then click Virus Hoaxes.

TIPS FOR PREVENTING VIRUS, WORM, AND TROJAN HORSE INFECTIONS

1. Never start a computer with removable media inserted in the drives or plugged in the ports, unless the media are uninfected.
2. Never open an e-mail attachment unless you are expecting it *and* it is from a trusted source. Turn off message preview.
3. Set the macro security in programs so you can enable or disable macros. Enable macros only if the document is from a trusted source and you are expecting it.
4. Install an antivirus program on all of your computers. Update the software regularly. Obtain updates to the virus signature files on a regular basis.
5. Check all downloaded programs for viruses, worms, or Trojan horses. This malware often is placed in seemingly innocent programs, so it will affect a large number of users.
6. If the antivirus program flags an e-mail attachment as infected, delete the attachment immediately.
7. Before using any removable media, use the antivirus scan program to check the media for infection. Incorporate this procedure even for shrink-wrapped software from major developers. Some commercial software has been infected and distributed to unsuspecting users this way.
8. Install a personal firewall program.

FIGURE 11-6 With the growing number of new viruses, worms, and Trojan horses, it is crucial that users take steps to protect their computers.

Botnets

A **botnet** is a group of compromised computers connected to a network such as the Internet that are being used as part of a network that attacks other networks, usually for nefarious purposes. A compromised computer, known as a **zombie**, is one whose owner is unaware the computer is being controlled remotely by an outsider. A *bot* is a program that performs a repetitive task on a network. Cybercriminals install malicious bots on unprotected computers to create a botnet, also called a *zombie army*. The perpetrator then uses the botnet to send spam via e-mail, spread viruses and other malware, or commit a distributed denial of service attack, which is discussed in the next section.

FAQ 11-2

How can I tell if my computer is a zombie or in a botnet?

Your computer may be a zombie or part of a botnet if you notice unusually high disk activity, a slower than normal Internet connection, or devices connected to your computer becoming increasingly unresponsive. The chances of your computer becoming a zombie or part of a botnet greatly increase if you do not have effective firewall software installed. For more information, visit scsite.com/dc2008/ch11/faq and then click Zombies and Botnets.

Denial of Service Attacks

A **denial of service attack**, or **DoS attack**, is an assault whose purpose is to disrupt computer access to an Internet service such as the Web or e-mail. Perpetrators carry out a DoS attack in a variety of ways. For example, they may use an unsuspecting computer to send an influx of confusing data messages or useless traffic to a computer network. The victim computer network eventually jams, blocking legitimate visitors from accessing the network.

A more devastating type of DoS attack is the *DDoS (distributed DoS) attack*, in which multiple unsuspecting computers are used to attack multiple computer networks. DDoS attacks have been able to stop operations temporarily at numerous Web sites, including powerhouses such as Yahoo!, Amazon.com, eBay, and CNN.com.

Back Doors

A **back door** is a program or set of instructions in a program that allow users to bypass security controls when accessing a program, computer, or network. Once perpetrators gain access to unsecure computers, they often install a back door or modify an existing program to include a back door which allows them to continue to access the computer remotely without the user's knowledge. Some worms leave back doors, which have been used to spread other worms or to distribute junk e-mail from the unsuspecting victim computers.

Programmers often build back doors into programs during system development. These back doors save development time because the programmer can bypass security controls while writing and testing programs. If the programmer fails to remove the back door before releasing the software, a perpetrator could use the back door to gain entry to a computer or network.

FAQ 11-3

How can I tell if my computer has a back door?

Back doors are difficult to identify unless an intruder maliciously affects your computer. If you notice that programs mysteriously appear and disappear, or the performance of your computer decreases, you may be experiencing symptoms of a back door. Utility programs are available that are able to identify some, but not all, back doors. If you are suspicious that a program you have installed contains a back door that hackers are taking advantage of, you either should update the program with the latest patches or completely uninstall the program. For more information, visit scsite.com/dc2008/ch11/faq and then click Back Doors.

Spoofing

Spoofing is a technique intruders use to make their network or Internet transmission appear legitimate to a victim computer or network. Several types of spoofing schemes exist. One type, called *e-mail spoofing*, occurs when the sender's address or other components of the e-mail header are altered so it appears the e-mail originated from a different sender.

E-mail spoofing commonly is used for spam and phishing scams, discussed later in the chapter.

Another type, called *IP spoofing*, occurs when an intruder computer fools a network into believing its IP address is associated with a trusted source. Perpetrators of IP spoofing trick their victims into interacting with the phony Web site. For example, the victim may provide confidential information or download files containing viruses, worms, or other malware.

Safeguards against Botnets, DoS Attacks, Back Doors, and Spoofing

Some of the latest antivirus programs include provisions to protect a computer from DoS and DDoS attacks. To further defend against these and other Internet and network attacks, users can implement firewall solutions, install intrusion detection software, and set up honeypots.

Firewalls

A **firewall** is hardware and/or software that protects a network's resources from intrusion by users on another network such as the Internet (Figure 11-7). All networked and online computer users should implement a firewall solution.

FIGURE 11-7 A firewall is hardware and/or software that protects a network's resources from intrusion by users on another network such as the Internet.

Companies use firewalls to protect network resources from outsiders and to restrict employees' access to sensitive data such as payroll or personnel records. Businesses can implement a firewall solution themselves or outsource their needs to a company specializing in providing firewall protection.

Large companies often route all their communications through a proxy server, which typically is a component of the firewall. A *proxy server* is a server outside the company's network that controls which communications pass into the company's network. That is, the proxy server carefully screens all incoming and outgoing messages. Proxy servers use a variety of screening techniques. Some check the domain name or IP address of the message for legitimacy. Others require that the messages have digital signatures. A section later in this chapter discusses digital signatures.

Home and small office/home office users often protect their computers with a personal firewall. As discussed in Chapter 8, a **personal firewall** is a utility that detects and protects a personal computer and its data from unauthorized intrusions. Personal firewalls constantly monitor all transmissions to and from the computer and inform you of any attempted intrusion. Some operating systems, such as Windows Vista, include personal firewalls. For enhanced firewall protection, many users purchase stand-alone personal firewall software (Figure 11-8), usually for less than $50.

Some small office/home office users purchase a hardware firewall, such as a router or other device that has a built-in firewall, in addition to or instead of personal firewall software. Hardware firewalls stop intrusions before they break in your computer.

WEB LINK 11-3

Personal Firewall Software

For more information, visit scsite.com/dc2008/ch11/weblink and then click Personal Firewall Software.

STAND-ALONE PERSONAL FIREWALL SOFTWARE
BlackICE PC Protection
CA Personal Firewall
McAfee Personal Firewall Plus
Norton Personal Firewall
Webroot Desktop Firewall
ZoneAlarm Pro

FIGURE 11-8 Popular personal firewall software.

Intrusion Detection Software

To provide extra protection against hackers and other intruders, large companies sometimes use intrusion detection software to identify possible security breaches. *Intrusion detection software* automatically analyzes all network traffic, assesses system vulnerabilities, identifies any unauthorized intrusions, and notifies network administrators of suspicious behavior patterns or system breaches.

To utilize intrusion detection software requires the expertise of a network administrator because the programs are complex and difficult to use and interpret. These programs also are quite expensive. This software, however, when combined with a firewall, provides an added layer of protection to companies with highly sensitive data such as credit card databases.

Honeypots

Some companies and organizations use honeypots so they can analyze an attack being perpetrated. A *honeypot* is a vulnerable computer that is set up to entice an intruder to break into it. These computers, which appear real to the intruder, actually are separated safely from the company or organization's network. Honeypots allow the company or organization to learn how intruders are exploiting their network and also attempt to catch perpetrators who have been doing damage elsewhere on their network. Large Web hosting companies, such as Yahoo! and AT&T, and law enforcement agencies frequently use honeypots.

UNAUTHORIZED ACCESS AND USE

Another type of computer security risk is unauthorized access and use. **Unauthorized access** is the use of a computer or network without permission. **Unauthorized use** is the use of a computer or its data for unapproved or possibly illegal activities. Unauthorized use includes a variety of activities: an employee using an organization's computer to send personal e-mail messages, an employee using the organization's word processing software to track his or her child's soccer league scores, or someone gaining access to a bank computer and performing an unauthorized transfer. For the home user, most unauthorized use occurs on computers that have always-on Internet connections, such as through Internet cable or DSL.

Why do hackers and other intruders want to access my home computer?

Some hackers and other intruders access home computers to use the computer's resources to spread malicious code, carry out a DoS attack, turn your computer into a zombie, or get away with other nefarious acts. Once they break into your home computer, these intruders often install a back door so they can continue to use your computer as a launching pad for their activities. For more information, visit scsite.com/dc2008/ch11/faq and then click Protecting Home Computers.

Safeguards against Unauthorized Access and Use

Companies take several measures to help prevent unauthorized access and use. At a minimum, they should have a written acceptable use policy (AUP) that outlines the computer activities for which the computer and network may and may not be used. A company's AUP should specify the acceptable use of computers by employees for personal reasons. Some companies prohibit such use entirely. Others allow personal use on the employee's own time such as a lunch hour. Whatever the policy, a company should document and explain it to employees.

To protect your personal computer from unauthorized intrusions, you should disable file and printer sharing on your Internet connection (Figure 11-9). This security measure attempts to ensure that others cannot access your files or your printer. To open the window shown in Figure 11-9 in Windows Vista, click the Start button on the taskbar, click Control Panel on the Start menu, and then click the Set up file sharing link in the Network and Internet area of the dialog box.

Other measures that safeguard against unauthorized access and use include firewalls and intrusion detection software, which were discussed in the previous section, and identifying and authenticating users.

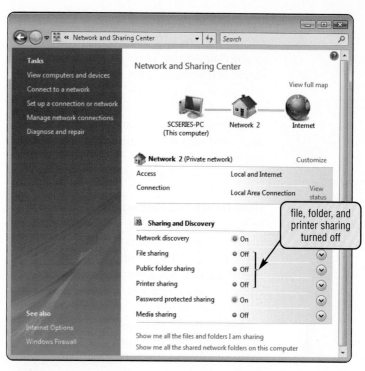

FIGURE 11-9 To protect files on your local hard disk from hackers and other intruders, turn off file and printer sharing on your Internet connection.

Identifying and Authenticating Users

Many companies use access controls to minimize the chance that a perpetrator intentionally may access or an employee accidentally may access confidential information on a computer. An *access control* is a security measure that defines who can access a computer, when they can access it, and what actions they can take while accessing the computer. In addition, the computer should maintain an **audit trail** that records in a file both successful and unsuccessful access attempts. An unsuccessful access attempt could result from a user mistyping his or her password, or it could result from a hacker trying thousands of passwords.

Companies should investigate unsuccessful access attempts immediately to ensure they are not intentional breaches of security. They also should review successful access for irregularities, such as use of the computer after normal working hours or from remote computers. In addition, a company regularly should review users' access privilege levels to determine whether they still are appropriate.

Many systems implement access controls using a two-phase process called identification and authentication. *Identification* verifies that an individual is a valid user. *Authentication* verifies that the individual is the person he or she claims to be. Three methods of identification and authentication include user names and passwords, possessed objects, and biometric devices. The technique(s) a company uses should correspond to the degree of risk associated with the unauthorized access. The following paragraphs discuss each of the identification and authentication methods.

USER NAMES AND PASSWORDS A **user name**, or *user ID* (identification), is a unique combination of characters, such as letters of the alphabet or numbers, that identifies one specific user. A **password** is a private combination of characters associated with the user name that allows access to certain computer resources.

Most multiuser (networked) operating systems require that users correctly enter a user name and a password before they can access the data, information, and programs stored on a computer or network. Many other systems that maintain financial, personal, and other confidential information also require a user name and password as part of their logon procedure (Figure 11-10).

Some systems assign a user name or user ID to each user. For example, a school may use the student identification number as a user ID. Some Web sites use your e-mail address as the user ID. With other systems, users select their own user name or user ID. Many users select a combination of their first and last names.

Most systems require that users select their own passwords. Users typically choose an easy-to-remember word or series of characters for passwords. If your password is too obvious, however, such as your initials or birthday, others can guess it easily. Easy passwords make it simple for hackers and other intruders to break into a system. Hackers use computer automated tools to assist them with guessing passwords. Thus, you should select a password carefully. Longer passwords provide greater security than shorter ones. Each character added to a password significantly increases the number of possible combinations and the length of time it might take for someone or for a hacker's computer to guess the password (Figure 11-11).

In addition to a user name and password, some systems ask users to enter one of several pieces of personal information. Such items can include a spouse's first name, a birth date, a place of birth, or a mother's maiden name. As with a password, if the user's response does not match information on file, the system denies access.

FIGURE 11-10 Many Web sites that maintain personal and confidential data require a user to enter a user name (e-mail address, in this case) and password.

FAQ 11-5

How can I protect my password?

Once you select a password, change it frequently. Do not disclose it to anyone or write it on a slip of paper kept near the computer, especially taped to the monitor or under the keyboard. E-mail and telemarketing scams often ask unsuspecting users to disclose their password, so be wary if you did not initiate the inquiry or telephone call. For more information, visit scsite.com/dc2008/ch11/faq and then click Protecting Passwords.

PASSWORD PROTECTION

Number of Characters	Possible Combinations	AVERAGE TIME TO DISCOVER	
		Human	Computer
1	36	3 minutes	.000018 second
2	1,300	2 hours	.00065 second
3	47,000	3 days	.02 second
4	1,700,000	3 months	1 second
5	60,000,000	10 years	30 seconds
10	3,700,000,000,000,000	580 million years	59 years

- Possible characters include the letters A–Z and numbers 0–9
- Human discovery assumes 1 try every 10 seconds
- Computer discovery assumes 1 million tries per second
- Average time assumes the password would be discovered in approximately half the time it would take to try all possible combinations

FIGURE 11-11 This table shows the effect of increasing the length of a password that consists of letters and numbers. The longer the password, the more effort required to discover it. Long passwords, however, are more difficult for users to remember.

POSSESSED OBJECTS A *possessed object* is any item that you must carry to gain access to a computer or computer facility. Examples of possessed objects are badges, cards, smart cards, and keys. The card you use in an automated teller machine (ATM) is a possessed object that allows access to your bank account (Figure 11-12).

Possessed objects often are used in combination with personal identification numbers. A **personal identification number** (**PIN**) is a numeric password, either assigned by a company or selected by a user. PINs provide an additional level of security. An ATM card typically requires a four-digit PIN. Most debit cards and some credit cards use PINs. If someone steals these cards, the thief must enter the user's PIN to access the account. PINs are passwords. Select them carefully and protect them as you do any other password.

BIOMETRIC DEVICES As Chapter 5 discussed, a **biometric device** authenticates a person's identity by translating a personal characteristic, such as a fingerprint, into a digital code that then is compared with a digital code stored in the computer verifying a physical or behavioral characteristic. If the digital code in the computer does not match the personal characteristic code, the computer denies access to the individual.

Biometric devices grant access to programs, computers, or rooms using computer analysis of some biometric identifier. Examples of biometric

FIGURE 11-12 The card you use in an automated teller machine (ATM) is a possessed object that allows access to your bank account.

devices and systems include fingerprint scanners (Figure 11-13), hand geometry systems, face recognition systems, voice verification systems, signature verification systems, iris recognition systems, and retinal scanners. Read Looking Ahead 11-1 for a look at the next generation of face recognition systems.

Biometric devices are gaining popularity as a security precaution because they are a virtually foolproof method of identification and authentication (read Ethics & Issues 11-2 for a related discussion). For example, many grocery stores, retail stores, and gas stations now use *biometric payment*, where the customer's fingerprint is read by a fingerprint scanner that is linked to a payment method such as a checking account or credit card.

Users can forget their user names and passwords. Possessed objects can be lost, copied, duplicated, or stolen. Personal characteristics, by contrast, are unique and cannot be forgotten or misplaced.

Biometric devices do have disadvantages. If you cut your finger, a fingerprint scanner might reject you as a legitimate user. Hand geometry readers can transmit germs. If you are nervous, a signature might not match the one on file. If you have a sore throat, a voice recognition system might reject you. Many people are uncomfortable with the thought of using an iris scanner.

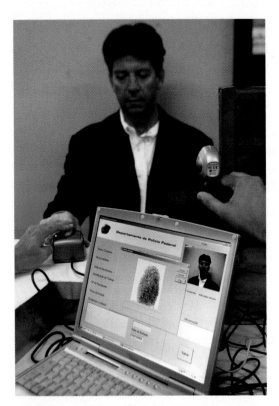

FIGURE 11-13 A fingerprint scanner verifies this traveler's identity.

ETHICS & ISSUES 11-2

Should Schools Use Biometric Devices?

Several school systems now require that students use a biometric thumbprint to pay for their school lunches. The school administrators cite the need to better track the number of free and subsidized lunches that the schools provide. In an attempt to increase security and track attendance, other school districts require thumbprint identification to enter classrooms or participate in school activities. In most cases, the schools promise to provide digital ID cards for those who oppose the system and refuse to take part. Some experts feel that children are being trained very early to expect no privacy when they are adults. Others also are concerned that student eating habits can be tracked and then used against them in the future, or that the information could end up in the wrong hands. Some people are concerned about the sanitary issue of students passing germs to each other over the biometric devices. Should children be required to provide biometric information to engage in common public school-related activities? Why or why not? Do the school boards' reasons for the measures justify them? Why or why not? What are the privacy and sanitary issues involved and should they be a concern?

LOOKING AHEAD 11-1

Three-Dimensional Facial Recognition Software — A Step Forward for Security

Your next cellular telephone may contain an added feature: built-in facial recognition software that prevents unauthorized people from using your telephone. All you will need to do to set up this system is use the phone to take a few photographs of yourself.

The facial recognition software market is expected to grow from $228 million in 2005 to $802 million in 2008 according to the International Biometric Group. Leading the way are three-dimensional systems that measure the width, height, and depth of an individual's face and then compare the dimensions to the original photographs. The software can identify an individual positively in a dark room or in a different pose than when the photographs were taken. For more information, visit scsite.com/dc2008/ch11/looking and then click Facial Recognition.

FAQ 11-6

How many people are victims of identity theft each year?

Studies reveal that identity theft is the fastest growing crime in the United States. More than 260,000 identity theft complaints currently are reported each year, with that number rapidly rising. The following chart illustrates the reported number of identity theft cases grouped by age. For more information, visit scsite.com/dc2008/ch11/faq and then click Identity Theft.

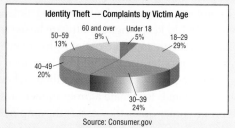

Identity Theft — Complaints by Victim Age

60 and over 9%
Under 18 5%
18–29 29%
30–39 24%
40–49 20%
50–59 13%

Source: Consumer.gov

Test your knowledge of pages 556 through 568 in Quiz Yourself 11-1.

QUIZ YOURSELF 11-1

Instructions: Find the true statement below. Then, rewrite the remaining false statements so they are true.

1. A back door attack is an assault whose purpose is to disrupt computer access to an Internet service such as the Web or e-mail.

2. All networked and online computer users should implement a firewall solution.

3. A biometric device translates a personal characteristic into an analog code that then is compared with a digital code stored in the computer.

4. Computer viruses, worms, and Trojan Horses are malware that acts with a user's knowledge.

5. Perpetrators of cybercrime and other intrusions fall into seven basic categories: hacker, cracker, CERT/CC, corporate spy, unethical employee, trusted source, and cyberterrorist.

6. Shorter passwords provide greater security than longer ones.

7. Updating an antivirus program's quarantine protects a computer against viruses written since the antivirus program was released.

Quiz Yourself Online: To further check your knowledge of security risks; safeguards against viruses, worms, Trojan horses, botnets, denial of service attacks, back doors, and spoofing; and preventing unauthorized computer access and use, visit scsite.com/dc2008/ch11/quiz and then click Objectives 1 – 3.

HARDWARE THEFT AND VANDALISM

Hardware theft and vandalism are other types of computer security risks. **Hardware theft** is the act of stealing computer equipment. **Hardware vandalism** is the act of defacing or destroying computer equipment. Hardware vandalism takes many forms, from someone cutting a computer cable to individuals breaking into a business or school computer lab and aimlessly smashing computers.

Hardware theft and vandalism do not really pose a threat to the home desktop computer user. Companies and schools and other organizations that house many computers, however, are at risk to hardware theft and vandalism.

Mobile users also are susceptible to hardware theft. It is estimated that more than two million notebook computers are stolen each year. The size and weight of these computers make them easy to steal. Thieves often target notebook computers of company executives, so they can use the stolen computer to access confidential company information illegally. In this case, hardware theft is combined with software and information theft.

Safeguards against Hardware Theft and Vandalism

To help reduce the chances of theft, companies and schools use a variety of security measures. Physical access controls, such as locked doors and windows, usually are adequate to protect the equipment. Many businesses, schools, and some homeowners install alarm systems for additional security. School computer labs and other areas with a large number of semifrequent users often attach additional physical security devices such as cables that lock the equipment to a desk (Figure 11-14), cabinet, or floor. Small locking devices also exist that require a key to access a hard disk or CD/DVD drive.

FIGURE 11-14 Using cables to lock computers can help prevent the theft of computer equipment.

Mobile computer users must take special care to protect their equipment. The best preventive measures are common sense and a constant awareness of the risk. Some users attach a physical device such as a cable to lock a mobile computer temporarily to a stationary object. For example, a hotel guest could lock a notebook computer to a desk or table in a hotel room when he or she leaves the room. Other mobile users install a mini-security system in the notebook computer. Some of these security systems shut down the computer and sound an alarm if the computer moves outside a specified distance. Notebook computer security systems and tracking software can track the location of a stolen notebook computer.

Some notebook computers use passwords, possessed objects, and biometrics as methods of security. When you boot up these computers, you must enter a password, slide a card in a card reader, or press your finger on a fingerprint scanner before the hard disk unlocks. This type of security does not prevent theft, but it renders the computer useless if it is stolen.

You also can password-protect many PDAs and smart phones. This allows only authorized users to access the device's data. You usually can instruct the password screen to display your name and telephone number, so a Good Samaritan can return it to you if lost. Several models also allow you to encrypt data in the device. A later section in this chapter discusses encryption.

SOFTWARE THEFT

Another type of computer security risk is software theft. **Software theft** occurs when someone (1) steals software media, (2) intentionally erases programs, or (3) illegally copies a program.

The first type of software theft involves a perpetrator physically stealing the media that contain the software or the hardware that contains the media, as described in the previous section. For example, an unscrupulous library patron might steal the Microsoft Encarta Encyclopedia DVD.

The second type of software theft can occur when a programmer is terminated from, or stops working for, a

company. Although the programs are company property, some dishonest programmers intentionally remove the programs they have written from company computers.

The third type of software theft occurs when software is stolen from software manufacturers. This type of theft, called piracy, is by far the most common form of software theft. Software **piracy** is the unauthorized and illegal duplication of copyrighted software.

Safeguards against Software Theft

To protect software media from being stolen, owners should keep original software boxes and media in a secure location, out of sight of prying eyes. All computer users should back up their files and disks regularly, in the event of theft. When some companies terminate a programmer or if the programmer quits, they escort the employee off the premises immediately. These companies believe that allowing terminated employees to remain on the premises gives them time to sabotage files and other network procedures.

To protect themselves from software piracy, software manufacturers issue users license agreements. A **license agreement** is the right to use the software. That is, you do not own the software. The license agreement provides specific conditions for use of the software, which a user must accept before using the software (Figure 11-15). These terms usually are displayed when you install the software. Use of the software constitutes acceptance of the terms on the user's part.

WEB LINK 11-4

Software Piracy

For more information, visit scsite.com/dc2008/ch11/weblink and then click Software Piracy.

Google Earth - InstallShield Wizard

License Agreement
Please read the following license agreement carefully.

Thank you for using Google Earth! By downloading, installing or using Google software or any portion thereof ("Google Software") you agree to the following terms and conditions (the "Terms and Conditions"). The Google Software, and any portion thereof, are referred to herein as the "Software."

1.   USE OF SOFTWARE
The Software is made available to you for your personal, non-commercial use only. You may not use the Software or the geographical information made available for display using the Software, or any prints or screen outputs generated with the Software in any commercial or business environment or for any commercial or business purposes for yourself or any third parties. You may not use the Google Software in any manner that could damage, disable, overburden, or impair Google's services (e.g., you may not use the

◉ I accept the terms of the license agreement

◯ I do not accept the terms of the license agreement   Print

InstallShield

< Back   Next >   Cancel

FIGURE 11-15 A user must accept the terms in the license agreement before using the software.

The most common type of license included with software purchased by individual users is a *single-user license agreement*, also called an *end-user license agreement* (*EULA*). A single-user license agreement typically includes many of the following conditions that specify a user's responsibility upon acceptance of the agreement.

Users are permitted to:

- Install the software on only one computer. (Some license agreements allow users to install the software on one desktop computer and one notebook computer.)
- Make one copy of the software as a backup.
- Give or sell the software to another individual, but only if the software is removed from the user's computer first.

Users are not permitted to:

- Install the software on a network, such as a school computer lab.
- Give copies to friends and colleagues, while continuing to use the software.
- Export the software.
- Rent or lease the software.

Unless otherwise specified by a license agreement, you do not have the right to copy, loan, borrow, rent, or in any way distribute software. Doing so is a violation of copyright law. It also is a federal crime. Despite this, some experts estimate for every authorized copy of software in use, at least one unauthorized copy exists.

Software piracy continues for several reasons. In some countries, legal protection for software does not exist. In other countries, laws rarely are enforced. In addition, many buyers believe they have the right to copy the software for which they pay hundreds, even thousands, of dollars. Finally, software piracy is a fairly simple crime to commit.

Software piracy, however, is a serious offense. For one, it introduces a number of risks into the software market. It increases the chance of spreading viruses, reduces your ability to receive technical support, and drives up the price of software for all users. Further, software companies take illegal copying seriously. In some cases, offenders have been prosecuted to the fullest extent of the law with penalties including fines up to $250,000 and five years in jail.

To promote a better understanding of software piracy problems and, if necessary, to take legal action, a number of major worldwide software companies formed the *Business Software Alliance* (*BSA*). The BSA operates a Web site and antipiracy hotlines in the United States and more than 80 other countries.

In an attempt to prevent software piracy, Microsoft and other manufacturers have incorporated an activation process into many of their consumer products. During the **product activation**, which is conducted either online or by telephone, users provide the software product's 25-character identification number to receive an installation identification number unique to the computer on which the software is installed. Usually, the software does not function or has limited functionality until you activate it via the Internet or telephone.

Many organizations and businesses also have strict written policies governing the installation and use of software and enforce their rules by checking networked or online computers periodically to ensure that all software is licensed properly. If you are not completely familiar with your school or employer's policies governing installation of software, check with the information technology department or your school's technology coordinator.

WEB LINK 11-5

Business Software Alliance

For more information, visit scsite.com/dc2008/ch11/weblink and then click Business Software Alliance.

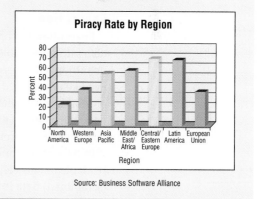

FAQ 11-7

How prevalent is software piracy?

A recent study showed that approximately 35 percent of packaged software installed on personal computers worldwide was illegal. The chart below outlines some of the piracy rates around the world. For more information, visit scsite.com/dc2008/ch11/faq and then click Software Piracy.

Piracy Rate by Region

Source: Business Software Alliance

INFORMATION THEFT

Information theft is yet another type of computer security risk. **Information theft** occurs when someone steals personal or confidential information. If stolen, the loss of information can cause as much damage as (if not more than) hardware or software theft.

Both business and home users can fall victim to information theft. An unethical company executive may steal or buy stolen information to learn about a competitor. A corrupt individual may steal credit card numbers to make fraudulent purchases. Information theft often is linked to other types of computer crime. For example, an individual first might gain unauthorized access to a computer and then steal credit card numbers stored in a firm's accounting department.

Information transmitted over networks offers a higher degree of risk because unscrupulous users can intercept it during transmission. Every computer along the path of your data can see what you send and receive.

Safeguards against Information Theft

Most companies attempt to prevent information theft by implementing the user identification and authentication controls discussed earlier in this chapter. These controls are best suited for protecting information on computers located on a company's premises.

To protect information on the Internet and networks, companies and individuals use a variety of encryption techniques to keep data secure and private.

Encryption

Encryption is a process of converting readable data into unreadable characters to prevent unauthorized access. You treat encrypted data just like any other data. That is, you can store it or send it in an e-mail message. To read the data, the recipient must **decrypt**, or decipher, it into a readable form.

In the encryption process, the unencrypted, readable data is called *plaintext*. The encrypted (scrambled) data is called *ciphertext*. To encrypt the data, the originator of the data converts the plaintext into ciphertext using an encryption key. In its simplest form, an *encryption key* is a programmed formula that the recipient of the data uses to decrypt ciphertext. For a more technical discussion about encryption keys, read the High-Tech Talk article on page 592.

Many data encryption methods exist. Figure 11-16 shows examples of some simple encryption methods. An encryption key (formula) often uses more than one of these methods, such as a combination of transposition and substitution. Most organizations use available software for encryption. Others develop their own encryption programs. With Windows Vista's *Encrypting File System*, you easily can encrypt the contents of files and folders. To display the Windows Vista dialog box shown in Figure 11-17, right-click the file or folder name in Explorer, click Properties on the shortcut menu, click the General tab, and then click the Advanced button in the Properties dialog box. Windows Vista also includes a feature called *BitLocker* that allows you to encrypt all files on a drive.

When users send an e-mail message over the Internet, they never know who might intercept it, who might read it, or to whom it might be forwarded. If a message contains personal or confidential information, users can protect the message by encrypting it or signing it digitally. One of the more popular e-mail encryption programs is called *Pretty Good Privacy* (*PGP*). PGP is freeware for personal, noncommercial users. Home users can download PGP from the Web at no cost.

A **digital signature** is an encrypted code that a person, Web site, or company attaches to an electronic message to verify the identity of the message sender. The code usually consists of the user's name and a hash of all or part of the message. A *hash* is a mathematical formula that generates a code from the contents of the message.

SAMPLE ENCRYPTION METHODS

Name	Method	Plaintext	Ciphertext	Explanation
Transposition	Switch the order of characters	SOFTWARE	OSTFAWER	Adjacent characters swapped
Substitution	Replace characters with other characters	INFORMATION	WLDIMXQUWIL	Each letter replaced with another
Expansion	Insert characters between existing characters	USER	UYSYEYRY	Letter Y inserted after each character
Compaction	Remove characters and store elsewhere	ACTIVATION	ACIVTIN	Every third letter removed (T, A, O)

FIGURE 11-16   This table shows four simple methods of encryption. Most encryption programs use a combination of these four methods

FIGURE 11-17 Through this Windows Vista dialog box, you can encrypt files and folders. Only the user that encrypted the files and folders can access them.

WEB LINK 11-6

BitLocker
For more information, visit scsite.com/dc2008/ch11/weblink and then click BitLocker.

Thus, the hash differs for each message. Receivers of the message decrypt the digital signature. The recipient then generates a new hash of the received message and compares it with one in the digital signature to ensure they match.

Digital signatures often are used to ensure that an impostor is not participating in an Internet transaction. That is, digital signatures help to prevent e-mail forgery. A digital signature also can verify that the content of a message has not changed.

Many Web browsers also use encryption. Some browsers offer a protection level known as *40-bit encryption*. Many also offer *128-bit encryption*, which is an even higher level of protection because it has a longer encryption key. Applications requiring more security, such as banks, brokerage firms, or online retailers that use credit card or other financial information, require 128-bit encryption.

A Web site that uses encryption techniques to secure its data is known as a **secure site**. Secure sites use digital certificates along with a security protocol. Two popular security protocols are Secure Sockets Layer and Secure HTTP. The following paragraphs briefly discuss digital certificates and these security protocols.

DIGITAL CERTIFICATES A **digital certificate** is a notice that guarantees a user or a Web site is legitimate. E-commerce applications commonly use digital certificates. Web browsers, such as Internet Explorer, often display a warning message if a Web site does not have a valid digital certificate.

A *certificate authority* (*CA*) is an authorized person or a company that issues and verifies digital certificates. Users apply for a digital certificate from a CA (Figure 11-18). A digital certificate typically contains information such as the user's name, the issuing CA's name and signature, and the serial number of the certificate. The information in a digital certificate is encrypted.

WEB LINK 11-7

Digital Certificates
For more information, visit scsite.com/dc2008/ch11/weblink and then click Digital Certificates.

FIGURE 11-18 A certificate authority issues and verifies digital certificates.

SECURE SOCKETS LAYER *Secure Sockets Layer (SSL)* provides encryption of all data that passes between a client and an Internet server. SSL requires the client have a digital certificate. Once the server has a digital certificate, the Web browser communicates securely with the client. Web addresses of pages that use SSL typically begin with https, instead of http (Figure 11-19). SSL is available in both 40-bit and 128-bit encryption.

indicates secure Web page

FIGURE 11-19 Web addresses of secure sites often begin with https instead of http. Secure sites also often display a lock symbol in the window.

SECURE HTTP *Secure HTTP (S-HTTP)* allows users to choose an encryption scheme for data that passes between a client and a server. With S-HTTP, the client and server both must have digital certificates. S-HTTP is more difficult to use than SSL, but it is more secure. Applications that must verify the authenticity of a client, such as for online banking, use S-HTTP.

Mobile users today often access their company networks through a virtual private network. When a mobile user connects to a main office using a standard Internet connection, a *virtual private network (VPN)* provides the mobile user with a secure connection to the company network server, as if the user has a private line. VPNs help ensure that data is safe from being intercepted by unauthorized people by encrypting data as it transmits from a notebook computer, Tablet PC, smart phone, PDA, or other mobile device.

SYSTEM FAILURE

System failure is yet another type of computer security risk. A *system failure* is the prolonged malfunction of a computer. System failure also can cause loss of hardware, software, data, or information. A variety of causes can lead to system failure. These include aging hardware; natural disasters such as fires, floods, or hurricanes; random events such as electrical power problems; and even errors in computer programs.

One of the more common causes of system failure is an electrical power variation. Electrical power variations can cause loss of data and loss of equipment. If the computer equipment is networked, a single power disturbance can damage multiple systems. Electrical disturbances include noise, undervoltages, and overvoltages.

Noise is any unwanted signal, usually varying quickly, that is mixed with the normal voltage entering the computer. Noise is caused by external devices such as fluorescent lighting, radios, and televisions, as well as by components within the computer itself. Noise generally is not a risk to hardware, software, or data. Computer power supplies, however, do filter out noise.

An **undervoltage** occurs when the electrical supply drops. In North America, a wall plug usually supplies electricity at approximately 120 volts. Any significant drop below 120 volts is an undervoltage. A *brownout* is a prolonged undervoltage. A *blackout* is a complete power failure. Undervoltages can cause data loss but generally do not cause equipment damage.

An **overvoltage**, or **power surge**, occurs when the incoming electrical power increases significantly above the normal 120 volts. A momentary overvoltage, called a *spike*, occurs when the increase in power lasts for less than one millisecond (one thousandth of a second). Uncontrollable disturbances such as lightning bolts cause spikes. Overvoltages can cause immediate and permanent damage to hardware.

Safeguards against System Failure

To protect against overvoltages, use a surge protector. A **surge protector**, also called a *surge suppressor*, uses special electrical components to smooth out minor noise, provide a stable current flow, and keep an overvoltage from reaching the computer and other electronic equipment (Figure 11-20). Sometimes resembling a power strip, the computer and other devices plug in the surge protector, which plugs in the power source. The surge protector absorbs small overvoltages — generally without damage to the computer and equipment. To protect the computer and other equipment from large overvoltages, such as those caused by a lightning strike, some surge protectors completely stop working when an overvoltage reaches a certain level.

No surge protectors are 100 percent effective. Large power surges can bypass the protector. Repeated small overvoltages can weaken a surge protector permanently. Some experts recommend replacing a surge protector every two to three years. Typically, the amount of protection offered by a surge protector is proportional to its cost. That is, the more expensive, the more protection the protector offers. Be sure to review the manufacturer's guarantee when deciding which surge protector to buy. Some will replace equipment damaged by a power surge, if the equipment was connected to their surge protector.

The surge protector you purchase should meet the safety specification for surge suppression products. This specification, which is called the *Underwriters Laboratories (UL) 1449 standard*, allows no more than 500 maximum volts to pass through the line. The response time of the surge protector should be less than one nanosecond. The surge protector also should have a Joule rating of at least 200. A *Joule* is the unit of energy a surge protection device can absorb before it can be damaged. The higher the Joule rating, the better the protection.

If your computer connects to a network or the Internet, also be sure to have protection for your modem, telephone lines, DSL lines, Internet cable lines, and network lines. Many surge protectors include plug-ins for telephone lines and other cables. If yours does not, you can purchase separate devices to protect these lines.

For additional electrical protection, some applications connect an uninterruptible power supply to the computer. An **uninterruptible power supply** (**UPS**) is a device that contains surge protection circuits and one or more batteries that can provide power during a temporary or permanent loss of power (Figure 11-21). A UPS connects between your computer and a power source.

Two types of UPS devices are standby and online. A *standby UPS*, sometimes called an *offline UPS*, switches to battery power when a problem occurs in the power line. The amount of time a standby UPS allows a user to continue working depends on the electrical requirements of the computer and the size of the batteries in the UPS. A UPS for a personal computer should provide from 10 to 50 minutes of use in the event of a total power loss. This should be enough time to save current work and shut down the computer properly. An *online UPS* always runs off the battery, which provides continuous protection. An online UPS is much more expensive than a standby UPS.

WEB LINK 11-8

Uninterruptible Power Supply

For more information, visit scsite.com/ dc2008/ch11/weblink and then click Uninterruptible Power Supply.

FIGURE 11-20 Circuits inside a surge protector safeguard against overvoltages and undervoltages.

FIGURE 11-21 If power fails, an uninterruptible power supply (UPS), uses batteries to provide electricity for a limited amount of time.

Some companies use duplicate components or computers to protect against system failure. A *fault-tolerant computer* has duplicate components so it can continue to operate when one of its main components fail. Companies that must have their computers operational at all times may have two separate duplicate computers running simultaneously. Airline reservation systems, communications networks, and automated teller machines are examples of systems that duplicate components or computers to ensure that no data is lost in the event of a system failure.

FAQ 11-8

Should I use a surge protector on electronic equipment, appliances, or even my entire house?

It is a good idea to use a surge protector on high-end, expensive electronic equipment such as entertainment systems, DVD players, fax machines, and copy machines, and also on any household appliance or device that includes a circuit board or computer such as a stove, dishwasher, and microwave. You also can hire an electrician to install a surge protector that protects your entire house. This type of surge protector is installed where the power lines connect to your house's electrical system. A lightning strike or other substantial power surge could damage electrical devices in your house. For more information, visit scsite.com/dc2008/ch11/faq and then click Surge Protectors.

BACKING UP — THE ULTIMATE SAFEGUARD

To prevent against data loss caused by system failure or hardware/software/information theft, computer users should back up files regularly. A **backup** is a duplicate of a file, program, or disk that can be used if the original is lost, damaged, or destroyed. Thus, to **back up** a file means to make a copy of it. In the case of system failure or the discovery of corrupted files, you **restore** the files by copying the backed up files to their original location on the computer.

You can use just about any media to store backups. Be sure to use high-quality media. A good choice for a home user might be CD-RWs or DVD+RWs.

Keep backup copies in a fireproof and heatproof safe or vault, or offsite. *Offsite* means in a location separate from the computer site. Home and business users keep backup copies offsite so that a single disaster, such as a fire, does not destroy both the original and the backup copy of the data. An offsite location

can be a safe deposit box at a bank or a briefcase. A growing trend is to use online storage as an offsite location. As discussed in Chapter 7, online storage is a service on the Web that provides storage to computer users.

Most backup programs for the home user provide for a full backup and a selective backup. A *full backup* copies all of the files in the computer. With a *selective backup*, users choose which folders and files to include in a backup.

Some users implement a *three-generation backup* policy to preserve three copies of important files. The *grandparent* is the oldest copy of the file. The *parent* is the second oldest copy of the file. The *child* is the most recent copy of the file.

Backup programs are available from many sources. Most operating systems include a backup program. Backup devices, such as tape and removable disk drives, also include backup programs. Numerous stand-alone backup utilities exist. Many of these can be downloaded from the Web at no cost.

Some companies choose to use an online backup service to handle their backup needs. An *online backup service* is a Web site that automatically backs up files to its online location. These sites usually charge a monthly or annual fee. If the system crashes, the online backup service typically sends the company one or more CDs that contains all of its backed up data. Users with high-speed Internet connections opt for online backup services. For slower connections, these services are not practical.

WIRELESS SECURITY

Wireless technology has made dramatic changes in the way computer users communicate worldwide. Billions of home and business users have notebook computers, PDAs, smart phones, and other devices to access the Internet, send e-mail and instant messages, chat online, or share network connections — all without wires. Home users set up wireless home networks. Mobile users access wireless networks in hot spots at airports, hotels, schools, shopping malls, bookstores, restaurants, and coffee shops. Schools have wireless networks so students can access the school network using their mobile computers and devices as they move from building to building.

Although wireless access provides many conveniences to users, it also poses additional security risks. One study showed that about 80 percent of wireless networks have no security protection. Some perpetrators connect to other's wireless networks to gain free Internet access; others may try to access a company's confidential data.

To access the network, the individual must be in range of the wireless network. Some intruders intercept and monitor communications as they transmit through the air. Others connect to a network through an unsecured wireless access point (WAP). In one technique, called *war driving*, individuals attempt to detect wireless networks via their notebook computer while driving a vehicle through areas they suspect have a wireless network. Some individuals instead use *war flying*, where they use airplanes instead of vehicles to detect unsecured wireless networks. Once located, some individuals use a GPS device to add the WAP to a war driving access point map on the Internet (Figure 11-22), making the wireless network vulnerable.

In addition to using firewalls, some safeguards that improve the security of wireless networks include reconfiguring the wireless access point and ensuring equipment uses one or more wireless security standards such as Wired Equivalent Privacy, Wi-Fi Protected Access, and 802.11i.

- A wireless access point (WAP) should be configured so it does not broadcast a network name, known as an *SSID* (service set identifier). The WAP also should be programmed so only certain devices can access it.
- *Wired Equivalent Privacy* (WEP) is a security standard that defines how to encrypt data as it travels across wireless networks. WEP supports both 40-bit and 128-bit encryption.
- *Wi-Fi Protected Access* (WPA) is a security standard that improves on WEP by authenticating network users and providing more advanced encryption techniques.
- An *802.11i* network, the most recent network security standard, conforms to the government's security standards and uses more sophisticated encryption techniques than both WPA and WEP.

By implementing these security measures, you can help to prevent unauthorized access to wireless networks.

FAQ 11-9

Can you detect if someone is wirelessly accessing your home network?

Yes. If you notice that the speed of your wireless network connection is slower than normal, it may be a sign that someone else is accessing your network. You also may notice indicator lights on your wireless router flashing rapidly when you are not connected to your wireless network. Most wireless routers have a built-in utility that allows you to view the computers currently connected to your network. If you notice a computer that does not belong to you, consult your wireless router's documentation to determine how to remove it from the network. For more information, visit scsite.com/dc2008/ch11/faq and then click Wireless Home Networks.

FIGURE 11-22 This Web site marks all unsecured wireless networks located during a war drive.

Test your knowledge of pages 569 through 577 in Quiz Yourself 11-2.

QUIZ YOURSELF 11-2

Instructions: Find the true statement below. Then, rewrite the remaining false statements so they are true.

1. An end-user license agreement (EULA) permits users to give copies to friends and colleagues, while continuing to use the software.
2. Encryption is a process of converting ciphertext into plaintext to prevent authorized access.
3. Mobile users are not susceptible to hardware theft.
4. Overvoltages can cause immediate and permanent damage to hardware.
5. Three backup security standards are Wired Equivalent Privacy, Wi-Fi Protected Access, and 802.11i.
6. To prevent against data loss caused by a system failure, computer users should restore files regularly.

Quiz Yourself Online: To further check your knowledge of safeguards against hardware theft and vandalism, software piracy, encryption, protection against system failure, backing up resources, and wireless security, visit scsite.com/dc2008/ch11/quiz and then click Objectives 4 – 9.

ETHICS AND SOCIETY

As with any powerful technology, computers can be used for both good and bad intentions. The standards that determine whether an action is good or bad are known as ethics.

Computer ethics are the moral guidelines that govern the use of computers and information systems. Six frequently discussed areas of computer ethics are unauthorized use of computers and networks, software theft (piracy),

information accuracy, intellectual property rights, codes of conduct, and information privacy. The questionnaire in Figure 11-23 raises issues in each of these areas.

Previous sections in this chapter discussed unauthorized use of computers and networks, and software theft (piracy). The following pages discuss issues related to information accuracy, intellectual property rights, codes of conduct, and information privacy.

	Ethical	Unethical
1. A company requires employees to wear badges that track their whereabouts while at work.	☐	☐
2. A supervisor reads an employee's e-mail.	☐	☐
3. An employee uses his computer at work to send e-mail messages to a friend.	☐	☐
4. An employee sends an e-mail message to several coworkers and blind copies his supervisor.	☐	☐
5. An employee forwards an e-mail message to a third party without permission from the sender.	☐	☐
6. An employee uses her computer at work to complete a homework assignment for school.	☐	☐
7. The vice president of your Student Government Association (SGA) downloads a photograph from the Web and uses it in a flier recruiting SGA members.	☐	☐
8. A student copies text from the Web and uses it in a research paper for his English Composition class.	☐	☐
9. An employee sends political campaign material to individuals on her employer's mailing list.	☐	☐
10. As an employee in the registration office, you have access to student grades. You look up grades for your friends, so they do not have to wait for delivery of grade reports from the postal service.	☐	☐
11. An employee makes a copy of software and installs it on her home computer. No one uses her home computer while she is at work, and she uses her home computer only to finish projects from work.	☐	☐
12. An employee who has been laid off installs a computer virus on his employer's computer.	☐	☐
13. A person designing a Web page finds one on the Web similar to his requirements, copies it, modifies it, and publishes it as his own Web page.	☐	☐
14. A student researches using only the Web to write a report.	☐	☐
15. In a society in which all transactions occur online (a cashless society), the government tracks every transaction you make and automatically deducts taxes from your bank account.	☐	☐
16. Someone copies a well-known novel to the Web and encourages others to read it.	☐	☐
17. A person accesses a company's network and reports to the company any vulnerabilities discovered.	☐	☐

FIGURE 11-23 Indicate whether you think the situation described is ethical or unethical. Discuss your answers with your instructor and other students.

Information Accuracy

Information accuracy today is a concern because many users access information maintained by other people or companies, such as on the Internet. Do not assume that because the information is on the Web that it is correct. As Chapter 2 discussed, users should evaluate the value of a Web page before relying on its content. Be aware that the company providing access to the information may not be the creator of the information.

In addition to concerns about the accuracy of computer input, some individuals and organizations raise questions about the ethics of using computers to alter output, primarily graphical output such as retouched photographs. Using graphics equipment and software, users easily can digitize photographs and then add, change, or remove images (Figure 11-24).

One group that completely opposes any manipulation of an image is the National Press Photographers Association. It believes that allowing even the slightest alteration eventually could lead to misrepresentative photographs. Others believe that digital photograph retouching is acceptable as long as the significant content or meaning of the photograph does not change. Digital retouching is an area in which legal precedents so far have not been established.

Intellectual Property Rights

Intellectual property (IP) refers to unique and original works such as ideas, inventions, art, writings, processes, company and product names, and logos. **Intellectual property rights** are the rights to which creators are entitled for their work. Certain issues arise surrounding IP today because many of these works are available digitally.

A **copyright** gives authors and artists exclusive rights to duplicate, publish, and sell their materials. A copyright protects any tangible form of expression.

A common infringement of copyright is piracy. People pirate (illegally copy) software, movies, and music. Many areas are not clear-cut with respect to the law, because copyright law gives the public fair use to copyrighted material. The issues surround the phrase, fair use, which allows use for educational and critical purposes.

FIGURE 11-24 A digitally altered photograph shows sports legend Michael Jordan (born in 1963) meeting the famous scientist Albert Einstein (who died in 1955).

This vague definition is subject to widespread interpretation and raises many questions:

- Should individuals be able to download contents of your Web site, modify it, and then put it on the Web again as their own?
- Should a faculty member have the right to print material from the Web and distribute it to all members of the class for teaching purposes only?
- Should someone be able to scan photographs or pages from a book, publish them to the Web, and allow others to download them?
- Should someone be able to put the lyrics of a song on the Web?
- Should students be able to post term papers they have written on the Web, making it tempting for other students to download and submit them as their own work?

These issues with copyright law led to the development of *digital rights management* (DRM), a strategy designed to prevent illegal distribution of movies, music, and other digital content. Read Ethics & Issues 11-3 for a related discussion.

WEB LINK 11-9

Digital Rights Management

For more information, visit scsite.com/dc2008/ch11/weblink and then click Digital Rights Management.

ETHICS & ISSUES 11-3

Should It Be Illegal to Sell Programs That Copy Movies from DVDs?

Somewhere in the dark corners of the Internet, you can find almost any movie that has been released on DVD. Of course, the existence of these files is illegal but possible due to DVD copying programs. Movie production companies are furious that these programs exist. Movies on DVDs are encrypted with a system known as the *Content Scrambling System* (CSS), and this encryption was meant to stop anyone from ever copying movies from DVDs. Frustrated that he could not view DVD movies on the Linux operating system, several years ago a teenager and two of his acquaintances developed a program known as DeCSS. DeCSS decrypts DVD movies that are encrypted with CSS. Although the movie industry tried to stop DeCSS from being used or distributed, the simplicity of the DeCSS program meant that it quickly found its way into the hands of thousands of people. The movie industry claims that the Digital Millennium Copyright Act prohibits any attempt to break any type of encryption in a commercial product, which DeCSS and DVD copying programs do. They claim that the programs assist in the violation of their copyright and that sales of movies and the movie industry are harmed by the programs. Also, the industry cannot improve the encryption system to make it stronger because doing so would make all current DVD players obsolete. Proponents of DVD copying programs claim that once you purchase a movie, you should be able to make backup copies and have the ability to play the movie in any way you like. Should it be illegal to distribute programs that copy movies from DVDs? Why or why not? Just because a program can be used in an illegal manner, should the program be banned? Why or why not? What steps can the movie industry take to protect its copyrights?

Codes of Conduct

Recognizing that individuals need specific standards for the ethical use of computers, a number of computer-related organizations have established IT (information technology) codes of conduct (Figure 11-25). An IT **code of conduct** is a written guideline that helps determine whether a specific computer action is ethical or unethical.

IT CODE OF CONDUCT
1. Computers may not be used to harm other people.
2. Employees may not interfere with others' computer work.
3. Employees may not meddle in others' computer files.
4. Computers may not be used to steal.
5. Computers may not be used to bear false witness.
6. Employees may not copy or use software illegally.
7. Employees may not use others' computer resources without authorization.
8. Employees may not use others' intellectual property as their own.
9. Employees shall consider the social impact of programs and systems they design.
10. Employees always should use computers in a way that demonstrates consideration and respect for fellow humans.

FIGURE 11-25 Sample IT code of conduct employers may distribute to employees.

INFORMATION PRIVACY

Information privacy refers to the right of individuals and companies to deny or restrict the collection and use of information about them. In the past, information privacy was easier to maintain because information was kept in separate locations. Each retail store had its own credit files. Each government agency maintained separate records. Doctors had their own patient files.

Today, huge databases store this data online. Much of the data is personal and confidential and should be accessible only to authorized users. Many individuals and organizations, however, question whether this data really is private. That is, some companies and individuals collect and use this information without your authorization. Web sites often collect data about you, so they can customize advertisements and send you personalized e-mail messages. Some employers monitor your computer usage and e-mail messages.

Figure 11-26 lists measures you can take to make your personal data more private. The following sections address techniques companies and employers use to collect your personal data.

Electronic Profiles

When you fill out a form such as a magazine subscription, product warranty registration card, or contest entry form, the merchant that receives the form usually enters it into a database. Likewise, every time you click an advertisement on the Web or register software online, your information and preferences enter a database. Merchants then sell the contents of their databases to national marketing firms and Internet advertising firms. By combining this data with information from public sources such as driver's licenses and vehicle registrations,

HOW TO SAFEGUARD PERSONAL INFORMATION
1. Fill in only necessary information on rebate, warranty, and registration forms.
2. Do not preprint your telephone number or Social Security number on personal checks.
3. Have an unlisted or unpublished telephone number.
4. If Caller ID is available in your area, find out how to block your number from displaying on the receiver's system.
5. Do not write your telephone number on charge or credit receipts.
6. Ask merchants not to write credit card numbers, telephone numbers, Social Security numbers, and driver's license numbers on the back of your personal checks.
7. Purchase goods with cash, rather than credit or checks.
8. Avoid shopping club and buyer cards.
9. If merchants ask personal questions, find out why they want to know before releasing the information.
10. Inform merchants that you do not want them to distribute your personal information.
11. Request, in writing, to be removed from mailing lists.
12. Obtain your credit report once a year from each of the three major credit reporting agencies (Equifax, Experian, and TransUnion) and correct any errors.
13. Request a free copy of your medical records once a year from the Medical Information Bureau.
14. Limit the amount of information you provide to Web sites. Fill in only required information.
15. Install a cookie manager to filter cookies.
16. Clear your history file when you are finished browsing.
17. Set up a free e-mail account. Use this e-mail address for merchant forms.
18. Turn off file and printer sharing on your Internet connection.
19. Install a personal firewall.
20. Sign up for e-mail filtering through your Internet service provider or use an anti-spam program such as Brightmail.
21. Do not reply to spam for any reason.
22. Surf the Web anonymously with a program such as Freedom WebSecure or through an anonymous Web site such as Anonymizer.com.

FIGURE 11-26 Techniques to keep personal data private.

these firms create an electronic profile of individuals. The information in these electronic profiles includes personal details such as your age, address, telephone number, spending habits, marital status, number of dependents, ages of dependents, and so on.

Direct marketing supporters say that using information in this way lowers overall selling costs, which lowers product prices. Critics contend that the information in an electronic profile reveals more about an individual than anyone has a right to know. They claim that companies should inform people if they plan to provide personal information to others, and people should have the right to deny such use. Many companies today allow people to specify whether they want their personal information distributed (Figure 11-27).

selecting these options indicates you want to be contacted

FIGURE 11-27 Many companies today allow people to specify whether they want their personal information distributed.

Cookies

E-commerce and other Web applications often rely on cookies to identify users and customize Web pages. A **cookie** is a small text file that a Web server stores on your computer. Cookie files typically contain data about you, such as your user name or viewing preferences.

Web sites use cookies for a variety of purposes.
- Most Web sites that allow for personalization use cookies to track user preferences. On such sites, users may be asked to fill in a form requesting personal information, such as their name, postal code, or site preferences. A news Web site, for example, might allow users to customize their viewing preferences to display certain stock quotes. The Web site stores their preferences in a cookie on the users' hard disks.
- Some Web sites use cookies to store users' passwords, so they do not need to enter it every time they log in to the Web site.
- Online shopping sites generally use a *session cookie* to keep track of items in a user's shopping cart. This way, users can start an order during one Web session and finish it on another day in another session. Session cookies usually expire after a certain time, such as a week or a month.
- Some Web sites use cookies to track how regularly users visit a site and the Web pages they visit while at the site.
- Web sites may use cookies to target advertisements. These sites store a user's interests and browsing habits in the cookie.

Many commercial Web sites send a cookie to your browser, and then your computer's hard disk stores the cookie. The next time you visit the Web site, your browser retrieves the cookie from your hard disk and sends the data in the cookie to the Web site. Figure 11-28 illustrates how Web sites work with cookies.

Some Web sites do sell or trade information stored in your cookie to advertisers — a practice many believe to be unethical. If you do not want your personal information distributed, you should limit the amount of information you provide to a Web site.

You can set your browser to accept cookies automatically, prompt you if you want to accept a cookie, or disable cookie use altogether. Keep in mind if you disable cookie use, you may not be able to use many of the e-commerce Web sites. As an alternative, you can purchase software that selectively blocks cookies.

 FAQ 11-10

Can a Web site read data in all the cookie files on my computer's hard disk?

No, a Web site can read data only from its own cookie file stored on your hard disk. It cannot access or view any other data on your hard disk — including another cookie file. For more information, visit scsite.com/dc2008/ch11/faq and then click Cookies.

FIGURE 11-28   HOW COOKIES WORK

Step 1:
When you type the Web address of a Web site in your browser window, the browser program searches your hard disk for a cookie associated with the Web site.

Step 2:
If the browser finds a cookie, it sends information in the cookie file to the Web site.

cookies

Web server for www.company.com

Step 3:
If the Web site does not receive cookie information, and is expecting it, the site creates an identification number for you in its database and sends that number to your browser. The browser in turn creates a cookie file based on that number and stores the cookie file on your hard disk. The Web site now can update information in the cookie file whenever you access the site.

Spyware and Adware

Spyware is a program placed on a computer without the user's knowledge that secretly collects information about the user. Spyware can enter a computer as a virus or as a result of a user installing a new program. The spyware program communicates information it collects to some outside source while you are online.

Some vendors or employers use spyware to collect information about program usage or employees. Internet advertising firms often collect information about users' Web browsing habits by hiding spyware in adware. *Adware* is a program that displays an online advertisement in a banner or pop-up window on Web pages, e-mail messages, or other Internet services.

Another type of spyware, called a *Web bug*, is hidden on Web pages or in e-mail messages in the form of graphical images. Web businesses use Web bugs to monitor online habits of Web site visitors. Often, Web bugs link to a cookie stored on the hard disk. (Cookies are not considered spyware because you know they exist.)

To remove spyware, you can obtain a spyware remover that can detect and delete it. Some operating systems and Web browsers include spyware removers. Read Ethics & Issues 11-4 for a related discussion.

ETHICS & ISSUES 11-4

Should Spyware Be Legal?

Legitimate businesses and illegitimate hackers use a variety of techniques to secretly install spyware on unsecured computers. Spyware can perform a number of tasks, such as monitoring the Web sites that you visit or controlling a computer remotely. Some Web pages also have cookies that count visitors and gather basic statistical information about a visitor's location and Web browser. Online advertising agencies or Internet service providers frequently place spyware cookies as part of a promotion, sometimes without the knowledge of the Web page's sponsor. When the collected information is stored in a Web database and shared among several sites, the technology can track a visitor's travels around the Web. If a visitor completes a registration, that information also can be distributed to other advertisers. Spyware and cookies help advertisers reach their markets and refine their messages, but opponents say the technology is little more than electronic stalking. Legal experts say that the use of spyware is in a legal gray area, and stronger laws are needed to regulate it. Should spyware and/or cookies be banned, or is it the right of Web page owners and advertisers to collect information about visitors? Why? Should Web page authors and/or Web page visitors be made aware of spyware and cookies? Why or why not?

Spam

Spam is an unsolicited e-mail message or newsgroup posting sent to many recipients or newsgroups at once. Spam is Internet junk mail (Figure 11-29). The content of spam ranges from selling a product or service, to promoting a business opportunity, to advertising offensive material. One study indicates the average user receives more than 2,200 spam e-mail messages each year. Instead of via e-mail, some spam is sent through an instant massaging system and, thus, is called *spim*. Another type, called *spit*, is spam sent via Internet telephony.

Users can reduce the amount of spam they receive with a number of techniques. Some e-mail programs have built-in settings that allow users to delete spam automatically. Users also can sign up for e-mail filtering from their Internet service provider. **E-mail filtering** is a service that blocks e-mail messages from designated sources. These services typically collect the spam in a central location that users can view at anytime. An alternative to e-mail filtering is to purchase an **anti-spam program** that attempts to remove spam before it reaches your inbox. The

disadvantage of e-mail filters and anti-spam programs is that sometimes they remove valid e-mail messages.

Phishing

Phishing is a scam in which a perpetrator sends an official looking e-mail message that attempts to obtain your personal and financial information. Some phishing e-mail messages ask you to reply with your information; others direct you to a phony Web site, or a pop-up window that looks like a Web site, that collects the information. Read Ethics & Issues 11-5 for a related discussion.

If you receive an e-mail message that looks legitimate and requests you update credit card numbers, Social Security numbers, bank account numbers, passwords, or other private information, the FTC recommends you visit the Web site directly to determine if the request is valid.

To help deter spam and phishing scams, Microsoft and others are developing standards that require e-mail messages contain sender identification so recipients can verify the legitimacy of messages.

Pharming is a scam, similar to phishing, where a perpetrator attempts to obtain your personal and financial information, except they do so via spoofing. That is, when you type a Web address in the Web browser, you are redirected to a phony Web site that looks legitimate. The phony Web site requests you enter confidential information.

WEB LINK 11-10

Spam

For more information, visit scsite.com/ dc2008/ch11/weblink and then click Spam.

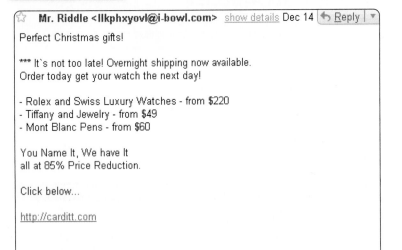

☆ **Mr. Riddle <llkphxyovl@i-bowl.com>** show details Dec 14 ↰ Reply | ▼

Perfect Christmas gifts!

*** It`s not too late! Overnight shipping now available.
Order today get your watch the next day!

- Rolex and Swiss Luxury Watches - from $220
- Tiffany and Jewelry - from $49
- Mont Blanc Pens - from $60

You Name It, We have It
all at 85% Price Reduction.

Click below...

http://carditt.com

FIGURE 11-29   An example of spam.

FAQ 11-11

What do I do if I have been caught in a phishing scam?

If you have been trapped in a phishing scam, visit http://www.ftc.gov or call the FTC help line at 1-877-FTC-HELP. For more information, visit scsite.com/dc2008/ch11/faq and then click Phishing Scams.

ETHICS & ISSUES 11-5

Who Should Protect You from Identity Theft?

If you respond to a phishing attempt, the information you submit ends up in the hands of a scammer, who then either uses the information to access your accounts and take money, or sells and trades the information with other criminals. Sadly, the result often is identity theft. Law enforcement agencies believe that many of the phishing schemes are related to organized crime. Approximately 15 percent of those targeted by phishing provide the requested information. This high level of response emboldens the scammers. Law enforcement agencies claim that these scams are difficult to stop and that people simply need to learn to ignore the requests for information. Computer users find that the scams often are impossible to distinguish from legitimate requests for information, and that the fault lies with Internet service providers or the makers of e-mail programs and Web browsers. Modern Web browsers include tools that fight phishing. Who should be responsible for stopping the phishing phenomenon? What can a person do to protect against phishing when e-mail messages are received from what appear to be legitimate organizations? What can be done to limit or stop the practice of phishing? Are companies and/or consumers to share in the blame for the success of phishing? Why or why not?

Privacy Laws

The concern about privacy has led to the enactment of federal and state laws regarding the storage and disclosure of personal data (Figure 11-30). Common points in some of these laws are outlined at the top of the next page.

Date	Law	Purpose
2003	CAN-SPAM Act	Gives law enforcement the right to impose penalties on people using the Internet to distribute spam.
2002	Sarbanes-Oxley Act	Requires corporate officers, auditors, and attorneys of publicly-traded companies follow strict financial reporting guidelines.
2001	Children's Internet Protection Act (CIPA)	Protects minors from inappropriate content when accessing the Internet in schools and libraries.
2001	Provide Appropriate Tools Required to Intercept and Obstruct Terrorism (PATRIOT) Act	Gives law enforcement the right to monitor people's activities, including Web and e-mail habits.
1999	Gramm-Leach-Bliley Act (GLBA) or Financial Modernization Act	Protects consumers from disclosure of their personal financial information and requires institutions to alert customers of information disclosure policies.
1998	Children's Online Privacy Protection Act (COPPA)	Requires Web sites protect personal information of children under 13 years of age.
1998	Digital Millennium Copyright Act (DMCA)	Makes it illegal to circumvent antipiracy schemes in commercial software; outlaws sale of devices that copy software illegally.
1997	No Electronic Theft (NET) Act	Closes a narrow loophole in the law that allowed people to give away copyrighted material (such as software) on the Internet without legal repercussions.
1996	Health Insurance Portability and Accountability Act (HIPAA)	Protects individuals against the wrongful disclosure of their health information.
1996	National Information Infrastructure Protection Act	Penalizes theft of information across state lines, threats against networks, and computer system trespassing.
1994	Computer Abuse Amendments Act	Amends 1984 act to outlaw transmission of harmful computer code such as viruses.
1992	Cable Act	Extends the privacy of the Cable Communications Policy Act of 1984 to include cellular and other wireless services.
1991	Telephone Consumer Protection Act	Restricts activities of telemarketers.
1988	Computer Matching and Privacy Protection Act	Regulates the use of government data to determine the eligibility of individuals for federal benefits.
1988	Video Privacy Protection Act	Forbids retailers from releasing or selling video-rental records without customer consent or a court order.
1986	Electronic Communications Privacy Act (ECPA)	Provides the same right of privacy protection for the postal delivery service and telephone companies to the new forms of electronic communications, such as voice mail, e-mail, and cellular telephones.
1984	Cable Communications Policy Act	Regulates disclosure of cable television subscriber records.
1984	Computer Fraud and Abuse Act	Outlaws unauthorized access of federal government computers.
1978	Right to Financial Privacy Act	Strictly outlines procedures federal agencies must follow when looking at customer records in banks.
1974	Privacy Act	Forbids federal agencies from allowing information to be used for a reason other than that for which it was collected.
1974	Family Educational Rights and Privacy Act	Gives students and parents access to school records and limits disclosure of records to unauthorized parties.
1970	Fair Credit Reporting Act	Prohibits credit reporting agencies from releasing credit information to unauthorized people and allows consumers to review their own credit records.

FIGURE 11-30 Summary of the major U.S. government laws concerning privacy.

1. Information collected and stored about individuals should be limited to what is necessary to carry out the function of the business or government agency collecting the data.
2. Once collected, provisions should be made to restrict access to the data to those employees within the organization who need access to it to perform their job duties.
3. Personal information should be released outside the organization collecting the data only when the person has agreed to its disclosure.
4. When information is collected about an individual, the individual should know that the data is being collected and have the opportunity to determine the accuracy of the data.

One law with an apparent legal loophole is the 1970 **Fair Credit Reporting Act**. The act limits the rights of others viewing a credit report to only those with a legitimate business need. The problem is that it does not define a legitimate business need. The result is that just about anyone can claim a legitimate business need and gain access to your credit report.

Social Engineering

As related to the use of computers, **social engineering** is defined as gaining unauthorized access or obtaining confidential information by taking advantage of the trusting human nature of some victims and the naivety of others. Some social engineers trick their victims into revealing confidential information such as user names and passwords on the telephone, in person, or on the Internet. Techniques they use include pretending to be an administrator or other authoritative figure, feigning an emergency situation, or impersonating an acquaintance. Social engineers also obtain information from users who do not destroy or conceal information properly. These perpetrators sift through company dumpsters, watch or film people dialing telephone numbers or using ATMs, and snoop around computers looking for openly displayed confidential information.

Employee Monitoring

Employee monitoring involves the use of computers to observe, record, and review an employee's use of a computer, including communications such as e-mail messages, keyboard activity (used to measure productivity), and Web sites visited. Many programs exist that easily allow employers to monitor employees. Further, it is legal for employers to use these programs.

A frequently debated issue is whether an employer has the right to read employee e-mail messages. Actual policies vary widely. Some companies declare that they will review e-mail messages regularly, and others state that e-mail is private. In some states, if a company does not have a formal e-mail policy, it can read e-mail messages without employee notification. One survey discovered that more than 73 percent of companies search and/or read employee files, voice mail, e-mail messages, Web connections, and other networking communications. Several lawsuits have been filed against employers because many believe that such internal communications should be private.

Another controversial issue relates to the use of cameras to monitor employees, customers, and the public. Many people feel that this use of video cameras is a violation of privacy.

Content Filtering

One of the more controversial issues that surround the Internet is its widespread availability of objectionable material, such as racist literature, violence, and obscene pictures. Some believe that such materials should be banned. Others believe that the materials should be filtered, that is, restricted. **Content filtering** is the process of restricting access to certain material on the Web. Content filtering opponents argue that banning any materials violates constitutional guarantees of free speech and personal rights.

Many businesses use content filtering to limit employees' Web access. These businesses argue that employees are unproductive when visiting inappropriate or objectionable Web sites. Some schools, libraries, and parents use content filtering to restrict access to minors.

One approach to content filtering is through a rating system of the *Internet Content Rating Association (ICRA)*, which is similar to those used for movies and videos. Major Web sites such as Yahoo!, AOL, and MSN use the rating system established by the ICRA. If content at the Web site goes beyond the rating limits set in the Web browser software, a user cannot access the Web site. Concerned parents can set the rating limits and prevent these limits from being changed by using a password.

Another approach to content filtering is to use filtering software. **Web filtering software** is a program that restricts access to specified Web sites. Some also filter sites that use specific words. Others allow you to filter e-mail messages, chat rooms, and programs. Many Internet security programs include a firewall, antivirus program, and filtering capabilities combined (Figure 11-31).

Computer Forensics

Computer forensics, also called *digital forensics*, *network forensics*, or *cyberforensics*, is the discovery, collection, and analysis of evidence found on computers and networks. Forensic analysis involves the examination of computer media, programs, data and log files on computers, servers, and networks. Many areas use computer forensics, including law enforcement, criminal prosecutors, military intelligence, insurance agencies, and information security departments in the private sector.

A computer forensics analyst must have knowledge of the law, technical experience with many types of hardware and software products, superior communication skills, familiarity with corporate structures and policies, a willingness to learn and update skills, and a knack for problem solving. For more information about computer forensics, read the Computer Forensics Special Feature that follows this chapter. For a look at the next generation of forensics, read Looking Ahead 11-2.

HEALTH CONCERNS OF COMPUTER USE

Users are a key component in any information system. Thus, protecting users is just as important as protecting hardware, software, and data.

The widespread use of computers has led to some important health concerns. Users should be proactive and minimize their chance of risk. The following sections discuss health risks and preventions, along with measures users can take to keep the environment healthy.

Computers and Health Risks

A **repetitive strain injury (RSI)** is an injury or disorder of the muscles, nerves, tendons,

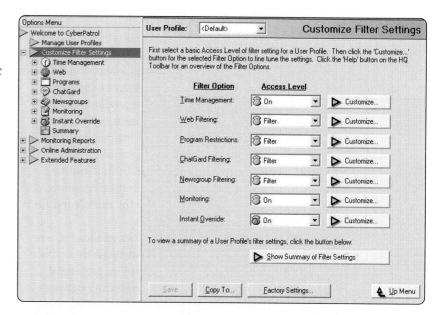

FIGURE 11-31 Many Internet security programs include content filtering capabilities, where users can block specified Web sites and applications.

LOOKING AHEAD 11-2

Computer Knowledge Assessment Using Brain Fingerprinting

A powerful forensic tool may one day replace the traditional lie detector test. Brain fingerprinting examines a subset of brain waves generated involuntarily when an individual recognizes familiar information.

To conduct the test, researchers place a strap equipped with sensors on an individual's head and then present a variety of relevant and irrelevant words, pictures, and sounds. If the stimulus is familiar, the brain generates unique brain waves 300 to 800 milliseconds after receiving the stimulus.

Computers store and then analyze the series of unique brain waves to determine if the person's brain has stored critical details of a situation, such as a fraudulent or criminal act. Researchers also have determined that brain fingerprinting could help identify the onset of Alzheimer's disease. For more information, visit scsite.com/dc2008/ch11/looking and then click Brain Fingerprinting.

ligaments, and joints. Computer-related RSIs include tendonitis and carpal tunnel syndrome. RSIs are the largest job-related injury and illness problem in the United States today. For this reason, OSHA (Occupational Safety and Health Administration) has developed industry-specific and task-specific guidelines designed to prevent workplace injuries with respect to computer usage.

WEB LINK 11-11

RSIs

For more information, visit scsite.com/dc2008/ch11/weblink and then click RSIs.

Tendonitis is inflammation of a tendon due to repeated motion or stress on that tendon. *Carpal tunnel syndrome* (*CTS*) is inflammation of the nerve that connects the forearm to the palm of the wrist. Repeated or forceful bending of the wrist can cause CTS or tendonitis of the wrist. Symptoms of tendonitis of the wrist include extreme pain that extends from the forearm to the hand, along with tingling in the fingers. Symptoms of CTS include burning pain when the nerve is compressed, along with numbness and tingling in the thumb and first two fingers.

Long-term computer work can lead to tendonitis or CTS. Factors that cause these disorders include prolonged typing, prolonged mouse usage, or continual shifting between the mouse and the keyboard. If untreated, these disorders can lead to permanent damage to your body.

You can take many precautions to prevent these types of injuries. Take frequent breaks during the computer session to exercise your hands and arms (Figure 11-32). To prevent injury due to typing, place a wrist rest between the keyboard and the edge of your desk. To prevent injury while using a mouse, place the mouse at least six inches from the edge of the

desk. In this position, your wrist is flat on the desk. Finally, minimize the number of times you switch between the mouse and the keyboard, and avoid using the heel of your hand as a pivot point while typing or using the mouse.

Another type of health-related condition due to computer usage is **computer vision syndrome** (*CVS*). You may have CVS if you have sore, tired, burning, itching, or dry eyes; blurred or double vision; distance blurred vision after prolonged staring at a display device; headache or sore neck; difficulty shifting focus between a display device and documents; difficulty focusing on the screen image; color fringes or after-images when you look away from the display device; and increased sensitivity to light. Eyestrain associated with CVS is not thought to have serious or long-term consequences. Figure 11-33 outlines some techniques you can follow to ease eyestrain.

People who spend their workday using the computer sometimes complain of lower back pain, muscle fatigue, and emotional fatigue. Lower back pain sometimes is caused from poor posture. Always sit properly in the chair while you work. Take a break every 30 to 60

HAND EXERCISES

- Spread fingers apart for several seconds while keeping wrists straight.
- Gently push back fingers and then thumb.
- Dangle arms loosely at sides and then shake arms and hands.

TECHNIQUES TO EASE EYESTRAIN

- Every 10 to 15 minutes, take an eye break.
  - Look into the distance and focus on an object for 20 to 30 seconds.
  - Roll your eyes in a complete circle.
  - Close your eyes and rest them for at least one minute.
- Blink your eyes every five seconds.
- Place your display device about an arm's length away from your eyes with the top of the screen at eye level or below.
- Use large fonts.
- If you wear glasses, ask your doctor about computer glasses.
- Adjust the lighting.

FIGURE 11-32 To reduce the chance of developing tendonitis or carpal tunnel syndrome, take frequent breaks during computer sessions to exercise your hands and arms.

FIGURE 11-33 Following these tips may help reduce eyestrain while working on a computer.

minutes — stand up, walk around, or stretch. Another way to help prevent these injuries is to be sure your workplace is designed ergonomically, which is discussed in the next section.

Ergonomics and Workplace Design

Ergonomics is an applied science devoted to incorporating comfort, efficiency, and safety into the design of items in the workplace. Ergonomic studies have shown that using the correct type and configuration of chair, keyboard, display device, and work surface helps users work comfortably and efficiently and helps protect their health. For the computer work space, experts recommend an area of at least two feet by four feet. Figure 11-34 illustrates additional guidelines for setting up the work area.

Computer Addiction

Computers can provide entertainment and enjoyment. Some computer users, however, become obsessed with the computer and the Internet. **Computer addiction** occurs when the computer consumes someone's entire social life. Computer addiction is a growing health problem.

Symptoms of a user with computer addiction include the following:
- Craves computer time
- Overjoyed when at the computer
- Unable to stop computer activity
- Irritable when not at the computer
- Neglects family and friends
- Problems at work or school

Computer addiction is a treatable illness through therapy and support groups.

viewing angle: 20° to center of screen
viewing distance: 18 to 28 inches

arms: elbows at about 90° and arms and hands approximately parallel to floor

keyboard height: 23 to 28 inches depending on height of user

adjustable height chair with 4 or 5 legs for stability

feet flat on floor

FIGURE 11-34   A well-designed work area should be flexible to allow adjustments to the height and build of different individuals. Good lighting and air quality also are important considerations.

Green Computing

Green computing involves reducing the electricity and environmental waste while using a computer. People use, and often waste, resources such as electricity and paper while using a computer. Society has become aware of this waste and is taking measures to combat it.

As discussed in Chapter 6, personal computers, display devices, and printers should comply with guidelines of the ENERGY STAR program. For example, many devices switch to standby or power save mode after a specified number of inactive minutes or hours.

Users should not store obsolete computers and devices in their basement, storage room, attic, warehouse, or any other location. Computers, monitors, and other equipment contain toxic materials and potentially dangerous elements including lead, mercury, and flame retardants. In a landfill, these materials release into the environment. Recycling and refurbishing old equipment are much safer alternatives for the environment. Manufacturers can use the millions of pounds of recycled raw materials to make products such as outdoor furniture and automotive parts.

Experts estimate that more than 700 million personal computers are obsolete. Because of the huge volumes of electronic waste, the U.S. federal government has proposed a bill that would require computer recycling across the country. Local governments are working on methods to make it easy for consumers to recycle this type of equipment. Many computer manufacturers, office supply stores, and other agencies offer free recycling to consumers and businesses.

To reduce the environmental impact of computing further, users simply can alter a few habits. Figure 11-35 lists the ways you can contribute to green computing.

WEB LINK 11-12

Green Computing

For more information, visit scsite.com/dc2008/ch11/weblink and then click Green Computing.

FAQ 11-12

Should I turn off my computer every night?

Manufacturers claim if you use the hibernate feature of your operating system or the sleep feature on your computer, you save about the same amount of energy as when you turn off the computer. The ENERGY STAR program, however, recommends turning it off. For more information, visit scsite.com/dc2008/ch11/faq and then click ENERGY STAR.

GREEN COMPUTING SUGGESTIONS

1. Use computers and devices that comply with the ENERGY STAR program.
2. Do not leave the computer running overnight.
3. Turn off the monitor, printer, and other devices when not in use.
4. Use paperless methods to communicate.
5. Recycle paper.
6. Buy recycled paper.
7. Recycle toner cartridges.
8. Recycle old computers and printers.
9. Telecommute (saves gas).

FIGURE 11-35   A list of suggestions to make computing healthy for the environment.

Test your knowledge of pages 578 through 590 in Quiz Yourself 11-3.

QUIZ YOURSELF 11-3

Instructions: Find the true statement below. Then, rewrite the remaining false statements so they are true.

1. A code of conduct gives authors and artists exclusive rights to duplicate, publish, and sell their materials.

2. Factors that cause CVS include prolonged typing, prolonged mouse usage, or continual shifting between the mouse and the keyboard.

3. Phishing is the discovery, collection, and analysis of evidence found on computers and networks.

4. Spam is Internet junk mail.

5. Users should store obsolete computers and devices in their basement or attic.

6. Web sites use electronic profiles to track user preferences, store users' passwords, keep track of items in a user's shopping cart, and track Web site browsing habits.

7. You can assume that information on the Web is correct.

Quiz Yourself Online: To further check your knowledge of information accuracy, intellectual property rights, codes of conduct, information privacy, and computer-related health disorders and preventions, visit scsite.com/dc2008/ch11/quiz and then click Objectives 10 – 12.

CHAPTER SUMMARY

This chapter identified some potential computer risks and the safeguards that schools, businesses, and individuals can implement to minimize these risks. Wireless security risks and safeguards also were discussed.

The chapter presented ethical issues surrounding information accuracy, intellectual property rights, codes of conduct, and information privacy. The chapter ended with a discussion of computer-related health issues, their preventions, and ways to keep the environment healthy.

CAREER CORNER   Computer Forensics Specialist

Computer forensics is a rapidly growing field that involves gathering and analyzing evidence from computers and networks. It is the responsibility of the *computer forensics specialist* to take several careful steps to identify and retrieve possible evidence that may exist on a suspect's computer. These steps include protecting the suspect's computer, discovering all files, recovering deleted files, revealing hidden files, accessing protected or encrypted files, analyzing all the data, and providing expert consultation and/or testimony as required. A computer forensics specialist must have knowledge of all aspects of the computer, from the operating system to computer architecture and hardware design.

In the past, many computer forensics specialists were self-taught computer users who may have attended computer forensics seminars, or they may have been trained in the use of one or more computer forensics tools by software vendors. The computer forensics specialist of today needs extensive training, usually from several different sources. A degree in Computer Science should be supplemented with graduate courses and university level professional development certificates. The most widely recognized certifications available to computer forensics professionals are the Certified Information Systems Security Professional (CISSP) and the Certified Computer Examiner (CCE).

Entry level salaries for computer forensics specialists range from $85,000 to $120,000. With experience and certifications, salaries can exceed $160,000. For more information, read the Computer Forensics Special Feature that follows this chapter or visit scsite.com/dc2008/ch11/careers and then click Computer Forensics Specialist.

High-Tech Talk

THE KEY(S) TO MAKING ENCRYPTION WORK

Every day, hundreds of thousands of people carry notebook computers to and from work, even as other computer users interact electronically, via e-mail, Web sites, ATMs, and cellular telephones. The increase of electronically transmitted information has led to an increased reliance on encryption, which helps ensure that unauthorized individuals cannot obtain the contents of these electronic transmissions.

The two basic types of encryption are private key and public key. With *private key encryption*, also called *symmetric key encryption*, both the originator and the recipient use the same secret key to encrypt and decrypt the data. The most popular private key encryption system is *advanced encryption standard* (*AES*), which was adopted officially as the U.S. government standard in May 2002.

Public key encryption, also called *asymmetric key encryption*, uses two encryption keys: a public key and a private key. Public key encryption software generates both your private key and your public key. A message encrypted with your public key can be decrypted only with your private key, and vice versa.

The public key is made known to those with whom you communicate. For example, public keys are posted on a Web page or e-mailed. A central administrator can publish a list of public keys on a public key server. The private key, by contrast, should be kept confidential. To send an encrypted e-mail message with public key encryption, the sender uses the receiver's public key to encrypt the message. Then, the receiver uses his or her private key to decrypt the message (Figure 11-36). For example, if Mae wants to send Jonah an encrypted message, she would use Jonah's public key to encrypt the message. When Jonah receives the encrypted message, he would use his private key to decrypt it. Jonah's encryption software generated his public and private keys. Mae uses Jonah's public key to encrypt the message. Thus, only Jonah will be able to decrypt the message with his private key.

Windows Vista includes a security feature called the *Encrypting File System* (*EFS*). EFS uses a combination of public key and symmetric key encryption to ensure that files are protected from almost any method of unauthorized access. When a user encrypts a file, EFS generates a random number for the file that EFS calls the file's file encryption key (FEK) to encrypt the data. EFS then uses FEK to encrypt the file's contents with an encryption algorithm. The FEK then is encrypted with the user's public key using the RSA public-key-based encryption algorithm, and the encrypted FEK then is stored with the file. Of course, the entire encryption process happens behind the scenes for the user, who simply completes a few mouse clicks to encrypt a folder or file. That is part of the elegance of EFS: while it is simple for a user, it is very difficult for any unauthorized user without the correct keys to crack the encryption. In the end, that is the key to keeping your data safe and sound. For more information, visit scsite.com/dc2008/ch11/tech and then click Encryption.

FIGURE 11-36   AN EXAMPLE OF PUBLIC KEY ENCRYPTION

Step 1:
The sender creates a document to be e-mailed to the receiver.

Step 2:
The sender uses the receiver's public key to encrypt a message.

Step 3:
The receiver uses his or her private key to decrypt the message.

Step 4:
The receiver can read or print the decrypted message.

```
CONFIDENTIAL
----------

The new
plant will
be located...
```
message to be sent

```
CONFIDENTIAL
----------

The new
plant will
be located...
```
decrypted message

sender (Mae)

receiver (Jonah)

public key

```
AA311C253
----------

43025OC
4CAD078
32EC8EF
```
encrypted message

private key

Companies on the Cutting Edge

MCAFEE
INTRUSION PREVENTION PRODUCTS DEVELOPER

Researchers in 17 cities in 12 countries are hard at work at *McAfee* laboratories trying to prevent computer intrusions. The Anti-Virus Emergency Response Team (Avert) protects desktop computers, servers, networks, and wireless devices by collecting and then disassembling malware. The researchers also monitor online bulletin board systems for suspicious messages and expect to find more than 18,000 new threats each year.

More than 70 million consumers, small- and medium-sized businesses, governmental agencies, and large corporations rely on McAfee's intrusion prevention products to shield them from viruses, worms, Trojan horses, spyware and adware, and phishing schemes. In 2006, *Popular Science Magazine* selected the Santa Clara, California, company to receive its "Best of What's New" award for the McAfee SiteAdvisor, which shields Internet users from dangerous and risky Web sites. For more information, visit scsite.com/dc2008/ch11/companies and then click McAfee.

SYMANTEC
COMPUTER SECURITY SOLUTIONS LEADER

Ninety percent of computer users have installed a virus protection program on their computers, but only twenty percent have a firewall to protect against malicious hackers, according to a survey conducted by Applied Marketing Research. *Symantec*'s line of Norton products, including AntiVirus, Personal Firewall, and AntiSpam, can provide these users with peace of mind knowing that their computers are as secure as possible.

Gordon Eubank founded Symantec in 1982. Since then, more than 120 million users worldwide have used that company's products, helping it grow to one of the world's premier Internet security technology companies with operations in more than 40 countries. Symantec opened its Phish Report Network in 2006 in an effort to track and stop cybercriminals from perpetrating additional phishing attacks. For more information, visit scsite.com/dc2008/ch11/companies and then click Symantec.

Technology Trailblazers

DONN PARKER
CYBERCRIME AUTHORITY

Computer criminals are troubled people, according to *Donn Parker*, so they violate the law in an attempt to solve their problems. In an attempt to fight cybercrime, Parker founded the International Information Integrity Institute (I-4), then interviewed hundreds of computer criminals and analyzed thousands of security crime cases during the past 30 years.

Security systems within corporations are critical, he says, but they should evolve constantly to defend against attackers. In a 2006 *ISSA Journal* article, Parker urges corporate managers to increase funding to replace their current risk-based security systems with practical and consistent processes, products, and techniques.

Parker has conducted security reviews for more than 250 companies and has written 6 computer security books. For more information, visit scsite.com/dc2008/ch11/people and then click Donn Parker.

CLIFFORD STOLL
COMPUTER PHILOSOPHER

Computers have become integrated in practically every phase of our lives, but *Clifford Stoll* wants us to think about their effect on our quality of life. He questions the benefits technology and the Internet presumably provide and the role computers play in schools.

In his books, *Silicon Snake Oil — Second Thoughts on the Information Highway* and *High Tech Heretic: Why Computers Don't Belong in the Classroom*, Stoll maintains that "life in the real world is far more interesting, far more important, far richer, than anything you'll ever find on a computer screen."

He first gained fame by tracking a hacker who was part of a spy ring selling computer secrets to the Soviet Union's KGB for money and drugs. For more information, visit scsite.com/dc2008/ch11/people and then click Clifford Stoll.

Chapter Review

The Chapter Review section summarizes the concepts presented in this chapter. To listen to the audio version of this Chapter Review, visit scsite.com/dc2008/ch11/review. To obtain help from other students regarding any subject in this chapter, visit scsite.com/dc2008/ch11/forum and post your thoughts or questions.

① What Are Types of Computer Security Risks?   A **computer security risk** is any event or action that could cause a loss of or damage to computer hardware, software, data, information, or processing capability. Common computer security risks include computer viruses, worms, Trojan horses, botnets, denial of service attacks, back doors, and spoofing; unauthorized access and use; hardware theft and vandalism; software theft; information theft; and system failure.

② How Can Users Safeguard against Computer Viruses, Worms, Trojan Horses, Botnets, Denial of Service Attacks, Back Doors, and Spoofing?   A computer **virus** is a potentially damaging program that affects, or infects, a computer negatively by altering the way the computer works. A **worm** is a program that copies itself repeatedly, using up resources and possibly shutting down the computer or network. A **Trojan horse** is a program that hides within or looks like a legitimate program. Users can take precautions to guard against this *malware*, short for *malicious software*. Do not start a computer with removable media in the drives or ports. Never open an e-mail attachment unless it is from a **trusted source**. Disable *macros* in documents that are not from a trusted source. Install an **antivirus program** and a personal firewall. Stay informed about any new virus alert or **virus hoax**. To defend against a **botnet,** a **denial of service attack**, improper use of a **back door**, and **spoofing**, users can install a **firewall**, install *intrusion detection software*, and set up a *honeypot*.

③ What Are Techniques to Prevent Unauthorized Computer Access and Use?
Unauthorized access is the use of a computer or network without permission. **Unauthorized use** is the use of a computer or its data for unapproved or illegal activities. A written acceptable use policy (AUP) outlines the activities for which the computer and network may and may not be used. A **firewall** consists of hardware and/or software that prevents unauthorized access to data, information, and storage media. *Intrusion detection software* analyzes network traffic, assesses vulnerability, identifies unauthorized intrusions, and notifies network administrators of suspicious behavior patterns or system breaches. An *access control* defines who can access a computer, when they can access it, and what actions they can take. Access controls include a **user name** and **password**, a *possessed object*, and a **biometric device**. An **audit trail** records in a file both successful and unsuccessful access attempts.

connect

Visit scsite.com/dc2008/ch11/qu or click the Quiz Yourself button. Click Objectives 1 – 3.

④ What Are Safeguards against Hardware Theft and Vandalism?   **Hardware theft** is the act of stealing computer equipment. **Hardware vandalism** is the act of defacing or destroying computer equipment. The best preventive measures against hardware theft and vandalism are common sense and a constant awareness of the risk. Physical devices and practical security measures, passwords, possessed objects, and biometrics can reduce the risk of theft or render a computer useless if it is stolen.

⑤ How Do Software Manufacturers Protect against Software Piracy?   Software **piracy** is the unauthorized and illegal duplication of copyrighted software. To protect themselves from software piracy, manufacturers issue a **license agreement** that provides specific conditions for use of the software. **Product activation** is a process during which users provide the product's identification number to receive an installation identification number unique to their computer.

⑥ What Is Encryption, and Why Is It Necessary?   **Information theft** occurs when someone steals personal or confidential information. **Encryption** prevents information theft by converting readable data into unreadable characters. To read the data, a recipient must **decrypt**, or decipher, it into a readable form.

Chapter Review

(7) What Types of Devices Are Available to Protect Computers from System Failure?

A *system failure* is the prolonged malfunction of a computer. A common cause of system failure is an electrical disturbance such as **noise**, an **undervoltage**, or an **overvoltage**. A **surge protector** uses special electrical components to smooth out minor noise, provide a stable current flow, and keep an overvoltage from reaching the computer. An **uninterruptible power supply** (**UPS**) contains surge protection circuits and one or more batteries that can provide power during an undervoltage.

(8) What Are Options for Backing Up Computer Resources?

A **backup** is a duplicate of a file, program, or disk that can be used to **restore** the file if the original is lost, damaged, or destroyed. Users can opt for a *full backup* or a *selective backup*. Most operating systems and backup devices include a backup program, and numerous stand-alone backup utilities exist.

(9) What Are Risks and Safeguards Associated with Wireless Communications?

Wireless access poses additional security risks. Intruders connect to other wireless networks to gain free Internet access or a company's confidential data. Some individuals intercept and monitor communications as they are transmitted. Others connect to a network through an unsecured wireless access point (WAP). Some safeguards include firewalls, reconfiguring the WAP, and ensuring equipment uses a wireless security standard, such as *Wired Equivalent Privacy* (WEP), *Wi-Fi Protected Access* (WPA), and *802.11i*.

connect
Visit scsite.com/dc2008/ch11/quiz or click the Quiz Yourself button. Click Objectives 4 – 9.

(10) What Are Issues Related to Information Accuracy, Rights, and Conduct?

Computer ethics govern the use of computers and information systems. Issues in computer ethics include the responsibility for information accuracy and the **intellectual property rights** to which creators are entitled for works that are available digitally. A **copyright** gives authors and artists exclusive rights to duplicate, publish, and sell their materials. An IT (information technology) **code of conduct** helps determine whether a specific computer action is ethical or unethical.

(11) What Are Issues Surrounding Information Privacy?

Information privacy is the right of individuals and companies to deny or restrict the collection and use of information about them. Issues surrounding information privacy include electronic profiles, cookies, spyware and adware, spam, phishing, social engineering, employee monitoring, and computer forensics. An electronic profile combines data about an individual's Web use with data from public sources, which then is sold. A **cookie** is a file that a Web server stores on a computer to collect data about the user. *Spyware* is a program placed on a computer that secretly collects information about the user. *Adware* is a program that displays an online advertisement in a banner or pop-up window. **Spam** is an unsolicited e-mail message or newsgroup posting sent to many recipients. **Phishing** is a scam in which a perpetrator sends an official looking e-mail that attempts to obtain personal or financial information. **Pharming** is a scam where a perpetrator attempts to obtain your personal and financial information, except they do so via spoofing. As related to the use of computers, **social engineering** is defined as gaining unauthorized access or obtaining confidential information by taking advantage of the trusting human nature of some victims and the naivety of others. **Employee monitoring** uses computers to observe, record, and review an employee's computer use.

(12) How Can Health-Related Disorders and Injuries Due to Computer Use Be Prevented?

A **repetitive strain injury** (**RSI**) is an injury or disorder of the muscles, nerves, tendons, ligaments, and joints. Computer-related RSIs include *tendonitis* and *carpal tunnel syndrome* (CTS). Another health-related condition is eyestrain associated with **computer vision syndrome** (CVS). To prevent health-related disorders, take frequent breaks, use precautionary exercises and techniques, and use *ergonomics* when planning the workplace. **Computer addiction** occurs when the computer consumes someone's entire social life. Computer addiction is a treatable illness through therapy and support groups.

connect
Visit scsite.com/dc2008/ch11/quiz or click the Quiz Yourself button. Click Objectives 10 – 12.

Key Terms

You should know the Primary Terms and be familiar with the Secondary Terms. Use the list below to help focus your study. To further enhance your understanding of the Key Terms in this chapter, visit scsite.com/dc2008/ch11/terms. See an example of and a definition for each term, and access current and additional information about the term from the Web.

Primary Terms

(shown in bold-black characters in the chapter)

anti-spam program (584)
antivirus program (560)
audit trail (565)
back door (562)
back up (576)
backup (576)
biometric device (567)
botnet (562)
code of conduct (580)
computer addiction (589)
computer crime (556)
computer ethics (578)
computer forensics (587)
computer security risk (556)
computer vision syndrome (588)
content filtering (586)
cookie (582)
copyright (579)
cracker (556)
cybercrime (556)
cyberextortionist (557)
cyberterrorist (557)
decrypt (572)
denial of service attack (562)
digital certificate (573)
digital signature (572)
DoS attack (562)
e-mail filtering (584)
employee monitoring (586)
encryption (572)
Fair Credit Reporting Act (586)
firewall (563)
green computing (590)
hacker (556)
hardware theft (569)
hardware vandalism (569)
information privacy (580)

information theft (571)
inoculate (561)
intellectual property rights (579)
license agreement (570)
noise (574)
online security service (558)
overvoltage (574)
password (566)
personal firewall (564)
personal identification number (PIN) (567)
pharming (584)
phishing (584)
piracy (570)
power surge (574)
product activation (571)
quarantine (561)
repetitive strain injury (RSI) (587)
restore (576)
script kiddie (556)
secure site (573)
social engineering (586)
software theft (570)
spam (584)
spoofing (563)
surge protector (574)
Trojan horse (558)
trusted source (560)
unauthorized access (564)
unauthorized use (564)
undervoltage (574)
uninterruptible power supply (UPS) (575)
user name (566)
virus (558)
virus definition (561)
virus hoax (562)
virus signature (561)
Web filtering software (587)
worm (558)
zombie (562)

Secondary Terms

(shown in italic characters in the chapter)

128-bit encryption (573)
40-bit encryption (573)
802.11i (577)
access control (565)
adware (583)
authentication (566)
biometric payment (568)
BitLocker (572)
blackout (574)
bot (562)
brownout (574)
Business Software Alliance (BSA) (571)
carpal tunnel syndrome (CTS) (588)
CERT/CC (558)
certificate authority (CA) (573)
child (576)
ciphertext (572)
Computer Emergency Response Team Coordination Center (558)
CVS (588)
cyberforensics (587)
DDoS (distributed DoS) attack (562)
digital forensics (587)
digital rights management (DRM) (580)
e-mail spoofing (563)
Encrypting File System (572)
encryption key (572)
end-user license agreement (EULA) (571)
ergonomics (589)
fault-tolerant computer (576)
full backup (576)
grandparent (576)
hash (572)
honeypot (564)
identification (565)
intellectual property (IP) (579)
Internet Content Rating Association (ICRA) (586)
intrusion detection software (564)

IP spoofing (563)
Joule (575)
macros (560)
malicious software (558)
malware (558)
network forensics (587)
offline UPS (575)
offsite (576)
online backup service (576)
online UPS (575)
parent (576)
payload (558)
plaintext (572)
possessed object (567)
Pretty Good Privacy (PGP) (572)
proxy server (564)
Secure HTTP (S-HTTP) (574)
Secure Sockets Layer (SSL) (574)
selective backup (576)
session cookie (582)
single-user license agreement (571)
spike (574)
spim (584)
spit (584)
spyware (583)
SSID (577)
standby UPS (575)
surge suppressor (574)
system failure (574)
tendonitis (588)
three-generation backup (576)
Underwriters Laboratories (UL) 1449 standard (575)
user ID (566)
virtual private network (VPN) (574)
war driving (577)
war flying (577)
Web bug (583)
Wi-Fi Protected Access (WPA) (577)
Wired Equivalent Privacy (WEP) (577)
zombie army (562)

SHELLY
CASHMAN
SERIES.
597

Select a chapter:
1 2 3 4 5 6 7 8 9 10 11 12 13 14 15

Checkpoint

Use the Checkpoint exercises to check your knowledge level of the chapter. The Beyond the Book exercises will help broaden your understanding of the concepts presented in this chapter. To complete the Checkpoint exercises interactively, visit scsite.com/dc2008/ch11/check.

Label the Figure

Identify these common computer security risks.

a. software theft
b. system failure
c. unauthorized access and use
d. information theft
e. hardware theft
f. Internet and network attacks

True/False

Mark T for True and F for False. (See page numbers in parentheses.)

_____ 1. Not all breaches to computer security are planned. (556)

_____ 2. Hackers often claim the intent of their security breaches is to improve security. (556)

_____ 3. Many methods exist to guarantee completely a computer or network is safe from computer viruses, worms, and Trojan horses. (560)

_____ 4. Cybercriminals install malicious bots on unprotected computers to create a zombie army. (562)

_____ 5. A honeypot is a computer that is set up to entice an intruder to break into it. (564)

_____ 6. Biometric payment involves a customer's fingerprint being read by a fingerprint scanner that is linked to a payment method such as a checking account or credit card. (568)

_____ 7. Encrypted (scrambled) data is called plaintext. (572)

_____ 8. A digitial signature is a mathematical formula that generates a code from the contents of the message. (572)

_____ 9. An online UPS switches to battery power when a problem occurs in a power line. (575)

_____ 10. Digital rights management (DRM) is a strategy designed to prevent illegal distribution of computer viruses, worms, and Trojan horses. (580)

_____ 11. A cookie is a small text file that a Web server stores on your computer. (582)

_____ 12. Green computing involves reducing the electricity while using a computer, but the practice increases environmental waste. (590)

Checkpoint

 Multiple Choice　　　　Select the best answer. (See page numbers in parentheses.)

1. A computer infected by a virus, worm, or Trojan horse may have any of the following symptoms except _____. (558)
   a. files become corrupted
   b. system properties change
   c. existing programs and files disappear
   d. available memory is more than expected

2. Malware is a term that can be used to describe _____. (558)
   a. worms
   b. spyware
   c. back doors
   d. all of the above

3. A _____ is a computer whose owner is completely unaware the computer is being controlled remotely by an outsider. (562)
   a. ghost
   b. zombie
   c. back door
   d. Trojan horse

4. _____ commonly is used for spam and phishing scams. (563)
   a. A back door
   b. E-mail spoofing
   c. IP spoofing
   d. A DoS attack

5. Physical access controls, such as locked doors and windows, usually are adequate to protect against _____. (569)
   a. software piracy
   b. unauthorized access
   c. hardware theft
   d. all of the above

6. Software piracy continues because _____. (571)
   a. in some countries, legal protection for software does not exist
   b. many buyers believe they have the right to copy software
   c. software piracy is a fairly simple crime to commit
   d. all of the above

7. Windows Vista includes a feature called _____ that allows you to encrypt all files on a drive. (572)
   a. Secure HTTP
   b. SSID
   c. Spim
   d. BitLocker

8. A(n) _____ is a notice that guarantees a user or a Web site is legitimate. (573)
   a. trusted source
   b. digital certificate
   c. surge protector
   d. end-user license agreement

9. A _____ is a prolonged undervoltage. (574)
   a. spike
   b. blackout
   c. joule
   d. brownout

10. A wireless access point (WAP) should be configured so it does not broadcast a(n) _____, known as an SSID. (577)
    a. overvoltage
    b. undervoltage
    c. WEP
    d. network name

11. A _____ gives authors and artists exclusive rights to duplicate, publish, and sell their materials. (579)
    a. copyright
    b. license
    c. password
    d. firewall

12. As related to the use of computers, _____ is defined as gaining unauthorized access or obtaining confidential information by taking advantage of the trusting human nature of some victims and the naivety of others. (586)
    a. phishing
    b. pharming
    c. a virus hoax
    d. social engineering

13. _____ involves the examination of computer media, programs, data and log files on computers, servers, and networks. (587)
    a. Forensics analysis
    b. E-mail filtering
    c. Encryption key
    d. Trusted source

14. _____ is inflammation of the nerve that connects the forearm to the palm of the wrist. (588)
    a. Carpal tunnel syndrome (CTS)
    b. Computer vision syndrome (CVS)
    c. Computer addiction
    d. Tendonitis

Checkpoint

Matching

Match the terms with their definitions. (See page numbers in parentheses.)

____ 1. cracker (556)

____ 2. virus (558)

____ 3. quarantine (561)

____ 4. botnet (562)

____ 5. personal firewall (564)

____ 6. password (566)

____ 7. biometric device (567)

____ 8. surge protector (574)

____ 9. spyware (583)

____ 10. adware (583)

a. spyware hidden on Web pages or in e-mail messages in the form of a graphical image

b. group of compromised computers connected to a network such as the Internet that is being used as part of a network that attacks other networks, usually for nefarious purposes

c. protects a personal computer and its data from unauthorized intrusions

d. private combination of characters associated with a user name

e. program that displays an online advertisement in a banner or pop-up window on Web pages, e-mail, or other Internet services

f. translates a personal characteristic into digital code

g. uses special electrical components to smooth out minor noise, provide a stable current flow, and keep an overvoltage from reaching the computer and other electronic equipment

h. someone who accesses a computer or network illegally with the intent of malicious action

i. contains an uninfected copy of key commands and startup information

j. potentially damaging computer program that affects, or infects, a computer negatively by altering the way the computer works without the user's knowledge or permission

k. area of the hard disk that holds an infected file until the infection can be removed

l. program placed on a computer without the user's knowledge that secretly collects information about the user

Short Answer

Write a brief answer to each of the following questions.

1. How do antivirus programs detect and identify a virus? _____ What is a virus hoax? _____

2. How is identification different from authentication? _____ What are three methods of identification and authentication? _____

3. What is product activation? _____ What might be the consequences of not activating software? _____

4. What is information privacy? _____ List five ways to protect your personal information. _____

5. Who uses content filtering and why? _____ Describe a rating system used for content filtering. _____

Beyond the Book

Read the following book elements, learn more about each using the Web, and then write a brief report.

1. Ethics & Issues — How Should Virus Authors Be Punished? (558), Should Schools Use Biometric Devices? (568), Should It Be Illegal to Sell Programs That Copy Movies from DVDs? (580), Should Spyware Be Legal? (583), or Who Should Protect You from Identity Theft? (584)

2. Career Corner — Computer Forensics Specialist (591)

3. Companies on the Cutting Edge — McAfee or Symantec (593)

4. FAQs (559, 562, 563, 565, 567, 569, 571, 576, 577, 582, 584, 590)

5. High-Tech Talk — The Key(s) to Making Encryption Work (592)

6. Looking Ahead — Three-Dimensional Facial Recognition Software — A Step Forward for Security (568) or Computer Knowledge Assessment Using Brain Fingerprinting (587)

7. Making Use of the Web — Environment (127)

8. Picture Yourself Avoiding Computer Risks (554)

9. Technology Trailblazers — Donn Parker and Clifford Stoll (593)

10. Web Links (558, 562, 564, 570, 571, 573, 575, 580, 584, 587, 590)

Learn It Online

Use the Learn It Online exercises to reinforce your understanding of the chapter concepts. To access the Learn It Online exercises, visit scsite.com/dc2008/ch11/learn.

① At the Movies — Attack of the Mobile Viruses

To view the Attack of the Mobile Viruses movie, click the number 1 button. Locate your video and click the corresponding High-Speed or Dial-Up link, depending on your Internet connection. Watch the movie and then complete the exercise by answering the question that follows. Take a look at the recent wave of viruses plaguing mobile phone users. How does a mobile device get a virus, and how can you protect your mobile device?

② Video and Audio: You Review It — Cybercrime

In this chapter you learned about cybercrime. Click the number 2 button to view the suggested links and begin your search for videos, podcasts, or vodcasts related to cybercrime. Choose a video, podcast, or vodcast that discusses cybercrime and is of interest to you, and then write a description of its contents. Explain why you chose this piece, what you liked about it, what you disliked about it, and whether you would recommend it to a fellow student. Finish your review by giving the video, podcast, or vodcast a rating of 1 – 5 stars. Submit your review in the format requested by your instructor.

③ Student Edition Labs — Protecting Your Privacy Online

Click the number 3 button. A new browser window will open, displaying the Student Edition Labs. Follow the on-screen instructions to complete the Protecting Your Privacy Online Lab. When finished, click the Exit button. If required, submit your results to your instructor.

④ Student Edition Labs — Computer Ethics

Click the number 4 button. A new browser window will open, displaying the Student Edition Labs. Follow the on-screen instructions to complete the Computer Ethics Lab. When finished, click the Exit button. If required, submit your results to your instructor.

⑤ Practice Test

Click the number 5 button. Answer each question. When completed, enter your name and click the Grade Test button to submit the quiz for grading. Make a note of any missed questions. If required, submit your results to your instructor.

⑥ Who Wants To Be a Computer Genius²?

Click the number 6 button to find out if you are a computer genius. Directions about how to play the game will be displayed. When you are ready to play, click the Play button. Submit your score to your instructor.

Learn It Online

7 Wheel of Terms

Click the number 7 button to reinforce important terms you learned in this chapter by playing the Shelly Cashman Series version of this popular game. Directions about how to play the game will be displayed. When you are ready to play, click the Play button. Submit your score to your instructor.

8 DC Track and Field

Click the number 8 button to use what you have learned in this chapter to compete against other students in three track and field events. Directions about how to play the game will be displayed. When you are ready to play, click the start first event button. If required, submit your score to your instructor.

9 You're Hired!

Click the number 9 button to use what you have learned in this chapter to embark on the path to a career in computers. Directions about how to play the game will be displayed. When you are ready to play, click the begin game button. If required, submit your score to your instructor.

10 Crossword Puzzle Challenge

Click the number 10 button, then click the Crossword Puzzle Challenge link. Directions about how to play the game will be displayed. Complete the puzzle to reinforce skills you learned in this chapter. When you are ready to play, click the Continue button. Submit the completed puzzle to your instructor.

11 Vista Exercises

Click the number 11 button. When the Vista Exercises menu appears, click the exercise assigned by your instructor. A new browser window will open. Follow the on-screen instructions to complete the exercise. When finished, click the Exit button. If required, submit your results to your instructor.

12 In the News

Why own the latest video game when you can rent it from the comfort of your personal computer? IGN Entertainment has agreements with leading video-game publishers — Ripcord Games, GameSpy.com, and FilePlanet.com — that will allow broadband users to download files from the IGN Entertainment Web site to play stand-alone or multiplayer games. The IGN Web site sends users all they need to get started playing the games, and as more bytes are needed, they are sent from the server to the users. Click the number 12 button and read a news article about online games and edutainment applications. What applications have been developed? Do you think the applications will be successful? Why or why not? Do you think online games will replace the traditional, local CD-ROM game?

13 Chapter Discussion Forum

Select an objective from this chapter on page 555 about which you would like more information. Click the number 13 button and post a short message listing a meaningful message title accompanied by one or more questions concerning the selected objective. In two days, return to the threaded discussion by clicking the number 13 button. Submit to your instructor your original message and at least one response to your message.

14 Buying Online

Click the number 14 button to learn how to use the Internet to purchase merchandise. Follow the instructions to use Amazon.com and Barnes & Noble's Web site to compare prices and reviews of David McCullough's *1776*. How did the prices of the book compare? Which site had more favorable reviews for the book? Which site would you recommend to a friend? Write a report summarizing your findings. Print the report and then submit it to your instructor.

Learn How To

Use the Learn How To activities to learn fundamental skills when using a computer and accompanying technology. Complete the exercises and submit them to your instructor. To see a video of a Learn How To activity, visit scsite.com/dc2008/ch11/howto.

LEARN HOW TO 1: Back Up Files on an Offsite Internet Server

Note: The service described in this exercise allows 15 days of free access. After that time, you may be billed automatically for service unless you cancel your service in the given time frame.

Backing up files stored on your computer on another disk or computer located in a different geographical location is the ultimate safeguard for data on your computer. A good way to back up data is to use one of the services available on the Web. A leading service is found at www.IBackup.com. To subscribe to the IBackup service, complete the following steps:

1. Start a Web browser, type the Web address **www.IBackup.com** in the Address bar, and then press the ENTER key.
2. When the IBackup Web page is displayed, click Sign Up on the top horizontal toolbar.
3. Enter your e-mail address in the E-mail Address text box, and then click the Send Registration E-mail button.
4. In a short period, you will receive a subscription e-mail message. Because you want to subscribe to the backup service, click the link to continue with the signup process. A form will be displayed in your browser (Figure 11-37).
5. Fill in the form. Select the plan you want in the Select a Storage Plan list. If you want to try the service for a short period of time before subscribing, select 5 GB Free Trial for 15 Days.
6. To continue, you must enter credit card information. If you select the 15 day trial, your credit card will not be charged, and an automatic billing at the end of 15 days will occur. After entering the required information, click the Continue button at the bottom of the page.
7. A message is displayed that confirms that you have signed up with IBackup, and also provides a link for you to download the IBackup for Windows application.
8. Click the Download button to download the IBackup for Windows application, and then follow the instructions to install the application on your computer.

IBackup window

FIGURE 11-37

After establishing an account, you can use it for the time for which you subscribed. Complete the following steps to use the service:

1. Start the IBackup for Windows application.
2. Enter your user name and password, and then click the Login button to display a window containing your files, as well as the contents of your IBackup folder (Figure 11-38).
3. To upload a file, locate the file in the left pane of the IBackup window, and drag it to the right pane. The Backup Progress dialog box will be displayed while the file is uploading. The file will be placed in the IBackup folder.
4. For further activities you can accomplish in this program for backing up your files, click the buttons on the top horizontal toolbar and experiment.

top horizontal

IBackup

files and folders on your computer

FIGURE 11-38

Learn How To

Exercise

1. Visit the IBackup Web site. Click View Demo and then follow the screen prompts to view all the services offered by IBackup. Which service is most appropriate for your home computer? Which service is most useful for the server that is used in the computer lab at your school? If you had critical data you needed to back up, would you use a service like this? Why or why not? Submit your answers to your instructor.
2. **Optional: Perform this exercise only for your own computer. Do not perform this exercise on a school computer.** Establish an account on IBackup.com. Upload two or more files from your computer. Download the files you uploaded back to your computer. Is this an efficient way to back up your files? Do you think the IBackup service would be useful for businesses? Submit your answers to your instructor.

LEARN HOW TO 2: Use the Windows Vista Firewall

When you use the Internet, data is sent both from your computer to the Internet and from computers on the Internet to your computer. A firewall is a barrier that checks information coming from the Internet and either turns it away or allows it to pass through to your computer, based on your firewall settings. It also checks data being sent from your computer to the Internet to ensure your computer is not sending unsolicited messages to other computers on the Internet. A firewall can be implemented using hardware or software.

Windows Vista contains a software firewall that starts automatically when you boot your computer. To control the firewall usage on your computer, complete the following steps:

1. Click the Start button on the Windows taskbar, and then click Control Panel on the Start menu.
2. In the Classic View of the Control Panel, double-click Security Center, and then click Windows Firewall in the Windows Security Center window to open the Windows Firewall window (Figure 11-39).
3. In the Windows Firewall window, click the Turn Windows Firewall on or off link to turn on or off the Windows firewall. The firewall automatically is on when you start your computer. You should NOT turn off the firewall unless you have a compelling reason to do so.
4. Click the Allow a program through Windows Firewall link to display the Exceptions sheet in the Windows Firewall Settings dialog box (Figure 11-40). The exceptions that are checked can communicate with the Internet without your clicking a link.
5. You may want to allow programs that routinely communicate with the Internet, such as sports programs that display updated game scores, to have full access to your computer. To add a program to the Exceptions list, in the Exceptions sheet click the Add program button. The Add a Program dialog box is displayed. Select a program and then click the OK button.

FIGURE 11-39

FIGURE 11-40

Exercise

1. Open the Windows Firewall window. Click the How does a firewall help protect my computer? link. Read the information about Windows firewall. What did you learn that you did not know? What is malicious software? What are some examples of malicious software? Submit your answers to your instructor.

Web Research

Use the Internet-based Web Research exercises to broaden your understanding of the concepts presented in this chapter. Visit scsite.com/dc2008/ch11/research to obtain more information pertaining to each exercise. To discuss any of the Web Research exercises in this chapter with other students, post your thoughts or questions at scsite.com/dc2008/ch11/forum.

(1) Scavenger Hunt Use one of the <u>search engines</u> listed in Figure 2-10 in Chapter 2 on page 78 or your own favorite search engine to find the answers to the questions that follow. Copy and paste the Web address from the Web page where you found the answer. Some questions may have more than one answer. If required, submit your answers to your instructor. (1) What is the current cost of a notebook computer security system? (2) What term is John Scoch credited with creating at the Xerox Palo Alto Research Center in the late 1970s? When this term was coined, what was its intended meaning? (3) What is EPEAT? (4) What company developed SSL? How does SSL differ from Secure HTTP (S-HTTP)? (5) At what university is the Computer Emergency Response Team Coordination Center (CERT/CC) located? What is one of the latest advisories or incident notes reported by this organization?

(2) Search Sleuth Internet subject directories are used to find information on specialized topics. One of the oldest and more popular subject directories is the **WWW Virtual Library (VL)**. This Web site is administered by a group of volunteers who are experts in particular topics. Visit this Web site and then use your word processing program to answer the following questions. Then, if required, submit your answers to your instructor. (1) Click the About link at the bottom of the page. What year was WWW Virtual Library established? Who created it? (2) Click the joining the VL link. What are some of the benefits Virtual Library members receive? (3) Click your browser's Back button or press the BACKSPACE key to return to the home page. Click the Computing and Computer Science link and then click the Digital Rights Management link. Click the Digital Rights Management Articles link at the bottom of the page, review two articles, and then write a 50-word summary that may be submitted to your instructor.

(3) Journaling Respond to your readings in this chapter by writing at least one page about your reactions, evaluations, and reflections on computer security, privacy, and ethics. For example, have you suffered from a **repetitive strain injury**? What steps have you taken to safeguard your personal computer? If you have installed an antivirus program on your computer, how often do you update and use it? Have you ever been trapped in a phishing or pharming scam? You also can write about the new terms you learned by reading this chapter. If required, submit your journal to your instructor.

(4) Expanding Your Understanding Thousands of hackers are attempting to gain unauthorized access to computer systems across the world, according to computer security experts. Some of these hackers are experienced programmers, while others are **script kiddies** who are using tools developed by sophisticated programmers. All computers are vulnerable to script-kiddie assaults, especially home computers with always-on, high-speed connections. A personal firewall can help thwart these invasions. Visit a software vendor and locate a personal firewall program. What is the name of this software? Who is the manufacturer? What is the cost? What are the system requirements? How is the software installed? What tasks does the software perform? Write a report summarizing your findings. If required, submit your report to your instructor.

(5) Ethics in Action **Radio frequency identification (RFID) tags** are expected to help merchants in many ways. By placing these tags on such items as prescription drugs, computer peripherals, and clothing, retailers hope to reduce theft, track inventory, reduce labor costs, and keep their shelves stocked. Privacy experts, however, claim the tags can store information about consumers' shopping habits and whereabouts. Law enforcement officials, lawyers, marketers, and even thieves could use this electronic detailed data to track people at all times of the day. View online sites that discuss using RFID tags in stores and the privacy issues that arise from their use. Write a report summarizing your findings, and include a table of links to Web sites that provide additional details about the developing field of RFID. If required, submit your report to your instructor.

Case Studies

Use the Case Studies to apply the concepts presented in the chapter to real-world situations. Visit scsite.com/dc2008/ch11/cases to obtain more information pertaining to each exercise. To discuss the Case Studies in this chapter with other students, visit scsite.com/dc2008/ch11/forum and post your thoughts or questions.

CASE STUDY 1 — Class Discussion   As manager of the information technology department, you are responsible for maintaining the company's **e-mail system**. Recently, you were sent a request by a member of the senior management team to make available for her review all e-mail messages sent and received by non-salaried employees over the past month. Your initial reaction was that such a request is not only unethical, but possibly illegal as well. Upon contacting the human resources department, you learn that an obscure statement in the employee handbook gives senior staff the right to read anything transmitted on media owned by the company without notifying the sender or recipient. Would you immediately honor the request, or would you first try to convince senior management that internal communications between employees should be private? Why or why not? Do you think such a policy is good for employee morale? Why or why not? Write a brief report and be prepared to discuss your recommendations in class.

CASE STUDY 2 — Class Discussion   Your best friend, Matthew, spends all his free time writing computer programs that interact with the Windows operating system. He recently informed you that over fall break he had written **malware** that randomly erases files and displays weird messages the day before Christmas (December 24) at exactly 1:00 p.m. He plans to distribute the Trojan horse, called Merry Christmas America, via an e-mail attachment. Also included with the e-mail is a hidden program that sends the same e-mail to all the e-mail addresses in the user's address list. The e-mail with the attachment will be sent as spam the day after finals in December, so it will have plenty of time to be distributed to millions of computers worldwide before December 24. Upon learning of Matthew's plan, what would you do? You know that a hefty reward of $250,000 is offered by a large software company for turning in unscrupulous programmers. Do you think it is right to inform on a friend when no profit is involved in the crime? Why or why not? Who would you notify (i.e., Matthew's parents, the dean of students, the police, or the software company offering the reward)? Write a brief report and be prepared to discuss your recommendations in class.

CASE STUDY 3 — Research   Computer viruses have cost companies billions of dollars in lost revenue. In a recent six-month period, the number of **new viruses and worms** aimed at Microsoft's ubiquitous Windows operating system rose from 1,000 a year to nearly 5,000. You work as a network analyst for a large manufacturing company that uses Windows. After the most recent virus attack, your manager asked you to investigate the feasibility of switching to a different operating system, such as Linux or UNIX. Use the Web and/or print media to research the advantages and disadvantages of switching operating systems. Are alternative operating systems as susceptible to viruses as Windows? Why or why not? What is Microsoft's approach to eliminating virus attacks? Why is Windows so prone to virus attacks? What types of costs are involved in changing operating systems? Submit your report or use PowerPoint to create a presentation and share your findings with your class.

CASE STUDY 4 — Research   Internet-based companies who take advantage of consumer trust are sneaking their spyware into computers for their own purposes. **Spyware** secretly collects information about a user's computer activities. The owner of a chain of fast-food restaurants, Burgers & Fries, where you are employed as an application analyst wants to purge spyware from the chain's computers. Use the Web and/or print media and compare the spyware remover programs available. For each program, answer the following questions. What is the program's function? What are the system requirements? How easy is the program to use? How do you obtain updates to the program? How much does the program cost? In your opinion, is the program worth the price? Why or why not? Which one would you recommend? Why? Write a brief report or use PowerPoint to create a presentation and share your findings with your class.

CASE STUDY 5 — Team Challenge   Your company has been hired by ABC Enterprises to create a **privacy information policy** for the company's Web site. You have been instructed to put together a policy that not only will respect an individual's privacy rights, but also will enable the company to collect data that can be used in targeted marketing. The company would like to collect the following information: who visits the Web site, how often they visit, what pages they view, and the amount of time they spend viewing a particular page. Using the Web and/or print media, create a policy that will include all of the preceding information. Have each team member justify a component within the policy and explain how the policy will not violate the individual's privacy rights. As a team, merge your findings into a team report and/or PowerPoint presentation and share your findings with your class.

Special Feature

COMPUTER FORENSICS

Forensics is the use of science to investigate and establish facts in criminal or civil courts. Forensic scientists are able to examine a set of clues and rebuild a sequence of events. Computer forensics is the newest and fastest growing discipline in this field. As described earlier in Chapter 11, computer forensics — also called digital forensics, network forensics, or cyber-forensics — is the discovery, collection, and analysis of evidence found on computers and networks. Computer forensics techniques include analyzing log files, analyzing storage media (including deleted files), analyzing chat logs, and tracking the routes of packets on a data network (Figure 1). This field of study integrates aspects of criminal justice, computer science, and computer and network investigative techniques.

(a) Analyze Log Files

```
1) Mar 13 03:11:55 watson ipop3d[16319]: pop3
   service init from 192.168.187.35

2) Mar 13 03:11:55 watson ipop3d[16319]: Login
   user=kumquat host=holmes.example.net
   [192.168.187.35] nmsgs=0/0

3) Mar 13 03:12:16 watson ipop3d[16319]: Logout
   user=kumquat host=holmes.example.net
   [192.168.187.35] nmsgs=0 ndele=0
```

(b) Analyze Deleted Files

Computer Forensics Examiner

(c) Analyze Chat Logs

```
Session Start: Tue Mar 23 15:50:33 2008
Session Ident: #Strong&40
Now talking in #Strong&40
Topic is 'Welcome to the BEST little channel on the net!   www.40plus.com.html  '
Set by Bunni on Tue Mar 23 10:31:01
BettyF> It sure beats the 20's we've been having, Cary
`Cary> Hi, billy
billy89> Hi
abc_m> hi Cary:)
abc_m> hi billy89
`Cary> hey cd  how  be?
billy89> Hi
abc_m> not bad a bit cold but doing okay
BettyF> How ya doing, billy?
billy89> So... I'm just lookin' around irc...
BettyF> and lo and behold you found us
billy89> Doin' ok... also cold where I am... Minnesota... Where're you?
BettyF> Maine here
billy89> Yep... here I am ... :-)
abc_m> ottawa canada here
billy89> Sunny Ontario! :-)
BettyF> You had some really nasty spells in January, billy
`Cary> I gotta go again.. laters  yawl.. play safe
`Cary has left #Strong&40
billy89> Bitter cold in Jan. dumped on by TWO bad snow storms in December
BettyF> I talked with my old Ottawa friend a few days ago, cdn -- but only for
about a minute -- I think he had a date. lol
abc_m> ohhhhhhhhhhhhh
abc_m> they have those out here?
BettyF> I have a friend in St. Paul, billy -- she was in her house with her jacket
on in January.
```

(d) Track Packet Routes

FIGURE 1 Computer forensics is the discovery, collection, and analysis of evidence found on computers and networks.

THE SCOPE OF COMPUTER FORENSICS

Computer forensics focuses on computers and networks. The forensic analysis of computers specifically involves the examination of computer media, programs, and data and log files to reconstruct the activity in which a computer was engaged, such as instant messaging conversations, Internet chats, e-mail messages, Web sites visited, documents and spreadsheets opened, and image and audio files viewed. The forensics analysis of networks focuses more on the activity of a network and includes the analysis of server contents, server and router log files, packet traffic, and information obtained from Internet service providers.

The science of computer forensics covers several overlapping areas (Figure 2). It is critical for law enforcement as an evidence gathering and criminal investigation tool. It is an increasingly important tool used for civilian and military intelligence gathering — including activities related to homeland security. It is becoming widely employed by businesses and other private sector organizations for combating information security attacks. The core tools and skills are the same regardless of the application.

A computer forensics specialist also must have knowledge of the law regardless of whether the investigation is for law enforcement or civilian purposes. Additional complexity in this area exists because computer crime statutes and users' legitimate expectation of privacy vary widely from state to state and nation to nation. With the Internet and World Wide Web, jurisdictional boundaries are blurred, and an individual in one country can commit crimes almost anywhere in the world without ever leaving his or her keyboard.

Although most computer forensic specialists today are engaged in law enforcement investigations, the field is not by any means limited to finding evidence of criminal guilt. Computer forensics also is a rapidly growing subspecialty for information security professionals. The traditional information security manager is responsible for proactively protecting the information technology assets within an organization. Security intrusions and other events are inevitable, however, and the computer forensics specialist often leads the incident response function to learn how an event occurred, who was behind it, and how to prevent a recurrence. Computer forensics techniques increasingly are being used by third-party firms for policy auditing and compliance enforcement for issues ranging from an organization's Appropriate User Policies (AUPs) to regulations such as Sarbanes-Oxley (SOX) and Health Insurance Portability and Accountability Act (HIPAA).

Computer forensics also is part of the toolkit of today's computer scientist. Many information security researchers purposely place a honeypot (vulnerable computer) on their networks for the specific purpose of analyzing the attacks that eventually will be perpetrated on those systems. Carefully examining the way in which a honeypot has been attacked can provide significant insight into new forms of attack, which then can be translated into new defensive tools and strategies.

THE IMPORTANCE OF COMPUTER FORENSICS

Computer forensics is a rapidly growing field for the simple reason that computers and the Internet are the fastest growing technology used for criminal activity. As computers become smaller, lighter, cheaper, and easier to use, they appear at nearly every crime scene that police investigate. Some activities, such as illegal gambling and the distribution of worms and viruses, have been given new life because of the pervasiveness of computers and the Internet.

Cybercrimes are growing rapidly in both the number of incidents as well as the cost in dollars, largely because these crimes are safer and more lucrative than crimes in the "real" world. The average bank robber, for example, nets only a few thousand dollars, and most are caught and sent to jail. Conversely, white collar computer crimes such as auction fraud, credit card theft, identity theft, and other financial scams tend to net a much larger sum of money, and the perpetrators are more difficult to catch and convict. In addition, computer criminals tend to generate more sympathy with judges, juries, and the public than violent offenders. Compounding the problem is the fact that access to corporate network resources makes insider jobs by employees easier and easier. Figure 3 shows the dollar loss reported by 269 large companies in a recent year due to telecom and financial fraud, insider abuse, unauthorized network access, theft of proprietary information, and other computer-related crimes.

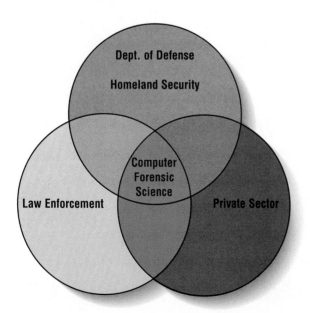

FIGURE 2 The domain of computer forensics is multidisciplinary, spanning the needs of the military and homeland security, law enforcement, and the private sector.

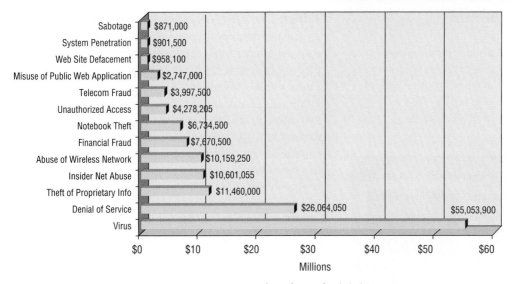

FIGURE 3
Total computer security losses of $141,496,560 reported by 269 respondents in a recent year.

Source: Computer Security Institute

Computer forensics is being used not just to combat cybercrime. Terrorists around the world are known to use computers and other digital devices, so computer forensics analysis is important as an antiterrorism tool for both criminal prosecution and intelligence gathering. All organizations that employ computers, ranging from nonprofit agencies and major corporations to government agencies and utility companies, are at risk. As more information is stored digitally and more aspects of our society are under computer control, we all face increased exposure and vulnerability. Computer forensics is an important tool in understanding our digital information systems and keeping them safe, as well as tracking down the people who abuse those systems.

THE COMPUTER FORENSICS PROCESS

The computer forensics process can be simple or complex, depending upon the circumstances causing the investigation in the first place. The computer forensics specialist may be part of an investigative team, and the analysis of digital evidence may be just one part of the investigation as a whole. The specialist will look for information pertinent to the incident or event being investigated, which may be limited by a search warrant, time, and/or other circumstances.

The first step in the process is to gather the materials to analyze. This may not be quite as easy as it sounds. Law enforcement personnel will be guided by a search warrant in the seizure of materials while a corporate forensics specialist may be guided by what equipment is owned by the company. Even with clear guidelines, many items need to be considered for collection and examination as described in the following sections.

Computer Media

Computer media can be found in many places these days (Figure 4). This includes the obvious hard disk, Zip disk, floppy disk, and optical disc (CDs and DVDs). Also included are physically small, high-capacity memory devices such as USB flash drives (including the versions where the device is embedded in a watch, pen, or Swiss Army knife) and flash memory cards.

(a) hard disk
(b) Zip disk
(c) USB flash drives
(f) optical disc
(e) flash memory card
(d) floppy disk

FIGURE 4 Computer forensics experts analyze the data stored on various types of media.

Computers and Peripherals

Every part of the computer needs to be considered for examination, and it is generally important to take possession of all of the equipment. The specialist cannot assume that the spare keyboard back in the lab will fit the computer being seized. The computer shown in Figure 5 has the basic hardware one might expect to see at a crime scene.

FIGURE 5 A typical scene a computer forensics specialist encounters.

Other Computer and Network Hardware

The word computer should be interpreted broadly in computer forensics to include not only traditional desktop, notebook, and server systems, but any digital device, including routers, digital cameras, mobile phones, and PDAs (Figure 6). Homes with broadband network connections increasingly have networks and, therefore, multiple computers and a router. Wireless networks make it relatively easy to hide a networked computer; a computer using a home's wireless network could be as far as 100 yards or so from the wireless access point, and thus be situated far outside of the immediate structure.

Computer Software

Although the computer forensics specialist generally will not run software directly from the suspect drive, it may be impossible to examine files without the proper application software. In some cases, the user of a suspect computer might have installed specialized, custom, or very old software to which the specialist generally will not have access; in that case, the specialist may have to install software found at the suspect site on a forensics lab computer. This is one reason to look around the site where the computer is found and consider seizing distribution media and manuals of any software with which the specialist is not familiar. The papers and books found near the computer also will give the specialist a clue as to the sophistication of the user and the possible types of applications to be found on the system.

(a) desktop computer (b) notebook computer (c) router (d) rack-mounted server (j) smart phone (h) answering machine (f) GPS receiver (e) PDA (g) residential broadband router (i) digital camera

FIGURE 6 Common digital hardware devices examined by a computer investigator.

In the Computer Forensics Lab

Once the materials are in the computer forensics lab, the investigation can begin. The basic steps of a computer forensics analysis are:

1. **Preserve the media** — Computer forensics analysis never should be performed on the original media except under the most extraordinary circumstances because of the potential of accidentally making a change to the original evidence. The copy also needs to be made in such a way that the original information is not altered in any way and that it can be authenticated as containing the same information as the original. This process is known as **imaging a drive**.

2. **Extract evidence** — Based upon the guidelines of the investigation, the specialist needs to determine what kind of information on the computer is pertinent to the case. Clues as to what to search for will depend upon the type of case. Spreadsheets, for example, would be highly relevant to a business fraud case, while images are important for a case of suspected child pornography, and chat and e-mail logs are of use in a case of cyberstalking. Keywords, such as pertinent phrases, slang words, names, locations, etc., must be provided to the computer forensics specialist on the case.

3. **Analyze computer media** — The actual analysis of evidence and/or the root cause of the event is the most time-consuming aspect of the process. It is important to note that the information retrieved from the computer either can be incriminating (indicating guilt) or exculpatory (indicating innocence). In addition, the specialist has to look at the entire capacity of the medium because information can be hidden anywhere. Figure 7 summarizes the common items examined during a computer forensics investigation.

4. **Document results** — The results of a computer forensics exam must be documented thoroughly, particularly if the examination is being performed for legal purposes. Everything must be written down, from the configuration of the computer and BIOS settings to each and every step taken by the computer forensic specialist and any pertinent evidence that is found. All computer equipment, media, peripherals, or other items seized must be logged, and photographs should be taken of external and internal connections, if possible. The handling of the evidence also has to be logged carefully to demonstrate that no tampering occurred. Sample computer forensics evidence worksheets are shown in Figure 8. Figure 8a is an evidence worksheet used with a computer. Figure 8b is an evidence worksheet used with a hard drive.

1. Visited Web sites
2. Downloaded files
3. Dates when files were last accessed and modified
4. Attempts to conceal, destroy, or fabricate evidence
5. Deleted or overwritten files
6. Data from RAM
7. Use of cryptography or steganography
8. File directory structure
9. Image, movie, and sound files
10. Keyword search hits
11. Contents of system files, such as the print spool and swap files
12. Installed programs
13. E-mail, chat logs, instant messaging logs
14. Registry entries
15. Contents of the Recycle Bin and unallocated space
16. Antivirus, personal firewall, and spyware detection software, as well as the presence of viruses, Trojan horses, and spyware

FIGURE 7 Common items examined during a computer forensics investigation.

(a) Computer evidence worksheet

(b) Hard drive evidence worksheet

FIGURE 8 Computer Evidence and Hard Drive Evidence Worksheets (from *Forensic Examination of Digital Evidence: A Guide for Law Enforcement*, National Institute of Justice).

In general, specialized computer forensics tools are used to perform an analysis to ensure that no information is modified on the target media and that the examination is thorough. Booting a computer changes hundreds of registry, log, and/or data files; therefore, the original hard disk never should be used to boot a computer. In addition, many operating systems, such as Linux and Windows, maintain a number of time stamps associated with every file, including the creation, last access, and last modified dates; using ordinary operating system tools to examine the contents of files usually will cause at least the last-access date to be altered. Use of specialized analysis tools maintains the integrity of the original data so that the specialist can be sure that the results of the analysis are legally and technically valid. It is important that no harm be done to the original evidence.

In some cases, specialists prefer to image hard disks in the field rather than transporting entire computers to the lab; this often is the preferable approach when the device to be imaged is a company's critical server where seizing the computer might cause undue economic hardship to the owner. Devices such as Intelligent Computer Solutions' Road MASSter-II (Figure 10) is such a device; note that it fits in a small carrying case.

Notebook computers represent a particular challenge for forensic analysis because many notebook computer hard disks have proprietary or specialty interfaces; additional hardware is available specifically for imaging drives from various models of Dell, Gateway, HP, IBM, NEC, Toshiba, and other brands of notebook computers. Other specialized hardware allows for the imaging of PDAs, smart phones, and other digital devices.

COMPUTER FORENSICS TOOLS

A wide variety of computer forensics tools are available, each with its own applications, strengths, and weaknesses. Several companies make computer forensics hardware, primarily for purposes of disk imaging. Digital Intelligence, for example, makes several forensics hardware devices, including:

- The Forensic Recovery of Digital Evidence (FRED) hardware (Figure 9a) is a stand-alone forensics workstation that can acquire data from all types of hard disk media, including IDE, ATA, SATA, and SCSI hard disks as well as floppy and Zip disks. This system includes fixed hard disks for the workstation's operating system and analysis tools plus a number of bays for other drives to be inserted and removed. For imaging applications, the contents of the suspect disk are copied to a blank disk; the analysis then is performed on the newly copied disk.
- The FireChief hardware (Figure 9b) has two removable hard disk bays, one of which is write-protected (for the original disk). This device can be used to copy the contents of one disk to another. It is connected to a computer via a FireWire connection and is ideal for building a low-cost forensics workstation.
- The FireFly hardware (Figure 9c) can plug directly into an IDE or SATA hard disk and attach to the forensics computer via a FireWire connection.

(a) Forensic Recovery of Digital Evidence (FRED) forensics workstation

(b) FireChief hard disk replication and examination hardware

(c) FireFly hard disk examination hardware

FIGURE 9 Three computer forensics devices manufactured by Digital Intelligence, Inc.

(a) Details of the keyboard and working area of the Road MASSter

USB connectors for additional peripheral attachment

connector for evidence drive

auxiliary VGA video connector

platform for evidence drive

A.C. power jack

serial port for printing an evidence report on the thermal printer or seizing data from personal data assistants

power for CD-ROM and floppy drive

10/100 Base T connector for Ethernet connectivity

voltage selector switch

(b) The Road MASSter case

ECP parallel port for use with LapLink™

connector for floppy disk drive

connector for suspect's drive

under keyboard storage compartment

full QWERTY mini keyboard

connector for CD-ROM

FIGURE 10 The Intelligent Computer Solutions' Road MASSter-II is a portable computer forensics laboratory.

The primary computer forensics analysis tool is software. The most widely-used specialty forensics programs today are Guidance Software's EnCase and AccessData's Ultimate Toolkit (Figure 11). No single program can perform all aspects of a computer forensics analysis, although several come close. These programs provide a broad range of forensics functions (Figure 12).

1. Create disk images
2. Recover passwords
3. Perform file access, modification, and creation time analysis
4. Create file catalogs
5. View system and application logs
6. Determine the activity of users and/or applications on a system
7. Recover "deleted" files and examine unallocated file space
8. Obtain network information such as IP addresses and host names, network routes, and Web site information
9. Track forensics activity and aid in documentation and report writing

(a) Guidance Software's EnCase

(b) AccessData's Ultimate Toolkit

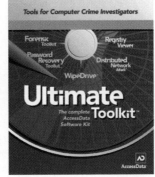

FIGURE 12 Common tasks handled by computer forensics software.

FIGURE 11 Popular computer forensics software.

COMPUTER FORENSICS AT WORK

A computer forensics specialist needs to have a working knowledge of a wide range of topics related to computers and networks. The most essential bit of knowledge concerns how files are stored on storage media and the various file systems that will be found. The following sections illustrate some of the tasks computer forensic specialists use to search for clues in an investigation.

Analyzing Deleted Files

Consider the scenario shown in Figure 13. Figure 13a shows the suspect displaying the names of the files involved in the criminal activity. Figure 13b shows the suspect deleting the files. Figure 13c shows the computer forensics specialist using special programs to retrieve the deleted files.

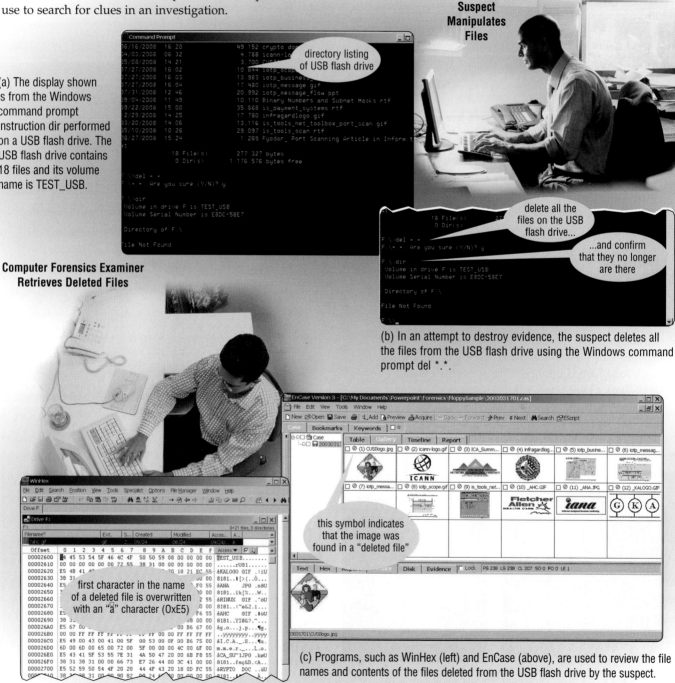

Suspect Manipulates Files

(a) The display shown is from the Windows command prompt instruction dir performed on a USB flash drive. The USB flash drive contains 18 files and its volume name is TEST_USB.

directory listing of USB flash drive

delete all the files on the USB flash drive...

...and confirm that they no longer are there

(b) In an attempt to destroy evidence, the suspect deletes all the files from the USB flash drive using the Windows command prompt del *.*.

Computer Forensics Examiner Retrieves Deleted Files

first character in the name of a deleted file is overwritten with an "a" character (0xE5)

this symbol indicates that the image was found in a "deleted file"

(c) Programs, such as WinHex (left) and EnCase (above), are used to review the file names and contents of the files deleted from the USB flash drive by the suspect.

FIGURE 13 The top portion of this figure shows the suspect (a) listing the files involved in criminal activity, (b) later deleting the files in an attempt to cover-up the illegal activity, and then the lower portion of the figure shows (c) the computer forensics specialist retrieving the deleted files using special programs.

Tracking Packet Routes

Knowledge of the Internet is another essential skill. Figure 14a shows the output from McAfee's Visual Trace, listing the intermediate packet routes between a local host computer (altamont) and a Web server (www.garykessler.net). Visual Trace is a graphical version of the tracert (DOS) and traceroute (Linux) command line utilities and lists the IP address of all hops along the path between the two computers. This display also shows the round-trip delay and can be used to show whois information about each packet route in the path. Visual Trace also can show a geographical map of the path (Figure 14b).

Analyzing Network Traffic

The ability to analyze network traffic also is an essential skill for a computer forensics specialist. E-mail headers are particularly important, as they provide many clues as to the origin and authenticity of e-mail messages. By now you should be familiar with the standard e-mail headers, such as To:, From:, and Subject:. But e-mail headers contain more information than what you see at the top of an e-mail; e-mail headers also can reveal the name and version of the e-mail program you use, the operating system, the name and version of your mail server, internal IP addresses, and the mail server path taken by this message.

(a) Route between two hosts, round-trip delay, and whois information.

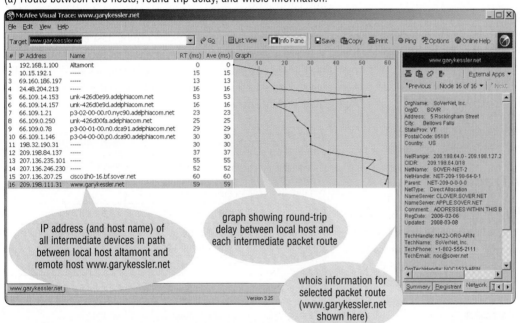

(b) Geographic map display of the route between two hosts.

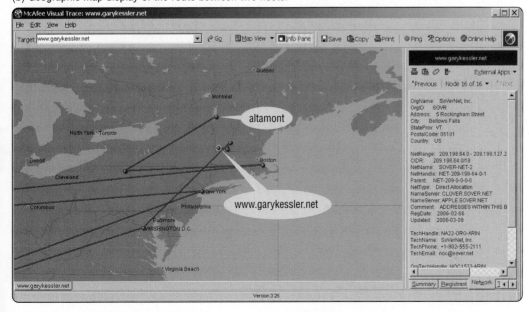

FIGURE 14 Tracing nodes between a local host computer (altamont) and a Web server using McAfee's Visual Trace.

Analyzing ISP Logs

During a computer forensics investigation, the specialist might request logs from an Internet service provider. The Internet service provider will deliver the logs, but they will be in the raw format in which they are saved.

While SMTP is used to forward e-mail across the Internet, other protocols are used to download e-mail by the client. One such protocol is the Post Office Protocol version 3 (POP3). Figure 1a on page 607 shows a set of three records from a POP3 server log showing a user logging on to check and download e-mail messages. All records show a date (March 13) and time stamp on a host named watson running the POP service (ipop3d) and access by a user on the host with IP address 192.168.187.35.

Analyzing Chat Logs

Analysis of chat logs is another important aspect of network analysis. The log shown in Figure 1c on page 607 is a conversation between BettyF, billy89, and other members of the Internet Relay Chat (IRC) Strong&40 channel. Although this conversation is relatively innocuous, analysis of logs such as these can turn up evidence of cyberstalking, criminal conspiracy, economic espionage, harassment, or other items of interest.

Analyzing a Packet Trace

Packet sniffers are an important software tool in the understanding of network traffic. A **packet sniffer** monitors all of the traffic seen on the network port of a computer and keeps a copy for later analysis. One of the most commonly used packet sniffers is tcpdump, a command line utility for UNIX/Linux; WinDump is the Windows version.

Analyzing Mobile Devices

Mobile phones, PDAs, and digital cameras increasingly are the focus of forensics examinations. Analysis of these devices is a growing subspecialty of computer forensics. In some ways, analysis of mobile devices is more problematic than analysis of traditional computers, because mobile devices have a large variety of physical connectors, operating environments, file structures, data formats, features, user interfaces, and operating modes. Mobile devices also can contain a variety of expansion cards ranging from flash memory to Subscriber Identity Module (SIM) cards.

LEARNING MORE ABOUT COMPUTER FORENSICS

Every action a user takes on a computer leaves a trail. Deleting files really does not erase information. Evidence of computer activity is stored in many places on the hard disk, some obvious and some very obscure. Information about network access potentially is logged on many computers throughout the local network and global Internet. Digital tracks are everywhere.

Computer forensics specialists must be technically knowledgeable and enjoy troubleshooting and solving puzzles. They must be aware of the legal constraints and organizational polices that guide what they can and cannot do.

Many sources for news and information about computer forensics are available online. Using the popular Web portals such as Google, Yahoo!, and others, you will find links to hundreds of computer forensics sites. Figure 15 lists sources for information about computer forensics and their Web addresses.

	WEB SITE	WEB ADDRESS
Computer Forensics Hardware Companies	Digital Intelligence, Inc.	digitalintelligence.com
	Intelligent Computer Solutions, Inc.	www.ics-iq.com
	WiebeTech	wiebetech.com
Computer Forensics Software	AccessData Corp. Ultimate Toolkit	accessdata.com
	Guidance Software EnCase	guidancesoftware.com
	STD — Security Tools Distribution	s-t-d.org
	SleuthKit & Autopsy	sleuthkit.org
	Technology Pathways ProDiscover	www.techpathways.com
	X-Ways Software Technology AG	winhex.com
Network Analysis Software	McAfee Personal Firewall Plus	us.mcafee.com
	tcpdump/libpcap	http://www.tcpdump.org
Additional Information	GCK Cybercrime and Cyberforensics-related URLs	www.garykessler.net/library/forensicsurl.html
	High Technology Crime Investigation Association (HTCIA)	htcia.org
	International Association of Computer Investigative Specialists (IACIS)	cops.org
	National White Collar Crime Center (NW3C)	nw3c.org

For an updated list, visit scsite.com/dc2008/ch11/computerforensics.

FIGURE 15 Online sources for information about computer forensics.

APPENDIX A

Coding Schemes and Number Systems

CODING SCHEMES

As discussed in Chapter 4, a computer uses a coding scheme to represent characters. This section of the appendix presents the ASCII, EBCDIC, and Unicode coding schemes and discusses parity.

ASCII and EBCDIC

Two popular coding schemes that represent characters in a computer are ASCII and EBCDIC. The **American Standard Code for Information Interchange**, or ASCII (pronounced ASK-ee), coding scheme is the most widely used coding scheme to represent data. Many personal computers and midrange servers use ASCII. The **Extended Binary Coded Decimal Interchange Code**, or EBCDIC (pronounced EB-see-dik), coding scheme is used primarily on mainframe computers and high-end servers. As shown in Figure A-1, the combination of bits (0s and 1s) is unique for each character in the ASCII and EBCDIC coding schemes.

When a computer uses the ASCII or EBCDIC coding scheme, it stores each represented character in one byte of memory. Other binary formats exist, however, that the computer sometimes uses to represent numeric data. For example, a computer may store, or pack, two numeric characters in one byte of memory. The computer uses these binary formats to increase storage and processing efficiency.

Unicode

The 256 characters and symbols that are represented by ASCII and EBCDIC codes are sufficient for English and western European languages but are not large enough for Asian and other languages that use different alphabets. Further compounding the problem is that many of these languages use symbols, called **ideograms**, to represent multiple words and ideas. One solution to this situation is Unicode. **Unicode** is a 16-bit coding scheme that has the capacity of representing all the world's current languages, as well as classic and historical languages, in more than 65,000 characters and symbols.

ASCII	SYMBOL	EBCDIC
00110000	0	11110000
00110001	1	11110001
00110010	2	11110010
00110011	3	11110011
00110100	4	11110100
00110101	5	11110101
00110110	6	11110110
00110111	7	11110111
00111000	8	11111000
00111001	9	11111001
01000001	A	11000001
01000010	B	11000010
01000011	C	11000011
01000100	D	11000100
01000101	E	11000101
01000110	F	11000110
01000111	G	11000111
01001000	H	11001000
01001001	I	11001001
01001010	J	11010001
01001011	K	11010010
01001100	L	11010011
01001101	M	11010100
01001110	N	11010101
01001111	O	11010110
01010000	P	11010111
01010001	Q	11011000
01010010	R	11011001
01010011	S	11100010
01010100	T	11100011
01010101	U	11100100
01010110	V	11100101
01010111	W	11100110
01011000	X	11100111
01011001	Y	11101000
01011010	Z	11101001
00100001	!	01011010
00100010	"	01111111
00100011	#	01111011
00100100	$	01011011
00100101	%	01101100
00100110	&	01010000
00101000	(	01001101
00101001	)	01011101
00101010	*	01011100
00101011	+	01001110

FIGURE A-1

A Unicode code for a symbol, as shown in Figure A-2, is obtained by appending the symbol's corresponding digit in the left-most column to the end of the symbol's corresponding three-digit code in the column heading. For

example, the Unicode for the capital letter C is 0043. In Unicode, 30,000 codes are reserved for future use, such as ancient languages, and 6,000 codes are reserved for private use. Existing ASCII coded data is fully compatible with Unicode because the first 256 codes are the same. Unicode is implemented in several operating systems, including Windows XP, Windows Vista, Mac OS X, and Linux. Unicode-enabled programming languages and software include Java, XML, Microsoft Office, and Oracle. Some experts believe that Unicode eventually will replace all other coding schemes.

Parity

Regardless of the coding scheme used to represent characters in memory, it is important that the computer store characters accurately. For each byte of memory, most computers have at least one extra bit, called a **parity bit**, that the computer uses for error checking. A parity bit can detect if one of the bits in a byte has been changed inadvertently. While such errors are extremely rare (most computers never have a parity error during their lifetime), they can occur because of voltage fluctuations, static electricity, or a memory failure.

Computers are either odd- or even-parity machines. In computers with odd-parity, the total number of on bits in the byte (including the parity bit) must be an odd number (Figure A-3). In computers with even parity, the total number of on bits must be an even number. The computer checks parity each time it uses a memory location. When the computer moves data from one location to another in memory, it compares the parity bits of both the sending and receiving locations to see if they are the same. If the computer detects a difference or if the wrong number of bits is on (e.g., an odd number in a computer with even parity), an error message is displayed. Many computers use multiple parity bits that enable them to detect and correct a single-bit error and detect multiple-bit errors.

	003	004	005	006	007
0	0 0030	@ 0040	P 0050	` 0060	p 0070
1	1 0031	A 0041	Q 0051	a 0061	q 0071
2	2 0032	B 0042	R 0052	b 0062	r 0072
3	3 0033	C 0043	S 0053	c 0063	s 0073
4	4 0034	D 0044	T 0054	d 0064	t 0074
5	5 0035	E 0045	U 0055	e 0065	u 0075
6	6 0036	F 0046	V 0056	f 0066	v 0076
7	7 0037	G 0047	W 0057	g 0067	w 0077
8	8 0038	H 0048	X 0058	h 0068	x 0078
9	9 0039	I 0049	Y 0059	i 0069	y 0079
A	: 003A	J 004A	Z 005A	j 006A	z 007A
B	; 003B	K 004B	[005B	k 006B	{ 007B
C	< 003C	L 004C	\ 005C	l 006C	| 007C
D	= 003D	M 004D	] 005D	m 006D	} 007D
E	> 003E	N 004E	^ 005E	n 006E	~ 007E
F	? 003F	O 004F	_ 005F	o 006F	DEL 007F

FIGURE A-2

FIGURE A-3

NUMBER SYSTEMS

This section of the appendix describes the number systems used with computers. Technical computer personnel require a thorough knowledge of this subject, but most users need only a general understanding of number systems and how they relate to computers.

The binary (base 2) number system is used to represent the electronic status of the bits in memory. It also is used for other purposes such as addressing the memory locations. Another number system commonly used with computers is **hexadecimal** (base 16). The computer uses the hexadecimal number system to communicate with a programmer when a problem with a program exists, because it would be difficult for the programmer to understand the 0s and 1s of binary code. Figure A-4 shows how the decimal values 0 through 15 are represented in binary and hexadecimal number systems.

DECIMAL	BINARY	HEXADECIMAL
0	0000	0
1	0001	1
2	0010	2
3	0011	3
4	0100	4
5	0101	5
6	0110	6
7	0111	7
8	1000	8
9	1001	9
10	1010	A
11	1011	B
12	1100	C
13	1101	D
14	1110	E
15	1111	F

FIGURE A-4

The mathematical principles that apply to the binary and hexadecimal number systems are the same as those that apply to the decimal number system. To help you better understand these principles, this section starts with the familiar decimal system, then progresses to the binary and hexadecimal number systems.

The Decimal Number System

The decimal number system is a base 10 number system (deci means ten). The base of a number system indicates how many symbols it uses. The decimal number system uses 10 symbols: 0 through 9. Each of the symbols in the number system has a value associated with it. For example, 3 represents a quantity of three and 5 represents a quantity of five.

The decimal number system also is a positional number system. This means that in a number such as 143, each position in the number has a value associated with it. When you look at the decimal number 143, the 3 is in the ones, or units, position and represents three ones (3×1); the 4 is in the tens position and represents four tens (4×10); and the 1 is in the hundreds position and represents one hundred (1×100). The number 143 is the sum of the values in each position of the number ($100 + 40 + 3 = 143$). The chart in Figure A-5 shows how you can calculate the positional values (hundreds, tens, and units) for a number system. Starting on the right and working to the left, the base of the number system, in this case 10, is raised to consecutive powers (10^0, 10^1, 10^2). These calculations are a mathematical way of determining the place values in a number system.

When you use number systems other than decimal, the same principles apply. The base of the number system indicates the number of symbols that it uses, and each position in a number system has a value associated with it. By raising the base of the number system to consecutive powers beginning with zero, you can calculate the positional value.

power of 10	10^2	10^1	10^0	1	4	3	=	
				(1×10^2) +	(4×10^1) +	(3×10^0)	=	
positional value	100	10	1	(1×100) +	(4×10) +	(3×1)	=	
number	1	4	3	100 +	40 +	3	=	143

FIGURE A-5

The Binary Number System

As previously discussed, binary is a base 2 number system (bi means two), and the symbols it uses are 0 and 1. Just as each position in a decimal number has a place value associated with it, so does each position in a binary number. In binary, the place values, moving from right to left, are successive powers of two (2^0, 2^1, 2^2, 2^3 or 1, 2, 4, 8). To construct a binary number, place ones in the positions where the corresponding values add up to the quantity you want to represent and place zeros in the other positions. For example, in a four-digit binary number, the binary place values are (from right to left) 1, 2, 4, and 8. The binary number 1001 has ones in the positions for the values 1 and 8 and zeros in the positions for 2 and 4. Therefore, as shown in Figure A-6, the quantity represented by binary 1001 is 9 (8 + 0 + 0 + 1).

The Hexadecimal Number System

The hexadecimal number system uses 16 symbols to represent values (hex means six). These include the symbols 0 through 9 and A through F (Figure A-4 on the previous page). The mathematical principles previously discussed also apply to hexadecimal (Figure A-7).

The primary reasons the hexadecimal number system is used with computers are (1) it can represent binary values in a more compact and readable form, and (2) the conversion between the binary and the hexadecimal number systems is very efficient.

An eight-digit binary number (a byte) can be represented by a two-digit hexadecimal number. For example, in the ASCII code, the character M is represented as 01001101. This value can be represented in the hexadecimal number system as 4D. One way to convert this binary number (4D) to a hexadecimal number is to divide the binary number (from right to left) into groups of four digits, calculate the value of each group, and then change any two-digit values (10 through 15) to the symbols A through F that are used in the hexadecimal number system (Figure A-8).

power of 2	2^3	2^2	2^1	2^0		**1**	**0**	**0**	**1**	**=**
						(1×2^3) +	(0×2^2) +	(0×2^1) +	(1×2^0) =	
positional value	8	4	2	1		(1×8) +	(0×4) +	(0×2) +	(1×1) =	
binary	1	0	0	1		8 +	0 +	0 +	1 =	9

FIGURE A-6

power of 16	16^1	16^0		**A**	**5**	**=**	
				(10×16^1) +	(5×16^0)	=	
positional value	16	1		(10×16) +	(5×1)	=	
hexadecimal	A	5		160 +	5	=	165

FIGURE A-7

	positional value	8421	8421
	binary	0100	1101
	decimal	4	13
	hexadecimal	4	D

FIGURE A-8

APPENDIX B

Quiz Yourself Answers

Following are possible answers to the Quiz Yourself boxes throughout the book.

Quiz Yourself 1-1

1. A computer is ~~a motorized~~an electronic device that processes ~~output~~input into ~~input~~output.
2. A storage device records (~~reads~~writes) and/or retrieves (~~writes~~reads) items to and from storage media.
3. An ~~output~~input device is any hardware component that allows you to enter data and instructions into a computer.
4. True Statement
5. Computers have the ~~dis~~advantages of fast speeds, ~~high~~low failure rates, producing consistent results, storing ~~small~~enormous amounts of data, and communicating with others.
6. Four commonly used ~~input~~output devices are a printer, a monitor, speakers, and a portable media player.

Quiz Yourself 1-2

1. A ~~resource~~network is a collection of computers and devices connected together via communications devices and transmission media.
2. True Statement
3. Popular ~~system~~application software includes Web browsers, word processing software, spreadsheet software, database software, and presentation graphics software.
4. The ~~Internet~~Web is one of the more popular services on the ~~Web~~Internet.
5. Two types of ~~application~~system software are the operating system and utility programs.

Quiz Yourself 1-3

1. A ~~desktop computer~~notebook computer (or laptop computer) is a portable, personal computer designed to fit on your lap.
2. True Statement
3. Each ~~large business~~home user spends time on the computer for different reasons that include budgeting and personal financial management, Web access, communications, and entertainment.
4. A ~~home~~power user requires the capabilities of a workstation or other powerful computer.
5. ~~Mainframes~~Supercomputers are the fastest, most powerful computers — and the most expensive.
6. The elements of an information system are hardware, ~~e-mail~~software, data, people, and ~~the Internet~~procedures.
7. With ~~embedded computers~~online banking, users access account balances, pay bills, and copy monthly transactions from the bank's computer right into their personal computers.

Quiz Yourself 2-1

1. True Statement
2. ~~A WISP~~An IP address (or Internet Protocol address) is a number that uniquely identifies each computer or device connected to the Internet.
3. ~~An IP address~~A domain name, such as www.google.com, is the text version of ~~a domain name~~an IP address.
4. Dial-up access takes place when the modem in your computer uses ~~the cable television network~~a standard telephone line to connect to the Internet.
5. The World Wide Web Consortium (W3C) oversees research and ~~owns~~sets standards and guidelines for many areas of the Internet.

Quiz Yourself 2-2

1. True Statement
2. A ~~Web browser~~subject directory classifies Web pages in an organized set of categories, such as sports or shopping, and related subcategories.
3. Audio and video files are ~~downloaded~~compressed to reduce their file sizes.
4. Popular ~~portals~~players include iTunes, RealPlayer, and Windows Media Player.
5. The more widely used ~~search engines~~Web browsers for personal computers are Internet Explorer, Netscape, Firefox, Opera, and Safari.
6. To develop a Web page, you do not have to be a computer programmer.
7. To improve your Web searches, use ~~general~~specific nouns and put the ~~least~~ most important terms first in the search text.

Quiz Yourself 2-3

1. True Statement
2. An e-mail address is a combination of a user name and ~~an e-mail program~~a domain name that identifies a user so he or she can receive Internet e-mail.
3. ~~Business~~Consumer-to-consumer e-commerce occurs when one consumer sells directly to another, such as in an online auction.
4. FTP is an Internet standard that permits file ~~reading~~uploading and ~~writing~~downloading with other computers on the Internet.
5. ~~Spam~~Internet telephony uses the Internet (instead of the public switched telephone network) to connect a calling party to one or more called parties.
6. Netiquette is the code of ~~un~~acceptable behaviors while on the Internet.
7. On a newsgroup, a ~~subscription~~thread (or threaded discussion) consists of the original article and all subsequent related replies.

Quiz Yourself 3-1

1. True Statement
2. ~~Public domain~~Packaged software is mass produced, copyrighted retail software that meets the needs of a wide variety of users, not just a single user or company.
3. To use ~~system~~application software, your computer must be running ~~application~~system software.
4. When a program is started, its instructions load from ~~memory~~a storage medium into ~~a storage medium~~memory.

Quiz Yourself 3-2

1. ~~Audio~~Video editing software typically includes ~~video~~audio editing capabilities.
2. ~~Enterprise computing~~Image editing software provides the capabilities of paint software and also includes the ability to modify existing images.
3. Millions of people use ~~spreadsheet~~word processing software every day to develop documents such as letters, memos, reports, fax cover sheets, mailing labels, newsletters, and Web pages.
4. Professional ~~accounting~~DTP (or desktop publishing) software is ideal for the production of high-quality color documents such as textbooks, corporate newsletters, marketing literature, product catalogs, and annual reports.
5. ~~Spreadsheet~~Presentation graphics software is application software that allows users to create visual aids for presentations to communicate ideas, messages, and other information to a group.
6. Two of the more widely used ~~CAD programs~~software suites are Microsoft Office 2007 and Sun StarOffice.
7. True Statement

Quiz Yourself 3-3

1. An ~~anti-spam~~antivirus program protects a computer against viruses by identifying and removing any computer viruses found in memory, on storage media, or in incoming files.
2. ~~Computer~~Web-based training is a type of ~~Web~~computer-based training that uses Internet technology and consists of application software on the Web.
3. True Statement
4. ~~Legal~~Personal finance software is a simplified accounting program that helps home users and small office/home office users balance their checkbooks, pay bills, track investments, and evaluate financial plans.
5. ~~Personal DTP~~Photo editing software is a popular type of image editing software that allows users to edit digital photographs.

Quiz Yourself 4-1

1. True Statement
2. Four basic operations in a machine cycle are: (1) ~~comparing~~fetching, (2) decoding, (3) executing, and, if necessary, (4) ~~pipelining~~storing.
3. Processors contain a ~~motherboard~~control unit and an arithmetic logic unit (ALU).
4. The ~~central processing unit~~motherboard, sometimes called a system board, is the main circuit board of the system unit.
5. The leading processor chip manufacturers for personal computers are ~~Microsoft~~Intel, AMD, IBM, Motorola, and Transmeta.
6. The pace of the system clock, called the clock speed, is measured by the number of ticks per ~~minute~~second.
7. The system unit is a case that contains ~~mechanical~~electronic components of the computer used to process data.

Quiz Yourself 4-2

1. True Statement
2. A gigabyte (GB) equals approximately 1 ~~trillion~~billion bytes.
3. Memory cache helps speed the processes of the computer because it stores ~~seldom~~frequently used instructions and data.
4. Most computers are ~~analog~~digital, which means they recognize only two discrete states: on and off.
5. Most RAM ~~retains~~loses its contents when the power is removed from the computer.
6. Read-only memory (ROM) refers to memory chips storing ~~temporary~~permanent data and instructions.

Quiz Yourself 4-3

1. A ~~bus~~port is the point at which a peripheral attaches to or communicates with a system unit so the peripheral can send data to or receive information from the computer.
2. An ~~AC adapter~~expansion slot is a socket on the motherboard that can hold an adapter card.
3. Built into the power supply is a ~~heater~~fan that keeps components of the system unit ~~warm~~cool.
4. ~~Serial~~USB ports can connect up to 127 different peripherals together with a single connector type.
5. The higher the bus clock speed, the ~~slower~~faster the transmission of data.
6. True Statement

Quiz Yourself 5-1

1. A keyboard is an ~~output~~input device that contains keys users press to enter data in a computer.
2. A ~~light pen~~graphics tablet is a flat, rectangular, electronic plastic board.

3. A ~~trackball~~ touch pad is a small, flat, rectangular pointing device commonly found on notebook computers.
4. True Statement
5. Operations you can perform with a ~~wheel~~ mouse include point, click, right-click, double-click, triple-click, drag, right-drag, rotate wheel, free-spin wheel, press wheel button, and tilt wheel.
6. ~~PDAs~~ Tablet PCs use a pressure-sensitive digital pen, and ~~Tablet PCs~~ PDAs use a stylus.

Quiz Yourself 5-2

1. True Statement
2. DV cameras record video as ~~analog~~ digital signals.
3. ~~Instant messaging~~ Voice recognition (or speech recognition) is the computer's capability of distinguishing spoken words.
4. Many smart phones today have a built-in camera so users easily can send ~~text~~ picture messages.
5. The ~~lower~~ higher the resolution of a digital camera, the better the image quality, but the more expensive the camera.

Quiz Yourself 5-3

1. A fingerprint scanner captures curves and indentations of a ~~signature~~ fingerprint.
2. After swiping a credit card through ~~an MICR~~ a magstripe (or magnetic stripe card) reader, a POS terminal connects to a system that authenticates the purchase.
3. ATMs ask you to enter a password, called a ~~biometric identifier~~ PIN (or personal identification number), which verifies that you are the holder of the bankcard.
4. Four types of ~~source documents~~ scanners are flatbed, pen, sheet-fed, and drum.
5. Retail and grocery stores use the ~~POSTNET~~ UPC (Universal Product Code) bar code.
6. RFID is a technology that uses ~~laser~~ radio signals to communicate with a tag placed in an object, an animal, or a person.
7. True Statement

Quiz Yourself 6-1

1. A ~~lower~~ higher resolution uses a greater number of pixels and thus provides a smoother image.
2. An output device is any type of ~~software~~ hardware component that conveys information to one or more people.
3. Documents often include ~~text~~ graphics to enhance their visual appeal and convey information.
4. ~~LCD~~ CRT monitors have a larger footprint than ~~CRT~~ LCD monitors.
5. Types of ~~CRTs~~ flat-panel displays include LCD monitors, LCD screens, and plasma monitors.
6. True Statement

Quiz Yourself 6-2

1. A ~~laser~~ thermal printer generates images by pushing electrically heated pins against heat-sensitive paper.
2. A ~~photo~~ laser printer creates images using a laser beam and powdered ink, called toner.
3. An ink-jet printer is a type of impact printer that forms characters and graphics by spraying tiny drops of liquid ~~nitrogen~~ ink onto a piece of paper.
4. Printed information is called ~~soft~~ hard copy.
5. Two commonly used types of impact printers are ~~ink-jet~~ dot-matrix printers and line printers.
6. True Statement

Quiz Yourself 6-3

1. A digital light processing (DLP) projector uses tiny ~~lightbulbs~~ mirrors to reflect light.
2. True Statement
3. Many personal computer users add surround sound ~~printer systems~~ speakers to their computers to generate a higher-quality sound.
4. Multifunction peripherals require ~~more~~ less space than having a separate printer, scanner, copy machine, and fax machine.
5. Some joysticks, wheels, and gamepads include ~~real-time action~~ force feedback, which is a technology that sends resistance to the device in response to actions of the user.

Quiz Yourself 7-1

1. Miniature hard disks are a type of ~~optical disc~~ magnetic disk.
2. True Statement
3. SATA is a hard disk interface that uses ~~parallel~~ serial signals to transfer data, instructions, and information.
4. ~~Storage media~~ A storage device is the computer hardware that records and/or retrieves items to and from ~~a~~ storage ~~device~~ media.
5. Two types of ~~manual~~ magnetic disks are hard disks and floppy disks.
6. Users can move an ~~internal~~ external hard disk from computer to computer as needed by connecting the disk to a USB port or FireWire port on the system unit.

Quiz Yourself 7-2

1. A ~~CD-RW~~ CD-ROM is a type of optical disc on which users can read but not write (record) or erase.
2. A ~~DVD-RAM~~ Picture CD is a single-session disc that stores digital versions of film using a jpg file format.
3. DVDs have ~~the same~~ much greater storage capacities ~~as~~ than CDs.
4. Optical discs are written and read by ~~mirrors~~ a laser.

5. ~~Single session~~Multisession means you can write on part of the disc at one time and another part at a later time.
6. True Statement

Quiz Yourself 7-3

1. A smart card stores data on a thin ~~magnetic stripe~~microprocessor embedded in the card.
2. A USB flash drive is a flash memory storage device that plugs in a ~~parallel~~USB port on a computer or mobile device.
3. Flash memory cards are a type of ~~magnetic~~solid-state media, which means they consist entirely of electronic components and contain no moving parts.
4. Microfilm and microfiche have the ~~shortest~~longest life of any storage media.
5. Tape storage requires ~~direct~~sequential access, which refers to reading or writing data consecutively.
6. True Statement

Quiz Yourself 8-1

1. A ~~buffer~~driver is a small program that tells the operating system how to communicate with a specific device.
2. A ~~cold~~warm boot is the process of using the operating system to restart a computer.
3. A password is a ~~public~~private combination of characters associated with the user name that allows access to certain computer resources.
4. Firmware that contains the computer's startup instructions is called the ~~kernel~~BIOS.
5. The program you currently are using is in the ~~background~~foreground, and the other programs running but not in use are in the ~~foreground~~ background.
6. Two types of system software are operating systems and ~~application~~utility programs.
7. True Statement

Quiz Yourself 8-2

1. A ~~file manager~~firewall is a utility that detects and protects a personal computer from unauthorized intrusions.
2. ~~Fragmenting~~Defragmenting a disk is the process of reorganizing it so the files are stored in contiguous sectors.
3. Windows Vista Home Basic uses the Windows ~~Aero~~Vista Basic interface.
4. True Statement
5. ~~Flip3D~~Linux is a UNIX-type operating system that is open source software.
6. You should ~~uninstall~~back up files and disks regularly in the event your originals are lost, damaged, or destroyed.

Quiz Yourself 8-3

1. A ~~pop-up blocker~~file compression utility shrinks the size of a file(s).
2. An ~~anti-spam~~antivirus program protects a computer against viruses by identifying and removing any computer viruses found in memory, on storage media, or on incoming files.
3. True Statement
4. Pocket PCs use ~~Palm OS~~Windows Mobile as their operating system.
5. ~~Web filtering~~CD/DVD burning software writes text, graphics, audio, and video files to a recordable or rewritable CD or DVD.

Quiz Yourself 9-1

1. A ~~cybercafé~~hot spot is a wireless network that provides Internet connections to mobile computers and other devices.
2. A ~~Web folder~~GPS (global positioning system) is a navigation system that consists of one or more earth-based receivers that accept and analyze signals sent by satellites in order to determine the receiver's geographic location.
3. True Statement
4. ~~Receiving~~Sending devices initiate an instruction to transmit data, instructions, or information.
5. Users can send pictures, and sound files, as well as short text messages, with ~~text~~picture messaging.

Quiz Yourself 9-2

1. A wireless LAN is a LAN that uses no physical wires.
2. An intranet is an internal network that uses ~~video conferencing~~Internet technologies.
3. Five types of digital ~~dial-up~~dedicated lines are ISDN lines, DSL, FTTH/FTTB, T-carrier lines, and ATM.
4. In a client/server network, ~~servers~~clients on the network access resources on the ~~client~~server.
5. In a networked environment, any ~~un~~authorized computer user can access data and information stored on other computers on the network.
6. True Statement

Quiz Yourself 9-3

1. A ~~cable~~dial-up modem converts a computer's digital signals to analog signals before they are transmitted over standard telephone lines.
2. A ~~hardware firewall~~wireless access point is a communications device that allows computers and devices to transfer data wirelessly among themselves or to transfer data wirelessly to a wired network.
3. True Statement
4. ~~Analog~~Digital signals consist of individual electrical pulses that represent bits grouped together into bytes.

5. ~~Physical~~ Wireless transmission media send communications signals through the air or space using radio, microwave, and infrared signals.

6. The ~~lower~~ higher the bandwidth, the more data, instructions, and information the channel transmits.

7. Two types of wireless home networks are HomeRF and ~~powerline cable~~ Wi-Fi.

Quiz Yourself 10-1

1. A ~~coding scheme~~ check digit is a number(s) or character(s) that is appended to or inserted in a primary key value.

2. A ~~database~~ field is a combination of one or more related characters or bytes and is the smallest unit of data a user accesses.

3. A ~~record~~ database is a collection of data organized in a manner that allows access, retrieval, and use of that data.

4. ~~Data~~ Information is processed ~~information~~ data.

5. ~~Hierarchy of data~~ File maintenance procedures include adding records to, changing records in, and deleting records from a file.

6. True Statement

Quiz Yourself 10-2

1. A DBMS is ~~hardware~~ software that allows you to create, access, and manage ~~an operating system~~ a database.

2. A ~~query~~ data dictionary contains data about files and fields in the database.

3. ~~Backup and recovery procedures~~ Access privileges for data involve establishing who can enter new data, change existing data, delete unwanted data, and view data.

4. Strengths of the database approach include ~~increased~~ reduced data redundancy, ~~reduced~~ improved data integrity, shared data, easier access, and ~~increased~~ reduced development time.

5. To reduce data entry errors, well-designed forms should ~~rollback~~ validate data as it is entered.

6. True Statement

Quiz Yourself 10-3

1. Data warehouses often use a process called ~~OQL~~ data mining to find patterns and relationships among data.

2. ~~Object-oriented~~ Relational databases store data in tables.

3. True Statement

4. Relational database users refer to a file as a table, a record as a ~~column~~ row, and a field as a ~~row~~ column.

5. SQL is a ~~data modeling~~ query language that allows users to manage, update, and retrieve data.

6. The database ~~analyst~~ administrator requires a more technical inside view of the data than does the ~~database administrator~~ data analyst.

Quiz Yourself 11-1

1. A ~~back door~~ denial of service (DoS) attack is an assault whose purpose is to disrupt computer access to an Internet service such as the Web or e-mail.

2. True Statement

3. A biometric device translates a personal characteristic into ~~an analog~~ a digital code that then is compared with a digital code stored in the computer.

4. Computer viruses, worms, and Trojan horses are malware that acts with~~out~~ a user's knowledge.

5. Perpetrators of cybercrime and other intrusions fall into seven basic categories: hacker, cracker, ~~CERT/CC~~ script kiddie, corporate spy, unethical employee, ~~trusted source~~ cyberextortionist, and cyberterrorist.

6. ~~Shorter~~ Longer passwords provide greater security than ~~longer~~ shorter ones.

7. Updating an antivirus program's ~~quarantine~~ signature file protects a computer against viruses written since the antivirus program was released.

Quiz Yourself 11-2

1. An end-user license agreement (EULA) ~~permits~~ does not permit users to give copies to friends and colleagues, while continuing to use the software.

2. Encryption is a process of converting ~~ciphertext~~ plaintext into ~~plaintext~~ ciphertext to prevent authorized access.

3. Mobile users are ~~not~~ susceptible to hardware theft.

4. True Statement

5. Three ~~backup~~ wireless security standards are Wired Equivalent Privacy, Wi-Fi Protected Access, and 802.11i.

6. To prevent against data loss caused by a system failure, computer users should ~~restore~~ back up files regularly.

Quiz Yourself 11-3

1. A ~~code of conduct~~ copyright gives authors and artists exclusive rights to duplicate, publish, and sell their materials.

2. Factors that cause ~~CVS~~ tendonitis or CTS (carpal tunnel syndrome) include prolonged typing, prolonged mouse usage, or continual shifting between the mouse and the keyboard.

3. ~~Phishing~~ Computer forensics is the discovery, collection, and analysis of evidence found on computers and networks.

4. True Statement

5. Users should not store obsolete computers and devices in their basement or attic.

6. Web sites use ~~electronic profiles~~ cookies to track user preferences, store users' passwords, keep track of items in a user's shopping cart, and track Web site browsing habits.

7. You cannot assume that information on the Web is correct.

APPENDIX C
Computer Acronyms

Acronym	Description	Page
0NF	zero normal form	540
1NF	first normal form	540
2NF	second normal form	540
3NF	third normal form	540
AA	Audible Audio	87
AAC	Advanced Audio Coding	87
AC	alternating current	213
ADA	Americans with Disabilities Act	266
ADC	analog-to-digital converter	38
ADSL	asymmetric digital subscriber line	482
AES	advanced encryption standard	592
AGP	Accelerated Graphics Port	212
AIFF	Audio Interchange File Format	87
ALU	arithmetic logic unit	188
AMD	Advanced Micro Devices	219
AOL	America Online	72, 82
ARPA	Advanced Research Projects Agency	69
ARPANET	Advanced Research Projects Agency network	69
ASCII	American Standard Code for Information Interchange	195, 518
ASF	Advanced Streaming (or Systems) Format	87
ASP	application service provider	164
ATC	advanced transfer cache	201
ATM	Asynchronous Transfer Mode	482, 483
ATM	automated teller machine	262
AUP	acceptable use policy	565
B2B	business-to-business	92
B2C	business-to-consumer	91
BD-R	Blu-ray Disc recordable	373
BD-RE	Blu-ray Disc rewritable	373
BD-ROM	Blu-ray Disc read-only memory	372
BIOS	basic input/output system	400
Bit	binary digit	195, 518
BLOB	binary large object	518
BMP	bit map	85
BSA	Business Software Alliance	571
BTW	by the way	100
C2C	consumer-to-consumer	92
CA	certificate authority	573
CAD	computer-aided design	151, 327
CAI	computer-aided instruction	160
CAM	computer-aided manufacturing	36
CATV	cable television	482
CBT	computer-based training	160
CCD	charge-coupled device	251
ccTLD	country code top-level domain	74
CD	compact disc	8, 9, 17, 27, 89, 357
CDMA	Code Division Multiple Access	494, 499
CD-R	compact disc-recordable	370
CD-ROM	compact disc read-only memory	369–70
CD-RW	compact disc-rewritable	371, 576
CERT/CC	Computer Emergency Response Team Coordination Center	558

Acronym	Description	Page
CF	CompactFlash	376
CIPA	Children's Internet Protection Act	480, 585
CMOS	complementary metal-oxide semiconductor	203
Coax	coaxial cable	493
COBOL	COmmon Business-Oriented Language	53
COM port	communications port	207
COPPA	Children's Online Privacy Protection Act	585
CPU	central processing unit	8, 187
CRT	cathode-ray tube	308
CSC	common short code	463
CSS	Content Scrambling System	580
CST	Computer Service Technician	381
CTS	carpal tunnel syndrome	588
CVS	computer vision syndrome	588
DA	database analyst	538
DAC	digital-to-analog converter	38
DBA	database administrator	538
DBMS	database management system	515
DDoS attack	distributed denial of service attack	562
DDR SDRAM	double data rate synchronous dynamic random access memory	199
DHCP	Dynamic Host Configuration Protocol	102
DIMM	dual inline memory module	199
DL	distance learning	166
DLP projector	digital light processing projector	324
DMCA	Digital Millennium Copyright Act	87, 585
DNS	domain name system	74
DOS	Disk Operating System	417
DoS attack	denial of service attack	562
Dpi	dots per inch	252, 313
DRAM	dynamic random access memory	199
DRM	digital rights management	86
DSL	Digital Subscriber Line	70, 449, 482, 486
DSP	digital signal processor	38
DTP	desktop publishing	152
DTV	digital television	307
DV camera	digital video camera	253
DVD	digital versatile disc or digital video disc	8, 17, 59, 89, 357
DVD+R	digital versatile disc or digital video disc recordable	373
DVD-R	digital versatile disc or digital video disc recordable	373
DVD+RAM	digital versatile disc or digital video disc + random access memory	373
DVD-ROM	digital versatile disc or digital video disc read-only memory	9, 372
DVD+RW	digital versatile disc or digital video disc + rewritable	373
DVD-RW	digital versatile disc or digital video disc + rewritable	373
DVI	Digital Video Interface	305
EB	exabyte	356

Appendix C Computer Acronyms

Acronym	Description	Page
EBCDIC	Extended Binary Coded Decimal Interchange Code	195, 518
E-book	electronic book	61, 303
E-commerce	electronic commerce	28, 30, 60, 61, 91–92
ECPA	Electronic Communications Privacy Act	585
EDGE	Enhanced Data GSM Environment	494
EDI	electronic data interchange	470
EEPROM	electrically erasable programmable read-only memory	202
E-form	electronic form	530
EFS	Encrypting File System	592
EFT	electronic funds transfer	470
EIDE	Enhanced Integrated Drive Electronics	364
E-mail	electronic mail	12, 31, 69, 92–95, 101, 161, 462
EMR	electromagnetic radiation	308
ENIAC	Electronic Numerical Integrator and Computer	52
EP	Enterprise Portal	541
eSATA	external Serial Advanced Technology Attachment	210
EULA	end-user license agreement	571
EVDO	Evolution Data Optimized	495
FAQ	frequently asked questions	6, 100
Fax	facsimile	322–23
FORTRAN	FORmula TRANslator	53
FRED	Forensic Recovery of Digital Evidence	612
FSB	front side bus	212
FTP	File Transfer Protocol	68, 96, 134, 161, 462
FTTB	Fiber to the Building	483
FTTH	Fiber to the Home	483
FWIW	for what it's worth	100
FYI	for your information	100
GB	gigabyte	197, 356
Gbps	giga [billion] bits per second	476
GHz	gigahertz	189
GIF	Graphics Interchange Format	85
GIGO	garbage in, garbage out	10, 516
GIS	geographic information system	534
GLBA	Graham-Leach-Bliley Act	585
GPRS	General Packet Radio Service	494
GPS	global positioning system	466, 513
GPU	graphics processing unit	305
GSM	Global System for Mobile Communications	494
gTLD	generic top-level domain	73
GUI	graphical user interface	15, 137, 403, 420, 421
HD	high density	364
HD DVD-R	high-density DVD-recordable	373
HD DVD-RW	high-density DVD-rewritable	373
HD DVD-ROM	high-density DVD read-only memory	372
HDTV	high-definition television	307
HIPAA	Health Insurance Portability and Accountability Act	381, 585
HomeRF network	home radio frequency network	490
HP	Hewlett-Packard	329
HT	Hyper Threading	190
http	Hypertext Transfer Protocol	76, 477
Hz	hertz	189
I-4	International Information Integrity Institute	593
IBM	International Business Machines	53, 54, 55, 138

Acronym	Description	Page
IC	integrated circuit	186
ICANN	Internet Corporation for Assigned Names and Numbers	74
ICRA	Internet Content Rating Association	587
IM	instant messaging	98
IMDb	Internet Movie Database	536
IMHO	in my humble opinion	100
Interactive TV	interactive television	307
IP	intellectual property	579
IP address	Internet Protocol address	73, 102
IPng	Internet Protocol Next Generation	102
IPv6	Internet Protocol version 6	102
IR	infrared	494
IrDA	Infrared Data Association	210, 478
IRQ	interrupt request	409
IS	information system	25
ISDN	Integrated Services Digital Network	482
ISP	Internet service provider	72
IT	information technology	25
JPEG	Joint Photographic Experts Group	85, 345
K	kilobyte	197
KB	kilobyte	197, 356
KBps	kilobytes per second	357, 369
Kbps	kilo [thousand] bits per second	478
L1 cache	Level 1 cache	201
L2 cache	Level 2 cache	201
L3 cache	Level 3 cache	201
LAN	local area network	55, 471
LCD	liquid crystal display	304
Mac OS	Macintosh Operating System	19
Mac OS X	Macintosh Operating System X	39, 135, 195, 420
MAN	metropolitan area network	472
MB	megabyte	197, 356
MBps	megabytes per second	357, 364
Mbps	megabits per second	365, 476, 492, 494
M-commerce	mobile commerce	91
MHz	megahertz	203
MIB	Medical Information Bureau	381, 581
MICR	magnetic-ink character recognition	260
MIDI	Musical Instrument Digital Interface	209, 246
MIPS	millions of instructions per second	190
MMS	multimedia message service	464
Modem	modulate/demodulate	9, 462, 485–86
MP	million pixels	252
MP3	Moving Pictures Experts Group Audio Layer 3 (MPEG-3)	86, 87, 89, 202
MPEG	Moving Pictures Experts Group	88
MRAM	magnetoresistive random access memory	199
µs	microsecond	203
ms	millisecond	203
MS-DOS	Microsoft Disk Operating System	417, 430
MSN	Microsoft Network, The	72, 82
MT/ST	Magnetic Tape/Selectric Typewriter	54
NET Act	No Electronic Theft Act	585
Netiquette	Internet etiquette	100
NIC	network interface card	486
NLQ	near letter quality	318

Acronym	Description	Page
ns	nanosecond	203
NSF	National Science Foundation	70
OCR	optical character recognition	257
OLE	object linking and embedding	57
OLED	organic light emitting diode	304
OMR	optical mark recognition	257
OODB	object-oriented database	534
OQL	object query language	535
OS	operating system	15-16, 398–425
OSI reference model	Open Systems Interconnection reference model	498
OSP	online service provider	72
P2P	peer-to-peer	473–74
PATA	parallel Serial Advanced Technology Attachment	447
PATRIOT Act	Provide Appropriate Tools Required to Intercept and Obstruct Terrorism Act	585
PB	petabyte	356
PC	personal computer	19–20, 445
PC-DOS	personal computer Disk Operating System	417
PCI bus	Peripheral Component Interconnect bus	212
PCL	Printer Control Language	316
PCMCIA	Personal Computer Memory Card International Association	205
PCS	Personal Communications Services	495
PC-to-TV port	personal computer-to-television port	453
PDA	personal digital assistant	21, 31, 265, 282, 325
PDF	Portable Document Format	150
PDL	page description language	316
PGP	Pretty Good Privacy	572
PIM	personal information manager	148
PIN	personal identification number	262, 567
Pixel	picture element	252, 304
PNG format	Portable Network Graphics format	85
POP	point of presence	72
POP	Post Office Protocol	95, 477
POP3	Post Office Protocol 3	95
POS	point of sale	261
POST	power-on self test	400
ppi	pixels (picture elements) per inch	252
PROM chip	programmable read-only memory chip	202
ps	picosecond	203
PSTN	public switched telephone network	481
QBE	query by example	528
QT	QuickTime	87
RA	RealAudio	87
RAID	redundant array of independent disks	362
RAM	random access memory	197, 198–200
RDRAM	Rambus dynamic random access memory	199
REMSAT	Real Time Emergency Management Via Satellite	496
RFID	radio frequency identification	259, 476, 479
RIAA	Recording Industry Association of America	63
RIMM	Rambus inline memory module	199
ROM	read-only memory	201–2
Rpm	revolutions per minute	360
RSI	repetitive strain injury	587
RSS 2.0	Really Simple Syndication	84
SATA	Serial Advanced Technology Attachment	364

Acronym	Description	Page
SCSI	small computer system interface	210, 364
SD	Secure Digital	376
SDRAM	synchronous dynamic random access memory	199, 203
S-HTTP	secure hypertext transfer protocol	574
SIMM	single inline memory module	199
SMS	short message service	463
SMTP	simple mail transfer protocol	94, 477
SOHO	small office/home office	28
SQL	Structured Query Language	534
SRAM	static random access memory	199
SSID	service set identifier	577
SSL	Secure Sockets Layer	574
SVGA	Super Video Graphics Array	306
SXGA	Super Extended Graphics Array	306
TB	terabyte	197, 356
TCP/IP	Transmission Control Protocol/Internet Protocol	477
TFT display	thin-film transistor display	304
TIFF	Tagged Image File Format	85, 345
TLD	top-level domain	73
TRACERT	traceroute	430
TTFN	ta ta for now	100
TYVM	thank you very much	100
U-HDTV	ultra high-definition television	324
UL 1449 standard	Underwriters Laboratories 1449 standard	575
ULV	Ultra Low Voltage	193
UMD	Universal Media Disc	372
UMPC	Ultra-Mobile PC	21
UMTS	Universal Mobile Telecommunications System	494
UNIVAC I	UNIVersal Automatic Computer	52
uPC	ultra personal computer	21
UPC	Universal Product Code	258
UPS	uninterruptible power supply	451, 575
URL	Uniform Resource Locator	76
USB	universal serial bus	208, 212
User ID	user identification	410, 566
UWB	ultra-wideband	478
UXGA	Ultra Extended Graphics Array	305
VAN	value-added network	470
VCD	video CD	371
VoiceXML	Voice eXtensible Markup Language	528
VoIP	voice over Internet Protocol	99, 160
VPN	virtual private network	574
VR	virtual reality	88
W3C	World Wide Web Consortium	70, 327, 528
WAN	wide area network	472
WAP	Wireless Application Protocol	480
WAV	Windows waveform	87
WBT	Web-based training	165
WEP	Wired Equivalent Privacy	577
Wi-Fi	wireless fidelity	478
WiMAX	Worldwide Interoperability for Microwave Access	479
WinFS	Windows Future Storage	382
WISP	wireless Internet service provider	72, 463
WLAN	wireless local area network	471

Appendix C   *Computer Acronyms*

Acronym	Description	Page
WMA	Windows Media Audio	87, 89, 202
WPA	Wi-Fi Protected Access	577
WQXGA	Wide Quad Extended Graphics Array	306
WSXGA	Wide Super Extended Graphics Array	306
WUXGA	Wide Ultra Extended Graphics Array	306
WWW	World Wide Web	75, 103

Acronym	Description	Page
WXGA	Wide Extended Graphic Array	306
XGA	Extended Graphics Array	306
XML	eXtensible Markup Language	468
YB	yottabyte	356
ZB	zettabyte	356

INDEX

bility of performing some functions independent of the host computer. **261**

SMS (short message service): Short message service; service that allows users to send and receive short text messages on a phone or PDA. **463.** *See also* **Text messaging**

SMTP (simple mail transfer protocol): Communications protocol used by some outgoing mail servers. **94**, 477

SoBig virus, 63

Social engineering: Act of gaining unauthorized access or obtaining confidential information by taking advantage of the trusting human nature of some victims and the naivety of others. **586**

Social networking Web site: Web site that encourages members to share their interests, ideas, stories, photos, music, and videos with other registered users. **14.** *See also* **Online social network**

Social Security number, protecting, 581

Society
computer applications in, 32–37
ethics and, 578–80

Soft copy: Temporary output presented on a display device. **302**

Software: Series of instructions that tells a computer what to do and how to do it. **15–18.** *See also* **Computer program; program**
bundled, 446
communications, 480
compatibility, 445
copyrighted, 579–80
custom, 135
defective, 416
development of, 18
filtering, 480
forensics, used in, 610
installing new, 400
integrated, 156
license agreement, 570–71
network license, 470
open source, 421, 425, 431
packaged, 134
purchasing desktop computer and, 445
system, 15–16
system failure and, 574
trial versions of, 154

Software manufacturers, liability, 416

Software piracy, 570, 579

Software suite: Collection of individual programs sold as a single package. Business software suites typically include word processing, spreadsheet, e-mail, and

presentation graphics software. **148,** 156, 446

Software theft: Computer security risk that occurs when someone (1) steals software media, (2) intentionally erases programs, or (3) illegally copies a program. 570–71, 579

SOHO, 28. *See also* **Small office/home office**

Solaris: A version of UNIX developed by Sun Microsystems that is a network operating system designed specifically for e-commerce applications. **423**

Solid-state media: Term used to refer to components that consist entirely of electronic components and contain no moving parts. **376**

Son, Masayoshi, 169

Song lyrics, on the Web, 580

Sony, 269

Sound, 86, 246. *See also* **Audio; Microphone; Music; Sound card; Speakers**

Sound card: Adapter card that enhances the sound generating capabilities of a personal computer by allowing sound to be input through a microphone and output through external speakers or headset. 186, **204**
audio input and, 246
bus connection, 212
MIDI standard, 209
operation of, 328
purchasing desktop computer and, 448

Source document: Document that contains the original form of data to be processed. **255**

Spam: Unsolicited e-mail message or newsgroups posting sent to many recipients or newsgroups at once. 65, **100, 427**, 581, **584**

Speaker-dependent software: Software that makes a profile of a user's voice, which requires the user to train the computer to recognize his or her voice. 246, 263

Speaker-independent software: Software that has a built-in set of word patterns so that a user need not train the computer to recognize his or her voice. **246**

Speakers: Audio output devices that generate sound. 8, **320**

Specialist ASP: Application service provider that delivers applications to meet a specific business need, such as human resources or project management. **164**

Special-purpose terminal, 261–62

Speech, 86
continuous, 246
discrete, 246

Speech recognition: Computer's capability of distinguishing spoken words. 140, **245.** *See also* **Voice recognition**

Speed
access times, 203
bus, 212
bus width, 211
cache, 201
of computers, 10
processor, 190–91
RAM, 199–200
of storage devices and memory, 357, 362
system clock influence on, 189
word size, 211

Spelling checker: Feature in some application software that reviews the spelling of individual words, sections of a document, or the entire document. **139**

Spider: Program used to build and maintain lists of words found on Web sites. **81**

Spike: Electrical disturbance that occurs when an overvoltage lasts for less than one millisecond (one thousandth of a second). **574**

Spim: Spam sent through an instant messaging service. 65, **584**

Spit: Spam sent via Internet telephony. 65, **584**

Splitting, 350

Spoiler: Message that reveals a solution to a game or ending to a movie or program. **100**

Spoofing: Technique intruders use to make their network or Internet transmission appear legitimate to a victim computer or network. **563**

Spooling: Operating system process that sends print jobs to a buffer instead of sending them immediately to the printer. The buffer then holds the information waiting to print while the printer prints from the buffer at its own rate of speed. **407**

Sports, Web site and, 124

Spreadsheet software: Application software that allows a user to organize data in rows and columns and to perform calculations on the data. 16, **142–44**

Spyware: Program placed on a computer without the user's knowledge that secretly collects information about the user. 65, **427, 583**

PHOTO CREDITS

Chapter 1: 1a Courtesy of Hewlett-Packard Company; 1b Courtesy of Hewlett-Packard Company; 1c Courtesy of Apple; 1d Darrin Klimek/Getty Images; 4a Courtesy of Hewlett-Packard Company; 4b Courtesy of SanDisk Corporation; 4c Courtesy of Hewlett-Packard Company; 4d Courtesy of Avid Technology; 4e Courtesy of Seagate Technology; 4f Courtesy of Hewlett-Packard Company; 4g Courtesy of Logitech; 4h Courtesy of Microsoft Corporation; 4j Courtesy of Zoom Technologies Inc; 4k Courtesy of ViewSonic Corporation; 4l Courtesy of Microsoft Corporation; 4m Courtesy of Hewlett-Packard Company; 4n Courtesy of Hewlett-Packard Company; 4o Courtesy of Intel Corporation; 4p Courtesy of Kingston Technology; 4q Courtesy of UMAX; 4s Courtesy of Logitech; 4t Courtesy of Logitech; 4u Courtesy of SanDisk; 4v Courtesy of 3Com Corporation; 4w Courtesy of D-Link Corporation/D-Link Systems, Inc; 12 PRNewsFoto/Mindjet LLC; 13 Courtesy of Fujitsu-Siemens Computers; 14 Courtesy of InFocus Corporation; 15 © Digital Archive Japan / Alamy; 16 © Patrick Olear / PhotoEdit; 19 Courtesy of Motion Computing; 21 Courtesy of Motion Computing; **Special Feature 1:** 1937 Courtesy of Iowa State University; 1937 Courtesy of Iowa State University; 1937 Courtesy of Iowa State University; 1943 Photo courtesy of The Computer History Museum; 1943 Photo courtesy of The Computer History Museum; 1945 Courtesy of the Archives of the Institute for Advanced Study; 1946 From the Collections of the University of Pennsylvania Archives; 1947 © IBM Corporate Archives; 1947 © IBM Corporate Archives; 1951 Courtesy Unisys Corporation; 1952 Courtesy of Hagley Museum and Library; 1953 © IBM Corporate Archives; 1957 © IBM Corporate Archives; 1957 © IBM Corporate Archives; 1957 Courtesy of the Department of the Navy; 1958 Courtesy of Texas Instruments; 1958 Courtesy of Texas Instruments; 1958 Courtesy of Texas Instruments; 1959 © IBM Corporate Archives; 1960 Courtesy of Hagley Museum and Library; 1964 © IBM Corporate Archives; 1964 © IBM Corporate Archives; 1964 © IBM Corporate Archives; 1965 Courtesy of Dartmouth College; 1965 Courtesy of Digital Equipment Corporation; 1969 Courtesy of IBM Corporation; 1970 © IBM Corporate Archives; 1971 Courtesy of Intel Corporation; 1971 Courtesy of Intel Corporation; 1975 Photo courtesy of Computer History Museum; 1975 Courtesy of InfoWorld; 1976 Courtesy of Apple; 1976 © Bettmann/CORBIS; 1979 Photo courtesy of Computer History Museum; 1980 Courtesy of Microsoft Corporation; 1981 © IBM Corporate Archives; 1982 Courtesy of Zoom Telephonics, Inc; 1983 © Time Life Pictures/Getty Images; 1983 © IBM Corporate Archives; 1984 Courtesy of Apple; 1984 Courtesy of Hewlett-Packard Company; 1989 © 1997-1998W3C (MIT, INRIA, Keio); 1989 Courtesy of Intel Corporation; 1992 Courtesy of Microsoft Corporation; 1993 Courtesy of Intel Corporation; 1993 Courtesy of Microsoft Corporation; 1993 © Costa Cruise Lines/Getty Images; 1994 Courtesy of Netscape Communications Corporation; 1994 Courtesy of Larry Ewing and The Gimp; 1995 Courtesy of Sun Microsystems, Inc; 1995 Courtesy of Microsoft Corporation; 1996 Courtesy of Microsoft Corporation; 1996 Courtesy of Palm, Inc; 1997 Motion Picture & Television Archives; 1997 Courtesy of Denon Electronics; 1997 Courtesy of Intel Corporation; 1998 © Andersen Ross/Getty Images; 1998 Courtesy of Apple; 1998 Courtesy of Microsoft Corporation; 1999 Courtesy of Microsoft Corporation; 2000 Courtesy of Microsoft Corporation; 2000 Courtesy of Microsoft Corporation; 2000 © B Busco/Getty Images; 2000 Courtesy of Intel Corporation; 2001 Courtesy of Microsoft Corporation; 2001 Courtesy of Microsoft Corporation; 2002 Courtesy of RCA/Thomson Consumer Electronics; 2002 Courtesy of Sharp Electronics; 2002 Courtesy of Intel Corporation; 2003 Courtesy of ViewSonic Corporation; 2002 Courtesy of Intel Corporation; 2002 © Scott Goodwin Photography; 2002 Courtesy of Handspring, Inc; 2003 ©LWA- JDC/CORBIS; 2003 © Royalty-Free/CORBIS; 2003 © Jim Cummins/CORBIS; 2003 © Ed Bock/CORBIS; 2003 © Koichi Kamoshida/Getty Images; 2003 Courtesy of Microsoft Corporation; 2003 © Getty Images; 2003 © REUTERS/Mannie Garcia; 2004 Courtesy of Sony Electronics Inc; 2004 Courtesy of SanDisk Corporation; 2004 Courtesy of Apple; 2004 Courtesy of Palm, Inc. 2005 Courtesy of Apple; 2005 Courtesy of Microsoft Corporation; 2005 © PRNewsFoto/Microsoft Corp; 2006 AP Images; 2006 AP Topic Gallery Photo; 2006 Mitchell Funk/Getty Images; 2006 Courtesy of Facebook; 2006 Courtesy of Intel Corporation; 2006 Courtesy of Intel Corporation; 2006 Courtesy of Microsoft Corporation; 2007 Courtesy of Belkin International; 2007 Courtesy of Intel Corporation; 2007 Courtesy of CinemaNow; 2007 Courtesy of Acer America; 2007 Courtesy of Microsoft Corporation; 2007 Courtesy of Microsoft Corporation; 2007 Courtesy of Memorex; **Chapter 2:** PY-2 © Erik Freeland/Corbis PY-2 © WireImageStock/Masterfile; PY-2 © image100 / Alamy; PY-2 © Donna Day / Imagestate; PY-2 Stephen Roberts / Alamy; PY-2 © AP Wide World Photos; PY-2 © Martin Rogers/Workbook Stock/Getty Images; PY-2 © PM Images/Getty Images; PY-2 Courtesy of Nokia; 2-1f ©David Young-Wolff / Photo Edit; 2-1g Courtesy of Skype; Looking Ahead 2-1 Courtesy of Internet2; 2-2a © Rob Lewine/CORBIS; 2-2b © Royalty-Free/Corbis; 2-2c ©LWA-Dann Tardif/CORBIS; 2-2d ©LWA-Dann Tardif/CORBIS; 2-2e © Paul C. Chauncey/CORBIS; 2-2f © Jiri Rezac / Alamy; 2-2g Courtesy of Motorola, Inc; 2-3, Step 2 Courtesy of Motorola, Inc; 2-3, Step 3 Courtesy of Terayon Communication Systems, Inc; 2-3, Step 4 © Stephen Chernin/Getty Images; 2-3, Step 6 Courtesy of Fujitsu Siemens Computers; 2-7a Courtesy of Hewlett-Packard Company; 2-7b Courtesy of Nokia; Looking Ahead 2-2 Courtesy of Identix Incorporated; 2-20, Step 2 © Stephen Chernin/Getty Images; Courtesy of Fujitsu- Siemens Computers; 2-20, Step 3a Courtesy of Fujitsu Siemens Computers; 2-20, Step 3b © Swerve / Alamy; 2-24a © MedioImages; 2-24b © MedioImages; 2-24c © Inmagine / Alamy; 2-25 © Noel Hendrickson/Getty Images; Looking Ahead 2-3 © Darren McCollester/Getty Images; 2-27 ©Royalty-Free Corbis; 2-28 Step 1 and 4 Courtesy of Acer America Corp; 2-28, Step 2 Copyright 2005 Sun Microsystems, Inc. All Rights Reserved. Used by permission; 2-28 Step 3 Courtesy of Juniper Networks, Inc; 2-32 center © Blend Images / Alamy; 2-32a Courtesy of Acer America Corp; 2-32b Courtesy of Sony Electronics Inc; 2-32c © Gateway, Inc; 2-33 Step 2 Courtesy of Acer America Corp; 2-33 Step 4 and 5 Courtesy of Hewlett-Packard Company; 2-34a Courtesy of D-Link Systems; 2-34b Courtesy of Vonage; 2- 34c Courtesy of Hewlett-Packard Company; Career Corner © Manchan/Getty Images; Technology Trailblazer 1 © EPA /Landov; Technology Trailblazer 2 © LAURENT FIEVET/AFP/Getty Images; **Special Feature 2:** Opener1 © Justin Sullivan/Getty Images; Opener2 © DAVID HECKER/AFP/Getty Images; Opener3 © Muntz/Getty Images; Opener4 Courtesy of Siemens AG, Munich/Berlin; Opener 5 © Stockbyte/Getty Images; Opener 6 © Dominic DiSaia/Getty Images; Opener 7 © Purestock/Getty Images; **Chapter 3:** PY-3 Lambert/Getty Images; PY-3 Courtesy of Adobe Systems Incorporated; PY-3 Courtesy of Microsoft Corporation; PY-3 David Young-Wolff/PhotoEdit; PY-3 Courtesy of Hewlett-Packard Company; PY-3 © Mary Kate Denny / PhotoEdit; PY-3 Courtesy of Intuit; PY-3 Courtesy of Microsoft Corporation; 3-2a © John Feingersh/Masterfile; 3-2b Courtesy of Xerox Corporation; 3-2c Courtesy of Intel Corporation; Looking Ahead 3-1 Courtesy of IO2Technology; 3-14 Courtesy of Agilix; 3-15 Courtesy of Sendo; 3-16 Courtesy of Computer Systems Odessa Corp; 3-17 Courtesy of Sage Software; 3-20 Courtesy of Bentley Systems; 3-21 David Young-Wolff/PhotoEdit; 3-22 Screen shots are Copyright 2003 Corel Corporation and Corel Corporation Limited, reprinted by permission. Artwork © 2004 Cher Threinen-Pendarvis. 3-23 Courtesy of Adobe Systems Incorporated; 3-24 Courtesy of Ulead Systems, Inc; 3-25 Courtesy of SumTotal Systems, Inc; 3-26 Courtesy of Microsoft Corporation; 3-28a Courtesy of Intuit Inc; 3-28b © Digital Vision; 3-29 © 2003 Riverdeep Interactive Learning Limited, and its licensors; 3-30 Courtesy of Intuit Inc; 3-31, 32, 33 Screen shot(s) are © Copyright 2006 Corel Corporation and Corel Corporation Limited, reprinted by permission. 3-34 Used with permission. All TM and © 2006 Riverdeep Interactive Learning Limited, and its licensors. All rights reserved. www.riverdeep.net; 3-36 Courtesy of Punch! Software; 3-37 Courtesy of Merriam-Webster Inc; 3-38 Courtesy of Ubisoft; Looking Ahead 3-2 Photo © Chris Armstrong/Courtesy of Brigham Young University; 3-43 © Gary Herrington Photography; 3-44 Courtesy of Blackboard Inc. and Dallas Baptist University; Career Corner © Royalty-Free/CORBIS; Technology Trailblazer 1 © Louis Fabian Bachrach/Daniel Bricklin; Technology Trailblazer 2 © Tom Wagner/Corbis; **Chapter 4:** PY-4 © Marc Rochon/Getty Images; PY-4 Courtesy of Seagate Technology; PY-4

Courtesy of Intel Corporation; PY-4 Courtesy of ATI Technologies Inc; PY-4 Courtesy of Hewlett-Packard Company; PY-4 Courtesy of Kingston Technology; PY-4 Courtesy of Hewlett-Packard Company; PY-4 Artifacts Images/Getty Images; 4-1a Courtesy of Hewlett-Packard Company; 4-1b Courtesy of Apple; 4-1c Courtesy of Microsoft® Corporation; 4-1d © 2006 Sony Computer Entertainment Inc. All Rights Reserved; 4-1e Courtesy of Sony Ericsson Mobile Communications AB. All Rights Reserved; 4-1f Courtesy of Motion Computing; 4-1g Courtesy of Hewlett-Packard Company; 4-1h Courtesy of Acer America Corp; 4-1i Courtesy of Sony Electronics Inc; 4-2a Courtesy of Intel Corporation; 4-02b Courtesy of Hewlett-Packard Company; 4-2c Courtesy of SMART Modular Technologies, Inc. © 2002; 4-2d Courtesy of Creative Labs, Inc. Copyright © 2003 Creative Technology Ltd. (SOUND BLASTER AUDIGY 2S). All rights reserved; 4-2e Courtesy of Matrox Graphics Inc; 4-03 © Kirsty Pargeter /istockphoto.com; 4-5, Step 1 © imagebroker / Alamy; Looking Ahead 4-1 Courtesy of IBM Corporation; 4-8a1 Courtesy of Intel Corporation; 4-8a2 Courtesy of Intel Corporation; 4-8a3 Courtesy of Advanced Micro Devices, Inc; 4-8b1 Courtesy of Intel Corporation; Figure 4-8b2 Courtesy of Intel Corporation; 4-8b3 Courtesy of Advanced Micro Devices, Inc; 4-8b4 Courtesy of Advanced Micro Devices, Inc; 4-8c1 Courtesy of Intel Corporation; Figure 4-8c2 Courtesy of Advanced Micro Devices, Inc; 4-8d1 Courtesy of Intel Corporation; 4-8d2 Courtesy of Transmeta Corporation; 4-8d3 Courtesy of Advanced Micro Devices, Inc; 4-9 © Gary Herrington Photography; 4-14 Step 1 Courtesy of Microsoft Corporation; 4-14 Step 2 Courtesy of Hewlett-Packard Company; 4-14 Step 4 Courtesy of Fujitsu- Siemens; 4-15 © Jeremy Walker/Getty Images; 4-17a Courtesy of Seagate Technology; 4-17b Courtesy of Kingston Technology Company, Inc; 4-17c Courtesy of ViewSonic Corporation; 4-18a © Gary Herrington Photography; 4-18b Courtesy of Kingston Technology Company, Inc.; 4-21 Courtesy of MPIO America; 4-23 © WireImageStock/Masterfile; 4-23 © WireImageStock/Masterfile; 4-25 © Gary Herrington Photography; 4-26 Courtesy of Kingston Technology Company, Inc; 4-27 © 2006 Personal Computer Memory Card International Association; 4-28 Courtesy of Hewlett-Packard Company; 4-28 © Tim Gilman Photography; 4-33a Courtesy of Acer America Corp; 4-33b Courtesy of Nokia; 4-33c Courtesy of Nokia; 4-34 Courtesy of Sony Ericsson Mobile Communications AB. All Rights Reserved; 4-35b Courtesy of Intel Corporation; 4-35b Courtesy of Kingston Technology Company, Inc; 4-36 Courtesy of Fujitsu Siemens Computers; 4-37 Courtesy of Hewlett-Packard Company; 4-37b Courtesy of ASUSTeK Computer Inc; 4-37c Courtesy of Sendo; 4-38 Courtesy of Fujitsu Siemens Computers; 4-39 Courtesy of Acer America Corp; Looking Ahead 4-2 © Dorling Kindersley; 4-40a © Comstock Images;4-40b © Paul Barton/CORBIS; 4-40c © C. Görling/zefa/Corbis; 4-40d © Mark Harmel / Alamy; 4-40e © Dynamic Graphics Group / IT Stock Free / Alamy; 4-41a Courtesy of Fellowes, Inc; 4-41b Courtesy of First-Aid- Product.com, a division of American CPR; Figure 4-41c Courtesy of Belkin International; 4-41d Courtesy of Fellowes, Inc; 4-41e © Gary Herrington Photography; Career Corner © Stephen Derr/Getty Images; Technology Trailblazer 1 © CORBIS SYGMA; Technology Trailblazer 2 © Andy Rain/Bloomberg News /Landov; **Chapter 5:** PY-5 © AP Photo; PY-5 © Jeff Greenberg / Alamy; PY-5 Courtesy of Sony Electronics Inc; PY-5 © Mario Tama/Getty Images; PY-5 © REUTERS/Jeff Zelevansky /Landov; PY-5 ©David Young-Wolff / Photo Edit; PY-5 Courtesy of Logitech; PY-5 © Royalty-Free/Corbis; PY-5 © Raquel Ramirez / PhotoEdit; PY-5 Courtesy of Logitech; PY-5 Courtesy of Sony Electronics Inc; 5-1a © Stockbyte/Getty Images; 5-1b © Ciaran Griffin/Stockbyte Platinum; 5-1c © Royalty-Free/Corbis; 5-1d AP Images; 5-1e © Rebecca McAlpin/Bloomberg News /Landov; 5-1f © Thinkstock / Alamy; 5-1g © Scott Olson/Getty Images; 5-1h1 © DAVID HECKER/AFP/Getty Images; 5-1h2 © Medioimages / Alamy; 5-1i Courtesy of Wacom Technology; 5-1j © Insy Shah/Getty Images; 5-1l1 Courtesy of Hewlett-Packard Company; 5-1l2 Courtesy of Hewlett-Packard Company; 5-1l3 Courtesy of Hewlett-Packard Company; 5-1m © Jose Luis Pelaez, Inc./CORBIS; 5-1n Courtesy of Sony Electronics Inc; 5-1o Courtesy of Hewlett-Packard Company; 5-1p1 © D. Hurst / Alamy; 5-1q1 ©Susan Van Etten / PhotoEdit; 5-1q2 © AP Photo; 5-1r © Tim Boyle/Newsmakers/Getty Images; 5-1s © James Nazz/CORBIS 5-1t © David Young-Wolff / Alamy 5-1u ©Bill Aron / Photo Edit; 5-1v © Ingram Publishing / SuperStock; 5-1w © Blend Images / Alamy; 5-1x1 © Peter Macdiarmid/Getty Images; 5-1x2 © MICHAEL CARONNA/BLOOMBERG NEWS /Landov; 5-1x3 © Peter Macdiarmid/Getty Images; 5-2 Courtesy of Microsoft Corporation; 5-4 Courtesy of Hewlett-Packard Company; 5-4 Courtesy of Belkin International; 5-6 Courtesy of Microsoft Corporation; 5-8 Courtesy of Logitech; 5-9 © Yo/Getty Images; 5-10 Courtesy of IBM Corporation; 5-11 © Frances M. Roberts / Alamy; 5-12 Courtesy of Sony Ericsson Mobile Communications AB. All rights reserved; 5-13 Courtesy of Wacom Technology Corp; 5-14a Courtesy of Wacom Technology Corp; 5-14b © Comstock Images; 5-15 Courtesy of Nyko; 5-15 Courtesy of Logic3 plc; 5-15 Courtesy of Logic3 plc; 5-15 Courtesy of Nintendo; 5-15 Courtesy of Logitech; 5-15 Courtesy of Logitech; 5-15 Courtesy of Logitech; 5-16 AP Image; 5-17 Courtesy of Nuance; 5-18 © ICP / Alamy; 5-19 Courtesy of Veo Intl; 5-19 Courtesy of Socket Communications Inc; 5-19 © Gustaf Brundin/istockphoto.com; 5-19 Courtesy of Hewlett-Packard Company; 5-20 Courtesy of Think Outside, Inc; 5-21 Courtesy of Nokia; 5-22 © Kaluzny-Thatcher/Getty Images; 5-23 Courtesy of Motion Computing, Inc; 5-24 © John Lawrence/Getty Images; 5-26 © Andersen Ross/Getty Images; 5-27 Courtesy of Sony Electronics Inc; 5-28a © Noel Hendrickson/Masterfile; 5-29a © Steve Chenn/CORBIS; 5-30 Courtesy of Hewlett-Packard Company; 5-30b Courtesy of C Technologies AB; 5-30c Courtesy of Visioneer, Inc; 5-30d Howtek HiResolve 8000 Drum Scanner, image courtesy of Howtek, Inc; 5-31 Step 1 Courtesy of Umax Systems GmbH; 5-31 Courtesy of Acer America Inc; 5-34a ©Colin Young-Wolff / Photo Edit; 5-34b Courtesy of Research In Motion; 5-34c ©Susan Van Etten / Photo Edit; 5-36 Courtesy of Tibbett & Britten Group; Looking Ahead 5-1 © Silvia Otte/Getty Images; 5-37 ©Spencer Grant / Photo Edit ; 5-39 Courtesy of Symbol Technology; 5-40 © KARLHEINZ SCHINDLER/dpa /Landov; 5-41 © Steve Dunwell / Index Stock Imagery; 5-42a © AP/WIDE WORLD PHOTOS; 5-42b Courtesy of Microsoft Corporation; 15827 Courtesy of Recognition Systems, Inc; 5-44 © BORIS ROESSLER/dpa /Landov; 5-45 Courtesy of Athena Smartcard Solutions - www.athena-scs.com; 5-47 Courtesy of www.keytools.com; 5-49 Courtesy of NaturalPoint, Inc. Looking Ahead 5-2 © Caroline von Tuempling/Getty Images; Career Corner © Romilly Lockyer/Getty Images; Technology Trailblazer 1 © 2002 Gary Reyes/San Jose Mercury News. All rights reserved; Technology Trailblazer 2 © AP Images; **Special Feature 5:** 1a Courtesy of OQO, Inc; 1b © Purestock/Getty Images; 1c Courtesy of Nokia; 1d Courtesy of Cingular; 2a Courtesy of Palm, Inc; 2b Courtesy of Hewlett-Packard Company; 2c Courtesy of Microsoft Corporation; 2d Courtesy of Nokia; 2e Courtesy of HTC; 2f Courtesy of Research In Motion; 2g Courtesy of Apple; 2h Courtesy of Sony Electronics; 2i Courtesy of Garmin Ltd; 2j Courtesy of Nintendo; 3b Courtesy Hewlett-Packard Company; 3c Courtesy of Garmin Ltd; 3d Courtesy of Think Outside Inc; 3e Courtesy of Griffin Technology; Fig 4 Courtesy of Microsoft Corporation; Fig 4 Courtesy of PocketGear; Fig 4c Courtesy of PocketGear; Fig 4d Courtesy of PocketGear; Fig 4e Courtesy of Microsoft Corporation; page 287 left Courtesy of Microsoft Corporation; page 287 right © Art Vandalay/Getty Images; 6a Courtesy of Microsoft Corporation; 6b Courtesy of Microsoft Corporation; 6c Courtesy of Handango; 6d Courtesy of PocketGear; 6e Courtesy of LandWare Inc; page 288 © Peter Griffith/Masterfile; page 288 © Hugh Threlfall / Alamy; page 288 Courtesy of Symbol Technologies; page 289 Courtesy of COMPELSON Laboratories; page 289 © CRIS BOURONCLE/AFP/Getty; page 289 Courtesy of Skyline Software Systems, Inc; page 290 © Dynamic Graphics Group / Creatas / Alamy; page 290 Courtesy of PocketGear; page 290 Courtesy of Symbol Technologies; page 291 © Orbit/Masterfile; page 291 Courtesy of Handango; page 291 Courtesy of PocketGear; page 291 Courtesy of PocketGear; page 291 Courtesy of PocketGear; page 291 Courtesy of PocketGear; page 291 Courtesy of PocketGear; page 292 top © Erik Dreyer/Getty Images; page 292 top Courtesy of PocketGear; page 292 Courtesy of PocketGear; page 292 Courtesy of PocketGear; page 292 Courtesy of Handango; page 293 top ©Michael Newman / Photo Edit; page 293 top Courtesy of Trusmart Technologies Corp; page 293 top page 293 bottom © AP Images; page 294 top Courtesy of Microsoft Corporation; page 294 top Courtesy of Nokia; page 294 bottom Courtesy of Namco Networks; page 296 Courtesy of Motorola; **Chapter 6:** PY6 © LWA/Getty Images; PY6 James Woodson/Getty Images; PY6 © imagebroker / Alamy; PY6 Steve Cole/Getty Images PY6 AP Images; PY6 © David Young-Wolff / Alamy; PY6 © Jim West / Alamy; PY6 © Jack Sullivan / Alamy; PY6 ©Andre Jenny / The Image Works; PY6 Courtesy of Hewlett-Packard Company; PY6 Courtesy of Hewlett-Packard Company; PY6 Courtesy of Belltech Systems, LLC; 6-1a1 Courtesy of T-Mobile SDA; 6-1a2

Courtesy of Microsoft Corporation; 6-1b Courtesy of Xerox Corporation; 6-1c Courtesy of Fujitsu-Siemens Computers; 6-1d Courtesy of Logitech; 6-1e Courtesy of SanDisk Corporation; 6-1f Courtesy of Tatung Science and Technology, Inc; 6-1g Courtesy of Creative Technology Ltd; 6-1h Courtesy of Hewlett-Packard Company; 6-1i Courtesy of Hewlett-Packard Company; 6-1j Courtesy of Nokia; 6-2 Courtesy of Hewlett-Packard Company; 6-3 Courtesy of ViewSonic Corporation; 6-4a Courtesy of Acer America Corp; 6-4b Courtesy of Acer America Corp; 6-4c Image courtesy of TabletKiosk; 6-4d Courtesy of Archos; 6-4e Courtesy of Nokia; 6-4f Courtesy of Palm, Inc; Looking Ahead 6-1 Courtesy of Philips Polymer Vision; 6-6 Courtesy of AMD; 6-8 Courtesy of Panasonic; 6-9 © BananaStock / Alamy; 6-10 Courtesy of NEC-Mitsubishi Electronics Display of America Inc; 6-13a Raimund Koch/Getty Images; 6-13b Courtesy of Hewlett-Packard Company; 6-13c © OSHIKAZU TSUNO/AFP/Getty Images; 6-13d Courtesy of Nokia; 6-13e Courtesy of Sony Electronics Inc; 6-13g Courtesy of Epson America, Inc; 6-13h QV3000EX camera photo courtesy of Casio Inc; 6-13i Courtesy of Eastman Kodak Company; 6-13j © Najlah Feanny/Corbis; 6-14 Courtesy of Hewlett-Packard Company; 6-14 Courtesy of Xerox Corporation; 6-14 Courtesy of Epson America, Inc; Figure 6-16 © Gary Herrington Photography; 6-17a Courtesy of Lexmark International, Inc; 6-17b Courtesy of Hewlett- Packard Company; 6-18a Courtesy of Xerox Corporation; 6-18b Courtesy of Xerox Corporation; 6-20a Courtesy of Mitsubishi Digital Electronics America, Inc; 6-21 Courtesy of Canon U.S.A, Inc; 6-22 Courtesy of Seiko Instruments USA Inc; 6-23 Courtesy of MacDermid ColorSpan Inc; 6-24 Courtesy of Oki Data Amercas, Inc; 6-25 Courtesy of IBM Corporation; 6-26 Courtesy of Logitech; 6-27 © Bill Aron / PhotoEdit; 6-29 © Tony Freeman/PhotoEdit; 6-30c Courtesy of MPC Computers, LLC; 6-30b Courtesy of U.S. Robotics Corporation; 6-30a ©Spencer Grant / PhotoEdit; 6-30d Courtesy of MPC Computers, LLC; 6-31 Courtesy of Lexmark International; 6-32a Courtesy of InFocus Corporation; 6-32b Courtesy of InFocus Corporation; Looking Ahead 6-2 AP Images; 6-33a & b © 2005 Guillemot Corporation S.A. All rights reserved. Thrustmaster® is a registered trademark of Guillemot Corporation S.A. Ferrari® is a registered trademark of Ferrari S.p.A. All other trademarks and brand names are hereby acknowledged and are property of their respective owners; 6-36a Courtesy of Enabling Technologies; 6-36b © Don Farrall/Getty Images; Career Corner © David Young-Wolff/PhotoEdit; 6-37a Courtesy of Intel Corporation; 6-37b Gustaf Brundin/istockphoto.com; Technology Trailblazer 1 © Fujifotos / The Image Works; Technology Trailblazer 2 © AP Images; **Special Feature 6:** Opener © Photo Resource Hawaii / Alamy; Opener ©Masterfile (Royalty-Free Div.); Opener © Design Pics Inc. / Alamy; 1a © Antonio Mo/Getty Images; 1b Courtesy of Sony Electronics. Inc; 1c © Larry Gatz/Getty Images; 1d Courtesy of Sony Electronics. Inc; 1e © Digital Vision/Getty Images; 1f Courtesy of Pioneer Electronics; 1g Courtesy of Hewlett-Packard Company; 1i Courtesy of Hewlett-Packard Company; 2a Courtesy of Hewlett-Packard Company; 2 Courtesy of FujiFilm USA Inc; 2 Courtesy of Nikon Inc; 5b Courtesy of SanDisk Corporation; 5a Courtesy of SanDisk Corporation; 5c Courtesy of SanDisk Corporation; 6 Courtesy of Iogear Inc; 8 Courtesy of Hewlett-Packard Company; 10a Courtesy of Sony Electronics. Inc; 10b Courtesy of JVC; 10c © Royalty-Free/CORBIS; 11 © John Giustina/Getty Images; 12 © Peter Moynes/Getty Images; 13 Courtesy of Apple; 15 Courtesy of DeskShare; 16 Courtesy of Ulead Systems Inc; 17 Courtesy of Ulead Systems Inc; 18 Courtesy of DeskShare; **Chapter 7:** PY7 © Richard Levine/Alamy; PY7 © Jeff Greenberg/Alamy; PY7 Courtesy of SanDisk Corporation; PY7 Courtesy of Seagate Technology; PY7 © Mark Boulton/Alamy; PY7 © walik/istockphoto.com; PY7 ©David Joel/Getty Images; PY7 © Keith Dannemiller/Alamy; PY7 Courtesy of Western Digital; PY7 © David McGlynn / Alamy; 7-1a Courtesy of Hewlett-Packard Company; 7-1b Courtesy of Hitachi Global Storage; 7-1c Courtesy of Seagate Technology; 7-1d Courtesy of Seagate Technology; 7-1e Courtesy of Iomega; 7-1f © Tetra Images / Alamy; 7-1g Courtesy of Hewlett-Packard Company; 7-1i Courtesy of PCMCIA; 7-1h Courtesy of Netgear; 7-1j Courtesy of SanDisk Corporation; 7-1k Courtesy of Hewlett-Packard Company; 7-1l © vario images GmbH & Co.KG / Alamy; 7-1m ©Aaron Flaum/Alamy; 7-6 Courtesy of Seagate Technology; 7-6 ©Tim Gilman Photography; Looking Ahead 7-1 Courtesy of IBM Zurich Research Laboratory. Unauthorized use not permitted; 7-8 Courtesy of Maxtor Corporation; 7-11 Courtesy of Intel Corporation; 7-12 Courtesy of Hitachi Global Storage; 7-13 Courtesy of Western Digital; 7-14 Courtesy of Iomega; 7-14 Courtesy of Western Digital; 7-16 Photo Courtesy of Iomega Corporation. Copyright © 2005 Iomega Corporation. All Rights Reserved. Zip is a registered trademark in the United States and/or other countries. Iomega, the stylized "i" logo and product images are property of Iomega Corporation in the United States and/or other countries; 7-17 © Gary Herrington Photography; 7-21a Courtesy of Merriam-Webster Inc; 7-21b Courtesy of Memorex Products, Inc; 7-21c Courtesy of Memorex Products, Inc; 7-21d1 Courtesy of DeLorme; 7-21d2 Courtesy of DeLorme; 7-21e1 Courtesy of Memorex Products, Inc; 7-21e2 Courtesy of Memorex Products, Inc; 7-21f1 Courtesy of Memorex Products, Inc; 7-21f2 Courtesy of Memorex Products, Inc; 7-21f3 Courtesy of Memorex Products, Inc; 7-21 Courtesy of Memorex Products, Inc; LA 7-2 Courtesy of Purdue News Service; 7-22 Courtesy of Encyclopaedia Britannica; 7-22 Courtesy of Microsoft Corporation; 7-22 © Gary Herrington Photography; 7-23c Courtesy of NEC Solutions (America), Inc; 7-23c AP Images; 7-24 © 2005 Dell Inc. All Rights Reserved; 7-24 Courtesy of DeLorme; 7-26 GamesareFun.com; 7-27 Courtesy of Sony Electronics Inc; 7-28 Courtesy of PCMCIA; 7-29 © Sam Lee/istockphoto.com; 7-29 © Marianna Day Massey/ZUMA/Corbis; 7-29 Courtesy of Hewlett-Packard Company; 7-29 Courtesy of Hewlett-Packard Company; 7-29 Scrambled/istockphoto.com; 7-30 Courtesy of SanDisk Corporation; 7-30 Courtesy of SanDisk Corporation; 7-30 Courtesy of SanDisk Corporation; 7-30 Courtesy of SanDisk Corporation; 7-31 Courtesy of Delkin Devices, Inc; 7-31 Courtesy of Kingston Technology; 7-32 Toshiba America Information Systems, Inc; 7-32 Toshiba America Information Systems, Inc; 7-33 ITAR-TASS/Alexander Bundin /Landov; 7-34 ©Bill Aron / PhotoEdit; 7-34 ©Bill Aron / Photo Edit 7-36 © Wes Thompson/CORBIS; Career Corner © Noel Hendrickson/Masterfile; Technology Trailblazer 1 Courtesy of Al Shugart International; Technology Trailblazer 2 Courtesy of IBM Research; page 386 Courtesy of SanDisk Corporation; **Chapter 8:** PY8 © imagebroker / Alamy; PY8 © JupiterMedia / Alamy; PY8 Daisuke Morita/Getty Images; PY8 © M. Timothy O'Keefe / Alamy; PY8 © Mark Sykes / Alamy; PY8 Flying Colours Ltd/Getty Images; PY8 Courtesy of Symantec; PY8 Courtesy of Symantec; PY8 Colin Young- Wolff/PhotoEdit; 8-1a Alex Nikada/istockphoto; 8-1c Courtesy of Hewlett-Packard Company; 8-1d Courtesy of Hewlett-Packard Company; 8-9a Courtesy of Hewlett-Packard Company; 8-9b Courtesy of Hewlett-Packard Company; 8-26 Courtesy of Microsoft Corporation; 8-28 Courtesy of Apple; Looking Ahead 8-1 AP Images; 8-31 Courtesy of BERNINA® of America, Inc.; 8-32b Courtesy of Audiovox; 8-33 Courtesy of Palm Inc; 8-34 Courtesy of Research in Motion; 8-35 Courtesy of Sony Ericsson; 8-39 "Nero" is a trademark of Nero AG. Image courtesy of Nero Inc; 8-40 Courtesy of Symantec; Career Corner © MTPA Stock/Masterfile; 8-41 Tanya Constantine/Getty Images; Technology Trailblazer 1 © AP Images; Technology Trailblazer 2 © Kim Kulish/CORBIS; **Special Feature 8:** 1a Courtesy of Hewlett-Packard Company; 1b Courtesy of Hewlett-Packard Company; 1c Courtesy of Apple; 1d Darrin Klimek/Getty Images; 4a Courtesy of Hewlett-Packard Company; 4b Courtesy of SanDisk Corporation; 4c Courtesy of Hewlett-Packard Company; 4d Courtesy of Avid Technology; 4e Courtesy of Seagate Technology; 4f Courtesy of Hewlett-Packard Company; 4g Courtesy of Logitech; 4h Courtesy of Microsoft Corporation; 4j Courtesy of Zoom Technologies Inc; 4k Courtesy of ViewSonic Corporation; 4l Courtesy of Microsoft Corporation; 4m Courtesy of Hewlett-Packard Company; 4n Courtesy of Hewlett- Packard Company; 4o Courtesy of UMAX; 4s Courtesy of Logitech; 4t Courtesy of Logitech; 4u Courtesy of SanDisk Corporation; 4v Courtesy of 3Com Corporation; 4w Courtesy of D-Link Corporation/D-Link Systems, Inc; 12 PRNewsFoto/Mindjet LLC; 13 Courtesy of Fujitsu-Siemens Computers; 14 Courtesy of InFocus Corporation; 15 © Digital Archive Japan / Alamy; 16 © Patrick Olear / PhotoEdit; 19 Courtesy of Motion Computing; 21 Courtesy of Motion Computing **Chapter 9:** PY-9 Courtesy of Nokia; PY-9 Courtesy of Nokia; PY-9 Courtesy of Research in Motion; PY-9 Image Source/Getty Images; PY-9 Katja Heinemann/Getty Images; PY-9 Tom Brakefield/Getty Images; PY-9 © ImageState / Alamy; PY-9 © Mint Photography / Alamy; PY-9 © Todd Bannor / Alamy; PY-9 Courtesy of Handango; 9-1a Courtesy of IBM Corporation; 9-1b Courtesy of IBM Corporation; 9-1c Courtesy of Fujitsu-Siemens Computers; 9-1d Courtesy of Hewlett-Packard Company; 9-1e Engin Communications/istockphoto.com; 9-1f Courtesy of Nokia; 9-1f2 Courtesy of Nokia; 9-1g Courtesy of Hewlett-Packard Company; 9-1h

Courtesy of Toyota; 9-1h Courtesy of Garmin Ltd; 9-1 Jason Reed/Getty Images; 9-1 © Digital Stock; 9-1 © Digital Stock; 9-1 © Digital Stock; 9-3 Courtesy of Handango; 9-3 © Kaz Mori/Getty Images; 9-3 © Royalty- Free/Corbis; 9-3 © Digital Vision; 9-4 Courtesy of Intel Corporation; 9-4 Courtesy of D-Link; 9-4 Courtesy of 3Com Corporation; 9-4 © James Leynse/Corbis; 9-4 © Justin Sullivan/Getty Images; 9-5 © Alex Segre / Alamy; 9-6 Courtesy of Garmin Ltd; 9-6 © George Simhoni/Masterfile; 9-6 Courtesy of Wherify Wireless, Inc; 9-6 Courtesy of Wherify Wireless, Inc; 9-6 © Siemens AG Press Pictures; 9-6 © Jasper James/Getty Images; 9-6 Courtesy of Garmin Ltd; 9-6 © Ron Chapple/Getty Images; 9-6 © Dante Burn-Forti/Getty Images; 9-6 Courtesy of GPS Tracks, Inc; 9-7 Courtesy of WebEx; 9-8a © Javier Pierini/Getty Images; 9-8b © Jon Feingersh/CORBIS; 9-8c © Andersen Ross/Brand X Pictures; 9-8d Courtesy of Sun Microsystems; 9-8d2 Courtesy of Sun Microsystems; 9-9 Courtesy of Symantec; 9-10 © Image Source/Imagestate; 9-11 Courtesy of Hewlett-Packard Company; 9-11 Courtesy of Netgear; 9-11 Courtesy of Hewlett- Packard Company; 9-18 Courtesy of Linksys; 9-19 YUJI MORI/Getty Images; 9-19b Courtesy of Fujitsu Siemens Computers; 9-21 Step 1 © James Leynse/CORBIS; 9-21 Step 2 © James Leynse/CORBIS; 9-21 Step 3 © E-ZPass/Getty Images; 9-21 Step 3 Courtesy of Hewlett- Packard Company; 9-22 Courtesy of Nokia; 9-25 Courtesy of Hewlett-Packard Company; 9-25 Courtesy of Zoom Technologies, Inc; 9-27 Courtesy of Motorola; 9-28a © Erik S. Lesser/Bloomberg News /Landov; 9-28b Courtesy of Motorola, Inc; 9-28c Courtesy of Saenix Technology Inc; 9-28d Courtesy of Panasonic; 9-28e © image100 / Alamy; 9-29 Courtesy of Sierra Wireless Inc; 9-30a Courtesy of Linksys; 9-30b Courtesy of Belkin International, Inc; 9-31a Courtesy of Linksys; 9-31b ©Bonnie Kamin / PhotoEdit; 9-31c ©CLEO PHOTOGRAPHY / PhotoEdit; 9-31d ©Michael Newman / PhotoEdit; 9-31e Courtesy of Linksys; 9-31f © F64/Getty Images; 9-32a Courtesy of D-Link Systems; 9-32b Courtesy of D-Link Systems; 9-33 Courtesy of D-Link Systems; 9-34a Courtesy of Hewlett-Packard Company; 9-34b Courtesy of D-Link Systems; 9-34c Courtesy of Palm, Inc; 9-34d Courtesy of Motorola; 9-35 Step 4 Courtesy of IBM Corporation; Looking Ahead 9-1 © Jon Feingersh/Masterfile; 9-42 © Vince Streano/CORBIS; 9-43 © William Whitehurst/CORBIS; Looking Ahead 9-2 NASA Glenn Research Center (NASA-GRC); Career Corner © Dana Hursey/Masterfile; Technology Trailblazer 1 © Kim Kulish/Corbis; Technology Trailblazer 2 © WOLFGANG VON BRAUCHITSCH/BLOOMBERG NEWS /Landov; **Chapter 10:** PY-10 © James Hughes / Alamy; PY-10 © eStock Photo Alamy; PY-10 © graham lawrence / Alamy; PY-10 © Rick Friedman/Corbis; PY-10 © Getty Images; PY-10 ©Jonathan Nourok/Photo Edit; PY-10 © David Young-Wolff/Photo Edit; PY-10 © David Young-Wolff/Photo Edit; PY-10 © Spencer C. Grant/Photo Edit; PY-10 © Bill Bachmann/Photo Edit; 10-1a © Red Chopsticks/Getty Images; 10-1b © Jeff Zelevansky/Reuters/Corbis; 10-1c Courtesy of Hewlett-Packard Company; 10-1d Courtesy of Hewlett-Packard Company; 10-1e Courtesy of Hewlett-Packard Company; 10-1f Courtesy of Hewlett-Packard Company; 10-1g Courtesy of Fargo Electronics; 10-2 © Getty Images; 10-7 © Richard Schultz/Getty Images; 10-9 © Jack Smith/Bloomberg News /Landov; 10-9 AP Images; Looking Ahead 10-1 Courtesy of Microsoft Corporation; 10-25 Courtesy of Symbol Technologies; Looking Ahead 10-2 © Lester Lefkowitz/CORBIS; Career Corner © Yang Liu/CORBIS; Technology Trailblazer 1 Courtesy of the National Academy of Engineering; Technology Trailblazer 2 © Justin Sullivan/Getty Images; **Chapter 11:** PY-11 Courtesy of Kingston Technology; PY-11 Papado/Getty Images; PY-11 Neil Leslie/Getty Images; PY-11 Andreas Pollok/Getty Images; PY-11 Ewan Stevenson / Alamy; PY-11 Courtesy of Hewlett-Packard Company; PY-11 Courtesy of Hewlett-Packard Company; PY-11 Michael Newman/Photo Edit; PY-11 Michael Newman/Photo Edit; 11-1a Courtesy of Hewlett-Packard Company; 11-1b Courtesy of ViewSonic Corporation; 11-1c © Comstock Images / Alamy; 11-1d © Comstock Images / Alamy; 11-1e © Alistair Berg/Getty Images; 11-1f © GOODSHOOT - JUPITERIMAGES FRANCE / Alamy; 11-1g © Hugh Threlfall / Alamy; 11-1h Courtesy of Fujitsu-Siemens Computers; 11-2 Step 3a Jason Todd/Getty Images; 11-2 Step 3b Mike Hill / Alamy; 11-5 Courtesy of McAfee; 11-7a Courtesy of Fujitsu-Siemens Computers; 11-7b Courtesy of Hotbrick 11-7c eIQnetworks, Inc.; 11-12 © Image Source/Imagestate; 11-13 © PAULO WHITAKER/Reuters /Landov ; 11-14 Courtesy of Kensington Computer Products Group; 11-20 Courtesy of American Power Conversion Corp; 11-21 Courtesy of MGE UPS SYSTEMS; 11-28 Courtesy of Hewlett-Packard Company; 11-31 Courtesy of Surf Control; Looking Ahead 11-2 © Pete Saloutos/CORBIS; 11-34 © C Squared Studios/Getty Images; Career Corner Box © AP/Wide World Photos; Technology Trailblazer 1 © Roger Ressmeyer/CORBIS; Technology Trailblazer 2 © Maggie Hallahan Photography; **Special Feature 11:** Top Opener a © altrendo images/Getty Images; Top Opener b © Kim Steele/Getty Images; Top Opener c Courtesy of Intelligent Computer Solutions, Inc; Opener 1 Courtesy of SanDisk Corporation; Opener 2 Courtesy of Hewlett-Packard Company; Opener 3 Courtesy of Hewlett-Packard Company; Figures: 1 center © Rubberball/Alamy; 1a Courtesy of LAKS GmbH; 1b Courtesy of Intelligent Computer Solutions, Inc; 1c Courtesy of Guidance Software; 1d Courtesy of Victorinox®; Figure 4a Courtesy of Western Digital Corporation; 4b Courtesy of Iomega Corporation; 4c © Getty Images; Courtesy of LAKS GmbH; © Josef Philipp/istockphoto.com; 4d © C Squared Studios/Getty Images; 4e Courtesy of SanDisk Corporation; 4f © Helene Rogers/Alamy; 5 © david martin hughes/ Alamy; 6a Courtesy of Hewlett- Packard Company; 6b Courtesy of Hewlett-Packard Company; 6c Courtesy of Juniper Networks; 6d Courtesy of Fujitsu-Siemens Computers; 6e Courtesy of Hewlett-Packard Company; 6f Courtesy of Lowrance; 6g Courtesy of Netgear; 6h Courtesy of AT&T; 6i Courtesy of Hewlett-Packard Company; 6j Reproduced with Permission from Motorola, Inc. © 2006 Motorola, Inc; 9a Courtesy of Digital Intelligence, Inc; 9b Courtesy of Digital Intelligence, Inc; 9c Courtesy of Digital Intelligence, Inc; 10a and 10b Courtesy of Intelligent Computer Solutions, Inc; 11a and 11b Courtesy of Guidance Software; 11b Courtesy of Access Data; 13b © Alistair Berg/Getty Images; 13c © Anthony Harvie/Getty Images